Lincoln Christian College

P9-DDZ-662

UNDERSTANDING
CHRISTIAN MISSIONS

UNDERSTANDING CHRISTIAN MISSIONS

By

J. HERBERT KANE

School of World Mission
Trinity Evangelical Divinity School
Deerfield, Illinois

Baker Book House
Grand Rapids, Michigan

Copyright 1974 by
Baker Book House Company
ISBN: 0-8010-5344-7

Library of Congress Catalog
Card Number: 74-81783

Third printing, December 1976

The Scripture quotations in this publication are from the Revised Standard Version
Bible, copyright 1946, 1952, and 1971 by the Division of Christian Education,
National Council of the Churches of Christ in the U.S.A. and used by permission.

Portions of the section on Europe in chapter 5, "Cultural Penetration," are excerpts
(updated where necessary) from the author's book, A Global View of Christian
Missions, copyright 1971 by Baker Book House, and used with the permission of
the publisher..

The content (updated where necessary) of chapter 9, "Recent Developments," was
taken from the author's book, Winds of Change in the Christian Mission, copyright
1973 by Moody Press, and used with the permission of the publisher.

Permission from the following publishers for use of short excerpts from their copy-
righted publications is gratefully acknowledged: EPWORTH PRESS, London: Christian
Missions and Social Ferment (1964) by Norman Goodall; FORTRESS PRESS, Philadelphia: Call to Mission (1970) by Stephen Neill; HARPER & ROW, New York:
Christendom and Islam (1937) by W. Wilson Cash, The Christian Understanding
of God (1951) by Nels Ferré, Christ in Bangladesh (1973) by James and Marti
Hefley, Re-Thinking Missions: A Laymen's Inquiry by William E. Hocking, Ecu-
menical Foundations (1952) by W. R. Hogg, The Great Century in the Americas,
Australasia, and Africa (1943) by K. S. Latourette, and The Far Eastern Crisis
(1936) by Henry L. Stimson; McGRAW-HILL, New York: Colonialism and Chris-
tian Missions (1966) by Stephen Neill; PRINCETON UNIVERSITY PRESS: Christian
Missionaries and the Creation of Northern Rhodesia, 1880-1924 (1965) by Robert
J. Rotberg and Missionaries, Chinese and Diplomats: The American Protestant
Missionary Movement in China, 1890-1952 (1958) by Paul A. Varg.

Printed in the United States of America

266.09
K14
c.2

TO MY THREE SONS
Stanley
Douglas
Norman

58048

Foreword

The title accurately describes this book. Professor Kane examines the tremendous enterprise, presenting truly how it came to be, its biblical and theological roots, its relationship to the ebb and flow of economic and political power, its failures, and its successes. He knows that the missionary enterprise is different in different countries and fluctuates with the fervor of the sending churches and the strength of the religions and cultures in which the enterprise is carried on.

He explains how it is that, while constantly misunderstood and in the midst of confident prophecies of its early demise, it is stronger today than at any previous period of history. Rather than dying with the end of European empires, obedience to the Great Commission is becoming habitual among the churches now multiplying in Asia, Africa, and Latin America. They are sending their own sons and daughters out as missionaries to other lands.

While Professor Kane draws heavily on the history of missions and presents them in historical perspective, he sets forth their contemporary difficulties and opportunities. He shows missions standing at the forks of many roads and describes accurately the options involved. He constantly evaluates the enterprise, giving the favorable and the unfavorable aspects of its several parts. For example under two rubrics —"What They Did Wrong," and "What They Did Right"—he discusses numerous aspects of these heralds of the new day—the missionaries.

Here is a book which every student thinking of missions, every missionary in training, every chairman of the missions committee of the local church, and most executive secretaries of missionary societies could read with profit. I particularly commend the book to leaders of missionary societies in Latfricasia. As they send out their own sons and daughters from Latin America, Africa and Asia, they need to see the tremendous sweep and glory of the missionary enterprise—and the many errors and dangers they ought to avoid. Pastors and lay leaders in North America and Europe also can read this volume with profit.

The closing quarter of the twentieth century, now hard upon us, can see tremendous spread of the liberating, uplifting Gospel of Jesus Christ. A merit of this book is that the author, while giving full weight to the obstacles and opponents encountered by Christian missions, describes well the remarkable openness to Jesus Christ which marks so many of the world's populations. He sees the big picture. He knows the total score. He has determined not to let local setbacks, the malaise which has beset the churches in Europe, and the pervasive secularism of the day obscure the unprecedented advance of the Christian religion in numerous regions of the world.

For a balanced understanding of the missionary enterprise, read this book. And send a copy to a friend!

August first 1974 *Donald McGavran*

Senior Professor of Missions
School of World Mission and
Institute of Church Growth
Fuller Theological Seminary
Pasadena, California

Preface

The Christian world mission is without doubt the most magnificent enterprise the world has ever seen. The Peace Corps, launched with great enthusiasm by the United States government barely ten years ago, is already showing signs of slowing down. On the contrary the modern missionary movement, now more than 250 years old, is forging ahead on all fronts. More than fifty thousand Protestant missionaries are serving in over one hundred countries of the world. Total contributions in North America alone amount to 400 million dollars a year.

For the most part these missionaries are men and women of like passions with ourselves. Regarded by some as heroes and by others as troublemakers, they regard themselves as "servants of Jesus Christ," concerned only for the glory of God and the good of their fellowmen. In spite of their bluff and blunder—and there has been plenty of both—these dedicated missionaries have achieved a success out of all proportion to their wealth, influence, or numbers. Outnumbered by hostile forces abroad and often forgotten by their trusted friends at home, they have labored on decade after decade in the face of overwhelming odds until today the Christian church is the most universal institution in the world.

This modern miracle is all the more remarkable when it is remembered that the entire enterprise operates in a free society on a voluntary basis. Nobody is ever forced into missionary work; and any missionary can quit any time he wants. And the money—all 400 million dollars—comes from freewill offerings, mostly from small churches supported by middle-class Americans.

Until the nineteenth century Christianity was largely a Western religion. Today it is truly universal. There are a half-dozen small countries (mostly Muslim) that are still without a Christian church; but there is not a country in the world without a Christian witness of one kind or another. These churches now emerging in the Third World are growing in strength and numbers, so that today they compare favorably with the finest churches in the West. Indeed, many of them put our churches to shame. One of the most exciting facets of the missionary movement is the way in which the national churches overseas are beginning to assume their share of responsibility for the evangelization of the world—both theirs and ours.

Far from dying out, the missionary movement is experiencing a new surge of life and a new sense of direction and purpose. For the first time since Pentecost it is now possible to speak responsibly of completing the task of world evangelization in a single generation. We have the tools and the techniques, the men and the money. Old forms of mission are disappearing, but in their place new forms are emerging. For every door that closes another opens. In all parts of the world exciting things are happening. People are turning to Christ in ever increasing numbers. For the time being at least there seems to be an almost universal hunger for spiritual reality, quite without precedent in the history of modern missions. No one knows how long this situation will last, but while it does it behooves us to be up and doing.

No intelligent Christian can afford to be ignorant of the missionary enterprise of our day. He may never himself become a professional missionary. That makes no difference. If he is only a church member he should have a working knowledge of the church's greatest task— the evangelization of the world. Emil Brunner said that the church exists by mission as fire exists by burning. If this is true then every church member should be conversant with the broad outlines of mission history, theology, philosophy, and strategy. He should know something of the progress of the past, the problems of the present, and the prospects for the future.

It is not enough to support the Christian mission with our prayers and gifts. To be effective our prayers should be intelligent; and our giving should be as intelligent as our praying. Christian stewardship demands more than the signing of a monthly check or the offering of an occasional prayer. If the Christian mission is worthy of our support, surely it merits our understanding.

A word of caution may be in order: This book will not make the reader an expert in missions. It is simply an introduction to the vast subject of missiology. Many important aspects of the subject have been omitted. Others have been mentioned only in passing, without giving them the attention they deserve. The subject is simply too great to be treated adequately in one volume. In fact, any one of these chapters could have been developed into a book.

Hopefully, this book will provide a basic understanding of Christian missions and be the stimulus to further and deeper study.

I wish to express my heartfelt thanks to my wife for the hundreds of long and sometimes tedious hours she devoted to reading, correcting, and generally enhancing the manuscript and the galleys. Without her untiring help the book could not have been produced.

June 1974   *J. Herbert Kane*

Contents

1

The Making of the Missionary

David Livingstone said, "God had only one Son and He made that Son a missionary." Every missionary follows in the steps of the Son of God, who visited this planet two thousand years ago on a mission of redemption. He came to seek and to save and to give His life a ransom for many. Upon the completion of His mission He returned to His Father in heaven; but before He left He said to His apostles, "As the Father has sent me, even so I send you" (Jn 20:21).

The worldwide mission of the Christian church is rooted in the Incarnation and is part of God's redemptive purpose for the world. God is a missionary God. The Bible is a missionary book. The gospel is a missionary message. The church is a missionary institution. And when the church ceases to be missionary minded, it has denied its faith and betrayed its trust.

Every Christian is a witness; but not every Christian is a missionary in the professional sense of the term. Many are called but few are chosen. Missionaries are made, not born; and as in every worthwhile vocation the making process is long and difficult. It can even be discouraging; but those who persevere to the end find it to be a rewarding occupation, second to none in valor, excitement, and achievement.

Never were the demands on the missionary greater than they are today. We need men of wisdom, vision, courage, patience, sincerity, and humility. These qualities and others must be acquired and developed before the missionary ever sets his foot on foreign soil.

Part of his training is to acquire an understanding of Christian missions in all major aspects of the undertaking at home and overseas. He should know both the strengths and the weaknesses, the successes and the failures. Only so will he be able to avoid the mistakes of the past.

Myths Regarding Missions

There is a great deal of confused thinking these days with regard to various aspects of Christian missions. Church members continue to support missions, mostly with their money, sometimes with their prayers; but they seldom read literature dealing with missionary strategy and policy. Most of them know little or nothing about the progress of the past or the nature and extent of the problems that remain. Much of their information comes through the annual missionary conference, and that is usually more inspirational than informational. Hence the myths persist. In this section we can deal only with the more obvious myths.

1. **The myth of the vanishing missionary.** Many people believe that the missionary era is over and that the missionary belongs to a species soon to become extinct. The reasoning goes something like this: When the modern missionary movement got under way 250 years ago, it coincided with the thrust of Western imperialism into Asia, Africa, and Oceania. During the heyday of imperialism Christian missions worked in cooperation with the colonial governments, implementing and supplementing their programs of educational and social reform. World War II marked the end of the colonial period; and except for a few pockets of colonialism here and there the system is forever dead. The gunboats have been recalled and the white sahibs have all gone home. The Christian missionaries should do the same. This reasoning is common.

Every time there is a riot or a revolution with anti-Western overtones, someone is sure to demand the withdrawal of the missionaries. Even without riot and revolution there are those who insist that the missionaries represent the last vestiges of Western imperialism, and as such should be recalled. To clinch the matter they ask: "If the national governments can function without the colonial administrators, why can't the national churches get along without the missionaries?" To all such people the missionaries at best are superfluous; at worst, they are downright dangerous. In either case, they should have the good sense to come home; or they should be recalled.

Our reply is twofold. First, the missionary's identification with imperialism was one of the unfortunate accidents of history. They did not plan it that way and were happy when the unholy alliance was terminated. If, as the critics say, it was a mistake for them to go in with the colonialists, surely it would have been a mistake to come out with them. Two wrongs don't make a right. To have come out with the colonialists would have confirmed what the nationalists and the Communists have been saying all along.

Second, the missionary task has not been completed. There is still an enormous amount of work to be done. To call it quits now would be to jeopardize all that has been accomplished up to this point. To compare the national government with the national church is grossly unfair to the latter. The former is in control of the entire country and has the support of all the people. Moreover, it has access to sufficient funds to implement its programs regardless of the cost. By contrast the national church in some countries represents only 1 or 2 percent of the population. To maintain its existing work strains the budget to the limit. In all such places the missionary will be needed and wanted for years to come. In many parts of the non-Christian world church membership is barely keeping up with the population growth; in other parts it is falling behind. There are twice as many non-Christians in India today as there were when William Carey arrived in 1793. By no stretch of the imagination is the missionary a vanishing species.

2. The myth of the foreign missionary. Jesus told us that the field is the world (Mt 13:38); but we have divided the field into two parts, home and foreign. In the popular mind a missionary is a person who is called by God to preach the gospel in a *foreign* country. The fellow who does the same kind of work at home must settle for a less exotic appellation.

> This mythology projected the illusion that the primary missionary frontier was geographical. And so developed what might be called the mystical doctrine of salt water. The mission of the church was so closely identified with geographical expansion, and the missionary enterprise so exclusively considered in terms of geographical frontiers, that the term "mission" inevitably had a foreign connotation. Traveling over salt water was thereby gradually changed from being the obvious concomitant of *some* kinds of missionary service, to being the *sine qua non* of *any* kind of missionary endeavor, and finally to being the final test and criterion of what in fact was missionary. Being transported over salt water, the more the better, was given a certain absolute theological and spiritual value.[1]

---

[1] Keith R. Bridston, *Mission Myth and Reality* (New York: Friendship Press, 1965), pp. 32-33.

There is, of course, a great difference between preaching the gospel to Americans in Chicago, Los Angeles, or New York and preaching to the Auca Indians of Ecuador. The latter requires insights, attitudes, and skills not necessary for the successful prosecution of the former. In that sense and to that degree there is something "special" about the missionary who serves in a cross-cultural situation. It does not, however, justify the degree to which we have exalted the foreign missionary and played down the home missionary. Both are missionaries in the true sense of the word and deserve similar treatment.

The preference we show for foreign missions can be seen in our treatment of missionary candidates. Most candidates are required to raise their own support before proceeding to the field. Candidates looking forward to foreign service generally raise their support without much difficulty. Home mission candidates usually take much longer.

Somehow the home churches have surrounded foreign missions with an aura of sacredness not granted to any other form of Christian service. This is unfortunate, for it not only violates the principles of the New Testament, but it also polarizes the missionary enterprise into two separate entities, one superior to the other.

American churches give tens of thousands of dollars every year to mission projects in every continent except North America. Church members will travel thousands of miles to Quito, Ecuador, to see Radio Station HCJB that they have been helping to support, but they feel no obligation to support WMBI in Chicago. The only difference is that one represents foreign missions and the other home missions, and foreign missions usually win out.

It is becoming increasingly difficult to maintain the arbitrary difference between home and foreign missions. We used to think that foreign missions was more difficult and dangerous than home missions, and that a person took his life in his hand if he went to the jungles of Borneo, Amazon, or New Guinea. Today there are few places on the mission field as difficult or dangerous as the ghettos of our large American cities. Any pastor who leaves a wealthy suburban church for Christian service in the inner city is by any definition a missionary. Such an assignment is likely to require more courage, more faith, and more perseverance than most posts on the foreign field.

3. The myth of the ugly missionary. The term *missionary* was once a cherished word. Today it has lost its glamor. Indeed, there are those who suggest that the term should be dropped. It smacks too much, they say, of colonialism. Strange as it may seem, the friends at home are the only ones that have this hang-up. Apparently the term is not a dirty word in the Third World. The church leaders there certainly have no objection to it.

In 1964 Daniel T. Niles, outstanding leader of the Younger Churches of Asia, made a strong plea for "old-time missionaries" not only to remain in Asia but to take the initiative in church affairs. He said:

> We are not looking for fraternal helpers. We want missionaries. We know that you cannot find too many of them, but at least send us some. I am not against fraternal helpers. I am only protesting that they are not missionaries. They are helpers. We need any amount of help; but it is the missionary that is wanted, and wanted badly.[2]

The same is true of the political leaders. When the African colonies got their independence in the 1960s leader after leader went on public record thanking the missionaries for their contribution to independence and asking them to remain at their posts to help build the new nation. Of all the expatriates living in the Third World, the missionaries and the Peace Corps are the only ones there to give and not to get, and the national leaders know this.

The missionary, though held in high esteem by his friends and converts on the mission field, has never stood very high in the social register in his own hometown. The mental image conjured up by the word *missionary* was anything but flattering. The usual cartoon depicted him as wearing knee sox, Bermuda shorts, and a beat-up pith helmet. The word *missionary* needn't appear; the identity was complete. The missionary wife looked even worse. She was expected to have flat heels, long skirt, white blouse, and a bun at the back of her neck. The children, with their hand-me-downs, scuffed shoes, and unruly behavior, completed the picture.

Intellectually the picture wasn't much brighter. Not many missionaries had college degrees. For this reason the critics assumed that they were doomed to mediocrity. Some even went so far as to suggest that they volunteered for overseas service because they couldn't make the grade at home. Brainy men and pretty women were not supposed to be missionaries!

The fact of the matter is that missionaries are neither dumb nor dowdy. Immediately upon return to the States the entire family in many cases is given a clothing allowance which enables them to get a whole new wardrobe. Today it is virtually impossible to spot a visiting missionary in a Sunday morning service unless he is on the platform. The womenfolk are smartly dressed and compare favorably with their homeside sisters. As for the MKs, their problem is to figure out a way to look as unkempt as their city cousins!

When it comes to intellectual prowess the missionary is not one whit behind the average American. A missionary without a college

---

[2] Dougles Webster, *Yes to Mission* (New York: Seabury Press, 1966), p. 31.

degree is a rare person today. Many have two or three degrees. He may not remember whether the New York Mets are in the American League or the National League; but he knows more about geography, history, and world affairs than we do. While away from our affluent society he acquired a genuine appreciation for the simpler, finer things of life. He can converse intelligently on a wide range of subjects and is an expert on his adopted country—its history, people, and culture.

As for the MKs, they may be less sophisticated than our youngsters, but they are more mature. They have read more books, visited more places, talked to more people, and made more friends. They are usually bicultural and can speak at least two languages fluently. They are accustomed to world travel, which in itself is an education. They have experienced in real life the exciting and exotic things available to us only on television. The number of MKs who go on to college, and do well when they get there, is considerably higher than for the population as a whole. Most of them go into the professions—law, medicine, politics, the pastorate, and teaching. Not a few return to the field as missionaries. Very few have any desire to go into business simply to make money and live well.

4. The myth of the spiritual missionary. We have placed the missionary on a pedestal. We have admired his zeal, his courage, his dedication, and his humility. We have praised him for his spirit of sacrifice, his sense of duty, his willingness to take joyfully the spoiling of his goods and the destruction of his property. And the ultimate in self-sacrifice was his willingness to part with his children at the tender age of six in order to pursue a missionary career. To cap it all he lived by faith, looking to the Lord alone for the supply of his daily needs; and he did all this quietly and joyfully with no thought of reward.

We took for granted that anyone who could do all these things must be a spiritual giant. He must live always in fellowship with God. Prayer must indeed be his vital breath, his native air. Surely he must have achieved such a high degree of personal holiness as to be beyond the temptations that assail the common Christian. He must long since have gained the victory over the world, the flesh, and the devil. Such a person, we concluded, must be a saint.

Well, we were wrong, and the missionary would be the first to acknowledge the fact. There were, and are, spiritual giants among them, but the *average* missionary is a man of like passions with ourselves (Ja 5:17). He is fashioned from the same clay and he, like us, has the treasure of the gospel in an earthen vessel (2 Co 4:7). He may have a heart of gold, but he has feet of clay. When he lets his hair down he looks very much like the rest of us. He is basically a spiritual man, but he has his full share of idiosyncrasies. He has his headaches and his hang-ups, his blind spots and his pet peeves, his prejudices and his passions. He even has his doubts and fears. Touch him and he's touchy. Cross him and he gets cross. There are limits to his endurance. He has cracked up physically, mentally, morally, and spiritually and has had to come home to an unsympathetic constituency devoid of understanding. He has been known to fall into sin, including adultery, homosexuality, and suicide. Not all missionaries are happily married; they have domestic problems. Not all MKs turn out well. Some of them go astray. Some resent the fact that their parents are missionaries. Some become rebellious and join the hippies. A few have been known to end up as agnostics or alcoholics.

The missionary, like the apostle Paul, lives by the grace of God (1 Co 15:10) and cherishes the hope that by a process of divine alchemy the infirmities of his flesh will become an occasion for the manifestation of the power of Christ (2 Co 12:9). In and of himself he can do nothing (Jn 15:5). With and through Christ he can do all things (Ph 4:13). Others may have illusions about the missionary; he has none about himself. He understands all too well the truth of those lines by Henry Twells:

> O Savior Christ, our woes dispel;
> For some are sick, and some are sad,
> And some have never loved Thee well,
> And some have lost the love they had.

> And none, O Lord, have perfect rest,
> For none are wholly free from sin;
> And they who fain would serve Thee best
> Are conscious most of wrong within.

5. The myth of the specialized missionary. We hear much these days about specialization in all fields of human endeavor. Automation and cybernation make it possible for more and more tasks to be performed by fewer and fewer highly skilled people in key positions. Before long only the specialists will be able to find employment. By the year 2000 only 10 percent of the work force will be employed. The other 90 percent will be paid by the government to do nothing!

There is no doubt about it—specialization is the name of the game. Wherein then lies the myth? There are really two myths, not one, so far as missionary work is concerned.

The first myth is the idea that the day of the general missionary is over; now only specialists need apply. Indeed, there seems to be a conspiracy to downgrade the general missionary in favor of the specialist. The general missionary is regarded as a jack-of-all-trades and therefore master of none. As such he is definitely a second-class worker in the vineyard of the Lord.

There is some misunderstanding at this point. The truth of the matter is that from the beginning of the missionary movement we have had both general and specialized missionaries. There is no rivalry between them. The one supplements and complements the other.

What people don't understand is that the East is still several decades behind the West and the need for specialists there is not so great as it is here. Moreover, there are not enough missionaries to permit the missions to indulge in the luxury of specialization.

A good seminary in the United States will probably have two or three professors in the New Testament department, and the Old Testament department will have the same. These men teach only in the area of their concentration. But on the mission field, where the average seminary has twenty-five students and only two or three full-time faculty members, it is obvious that specialization, however desirable, is out of the question. The Old Testament professor will be asked to teach homiletics and apologetics in addition to Old Testament. The church history man will be required to teach evangelism and missions as well as church history.

For this reason mission executives prefer men who are versatile and flexible. Indeed, versatility is the greatest single human virtue any missionary can possess. Without it he may feel like a square peg in a round hole and blame the mission for his feelings of frustration.

The same goes for the medical missionary. The doctor on the mission field must be both a physician and a surgeon, for often he is the only doctor on the hospital staff. The heart, eye, and bone specialists will have ample scope for their special skills, but they must be prepared to function as general practitioners. Indeed, most mission doctors have to pitch in and help solve the problem when there is a short in the electrical system or when the incubator, the jeep, or the X-ray machine breaks down. At such times versatility is a priceless asset. Some doctors have been known to build their own hospitals!

The other myth is the idea that only doctors, nurses, teachers, radio technicians, agriculturalists, etc., are specialists. All others are lumped together and referred to as general missionaries. Is the evangelist not a specialist? What about the seminary professor, the youth worker, the business manager, or the area superintendent? Are they not specialists? If a man has four years of medical school we call him a specialist. If another man spends three or four years in a seminary, he is a general missionary. This doesn't make sense.

6. The myth of the primitive life. There are people who believe that missionaries live in primitive conditions with barely enough to keep body and soul together. They still think of them as hacking their way through snake-infested jungles and living in thatched houses with furniture made from packing cases.

There are, of course, some missionaries who live that way. Wycliffe Bible Translators and the New Tribes Mission, because of the nature of their work, have most of their missionaries living and working in primitive conditions. In fact, part of their training takes place in a jungle camp where they are required to survive for several weeks in the jungle equipped only with a sleeping bag, a machete, a compass, a few simple medicines, and a box of matches.

But they are the exception. The great majority of present-day missionaries enjoys a standard of living considerably higher than they ever anticipated. They are located in modern cities where they drive their own cars, shop in department stores and supermarkets, and have access to four-lane highways, airports, public libraries, golf courses, and tennis courts. Even the missionaries living in bush country usually congregate in central stations built for the purpose, where they have the basic amenities of Western civilization—simple but adequate housing, running water, and indoor plumbing. Most of them have electricity even if they have to generate it themselves. This enables them to make use of various kinds of electrical appliances brought from home. Food, mail, medicine, gasoline, and other supplies are flown in periodically by Mission Aviation Fellowship planes.

A young missionary couple that went to Ethiopia only last summer wrote in their first prayer letter:

> The S.I.M. station is beautiful. Gardens abound with all the familiar fruits and vegetables plus such things as bananas, pineapples, and papayas. Flowers are abundant. One can view Jimma five km. away with several mountain ranges in the background. The homes have electricity, running water, flush toilets, and refrigerators. Carey and Livingstone should have seen this day![3]

In former days the missions acquired land and built homes for their missionaries which were rent free. These were invariably Western in architectural style and interior decoration. They were large, airy, and comfortable. In fact some of these homes were better than some parsonages here in the United States.

In more recent years it has become a practice for missionaries to live in rented premises. These are usually located in the more attractive part of town and would compare favorably with middle-class housing in urban America.

---

[3] Letter from Art and Sue Volkmann, September 1973.

God forbid that we should base our missionary appeal to modern youth on creature comforts; but truthfulness demands that we tell it like it is. When most missionaries first leave for the field they are prepared to live and work under any circumstances; but when they get there they are pleasantly surprised to find conditions much better than they had ever dreamed.

7. The myth of the hungry heart. Few Christians have an adequate understanding of the enormous difficulties inherent in the conversion of the non-Christian peoples of the world. It is assumed that the "heathen" in their moral and spiritual degradation are expectantly awaiting the coming of the missionary; his arrival will be the signal for them to abandon their evil ways and embrace the gospel.

Missionary speakers, literature, and hymns have all contributed to this view. The "heathen" have been depicted as sitting in darkness, living in fear, and dying without hope. They have been variously described as forsaken, benighted, depraved, debauched, and deluded. Much has been made of the phenomenon of fear—fear of sickness, ancestors, evil spirits, angry gods, natural disasters, and finally, death.

Surely these people in their more sober moments must be aware of their plight. Given an opportunity they will readily accept the Christian message with its offer of life, health, joy, peace, and power.

What are the facts? That the non-Christian peoples of the world are lost in the darkness of sin, living in fear, and dying without hope is true. That they are ready and eager to accept Christ is not true. From time to time missionaries have come across certain individuals who believed the gospel the first time they heard it. They are the exception, not the rule. The overwhelming majority of non-Christian peoples must be included in Paul's statement: "None is righteous, no, not one; no one understands, no one seeks for God. All have turned aside, together they have gone wrong; no one does good, not even one" (Ro 3:10-12).

There is no evidence to support the view expressed in a well-known missionary hymn to the effect that "the heathen in his blindness" is calling on us to "deliver him from error's chain." He is not aware of his blindness, nor does he feel the weight of any chain. The Hindu, the Buddhist, the Muslim, and the Confucianist all consider their religion superior to ours; hence they are in no hurry to give it up. As for the peasant in his paddy field, he is so engrossed in the problem of feeding his large family that he has neither time nor thought for the needs of his soul. His chief concern is not where he will spend eternity, but how he and his children will survive until harvest. The same goes for the shopkeeper in the bazaar, the worker in the factory, and the housewife in the home. And if the time comes when they do need the comforts of religion, they will turn to their own priests and gods, not to the foreign missionary.

If anyone is inclined to doubt these remarks, he need only recall the fact that after a hundred years of missionary work in Japan, there are only one million professing Christians out of a population of 107 million. The figures for other countries in Asia are not much better; in some instances they are worse. We take to these people the bread of life only to find they're not hungry. We offer them the water of life only to discover they're not thirsty.

8. The myth of the closing door. In this postcolonial period a great deal has been said about closing doors. Books and magazine articles have discussed the problem from every conceivable angle. Missionaries on furlough have added to the confusion by warning us that we have "five more years" in one part of the world and "ten more years" in another. We seem to have developed a pathological preoccupation with this particular problem. In fact we have talked so long and loudly about closing doors that we have come to believe our own story.

It would be foolish, of course, to deny that some doors have already closed or that others will close in the future. What we do deny is that sooner or later *all* doors will close and the missionaries will find themselves without employment. Neither the lessons of history nor the statements of Scripture oblige us to accept that melancholy conclusion.

If one takes the trouble to enumerate all the countries that during the past twenty-five years have closed their doors to Christian missionaries, he will find that his list is rather short. In Asia it will include China, North Korea, North Vietnam, and Burma. In the Middle East it will include Libya, Syria, Iraq, and Southern Yemen. To his surprise he will find not a single closed country in Black Africa, Latin America, or Oceania. So his list will include only eight or ten countries, and there are 135 countries in the United Nations.

Some Muslim countries, such as Malaysia, Morocco, Algeria, and Sudan are not happy with the missionaries now in those countries and may expel them in the days to come. On the other hand some countries, such as Nepal, Somalia, and Yemen have in recent years accepted missionaries for the first time. Somalia has had second thoughts and more recently has terminated mission work. Afghanistan is closed to professional missionaries but has allowed over one hundred nonprofessional missionaries to engage in medical and educational work.

Some countries, such as Indonesia, Kenya, and India, that we feared would close, are still open. Others, such as Ethiopia and Colombia, that were closed for several years, are open again. It is quite possible that other countries may do the same. We dare not write off even Red China.

And what shall be said about the 100-plus countries that are open? In some of them the work is difficult and the response is disappointing, but in many of them the missionaries describe the opportunities as "fabulous" and "fantastic." The American Bible Society is publishing and distributing the Scriptures in over 100 countries. The Assemblies of God Mission has work in 92 countries. The Moody Literature Mission is producing and distributing gospel literature in 184 languages in over 100 countries. In addition the Moody Institute of Science has made its films available in 21 languages to missionaries in 120 countries of the world. If worldwide missionary activity is any criterion, it doesn't look as if the doors are closing.

9. The myth of the finished task. Missionary speakers have much to say these days about the indigenous churches on the mission field which are reported to be self-governing, self-propagating, and self-supporting. And the question is raised: If the national churches are able to stand on their own feet, pay their own way, and manage their own affairs, why are missionaries still needed? This is a good question.

We should blush with shame should we have to confess that after 250 years of missionary work we had not yet produced any indigenous churches. The indigenous churches are indeed a fact. Some are large and strong; others are small and weak. We thank God for every one of them. When we remember the enormous difficulties of the pioneer days, we are amazed that so much was accomplished by so few. Every indigenous church is a monument to the grace of God and the power of the gospel.

But having said that, we must go on to state that the missionary mandate has not been fulfilled when we have established indigenous churches. The original mandate called for the evangelization of the world, which includes preaching the gospel to *every* creature and making disciples of *all* nations. And this performance must be repeated in every succeeding generation. *That* task is far from complete.

In some countries, such as Korea and Indonesia, the national churches are large and strong; but even there the Christians represent not more than 10 percent of the population. These churches are certainly able to maintain their own existence, but can they be expected to win the other 90 percent of the population without outside help?

And what about the other countries where the churches are small and weak and the Christians account for only 2 or 3 percent of the population? The churches in Japan are strong from some points of view, but weak from others; the Christians there represent less than 1 percent of the total population. The Japanese church lacks evangelistic vision and zeal. Even the evangelical churches insist that the missionaries make the best evangelists.

In Thailand the situation is even less hopeful. For every Christian there are 999 Buddhists, most of whom are still without a knowledge of Jesus Christ. The Baptist church in Burma is very strong, but it is composed entirely of tribespeople, converts from animism. The 28 million Burmese who are Buddhists are practically untouched after 160 years of Christian work. Not more than 10,000 of them are Christians.

The Scriptures have been translated into 1,526 languages and dialects, but the complete Bible is available in only 257 languages. This means that millions of church members in the Third World have only the New Testament, and many of them don't even have that. Wycliffe Bible Translators estimates that there are 2,000 tribes, representing 160 million people, who are still without any portion of the Word of God. Indeed, their languages have not yet been reduced to writing.

According to the most reliable estimates world Christianity is not holding its own against the non-Christian religions. In 1960 the Christians represented about 34 percent of the world's population. Today the figure is around 30 percent and it continues to drop slowly year by year. There are more non-Christians in the two countries of China and India than there are Christians in the entire world.

Obviously the task of world evangelization is not complete. The indigenous churches still need help. In spite of all we have accomplished in the last 250 years we have barely scratched the surface.

What Is a Missionary?

The word *missionary* comes from the Latin word *mitto*, which means "to send." It is the equivalent of the Greek word *apostello*, which also means "to send." The root meaning of the two words is identical.

The word *apostle* occurs more than eighty times in the New Testament. In one place it refers to Christ (He 3:1). Jesus Christ was the first Apostle. He was also the chief Apostle. He derived His apostleship from the Father who, He said on many occasions, "sent" Him into the world on a mission of redemption.

From among His disciples Jesus chose twelve men whom He called "apostles." These men were taught and trained by Him, endowed with apostolic authority, and after the Resurrection were sent out to make disciples of all nations (Mt 28:18-20). There was a direct connection between His mission and theirs (Jn 20:21). These men came to be known as "The Twelve." They were undoubtedly a unique group of men with unique privileges and responsibilities. But there were others in the New Testament who came to be referred to as "apostles." Included in this second group were such well-known men as Barnabas, Timothy, Silas, and others.

In The Acts the apostles are sent out by the Holy Spirit (Acts 13:4) *and* the church (Acts 13:3). Most of Luke's account is built around the activities of the apostles, though they were by no means the only ones who preached the gospel (Acts 8:4; 11:19).

To whom should the term *missionary* be applied? Obviously today's missionary is not in the same class with the twelve apostles, who must forever remain in a class by themselves (Lk 22:30; Re 21:14). They do, however, have much in common with the "second-string" apostles who were sent out by the various churches on teaching and preaching missions to all parts of the Roman Empire. They did not remain long in any one place, but moved about as the Spirit directed them (Acts 8:26, 29, 39; 16:6-7).

It is impossible to come up with a scientific definition of the term *missionary* that will meet all the conditions and satisfy all the demands. It is possible to punch holes in any definition on which we might settle. In the traditional sense the term *missionary* has been reserved for those who have been called by God to a full-time ministry of the Word and prayer (Acts 6:4), and who have crossed geographical and/or cultural boundaries (Acts 22:21) to preach the gospel in those areas of the world where Jesus Christ is largely, if not entirely, unknown (Ro 15:20). This definition, though by no means perfect, has the virtue of being Biblical.

The problem is more than a semantic one and must be seen in a much larger frame of reference. There are those who refuse to buy the idea of "full-time Christian service" as applied to pastors, evangelists, and missionaries. By their definition every dedicated Christian, regardless of his vocation, is in full-time Christian service. If every Christian is in full-time service, then it is only a step to saying, as many do today, that every Christian is a missionary.

There is abroad in evangelical circles a move to do away with all "artificial distinctions." Today's Christians are challenged to rethink their position and give up their narrow view of the Christian life with its rigid categories of black and white and right and wrong, and to embrace a more sophisticated view of the wholeness of life. Gone are the former dichotomies between the secular and the sacred, work and prayer, and service and witness. As for any special missionary call—forget it. All Christians are missionaries.

The above point of view is not entirely wrong. It contains an element of truth that needs to be acknowledged and emphasized. On the other hand, if pushed too far it can become dangerous. Take the matter of tithing. There are those who assert that tithing is too legalistic an approach to Christian stewardship. They claim that "everything belongs to God" and they would not think of giving Him only a tenth of their income. Such talk sounds very spiritual and certainly it is not contrary to the Word of God; but what really matters is the end result. When December 31 comes around, how much of one's income has actually been spent on oneself and how much has been given to the work of the Lord? It is difficult to understand how $2,000 spent on a winter vacation in Acapulco or $50,000 spent on a beautiful yacht can be regarded as going into the Lord's work. James, the leader of the Jerusalem church, had some harsh words for Christians who spend their money on luxury and pleasure (Ja 5:1-5). There is no suggestion that God regards such money as going into His work. It is better to settle for a "legalistic" system of tithing and see to it that God actually gets His tenth, than to make all kinds of pious protests about everything belonging to the Lord and ending up by giving Him less than He demands.

The same principle applies to the use of the term *missionary*. There are those who advocate that we drop the word altogether. Others insist that it should be applied to all committed Christians. Stephen Neill has warned that if everybody is a missionary, nobody is a missionary. The Chinese have a proverb: "If two men feed a horse, it will lose weight; if two men keep a boat, it will soon leak." What is everybody's job is nobody's job. If every Christian is a missionary, missionary work is bound to suffer. It is correct to say that every Christian is, or should be, a witness. It is not correct to say that every Christian is a missionary.

An illustration may help at this point. During World War II there was in this country total mobilization. No sector of the economy, private or public, was exempt from the war effort. Whether a person was driving a truck, or digging ditches, or filing vouchers, he was part of the total war effort. But none of these persons was in the same category as the men in uniform, who were known as "soldiers." This term was not applied to everyone, not even to the workers in the munitions factories. It was reserved for the twelve million men under arms in the various branches of the Armed Services. Many of them never saw combat; some never even went overseas. The fact remains that by government statute they were in a class by themselves and played a unique role in the conduct of the war. No one suggested that "everybody" was a soldier. Soldiers were soldiers and civilians were civilians, even though both were totally involved in the war effort and, win or lose, shared the same fate.

The same kind of distinction should be made in the spiritual warfare in which we are engaged. The total resources of the Christian church should be thrown into the battle for the souls of men on a global scale, and every member of that church should regard himself as being involved in the total mobilization required by such an operation. But not every church member is a missionary. That term should be reserved for those who, like the soldiers in Uncle Sam's army, necessarily fill a unique role in the overall operation. In this sense it is helpful to retain the term *missionary* and to invest it with full and proper significance.

When we say that the missionary fills a unique role we do not imply that he is better than others, simply that he is different. He is not necessarily more spiritual than the pastor, or even the layman, who remains at home. Nor will his reward at the judgment seat of Christ be any greater. He is the servant of Christ and will be asked the same questions and judged on the same basis as anyone else. Did he seek to promote his own glory or was he concerned solely for the glory of God (1 Co 10:31)? Was he motivated by some personal considerations or was he constrained by the love of Christ (1 Co 13:1-3)? Did he do his work in the energy of the flesh or in the power of the Holy Spirit (Acts 1:8)? If he can answer all three questions correctly he will have his reward; otherwise his work will be judged to be wood, hay, and stubble to be consumed in the fire (1 Co 3:12-15). The missionary is not better than his fellow workers, just different.

The missionary in a cross-cultural situation finds himself filling several important roles.

1. He is an ambassador for Christ. The American missionary carries a little green book called a passport. It is issued by the State Department in Washington. It is his most precious possession. Without it he couldn't enter the country of his choice or get back into the United States. The American missionary is proud to be an American and is grateful for the services his government is prepared to offer, especially in time of war or revolution. That he is an American citizen is quite incidental to his mission. He might just as well be a Canadian or a Norwegian. More important is the fact that he is an ambassador for Christ.

His Sovereign is the Son of God who, in the Incarnation, became the Son of Man, that through His death and resurrection He might become the Savior and Sovereign of the world. One purpose of the incarnation was to bind the Strong Man, Satan (Mt 12:25-29), to destroy his works (1 Jn 3:8), his power (He 2:14), and ultimately his person (Re 20:10). By virtue of His glorious ascension He is now sitting on the right hand of the Majesty on high, far above all principality, and power, and might, and dominion (Eph 1:21). All power in heaven and on earth has been given to Him (Mt 28:18). By raising Him from the dead and exalting Him at His own right hand, God has forever established the universal Lordship of Jesus Christ (Acts 2:36). He is not only the Head of the church; He is also the Lord of history, the King of the nations, and the Judge of all the earth. In short, Jesus Christ is King of kings and Lord of lords. Sooner or later all men and nations must come to terms with Him (Ph 2:9-11).

To this end the King has given orders to His ambassadors. They are to go into all the world, preach the gospel to every creature, and make disciples of all nations (Mt 28:19). All men everywhere are required to repent and believe the gospel (Acts 17:30). Only by so doing can they be delivered from the dominion of darkness and be transferred to the kingdom of light (Co 1:13). Nothing short of world conquest is the ultimate goal, and the King has given assurance that one day the kingdoms of this world are to become the Kingdom of our Lord and of His Christ (Re 11:15). There is no ambiguity about the plan, no uncertainty about the outcome.

> Jesus shall reign where'er the sun
> Doth its successive journeys run;
> His Kingdom spread from shore to shore
> Till moons shall wax and wane no more.

The lowly missionary is the personal envoy of the Sovereign of the universe. His abode, even should it be a mud hut in Africa, a snow-covered house in Alaska, a cottage in the Amazon jungle, or a tent in the Gobi Desert, is the "residency over which waves the banner of his King and round which an angel keeps watch."

> This must ever be holy ground, even though all round be evil, for the Embassy is privileged land and here the Ambassador enjoys extra-territorial rights. No one may interfere in the correspondence and intercourse between him and his King. . . . His intercourse with his Sovereign is so safeguarded that no spy can overhear his reports or intercept his dispatches. At any moment of the day or night he may have audience with his King, secure His counsel, receive His instructions, and can never fail of His understanding sympathy.[4]

While the missionary has none of the outward accoutrements

---

[4] Mildred Cable and Francesca French, *Ambassadors for Christ* (London: Hodder and Stoughton, 1935), p. 153.

usually associated with diplomatic protocol, nevertheless his credentials are impeccable. He is the bearer of a divine revelation enshrined
in an infallible Book. He has the law of God in his mouth, the rod
of God in his hand, and the power of God in his life. His message,
given to him by his Sovereign, he delivers without fear, favor, or
flattery. The message itself is both clear and simple. In former times
God allowed all nations to walk in their own ways (Acts 14:16);
but since He has acted decisively in Jesus Christ He now commands
all men everywhere to repent (Acts 17:30), to turn from their dumb
idols to the true and living God (1 Th 1:9), and to acknowledge the
universal Lordship of Jesus Christ (Ph 2:9-11).

2. He is a herald of truth. Jesus Christ claimed to be the way, the
truth, and the life (Jn 14:6). He promised that men would know the
truth and the truth would make them free (Jn 8:32). He stated that
His purpose in coming into the world was to bear witness to the truth
(Jn 18:37). His kingdom is a kingdom of truth (Jn 18:36-37). It is
founded on an understanding of the truth (Jn 8:32). It is extended by
the preaching of the truth (Co 1:5-6). It is maintained by the practice
of the truth (1 Jn 4:1-6).

The missionary as an ambassador for Christ becomes a herald of
truth. When Jesus sent out the twelve apostles on their first preaching mission He gave them clear instructions: "What I tell you in the
dark, utter in the light and what you hear whispered, proclaim upon
the housetops" (Mt 10:27). The idea of a herald is that of a town
crier before the days of mass communications. He marched the length
and breadth of the town reading aloud a proclamation for the benefit
of the townsfolk. He did not invent or originate the message. He
simply proclaimed it. This is the responsibility of the missionary. He
does not invent his message any more than Paul did (Ga 1:1-10).
He has been told precisely what he is to teach and preach: all that
Jesus commanded (Mt 28:20). That includes all His major discourses,
public and private, including the Sermon on the Mount.

The modern missionary finds himself in an embarrassing situation.
In a pluralistic world it is becoming increasingly difficult to maintain
the truth of the gospel as over against the other faiths. It is considered
bad taste to suggest that one religion is true and all the other religions are partly or wholly false. No religion, we are told, has all
the truth and nothing but the truth; and to cling to such an outmoded
concept is to forfeit one's intellectual respectability. What is needed,
they say, is an eclectic religion that will incorporate the best elements
of the various faiths, including Christianity.

At the risk of being misunderstood the Christian missionary, in
all humility and sincerity, must insist on the truth of the gospel. If

other religions contradict Christianity they must be regarded as false, at least at the point of contradiction. Two contradictory statements on any subject cannot both be true. Both *may* be wrong. One *must* be wrong. The Christian faith is not true because the missionary says so, but because Jesus Christ, the King of truth, declared it to be so.

This question of truth is of immense importance. Stephen Neill said: "The only reason for being a Christian is the overpowering conviction that the Christian faith is true."[5]

That expression "overwhelming conviction" describes perfectly the mentality of the early church. The apostles believed with all their hearts that in the gospel of Christ they possessed the truth concerning God, man, sin, and salvation. By that truth they were determined to live; for that truth they were prepared to die. Jesus Christ was the way, the truth, and the life; and there was salvation only in Him. So far as the apostles were concerned there were many paths, but only one way; many prophets, but only one Savior; many religions, but only one gospel.

Their creed was simple but it was sufficient: "Jesus Christ is Lord." He stands in a class all by Himself. He occupies a solitary throne. He has no equals; He doesn't even have any rivals. And they came to this conclusion slowly, cautiously, painfully over a period of three years, during which time they saw Him under every conceivable condition of life. And the Resurrection clinched the matter for them. It was no "Easter story" that they believed, but a historic event of which they were eyewitnesses. They were there when it happened; it happened to them; and they were never the same again. The Resurrection is the keystone in the arch of the Christian faith. If it is a fact, Christianity is true; if it is not a fact, Christianity is false. The resurrection of Christ is one of the best authenticated facts of history. There is more and better evidence for the resurrection of Jesus than for the death of Socrates.

As a herald of truth it is the missionary's solemn but joyous task to proclaim to the entire non-Christian world the glorious news that Jesus Christ lived and died and rose again, and by so doing provided salvation for the whole human race. As a result whosoever will now call on the name of the Lord will be saved.

3. **He is an apostle of love.** Christianity is preeminently a religion of love. God loved the world and gave His Son (Jn 3:16). Jesus loved the world and gave Himself (Ga 2:20). Christians are called upon to do the same (1 Jn 3:16). Jesus said, "By this all men will know that you are my disciples, if you have love for one another" (Jn 13:35).

---

[5] Stephen Neill, *Call to Mission* (Philadelphia: Fortress Press, 1970), p. 10.

According to the apostle Paul love is the supreme virtue. It gives value to all the other virtues of the Christian life (1 Co 13:1-3). Indeed, without love the other virtues count for nothing.

As Christ was the embodiment of God's love, so the missionary is the embodiment of Christ's love. Jesus wept over the city of Jerusalem when it failed to respond to God's love. Paul could say of his unresponsive compatriots: "I have great sorrow and unceasing anguish in my heart. For I could wish that I myself were accursed and cut off from Christ for the sake of my brethren, my kinsmen by race" (Ro 9:2-3). And these very "kinsmen" were the ones who, time and again, tried to destroy him.

Missionaries have always been apostles of love. Count Zinzendorf, the greatest missionary statesman of the eighteenth century, said: "I have one passion, it is He and He alone." Hudson Taylor, who gave fifty years to the service of Christ in China, said: "If I had a thousand lives, I'd give them all to China." Alexander Mackay, writing to the Church Missionary Society, said: "My heart burns for the deliverance of Africa." Melville Cox died after being in Liberia only four months. His last words were: "Let a thousand fall before Africa be given up." Henry Martyn on his arrival in India said, "Now let me burn out for God." All these men were, like Paul, constrained by the love of Christ (2 Co 5:14) and they literally burned themselves out for God and man.

Nor was this love confined to a passion for *souls*. With the love of God poured into their hearts by the Holy Spirit (Ro 5:5), they overflowed with love to others—not just their souls, but their bodies as well. They loved them as persons, not just as potential converts; and they tried to minister to the needs of the whole man: body, mind, and soul.

The missionaries went where others would not go, and remained with the people they loved through famine, flood, plague, pestilence, and war. Often they endangered their own lives to save the lives of others. They may not have raised the dead; but they healed the sick, fed the poor, and clothed the naked. They cared for widows and orphans. They took in abandoned baby girls, fed, clothed, and educated them, and, when the time came, arranged suitable marriages for them.

Hundreds of missionaries became martyrs. In the Boxer Rebellion in China the Overseas Missionary Fellowship lost seventy-nine missionaries and their children in one year. When the storm blew over the remaining missionaries returned to their stations, asking for nothing but the privilege of serving the people who had killed their colleagues. When compensation was offered by the Chinese government it was refused.

During the Sino-Japanese War (1937-1945) hundreds of mission aries, many of them single ladies, opened their homes and compounds to Chinese women and girls in an effort to save them from the rapacious Japanese soldiers. Hector MacMillan, father of six children, was killed by the Simbas in Zaire in 1964. Undaunted, his wife returned to Zaire in 1966 to minister to the very people who had killed her husband. Rachel Saint and Betty Elliot took the gospel to the Auca Indians who murdered the brother of one and the husband of the other. Today the Aucas are Christians. Two of the children of the martyred missionaries were baptized by the men who murdered their fathers. Such is the power of Christian love.

During his exile on the Island of St. Helena, Napoleon remarked to a friend: "Alexander, Charlemagne, and myself all tried to found an empire on force and we failed. Jesus Christ is building an empire on love, and today there are millions of people who would gladly die for His sake." The missionary, more than anyone else, is helping to build that kingdom of love.

4. He is an envoy of peace. One of Christ's Messianic titles is Prince of Peace (Is 9:6). At His birth the angels sang about "peace on earth" (Lk 2:14). In His teachings He advocated peace (Mt 5:21-26). By His death He achieved peace between God and man (Co 1:20) and between man and man (Eph 2:14-15). Every kingdom known to man was founded on force and maintained by force. His kingdom was different. He would not resort to force nor permit His disciples to do so (Jn 18:36). He extolled the virtues of peace and pronounced a benediction on those who actively seek peace (Mt 5:9).

The kingdom that Jesus Christ is building on earth is a kingdom of peace (Ro 14:17), and the gospel that goes along with that kingdom is a gospel of peace (Eph 6:15). This peace has two dimensions, vertical and horizontal. Traditionally the conservatives have emphasized the first, the liberals the second. Both are part of the gospel; both belong to the kingdom.

The missionary, by virtue of his high calling, must be an envoy of peace. He bids men be reconciled first to God (2 Co 5:20) and then to one another (Ro 12:18). Sin brought discord into the world and set man against God (Eph 4:17-19). It also set man against man (Ro 3:15-18). The Fall not only separated Adam and Eve from God but produced enmity between Cain and Abel. Before man can be reconciled to man, he must first be reconciled to God.

The missionary, when he preaches the gospel of peace, hopes to achieve both dimensions of peace—the horizontal and the vertical. Consequently wherever he has gone he has tried to sow the seeds of peace between warring factions. He more than anyone else has been able to bridge the gap between the Jew and the Gentile, the Arab and the Jew, the Hindu and the Muslim.

Before the coming of the missionary, the South Sea Islanders constantly engaged in cannibalistic wars that decimated the population. Those wars suddenly ceased with the acceptance of the gospel. In the eighteenth century India was torn with strife caused by the contending European powers. Only one man, Lutheran missionary Christian Schwartz, was trusted and respected by the British, French, and Dutch on the one hand and the Hindu and Muslim leaders on the other. One of the Muslim princes, Hyder Ali, refused to deal directly with the British, saying, "Send me the Christian; he will not deceive me."

And what shall be said of China between 1910 and 1935, when warlords ravaged the countryside? During those years hundreds of missionaries were carried off by bandits. Some were held for ransom, others were killed, and still others died in captivity. Yet in the midst of all the turmoil the missionaries remained at their posts. On at least a half dozen occasions they offered their good services and effected a truce between the various warlords, thus preventing further destruction. In 1923 at the height of the troubles a group of missionaries signed the following declaration:

> The undersigned, American missionaries, are in China as messengers of the gospel of brotherhood and peace. . . . We therefore express our earnest desire that no form of military pressure . . . be exerted to protect us or our property; and that in the event of our capture by lawless persons or our death at their hands, no money be paid for our release, no punitive expeditions be sent out, and no indemnity be exacted.[6]

In more recent years the missionaries have continued their mission of peace. In civil wars in Nigeria, India, Pakistan, Burundi, Vietnam, and other countries they have protected national leaders, political as well as religious, organized and supervised refugee camps, and engaged in relief and rehabilitation. And working alongside the missionaries have been the national Christians, some of whom were themselves refugees.

5. He is a bearer of culture. In some circles this is a debatable subject. Anthropologists especially have been critical of the missionary for "interfering" with the indigenous culture. The missionary has been blamed for many things. Not content with saving their souls, he insisted that they wear clothes, learn English, cut out smoking, drinking, dancing, and carousing. In short, he presumed to change their whole life-style; and this, the anthropologists say, is bad.

First: In reply we would have to say that with or without intention

---

[6] R. Pierce Beaver, *Envoys of Peace* (Grand Rapids: Eerdmans, 1964), p. 29.

the missionary is *a bearer of culture*. It cannot be otherwise. No matter how hard he tries, he can never completely divest himself of his Western-Christian orientation. Sir James Jeans, leading astronomer in England in the 1930s, wrote a fascinating book, *The Universe Around Us*, in which he said that when a baby throws its rattle on the floor, it disturbs the molecular motion of every star in the universe! The author cannot vouch for the veracity of that statement; but he does know that something similar takes place when a missionary resides for any length of time in a "primitive" culture. Almost by a process of osmosis a transfer of culture takes place. He cannot walk down the street without arousing the curiosity of the populace. They are bound to ask questions, and from his answers they will make certain deductions. Already they are well on their way to being indirectly affected by the new culture that has appeared in their midst. Before long they will visit in his home, and they will be most unusual people if they don't want what they see there. The missionary's problem is not how to talk them into accepting his culture, but how to dissuade them from wanting it in the first place.

Second: It is simply not true that missionaries set out deliberately to change the indigenous culture. There were, of course, some who did this; but they should not be regarded as the norm for missionary behavior. The vast majority of missionaries were interested primarily in spiritual and moral renewal, not in cultural change *per se*.

Third: If the missionary only preaches the gospel and does nothing to help solve the social and economic problems of a backward people, he is accused of being pietistic and interested only in personal salvation. If on the other hand he introduces new tools and time-saving, money-making devices he is accused of interfering with the culture. Either way he is faulted.

Fourth: Is all cultural change bad? If the missionaries did wrong to share the good things of Western civilization with the Africans, the Africans now have their own sovereign, independent states and are free to revert to the kind of indigenous culture they enjoyed before the coming of the missionary. One does not observe any stampede in that direction. In fact, there is plenty of evidence that our friends in the Third World are determined to catch up with the West as fast as they can. At present there are 200,000 of them in Western countries studying our "advanced" civilization with a view to raising their own standards of living. They want all the mechanical gadgets of our technology from Parker pens to Phantom jets.

Fifth: Is the missionary not under obligation to minister to the needs of the whole man? Can he save his soul and refuse to heal his body or inform his mind? Should he leave the people to the tender mercies of the witch doctor or should he make available to them the marvelous discoveries of modern medicine? Is it wrong to teach people to build better and more durable houses, to use better seed and reap a bigger harvest? Is it wrong to eliminate malaria, typhus, yellow fever, and other equally devastating diseases? Is it wrong to teach a child to read?

To ask these questions is to answer them. The missionary made no mistake. He *is* the bearer of culture. He has not only an evangelistic mandate; he has a cultural mandate as well. He *is* his brother's keeper. The good things of life that he enjoys are not really his. They are God's gifts to mankind. It so happens that they occur in greater abundance in the Western world. This does not give us the right to keep them to ourselves. As followers of Jesus Christ we are duty bound to love our neighbors as ourselves (Mt 22:39), and we must love them in deed and in truth, not simply in word or speech (1 Jn 3:18).

If there is any doubt in our minds on this score, we have only to recall the teachings of our Lord, especially the parable of the Good Samaritan (Lk 10). The same emphasis is found in other parts of the New Testament. Paul declares that it is incumbent on Christians to do good to all men (Ga 6:10). The apostle John asks the question: "If any one has the world's goods and sees his brother in need, yet closes his heart against him, how does God's love abide in him?" (1 Jn 3:17).

Sixth: The missionary need not be either defensive or apologetic about being an agent of culture change. He is simply following in the footsteps of the Master.

> The fact is that the greatest cultural transformation in the history of mankind was brought about by a single Missionary, the Divine Legate Himself, Who declared Himself to be nothing less than "the Light of man" (John 1:4) and "the Way, the Truth, and the Life" (John 14:6), Whose mission it was "to cast fire" upon the earth until every tribe and nation, even those in the remotest corners of the earth, would be consumed by that "fire" (Luke 12:49).[7]

How Important Is a Call?

No aspect of the Christian mission is more puzzling than this problem of a call. It is the biggest hang-up that young people have as they face the claims of the mission field. At every panel discussion on missions the questions come thick and fast: "What exactly is a missionary call?" "How can I know that I have a call?" "Can I be

---

[7] Louis J. Luzbetak, *The Church and Cultures* (Techny, IL: Divine Word Publications, 1970), p. 5.

a missionary without a call?" These questions are asked by dedicated Christians who take the Great Commission seriously and genuinely desire to know and do God's will. The questions are fair questions; they deserve honest answers.

In dealing with this most important subject we must avoid two extreme positions. On the one hand there are those who insist that everyone must have what they call a "Macedonian call" such as Paul experienced at Troas (Acts 16:9-10). This is usually thought to be associated with voices, visions, dreams, and other mysterious happenings whereby a clear knowledge of God's will is directly and infallibly imparted to the consciousness of the seeking soul. Without this kind of esoteric experience it is impossible to receive a missionary call. Therefore everyone ought to seek such an experience and wait patiently until it comes.

At the other end of the spectrum are those who maintain that because all Christians are missionaries, no call of any kind is required. Missionary work is not different from any other kind of Christian service. Indeed, there is no essential difference between a missionary and a butcher, or a baker, or a candlestick maker. If you want to be a missionary, hop a plane, go where you like, and do your own thing when you get there. Don't get uptight about such trivial matters as time, call, place, board, ministry, etc. Just hang loose and assume that the Lord will guide.

Needless to say both positions are wrong. Those who advocate the first frequently end up by staying at home. Those who practice the second often do more harm than good on the mission field, and come home with a feeling of failure and frustration. The truth lies somewhere between the two extremes. This leads us to the first question.

IS A CALL NECESSARY?

Much depends on the kind of call one has in mind. The word *call* is used in many different ways in the New Testament. In most instances it refers to Christian life, not service. There is a general call of God (Ro 9:24-26) which became articulate in Christ (Lk 5:32). All believers are called to be saints (Ro 1:7), and the ultimate purpose of such a call is that they might be conformed to the image of Jesus Christ (Ro 8:30). In the meantime *all* believers are called to grace (Ga 1:6), peace (1 Co 7:15), light (1 Pe 2:9), hope (Eph 4:4), glory (1 Th 2:12), holiness (1 Th 4:7), liberty (Ga 5:13), and suffering (1 Pe 2:20-21).

In addition there is a second kind of call—a call to Christian service. This is not addressed to all, but only to those who are called upon to leave their ordinary occupation and devote themselves full time to what Peter called "prayer and the ministry of the Word" (Acts 6:4). All are called to be saints (Ro 1:7); not all are called to be apostles (1 Co 12:29). Paul in his epistles is careful to point out that he was a genuine apostle (1 Co 9). Moreover he insisted that he was an apostle by the will (1 Co 1:1) and calling (Ro 1:1) of God. He did not choose this high calling (1 Co 9:16-18), nor was it conferred on him by others (Ga 1:1).

He was an apostle "by the will of God," and he described himself as having been *made* a minister of the gospel (Eph 3:7). He was *appointed* to be a preacher, apostle, and teacher (2 Ti 1:11). It is true, of course, that he labored with his hands to support himself and his colleagues (Acts 20:34); but he did not regard tent-making as his vocation. He never referred to himself as a "tent-maker by the will of God," though certainly he did not take himself out of the will of God by resorting now and again to his old trade. He *was* an apostle; he made tents simply to pay the bills. And to his dying day Paul could never adequately express his utter amazement at the grace of God that made him a preacher and an apostle (1 Co 15:9-10; 1 Ti 1: 12-14).

The so-called Macedonian call (Acts 16:9-10) wasn't a missionary call at all. Paul had been a missionary for years before that. His call to missionary service coincided with his conversion, when God said to Ananias, "He is a chosen instrument of mine to carry my name before the Gentiles and kings and the sons of Israel" (Acts 9:15). This call was later confirmed by the Holy Spirit when He said to the leaders of the church in Antioch: "Set apart for me Barnabas and Saul for the work to which I have called them" (Acts 13:2).

What then was the nature of the Macedonian call? It was not a divine call at all; it was simply a human call for help. The call came not from God but from a "man of Macedonia." The plea was, "Come over to Macedonia and help us." This episode had nothing whatever to do with a missionary call. It was simply a matter of guidance to a man already in full-time missionary service. Paul had reached the extreme western end of the continent of Asia and had several options open to him. Apparently he had not given any thought to crossing over into Europe. Instead he attempted to turn eastward again, first into the Roman province of Asia and then into Bithynia; but the Holy Spirit prevented him in both instances. Where should he go? Obviously he was in need of special guidance if he were to take the gospel for the first time into Europe. The decision he was about to make was of such momentous importance that he required unusual guidance. This God gave him in the vision of the man from Macedonia. It is a great pity that this so-called Macedonian call should ever have been equated with a missionary call.

The term *missionary call* should never have been coined. It is not Scriptural and therefore can be harmful. Thousands of youth desiring to serve the Lord have waited and waited for some mysterious "missionary call" that never came. After a time they became weary in waiting and gave up the idea of going to the mission field.

Does this mean that there is no such thing as a call of any kind? No, indeed. There is a call, a very definite call, to the service of God on a full-time basis. Jesus "called" Peter and Andrew to follow Him. "Immediately they left their nets and followed him" (Mt 4:20). Later He "called" James and John. "Immediately they left the boat and their father, and followed him" (Mt 4:22). When Luke describes the same event, he says: "And when they had brought their boats to land, *they left everything* and followed him" (Lk 5:11).

It seems clear from this passage that this "call" involved a clean break with their previous occupation and launched them into a brand new occupation, that of "fishers of men." Apparently it was not possible for them to be fishers of fish and fishers of men at the same time. This does not mean that there was anything wrong with their previous occupation or that their new occupation was to be regarded as "higher" or "holier." It was a completely different occupation that would require all their time and energy. In present-day parlance it would be "full-time Christian service." It is worth noting that these four men and the other apostles never went back to their old occupations.

This idea of a call to Christian service is further strengthened by our Lord's attitude toward those who took it upon themselves to volunteer for His service. One fellow in a moment of enthusiasm said, "I will follow you wherever you go." Jesus replied: "Foxes have holes, and birds of the air have nests; but the Son of man has nowhere to lay his head" (Lk 9:57-58). Apparently the man withdrew his offer at that point.

Another person volunteered, "I will follow you, Lord; but let me first say farewell to those at home." Jesus replied: "No one who puts his hand to the plow and looks back is fit for the kingdom of God" (Lk 9:61-62).

There are those who object to the terms *secular* and *sacred* as applied to the vocational life of the Christian. To the dedicated Christian, they say, all vocations are sacred because whatever he does, he does it unto the Lord (Co 3:23). This, of course, is true. It does not, however, invalidate the distinction that the New Testament seems to make between secular and sacred ministries.

In several passages of his epistles Paul seems to make a distinction between the "spiritual" and the "secular" or "material" (Ro 15:27; 1 Co 9:11). In his own case Paul was conscious of having been appointed to a special ministry (1 Ti 1:12), that of teaching and preaching the Word (2 Ti 1:11). Moreover, he recognized the possibility that he might fail in the ministry (1 Co 9:27) and expressed the hope that he would be able to complete it (Acts 20:24), which he seems to have done (2 Ti 4:7).

He spoke of Epaphras as a "faithful minister of Christ" (Co 1:7; 4:12), a description he obviously did not apply to everyone. He reminded Timothy of his consecration to the gospel ministry when the elders laid their hands on him (1 Ti 4:14). There is nothing in the New Testament to suggest that men in secular employment were ever set apart to their work by the laying on of hands. This seems to have been reserved for those whose lifework was directly connected with the preaching of the gospel and the life of the church.

Apparently the apostles felt that there was something "sacred" or "special" about their ministry, for when the daily distribution of food threatened the unity of the church in Jerusalem, they refused to get involved in "serving tables." They said, "It is not right that we should give up preaching the word of God to serve tables" (Acts 6:2). Instead they decided that they would continue to devote themselves to "prayer and to the ministry of the word."

It is difficult to escape the conviction that the early church regarded "prayer and the ministry of the word" as being the equivalent of what we now call "full-time Christian service." All Christians are expected to work and witness for Christ regardless of their vocation; but only a few are called to leave everything and follow Christ in order to give themselves unreservedly to prayer and the ministry of the Word. It is important to preserve this distinction in a day when egalitarianism threatens to do away with *all* distinctions between the clergy and the laity in the Christian church.

WHAT CONSTITUTES A CALL
TO CHRISTIAN SERVICE?

The call to Christian service seldom comes as a meteor out of the blue. More often it is a growing conviction based on certain well-defined principles laid down in the Word of God. As one walks with the Lord in the light of His Word, he discovers that step by step he is led to the place where he hears the still small voice behind him saying, "This is the way, walk in it" (Is 30:21).

1. Acknowledgment of the claims of Christ. The very first step in the process is the recognition of the Lordship of Christ. "Jesus Christ is Lord," was the great affirmation of the early church. That one great fact ought to settle everything. He created me for His glory.

He redeemed me with His blood. He saved me by His grace. He keeps me by His power. Therefore He has first claim on my life. I am His personal property. Body, mind, and soul I belong to Him. He has the right to do with me exactly what He likes. I am His obedient servant. When He speaks, I listen. When He calls, I answer. When He commands, I obey. I have only one pertinent question to ask of Him: "Lord, what wilt Thou have me to do?" If He wants me in Christian service, I have no option but to obey.

2. **Understanding of the will of God.** God's will is twofold, general and specific. His general will embraces His plan and purpose for the whole creation. This is spelled out in broad outlines in the Scriptures. There is no mystery about it. It is plain for all to see. For instance, we know that God is not willing that any should perish, but that all should come to repentance (2 Pe 3:9). When we pray for the salvation of our loved ones and add, "If it be Thy will," we weaken our prayer. God has already told us that it *is* His will. With regard to His own children, we know that it is His will that *all* of them should be holy in character and conduct (1 Th 4:3). There can be no doubt about this.

In addition God has His specific will which differs with each individual Christian. "We are his workmanship, created in Christ Jesus for good works, which God prepared beforehand, that we should walk in them" (Eph 2:10). God has a tailor-made plan for the life of every believer. The details, of course, are not spelled out in the Scriptures. To ascertain the specific will of God the mind of the believer must be renewed day by day by an act of continual consecration (Ro 12:1-2). When discovered, that will proves to be "good and acceptable and perfect."

It is not easy to ascertain God's specific will. It takes time and discipline. Moreover, it is impossible to know God's specific will unless we are willing to bring our lives into conformity with His general will. Only when we do His general will, which we know, will He give us light regarding His specific will, which we don't know. It is at this point that many Christians go wrong. They pay little attention to what God has revealed regarding His general will, but spend much time and thought trying to ascertain His specific will.

3. **Susceptibility to the leading of the Holy Spirit.** What constitutes a call to Christian service? It is easier to ask that question than to answer it. Indeed, it is probably impossible to answer it to the satisfaction of everyone, for the simple reason that the call is communicated to the soul by the Holy Spirit, who works in different ways with different people. Speaking of the regenerating work of the Holy

Spirit Jesus said, "The wind blows where it wills, and you hear the sound of it, but you do not know whence it comes or whither it goes; so is everyone who is born of the Spirit" (Jn 3:8). The same element of mystery accompanies the consecrating work of the Holy Spirit. He works, moves, directs, and controls in His own sovereign way, and no one can be sure just when, where, or what His next move will be. For this reason it is dangerous to compare one Christian's experience with another's.

No two Christians are alike either in their conversion experience or in the matter of guidance that comes later. The Holy Spirit deals with each believer in a manner best suited to his needs and interests, his attitudes and aptitudes. It is therefore difficult to tell another person how the Holy Spirit is likely to lead him.

To most serious-minded Christians Jesus Christ is a "living, bright reality." Not so the Holy Spirit. He seems to be so distant, so ethereal, so unreal that many Christians aren't even on speaking terms with Him. John E. Skoglund calls Him "the missing person."[8] Indeed, that is precisely what He is to many Christians. Some of them would have to confess with the believers in Ephesus: "We have never even heard that there is a Holy Spirit" (Acts 19:2).

To the early church the Holy Spirit was not simply a power to be employed but a person to be loved, trusted, consulted, and obeyed. When the first church council wrote up its final report it said: "It has seemed good to the Holy Spirit and to us" (Acts 15:28). Imagine any church council talking that way today!

The Holy Spirit was as real to the early church as Jesus was to His disciples in the days of His flesh. He was indeed the "other Comforter" sent to take the place of the risen, ascended Lord (Jn 14:16). The early Christians had little difficulty in getting guidance. They lived on such a high spiritual plane that communion with the Holy Spirit was a matter of course. They confided in Him and He spoke to them. Their ears were attuned to the sound of His voice. When He spoke they listened and obeyed. One problem with present-day Christians is that we have failed to develop our spiritual faculties. We are so busy running here and there to get counsel and advice from pastors, teachers, and guidance counselors that we have neglected to listen for the still, small voice of the Holy Spirit. He speaks, but we are not listening. And all the while we wonder why we don't get a call to Christian service.

4. Confirmation by the local church. This is an aspect of the call to Christian service that is prominent in the New Testament but is

---

[8] John E. Skoglund, *To the Whole Creation* (Valley Forge: Judson Press, 1962), chap. 5.

almost completely missing in church life today. The classic example is the command of the Holy Spirit to the church in Antioch: "Set apart for me Barnabas and Saul for the work to which I have called them" (Acts 13:2). If the Holy Spirit has already called them, is that not enough? Why does the church have to get in on the act?

The reason is that the church is the pillar and ground of the truth (1 Ti 3:15). It is the channel through which God's saving grace flows out to a needy world (Acts 1:8). The evangelization of the world is not the work of a few individuals but the responsibility of the church as a whole. Paul and Barnabas were sent out by the Holy Spirit *and* the local church, and when they returned they made their report to that church.

All of Paul's co-workers mentioned in the Acts of the Apostles were identified with local churches. Timothy was "well spoken of by the brethren at Lystra and Iconium" (Acts 16:2). Epaphras hailed from Colosse (Co 1:7), Gaius from Derbe, and Sopater from Berea (Acts 20:4). When the fledgling church in Antioch was just getting under way, the church in Jerusalem sent Barnabas to help the believers there to get established (Acts 11:22). In the early church there were no "independent" missionaries. Each one was a member of a local church, approved by that church, and sent forth and supported by that church.

The call to Christian service can come only from the Holy Spirit, but there should be some kind of confirmation on the part of the local church of which the individual is a member. That church will know him best, and if its leadership is what it ought to be it will be in a position to give its blessing to those going into full-time Christian service. If this were done it would greatly strengthen the hands and encourage the hearts of young candidates for the Christian ministry. It would help to confirm the leading of the Lord given directly to the person himself.

CALL VERSUS GUIDANCE

A clear distinction must be made between a call to full-time Christian service and guidance. We have already stated that the "Macedonian call" in Acts 16 was not a missionary call at all, but simply a matter of guidance. The call comes once in a lifetime; and once it is understood and obeyed, it need not be repeated. But guidance is something that is required throughout the whole of life.

Where does the Lord want His servant to serve? At home or overseas? He can't be in both places at the same time, so guidance is needed. And even when he knows he will be serving overseas, he still needs guidance regarding the country to which he will go and the mission under which he will serve. These important considerations are not left to chance or even to the choice of the individual. God deploys His servants according to His own wisdom. He sent Paul to the Gentiles and Peter to the Jews (Ga 2:7-8). He directed William Carey to India, David Livingstone to Africa, and Hudson Taylor to China.

The missionary is not the only one who needs guidance. Those who serve at home need it just as much. Does the Christian worker become a pastor, an evangelist, or a Christian education director? Or should he teach in a Bible college or seminary? And if he goes into the pastorate, where will he minister? In Maine or California or Colorado? And how long will he remain in any one church? Five years? Ten years? Or thirty years? In all these momentous decisions the Christian worker is dependent on God for guidance. But this kind of guidance should not be mistaken for a call.

HOW DOES ONE RECEIVE
A CALL TO CHRISTIAN SERVICE?

God is sovereign in His choice of the servants who will serve Him. This does not mean that we sit down with folded hands and wait for some miraculous event to catapult us into the service of Jesus Christ. There must be on our part an attitude of receptivity and readiness so that when the call comes we will be in a position to hear and answer. The chances of our getting a call will be greatly enhanced if we meet certain conditions. Among these are the following:

1. **An open mind.** Everybody prides himself on having an open mind but few actually achieve it. Man's capacity for self-deception is enormous. We think we have an open mind while all along we are victims of our own prejudices and predilections. We have long ago decided that there are certain things we will not do. We wouldn't dare say it to God; but in our own minds we have decided, "Anything but Christian service," or "Anywhere but the foreign field." So long as we harbor preconceived negative notions about the will of God or the work of the church we shall wait in vain for a call.

It is incumbent on every young Christian to be absolutely honest in his dealings with God, to keep his options open, to allow the Holy Spirit to take full control of his mental faculties. This is by no means easy. In fact it is a never-ending battle. J. B. Phillips expresses it well: "Our battle is to bring down every deceptive fantasy and every imposing defense that men erect against the true knowledge of God. We even fight to capture every thought until it acknowledges the authority of Christ" (2 Co 10:5).

2. An attentive ear. An open mind is a great achievement, but it may still fall short unless it is accompanied by an attentive ear. It is not enough to rid one's mind of all "deceptive fantasies." We must also have our ear open to the voice of the Holy Spirit.

We know all too well that the hearing faculty can be turned on or off almost at will. It doesn't take much practice to sharpen one's sense of hearing provided there is sufficient motivation. In the dead of night the young mother can hear the cry of her firstborn son and is instantly on her feet to prepare the two o'clock feeding, while the father in the same room sleeps blissfully through the entire operation. What makes the difference? Do not both parents have the same hearing faculty? The maternal instinct in one parent sharpened her sense of hearing to the point where the slightest cry from the little one in the crib brought her out of bed. She slept, as we say, with "one ear open" while her husband slept with both ears closed.

The same thing can happen in the spiritual realm. With a little practice we can train ourselves to detect the slightest whisper of the Holy Spirit when He speaks to us. On the other hand we can turn a deaf ear to His entreaties. We need do this only two or three times and our hearing faculty will be so impaired that we will be beyond the reach of His voice.

Christians have been known to complain: "How is it that God speaks to others, but never to me?" It may be that God did speak, not once but many times, but they were not listening. Effective communication is possible only when the speaker and the listener are in direct contact. If only one is operating there can be no communication.

3. A pure heart. Understanding God's truth, or ascertaining God's will, is not a purely intellectual exercise. It has a moral dimension to it. God does not reveal Himself to every Tom, Dick, or Harry whose interest in His truth takes the form of intellectual curiosity. God reveals His truth not to those who want to *know* it but to those who are prepared to *do* it. The Jews of Jesus' day had difficulty in deciding the true origin of His teaching, whether it was from God or from man. Jesus said to them, "If any man's will is to *do* his [God's] will, he shall know whether the teaching is from God or whether I am speaking on my own authority" (Jn 7:17).

In the Hall of Science at the Century of Progress World's Fair in Chicago in 1933-34 there was a huge motto which read: "Nature reveals her secrets only to those who obey her laws." Every scientist knows the truth of those words. This truth, however, is not confined to the physical realm of science. It is likewise true in the metaphysical realm of theology. God reveals His truths only to those who obey His laws. One of His laws is that since He is holy (Ps 99:5) all who wish to have fellowship with Him must likewise be holy (He 12:14). King David asked: "Who shall ascend the hill of the Lord? And who shall stand in his holy place?" And the answer came back: "He who has clean hands and a pure heart, who does not lift up his soul to what is false, and does not swear deceitfully" (Ps 24:3-4). A pure heart is absolutely essential to communication between God and man—in either direction. The psalmist said: "If I had cherished iniquity in my heart, the Lord would not have listened" (Ps 66:18).

The person with unconfessed sin in his life will wait in vain for any call from the Lord, other than the call to repent (Is 55:7). For the Christian waiting for God's call it is not enough to have an open mind and an attentive ear; he must also have a pure heart, for only the pure in heart will ever see God (Mt 5:8).

4. Busy hands. There is a common saying that Satan is sure to find some work for idle hands to do. Doubtless there is some truth in the statement. If Satan prefers idle hands, God certainly does not. If the Scriptures are anything to go by, God's call comes to those who are busy, not idle. Moses, David, Peter, Matthew, and Paul were all engaged in some demanding work when the call of God came. He wants workers, not loafers, in His vineyard. Jesus Himself was the great Worker. He said, "My Father is working still, and I am working" (Jn 5:17). Again He said, "We must work the works of him who sent me while it is day; night comes when no man can work" (Jn 9:4).

Any person contemplating even the possibility of a call should begin by getting involved in some kind of work for the Lord. How is God going to call a person into full-time service if that person has never engaged in any kind of Christian work? One could begin by teaching a Sunday school class, or engaging in open-air work, or home visitation, or tract distribution, or rescue mission work, or leading a youth group, or helping in a vacation Bible school, or doing any one of the many things that need to be done in the local church.

In this connection it is instructive to observe that the vast majority of missionary candidates come from the Bible colleges, not from the Christian liberal arts colleges or the secular universities. Why is this? Doubtless the most important reason is that the Bible colleges require all students to engage in practical Christian work during their four years in college. During that time they gain courage, experience, and expertise. As a result they acquire a taste for Christian service, which they might never have done under different circumstances.

It is tragically possible for a student to spend four years in a Christian liberal arts college and never accept a single Christian service assignment, or attend a single missionary prayer meeting, or read a single missionary biography or periodical, or talk personally with a visiting chapel speaker, or even give his testimony in a class meeting. It is fair to ask: How is the Holy Spirit to reach that student with a call to Christian service?

5. Ready feet. The psalmist said: "I will run in the way of thy commandments" (Ps 119:32). Isaiah said: "How beautiful on the mountains are the feet of him who brings good tidings, who publishes peace" (Is 52:7). The time is short (1 Co 7:29) and the king's business requires haste (1 Sa 21:8). Indecision and procrastination have more than once played havoc with a call to Christian service.

Young people facing Christian service encounter two temptations. One is to run before the Lord; the other is to lag behind; for every one who succumbs to the first temptation there are ten who fall before the second. There are people who can't bring themselves to make a major decision such as that required to enter full-time Christian service. They examine all aspects of the situation; they pray about the matter; they discuss it with others; they do everything but come to a conclusion.

One problem is that they don't understand the true nature of divine guidance; consequently they are not prepared to step out in faith. They want to wait until their guidance is 100 percent certain; and that, of course, never happens. Guidance as granted by God is always perfect; but once it has filtered through the human mind it is no longer perfect. If one waits until he is *absolutely* sure of the Lord's leading, he will wait forever. Divine guidance is never 100 percent certain; if it were, where would faith come in? We must remember that the Christian walks by faith and not by sight (2 Co 5:7); which means that he must be willing to act on the guidance God has given and expect Him to be responsible for all the consequences that flow from his obedience.

Even Paul, when giving instructions regarding Christian marriage, was obliged to say, "I *think* that I have the Spirit of God" (1 Co 7:40). And after he received the so-called Macedonian call, Luke says, "Immediately we sought to go into Macedonia, *concluding* that God had called us to preach the gospel to them" (Acts 16:10).

Somewhere along the line the individual must make up his mind to act, to get going. It is always easier to steer a moving vehicle than a stationary one. Some would-be missionaries give the impression that they are waiting for God to pack their trunks, buy their tickets, and see them off at the airport.

2

Matters Relating to Recruitment

In North America there are almost five hundred missionary agencies involved in overseas operations. A small number of these occupy a supportive role and do little more than collect and distribute mission funds. The overwhelming majority are sending agencies that require both men and money.

Recruitment is a perennial problem with the sending agencies. To begin with, all missions have their share of dropouts. Although these are not as numerous as generally assumed, they do pose a problem. The average dropout rate is about 2.5 percent per year. The membership of the older missions is further depleted each year by two additional factors, deaths and retirements. Taken together these three factors represent an annual attrition rate of about 10 percent. This means that a large mission with eight hundred members requires eighty new missionaries every year just to maintain its existing work. If expansion is contemplated, additional recruits will be needed.

Recruitment is a long and costly process, especially for the interdenominational missions that do not have their own denomination on which they can rely for recruits. The candidate secretary has to visit ten or twenty colleges each year, speak in chapel, interview interested students, write follow-up letters, prepare literature, conduct seminars, process application papers, and finally make arrangements for candidate school in June. Very few missions are getting recruits in sufficient numbers to permit them to expand their program. If they manage to hold their own they are doing well. If it were not for the short-term missionaries the situation would be critical indeed. The short-terms-abroad program has become so popular that in some missions half the new missionaries going out each year are short-termers.

Most of the missions are now accepting short-term workers, who spend anywhere from one to three years overseas. This new program adds enormously to the burdens of recruitment, for it takes just as long to process the application of a short-termer as it does that of a career missionary. In the initial stages the new program works well; but after five or ten years the homebound traffic gets rather heavy. Instead of having to replace only 10 percent of the membership each year, it will become necessary to raise that to 20 percent.

If this trend continues the missions will have to devote more time and money to the task of recruitment.

Hang-ups Regarding Missionary Life

Of all the forms of Christian service the missionary vocation seems to inspire the greatest fear. Many a dedicated Christian has said in his heart, "I am willing, Lord, to be anything but a missionary." Somehow missionary work seems to be so difficult and so demanding that only the most courageous souls are willing to join up.

Missionary work, like many other things in life, looks more forbidding at a distance than it does close up. The hill that appears to be very steep from a distance has a way of flattening out as one approaches it. There are very few missionaries who would not have to confess that in the beginning of their career they had misgivings of one kind or another; but as they got into the work they discovered to their surprise that one by one the misgivings disappeared.

In this section we shall discuss only the more prominent hang-ups that trouble Christian youth today. These hang-ups, it should be noted, loom much larger for the career missionary than for the short-termer. One can endure almost anything if he knows beforehand it will last for only a year or two. One reason for the popularity of the Peace Corps is the fact that the term of service is only twenty-one months and then it's all over; but the volunteer has the satisfaction of knowing that he devoted two good years to helping others.

1. **Unconditional surrender.** The very phrase scares some people. The word *surrender* has a rather unfortunate connotation. For most people it carries with it the idea of conflict, crisis, and capitulation leading to permanent subjugation. Paul Little has suggested that we drop the word altogether and speak of *affirming*, rather than surrender-

ing to, the will of God. He may have a point. And the adjective *un-conditional* makes the idea more horrendous still.

The New Testament makes it clear that Jesus Christ is Lord and His Lordship extends to all of life. Either He is Lord of all or He isn't Lord at all. He won't play second fiddle to anyone. He even went so far as to say, "He who loves father or mother more than me is not worthy of me; and he who loves son or daughter more than me is not worthy of me" (Mt 10:37). In the New Testament we find the two words *master* and *servant* used in juxtaposition and the combination scares some people. These two words don't sit too well with modern man. They seem to be outmoded ideas.

The real question, however, is not semantic but spiritual. It has its roots in a false concept of the character of God. People seem to have the idea that God is a tyrant who takes sinister delight in inflicting His will on His children. He is just waiting for them to surrender. Then He will move in with all the power at His command, break their wills, destroy their plans, and forever crush their hopes beneath His feet; and for the rest of their days they will be required to grovel in the dust. They have a sneaking suspicion that they can't be a follower of Christ and have fun at the same time. If they once allow God to put them into a strait jacket, they will be doomed to a life of perpetual frustration.

That is one of the greatest lies ever perpetrated by the devil. He has succeeded in getting millions of Christians to believe that lie; and the result has been catastrophic, both for the individuals concerned and for the church as a whole.

It is true that Jesus spoke of self-denial, but *only as a way to self-fulfillment.* He said, "He who finds his life will lose it, and he who loses his life for my sake will find it" (Mt 10:39). Modern man, aided and abetted by the insights of psychology, is striving with all his might and main to achieve self-fulfillment; but he is going about it in the wrong way. He is seeking it directly and for its own sake; and it continues to elude him. For the Christian the way to self-fulfillment is by way of self-denial. This is one of the many paradoxes of the Christian life.

Far from being a tyrant, God is a loving heavenly Father. His lovingkindness is better than life; and His tender mercies are over all His works. Nothing is too great for His power; nothing is too small for His love. He desires our highest good; and to this end He plans for us in love. He would no more crush our hopes than an earthly father would crush the hopes of his children.

He knows all about our training and our talents. He knows us better than we know ourselves. He knows that we function best when we are well adjusted, not maladjusted. Certainly He doesn't have less compassion or less common sense than we do. It would hardly serve His purpose to have us end up as square pegs in round holes.

The most miserable person alive is not the sinner enjoying the pleasures of sin, but the child of God who is trying desperately to serve two masters. There is nothing in the world more frustrating. For the Christian there is only one road to self-fulfillment and that is by way of self-denial. His yoke *is* easy; His burden *is* light (Mt 11:30). His ways are ways of pleasantness and all His paths are peace (Pr 3:17). God's will is good, acceptable, and perfect (Ro 12:2). Samuel Rutherford said, "What a beautiful yoke are youth and grace, Christ and a young man." No man who followed Christ ever lived to regret his decision. Call it "unconditional surrender," or just "plain obedience," or anything you wish; it doesn't make much difference. To follow Christ is to walk in light (Jn 8:12).

2. Loss of personal freedom. We in the Western world are living in a period of unprecedented personal freedom. Today's youngsters don't want anybody—including their parents—to tell them what to do. And it all begins at an early age. The four-year-old boy accompanies his mother to the supermarket where he is allowed to choose one of twenty-nine kinds of cereal or one of fifty-seven varieties of cookies. When he gets home he may change his mind and refuse to eat them, in which case he will be given a second choice the following week. In this way he never learns to accept discipline, to knuckle down to authority, or to take "no" for an answer. After twenty-five years of this kind of treatment the young man can be forgiven if he has serious misgivings about joining a mission.

Today's youth are wary of anything belonging to the establishment. Missions, being part of the establishment, come in for their share of distrust. They are reputed to be conservative, paternalistic, even reactionary. They are accused of thinking in old categories and being unwilling to change with the changing times. They cling tenaciously to the outmoded principles and practices of the past and refuse to experiment with new methods and policies. Consequently the youth are turned off.

Mission boards are part of the establishment, all right; and most of the mission executives, through no fault of their own, are on the wrong side of thirty; but that does not mean that they are necessarily inflexible. The mission leaders with whom the author is acquainted are among the most progressive men in Christian service today. They are anything but inflexible. They are conservative in their theology but not in their methodology. Because they are committed to progress, they are open to change. With few exceptions they are aggressive, innovative, and dynamic. They don't pretend to have all the answers. They are just as eager to listen and learn as they are to speak and act. They welcome suggestions from all and sundry, including recent recruits.

A former student of mine spent a year in Japan as a short-term worker. He was amazed when he attended his first prayer meeting to hear a mission leader pray, "Lord, if we're doing anything wrong, show us, and we'll set it right." He soon discovered to his delight that this was the prevailing mood among the missionaries in Japan.

This is not to suggest that every missionary is a law unto himself and does that which is right in his own eyes. Every mission has its principles and practices which have developed over a long period of time. Policies hammered out on the anvil of experience are usually both sound and sane and in time will commend themselves to the new recruit. But there is nothing particularly sacred about such policies. They can be altered. Indeed they are altered from time to time. Most missions hold a top-level consultation at least once every five years, when anything and everything comes under review. Outmoded policies are discarded. New and innovative ideas are discussed and, if found to be workable, adopted.

As for the individual within a mission, it is fair to say that the missionary on the field has at least as much, maybe more, personal freedom than the pastor at home. He is expected to be in sympathy with the aims and policies of the mission, or he wouldn't have joined in the first place; but he is not placed in a strait jacket. There is an honest effort to reconcile group guidance with personal guidance; and if a worker is genuinely unhappy with his assignment, every effort will be made to accommodate him. If necessary he will be transferred to another city or another institution, or assigned to another kind of work. No one is required to remain at the same job year after year if he really believes he is out of the will of God.

It is interesting in this respect to learn that the missionary has much more freedom than does the Peace Corps volunteer. In the Peace Corps it is virtually impossible to have one's assignment changed. This is a source of great frustration.

3. Raising one's own support. The mainline denominations have a unified budget which takes care of all their missionaries; consequently no one is expected to raise his own support. Among the smaller, conservative missions, both denominational and interdenominational, the practice is for each recruit to raise his own support before proceeding to the field. Exceptions to this rule include the Christian and Missionary Alliance, Overseas Missionary Fellowship, and maybe one or two others. This policy of raising one's own support is a major hang-up with a growing number of potential missionaries.

They can't bear the thought of going from church to church, cup in hand like a mendicant, "begging" for support. It is embarrassing for the churches and humiliating for the candidates. At least this is what many people think. What are the facts?

It should be acknowledged that for many people this is a real hurdle that they are not sure they can clear. Some people by temperament find it distasteful to ask for help of any kind. They detest asking for money. Somehow it goes against the grain.

Raising support can be a long, tedious, discouraging pursuit, depending on the candidate's background and connections, his personality and speaking ability, the reputation of his mission, and the kind of work into which he is going.

There are just so many evangelical, missionary-minded churches to which the candidates can appeal. Many of them are fully committed already and cannot find room in their budget for another missionary. Not every church will give him a hearing; and not all churches in which he speaks will take on his support. Some won't even give him an offering to defray his expenses.

Raising one's support is costly in time and money. It may take twelve or eighteen months to complete the job. In the process it may be necessary to travel thousands of miles to reach the churches. During all this time where does he live and how does he support himself? If he is married and has a family his problems are compounded.

Some missionary candidates—not many—never succeed in raising their full support. After many months of fruitless effort they become discouraged and give up. They conclude that the mission field is not for them. This is not necessarily a bad thing. It may be God's way of indicating His will. In all his long experience the author has known only three persons in this category, and in each case there was a valid reason for the failure.

What shall be said about the positive side?

The vast majority of candidates succeed in raising their support without much trouble. Some complete the task in a matter of weeks; others take considerably longer. The important thing is that they make the grade.

Almost to a man those who succeed testify that the experience is enriching and rewarding from every point of view. They learn lessons of faith; they get answers to prayer; they have opportunities for witness they never dreamed of. When the ordeal is over they are better and stronger Christians.

In addition to raising their support, they make friends and acquire prayer partners who will stand by them for all the days to come. They may end up with two or three hundred names for their prayer letter list. This kind of support is as important as financial backing.

Contrary to popular opinion the candidate is not entirely on his own, nor does he have to start from scratch. Most of the larger missions have a candidate secretary who is responsible to help the candidate secure his support in the shortest time. The mission will not only stand behind him, it will go before him—writing letters of introduction, contacting pastors, arranging meetings, providing literature, slides, and other helps. Some of the larger churches take on the support of one or two new missionaries each year. To do this they usually get in touch with various mission boards asking for the names of prospective missionaries. In this way some candidates pick up half their support in one church.

There is no reason why the candidate should be embarrassed to make his needs known. When he does so he is on solid Biblical grounds. Moreover, he confers a privilege on the church when he makes it possible for its members to contribute to his support. The churches need to be constantly reminded of the word of our Lord: "It is more blessed to give than to receive" (Acts 20:35). When church members give to the support of a missionary they are laying up treasure in heaven. What they spend on themselves is lost forever.

One important aspect of deputation work that is often overlooked is the ministry the candidate has to the churches he visits. He goes to give as well as to get. It is always thrilling to see a young person in the glow of his first love preparing to go to the mission field. His testimony is bound to make an impression on the audience, especially any young people who may be present.

4. Inadequate financial remuneration. It is common knowledge that missionaries are among the lowest paid people in the world. Their support level is considerably lower than the income of a middle-class American family. What's worse, they don't always get their full support. Consequently they have to "live by faith," with a little help from the "missionary barrel."

Such a prospect is frightening to American youth who have been brought up in the lap of luxury and have been able to acquire anything their hearts desired. Money is no problem. Either they have their own or they can "borrow" from their parents. Teen-age America now has billions of dollars at its disposal annually, and it has created a subculture of its own. And the older generation is no better. They too are interested in shorter hours, longer vacations, and higher salaries. Compared with affluent Americans the missionary appears to be poverty-stricken.

Another unattractive feature is the practice of giving all missionaries the same allowance regardless of their position in the mission or their years of experience. There are those who advocate that this policy of equal remuneration for all should be abolished. Every missionary, they say, should be paid what he is worth. Only when such incentives are provided will we get the caliber of missionary we want.

Not many people are aware of the significant progress that has been made along these lines in recent years. In the first place it should be noted that the missionaries are better cared for than ever before. They will never get rich on what they are making, but their allowance permits them to live quite comfortably *in the society in which they reside*. To say that a missionary to India gets only two thousand dollars a year sounds incredibly low; but when it is remembered that the average per capita annual income in India is not much more than one hundred dollars, the picture changes drastically. It *is* possible for a single person to live comfortably in India on two thousand dollars a year.

This is not to say that the missionary on the foreign field enjoys all the amenities that go to make up the American way of life. Nor is it desirable that he should. His standard of living may be low by American standards, but in most cases it is high by the standards of the host country.

The missionary must be prepared to live the incarnational life and get as close to the people as possible; only then is he following in the footsteps of the Master who, though He was rich, for our sakes became poor that we through His poverty might be rich (2 Co 8:9). He warned us that a man's life does not consist in the abundance of things that he possesses (Lk 12:15).

It is difficult for the American Christian, accustomed as he is to his affluence, to take Jesus seriously. It is amazing what people can get along without and be happy. After only two years in China the author and his wife lost all their earthly goods and chattels in one day—thanks to the Japanese air force. They remained in China for another seven years without their possessions and never missed them. There are two ways in which a person may be rich. One is in the multiplicity of his possessions. The other is in the simplicity of his wants. Madison Avenue has brainwashed the American people, including not a few Christians, into believing that modern man cannot be happy without the toys and trinkets produced by a technological civilization. If nobody else is prepared to explode the myth surely the missionary should be.

5. Separation from children. This is the greatest single hang-up, especially for young mothers. They cannot bring themselves to contemplate the possibility of sending their children off to boarding school at the tender age of six or seven, after which they will see them only once or twice a year for short vacation periods. It seems to be so unnatural and unnecessary. Moreover, they have been led to believe that MKs have warped personalities and are not a very good advertisement for the gospel or the missionary vocation. Besides, one's first responsibility is to one's own family, not to the church, or the world; or even the work.

Having been through the experience of parting with his own two boys when they both went away to school at the same time, the author has no desire to deny the magnitude of this problem. It was the only thing he and his wife ever did in fifteen years in China that they thought of as a sacrifice. Having said that, it is necessary to place the problem in proper perspective.

To begin with, we must go back to the Scriptures and discover what Christ had to say about the matter. Few of His statements are stronger or clearer than His statement on family ties. "He who loves father or mother more than me is not worthy of me; and he who loves son or daughter more than me is not worthy of me" (Mt 10:37). However difficult it is to work it out in practice, we are forced to confess that all horizontal relationships must be subservient to the vertical relationship between Christ and the disciple. Nobody, not even the dearest person on earth, must be allowed to come between the disciple and his Lord. Jesus Christ must have first place in our affections as well as in everything else. Otherwise the Lordship of Christ is a meaningless cliché. This does not mean that we abandon our children or repudiate our parents (1 Ti 5:8); but it does mean that *in principle* we recognize the supremacy of Jesus Christ in *all* relationships of life.

Some missions permit the parents to choose for themselves how and where their children will be educated; others require the children to attend the mission school. The separation is not nearly so traumatic as some people imagine, either for the parents or for the children. If the children have been psychologically prepared for the event they may actually look forward to going to school. They not only survive; they enjoy life in school. In fact, the act of separation is usually harder on the parents than on the children.

Once the child makes the initial adjustment, which usually takes only a few days, he settles down to a life of comfort and contentment. He has other children of his own age, language, and culture with whom he can study and play. Classes are small enough to permit individual tutoring where necessary. Teachers are dedicated as well as competent. Homework is done together under supervision, which means that no one falls behind. And best of all—there is no television!

Houseparents are in charge of the dormitories and give themselves unstintingly to the children under their care. Each school has an infirmary with a registered nurse on call twenty-four hours around the clock. The larger schools have their own doctor on the staff. Everything possible is done to provide the children with a home away from home. It is no exaggeration to say that the MKs in a mission school are given more attention and security than the children in American suburbia.

There are several advantages to communal life. Discipline is no problem when it is applied across the board and everyone is doing the same thing at the same time. Children reared in that environment are apt to be less possessive, for they must share their things with others; they are more self-reliant, for they must make their own beds, clean their own rooms, and be responsible for their share of the daily chores. The author had two sons reared in China and one in the United States. He has no doubts about the relative merits of the two systems.

Schools for missionaries' children are not penal institutions nor are they reformatories. They are a combination of home, school, and church where the prevailing atmosphere is surcharged with Christian love. There is no need to shed any tears for the MKs on the mission field. They should be reserved for the "underprivileged" kids at home.

6. The lot of the single woman. Every woman, sometime in her life, entertains the hope of getting married and raising a family. This is her God-given right and privilege. Paul tells us that the man is not independent of the woman, nor the woman of the man (1 Co 11:11). They were made for each other and, other things being equal, function better as man and wife than as separate individuals. And this includes a great deal more than sex.

In the missionary body the women outnumber the men three to two, which means that one out of every three women missionaries is doomed to single blessedness for the rest of her life. Such a prospect can hardly be pleasing to the woman who goes out single. Her chances of getting married after she gets to the field are rather slim. With some women the desire to have a family is so strong that it overrides every other consideration. For all such persons the thought of going to the mission field single is horrendous. Single blessedness is not for everyone. Jesus said as much in Matthew 19:12. So did Paul in 1 Corinthians 7:9. No one should be criticized for leaving missionary service to get married. This is a matter between the individual and God. One missionary, after a frustrating term of service in Africa, came home on furlough vowing that she would not return to the field without a husband. She meant business, for when she failed to get a husband she refused to go back. Later on she achieved her ambition. She married a widower with three children and today is a pastor's wife and very happy. Who is to say that she did wrong—either in going to the field the first time or in refusing to go the second time? The final judgment in all such cases must rest with the Lord (1 Co 4:5).

On the other hand let no one jump to the conclusion that the single women on the mission field are pining for a husband. If marriage is what they wanted most they could have had it long ago. Hundreds of them had offers of marriage here in the homeland before they ever went to the field, but turned them down because they were convinced that the Lord wanted them in missionary work. Having once put their hand to the plow they refused to turn back.

And how does it work out when they sublimate their desire for marriage to the greater glory of God? For the most part it works out amazingly well. These single women are among the finest missionaries to be found anywhere. In spite of the handicaps under which they live, they do a remarkably good job. They are well-integrated personalities. They adjust readily to new circumstances and situations. They are cheerful, conscientious, hard-working, and co-operative. They have hardly any household duties to perform and no children to worry about; consequently they have more time to devote to the Lord's work. They are free to come and go as they wish. It is much easier for them than for married women to keep open house. In this way they get closer to the people, especially the women and children. Having more time to devote to language study, they usually become better speakers than the married women.

It is interesting to note in this connection that those missions that are working in the more primitive regions of the world, where both life and work are hard, usually have a higher than average ratio of women to men. In some missions they outnumber the men two and three to one. Pioneer work used to be reserved for single men; but now that they are a vanishing breed, much pioneer work has to be done by the single women. In fact, in many parts of the world they are doing the kind of work that should be required only of men. But they do it cheerfully as unto the Lord and ask no questions.

There are, of course, some disadvantages under which the single ladies must work. The first of these is a certain stigma that is associated with the single state in a culture where celibacy is unknown. The single person naturally sticks out like a sore thumb. Curiosity is aroused and embarrassing questions may be asked. However, this is not as troublesome as it might appear. When the questions have all been answered and rapport has been established, the single missionary fits into the landscape without much difficulty. Certainly in church circles her celibacy is understood. Then again, in the Buddhist countries of Southeast Asia and the Far East male and female celibacy is practiced in the *Sangha*—the monastic order. So in that part of the world religious celibates pose no problem.

In some parts of the world, especially where the Confucian ethic has spread, there is a clear line of demarcation between the sexes. Men fellowship with men, and women with women. In such a culture the single women missionaries find that much of their work is confined to the women and children. But this is no great drawback. The male missionaries can't very well minister to the womenfolk; so the single ladies concentrate on that segment of the population. So it works out quite well—the men missionaries ministering to the men and the women missionaries working with the women.

There is one other problem. In most parts of the Third World the Women's Liberation Movement is still unknown. Society is still dominated by the menfolk and the women are happy to have it that way. This means that when a church comes into being it too will be dominated by men. Naturally the leaders will have some difficulty in adjusting to the presence of women missionaries in the church. The latter will have to be as wise as serpents and as harmless as doves to work harmoniously with church leaders who are unaccustomed to dealing with women on a basis of equality.

When all is said and done, single women missionaries have a strategic role to play on the mission field, and with few exceptions they play it well. Young women looking forward to the mission field have nothing to fear. If they go at God's command, He will have a place for them to fill.

7. Fear of failure. So much has been said of the hardships of missionary life and the high qualifications for missionary service that many young Christians have been turned aside. They say to themselves: "If missionary life is that difficult, I might as well forget about it. I just don't have what it takes." The fear of failure is very real and acts as a strong deterrent. Through the years thousands of young people have been kept from going into missionary work because of a sense of inadequacy.

What about hardships? Are they really as great as we have been led to believe? Much depends on what part of the world one has in mind. The missionaries in Japan have all the amenities of modern life that we enjoy here in the United States. The climate is moderate; the food plentiful and nutritious. The trains are newer, cleaner, and faster than ours. The literacy rate is the highest in the world. The architecture and the gardens are exquisitely beautiful. The people are clever, courteous, industrious, and immaculately clean. Hardship? The two thousand missionaries in Japan don't know what it is.

There are, of course, other parts of the world where life is not quite so pleasant; but even there the picture has often been overdrawn. Most missionaries would have to acknowledge that upon arrival in the host country they found conditions better than they expected. Even in very primitive areas the missionaries manage to surround them selves with some of the *basic* comforts and conveniences of life.

More important is the fact that the human organism possesses an amazing capacity for survival. It does not die easily! Given time and patience the individual can adjust both physically and psychologically to almost any kind of environment. Upon arrival the appalling poverty that abounds on every hand seems to rise up and smite the new missionary in the face. The fact that the missionary with his meager resources cannot possibly alleviate the poverty only serves to aggravate the situation. But after a while he becomes inured to the strange sights and sounds and doesn't even notice them. That is nature's way of protecting the sensitive soul from the abrasive elements in the environment.

In addition to nature's healing ways there is the grace of God. Paul found it sufficient for him in his day, even with his thorn in the flesh (2 Co 12:9). Thousands of veteran missionaries can testify to the fact that Hudson Taylor, who spent fifty years in China, hit the nail on the head when he expressed his missionary creed in four clauses: "There is a living God. He has spoken in His Word. He means what He says. And He always keeps His promise."

The missionary does not go out alone, nor in his own strength. He is sent by the living Lord (Jn 20:21), who has promised to be with him to the end of the age (Mt 28:20). The Captain of his salvation is the same yesterday, today, and forever (Heb 13:8), and He has promised never to leave him nor forsake him (He 13:5). He will perfect that which concerns him (Ps 138:8). He will deliver him from every evil work and preserve him unto His heavenly kingdom (2 Ti 4:18).

If the misisonary is a missionary by the will of God, as Paul said he was, he need have no fear of failure. God will lead him in triumph (2 Co 2:14) and give him the victory (1 Co 15:57). It makes no difference whether it is a matter of learning a difficult language, or adjusting to a strange culture, or living with loneliness, the grace of God and the power of Christ can make the missionary more than conqueror (Ro 8:37) .

Obstacles to a Missionary Career

When the potential missionary has exploded all the myths and gotten rid of all the hang-ups, he is still not out of the woods. Even after he has dedicated his life to the Lord for missionary service there may still be obstacles in his way. As we sometimes say—there is many a slip 'twixt the cup and the lip. So there are many pitfalls between the decision to be a missionary and arrival on the field.

It has been estimated that for every hundred persons who dedicate their lives for missionary work only one actually gets to the field. It is impossible to say how accurate that figure is, for there is no possible way to check it; but it is safe to say that only a fraction of those who declare their willingness to go to the mission field ever get there.

There are many reasons for this. In the first place time is always a factor. Many persons register a decision in their teens before they realize what it is all about. Such a decision may not have been of the Lord to begin with. Others make the decision in good faith only to find it fade with the passing of time. Still others, for no particular reason, drift along with the crowd and eventually end up in secular work. And still others get into Christian work at home. The reasons are legion. We shall discuss only some of the more common obstacles.

1. Advanced education. Education is a splendid thing and every prospective missionary should get as much as he possibly can before going to the field. Most Americans contemplating missionary service will want to have at least a college degree. Up to this point they are fairly safe; but for every year they remain in this country after that their chances of getting to the field are correspondingly diminished. What is the reason for this?

It usually requires two full years to get an M.A. degree. During that time many things may happen to the prospective missionary. He may become so absorbed in his studies that he loses sight of the mission field and ends up in a teaching position here at home. If he goes off to seminary it will take him three years to graduate. During his seminary years he will be exposed more to the opportunities of the pastorate than to the claims of the mission field. He may decide that the Lord has called him to be a pastor, not a missionary.

And if he stays around long enough to get a Ph.D. his chances of getting to the mission field are drastically reduced. By this time he will have become a scholar, more interested in the pursuit of knowledge than in the propagation of the gospel. It *need* not be that way; it *should* not be that way; but in fact it often turns out that way. Most evangelists are not scholars; most scholars are not evangelists. The ideal missionary is one who has the mind of a scholar and the heart of an evangelist. Alas, that combination is very rare.

The person with advanced degrees may easily assume that the mission field does not offer sufficient scope for his many talents. To make the best use of his education he should remain at home where he can teach in a prestigious university.

This does not mean that any of these persons is necessarily out of the will of God. The Lord may have called them to teach in a university or to pastor a church. If so, there can be no quarrel with them. The fact remains—they are lost to the mission field.

2. **Accumulation of debts.** "Buy now and pay later" is the foundation stone of the American free enterprise system. With every passing year it becomes easier and easier to do just that. The only exception to this rule is the funeral service! And before long they may devise a way of taking care of that too.

The cost of higher education has risen so much in the last decade that tens of thousands of college students have been obliged to borrow money to put themselves through school. Uncle Sam doesn't charge any interest on his loans until after graduation; and if the borrower teaches public school his loan is reduced by 10 percent each year. With inflation as rampant as it is, it pays the student to borrow money rather than work for it.

This kind of arrangement is excellent for the average student. With a college degree under his belt he will be able to command a good salary and repay his loan in two or three years. But what about the prospective missionary who majors in Bible or missions? When he graduates he goes into Christian service where the salary scale is much lower than in business or the professions. If he has accumulated a sizable loan it may take him five or six years to liquidate it. By that time he may have settled down in the pastorate and decided to stay.

No reputable mission board will accept a candidate with a debt over his head. He must be free of all debts before he is permitted to proceed to the field. One candidate secretary has gone on record saying that he personally never knew of a single missionary candidate with a sizable debt who ever got to the mission field. It takes too long for Christian workers to liquidate their debts.

Prospective missionary doctors are particularly vulnerable at this point, and for two reasons. First, their academic career is so long that they are pushing thirty by the time they are ready to practice. Second, the cost of that kind of education may run as high as forty or fifty thousand dollars. Unless he has a rich uncle the medical student will have to borrow most of that money; and it will take him years before he is free of debt. By that time he will be pushing thirty-five, will have begun to raise a family, and will have established his own practice. To pull up stakes at that point and give up a lucrative profession to move to the mission field is a difficult decision to make. This is why medical missionaries today are in such short supply, and why mission after mission is crying out for them.

3. Love and marriage. Only the Lord knows exactly how many people have fallen by the way on this account. But the number must be very high. According to several recent studies a significant number of persons who opt for the mission field make their decision during their teens before they ever get to college. While in college they make many friends and in the process may fall in love. The other partner may be a good Christian but one who has no call to full-time Christian work and certainly no intentions of going to the mission field.

Occasionally the missionary-minded student will win the other partner to his or her point of view, and together they will prepare for missionary service. They may even get married before leaving for the field. But that is the exception, not the rule. Oftener than not the missionary-minded one gradually loses his missionary vision and is lost to the mission field.

There are, of course, some shining exceptions. The author personally knows of a number of persons whose dedication to the Lord and His service was strong enough to overcome every other consideration. Some of these went to the mission field at great sacrifice to themselves only to find that the Lord had someone waiting for them when they got there. Others have waited patiently for years until the Holy Spirit spoke to the reluctant partner and he or she eventually joined them on the mission field.

Others get married when they are quite young and by the time they are ready to go to the field they have two or three children. This may pose a problem, depending on the mission of one's choice. A generation ago this problem did not not exist. At that time the vast majority of candidates were young and single. Today's youth are marrying at a younger age, many of them while still in college. Moreover, more of them are remaining at home for an extra year or two to pick up an advanced degree. Consequently it is not uncommon for candidates to have one or two children by the time they apply to the mission.

As might be expected, policy differs from mission to mission. There are not more than one or two boards that will accept a couple regardless of the number of children they have. Most boards draw the line at two; some reduce it to one. There are a few boards that refuse to accept a couple with even one child.

In this, as in most other things, the mission boards have good reasons for the policies they adopt. Experience has taught them that adjustment to a different culture and the learning of a foreign language are achieved with greater facility and success if the persons involved can give all their time and thought to the business at hand. Young mothers with children seldom achieve either accuracy or fluency in a foreign tongue; and this, of course, hampers their usefulness for the whole of their missionary career.

4. Parental opposition. This is a greater obstacle than most people think. There are two kinds of opposition. One kind comes from non-Christian parents who have no use for religion, much less missions. The other comes from Christian parents, some of them evangelical, who believe in missions but are unhappy when *their* children become involved.

In the case of non-Christian parents, sometimes the opposition assumes violent, almost paranoiac, proportions. The author is personally acquainted with fellows and girls who have been locked out of their own homes for no other offense than announcing their intention to become missionaries. Some have been completely disowned by their families. Others have had their names removed from their father's will.

One mother was so sick at the thought of her daughter's going to the mission field that when it came time for her to leave the mother went to bed, turned her face to the wall, and refused to say good-bye. For seven years the daughter wrote regularly to her mother; but she didn't get so much as a postcard in reply. It was not until she returned on furlough that the mother finally relented and was reconciled to her daughter. This is by no means an unusual case.

The opposition that comes from Christian parents is more silent and more subtle but none the less damaging. Such parents are in favor of Christian missions and give generously to the cause; but they are less than happy when their *own* son or daughter decides on a missionary career. That brings the matter a little too close to home. Missions is all right for the other fellow's son or daughter but not for theirs. They have grandiose plans for their children and these don't include the mission field. The father may want his son to succeed him in the business, which may have been in the family for several generations. The pressure generated by this kind of situation is sometimes harder to resist than the outright opposition of non-Christian parents.

What should young people do when they find themselves in that kind of predicament? Filial piety is a Christian virtue, and under ordinary circumstances children are obliged to obey their parents, especially when they are Christians. But nowhere does the Bible suggest that parents, Christian or non-Christian, have the right to come between their children and the will of God. From a purely human point of view it is wrong for parents to force their plans on their children. It is doubly wrong when those plans run contrary to the will of God.

If the parents are old, or ill, or poor, or for some other reason are absolutely dependent on their son or daughter for their livelihood, then the young person should give serious consideration to what Paul had to say to Timothy: "If any one does not provide for his relatives, and especially for his own family, he has disowned the faith and is worse than an unbeliever" (1 Ti 5:8). After much prayer and soul-searching he may decide that the Lord would have him remain at home, at least for the time being, to fulfill his Christian duty to his parents. Missionaries in mid-career have been known to remain at home for five or ten years to minister to the needs of aging parents. But 1 Timothy 5:8 should not be applied to well-meaning but self-centered parents who are unwilling to give their children to the Lord for His service.

In that case the young person should be guided by the words of Christ: "He who loves father or mother more than me is not worthy of me; and he who loves son or daughter more than me is not worthy of me" (Mt 10:37).

It should, however, be borne in mind that when we obey the teaching of Scripture the Lord has a way of working on our behalf and giving us the desire of our hearts (Ps 37:4). And in the case of those who have left family and loved ones He has given His word of promise: "Truly, I say to you, there is no one who has left house or brothers or sisters or mother or father or children or lands, for my sake and for the gospel, who will not receive a hundredfold now in this time ... and in the age to come eternal life" (Mk 10:29-30).

God is no man's debtor. He has said, "Those who honor me I will honor" (1 Sa 2:30). If we obey Him, He will be responsible for all the consequences that flow from our obedience. Missionaries have given their children to the Lord only to find that He takes better care of them than they themselves could have done. There are missionaries who have given up parents only to find that He makes ample provision for them, far exceeding anything the missionaries could have asked or thought (Eph. 3:20).

On the other hand, parents have refused to allow their children to go to the mission field only to find that the children turned out to be a sorrow to them in their old age.

5. Health problems. Most mission boards maintain high health standards and anyone who falls below them is rejected. The health standards maintained by the Peace Corps are considerably lower than those demanded by the average mission board. The Peace Corps volunteer spends only twenty-one months overseas, whereas the missionary usually serves for life; and this makes a big difference.

Mission boards have been criticized for rejecting people on health grounds; but experience has taught them that a poor risk can turn out to be very costly, not only for the mission but also for the missionary. Missions are supported by the churches, and they feel an obligation to be faithful in the exercise of their stewardship.

The average missionary doesn't reach his full potential until his second term of service. To send a family to the field, and keep them there for four years, is a costly undertaking. It might run as high as $30,000. If for any reason the family doesn't return for a second term that huge investment is lost. Little wonder that the mission boards are reluctant to take the risk of accepting a person with a health problem.

Mission boards are not infallible, and so they make mistakes. One man from Scotland was turned down by the China Inland Mission but accepted by the British and Foreign Bible Society, with whom he served for thirty years in Singapore. On the other hand missions have been known to accept persons who seemed to be in good health only to discover that they cracked up within a year.

It is always disappointing for a young person to pass all the other tests and then to be rejected on health grounds. More than one young lady has dissolved into tears when the final verdict became known. It is equally disappointing for the mission. Good candidates are not so plentiful that mission boards can afford to turn them down. It is an agonizing decision to make.

The candidate who has offered for overseas service and has been rejected at least has the satisfaction of knowing that he followed the Lord to the end of the trail and gave up only when the way was closed. Such people usually find their way into some form of full-time Christian service at home. They never lose their interest in missions and quite frequently are instrumental in sending others to the field. So the venture is by no means lost. And the Lord will say to all such persons, as He said to David, "You did well that it was in your heart" (1 Kg 8:18).

6. Lack of direction. Modern youth is restive, uncertain, confused, and sometimes frightened. Human problems are so enormous that they defy solution. Personal options are so numerous that they cause confusion. And today's young people are caught between the problems and the options and hardly know how to relate the one to the other. In such a complex situation it is difficult to make up one's mind. It is not uncommon for students to reach their senior year and still not know what they are going to do. By the time June rolls round they are in the throes of "senior panic."

One problem is that today's students, with their knowledge of psychology, anthropology, and sociology, are tempted to lean on their own understanding (Pr 3:5) rather than look to the Lord for His direction and guidance. Some years ago a student of mine was approaching graduation and was still uncertain about his future. He was a good Christian fellow who, when he entered college, had definite plans to enter the ministry. Now he was not so sure. So I asked him, "Jim, do you ever pray about this matter? Have you ever asked the Lord to guide you with regard to your lifework?"

He replied, "Oh, I take God for granted. He is always in the back of my mind. I make my decisions as best I can in the light of what I know about myself, and I trust Him to keep me from going wrong."

Then again, there is the problem of understanding what Christian missions is all about. There are many fine Christian students today who have a passing interest in missions and from time to time have an urge to participate; but they don't have sufficient information to enable them to make an intelligent decision one way or the other. Their knowledge of missions is derived largely from missionary speakers in church or chapel whose messages tend to center around their own local work. Seldom do they hear a message that deals with the major issues of Christian missions on anything like a global scale. Consequently their knowledge of missions is fragmentary and superficial. What they know seems to intrigue them; but they don't know enough to enable them to make a definite commitment.

There is no substitute for knowledge. The best form of inspiration is information. Alas, it is possible for students to attend a Christian liberal arts college for four years and never be required to read a single book on church history or world missions. It is pertinent to ask: "In what sense is a college Christian if it does not include in its offerings those courses which might conceivably lead the graduates into full-time Christian service, either at home or overseas?" This is usually left to the inspiration provided by chapel services, prayer meetings, and spiritual emphasis week. These are good, to be sure, but hardly provide a solid foundation on which to build a missionary vocation.

7. Lack of Bible training. The conservative mission boards require their candidates to have a working knowledge of the Bible. The absolute minimum is one year of formal Bible training. Some Bible colleges have a special one-year program designed to meet this particular need. Several seminaries now have a one-year program in Biblical studies leading to a Master of Arts in Religion degree. The ideal preparation for missionary service is four years of liberal arts and three years of seminary with a concentration in missions. In this way the candidate gets a good foundation in all three major areas: liberal arts, theological studies, and missiology. Another very acceptable program is that offered by the four-year Bible colleges. Traditionally they have provided the lion's share of missionary candidates for the conservative missions.

Even specialists, such as doctors and nurses, are required to have *some* Bible training. The rationale for this requirement is that the candidate is first a missionary and only secondarily a doctor or a nurse or some other specialist. Consequently he is expected to have a good grasp of the major doctrines of the Christian faith and be able to explain them to others. The year of extra study will also provide an opportunity to pick up some courses in personal evangelism, non-Christian religions, and cross-cultural communications, all designed to help him articulate his faith when he gets to the mission field. Without this additional training he may be a competent doctor, but he will be a poor communicator. To be a *missionary* doctor he ought to be good at both.

The problem arises when a graduate of the secular university offers for missionary service. His academic record may be impeccable, but because he lacks Bible and theology he is disqualified. Even a person from a Christian liberal arts college will run into trouble at this point. Unless he has majored in Bible he will have only two or three Bible survey courses to his credit, and that is not enough. So the mission board says to the candidate: "Fine, you have a good, sound liberal arts education; now you must go back to school to get at least one year of concentrated Bible and theology."

With some people this is no great problem. They understand the reason for the requirement and are quite willing to cooperate. They are still young and consequently not averse to returning to school for another year. With others it may be a problem, depending on age, finances, and family circumstances, etc. Some people have been in school so long that the thought of another year of the academic rat race is not a pleasant prospect. Others simply balk at the requirement and withdraw their offer for missionary service.

8. Lack of practical experience. There is a growing recognition on the part of educators of the importance of in-service training. The American Association of Theological Schools is now insisting that all its member schools strengthen their field education programs. The minimum requirement is nine hours of field education under proper supervision. To put teeth into the program academic credit is given.

One of the outstanding features of the Bible college movement has been the insistence on Christian service. Every student is required to engage in some form of Christian service during his entire course of study. Up to this point it has not carried academic credit; but it has been required right across the board. The theories learned in the classroom are tested in the laboratory of experience. In this way the student gains valuable experience while he is learning. In fact, learning by doing is now an accepted principle of modern pedagogy. The student with three or four years of experience in Christian service makes a better missionary candidate.

Most Christian liberal arts colleges have a Christian service department. While Christian service is not required, it is definitely encouraged. It is estimated that about 50 percent of the students engage in some form of Christian service during the course of the academic year.

It goes without saying that the secular universities have no such program. Christian students in these institutions can, if they wish, find their own Christian service; but not many go to the trouble.

The missionary candidate who has had little or no practical experience will encounter grave difficulty when he meets the mission board. Even if he is qualified in all other respects he will not be accepted without sufficient practical experience. What usually happens is that the board will accept him *tentatively* on condition that he spend eight or nine months at Missionary Internship in Detroit. There he will be placed in a church where he will work closely with the pastor and engage in the various kinds of ministry usually connected with the local church. During this time he will be under the supervision of Missionary Internship personnel. When the period is over MI will evaluate his work and send a report to the mission. If the report is favorable his tentative acceptance will be changed to total acceptance; if not, he will be turned down. It is important that young people looking forward to missionary service should get as much practical training as possible during their college career.

So important is Christian service training that some mission boards now require all candidates, regardless of their background or experience, to spend two years in the pastorate before going overseas. This is particularly true of all missionaries looking forward to church-planting work.

9. Attractive offers at home. This is the final hurdle and many a young man has failed to clear it successfully.

It is an excellent idea to get two years of experience in some form of ministry in the homeland before proceeding to the field; *but* during that time many things can happen. Some candidates get married to a person who does not share their missionary vision. Others become so absorbed in the work they are doing that they lose contact with the mission and by and by lose their missionary burden. Still others are so successful that the churches are reluctant to release them when the two years are up. Not all churches are as magnanimous as the one in Antioch, which was willing to part with its best teachers,

Barnabas and Saul, when the Holy Spirit called them into missionary service (Acts 13.1-3).

Not a few missionary candidates have ended up in the pastorate here because of the pressure brought to bear on them by well-meaning but short-sighted churches. The author knows of one large church that offered its youth director a substantial increase in salary if he would give up the idea of going to Africa. Fortunately he had the fortitude to stick to his guns and do what he believed the Lord wanted him to do.

The longer the missionary candidate remains in Christian work at home and the more successful he is, the greater is the temptation to remain in this country.

Qualifications for Missionary Service

In the nineteenth century the missionary was regarded as a hero. It was assumed that he was an intellectual and spiritual giant, more dedicated, more courageous, and more spiritual than his counterpart, the pastor here at home. Today the pendulum has swung in the opposite direction, and today's missionary is in danger of being reduced to the status of a "humdrum worker in the vineyard of the Lord." Students returning from a summer of missionary work overseas report that their greatest discovery was that missionaries are human after all. In our reaction against the adulation of the past we may be in danger of underestimating the qualities of today's missionary.

Stephen Neill, himself a missionary of no mean stature, wrote:

> I may place on record my conviction that the needs of the mission field are always far greater than the needs of the Church at home, that no human qualifications, however high, render a man or woman more than adequate for missionary work, that there is no career which affords such scope for enterprise and creative work, and that in comparison with the slight sacrifice demanded, the reward is great beyond all measuring.[1]

Most mission societies screen their candidates very carefully. This they do for two reasons. First, they want to reduce as far as possible the number of dropouts. Second, they want to be sure that they get the highest possible caliber of missionary. The best is none too good for the mission field.

There are almost five hundred missionary agencies based in North America. Naturally they don't all have the same standards. Some accept only seminary graduates. Others will accept college graduates.

---

[1] Stephen Neill, *Builders of the Indian Church* (London: Edinburgh House Press, 1934), p. 4.

Still others, with lower standards, accept Bible school graduates. Some insist on very high academic qualifications but don't worry too much about spiritual qualifications. Others are very particular about spiritual qualifications but don't hassle over academic qualifications. There are others that do their best to maintain high standards in both areas.

The perfect missionary has not yet appeared on the scene; and it would be foolish and futile to insist on standards bordering on perfection. On the other hand it would be a grave mistake to suggest that any Tom, Dick, or Harry, without any special training or any particular qualifications, can make an acceptable missionary. He need not be a genius; but he had better not be a dunce either.

The qualifications of a good missionary break down into several categories.

1. Physical qualifications. High schools, colleges, the Peace Corps, and the United States Army all require a physical examination before accepting the applicant. The reasons for this are obvious. Mission boards have additional reasons to be careful about the health of their applicants. Life on the mission field, with few exceptions, is harder on one's health than life here at home. Contributing factors include hot, humid climate, poor food, contagious diseases, and lack of public sanitation. Medical facilities are either nonexistent or in short supply. Some families live in isolated areas where the nearest doctor or hospital may be a three-day journey away. When casualties occur they are very costly to both the missionary and the mission.

For this reason all missions require a complete medical checkup. They are particularly wary of any signs of high blood pressure, impaired sight or hearing, nervous disorders, allergies, etc. Physical deformities such as blindness, deafness, artificial limbs, etc., are almost sure to disqualify the applicant. Some physical defects can be removed by surgery, after which the applicant will be accepted. The candidate doesn't have to be a physical giant or have a near-perfect physique; but he must have a good, consistent, all-round health record. Any chronic ailment, however slight, is apt to be aggravated on the mission field. It is always a tragedy when an otherwise fully qualified candidate is rejected for health reasons.

2. Academic qualifications. For the most part the mainline denominations have maintained fairly high academic standards. Even in the nineteenth century most of their missionaries were college or seminary graduates. When Hudson Taylor came along and started the faith missions movement he appealed for those "of little formal education." When the Bible schools got under way on this continent in the last decades of the nineteenth century they too accepted those of little formal education, and gave them enough Bible training to enable them to become effective lay workers in the Christian church. It comes as no surprise to learn that most of the Bible school graduates who went overseas joined the faith missions. In recent decades both the Bible schools and the faith missions have raised their academic standards. Most of the larger schools are now degree-granting institutions.

Most missions prefer their candidates to have at least a college education. Beyond that the higher they go the better. The demands on today's missionary are so great that he should get as much education as he possibly can before going to the field. Only so will he be able to cope with the intellectual, social, political, and religious problems he is likely to encounter in the course of his missionary career. This is especially true if he plans to work among students and other intellectuals.

At the same time it should be recognized that a college or seminary education is no guarantee of genuine intellectual prowess—at least not here in the United States, where higher education is accessible to all. On the mission field there are hundreds of older missionaries who never had a chance to go to college, but they have something that no college can impart, intellectual capacity. They are largely self-educated but can hold their own with the best of them. The real test of a person's intellectual prowess is whether he keeps on growing after his formal education has ceased.

3. Vocational qualifications. We hear a great deal today about specialization, not only at home but also on the mission field. Most missionaries need some technical or vocational training over and above their liberal arts education. All missionaries, regardless of their area of specialization, should have a thorough understanding of missiology, including the history, theology, philosophy, and methodology of missions, non-Christian religions, cross-cultural communications, missionary anthropology, area studies, church planting, etc. Those going into Bible translation work should have a mastery of Greek and Hebrew and be completely conversant with the language and culture of the host country. This has not always been the case.

> Out of some 1,500 evangelical missionaries in Japan recently not one could be found who was competent enough in both languages to check a new Japanese translation against the original Hebrew. Liberals and Roman Catholics could have done it—but not the evangelicals.[2]

---

[2] Michael Griffiths, *Give Up Your Small Ambitions* (London: Inter-Varsity Press, 1970), p. 50.

Much depends, of course, on the kind of work into which the specialist goes. The larger missions have room for all kinds of specialists in the areas of theology, teaching, medicine, evangelism, radio and television, literature, journalism, youth work, business, finance, accounting, secretarial work, linguistics, aviation, etc. There is a crying need for specialists in all these areas. The tragedy is that in many instances these roles are now being filled by persons without any special or technical training for the tasks they are performing. They mean well; they work long and hard; and they are doing a tolerably good job; but they lack professional competence and the work suffers accordingly. The time is long past when we can do a second-rate job and expect to get away with it.

Topflight theologians are desperately needed on the mission field. Until such time as they are forthcoming it will be necessary for church leaders from the Third World to come to the West for their theological training. It would be much better, and certainly much cheaper, to educate them in their own countries.

4. Psychological qualifications. By psychological qualifications we really mean personality traits. Personality traits are more important in some roles than in others.

> A bookkeeper doesn't have to worry about the impression he makes on anybody but the boss. The main thing is to have his records neat and accurate. That's not true of the salesperson, however. The volume of his sales and the commission he gets may depend on such impressions. A research scientist may be a very disagreeable person to meet, at the same time that he is highly regarded for his contribution to science. But a minister of the Gospel can't even get a hearing for his message if he continually rubs people the wrong way.[3]

Rubbing people the wrong way is a greater danger on the mission field than here at home, for the simple reason that missionaries have to live at close quarters. Some of them live on "stations" or "compounds" where they are thrown together with other missionaries twelve hours a day, seven days a week. If one person in the group is abrasive, he can make life miserable for the others. Nowhere are interpersonal relations more important than on the mission field. For this reason many missions are now administering psychological as well as medical tests to all candidates.

No matter how hard we try we will not be able to achieve the perfectly integrated personality; but human relations are greatly facilitated if the persons involved possess certain desirable personality traits.

---

[3] Harold C. Cook, *An Introduction to the Study of Christian Missions* (Chicago: Moody Press, 1954), p. 112.

a. Emotional stability. The wear and tear of life on the mission field is considerably greater than here at home. The difficulty lies not in the big crack-ups that come once or twice a decade but in the hundred-and-one little irritations that are part of everyday life. Over the long haul these can completely upset one's emotional equilibrium. Persons who are given to introspection, or have an inferiority complex, or are afflicted with phobias and frustrations of various kinds usually have a difficult time adjusting to the kind of communal life found in some parts of the mission field. Mental health and emotional immaturity account for 10.9 percent of all the dropouts on the mission field.

b. Adaptability. Confucius said on one occasion, "When you enter a new territory, be sure to inquire concerning its customs." The Western counterpart of that is, "When in Rome do as the Romans do." When the missionary from the West arrives in the East he finds himself in an entirely different world. Everything is different—climate, food, dress, language, religion, and customs. In a word, the entire culture is different from anything he has known up to that point.

Obviously if he is going to be a success he must adapt to the mores of the host country. This is absolutely necessary if he wants to make friends and influence people. Otherwise he will be just another "ugly American." The person who is unable to change his ways will probably not last more than a year or two on the mission field.

c. Sense of humor. Missionary work is serious business. It is the King's business and requires haste; but the missionary himself must not be *too* serious. He must not take his fellow missionaries too seriously. Above all he ought to be able to laugh at himself. Many a tense and potentially explosive situation can be avoided if he sees the humorous side of the picture.

Particularly irksome to some missionaries is the universal practice in the East of "talking price." On one occasion I was at the mercy of a group of rickshaw coolies in Nanking. I was escorting eight children with all their baggage back to school after the Christmas break. We needed nine rickshaws to take us from the ferry to the railway station, a distance of about three miles. To make matters worse it was raining. Knowing my predicament they began by asking an exorbitant price. We haggled back and forth for several minutes but they refused to come down to a reasonable figure. Finally I said to the leader, "Venerable Brother, you misunderstand me. I don't want to *buy* the rickshaws; I just want to *hire* them!" That brought the house down. The other coolies burst into laughter, and the leader said, "Okay. Okay. Let's go." And away we went to the railway station.

d. Spirit of cooperation. The missionary is a member of a team.

On the team are missionaries and nationals; he must learn to work harmoniously with both. He cannot be a lone eagle. There are too many jobs to be done, too many roles to be filled. He must be willing to step into the breach and do a job for which he may not be particularly well qualified. He cannot refuse to teach Old Testament in the Bible school because he did his graduate work in New Testament. He may even be asked to teach homiletics, not because the mission wants to punish him, but because it must be taught and there is no one else to do it.

It is at this point that members of the younger generation who insist on doing their own thing get into trouble. All of us need to give heed to the admonition of Paul: "Let each of you look not only to his own interests, but also to the interests of others" (Ph 2:4).

e. *Willingness to take orders.* Much of the paternalism has gone out of the missionary movement, and that is a good thing; but so long as there is a structured organization with a chain of command, somebody has to give the orders and others must accept them. Major decisions and policies must be made at the top and carried out by those lower down. This does not preclude the desirability of input at all levels; but the final decision must be made by the leaders, after which the rank and file are expected to fall into line.

In all well-ordered missions every effort is made to canvass the opinions of the membership; and annual conferences are held on the various fields when the missionaries have ample opportunity to air their grievances and present their points of view; but the responsibility for policy making rests with the leadership on the field. Above the field council is the home council or, in some missions, the international council, which is responsible for the total operation of the entire mission at home and overseas. The field council members must be willing to implement the policies laid down by the international council; and the missionaries must be prepared to abide by the decisions of the field council. There is no other way to operate an international organization.

f. *Ability to endure hardness.* The Chinese call it "eating bitterness." There is no doubt that the affluent society in which we live has produced in all of us a love of ease and comfort that is the hallmark of the American way of life. We have central heating in the winter and air conditioning in the summer and twenty-eight varieties of ice cream the year round. Physical well-being, financial security, material prosperity, peace and contentment, law and order—these are the main ingredients that go to make up the affluent society that is America. The individual is pampered and protected from the cradle to the grave. Dentistry, surgery, and now childbirth, are all rendered painless. Even Band-Aids must be "ouchless." The energy crisis that now threatens to change drastically the American life-style is perhaps the best thing that has happened to us since Thomas Edison invented the incandescent lamp.

The American missionary, more than any other, finds it difficult to knuckle down to the simple life-style in most parts of the Third World. Like the Children of Israel who hankered after the "leeks and onions of Egypt," he wants to retain as much as possible of the American standard of living. That is why some of them take tons of household stuff, including canned goods, when they leave for the field. In this respect the Peace Corps volunteers put the missionaries to shame. They live at the level of the people they serve. They are not allowed to own jeeps, cars, or even bicycles. They use public transportation, second class where available.

Most missionaries are married and have families, so they cannot be expected to compete with the Peace Corps; but they must be prepared to endure hardness, like good soldiers of Jesus Christ, in order to identify with the people they are seeking to win. The gap between the "have" nations and the "have not" nations is altogether too great. The Christian missionary by himself cannot close that gap no matter what he does, but he can help to bridge it at the local level if he is willing to "eat bitterness."

g. *Patience and perseverance.* The missionary is not going to change the world overnight. The East is agonizingly slow. The West is ridiculously fast. A man's whole day can be spoiled if the elevator in the office building takes him one floor beyond where he wants to go.

One of the most difficult adjustments for the missionary is to s-l-o-w d-o-w-n. In thirty-six hours he goes from the jet age to the ox age, and the sudden change can be traumatic. In all aspects of his life and work he will have need of patience and perseverance. Without these virtues he is almost sure to crack up. He may try to circumvent the problem by operating his own jeep; but he will still need patience when the jeep bogs down in two feet of mire or he comes to a river that has no bridge and the ferry is not operating. If he decides to go by bus he may find that the bus driver has decided to take the day off.

Government officials, church leaders, and the people in general are in no great rush to get things done. The missionary may have to wait nine months to get his car through Customs and another two years to get his driver's license. Church leaders also take their time in making decisions, and having made them are often slow in executing them. They see no need for haste and can't understand why the missionary should be upset by the delay. What isn't accomplished today can always be undertaken tomorrow—or the next day, or the next day after that. In the meantime they may discover that the decision wasn't a wise one to begin with and therefore need not be implemented at all. And all the while the American missionary is fussing and fuming, and sometimes fulminating.

h. Without a superiority complex. In the words of Kenneth Scott Latourette, the nineteenth-century missionary was "serenely convinced of the superiority of Western culture." In the missionary literature of that period the words "Christianity" and "civilization" were used almost interchangeably. The missionaries conceived of themselves as playing a civilizing as well as a Christianizing role. That day is gone. No missionary today would entertain such naive notions. Hopefully we know better.

That does not mean that we have licked the problem. It is still with us, albeit in more subtle forms. There are a hundred-and-one little ways in which the missionary may unconsciously reveal his superiority complex. There is an almost irresistible temptation to compare local products with their counterparts in the United States. Quite frequently they appear to be inferior in quality and craftsmanship. They don't work as well. They don't last as long. The missionary tosses them aside with some remark about "the crazy gadgets that don't work." His remarks may be heard only by his household servants; but that is enough. The word soon spreads throughout the community that the missionary doesn't like native products.

Indeed, the very fact that he arrives from the United States with nineteen drums of personal effects conveys the impression that American goods are superior to all others, else why would he go to all that trouble and expense?

The peoples of the Third World are doing their best to catch up with the technology of the West and are very self-conscious about the gap that still exists. Understandably they are touchy on these points and appreciate the missionary who has a genuine appreciation of them and their culture.

In most parts of the world the missionary is still treated with a certain degree of deference, partly as a carry-over from the past and partly because the Third World culture has always shown kindness and hospitality to strangers. It is very easy for the missionary to come to *expect* this kind of treatment and take offense if it is not forthcoming.

The missionary with his advanced degrees and his expertise may easily get a swelled head and think that he has all the answers and that the national leaders should listen to him and follow his advice. An attitude of superiority is something the missionary must guard against all the days of his life. It was bad enough in the nineteenth century; it is quite insufferable now.

i. Without racial prejudice. The white race has no monopoly on racial prejudice. The ancient Greeks divided the world into Greeks and barbarians. The Chinese called their country the "Middle Kingdom" and referred to all foreigners as barbarians. There is hardly a country in the world that does not have some form of racial prejudice.

On one occasion when riding the subway in New York City I saw an ad which contained only one word printed in large black letters on a white background—ECIDUJERP. For several minutes I could not figure out what it was all about. Then at the bottom of the ad, in small letters barely discernible, I read: "This word is PREJUDICE spelled backwards. Whichever way you spell it, it doesn't make sense." But sense or nonsense, it still persists in almost every society.

The problems relating to racism in the United States have been published in all the major newspapers of the world. There are people in the Third World who have never heard of Chicago or San Francisco who are well acquainted with Little Rock and Birmingham. Martin Luther King is almost as well known as John F. Kennedy.

It wouldn't be so bad if racism were confined to American society, but it has infected the churches as well. Indeed, the eleven o'clock hour on Sunday morning is the most segregated hour of the week. This sad fact has not gone unnoticed by foreign nationals in this country. Racism in America is a millstone around the neck of the missionary, especially in Africa.

In its more blatant forms racism has disappeared from the mission field; but there are a hundred-and-one subtle ways in which it can still be seen. It comes out not so much in the conduct of his work as in various aspects of his social life. It is one thing to *work* with the nationals on a basis of equality; it is another to *play* with them on the same basis. There is still a tendency for missionaries to seek the company of fellow missionaries or other Americans residing in a large city. The real test of a missionary's love for the people will be shown in the friends with whom he shares his leisure time.

Racial prejudice is particularly unfortunate in the Christian missionary—for two reasons. First, it is a denial of the teachings of Christ. Second, it alienates the very people he is trying to win.

5. Spiritual qualifications. If the missionary is not in every sense of the word a "man of God" he might as well remain at home. "It cannot be too positively asserted that missionary work is a spiritual enterprise, undertaken for spiritual results to be achieved only by spiritual means. It follows, therefore, that the essential qualifications are spiritual."[4]

a. Genuine conversion experience. It is hardly necessary to belabor this point. To be a missionary a person must have an evangelical fervor

---

[4] Rowland Hogben, *In Training* (Chicago: Inter-Varsity Christian Fellowship, 1946), p. 30.

growing out of a conversion experience. This is very important in a so-called Christian society where everyone whose name appears on a church roll is assumed to be a Christian. Some of the most zealous missionaries are those from a "pagan" background who were soundly converted to Christ after they reached college. Inter-Varsity Christian Fellowship and Campus Crusade for Christ play a major role at this point. The missionary who is not sure of his own salvation is not likely to lead others to a saving knowledge of Christ.

b. Knowledge of the Scriptures. The missionary's chief task is to share Jesus Christ with the non-Christian world. All he knows about Christ he learned from the Bible. Therefore it behooves him to have a thorough working knowledge of the Scriptures, which are able to make men wise unto salvation (2 Ti 3:15). No amount of worldly wisdom can substitute for a knowledge of the Scriptures. The missionary not only should know their contents but also have a thorough understanding of the major doctrines concerning God, man, sin, salvation, etc.

Moreover, the Scriptures are the source from which he gets the sustenance necessary for his spiritual life. They provide him with his message and his mandate. They are his chart and compass. They are his trustworthy guide in all matters pertaining to faith and morals. From them he derives wisdom, counsel, comfort, encouragement, and cleansing. In short, the Bible is the foundation on which he builds both his life and his work. Without a thorough knowledge of it the missionary is at a serious disadvantage.

c. Assurance of divine guidance. Missionary work is not getting any easier. Some of the physical hardships have been eliminated, but in their place is a whole host of other difficulties, psychological, ideological, and interpersonal. The short-termer may be able to get along fairly well without any great "sense of call," but the career missionary will find it mighty handy when the going gets rough. It will help him immensely if he can say, "I am a missionary by the will of God."

Two journalists, both agnostics, spent three months with missionaries in East Africa to see what makes them tick. In their report they made the following observation. "It is obvious when you talk to missionaries, and still more obvious on reflection, that the phenomenon of missionary work really makes sense only if their belief in a calling is taken at its face value. . . . Virtually everyone we met really did feel that in some deep sense they had surrendered their own will for that of another way of life—for their Lord, as they would put it."[5]

If a missionary has a deep, abiding conviction that he is in Brazil, or Borneo, or Burundi by the will of God he will not turn and run

---

[5] Helen and Richard Exley, *In Search of the Missionary* (London: Highway Press, 1970), p. 38.

at the first sight or sound of danger, nor will he give up when the difficulties multiply and the frustrations almost drive him crazy. He will go the second mile and stay on the job long after the sun has gone down only if he is sure that he is in the will of the Lord.

d. *Strong devotional life.* The devotional life of the missionary is all-important. He neglects it at his peril. He will be a man of God only if his spiritual life is systematically developed by daily Bible study, prayer, meditation, and worship.

Here at home, especially in seminary or Bible college, the student is buoyed up and carried along by the spiritual support provided by the Christian community of which he is a part: prayer meetings, chapel services, dorm fellowships, rap sessions, etc. On the mission field these props are largely missing. The missionary is on his own. He can't depend on others for fellowship or growth. He must know how to cultivate his own spiritual life without any outside help. Like the date tree whose taproot enables it to flourish even in the desert, he must have roots that go down deep. Otherwise his spiritual life will wither and die.

Hudson Taylor was one of the missionary giants of the nineteenth century whose name is a household word in evangelical circles. It was said of him that never once in fifty years did the sun rise in China without finding Hudson Taylor on his knees.

Most missionaries would have to confess that this is one of their greatest problems. They are constantly ministering to others; nobody ministers to them. If they don't set aside and jealously guard the "quiet time" each morning they will soon find themselves robbed of their joy as well as their power.

e. *Self-discipline.* Discipline seems to be essential to the ongoing of human society. Without it community life tends to disintegrate. There are two kinds of discipline. One is imposed from without; the other is cultivated from within. Most people have to rely on the first because they possess so little of the second. This is why we hear so much talk about "law and order." Apparently it is impossible to achieve the one without the other.

The missionary, more than anyone else, is dependent on *self-discipline.* Even the pastor at home is not in the same class with the missionary. The pastor is constantly under the surveillance of the people who pay his salary. If he falls down on the job he will be called before the church board to give an account of himself. More than one pastor has been asked to terminate his service for that reason. What about the missionary? Who is to check up on him? He may not see the field director more than once a year. If he loafs on the job or becomes lazy in body or mind he can easily get away with it.

Self-discipline is listed by Paul as one of the fruits of the Spirit in Galatians 5:23, where it is called "self-control." Even the great apostle had problems along this line. He said, "Every athlete exercises self-control in all things. They do it to receive a perishable wreath; but we an imperishable. Well, I do not run aimlessly, I do not box as one beating the air; but I pommel my body and subdue it, lest after preaching to others I myself should be disqualified" (1 Co 9:25-27).

f. A heart of love. Love is the hallmark of the Christian life (Jn 13:34-35) and the *sine qua non* of Christian service (1 Co 13:1-3). Jesus Christ, as the first and chief Missionary, came into the world to express the Father's love (Jn 3:16). The missionary goes into the world to express Christ's love. Paul and the other apostles were so controlled by the love of Christ (2 Co 5:14) that they were willing to risk their lives for the sake of the Lord Jesus Christ (Acts 15:26).

Writing to the little mission church in Thessalonica, Paul could say, "So being affectionately desirous of you, we were ready to share with you not only the gospel of God but also our own selves, because you had become very dear to us" (1 Th 2:8). Missionaries don't have to be bright or brave to be successful (though both are very desirable qualities), but they *must* be loving. The nationals will overlook many weaknesses and forgive many blunders if they are persuaded that the missionary has a heart of love.

g. Some success in Christian service. Important as the above-mentioned qualifications are, they are not sufficient. In addition there should be some evidence of fruitfulness in Christian service here at home. Before setting out for distant shores he should have proved himself in church or mission work at home. If he can't win souls in his own culture, what reason is there to believe he will do better in a foreign culture? Is he going to be an evangelistic missionary? Then there should be some evidence that he has the gift of evangelism. Does he hope to be a Bible teacher? Then he should have demonstrated that he possesses the gift of teaching.

There should be some evidence of God's blessing in his life and some proof of the power of the Holy Spirit in his ministry before he ventures overseas. Of one thing he can be sure: Success will not come more easily on the mission field.

3
Theological Issues

The Christian mission is rooted in the Holy Scriptures. They and they alone are able to make man "wise unto salvation" (2 Ti 3:16). From them we derive our message, our mandate, our motivation, and our methodology. Apart from the Word of God the missionary movement has neither meaning nor sanction.

It is imperative that today's missionary have an adequate grasp of Christian theology, especially as it relates to the worldwide proclamation of the gospel in a cross-cultural situation in a rapidly changing world. In the nineteenth century almost all missionaries held to a conservative interpretation of Scripture. This is no longer true. The ancient landmarks are being removed. As a result we have the "new theology" and the "new evangelism," both of which threaten to change the force and thrust of the Christian mission.

In our day the ideas of men are being substituted for the Word of God. Anthropology and sociology are rapidly replacing theology, with disastrous results. The vertical dimension of the Christian mission has been lost and all that remains is the horizontal.

According to the "new theology" man is not eternally lost, for the simple reason that a loving Heavenly Father would never consign even a Hitler to hell. His all-conquering love and His irresistible grace will finally win the day, and all men will be saved. Indeed, they are already saved by virtue of the universal application of the saving merit of Jesus Christ to all and sundry, regardless of their attitude or understanding.

The task of today's missionary, according to this "new theology," is simply to inform the non-Christian world that without their knowledge or consent all men are "in Christ," and as such are part of the new humanity of which He is the Head.

This gives to salvation an altogether new twist. Salvation today is no longer personal but societal. Humanization and not redemption is the watchword. Man needs to be delivered, not from the penalty and power of his own sins, but from the demonic power structures that have destroyed his authentic manhood and alienated him from his neighbor.

Missionaries, pastors, and all who have a vital interest in the evangelization of the world, have an obligation to search the Scriptures in order to come to an understanding of the Biblical basis of the Christian mission. Here in this short chapter we can deal with only five facets of the subject.

Missions and the Sovereignty of God

One of the great doctrines of the Bible is the sovereignty of God. The Scriptures clearly teach that God is the Creator, Sustainer, and Ruler of the universe. Heaven is His throne and earth is His footstool (Is 66:1). The earth is the Lord's and the fullness thereof, the world and they that dwell therein (Ps 24:1). He is the giver of every good and perfect gift (Ja 1:17). Day by day He opens His hand and satisfies the desire of every living thing (Ps 145:16). In Him we live and move and have our being (Acts 17:28). He has a plan and purpose for the church and the world (Eph 1:9-10). He knows the end from the beginning (Is 46:10) and is working all things after the counsel of His own will (Eph 1:11), not only among the hosts of heaven but also among the inhabitants of the earth (Da 4:35). Paul sums it up in those majestic words: "O the depth of the riches and wisdom and knowledge of God! How unsearchable are his judgments and how inscrutable his ways! 'For who has known the mind of the Lord, or who has been his counselor?' 'Or who has given a gift to him that he might be repaid?' For from him and through him and to him are all things. To him be glory for ever. Amen" (Ro 11:33-36).

The sovereignty of God is based on three outstanding attributes which in their fullness belong only to God: His almighty power (Is 40:12-31), His perfect wisdom (Ro 11:33-36), and His intrinsic goodness (Ps 145:17). All three of these great attributes are essential to the concept of sovereignty. It is not enough to say, "I believe in God the Father almighty." If God were all powerful but not all wise, He might conceivably use His power in foolish and futile pursuits. If He were all powerful but not all good, He might abuse His power to the everlasting detriment of His helpless creatures. This means that in the moral character of God there are built-in checks and balances which make Him a perfect Supreme Being worthy of our love and trust. His wisdom ensures that His power will always be used in a safe and sane manner. His goodness ensures that all His plans and purposes will be not only for His own glory but also for the ultimate and everlasting good of His creatures.

The sovereignty of God is seen in all three of His divine activities: creation (Re 4:11), redemption (Eph 1:5 9), and judgment (Re 15:3-4; 16:5-7; Ro 9:18-23). Everything God does He does according to His own plan and purpose, on His own initiative, by His own power, for His own glory. When human history has run its course and mankind stands before God, the unanimous verdict of a moral universe will be, "He has done all things well."

The Christian mission is part of God's sovereign activity in the realm of redemption. From first to last the Christian mission is God's mission, not man's. It originated in the heart of God. It is based on the love of God. It is determined by the will of God. Its mandate was enunciated by the Son of God. Its rationale is explained in the Word of God. For its ultimate success it is dependent on the power of God. Nowhere is the sovereignty of God more clearly seen than in the Christian mission, and this in several ways.

GOD'S DEALINGS
WITH THE MISSIONARY

1. God's choice of the man. We are accustomed to speaking of missionary "volunteers," and everyone knows what is meant by the expression. Is it Biblically correct? What about the great prophets of the Old Testament? Were any of them "volunteers?" Did Abraham, Moses, David, or Jeremiah volunteer for the service of God? The answer is No. At forty years of age Moses was a "volunteer" and offered his services to his people in slavery. His self-initiated attempt at saving his people ended in disaster and he had to flee for his life. Forty years later, when God's time had come, Moses was anything but a volunteer. He offered all kinds of excuses why God should get someone else.

Jeremiah was no better; he too tried to beg off. At first sight it looks as if Isaiah was a volunteer, for he said, "Here am I, send me" (Is 6:8), but a closer look at the passage will reveal the fact that he was simply responding to God's call, "Whom shall I send, and who will go for us?"

Jesus made it very plain: "You did not choose me, but I chose you and appointed you that you should go and bear fruit" (Jn 15:16). He found Peter and Andrew by the Sea of Galilee and issued the command, "Follow me." He did the same with James and John (Mt 4:18-

22). There is no reason to believe that these four fishermen, left to themselves, would have left their fishing business and followed Jesus. It was His idea, not theirs.

Paul is most emphatic on this point. He insisted that he was an apostle "by the will of God" (Co 1:1). It is unthinkable that the arch persecutor of the church would ever have volunteered to become its chief apostle. He would never have capitulated to the hated Nazarene unless he had been "apprehended" on the road to Damascus. At the beginning of his Christian life God spoke of him as a "chosen instrument" (Acts 9:15). And writing about his apostolic ministry Paul said: "For I take no special pride in the fact that I preach the Gospel. I feel compelled to do so; I should be utterly miserable if I failed to preach it. If I do this work because I choose to do so then I am entitled to a reward. But if it is no choice of mine, but a sacred responsibility put upon me, what can I expect in the way of reward?" (1 Co 9:16-17, Phillips).

In the four Gospels only one person ever "volunteered" to follow Christ, and he was dissuaded by the hardships involved (Lk 9:57-58). "Don't be a missionary if you can possibly avoid it" was the advice given to a young man by a veteran missionary. Taken at face value it sounds like queer advice; but there is enough truth in the statement to make us sit up and take notice.

Every Christian is called upon to be a witness for Christ in his daily life and work. Not everyone is called to be a full-time missionary in the professional sense of that term. Not all were apostles in Paul's day; not all are missionaries in our day; and whether or not a person becomes a missionary depends on the will of God, not the inclination of the individual.

2. The kind of ministry. Not only does God make sovereign choice of the man; He also decides on the kind of ministry in which the messenger will engage. One's ministry depends on the spiritual gifts he possesses. There is a necessary connection between the two. The gift equips the man for the ministry and the ministry depends for its success on the gift. And how does one acquire the gift? The spiritual gifts are bestowed on the believer by the Holy Spirit in His own sovereign way. After enumerating the various gifts of the Spirit, Paul goes on to say, "All these are inspired by one and the same Spirit, who apportions to each one individually as he wills" (1 Co 12:11). The same teaching is found in Ephesians 4.

Peter and Paul were both apostles by the will of God; but one was an apostle to the Jews and the other to the Gentiles. Who was responsible for the choice? Was the choice left to them or was it made for them? Paul makes bold to suggest that God Himself was responsible for this division of labor (Ga 2:8). Left to himself Paul would surely have preferred to be an apostle to the Jews, whom he loved so passionately that he was willing to be separated from Christ for their sake (Ro 9:3). But the choice was not his. God ordained that he should be an apostle to the Gentiles, and on more than one occasion He had to remind Paul of this fact (Acts 9:15; 22:21).

Even though Peter was officially known as an apostle to the Jews, it was he who preached the gospel to the Gentile, Cornelius. Was this left to Peter's discretion? Indeed not. When speaking at the council in Jerusalem when the fate of the Gentile Christians was in the balance, Peter reminded the assembly of the historic event recorded in Acts 10. "Brethren, you know that in the early days God made choice among you, that by my mouth the Gentiles should hear the word of the gospel and believe" (Acts 15:7). Left to himself Peter would never have preached the gospel to Cornelius. But God chose Peter and the Spirit bade him go (Acts 11:12). Only then was he willing to preach the gospel to the Gentiles.

In both cases—Peter and Paul—the choice was God's. Fortunately the two men had the good sense to acquiesce in the will of God.

3. The sphere of the ministry. The field is the world, and the apostles were told to go into all the world and preach the gospel to every creature. They were to begin at Jerusalem and proceed from there to Judea and Samaria, and ultimately to the ends of the earth. Obviously a person can work in only one place at a time. It would not be wise to have all the apostles in Judea or in Samaria. If the world is to be evangelized in an orderly fashion, there must be some overall plan of action.

Who decides on the plan of action? When Paul reached the western perimeter of Asia he tried to preach the gospel in the Roman province of Asia, but the Holy Spirit forbade him (Acts 16:6). He then tried to go into Bithynia, but again the Spirit interfered (Acts 16:7). In a nocturnal vision Paul saw a man of Macedonia saying, "Come over to Macedonia and help us" (Acts 16:9). Interpreting this to be the Lord's will for him at that time, Paul and his companions crossed over into Europe and planted the church in that continent. As a result Europe became a "Christian" continent and Asia remained "heathen."

What might have happened had Paul followed his own inclinations and gone east instead of west? It is intriguing to remember that Buddhism entered China from India about the time Paul arrived in Rome. There it took root and became one of the three great religions of China. Suppose Christianity instead of Buddhism had been taken to China at that time. Would Asia today be "Christian" and Europe "heathen"?

The fact remains that Paul in his missionary journeys was guided very definitely by the Lord, and the sphere of his ministry was necessarily restricted to those regions for which God had a purpose of grace. Wherever Paul went he knew he would go "in the fulness of the blessing of Christ" (Ro 15:29). Paul was not left to make his own travel plans. It is true that he used good common sense when he followed the Roman roads and concentrated on the large cities with their cosmopolitan populations. Nevertheless in all his travels he was conscious of the leading of the Lord, and no amount of danger could deter him from going forward if he conceived this to be the will of God for him (Acts 21:13). On the other hand a city as large and strategic as Ephesus would merit a visit only "if God will" (Acts 18:21).

4. The duration of the ministry. Some missionaries, such as William Axling (Japan) and Stanley Jones (India), rounded out sixty years in the service of Christ. Others, such as John and Betty Stam (China), were cut down during their first term of service. Circumstances enter into the picture to be sure, but even the circumstances are under God's control. When Peter asked Jesus about the ministry of John, Jesus replied, "If it is my will that he remain until I come, what is that to you?" (Jn 21:22). Stephen became the first Christian martyr; but his fellow deacon, Philip, served Christ for a whole generation (Acts 21:8). The apostle James was beheaded by Herod; but Peter, slated for the same fate, was miraculously delivered (Acts 12).

5. The success of the ministry. Who is to say what is "success" in the service of Christ? Jesus Christ is the Lord of the Harvest. It is He who deploys His workers in various parts of the vineyard. He ordains some to sow and others to reap (Jn 4:35-38). We identify success with those who reap. Every supporting church likes to hear a "success" story when the missionary returns on furlough. Given a choice, most missionaries would prefer to be among the reapers, not the sowers. Who wants to sow year after year and not see a harvest? But God has ordained that some of His servants will sow and others will reap. In the final analysis it is God who gives the increase (1 Co 3:6-9). John the Baptist recognized this fact and was content to leave the results with God (Jn 3:25-27). When Jesus' Messianic mission ended in failure, He fell back on the sovereignty of God and gave thanks for apparent failure (Mt 11:25-26). A thing is good only if it is good *in God's sight.*

GOD'S DEALINGS WITH THE SINNER

1. The fate of the sinner is decided by a judicial act of God. However difficult it may be for us to explain, the fact remains that God in

His sovereignty opens the eyes of some (Mt 13:14-17) and closes the eyes of others (Ro 11:8). The Scriptures tell us that God hardened Pharoah's heart (Ex 7:3) and opened Lydia's heart (Acts 16:14). The early church grew in strength and size not because people decided to join the church, but because they were added to the church by an act of God (Acts 2:47). The only ones who believed were those who were "ordained to eternal life" (Acts 13:48).

2. **Only those who are "drawn" by the Father will ever come to Christ.** The teaching of Christ is clear on this point. He said, "No one can come to me unless the Father who sent me draws him" (Jn 6:44). Left to himself the ungodly sinner will never forsake his wicked way and seek after God (Ro 3:10-18). Therefore God must take the initiative. Jesus Christ came into the world to seek and to save that which is lost (Lk 19:10). The Holy Spirit came into the world to convict the world of sin, righteousness, and judgment (Jn 16:8). Without the seeking Shepherd the sheep would never be found. Without the convicting Spirit the sinner would never be saved.

3. **The very faith by which a person believes is itself the gift of God.** Paul is very emphatic on this point. "For by grace you have been saved through faith, and this is not your own doing, it is the gift of God" (Eph 2:8).

> We must never forget that it is God who saves. It is God who brings men and women under the sound of the gospel, and it is God who brings them to faith in Christ. . . . If we forget that only God can give faith, we shall start to think that the making of converts depends, in the last analysis, not on God but on us.[1]

If God of His own free will does not give this faith, man cannot by the independent exercise of his own intellect "believe" in Christ. He can give intellectual assent to certain historic facts concerning Christ; but saving faith is something else. The insight that enabled Peter to confess Jesus as the Son of God came as a revelation from God (Mt 16:17). Paul informs us that no man can call Jesus "Lord" except by the Holy Spirit (1 Co 12:3).

4. **Only persons united to Christ by the Holy Spirit remain steadfast in the faith; the others fall away.** The way to God is through Jesus Christ (Jn 14:6). The way to Christ is through the Holy Spirit (Jn 16:13-14). He and He alone unites the soul to Christ (1 Co 12:13). Not all of Christ's disciples remained with Him to the end. In mid-

---

[1] J. I. Packer, *Evangelism and the Sovereignty of God* (London: Inter-Varsity Fellowship, 1961), p. 27.

career many of them left Him and went their way when they were introduced to His "hard sayings" (Jn 6:60, 66). Only those whose faith was God-given (Mt 16:17) and therefore genuine (Jn 6:69) remained with Him to the end (Jn 17:12).

The apostles were disturbed when the Pharisees took offense at the teachings of Christ. They feared that the "hard sayings" would alienate them and they expressed their fears to the Master. Jesus had no such fears. He replied: "Every plant which My heavenly Father has not planted will be rooted up" (Mt 15:13). Jesus had implicit faith in the sovereignty of God and refused to panic when the crowds began to dwindle. He believed that every soul "given" to Him by the Father would ultimately come to Him. None would be cast out (Jn 6:37). None would be uprooted (Mt 15:13). If they took offense and went away, that was proof that they had never been "given" or "planted" by the Father. If their roots were in God they would remain no matter what happened. If their roots were not in God sooner or later they were sure to be plucked up.

GOD'S ORDERING OF WORLD EVENTS

God is the Creator and Sustainer of the universe. This world is *His* world. In spite of all the evidence to the contrary, God is in full charge of human affairs and world events (Da 4:35). He is the God of history as well as the God of creation and redemption. The missionary movement is part of history and must continue to operate within the context of history regardless of how turbulent it may become. This is seen in the following ways:

1. The times and seasons are in God's control. The last question addressed to Christ by His disciples was, "Will you at this time restore the kingdom to Israel?" (Acts 1:6). Jesus replied, "It is not for you to know times or seasons which the Father has fixed by his own authority." In the course of church history there have been good times and bad. Indeed, we are informed that "for everything there is a season and a time for every matter under heaven" (Ec 3:1). There is a time to plant and a time to pluck up that which is planted. There is a time to break down and a time to build up. There is a time to keep and a time to cast away. There is a time for war and a time for peace (Ec 3:2-9). These times and seasons, bad as well as good, are fixed by the authority of God.

2. The opening and the closing of doors are the prerogative of God. We have heard much in this postwar period about closing doors, and the assumption is that these doors were closed by the nationalists, or the Communists, or the revolutionists; and behind all these, of course, was the devil. It is true that the devil delights in closing doors. It is also true that human agents are usually employed. The fact remains that when doors are closed they are closed by God and not by man or the devil.

This may sound like heresy but it has the sanction of Holy Scripture. In His letter to the church in Philadelphia Jesus Christ describes Himself as the One who opens and no man shuts and shuts and no man opens (Re 3:7). Most of us prefer open doors. We don't like closed doors. We tend to identify the former with God and His purposes; we associate the second with the devil and his diabolical schemes. This is because, like Peter, we have man's point of view and not God's (Mt 16:23).

The greatest reverse ever suffered by the modern missionary movement was the evacuation of mainland China in the 1950s. In the 1840s the Christian Church, like a mighty army, moved into China with its banners flying. On those banners were inscribed the words of Scripture: "I am He that openeth and no man shutteth." One hundred years later the Church was on the march again; but this time it was coming out of China. Its banners, tattered and torn, were dragging in the dust. But on those banners were inscribed the words of Scripture: "I am He that shutteth and no man openeth." By purely human definition the first event was a victory; the second was a tragedy. But both were engineered by God. It was He who opened the door in the 1840s. It was He who closed the door in the 1940s. If it had not been for the permissive will of God, all the armies of Red China could not have chased the missionaries out of that country. One can only conclude that when doors open, they open at His command; and when they close, they close at His behest. Closed doors are just as much a part of His plan as open doors.

3. Open and closed doors involve a great mystery; but God has explained the mystery in the Scriptures. After his great discourse on the history of Israel, past, present, and future, the apostle Paul exclaims, "O the depth of the riches and wisdom and knowledge of God! How unsearchable are his judgments and how inscrutable his ways! . . . For from him and through him and to him are all things. To him be glory for ever" (Ro 11:33-36).

We are living in an anthropocentric world where man is the measure of all things. The whole world, so we think, revolves around a center of gravity called man. Little by little God has been pushed from the center to the perimeter. What the church needs today is a fresh look at what the Scriptures have to say about the sovereignty of God. Surely He knows the end from the beginning and is even now working all things after the counsel of His own will (Eph 1:11). He has a plan and purpose for the Jews, the Gentiles, and the Church of God (1 Co 10:32). And when things get out of hand, He is able to make even the wrath of man to praise Him (Ps 76:10). When his sanity returned after seven years, King Nebuchadnezzar had to acknowledge that the Most High does "according to his will in the host of heaven and among the inhabitants of the earth; and none can stay his hand, or say to him 'What doest thou?' " (Da 4:35).

If we have difficulty in accepting this point of view, we should not be surprised. God has already warned us: "My thoughts are not your thoughts, neither are your ways my ways, says the Lord. For as the heavens are higher than the earth so are my ways higher than your ways and my thoughts than your thoughts" (Is 55:8-9). Should we be surprised if now and then Almighty God, Maker of heaven and earth, does something that our puny, finite minds cannot fully understand? To understand everything God does, we would have to be God.

It doesn't require much faith to believe in the sovereignty of God when the world situation is under control and everything is to our liking. It is when things go wrong and life breaks down that the Christian must take his stand on the Holy Scriptures and believe that in some mysterious way he cannot fully understand the purposes of God are being worked out according to His perfect plan.

The China debacle in the late 1940s was a heart-breaking experience for the thousands of missionaries there at that time. It was unthinkable that Chiang Kai-shek, a devout Christian, should be defeated by Mao Tse-tung, an avowed atheist whose hatred for religion was well known. Had God taken a poll of missionary opinion, almost to a man the missionary body would have supported Chiang Kai-shek and the Kuomintang. But God acted on His own without consulting the missionaries. And the result? By 1953 all of the missionaries were out of China. It was a bitter pill to swallow. The missionaries shook their heads. They could not believe their eyes. At least one mission leader had a nervous breakdown. The largest single mission field in all the world was closed to Christian missionaries. Worse than that, the institutional church has all but been destroyed. It takes great faith to believe that God has been in control of the situation in China during the last twenty-five years. But that is the verdict of Holy Scripture, and we had better believe it.

4. God's command to us is to get on with the job of world evangelization whether the circumstances be favorable or unfavorable. He was a wise Preacher who said, "He who observes the wind will not sow; and he who regards the clouds will not reap. . . . In the morning sow your seed, and at evening withhold not your hand; for you do not know which will prosper, this or that, or whether both alike will be good" (Ec 11:4-0).

World evangelization cannot wait for fair skies and calm seas. The king's business requires haste (1 Sa 21:8). In the world we will always have tribulation (Jn 16:33). Bonds and afflictions awaited Paul in every city (Acts 20:23), but he never allowed them to delay or deter him (Acts 21:13). He was always ready for service (Ro 1:15) or sacrifice (Ph 2:17). To live or die was all the same to him (Ph 1:20). His only concern was that he might glorify God (1 Co 10:31) and finish his course with joy (Acts 20:24; 2 Ti 4:7).

Some of the greatest events in mission history occurred when the times were least propitious. William Carey was pleading the cause of world missions during the French Revolution, which threatened to engulf the whole of Europe. The first American missionaries sailed for India in 1812, the year that war broke out between Britain and the United States. Hudson Taylor first arrived in China in 1853 as the Taiping Rebellion was getting under way—a rebellion that lasted fifteen years and took at least twenty million lives. In 1930, at the depth of the Depression, the China Inland Mission, now the Overseas Missionary Fellowship, called for two hundred new workers in two years—and got them.

In Ephesus Paul found "a wide door for effective work." He also discovered that there were "many adversaries" (1 Co 16:9). The one often accompanies the other. Paul had a very turbulent career. In nearly every city his preaching precipitated a citywide riot. Time and again he barely escaped with his life. Sometimes he was told to remain where he was in spite of danger, as in the city of Corinth (Acts 18:9-10). At other times he was told to flee, as was the case in Jerusalem (Acts 22:17-18). But whether he stayed or went was inconsequential. His chief concern was to preach Christ. He never allowed circumstances, good or bad, to determine his course of action. He got his guidance from God. Once he received the green light, he pressed forward without hesitation, knowing that God would hold Himself responsible for all the consequences that flowed from his obedience. He realized that safety and security are no guarantee of success. On the other hand he recognized that difficulty and danger do not necessarily spell disaster.

Missionary work must be carried on in fair weather and foul. The real tragedy does not lie in the closed countries that we can't enter but in the open countries that we don't enter. Closed countries are God's responsibility. We can safely leave them with Him. Open countries are our responsibility, and we neglect them at our peril. We should be up and doing. The time *is* short. The fields *are* white. The laborers *are* few. It is both foolish and futile to spend our time lamenting the few doors that are closed while we refuse to enter the many doors that are open.

Missions and the Responsibility of Man

There are two aspects to the Christian mission, the divine and the human. In the preceding section we have discussed the first; now we turn to the second. The Scriptures plainly teach the sovereignty of God. They just as plainly teach the responsibility of man. Properly understood, there is no conflict between these two concepts.

God is omnipotent, by which we mean that He is able to do anything that is in accord with His own nature, which is essentially holy. He is the sovereign Lord of the universe and works all things after the counsel of His own will, by His own power, and for His own glory. Of one thing we are sure—God is a moral Being, righteous in all His ways and kind in all His doings (Ps 145:17). His choices and decisions are always determined with reference to those eternal principles of righteousness, goodness, and truth of which His own nature is the eternal and absolutely perfect expression. His only limitations are those that he *chooses to place upon Himself.*

In all three of His works—creation, redemption, and judgment—God works according to His own plan and purpose. He is the self-existing, all-sufficient Supreme Ruler who upholds all things by the word of His power. Yet for reasons fully understood only by Himself He has agreed to place certain limitations on the exercise of His own sovereignty. He has ordained that certain prerogatives belong solely to Him. He has likewise ordained that certain responsibilities belong solely to man. In the work of creation described in Genesis 1 and 2 this division of labor is clearly seen. A simple diagram will illustrate the point.

GOD'S PART—MIRACLE	MAN'S PART—MANDATE
God created the heavens and the earth and prepared the latter for the advent of man.	Man was told to cultivate the garden and subdue the earth.
God created the first forms of plant and animal life.	Once created, these plants and animals reproduced "each after its own kind."
God created the first pair, Adam and Eve, in His own image.	By his own powers of procreation man was able to multiply and replenish the earth.

In each instance God's work involved supernatural power. In no instance did man's work involve supernatural power. The miracle therefore belongs to God; the mandate belongs to man.

Obviously man was the apex of God's creation. He was God's masterpiece. It was God's intention that man should live in conformity to the law of God and work in harmony with the purposes of God. God took man into partnership with Himself and made him His representative on the earth. To this end God gave him dominion over the fish of the sea, the fowl of the air, and the beasts of the field. All were placed under the rule and at the service of man. In making this arrangement God was, as it were, sharing a little of His sovereignty with man. In this sense man was crowned with glory and honor (Ps 8:5).

After the Flood God promised Noah that He would maintain on the earth certain physical and atmospheric conditions essential to the preservation of life (Ge 8:22); but this was on the assumption that man would do his part. He would sow the seed in the spring; only then would he reap a harvest in the fall. General Booth of the Salvation Army said, "It takes two to grow a potato—God and the farmer." God could, of course, grow potatoes on His own. He has never been known to do so. He has provided the sun, the soil, the rain, and the seed. He will do no more. Man must assume his responsibility. He must prepare the soil; he must sow the seed; he must harvest the crop. That is a law that runs uniformly throughout all of nature, and woe betide the farmer who ignores or defies that law.

God is most prodigal when it comes to dispensing His grace. He is most economical when it comes to exercising His power. If man can do the job on his own, God allows him to do so. Indeed, God insists that man use all the resources at his command. Only when these have been employed and have failed does God step in and work a miracle. There are those who deny that God ever works miracles. There are others who think that God should always work miracles and thus relieve them of the obligation to put forth any great effort on their own behalf. Both are wrong. God *created* the earth. Then He turned it over to man and instructed him to *subdue* it. The first required a miracle, for it was obviously beyond the power of man to achieve. The second was not a miracle; rather it constituted a mandate.

It stands to reason that there are some things that God does all on His own. It's just as well, because there isn't much that we could do to help Him. The seasons come and go and the tides rise and fall without any help from man. The stars in their courses, the planets in their orbits, the earth on its axis—all are maintained and controlled by His almighty power. Man is quite helpless to do anything in those areas.

If there is a human or natural way for God to achieve His purpose, however, He will go that route; and He expects man to follow. In so doing He confers on man a high honor as well as a great obligation, for then man becomes a co-worker with God (1 Co 3:9). It is a staggering thought that God has taken man into partnership with Himself.

This is true in the realm of redemption as well as in the realm of creation. The Old Testament is replete with examples of divine-human cooperation. God always achieves His purpose, but seldom without the active cooperation of His people. When God decided to destroy the world with the Flood, He commanded Noah to build an ark. When He decided to liberate His people from the bondage of Egypt, He commissioned Moses to be their emancipator. When the theocracy gave way to the monarchy, God raised up David, a man after His own heart, who did all His will. When God found it necessary to punish His people, He used a heathen king, Nebuchadnezzar, to carry them away into captivity. When He saved His people from national destruction, He saw to it that Queen Esther was on the throne at the right time. When He wanted to restore His people to the Promised Land after the captivity, He raised up Ezra, Nehemiah, and Zerubbabel.

When we turn to the New Testament we find the same division of labor in the realm of redemption that we noted in the early chapters of Genesis with regard to creation. Here again we find both miracle and mandate, the miracle being the work of God and the mandate being the work of man. The miracle involved three historic events—the incarnation of Jesus Christ, His atoning death, and His bodily resurrection.

The greatest event in the history of the world occurred when God visited this planet in the person of His Son, when He wrapped Himself round with the mantle of our humanity and appeared on earth in the humble guise of a tiny babe wrapped in swaddling clothes and cradled in a manger. In the Incarnation the Son of God became the Son of Man that through His death and resurrection He might reconcile the world to Himself (2 Co 5:19).

The New Testament is very clear concerning the purpose of the Incarnation. Jesus said: "The Son of man came to seek and to save the lost" (Lk 19:10). Paul said: "Christ Jesus came into the world to save sinners" (1 Ti 1:15). John said: "The Father has sent His Son as the Savior of the world" (1 Jn 4:14).

The salvation of the human race could not be effected by any other means. It required nothing less than the death and resurrection of the Son of God. The Gospels record with some detail the three-year public ministry of Christ, but the main emphasis is obviously on the last week —Passion Week, which ended with the crucifixion. His prime purpose in coming into the world was not to live but to die.

The crucifixion involved two kinds of suffering. During the first three hours on the cross His sufferings were physical, inflicted by the hand of man. They were an expression of man's hate. During the second three hours His sufferings were spiritual, inflicted by the hand of God. They were an expression of God's wrath. The former He bore without a murmur. Indeed, He rose triumphant above them and prayed for His tormentors. But the latter—the spiritual sufferings—were of an entirely different character. They were spiritual and they entered into the very sinews of His soul. It was during those three hours that His soul was made an offering for sin (Is 53:10). Peter said: "He himself bore our sins in his own body on the tree" (1 Pe 2:24). Paul went further and said that the sinless One was actually made "to be sin" on our behalf (2 Co 5:21). Here we come face to face with the mystery—miracle, if you like—of the Atonement. In some mysterious way that we cannot possibly understand Jesus Christ on the cross was so thoroughly and completely identified with us and our sin that He is said to have been "made sin for us." No theologian has ever been able to plumb the depths of that expression.

> We do not know, we cannot tell
> What pains He had to bear;
> But we believe it was for us
> He hung and suffered there.
>
> There was none other good enough
> To pay the price of sin;
> He only could unlock the gate
> Of heaven, and let us in.

The third great event was the Resurrection. If the gospel story had ended with the crucifixion, there would have been no salvation, no gospel, no church, and no mission. But it didn't end there; it went on to include the Resurrection. In the New Testament the death and resurrection of Christ are linked together. Paul said He "was put to death for our trespasses and raised for our justification" (Ro 4:25). These two events belong together. Both are essential to the gospel (1 Co 15:3-4).

The fact that nobody else ever rose from the dead is no reason for rejecting the miracle of the Resurrection, for it is one of the best authenticated facts of history. The Resurrection was not the only unique thing about Christ. Everything about Him was unique. His virgin birth, His sinless character, His atoning death, His victorious resurrection, and His glorious ascension into heaven—all were unique. He was the only one who ever rose victorious over life. Why should He not rise victorious over death? It is unthinkable that Jesus, who claimed to be the resurrection and the life and who raised others from the dead, should Himself finally succumb to its power. Everything Jesus ever said or did would lead us to expect a resurrection. If He didn't rise from the dead, He should have!

So much for the miracle of redemption. What about the mandate? This is where the apostles came in. Jesus came to *provide* redemption, not to *preach* it. That is part of the mandate and for that reason it belongs to the disciples. That is why Jesus did not remain on earth more than forty days after the Resurrection. He stayed only long enough to round up the discouraged disciples, confirm their faith, dispel their fears, and give them their marching orders for the days ahead. So far as we know, Jesus never engaged in public ministry after His resurrection. His redemptive mission, that part of it which involved a miracle and for which He alone was responsible, was accomplished, and He returned to heaven from whence He had come.

But before He left He gave the disciples the missionary mandate, the Great Commission, as recorded in one form or another in all four Gospels and repeated by Luke in Acts 1:8. He had done His part. Now they must do theirs. His part was to *provide* the gospel. Theirs was to *proclaim* it. They *could* not provide it. He *would* not proclaim it.

So important was this lesson that Jesus began teaching it to His disciples long before the crucifixion. From among His many disciples He chose twelve apostles that they might learn to bear His yoke (Mt 11:29) and ultimately come to share His mission (Jn 20:21). On these twelve men He lavished most of His time, thought, counsel, and prayer. He was training them for the part they were destined to play later on in His redemptive mission. He taught them to pray. He sent them out to preach. He gave them power to heal the sick and to cleanse the leper. They even cast out demons in His name.

Even in the working of His miracles He saw to it that His disciples were identified with Him. On certain occasions He used their resources rather than His own. When performing the very first miracle He enlisted the help of others. He could easily have made the wine out of nothing. He chose to take water and convert it into wine. And where did He get the water? From a nearby well. The servants could not turn the water into wine, but they could fill the waterpots with water and thus make it possible for Jesus to work the miracle. Jesus insisted on others doing what they could before He employed His power to do what they could not.

Again, when He fed the five thousand He was careful to solicit their cooperation. He performed the miracle in such a way as to teach them another lesson in divine-human cooperation. He began by asking for an inventory of their resources. They were meager to be sure—five loaves and two fishes. The disciples complained that they were insufficient. But they were finally persuaded to turn them over to Him. And with *their* resources He worked the miracle and the people were fed. He simply multiplied the loaves and fishes they had provided. He could easily have created food out of nothing or turned the stones into bread.

58048

Instead He chose to work with and through His disciples, thereby teaching them an important lesson.

The greatest of all miracles was the raising of Lazarus from the dead. Surely Jesus will work this miracle entirely on His own. But no; there were two things the others could do, and Jesus insisted that they do them. One preceded the miracle and the other followed; but both were part of the lesson He wanted to get across to them. So He said to Martha: "Roll away the stone." Why the command? Could He not have raised Lazarus with the stone in its place? Failing that, could He not have rolled away the stone by Himself, either by word or deed? Then why all the bother to get Martha in on the act? Because here, as on other occasions, He wanted to teach the lesson of divine-human cooperation.

And after Lazarus was raised from the dead there was one more act to the drama. So Jesus commanded: "Loose him and let him go." Again, Jesus could have done this by Himself with little or no effort; but He wanted to drive home the all-important lesson that they must be prepared to do everything that is humanly possible; then and only then will He perform the miracle.

Did the disciples learn the lesson well? For the answer we need only turn to the Acts of the Apostles. The miracle of redemption had been completed and Jesus had returned to heaven. The disciples, who in the Gospels were timid, fearful, stupid, and unbelieving, were now full-fledged apostles. The Holy Spirit had come and they had been endued with power from on high. As a result they now manifested a new insight into Scripture (Acts 2:16, 25-28, 34-35), a new courage in witnessing (Acts 4:13, 31), a new power in service (Acts 5:12-16), and a new initiative in action (Acts 5:1-11; 6:1-7).

They realized that the end of the miracle was the beginning of the mandate. Jesus Christ had gone but the Holy Spirit had come, and in His power they were prepared to take the gospel to the ends of the earth. They began, as Jesus told them, in Jerusalem; and before long they were accused of filling the city with their doctrine (Acts 5:28). From Jerusalem the gospel spread to Judea and Samaria, and in a few years there were churches throughout all Judea, Galilee, and Samaria (Acts 9:31). Peter preached the gospel to Cornelius and thus opened the door of the gospel to the Gentiles (Acts 10). Later on Paul appeared on the scene and almost single-handedly planted churches in four of the most populous provinces of the empire—Galatia, Asia, Macedonia, and Achaia—all in less than fifteen years.

It is clear from the Acts that the church was fully aware of the missionary mandate. In those days the church *was* mission. The history of the early church is the history of missions. The entire Book of Acts, with the possible exception of chapter 15, deals directly with the proc-

Lincoln Christian College

lamation of the gospel and the extension of the kingdom into all parts of the empire. And even chapter 15 has an indirect bearing on missions, for it records the momentous decision of the church to allow the Gentiles into the church as first-class citizens.

The apostles were eyewitnesses of the *miracle* of redemption (1 Jn 1:1-3). They were there when it happened (2 Pe 1:18), and to a man they were persuaded that God was in Christ reconciling the world to Himself (2 Co 5:19). They were equally sure that the *mandate* of redemption rested on them and that God had committed to them the ministry of reconciliation. Everywhere they went their testimony was the same. "We are ambassadors for Christ, *God making his appeal through us*. We beseech you on behalf of Christ, be reconciled to God" (2 Co 5:20).

The glorious fact of the gospel is that God loved the world (Jn 3:16), that Christ died for all (2 Co 5:15), that whoever calls on the name of the Lord shall be saved (Ro 10:13). But Paul asks: "How are men to call upon him in whom they have not believed? And how are they to believe in him of whom they have never heard? And how shall they hear without a preacher?" (Ro 10:14). That is logic, not rhetoric; and the logic is devastating. God has ordained that men should be saved through the preaching of the gospel, even though the gospel may be folly to the Greeks and a stumbling-block to the Jews (1 Co 1:23).

There is not a single line in the Book of Acts to suggest that God can save a human being without employing a human agent. On the contrary there are several examples of God's going to great lengths to secure the active cooperation of one or another of His servants.

The Ethiopian eunuch in chapter 8 is a classic example. A proselyte to Judaism, he had been to Jerusalem to worship in the temple. While there he acquired a copy of the Old Testament and was on his way home, still without a knowledge of Christ. Philip, the evangelist, was called away from a citywide crusade in Samaria and directed by the Holy Spirit to go south into the desert to intercept the eunuch as he traveled back to Ethiopia. Philip found the eunuch reading Isaiah 53. Philip's first question was: "Do you understand what you are reading?" and he replied, "How can I, unless someone guides me?" (Acts 8:30-31). In this case, even a copy of the Scriptures was not sufficient. He needed someone to explain them to him. This Philip did. The eunuch believed, was baptized, and went on his way rejoicing.

Perhaps the most notable example of the human agent in Christian witness was that of Peter and Cornelius in chapter 10. Cornelius was a Roman centurion, a proselyte to Judaism, and doubtless a seeker after truth. His prayers and his alms prompted God to act on his behalf and make it possible for him to hear the gospel. And how did He do it? He sent an angel all the way from heaven to Caesarea, and when he got there all he could do was give Cornelius the name and address of a *man* who would tell him the gospel. The angel had no mandate to preach—just to inform Cornelius where he could find a preacher.

What about Saul of Tarsus? At first sight it would seem that he was an exception to the rule. But this is more apparent than real. Actually, there were at least two human agents used in the conversion of Saul. One was Stephen and the other was Ananias.

Saul's first contact with Stephen came long before the latter was stoned (Acts 7:58). It is almost certain that these two men had more than one face-to-face confrontation in the synagogue of the Cilicians in Jerusalem (Acts 6:9). That Saul was a member, doubtless an elder, of that particular synagogue is a safe assumption. He hailed from Tarsus, the most important city in Cilicia. It is unthinkable that he was not a member of the synagogue made up of his compatriots from that province. If so, he must have been among those who "disputed with Stephen." It is said that Stephen preached with such convincing power that the leaders of the synagogue were unable to hold their own against him. Saul, as a leading rabbi, must have felt the sting of Stephen's words.

But that was not all. When Saul was struck blind at Damascus (chap. 9), a local Christian, Ananias by name, was commissioned by God to contact Saul, restore his sight, baptize him, and introduce him to the local church. So the mighty Saul of Tarsus, later to become the great apostle Paul, was initiated into the Christian faith by a humble, unknown disciple in Damascus.

The question naturally follows: Is this an invariable rule? If so, what happens when the church falls down on the job and missions are allowed to languish? What about the heathen who have never heard? Are they all lost? The final answer must rest with God, the Judge of all the earth (Ge 18:25), who is righteous in all His ways and holy in all His works (Ps 145:17). It would not be correct to say that Almighty God *cannot* impinge His saving truth directly on the minds of men with sufficient force to bring them to a knowledge of Himself; but we have no reason *from the Scriptures* to believe, or even to assume, that He ever does so. By precept and example the New Testament clearly teaches that the mandate to preach the gospel and make disciples of all nations has been given to the church, and only the church can assume and fulfill that mandate. When the church ceases to be a missionary church, it denies its faith and betrays its trust.

Some people have taken comfort from the hope that if one person falls down on his missionary obligation, God will raise up someone else to take his place. There is nothing in Scripture to warrant such a false hope. Jesus told us that God has given to every man his own work (Mk 13:34). Nowhere does the New Testament suggest that God has His back-up team to step into the gap when the original team fails to follow through. Every Christian has been appointed to his own task. If he is pulled out of line to fill the gap left by some delinquent, what happens to his work?

Then there are those whose understanding of God's sovereignty leads them to believe that come what may God will achieve His purpose, with or without man's help. God will take care of the heathen, they say. This was the prevailing view among the Reformers and the churches they established in Europe. For almost two hundred years there was practically no missionary outreach from Protestant Europe. As late as William Carey's day the church continued to have a blind spot in regard to world missions. When Carey, in a ministerial meeting, urged his brethren to undertake the conversion of the heathen world, he was politely told by the moderator: "Young man, sit down! When God decides to convert the heathen He will do so without your help or mine."

The moderator was dead wrong. God converted the heathen in India, but *not* without Carey's help. Carey spent almost forty years in India, during which time he helped to translate the Scriptures into thirty-five of the languages of that part of the world. Those thirty-five languages and the people who spoke them had been in existence for several thousand years. The Scriptures had been in existence for almost eighteen hundred years; but never until the nineteenth century were those Scriptures made available to those people. And without Carey, and the others who followed him, those people would still be without a knowledge of Jesus Christ.

To say, "God will take care of the heathen," and leave it there is to close one's eyes to the clear statements of the Bible and the hard, cold facts of history. The question is not whether God will take care of the heathen, but *how* He does it. He has made it abundantly clear in His Word that it is His will and purpose to care for the heathen *through the church*. The *miracle* of reconciliation was accomplished by the death and resurrection of Christ. The *ministry* of reconciliation has been committed to the church. If the church for any reason fails to fulfill its God-given ministry, the church, and not God, must bear the blame. The church cannot abrogate its responsibility and throw the burden back on God. World evangelization *can* be achieved by human means and manpower. It is both foolish and futile to expect God to achieve by supernatural means what the church can accomplish by human means.

The Uniqueness of the Christian Faith

In a pluralistic world it is becoming increasingly difficult to maintain the uniqueness of the Christian faith. We have the problem right here on the home front, where Bible reading and the Lord's Prayer have been banned from the public school system because of the presence of a small minority of Jews, agnostics, and others for whom Christianity is not a viable option.

It is impossible to open the United Nations sessions with prayer, not because the illustrious delegates are atheists or agnostics, but because they represent all the major religions of the world, each competing for its place in the sun. If prayer is offered, to whom should it be addressed—God, Allah, Jesus, Buddha, Vishnu, Krishna, or someone else? Everyone, of course, believes his religion to be the best, but he runs into trouble when he tries to impose this point of view on others.

The notion that one religion is true and the others are, to a lesser or greater degree, false is hardly in keeping with the insights of anthropology. According to anthropology religion is a purely social phenomenon, an integral part of culture. It is no longer considered in good taste to refer to certain cultures as "primitive" or certain religions as "pagan." To do so is to forfeit one's intellectual respectability in academic circles. Modern man is too sophisticated to speak in pejorative terms of other peoples and their cultures.

Even within Christendom the ancient landmarks are rapidly disappearing. In morality there is no such thing as sin; in theology there is no such thing as heresy. The only heresy is bigotry. Even the Supreme Court of the United States declares that it is impossible to define such terms as *pornography* or *obscenity;* so the movies and magazines are filled with both; and it will not be long before they invade the television industry.

When we move into the non-Christian world, where the missionary has to operate, we find that the exclusive claims of Christianity are vigorously challenged by the non-Christian religions now undergoing an unprecedented resurgence. It is safe to say that the most offensive aspect of twentieth-century Christianity is its exclusiveness. Such a claim does not make sense to the Hindu, the Buddhist, or the Confucianist.

Most of the great ethnic religions of the world hold certain doctrines in common. Most of them believe in the existence of a supreme being. They possess sacred scriptures. They have a well-defined doctrine of salvation. They believe in life after death. They have a system of ethics. They engage in religious rituals. They have human founders for whom they make certain claims. They have a priestly caste and religious orders. But they are not, generally speaking, exclusive, except, of course, Islam. Hinduism is reputed to be the most inclusive of them all. Buddhism prides itself on being tolerant of other systems. Christianity and Islam are exclusive, the latter militantly so.

It is only fair to point out that while these non-Christian religions are tolerant in theory, they are not always tolerant in practice. There are certain fundamental doctrines in Hinduism that are not open to debate. One of these is the doctrine that all matter, including *atman,* the individual soul, has no objective existence in fact. Another is that ultimate reality is spiritual and found only in *Brahman,* the world soul. Hinduism tolerates everything except conversion, and herein lies its inconsistency. If all religions are equally valid, as the Hindus maintain, why should they object when a Hindu becomes a Christian?

In this study we are not concerned to "prove" that Christianity is true or that the non-Christian religions are false. Nor are we saying that these other religions do not have *some* things in common with Christianity. We are simply trying to point out certain features of Christianity which, *taken together,* place it in a class by itself. Harry Emerson Fosdick, former high priest of American liberal theology, said on one occasion that there is nothing in Christianity that cannot be found in the other religions of the world. It is true that unusual births and strange resurrections are found in the non-Christian religions; but when one examines the details one is struck not with the similarities of the two accounts, but with the dissimilarities. What person in his right mind would want to suggest that the Resurrection story in the Gospels is to be placed in the same category with the resurrections found in the mystery religions so common in the Roman world of Jesus' day? They have about as much in common as ancient witchcraft and modern medicine.

THE CHARACTER OF GOD

The God of the Christian revelation, Jehovah or Yahweh, claims to be the one true God (Jn 17:3), Creator of heaven and earth (Is 40:28). Though His revelation was given through Israel and He was known as the God of Abraham, Isaac, and Jacob (Ex 3:6), He is never depicted as a tribal god. He is the King of all the earth (Ps 47:2). He is a great God and a great King above all gods (Ps 95:3); and all other gods are idols (Ps 96:5). There is no other god like Him (Ps 89:6). He deserves and demands the worship and service of all men (De 6:13-15).

1. He is an eternal Being. He is self-existent (Ex 3:14) and therefore eternal (De 32:40). All else exists because He willed its existence

(Co 1:16-17). He alone exists necessarily, from eternity to eternity (Jn 1:1).

2. **He is a personal Being.** He is eternally separate and distinct from all other beings. He is conscious of Himself as the Eternal Ego (Pr 8:22-23). He possesses the power of self-determination. He can love (Jn 3:16) and be loved (Mt 22:37).

3. **He is an infinite Being.** His attributes are infinite. He is all good (Ex 34:6), all wise (Ro 11:33), and all powerful (Is 40:18-26). He fills all heaven (Is 66:1). He fills all earth as well (Ps 139:7-10). He is not merely more wise, more just, and more good than any other being. He is infinitely wise, infinitely just, and infinitely good. He is both immanent (Acts 17:27-28) and transcendent (Is 55:8-9) at the same time. His only limitations are those that He has voluntarily imposed on Himself.

4. **He is a moral Being.** The Greek gods were more immoral than their devotees. Not so Jehovah. He loves righteousness and hates iniquity (He 1:9). He is righteous in all His ways and holy in all His works (Ps 145:17). He is both light (1 Jn 1:5) and love (1 Jn 4:8). His love is a holy love. His holiness glows with love and His love burns with holiness. He is a holy God (Ex 15:11; Is 6:3) and demands holiness of all His people (Le 19:2; He 12:14).

5. **He exists in three persons—Father, Son, and Holy Spirit.** They are three persons but only one God (Mt 28:19). All three persons are eternally coequal in wisdom, love, and power. Each has all the powers and prerogatives of the other two. All three persons have been and are engaged in the work of creation, redemption, and judgment.

6. **He has revealed Himself to man.** He is not a god afar off, who hides Himself. He rejoices in the inhabited world and delights in the sons of men (Pr 8:31). He has revealed Himself through general revelation, which includes creation (Ro 1:19-20) and conscience (Ro 2:14-15); and through special revelation, which includes the written Word (He 1:1) and the living Word (Jn 1:14, 18).

No other religion has a god who possesses all these characteristics. The Christian God, therefore, is unique.

THE PERSON OF CHRIST

All the great religions, except Hinduism and Shinto, have their founders. Some of them were good and great men; but none of them belongs in the same category with Jesus Christ. He stands alone in solitary grandeur among the sons of men. By almost universal consent He was the greatest character who ever lived. Even non-Christians gladly acknowledge the influence of His life and teaching. Jean Paul Richter expressed it well when he said, "He, being the mightiest among the holy and the holiest among the mighty, lifted with His pierced hands the gates of empires off their hinges, turned the streams of centuries out of their channels, and today rules the world."

No other religion, including Islam, is so completely identified with the life and teaching of its founder. Buddhism could exist and flourish if Gautama had never lived. The same can be said of Communism and Karl Marx. Confucius is by no means essential to the system that bears his name. This is not true of Christianity. Christianity stands or falls with Jesus Christ. Without Him there would be no salvation, no gospel, no New Testament, and no Christian church.

The uniqueness of Jesus Christ finds expression in six things:

1. His virgin birth. This is clearly taught in two of the four Gospels. It is true that miraculous births are claimed for other religious leaders, but the details are so vulgar and grotesque as to make them suspect. In Jesus' case the miraculous element was reduced to an irreducible minimum—conception. After that, nature took over and Jesus was born nine months later as any other child is born.

He was neither a physical giant nor a mental prodigy. The record tells us that he "increased in wisdom and in stature, and in favor with God and man" (Lk 2:52). If modern scholars have problems with the virgin birth, they can derive comfort from the fact that both Mary and Joseph did too. We should also remember that the Gospel writer who gives us the most details concerning the birth of Christ (Luke) was a physician. Moreover, the virgin birth was not added simply to embellish the story. It was a necessary part of the miracle of the Incarnation. It was essential to the preservation of His holy nature (Lk 1:35).

2. His sinless character. The matchless life of perfect love lived by Christ is a unique phenomenon in the history of the world. He was born without sin, and He lived without sin. On this point we have the testimony of both friends (2 Co 5:21; 1 Pe 2:22; 1 Jn 3:5) and foes (Lk 23:41; Jn 19:4, 6). He was the only man who ever lived whose inner life was white as snow, pure as sunlight, strong as steel. Never once did He depart from the path of rectitude. Never once did He succumb to the world, the flesh, or the devil. He was the only person who ever loved God with all His heart and could say, "I delight to do thy will, O my God" (Ps 40:8).

3. His atoning death. Without sin Himself, He died for the sins of others. He died not as a prophet, or a reformer, or even as a martyr.

He died as a Savior, the *only* Savior of the world (1 Pe 3:18). He gave His life and shed His blood for the remission of sins (Mt 26:28). His death, far from being an accident or incident of human history, was part of God's eternal plan and purpose (Acts 4:27-28) and could be brought about only in God's way, in God's time, and with God's consent (Jn 19:11). In death as well as in life He occupied a solitary throne.

4. His victorious resurrection. Not only did He claim to be "the resurrection and the life" (Jn 11:25); He rose from the dead on the third day as He had predicted. The Resurrection accounts as given by the four evangelists bear all the earmarks of a true story. They are all the more remarkable because the disciples did not expect ever to see Jesus alive again; and even when His resurrection was reported to them, they refused to believe it until they saw Him with their own eyes. And when they finally preached "Jesus and the resurrection" in the city that crucified Him they paid for it with their lives. To say that the disciples deliberately fabricated the story is sheer nonsense. To say that they believed something that didn't actually happen is also nonsense.

This historic event, one of the best-authenticated facts in history, is of the utmost significance to the Christian faith. It is the foundation stone. Remove this stone and the whole superstructure crumbles. Christianity stands or falls on the Resurrection. His virgin birth, His sinless character, His atoning death—all have no meaning apart from the Resurrection. Deny that and you have denied everything else.

5. His ascension into heaven. His entrance into the world was a miracle; His departure from the world was also a miracle. This is the way God intended it to be (Jn 16:28). Jesus did not intend to remain on earth indefinitely. He came simply to "tabernacle" among us (Jn 1:4). When His redemptive mission was accomplished it was fitting that He should return to heaven. The Resurrection and the Ascension are treated in the Pauline Epistles as two phases of one climactic event by which God raised Him from the dead and exalted Him to His own right hand, far above all principality and power and might and dominion (Eph 1:20-21; Ph 2:9-10). He is now the Prince of life (Acts 3:15), the Lord of glory (1 Co 2:8), and the Head of the church (Co 1:18). He now sits at the right hand of God, the place of power, where He is a living, reigning Lord and Savior, able to save all who come to God by Him (He 7:25). All power in heaven and on earth has been given to Him (Mt 28:18).

6. His second coming to earth. The New Testament clearly teaches that Jesus Christ will return to the earth to rapture the church (1 Th 4:16-17), to judge the world (Mt 25.31-46), and to establish His ever-lasting kingdom of justice and peace (Re 19:11—20:4).

These six aspects of His life and person place Jesus Christ in a class by Himself. He is a unique figure in the annals of history. Not one of these things can truthfully be said of any of the great figures of history or any of the founders of the non-Christian religions. Jesus would say of them what He said to His disciples: "You are from below, I am from above; you are of this world, I am not of this world" (Jn 8:23).

THE DOCTRINE OF SALVATION

All the great ethnic religions of the world have a doctrine of salva-tion. Indeed, salvation is the ultimate purpose of all religions. They use various terms and advocate different ways; but they all purport to deliver man from the human predicament in which he finds himself. The doctrine of salvation in Christianity differs fundamentally from the salvation offered by these other religions.

1. Salvation is the gift of God, not the work of man. In every other religion man seeks after God and tries by various ways and means to placate His wrath and secure His favor and protection. In Christianity it is God who seeks after man. Redemption is something accomplished by God and offered to man "without money and without price" (Is 55:1). Salvation is a free gift (Ro 6:23), bestowed by God on the principle of grace and received by man on the principle of faith (Eph 2:8).

2. Salvation is rooted in morality. God is a holy God. He cannot forgive sin simply by fiat. He cannot dispense mercy at the expense of justice. He must remain just at the same time that He justifies the sinner (Ro 3:26). He cannot save the sinner, however much He loves him, without first solving the moral problem of sin. The theology of redemption as taught in Scripture embraces several great laws or principles required by the holiness of God. (1) "The soul that sins shall die" (Ez 18:20). (2) "Without the shedding of blood there is no forgiveness of sins" (He 9:2). (3) "For the life of the flesh is in the blood; and I have given it for you upon the altar to make atonement for your souls; for it is the blood that makes atonement, by reason of the life" (Le 17:11) (4) "It is impossible that the blood of bulls and goats should take away sins" (He 10:4). (5) "He [Christ] entered once for all into the Holy Place, taking not the blood of goats and calves but his own blood, thus securing an eternal redemption" (He 9:12).

These five statements constitute the moral basis for the Christian doctrine of salvation. It is free, but not cheap. It cost God the lifeblood of His only Son. Now when God forgives sin He is not only good and kind (Ti 3:4), He is also faithful and just (1 Jn 1:9). No other religion offers a salvation that is rooted in morality and therefore consistent with the holiness of God.

3. Salvation is always deliverance from sin—both its penalty and its power. Other religions treat the symptoms, not the disease. Salvation for them is release from suffering, as in Buddhism; or ignorance, as in Hinduism. In Christianity salvation goes deeper and gets at the root cause of suffering, ignorance, and all the other ills that afflict mankind. The human predicament is the result of sin; and all man's fears, doubts, and frustrations stem from that. To get rid of *them*, one must first get rid of *it*.

Jesus Christ by His atoning death and victorious resurrection met all the demands of a holy God against the sinner. Jesus Christ, acting on our behalf, accepted the penalty, paid the price, and settled the account. The sinner who repents and believes is forever set free from the law of sin and death (Ro 8:2). Here and now he enjoys "peace with God" (Ro 5:1) and for him there is "no condemnation" (Ro 8:1).

But that is not all. Salvation in Christianity includes deliverance from the power as well as the penalty of sin. This is made possible by the presence of the Holy Spirit in the life of the believer. If the Christian walks in the power of the Spirit he will not fulfill the lusts of the flesh (Ga 5:16). The power of sin has been broken. Sin has no more dominion over him, since he is not under law but under grace (Ro 6:14). He is given not just a new leaf but a new life. He is now "in Christ," which means that he is a "new creation" (2 Co 5:17). Old things have passed away, and all things have become new.

4. Salvation includes the whole man—body, soul, and spirit. When man fell chaos was introduced into all parts of his constitution—spirit, soul, and body; mind, heart, and will. Theologians have called this "total depravity." Salvation, if it is to be effective, must attack and conquer sin in every part of man, not just his soul. This is precisely what Christian salvation does. It involves the whole man—spirit, soul, and body (1 Th 5:23). It also includes the mind (Ro 12:2; Ph 2:5; 2 Co 10:5), the heart (Ro 5:5; Co 3:15; He 10:22), and the will (Ro 7:9-25).

5. Salvation is a present possession as well as a future prospect. Christianity is the only religion which offers a here-and-now salvation. In all other religions the devotee must wait until the future life to dis-

cover whether or not he is a candidate for salvation. Buddhism and
Hinduism teach the doctrine of *samsara*—reincarnation. One can only
hope that his lot in the next life will be an improvement on this one.
But he is never sure. He may go up in the scale of life or he may go
down. Before he gets through he may have to pass through eight million
incarnations. And when Nirvana is finally reached what kind of salvation does he experience? The word *Nirvana* means to "blow out" like a
candle. The five *khandhas,* or states of being, are dissolved, and the
individual soul is lost in the universal soul. Like a drop of rain falling
back into the ocean, it loses its separate identity. Not only is there no
salvation for the body, but the personality itself is destroyed.

On the contrary, the Christian does not have to wait for the next
life. Here and now he can enjoy the forgiveness of sins (1 Jn 2:12) and
know that he has eternal life (1 Jn 5:13). Moreover, for the Christian
salvation is also a future prospect. What he has now is only a foretaste
of what's ahead. His body too is to be redeemed (Ro 8:23). In the
resurrection he will be given a new body, a "spiritual" body (1 Co
15:44), a "glorious" body (Ph 3:21), which will be free of sin and
endowed with new powers and properties (1 Co 15:42-44) quite beyond anything he has known in this life. Indeed, salvation will extend
to the "whole creation" (Ro 8:22-25) and will involve a new heaven
and a new earth from which all taint and trace of sin will have been
removed (Re 21).

6. Salvation involves not only the individual but society as well.
The gospel has social implications. "You shall love the Lord your God
with all your heart . . . [and] your neighbor as yourself" (Mt 22:37-39).
The gospel is first personal, then social. Both are important. Traditionally the liberals have preached a social gospel and the conservatives a
personal gospel. Both are right in what they include but wrong in what
they omit. To preach one aspect of the gospel and omit the other is to
preach an emasculated message.

The New Testament writers refused to settle for a dichotomy. In
Paul's Epistles faith and love are frequently mentioned in the same
verse (Co 1:4; 1 Th 1:3). John brings the two together in his First
Epistle (3:23). James insists that faith and works belong together and
goes so far as to say that without works faith is dead (Ja 2:14-26).
Genuine faith in Christ always leads to love for the brethren, and love
does not stop with the brethren; it goes on to embrace the world in all
its varied needs—physical, mental, material, and social, as well as
spiritual. When the question is asked, "Am I my brother's keeper?"
the Christian's answer is a resounding "Yes." He cannot, like the priest
and Levite, pass by on the other side (Lu 10:31-32). The love of Christ
will compel him to share his resources, however meager, with the

world round about him. His Master "went about doing good" (Acts 10:38) and he can do no less (Ga 6:10) He has no illusions that by his own efforts he can bring in the kingdom; but as the "salt of the earth" and the "light of the world" he will do his best to permeate society with the principles of the gospel, including social justice, civil rights, equal opportunity, brotherly love, and world peace.

Wherever missionaries have gone they have built churches, opened hospitals, operated schools, and in a hundred-and-one other ways have tried to follow in the steps of the Master, who had compassion on the multitudes, helped the helpless, fed the hungry, healed the sick, cleansed the leper, and raised the dead.

The non-Christian religions are now engaging in various kinds of social service and medical and educational work; but the impulse did not come from their religious beliefs. They have been forced into them by the competition afforded by Christian missionaries.

Each non-Christian religion has its own doctrine of salvation; but none of them can compare with the glorious salvation found in Jesus Christ.

THE HOLY SCRIPTURES

All the great religions have their sacred books. Some of them are older than the oldest parts of our Old Testament. Some claim to be inspired. Others claim to be revelations from God. Many of them contain fragments of high ethical teachings worthy of emulation. But when placed alongside the Christian Scriptures they leave much to be desired. Several important elements in the Christian Scriptures place them in a class by themselves.

1. **The human element.** The Holy Spirit is the Author of the Bible; but the individual books were written by human writers. Altogether there are sixty-six books with some forty different authors, all of whom can be readily identified as historic persons. In the Old Testament we have such outstanding persons as Moses, David, Isaiah, Jeremiah, Ezekiel, Daniel, and others. In the New Testament we have Matthew, Mark, Luke, John, Paul, Peter, James, and Jude. These men were not ghost writers. Though they wrote under the inspiration of the Holy Spirit (2 Ti 3:16), each was permitted to retain his own vocabulary and style. Yet in spite of a vast array of writers stretching over a period of fifteen hundred years, there is in the Scriptures an amazing degree of unity.

2. **The historical element.** A large portion of both Testaments is taken up with history. Bible history is the history of Israel; neverthe-

less it is genuine history, not legend or myth. And there are frequent references to the other great nations of antiquity—Egypt, Babylon, Assyria, Persia, Greece, and Rome. The four Gospels, while biographical in content, include historical references. The Book of Acts is made up entirely of history. Herod the Great, Herod Antipas, Herod Agrippa, Pontius Pilate, Caesar Augustus, Caiaphas, Gallio, and others, are well-known figures in Roman history. No other sacred scripture contains so many specific references to historic persons, places, and events.

3. The prophetic element. This is most prominent in the Old Testament. Coming events in Israel and in the Gentile world were foretold centuries before they came to pass. And this occurs not once or twice but many times. Genesis 15:13 predicted the four-hundred-year captivity of the Hebrews in Egypt. It also predicted their deliverance when the iniquity of the Amorites would be complete. Moses, in Deuteronomy 28, predicted the future of Israel, which included blessings if they obeyed and calamities if they disobeyed. It is most unusual for a people to record, much less predict, their failures and defeats. Jeremiah predicted that the Jews would be carried into Babylon, where they would remain in captivity for seventy years (Je 25:8-11). He also predicted that after seventy years they would be restored to their own land (Je 29:10). Both predictions came to pass.

Isaiah predicted the judgment of the heathen nations, and in each case the judgment came to pass. Hosea predicted that Israel would "dwell many days without king or prince, without sacrifice or pillar, without ephod or teraphim" (Ho 3:4). By all human reasoning the Jews as a people should long ago have perished from the earth; but they are still with us and in recent years have been restored to their homeland in Palestine. Daniel predicted the rise and fall of Babylon, Medo-Persia, Greece, and Rome with such detail and accuracy that liberal scholars insist that the Book of Daniel is history and not prophecy! In the New Testament Jesus predicted the destruction of Jerusalem and the temple (Mt 24:2), which happened in A.D. 70.

4. The Messianic element. The greatest of all predictions were those relating to the coming Messiah. The earliest reference is Genesis 3:15, where He is referred to as the seed of the woman. Later on further information was divulged. He was to be of the seed of Abraham (Ge 12:3), of the tribe of Judah (Ge 49:10), of the house of David (2 Sa 7:16). He was to be born of a virgin (Is 7:14) in the city of Bethlehem (Mi 5:2). His death by crucifixion was foretold in Psalm 22 long before crucifixion became an accepted form of execution. Many specific details of the crucifixion contained in that passage were fulfilled to the letter, as the Gospel writers were careful to point out.

5. The eschatological element. Voltaire said that history is nothing but a pack of tricks that we play on the dead. Matthew Arnold called history a "Mississippi of falsehoods." World history may not make sense to us; but it does to God. He is the King of the nations and He is the Lord of history. History is not moving in cycles but unfolding persistently and progressively towards its appointed goal. Nations come and go, kingdoms rise and fall, civilizations wax and wane, all at His command (Da 2:21).

God is both omnipotent and omniscient. He is in possession of all the facts. He is in control of every situation. He knows the end from the beginning and is working all things after the counsel of His own will (Eph 1:9-12). History will not run on forever. When it has run its appointed course God will step in and the curtain will close. This age will end with the second coming of Jesus Christ. We know almost nothing of the details relating to time and circumstance. We have been warned against setting dates, but the broad outlines have been drawn for us in the Scriptures. The world will not blow itself to smithereens, nor will it end in a nuclear holocaust. At the end of the age Jesus Christ will return to establish His kingdom (2 Th 1:5-10), the kingdom for which He told us to pray (Mt 6:10).

6. The dynamic element. We are accustomed to speaking of the living Word when referring to Christ and the written Word when referring to the Bible, and the distinction is a valid one; but we must not forget that the Bible is a living book (He 4:12). Jesus said, "The words that I have spoken to you are spirit and life" (Jn 6:63). The two agents that are used in the regeneration of the human soul are the Spirit of God and the Word of God (Jn 3:5). When the living Spirit applies the living Word to the heart and conscience of the sinner, life is imparted to the dead soul and the person is born anew.

As a profligate young man Augustine, walking in a garden in Milan, heard a voice saying to him: "Pick up the book and read." He opened the Bible and read:

> The night is far gone, the day is at hand. Let us then cast off the works of darkness and put on the armor of light; let us conduct ourselves becomingly as in the day, not in reveling and drunkenness, not in debauchery and licentiousness, not in quarreling and jealousy. But put on the Lord Jesus Christ, and make no provision for the flesh, to gratify its desires (Ro 13:12-14).

Augustine was immediately delivered from a life of sin and became the church's greatest theologian since Paul.

Martin Luther was gloriously liberated from a life of spiritual bondage when his mind was suddenly directed to the words: "The just shall live by faith" (Ro 1:17, KJV), and he became the great leader of the Protestant Reformation.

As a young man Charles Spurgeon wandered into a country chapel and heard a semiliterate preacher read with some difficulty this text: "Turn to me and be saved, all the ends of the earth! For I am God and there is no other" (Is 45:22). The verse so gripped Spurgeon's soul that he was converted on the spot and went on to become one of England's greatest preachers.

Wherever the Bible has gone it has transformed men, nations, and cultures. It is by far the most influential book in the world, and year after year it continues to be the best seller. It has been translated into more than fifteen hundred languages and dialects and is now available, in whole or in part, to 98 percent of the world's population. Among all the books of the world, religious and nonreligious, the Bible heads the list.

Voltaire wrote on one occasion: "A hundred years after my death you will not find a Bible outside the museums." Exactly one hundred years later the house in which Voltaire penned those words passed into the hands of the Geneva Bible Society and the walls were lined to the ceiling with Bibles.

The Missionary Mandate

The missionary mandate is usually restricted to the last words of Christ as recorded in the closing verses of the Gospel of Matthew. This familiar passage is known as the Great Commission, and not without reason; for it contains the marching orders given by the risen Christ to His disciples on the eve of His departure from the world. These words surely form part of the mandate, but should not be regarded as the whole mandate. There is much more to it than that.

There are at least three dimensions to the missionary mandate, only one of which is the Great Commission. The missionary mandate in its fullness is seen in the character of God, the command of Christ, and the condition of mankind.

1. **The Character of God.** The Christian mission, like the gospel, originated in the heart of God. It is His work, not man's; and it grows out of His essential character. If God were any other kind of God, there would be no Christian mission. The revelation of God in the Scriptures is not confined to His existence; it includes the *kind* of God He is. Indeed the Scriptures are not concerned to prove the existence of God; that is taken for granted. What the Bible reveals is the *character* of God. His person can never be divorced from His character. The

Scriptures have much to say about the attributes of God. Two of them are closely linked with the underlying concept of the world mission of the church. The apostle John in his First Epistle makes two great declarations concerning the character of God. "God is light" (1:5); and "God is love" (4:16).

These two attributes have always been an integral part of the character of God; but they were not fully manifest to the world until the coming of Christ. After spending three wonderful years in the company of the Son of God, John summed it all up in those majestic words: "This is the message we have heard from him and proclaim unto you, that God is light and in him is no darkness at all" (1 Jn 1:5).

The same is true of the other attribute, love. John says: "In this the love of God was made manifest among us, that God sent his only Son into the world, so that we might live through him. In this is love, not that we loved him but that he loved us and sent his Son to be the expiation for our sins" (1 Jn 4:9-10).

These two attributes, revealing as they do the true character of God, constitute an important dimension of the missionary mandate.

The world belongs to God (Ps 24:1). He loves that world (Jn 3:16). He is not willing that any should perish (2 Pe 3:9). He will have all men to be saved and to come to a knowledge of the truth (1 Ti 2:4). Why? Because the human race is one big family—His family (Acts 17:26). Man was made in the beginning *by* God, *for* God, and it was God's intention that man should find his highest happiness *in* God. God made man in His own image so that He could have an object worthy of His everlasting love.

God is love. This is the central fact of the gospel. We look up through nature and discover that God is law, responsible and dependable. We look up through Christ and discover that God is love, slow to anger and plenteous in mercy, full of pity and compassion, ready always to forgive.

God's love, like Himself, is eternal, inscrutable, and immutable. He loves mankind with an everlasting love (Je 31:3); and having once set His love upon man, He can never let him go. No matter how long the prodigal has remained in the far country, he is always free to return to the Father's house; and upon his return he will find the door open, the lamps burning, and the feast spread.

No one has expressed it more beautifully than Frederick Faber:

> There's a wideness in God's mercy
> Like the wideness of the sea;
> There's a kindness in His justice
> Which is more than liberty.

> For the love of God is broader
> Than the measure of man's mind,
> And the heart of the Eternal
> Is most wonderfully kind.

One of the greatest missionary books in the Old Testament is the Book of Jonah. The meaning and the miracle of that episode are not found in the story of the "great fish," but in the mercy of God that spared the wicked city of Nineveh when king and people repented. Jonah knew all along that that was precisely what God was likely to do. That's why he refused to go to Nineveh in the first place. He had a sneaking suspicion that, given half a chance, God would change His mind, forgive their sin, and spare the city. Jonah knew enough about God to know that He is essentially good and infinitely longsuffering, delighting not in the death of the wicked but desiring that man should turn from his wicked way and live.

This indestructible, all-inclusive love of God prompted Him to send Jesus Christ to be the Savior of the world (1 Jn 4:9). This is the Good News that constitutes the gospel. This great, glorious fact is the foundation of all missionary endeavor. Without it there would be no missionary mandate.

But that is not all there is to God's character. There is another side. God is *light* as well as love. *Light,* in Scripture, is a symbolic term and stands for three things. Physically, it stands for splendor or glory (2 Co 4:6, Re 21:23). Intellectually, it stands for truth (Ps 43:3). Morally, it stands for holiness (Ro 13:11-14). God is light; God is love. The two statements belong together.

God's love is a holy love. That is what makes it unique. It can never be compared with man's love. The difference between the two is not simply one of quantity, but one of quality as well. God's love is white as snow and pure as sunlight. Man's love, on the other hand, is a debased, corrupted form of love, streaked with selfishness and tainted with pride. This is why man has so much difficulty in understanding the true nature of love.

Everything pertaining to God speaks of the beauty of holiness. His law is perfect (Ps. 19:7). His commandment is holy and just and good (Ro 7:12). His throne is a throne of holiness (Ps 47:8). His kingdom is a kingdom of righteousness (Mt 6:33). His scepter is a scepter of equity (Ps 45:6). The psalmist summed it all up in one sentence when he spoke of Jehovah as being righteous in all His ways and holy in all His works (Ps 145:17).

Associated with God's holiness is His wrath, which is revealed from heaven against "all ungodliness and wickedness of men" (Ro 1:18). If man rejects God's love, he shuts himself up to God's wrath (Jn 3:36).

In our thinking about God we have tended to place these two attributes—love and wrath—in two separate compartments. His love, it is assumed, is reserved for His children, His wrath for His enemies. Not so. His love and His wrath cannot be separated. They are not two entities; rather they are two aspects of one entity—His holiness. His holiness glows with love. His love burns with holiness. He cannot express the one without at the same time expressing the other. His love goes out to the sinner just as much as to the saint, and for the same reason, namely, that both are creatures of His hand and therefore objects of His love. His anger is kindled against the saint as much as against the sinner, and for the same reason—He cannot tolerate sin no matter where it is found. When He punishes the sinner He acts in love; when He chastises the saint He likewise acts in love. The history of Israel in her declension and apostasy is ample evidence of that.

It has been said so often that it has become something of a cliché; but it is true nevertheless: God loves the sinner at the same time that He hates his sin. He loves righteousness *and* hates iniquity (He 1:9). The one is the corollary of the other. To love righteousness *is* to hate iniquity. This must be true in the very nature of the case. There is, therefore, no incompatibility between God's love and His wrath. His just wrath is an expression of His holy love.

If God were only love and not light, there would be no need of the Christian mission. He could save all men by a word, without faith or repentance. In that case there would be no need to preach the gospel. But Paul knew better. He declared, "Therefore, knowing the fear of the Lord, we persuade men" (2 Co 5:11). He also said, "Woe to me if I do not preach the gospel" (1 Co 9:16).

God's love makes it possible for the repentant sinner to be saved. God's holiness makes it inevitable that the unrepentant sinner will perish. Both are part of the gospel; both are part of the mandate. Without the love of God we would have no gospel. Without the wrath of God there would be no need for the gospel. So the missionary mandate is rooted in the character of God, who is light and who is also love.

2. The Command of Christ. This, of course, refers to the Great Commission, which is recorded in all four Gospels and the first chapter of Acts.

Here again the church has made the mistake of isolating one word —"go"—and building the entire missionary mandate on that. A closer look at the teachings of Christ will reveal the fact that He used not one word but three words to express the relationship of the disciples to Himself and His mission. These words were *Come, Follow, Go.* There is a sense in which everything Jesus said can be summed up in these three words. All three words are really part of the Great Commission.

Taken together they form an integral part of the missionary mandate.

The first word is COME. This was the word of invitation. It was addressed to the multitudes, to the publicans, harlots, lepers—in a word, to sinners. There is no more beautiful verse in the Bible than Matthew 11:28: "Come unto me, all who labor and are heavy laden, and I will give you rest." It was addressed to man in his alienation from God. The entire life of Christ on earth was a dramatic enactment of the call from Jehovah through Isaiah: "Let the wicked forsake his way and the unrighteous man his thoughts; and let him return to the Lord that he may have mercy on him, and to our God, for he will abundantly pardon" (Is 55:7). Men and women in all walks of life responded to the gracious invitation. They "came to Christ," and in coming they found exactly what He promised—life and health, joy and peace, all based on the forgiveness of sins.

The second word is FOLLOW. Having "come" to Christ, the person now becomes a believer. By an act of faith he has passed from death unto life, and is now a child of God, a member of Christ, and an inheritor of the Kingdom of Heaven.

Having responded to the invitation to come, he now hears a second word—"follow." Having become a believer, he is expected to take a second step and become a follower or disciple. Salvation is of grace by faith. It is a free gift. It does not depend on anything man can do. But discipleship is quite another matter. That is neither cheap nor easy. It is very difficult and very costly. In fact, in Jesus' day it was so costly that many people took offense when they heard the "hard sayings" of Jesus, and they went their way. Time and again Jesus said: "If any man would come after me, let him deny himself and take up his cross and follow me. . . . For whoever loses his life for my sake will find it" (Mt 16:24-25).

Matthew 11:28, which contains the Great Invitation, should never be divorced from Matthew 11:29—the Great Renunciation: "Take my yoke upon you, and learn from me; for I am gentle and lowly in heart, and you will find rest for your souls. For my yoke is easy and my burden is light." The Great Invitation was obviously addressed to the multitude. The Great Renunciation was demanded of those who had already allied themselves with Jesus but had gone no farther.

This is a challenge for the believer to become a disciple—one who follows Christ for the purpose of "learning" from Him. In evangelical circles we hear more about salvation than discipleship. We have settled for a cheap and ready form of "easy believism"; and to add to our sense of spiritual well-being we have tossed in the concept of eternal security for good measure. Once saved, always saved. In the meantime we go our own way and do our own thing. A. W. Tozer called this "instant Christianity."

It is hardly a matter of wonder that the country that gave the world instant tea and instant coffee should be the one to give it instant Christianity.... By instant Christianity I mean the kind found almost everywhere in gospel circles and which is born of the notion that we may discharge our total obligation to our own souls by one act of faith, or at most by two, and be relieved thereafter of all anxiety about our spiritual condition. We are saints by calling, our teachers keep telling us, and we are permitted to infer from this that there is no reason to seek to be saints by character.... By trying to pack all of salvation into one experience, or two, the advocates of instant Christianity flaunt the law of development which runs through all nature. They ignore the sanctifying effects of suffering, cross carrying and practical obedience. They pass by the need for spiritual training, the necessity of forming right religious habits and the need to wrestle against the world, the devil and the flesh.... Undue preoccupation with the initial act of believing has created in some a psychology of contentment, or at least of non-expectation.... It relieves them of the need to watch and fight and pray and sets them free to enjoy this world while waiting for the next.[2]

Tozer was right. Too often we have preached an emasculated gospel which has produced a watered-down version of Christianity. We have attached great importance to the positive aspects of the gospel —love, joy, and peace—but have said little about the less attractive features—alienation, humiliation, and persecution. Jesus warned His disciples that they would be hated by all men, that they would encounter all kinds of opposition and tribulation. He went so far as to say that the day would come when "whoever kills you will think he is offering service to God" (Jn 16:2). Paul exhorted his converts to continue in the faith and warned them that "through many tribulations we must enter the kingdom of God" (Acts 14:22).

In our preaching we have challenged young people to "give their hearts to Christ," and led them to believe that this is the end and aim of the Christian life. We have said little or nothing about allegiance to the person of Christ, obedience to the will of Christ, or involvement in the cause of Christ. We have talked about self-fulfillment. Jesus spoke about self-denial. Three times in one passage (Lk 14:25-33) He warned that if His followers were not prepared for self-denial in its severest form they *could not* be His disciples.

To be a disciple is to follow Christ. The whole idea underlying the word *disciple* is foreign to Western culture. The student in the West chooses the *school* to which he will go. Hopefully he will find good teachers when he gets there; but that is of secondary importance. His loyalty is first to the school; it is called "school spirit." After gradua-

---

[2] A. W. Tozer, *That Incredible Christian* (Harrisburg, Pa.: Christian Publications, 1964), pp. 23-25.

tion he becomes a loyal supporter of the school; but in four years in college he may never visit a single professor in his home.

For the real meaning of *disciple* we must go to India, where the disciple chooses a particular *guru* and proceeds to attach himself to his person, living under his roof, sitting at his feet, eating at his table, listening to his words, walking and talking with him in the bazaar or the marketplace, even helping with the household chores. In a word, he shares the total life of the *guru*. In the give-and-take of this intimate fellowship the disciple gradually takes on the character of his *guru*. Before long he finds himself thinking, talking, acting like him. When he gets through he is a carbon copy of the *guru*. That is discipleship.

This is what our Lord had in mind when He said, "Take my yoke upon you and learn from me." It is not enough to confess Christ as Savior. We must go on to acknowledge Him as our Teacher. We must attach ourselves to His person, enroll in His school, listen to His words, walk in His way, surrender to His will.

Slowly but surely we shall undergo a complete transformation of life and thought. As a result we shall come to have a new center of gravity, a new system of values, a new standard of morality, a new frame of reference, a new purpose in life. We are now His disciples because we have accepted His discipline. The two words come from the same root. As the discipline deepens something of His spirit rubs off on us—the spirit of humility, sincerity, service, and sacrifice. We become a carbon copy of Him. That is discipleship.

The third word is GO. Now the disciple is ready for another word—GO. He is not solely concerned for the cultivation of his own spiritual life. He must be concerned for others also. The time comes when he is ready to hear the word that will change him from a disciple to an apostle and send him into the world with the saving gospel of Jesus Christ. The true disciple will have the same compassion for the world that Jesus had. Indeed, this is one of the things he learns from his Teacher. Jesus was moved with compassion when He saw the multitudes as sheep without a shepherd, and He instructed His disciples to pray "the Lord of the harvest to send out laborers into his harvest" (Mt 9:38).

The central fact of the Christian faith is the Incarnation. Jesus leaves us in no doubt regarding its purpose. "The Son of man came to seek and save the lost" (Lk 19:10). By His death and resurrection Jesus procured salvation for the entire human race. The glorious truth of the gospel is that "God was in Christ reconciling the world to himself" (2 Co 5:19). That was the purpose of the Incarnation. Having achieved the victory over sin, death, and hell, Jesus returned to heaven; but before leaving He gave His disciples their marching orders for all time to come. "All authority in heaven and on earth is given to me.

Go therefore and make disciples of all nations" (Mt 28:18-19). In another passage He was careful to point out the vital connection between His mission and theirs. At His first meeting with the Twelve after His resurrection Jesus said: "As the Father has sent me, even so I send you" (Jn 20:21). The Great Commission is nothing new. It is part of the purpose of the Incarnation. As the Father sent Christ into the world on a mission of redemption, so Christ sends the church into the world on a similar mission.

By virtue of this third word—GO—the disciple now becomes an apostle—if you like, a missionary. The two words have the same root meaning, one derived from Greek and the other from Latin. In the early church they used the word *apostle*. Today we use the term *missionary*. The meaning is identical. An apostle, or a missionary, is simply a "sent one."

The order of these three words is important. One must first "come" to Christ before he can "follow," and one must learn to "follow" before he can "go." A great deal of frustration in Christian life and failure in Christian service have resulted from failure to observe the proper order of these words. Sincere people try to act like disciples without ever having become true believers. They try to order their lives by the Sermon on the Mount without being on speaking terms with the Savior of the Mount. There is nothing more frustrating than trying to cultivate a spiritual life that one does not possess. Likewise, there are those who undertake Christian service without ever having learned Christian discipline, and invariably they fail.

The missionary concept includes four ideas: the one who sends, the one who is sent, the ones to whom he is sent, and the message he is commanded to proclaim.

The One who sends is none other than Jesus Christ, who by virtue of His unquestioned obedience to the Father's will (Ph 2:8) is now invested with "all authority in heaven and on earth" (Mt 28:18). The Great Commission, then, is based on the supremacy and sovereignty of Jesus Christ, the Son of God, who in the Incarnation became the Son of Man, that through His death and resurrection He might become the Savior and the Sovereign of the world. He is not only the Head of the church and the Lord of the harvest; He is also the Lord of history, the King of the nations, and the Arbiter of human destiny. Sooner or later all men must come to terms with Him. He and He alone has the right to demand universal allegiance.

The one who is sent is the disciple who has accepted both the doctrine and the discipline of his Lord. He is commissioned to carry the gospel to the ends of the earth. In so doing he is prepared to hazard his life for the sake of the gospel. He knows both its preciousness and its power. He can share it with courage and conviction, knowing that "there is salvation in no one else, for there is no other name under heaven given among men by which we must be saved" (Acts 4:12).

And to whom is the missionary sent? In the Gospels the disciples were sent to the lost sheep of the house of Israel; but in the words of the Great Commission the apostles were to go into "all the world." They were to preach the gospel to "every creature." They were to make disciples of "all nations." The entire world was to be included and the message was to be addressed to all men. No distinction was to be made between Jew and Gentile, Greek and Roman. All men are lost; all men need to be saved; therefore all men must hear the gospel.

And what about the message? The message is the Good News: God loved the world; Christ died for all. Salvation is an accomplished fact. It is offered as a free gift. It can be a present possession. Salvation is bestowed by God on the principle of grace and received by man on the principle of faith (Eph 2:8). The early apostles and present-day missionaries have one and the same message—Jesus Christ and Him crucified (1 Co 2:2). That Jesus suffered under Pontius Pilate is a matter of history. That He died the just for the unjust to bring us to God is a matter of revelation (Ga 1:11-12). The missionary does not invent his message. He isn't even called upon to defend it. His chief task is to proclaim it.

This gospel, preached in the power of the Holy Spirit, calls for a response. The hearer of the message is called upon to repent and believe. In so doing he is saved. If he refuses he faces certain condemnation (Mk 16:16). Missionary work is serious business. To one group of listeners the missionary becomes a fragrance from life to life; to another a fragrance from death to death. Little wonder that Paul exclaims, "Who is sufficient for these things?" (2 Co 2:16). It is better for a person never to hear the gospel than having heard it to reject it.

3. The Condition of Mankind. This is the third dimension and it constitutes an integral part of the missionary mandate. If the condition of mankind were other than it is, there would be little or no need for the missionary enterprise.

The needs of the world are deep-seated and of long standing. They cry out for amelioration. The church, if it is to be loyal to Christ, cannot pass by on the other side as the priest and the Levite did (Lk 10:31-32).

The church cannot be true to its own gospel if it turns a deaf ear to the cry of need, whatever that need may be. When Jesus saw the multitudes as sheep without a shepherd He was moved with compassion; and His compassion always issued in action. Peter summed it all up in one beautiful phrase: "He went about doing good" (Acts 10:38). The Christian cannot do less.

There are those who contend that missionary work should be confined to the spiritual needs of the world. Consequently the missionary has no business engaging in medical and educational work. The practice of our Lord and the teaching of the early church do not seem to support this view. At the beginning of His public ministry our Lord declared, "The Spirit of the Lord is upon me, because he has anointed me to preach good news to the poor. He has sent me to proclaim release to the captives, and recovering of sight to the blind, to set at liberty those who are oppressed, to proclaim the acceptable year of the Lord" (Lk 4:18). According to Matthew's Gospel Jesus came preaching, teaching, and healing (4:23), a threefold ministry corresponding roughly to the threefold nature of man—soul, mind, and body. It is from such passages that we get the expression, "The whole gospel for the whole man."

Man's spiritual needs. No Christian would wish to deny that man's deepest and greatest needs are spiritual. If man is made in the image of God and possesses an immortal soul that will live as long as God lives, either in fellowship with God or alienated from God, it stands to reason that man's greatest need is to be saved. Certainly this was the teaching of Christ when He said, "What does it profit a man to gain the whole world and forfeit his life? For what can a man give in return for his life?" (Mk 8:36-37). The most profound question any man can ask during his life on earth is, "What must I do to be saved?" (Acts 16:30). On the answer to that question depends man's happiness here and hereafter.

The Scriptures clearly teach that mankind is alienated from God (Eph 4:18), hostile to God (Ro 5:10), and under the wrath of God (Jn 3:36). The sinner's only hope is to turn from his wicked way, repent, and believe the gospel. There is no other hope held out to him. He has no other option. It is, therefore, imperative that he hear and understand the gospel.

The missionary's first concern, then, is to preach the gospel, to be instant in season and out of season, to seize upon every opportunity to press home the claims of Christ. The fact that most men are not conscious of their spiritual needs only serves to underscore the gravity of the situation. The most perilous aspect of man's lostness is the fact that he doesn't know he is lost (2 Co 4:4). The fact that the "heathen" are lost and must hear the gospel in order to be saved is a major factor in the missionary mandate. If all men are not lost, or if God can somehow save them without a knowledge of Christ, the nerve of the Christian mission has been severed.

Man's intellectual needs. Man is not all soul. He has a mind as well. Consequently he has certain well-defined intellectual needs. If these are being met by other agencies, there is no need for the missionaries to duplicate the services provided by others. If, on the other hand, no one is caring for the intellectual needs of the people, the missionary is forced to do something about the situation. This is precisely what happened in Africa. When the missionaries first arrived they found more than eight hundred tribes, each with its own language. Not only were the people illiterate; their languages had never been reduced to writing. In that case the missionaries had no choice. They had to step into the breach and provide for the intellectual needs, first of their own converts and later of the people at large. What church can grow and become strong without a knowledge of the Word of God? The Bible must be translated into the vernacular; and the Christians must be taught to read their own language.

But more than that. Men's minds must be enlightened not simply in order to read the Bible, but also in order to take their place in life and make their contribution to society. Man is a rational creature; his powers of mind and reason must be developed if he is to be the kind of well-integrated personality God intended him to be. So in every country missionaries opened schools, reduced languages to writing, taught the people to read, published literature, and opened a whole new world of thought and ideas to people previously content to spend their time eating, sleeping, living, and mating. Such people were not really living; they were merely existing.

Man's physical needs. Most of the Oriental religions, especially Buddhism and Hinduism, are world-renouncing. To them the body is a highly undesirable thing, something that stands in the way of man's spiritual quest. To cultivate his soul he must neglect, if not abuse, his body. Salvation does not embrace the body; that is something to be sloughed off when the soul enters Nirvana.

In contrast to all this is Christianity, which is a world-affirming religion. To be sure, Jesus taught that man's most precious possession is his soul, and He warned that if that is lost, *all* is lost. But nowhere did Jesus deprecate either the body or its needs. He said, "Man shall not live by bread *alone*" (Mt 4:4); but he does need bread. In short, man has physical needs which are God given. Jesus went so far as to sanction the act of David and his guerrilla band when they ate the shewbread, which was to be eaten only by the priests (Mt 12:4). So essential is the life and health of the body that, under certain circumstances, the elemental needs of human nature take precedence over religious ritual.

Time and again Jesus asked, "Will you be made whole?" The word *whole* comes from an old Anglo-Saxon root *hal*, from which we get our words *health* and *holiness*. In order to be "whole" man needs both health and holiness. In his mundane existence man requires a body; in the resurrection he will have a glorified body. No religion places more honor on the body than does Christianity. Hence we find Jesus cleansing the leper, healing the sick, feeding the hungry, even raising the dead. Sickness, pain, weakness, and death are all part of the kingdom of Satan that He came to destroy. When He sent out the Twelve and again the seventy He gave them instructions to heal the sick and cleanse the leper.

When the missionary took the gospel to the ends of the earth in the nineteenth century, he too engaged in a healing ministry. It is true he did not work many miracles; but he took with him the findings and facilities of modern medicine and shared them not only with his converts but with all and sundry. He used modern medicine and surgery to bring health and healing to bodies hitherto racked with pain and deformed by disease.

Of course, others besides the missionary can minister to the intellectual and physical needs of the world; and this is being done more as the newly independent countries of the Third World introduce socialized medicine and universal, compulsory, free education. Consequently mission schools and hospitals are rapidly passing under government control. This is all to the good. The missionary should rejoice when he sees these things coming to pass. Instead of bemoaning his "loss" he should rejoice that he is now being set free for the spiritual work that *only he can perform.* The spiritual needs of mankind will never be met by the governments, foundations, or corporations, however wealthy and benign they may become. Relieved of his medical and educational institutions, which in former years ate up so many of his human and natural resources, today's missionary is free to concentrate on dispensing the True Bread which came down from heaven to give life to the world.

The Fate of the Heathen

Modern man finds it difficult if not impossible to accept the doctrine of eternal punishment. This doctrine becomes especially offensive when applied to the heathen who, having never heard the gospel, can hardly be blamed for rejecting it.

Before addressing ourselves to the fate of the heathen it will be helpful to discuss the lostness of man in general. Three questions are pertinent here. Is man lost or is he not? If he is lost, is he lost for time only or also for eternity? If perchance he finds himself lost in the next life, will he have a second chance?

It is easy to ask these questions; it is not easy to answer them. Indeed, man does not have the answers to these questions, nor is he capable of finding them. Man's ultimate fate rests in the hands of God.

Whether he is saved or lost depends entirely on Him. If God declares man to be lost, then he is lost. Left to his own intelligence and shut up to his own information, man has no way of knowing how he stands in the sight of God. Being a creature of time, he has no understanding of eternity. Being a denizen of earth, he has no knowledge of heaven —or of hell either, for that matter. It is, therefore, idle for him to speculate; it is dangerous for him to dogmatize. Concerning his own fate, man knows only what God has been pleased to reveal. It is an act of consummate folly for him to reject that revelation.

1. Is man lost? For the answer to that question we must turn to the Bible, the only book in the world that speaks to that point. And the answer we get comes through loud and clear: "Yes, man is lost." That statement embraces the entire human race. *All* men are lost. Jews and Gentiles, good men and bad, the pagans in America as well as the heathen in Africa—all have sinned and come short of the glory of God (Ro 3:23). All are children of wrath (Eph 2:3); all are under condemnation (Ro 3:19); all have a rendezvous with death (Ro 5:12, He 9:27). Upright, moral, decent men, such as Nicodemus and Cornelius—all are lost and need to be saved (Jn 3:3; Acts 11:13-14).

What does it mean to be lost? The Scriptures portray a dismal, dreadful picture of man in his lost condition. Man was made in the beginning by God for God, and God intended that man should find his highest happiness in fellowship with Himself. But man disobeyed. With his eyes wide open and knowing full well the awful and inevitable consequences of his act, Adam put forth his hand and partook of the forbidden fruit. Instantly something happened; sin came into his life and God went out. From that day to this man has wandered to and fro as a spiritual vagabond on the face of the earth. He has sailed the seven seas; he has traveled to the ends of the earth; he has even visited the moon; he has conquered the wilderness and made the desert to blossom like the rose; he has founded empires and dynasties; he has built cities and castles; he has heaped to himself riches and honor; but for all that, his soul is an orphan still. In his heart there is what H. G. Wells called a "God-shaped blank" that nothing on earth can ever fill. His spirit, like Noah's dove, flits back and forth between "rough seas and stormy skies." He is totally unable to find what Jesus called "rest for the soul."

With the vertical connection broken, all horizontal connections are at loose ends. He is not only at odds with his Maker, but with his neighbor as well.

The Bible describes him as being dead in trespasses and sins (Eph 2:1). He has plenty of physical, intellectual, and social life; but he is completely devoid of spiritual life. He is alienated from the life of

God (Eph 4:18), ignorant of the truth of God (Ro 1:25), hostile to the law of God (Ro 8:7), disobedient to the will of God (Ti 3:3), and exposed to the wrath of God (Jn 3:36). He has been separated from God so long that he has become naturalized in the unnatural, and actually loves darkness rather than light (Jn 3:19).

The virus of sin has penetrated into every part of his constitution. His mind has been darkened (Eph 4:18), his emotions vitiated (Ro 1:26-27), and his will enslaved (Jn 8:31-36). In the words of the theologians, he is "totally depraved." Even his body has been affected by the Fall, so that it is now subject to weakness, sickness, pain, and finally death (Ge 3:19).

As a result of the Fall all men are now members of a sinful, fallen race. Every man is born in sin and shapen in iniquity (Ps 51:5). He enters the world with a corrupt, sinful nature and finds himself afflicted with an inborn, inevitable propensity to sin. He takes to sin like a duck takes to water. His members and faculties he employs as "instruments of wickedness" (Ro 6:13)and his five physical senses are inlets and outlets for sin (Co 2:21). A hundred times a day he commits sins of omission as well as commission. He sins in thought (Ge 6:5), word (Ro 3:13-14), and deed (Ro 1:29-32); and all his so-called good deeds are as filthy rags (Is 64:6).

Man is not a sinner because he sins; he sins because he is a sinner. It is just as natural for man to sin as it is for a dog to bark, or a bird to fly, or a fish to swim. It is part of his nature (Ro 7:18); it comes from his heart (Mt 15:19); and his heart is "deceitful above all things and desperately corrupt" (Je 17:9). Or as Isaiah expressed it: "The whole head is sick and the whole heart faint. From the sole of the foot even to the head, there is no soundness in it, but bruises and sores and bleeding wounds; they are not pressed out, or bound up, or softened with oil" (Is 1:5-6).

Nowhere is the lostness of man more vividly portrayed than in the three parables spoken by Christ in Luke 15. There we have the lost coin, the lost sheep, and the lost son. J. Oswald Sanders says: "The coin was helplessly lost; the sheep was heedlessly lost; the son was wilfully lost."[3] Man has gone astray not like a bird but like a sheep (Is 53:6). He has no homing instinct. Left to himself he will always travel the downward road, farther and farther into the wilderness of sin (Lk 15:13).

2. If man is lost, is he lost for time only or also for eternity? The question has meaning only if man possesses immortality. If man's existence is confined to this life and he dies like the beasts of

---

[3] J. Oswald Sanders, *What of the Unevangelized?* (London: Overseas Missionary Fellowship, 1966), p. 27.

the field, it is useless to talk about his being saved or lost for eternity. Man's destiny is linked with his origin. According to the Biblical account, "The Lord God formed man of dust from the ground and breathed into his nostrils the breath of life; and man became a living being" (Ge 2:7). Man is the only earthly creature who is said to have been made in the image of God (Ge 1:26). As such he must possess immortality.

The Bible nowhere tries to prove the immortality of the soul any more than it tries to prove the existence of God, for the simple reason that both ideas are part of the innate consciousness of the human race. There is no tribe, however primitive, that does not have some consciousness of a Supreme Being and some hope of life beyond the grave. Doubtless this was what the Preacher had in mind when he wrote: "He [God] has made everything beautiful in its time; also he has put eternity in man's mind" (Ec 3:11).

The Bible clearly teaches that there are two destinies open to man. One involves everlasting happiness in the presence of God and the holy angels (Lk 15:10; Re 22:3-5; 1 Th 4:17); the other involves everlasting misery in the company of the Devil and his angels (Mt 25:41). The New Testament speaks of two gates—one strait and the other wide; two ways—one broad and the other narrow; two destinies—one life and the other destruction (Mt 7:13-14). In the day of judgment the sheep will be separated from the goats (Mt 25:31-46), the wheat from the tares (Mt 13:36-43), the good from the evil (Jn 5:29). And in the resurrection there will be a separation between the just and the unjust (Acts 24:15).

The doctrine of everlasting punishment, though taught in the Scriptures, is challenged by many today. The chief quarrel with the doctrine is twofold. First, the very idea is said to be repugnant to the modern mind. No man in his right mind, they say, would consign his worst enemy to hell. Not even a Hitler deserves that kind of punishment. Secondly, it is impossible to reconcile everlasting punishment with the all-embracing love of God. Nels Ferré speaks for all universalists when he says:

> The very conception of an eternal hell is monstrous and an insult to the conception of last things in other religions, not to mention the Christian doctrine of God's sovereign love. Such a doctrine would either make God a tyrant, where any human Hitler would be a third degree saint, and the concentration camps of human torture the king's picnic grounds. That such a doctrine could be conceived, not to mention believed, shows how far from any understanding of the love of God many people once were, and, alas, still are.[4]

---

[4] Nels Ferré, *The Christian Understanding of God* (New York: Harper and Brothers, 1951), p. vii.

It must be acknowledged that the idea of everlasting punishment *is* repugnant to the modern mind. So what? That is not the only Christian doctrine that is unacceptable to the humanistic, naturalistic mind of the twentieth century. The Christian must choose between the modern mind and the mind of Christ; for after all it was Christ who first taught this awful doctrine.

> Jesus Christ is the Person who is responsible for the doctrine of Eternal Perdition. He is the Being with whom all opponents of this theological tenet are in conflict. Neither the Christian Church nor the Christian ministry are the authors of it. The Christian ministry never would have invented the dogma; neither would they have preached it all the Christian centuries.[5]

The word *Gehenna* (hell) occurs twelve times in the New Testament; eleven times it came from the lips of Christ. It was not John the Baptist or the apostle Paul, or Martin Luther, or John Knox who first coined those awful words we would prefer to drop from our present-day preaching: "the unquenchable fire," "the worm that dieth not," "outer darkness," "weeping and gnashing of teeth," "he is comforted and thou art tormented." These are not the wild, irresponsible words of some flaming evangelist who goes up and down the country preaching hell, fire, and brimstone in an attempt to scare people into the kingdom. These words, terrible though they are, fell from the lips of the meekest Man who ever lived, the Friend of publicans and sinners, the Man who gave His life and shed His blood that men might be forgiven; and they were spoken, we may be sure, with a tear in the eye and a quiver in the voice.

No, we cannot evade the issue. Jesus taught the doctrine of everlasting punishment. He claimed to be the way, the truth, and the life; and we accept the claim. He knew the truth (Jn 2:24-25), He taught the truth (Jn 18:37), He lived the truth (Jn 1:14), He was the truth (Jn 14:6). Jesus Christ is the King of Truth. He cannot lie. What He says must be true. Whether we understand it or not, whether we like it or not, is really beside the point. It makes no difference to the truth of any statement that comes from Him. If He said it, it must be true. Otherwise the concept of the lordship of Christ becomes meaningless.

It might not be out of place to remind ourselves that all we know about eternal life and heaven we learned from Christ. Likewise, all we know about death and judgment we obtained from the same source. What right have we to accept His teaching on the one and reject it on the other? If He is an authority on heaven, He is also an authority on hell.

Some people talk as if love were the only truth Jesus ever taught.

---

[5] William G. T. Shedd, *Dogmatic Theology* (Grand Rapids, Michigan: Zondervan, 1953), Vol. II, p. 680.

Nothing could be farther from the facts. He taught love, all right. Indeed, He himself was the ultimate expression of God's love (Jn 3:16). It is true that God loved the world and that Christ died for all. It is true that God is ready and willing to reconcile the rebel, forgive the sinner, and receive the prodigal back from the far country. But what if the rebel spurns God's love and persists in his rebellion? What if the sinner refuses forgiveness? What if the prodigal elects to remain in the far country?

Jesus taught the love of God as no one else has ever done. He also spoke of sin, wrath, death, and judgment. He recognized that there is such a thing as recalcitrant sin, and He did not hesitate to declare that if men will not accept the mercy of God they shut themselves up to the wrath of God (Jn 3:36). Christianity has two symbols, the cross and the throne. One speaks of love, the other of judgment. Every man must make his own choice. God does not force His love on anyone. But let us make no mistake about it; the man who rejects God's love exposes himself to His wrath; and the one is commensurate with the other (Acts 17:30-31; Ro 2:3-5; 2 Th 1:7-10).

Must Almighty God, Ruler of heaven and earth, tolerate rebellion in His universe forever? To ask the question is to answer it. Christ's picture of the final judgment is completely realistic. He was too good and too honest to fool us. What He told us about the judgment to come is the simple, naked, unvarnished truth of God; and we alter or reject it at our peril.

We do not preach the wrath of God because we like to, but because Jesus taught it. Being followers of Christ we have no choice. What preacher does not understand the feelings of C. S. Lewis when he wrote: "There is no doctrine which I would more willingly remove from Christianity than this [hell], if it lay in my power. . . . I would pay any price to be able to say truthfully: 'All will be saved.' "[6]

Mark that phrase—"If it lay in my power." That is the crux of the whole matter. It clearly does not lie in our power to remove hell, or any other doctrine, from the corpus of Christian truth. If Jesus Christ is Lord of all life, it behooves us to "destroy arguments and every proud obstacle to the knowledge of God, and take every thought captive to obey Christ" (2 Co 10:5).

Those who reject Christ's teaching about everlasting punishment insist that the words He used are not to be taken at their face value. They are symbolic and not literal, and no longer mean what our forefathers of a cruder generation thought they meant. Be that as it may. If they are symbolic, they are symbolic of *something;* and whatever that something is, it must be unspeakably awful to require such sym-

---

[6] C. S. Lewis, *The Problem of Pain* (New York: MacMillan, 1962), p. 118.

bols to express it. Take the most liberal view, place on these stinging words the most charitable construction they can possibly bear; one cannot by any stretch of the imagination deny the fact that they describe a form of punishment more severe than any human being would wish to bear.

3. Is there a second chance after death? Here again we are totally dependent for our information on the New Testament.

There is nothing in the teachings of Christ to suggest the possibility of a second chance after death. In fact, in the parable of the rich man and Lazarus (Lk 16:19-31) the very opposite is clearly taught. The rich man in Hades made two requests of Abraham. One was that Lazarus might be sent to cool his tongue with water. The other was that he might be sent to warn his five brothers still on earth. Both requests were denied. In denying the first request Abraham explained the impossibility of any such arrangement, saying, "Son, remember that you in your lifetime received your good things, and Lazarus in like manner evil things; but now he is comforted here, and you are in anguish. And besides all this, between us and you a great chasm has been fixed, in order that those who would pass from here to you may not be able, and none may cross from there to us" (Lk 16:26-27).

It is clear from this passage that death seals the fate of both the believer and the unbeliever. Repentance is possible only in this life; after death there is only remorse.

The author of the Book of Hebrews says: "It is appointed for men to die once, and after that comes judgment"—not probation (He 9:27).

What about the heathen who have never heard the gospel and, therefore, cannot be charged with having rejected it? It is their fate that has caused the most controversy. The doctrine of everlasting punishment is bad enough when applied to the gospel-hardened sinner who deliberately rejects the gospel; but what about those in non-Christian lands who never had a chance to accept Christ? Is it fair to punish them for rejecting a Christ of whom they are completely ignorant? Many of them are seeking souls and doubtless would believe if they had an opportunity. Are all these people going to be forever lost through no fault of their own?

Before we attempt to answer that specific question, it is necessary to discuss the condition of the heathen in general—again from the viewpoint of the New Testament. Certain truths are made clear.

1. The heathen were not heathen to begin with. They *became* heathen when they deliberately gave up their knowledge of God.

"For although they knew God they did not honor him as God or give thanks to him, but they *became* futile in their thinking and their senseless minds were darkened. Claiming to be wise, they *became* fools, and exchanged the glory of the immortal God for images resembling mortal man, or birds, or animals, or reptiles" (Ro 1:21-23).

2. In their progressive apostasy the heathen did not lose all knowledge of God. They retained a knowledge of God's eternal power and deity which reached them through creation (Ro 1:20). "For that which can be known about God is plain to them, because God has shown it to them. Ever since the creation of the world his invisible nature, namely, his eternal power and deity, has been clearly perceived in the things that have been made" (Ro 1:20).

3. The revelation of God through creation is supplemented by another revelation through nature or providence. Speaking to the primitive people of Lycaonia, Paul said, "He [God] did not leave himself without witness, for he did good and gave you from heaven rain and fruitful seasons, satisfying your hearts with food and gladness" (Acts 14:17). Modern man with his food stamps and welfare programs was not the first to discover the connection between food and felicity. God knew it all along and made provision for both. Farmers the world over realize how susceptible they are to the vagaries of the weather; but back of the weather is God, the Creator and Sustainer of the world of nature. Nearly every heathen society has some kind of ritual whereby it celebrates a good harvest. Alas, the thank offerings on such occasions are usually made to the earth god, not the God of heaven and earth. But the recognition is there. God has not left Himself without witness.

4. There is still another form of revelation given to the heathen— the human conscience. The heathen have neither the light of the law nor the light of the gospel; but they do have the light of conscience. Paul says, "When the Gentiles who do not have the law do by nature what the law requires, they are a law to themselves, even though they do not have the law. They show that what the law requires is written on their hearts, while their conscience also bears witness and their conflicting thoughts accuse or perhaps excuse them" (Ro 2:14-15). Conscience is by no means a perfect instrument, and it can be abused to the point where it fails to function properly; but it still remains the divine monitor within the human breast. No man is so low in the moral scale that his conscience ceases to function.

This brings us to the crucial question: On what basis are the heathen to be judged? At this point there is a great deal of confused thinking. The popular argument goes something like this: There is only one way to be saved and that is through faith in Christ; the heathen, having never heard of Christ, cannot exercise faith; consequently he is doomed to everlasting punishment for something quite beyond his capability.

This line of thought is based on a false assumption that has no support in Scripture. The assumption is that all men will be judged on the same basis—namely, for failing to believe the gospel.

The second chapter of Romans makes it plain that all men will not be judged on the same basis. Rather they will be judged according to the light they had. In that chapter there are three groups: the Jew with the light of the law, the Gentile with the light of the gospel, and the heathen with the light of conscience. No man will be judged by light he did not possess. That would be grossly unfair. Every man possesses *some* form of light and he will be judged by that light and by no other.

The greater the light the heavier the responsibility. The man who all his life lived in sound of the church bell but never entered the church door will have the hardest time of all. He will be judged in the blazing light of the full revelation of God's saving grace in Jesus Christ (2 Co 4:4). He had Christian friends and neighbors. He possessed, or could easily have acquired, the Holy Scriptures, which are able to make him wise unto salvation (2 Ti 3:16). In his own home, on radio or television, he could have heard the gospel any Sunday in the year. The coins he carried in his pocket were inscribed with the words: "In God we trust." What excuse does that man have for failing to come to terms with Jesus Christ? If he goes to hell he will have no one to blame but himself; and his remorse will be all the greater when he remembers the thousand-and-one opportunities for salvation that he passed up.

The heathen on the other hand will have a much easier time. But he will not go scot free. He had the light of creation, providence, and conscience and will be judged by that light. If he is finally condemned it will not be because he refused to believe the gospel, but because he failed to live up to the little light he had. In that case he too must bear the responsibility for his own destiny. God does not consign him to hell; he goes there because that is where he belongs.

If the heathen is judged by his works, how will he fare? The question has often been asked: Do any of the heathen live up to the light they have? The teaching of Scripture and the testimony of the missionaries leave no room for hope in this regard. If the first chapter of Romans is an accurate picture of the heathen world, the individuals who make up that world are not likely candidates for salvation. The concept of the "noble savage" exists only in the mind of the skeptic.

J. Hudson Taylor, who spent fifty years in China, said that in all that time he never met anyone who claimed to have lived up to the light he had. Moral failure is a universal phenomenon.

What about Cornelius, described in Acts 10? Though a Gentile, he is described as a devout person, one who feared God with all his house, who gave alms liberally to the people, and engaged daily in prayer. When Peter arrived in Caesarea his first words to Cornelius were: "Truly I perceive that God shows no partiality, but in every nation any one who fears him and does what is right is acceptable to him" (Acts 10:34-35).

What did Peter mean? What are the key words in this statement? The statement must be taken in its historical context. Peter had always believed this was true of the Jews. Now, for the first time in his life, he becomes aware of the fact that it is true regardless of race. The key words, then, are "in every nation."

Peter was not prepared to have anything to do with the Gentiles, good or bad, God-fearing or God-hating. Fraternization with them was totally unacceptable to Peter prior to this time. Now he learns better. Indeed, the real reason why the story of Cornelius is included in the Book of Acts is not because of what the episode did for Cornelius but what it did for Peter. The story is really the "conversion" of Peter, not of Cornelius.

That Peter by these words did not mean to suggest that Cornelius was already a saved man comes out in his recital of the story on his return to Jerusalem. Peter's commission was to tell Cornelius words whereby he and all his house could be saved (Acts 11:14). Obviously, then, Cornelius was not saved prior to Peter's visit regardless of his piety and his prayers.

What about Romans 2:6-7, where Paul says: "For he will render to every man according to his works: to those who by patience in well-doing seek for glory and honor and immortality, he will give eternal life"? Does this verse hold out any hope that the "moral heathen" will one day win God's favor?

Paul Kanamori, the great Japanese evangelist of another day, had a very dear mother who was a devout Buddhist. Every morning she rose before dawn, lit the candles, burned incense, and prayed to Buddha. Alas, she died without ever hearing the gospel. Mr. Kanamori said that he expected to meet his mother in heaven. Sadhu Sundar Singh, the Indian Christian saint, also had a mother who longed and prayed and worked for salvation without ever hearing of Christ. Sundar Singh said that if he didn't find his mother in heaven he would request permission to go to hell to be with her.

One can admire the filial piety that prompted these two men to speak and feel the way they did. No person wants to think of his parents as being in hell. Momentous questions of this kind, however, cannot be answered on the basis of filial piety, family loyalty, or any other human sentiment. The Christian gospel says: "Everyone who calls on the name of the Lord will be saved" (Ro 10:13). Do we have the right to substitute the name of Buddha, or Vishnu, or Krishna for Christ? Most certainly not. "There is salvation in no one else, for there is no other name under heaven given among men by which we must be saved" (Acts 4:12). Jesus said, "I am the way, and the truth, and the life; no one comes to the Father but by me" (Jn 14:6). Paul says, "For no other foundation can anyone lay than that which is laid, which is Jesus Christ" (1 Co 3:11). Again he says, "For there is one God, and there is one mediator between God and men, the man Christ Jesus" (1 Ti 2:5). The above statements are clear, cogent, and categorical. They admit of only one interpretation. All other passages which are less clear and which are capable of more than one interpretation must be exegeted in the light of these statements. This is the broad teaching of the New Testament. This is the general principle on which the Christian mission must operate.

In the light of Romans 2:6-7, however, we must not completely rule out the possibility, however remote, that here and there throughout history there may have been the odd person who got to heaven without the full light of the gospel. In that case, *God* is the sole Judge. He is sovereign in the exercise of His grace. We are not called upon to pass judgment in such cases—if indeed they ever occurred. Here, as in many other instances, we must fall back on the sovereignty of God and say with Abraham, "Shall not the Judge of all the earth do right? (Ge 18:25).

4

Historical Development

Christianity is a historic religion founded on the life, work, and teachings of a historic person, Jesus Christ, who entered the stream of history in the days of Caesar Augustus and died under Pontius Pilate. The church which He founded is a historic institution. It had its beginnings at Pentecost and will run its course until the Second Advent. Between these two events the chief task of the church is to take the gospel into all the world and make disciples of all nations.

The Christian mission, then, has its locus in time and space. The New Testament lays down two terminal goals for the church and its mission. One relates to time and the other to space. The first is a matter of history and runs to the end of the age. The second is a matter of geography and extends to the ends of the earth. In this chapter we are concerned with history, not geography, and shall begin with the modern period.

Origin of Protestant Missions in the Eighteenth Century

One would naturally expect that the spiritual forces released by the Reformation would have prompted the Protestant churches of Europe to take the gospel to the ends of the earth during the period of world exploration and colonization which began about 1500. But such was not the case. The Roman Catholic Church between 1500 and 1700 won more converts in the pagan world than it lost to Protestantism in Europe. Why did the Protestant churches take so long to inaugurate their missionary program? What were some of the contributing factors.

1. **Perhaps the most potent factor was the theology of the Reformers.** They taught that the Great Commission pertained only to the original apostles; that the apostles fulfilled the Great Commission by taking the gospel to the ends of the then-known world; that if later generations were without the gospel, it was their own fault—a judgment of God on their unbelief; that the apostolate, with its immediate call, peculiar functions, and miraculous powers, having ceased, the church in later ages had neither the authority nor the responsibility to send missionaries to the ends of the earth.

2. **The sad plight of the Protestant churches of the sixteenth and seventeenth centuries inhibited mission work.** Compared with the Roman Catholic Church they were extremely small both in strength and numbers. Moreover, the Catholic Church launched the Counter Reformation and thereby regained much of the territory lost to the Reformation. The war against Rome was long and bitter and the outcome was by no means certain. The Thirty Years' War reduced Germany to economic and social chaos. The Protestant churches, preoccupied as they were with the problem of survival, may be excused for having neither the vision nor the vigor necessary for world evangelization.

Equally, if not more, enervating was the internecine warfare carried on between the Lutheran and Reformed churches themselves. If they had joined forces to present a united front to the common enemy, they might have done a better job with evangelism at home and missions overseas; but as it was they were torn asunder by ecclesiastical strife. They were united in only one thing, their hatred for the "papists." They no sooner broke with Rome than they fell to fighting one another.

3. **The isolation of Protestant Europe from the mission lands of Asia, Africa, and the New World deterred missionary activity.** Spain and Portugal, both Roman Catholic countries, were the great exploring and colonizing powers of the post-Reformation period. For more than a century they enjoyed complete mastery of the seas and a monopoly on world trade. Wherever their ships went they carried both merchants and missionaries. The kings of Portugal and Spain were deeply committed to the Christianization of their overseas colonies. Later on the Dutch and then the British got in on the act; but they were interested

primarily in commerce, not colonization. The Dutch East India Company, founded in 1602, stated that one of its objectives was to plant the Reformed faith in its territories overseas, but seldom did they work at it. The British East India Company entertained no such ambitions. While providing chaplains for its own personnel, it was adamantly opposed to missionary work among the indigenous population. Time and again it refused to transport missionaries in its ships and forbade missionaries to reside in its territories.

4. **The absence in the Protestant churches of the religious orders which played such a prominent role in the spread of the Catholic faith throughout the world slowed Protestant missions.** Referring to the worldwide missionary program of the Roman Catholic Church one of its historians says:

> As papal missionary agencies, even apart from the curia, the various Religious Orders engaged ever more energetically in the missions, and vied with one another in spreading the Gospel. In the first place, the older missionary Orders renewed their activities —the Franciscans and Dominicans, and also the Augustinians and Carmelites after their internal reform. . . . The new Orders included (besides the Capuchins) one which apart from its general fitness as a regular Order, was also adapted and impelled by its deepest nature and its most intimate aims to attain the summit, to speak relatively, in missionary achievement—the Society of Jesus. The qualities which fitted it for this work were especially its cosmopolitan character, its faculty of accommodation and mobility, its military organization and centralization, its absolute obedience and the complete submerging of the individual in the common cause.[1]

When the Protestant churches two centuries later launched their missionary enterprise they had nothing to compare with the religious orders of the Roman Catholic Church. The largest group were the Moravians—one of the so-called sects. With few exceptions their missionaries were unlettered men with more zeal than knowledge, artisans and farmers—married men, with ground to till, houses to build, and families to support. Fettered thus with family ties and domestic duties, the Protestant missionaries were no match for their Catholic counterparts. Certainly they had nothing to compare to the military discipline of the Society of Jesus.

The first Lutheran to attempt missionary work was an Austrian, Baron Justinian von Weltz, who about 1664 issued a clarion call to the church to assume its missionary responsibilities. In three pamphlets he set forth the missionary obligation of the church, called for the organi-

---

[1] Joseph Schmidlin, *Catholic Mission History* (Techny, IL: Divine Word Mission Press, 1933), p. 259.

zation of a missionary society or association to get the job done, and advocated the opening of a training school for missionary candidates. But the times were not propitious. The churches, though orthodox in doctrine, were lacking in spiritual life and missionary vision. Not content with remaining indifferent, his colleagues, almost to a man, rose in indignation against him, calling him a dreamer, a fanatic, and a heretic. "The holy things of God," they said, "are not to be cast before such dogs and swine."

Undeterred by opposition and ridicule the disconcerted baron proceeded to Holland, where he abandoned his baronial title. Following ordination as an "apostle to the Gentiles," he sailed for Dutch Guiana (Surinam), where he died an early death before he could reap a harvest. Another missionary adventure had failed. Before the Protestant churches could launch a continuing missionary endeavor they must be inwardly renewed.

The modern missionary enterprise was the direct outcome of the Pietist movement which began in Germany following the Thirty Years' War, which ended with the Peace of Westphalia in 1648. As the Protestant Reformation was a revolt against the false doctrines and corrupt morals of the Church of Rome, so the Pietist movement was a revolt against the barren orthodoxy and dead formalism of the state churches of Protestant Europe.

The father of Pietism was Philip Spener (1635-1705). As a Lutheran pastor, first in Strasbourg and later in Frankfort, Spener tried to raise the spiritual tone of his flock by the systematic cultivation of the spiritual life. Cottage meetings for prayer and Bible study supplemented the Sunday sermon and brought the members together in an atmosphere of fellowship hitherto unknown. The Pietists in their teaching emphasized three things: a genuine conversion experience leading to newness of life; the cultivation of the inner life by Bible study, prayer, and Christian fellowship; and missionary zeal. True religion for the Pietists is a matter of the heart, not the head; hence the emphasis on the cultivation of the spiritual life.

Like many reformers before him, Spener incurred the wrath of the hierarchy. Civil and ecclesiastical authorities denounced the man and his movement. But in spite of opposition and even persecution, Pietism proved contagious and won adherents in the Lutheran churches. When the universities of Saxony closed their doors to the new sect the Pietists opened their own university at Halle in 1694. For ten years Spener built up the school. Following his death in 1705 the most influential leader was August Francke (1663-1727), who had been dismissed from Leipzig University because, following a deep religious experience which changed his whole life, he conferred with Spener and wholeheartedly embraced Pietism. Largely through his influence Halle became the educational center of Pietism and the fountainhead of the missionary enterprise of the eighteenth century.

> The university was surrounded with other institutions; a pauper school, a boy's boarding school, an orphanage, a Latin school, a printing press, a pharmacy, a Bible Institute. Thousands of children were taught there; many became missionaries, and some six thousand pietist clergy were trained in the Halle theological faculty, which was the largest divinity school in Germany. Bogatzky was one of the most influential of the devotional writers of Halle, and Freylinghausen the chief hymn writer. Even the Reformed pietists in the Lower Rhine contributed regularly to Halle. Colonial Lutheranism in America was largely evangelized from Halle.[2]

Out of Halle University grew the first Protestant mission, the Danish-Halle Mission. The men and much of the support were furnished by Halle; the initial impetus originated in Denmark. Hence the name—Danish-Halle Mission.

In 1705 Dr. Franz Lütkens, court chaplain at Copenhagen, was commissioned by Frederick IV to recruit missionaries for the East Indies. Failing to find suitable men in Denmark, Lütkens conferred with Spener and Francke in Germany, hoping that the Pietist center at Halle could furnish volunteers. Two names were suggested, Bartholomew Ziegenbalg and Heinrich Plütschau, both of whom had studied at Halle under Francke.

From its inception the mission encountered opposition both in Europe and in India. The Lutheran churches in Germany failed to support it. Instead support, moral and material, came from Halle and interested individuals. Indeed, Warneck goes so far as to say that "but for Francke the Danish mission would soon have gone to sleep."[3] Owing to their Pietist convictions the two missionaries had difficulty in getting the Danish hierarchy to ordain them. Belatedly and somewhat reluctantly they were ordained and sailed for Tranquebar on November 29, 1705. Their departure raised a storm of protest in Lutheran circles in Germany. Some leaders, such as V. E. Loscher, were comparatively mild in their criticism and were content to sound a "cursory warning" against supporting the mission. Most of the critics were much more violent in their denunciation of the young mission. The faculty of theology at Wittenberg called the missionaries "false prophets" because their "orderly vocation was not ascertained."

The second missionary venture was that of the Moravians. The origin of the Moravian Church goes back to 1467 when the persecuted

---

[2] James H. Nichols, *History of Christianity, 1650-1950* (New York: Ronald Press, 1956), p. 84.
[3] Gustav Warneck, *History of Protestant Missions* (New York: Revell, 1904), p. 44.

followers of John Huss, with certain Waldensians and Moravians, banded together to form the *Unitas Fratrum* (United Brethren). After being almost wiped out by the Counter Reformation the remnant, under the leadership of Christian David, migrated in 1722 to Saxony, where they were given refuge by Count Zinzendorf on one of his estates near Dresden. Known as *Herrnhut* (The Lord's Watch), this colony became the source and center of a missionary movement destined to circle the globe.

Nicolas Ludwig Zinzendorf (1700-1760), godson of Spener and student at Francke's grammar school in Halle, decided as a young man to devote all his time and treasure to the cause of Christ. An ardent Pietist by parentage and profession, he declared: "I have one passion; it is He and He alone." He soon became the recognized leader of the colony and set about to organize its religious life. He became bishop of the Moravian Church in 1737. For thirty years he inspired and guided its worldwide missionary activities. He and Francke were by all odds the greatest missionary leaders of the eighteenth century.

Their first mission (1732) was to the Negro slaves on the Danish island of St. Thomas in the Virgin Islands. Greenland was next, in 1733, and St. Croix, also in the Virgin Islands, in 1734. Ten of this last group died in the first year; but it was not difficult to get recruits to fill up the depleted ranks. Other mission fields were opened: Surinam (1735), the Gold Coast and South Africa (1737), the North American Indians (1740), Jamaica (1754), and Antigua (1756). Between 1732 and 1760, 226 Moravians entered ten foreign countries.

> Within twenty years of the commencement of their missionary work the Moravian Brethren had started more missions than Anglicans and Protestants had started during the two preceding centuries. Their marvelous success was largely due to the fact that from the first they recognized that the evangelization of the world was the most pressing of all the obligations that rested upon the Christian Church, and that the carrying out of this obligation was the "common affair" of the community. Up to the present time [1930] the Moravians have sent out nearly 3,000 missionaries, the proportion of missionaries to their communicant members being 1 in 12.[4]

These two missions, the Danish-Halle and the Moravian, occupied the center of the stage throughout the whole of the eighteenth century. Towards the close (1797) the Netherlands Missionary Society got under way.

We generally regard British missions as beginning in 1792 with the famous William Carey. Strictly speaking, this is not correct. Prior to

---

[4] Charles H. Robinson, *History of Christian Missions* (New York: Scribners, 1930), pp. 49-50.

that time there were three societies, all of them designed originally to operate within the colonial framework of North America.

The first was the Society for the Propagation of the Gospel in New England, founded in 1649. As its name implies it was organized with the Indians of North America in mind. An original endowment of twelve thousand pounds was invested in land and the proceeds used to support missions in the New World. Its first missionary was John Eliot, who had been in Massachusetts since 1631 and who gave half a century to the evangelization of the Indians of that colony. The mission continued its work in New England until the War of Independence.

The Society for Promoting Christian Knowledge was organized in 1698 as an independent mission within the Anglican Church. A leading figure in its formation was Thomas Bray, rector of Sheldon and Commissary in Maryland of the Bishop of London. It was not intended in the beginning to be a missionary venture. Its original purpose was to strengthen the religious life of the white colonists in the New World. This was to be done by the dissemination of Christian literature and by augmenting the meager libraries of the colonial clergy. As it branched out into many different parts of the world it became, for all intents and purposes, a missionary agency.

Through the years the SPCK has engaged in a variety of activities, mostly in the fields of education and literature. During a time of crisis in the eighteenth century it came to the rescue of the Danish-Halle Mission in South India. For over 260 years it has been a supporting mission, providing an ever-increasing stream of high-grade Christian literature, not only for Anglicans but for others as well. Since 1835 it has been doing its own publishing. Today it has bookstores all around the world.

The Society for the Propagation of the Gospel in Foreign Parts, commonly known throughout the world as the SPG, is the oldest, and was for nearly a century the only specifically missionary agency of the Church of England. The major difference between the SPG and its equally famous sister mission, the Church Missionary Society, is that the former is High Church and the latter Low Church.

The SPG was founded by royal charter in 1701 with a twofold purpose: to minister to the spiritual needs of the English settlers overseas, many of whom were in danger of lapsing into heathen ways for lack of religious instruction; and to evangelize the indigenous population, who were heathen to begin with.

During the entire eighteenth century the SPG maintained a rather modest program on a very restricted budget. During that time its activities were confined to the American colonies and the West Indies. Nevertheless the SPG filled a pressing need for chaplains and missionaries in colonial America.

If Western colonialism is said to have begun with Vasco da Gama, Protestant missions may be said to have been launched by William Carey. What Luther was to the Protestant Reformation Carey was to the Christian missionary movement. Though there were missionaries before him it is altogether fitting that William Carey should be known as the father of modern missions.

Many factors prepared the way for the period of modern missions. The famous East India Companies tapped the riches of the Indies and laid the foundation of world trade. They also paved the way for European colonization which, in the providence of God, greatly facilitated the worldwide mission of the church. The invention of the steamboat made ocean travel faster and safer. Of more immediate interest to William Carey were the voyages of Captain James Cook.

Religious factors played an even more important role. The Pietist movement on the Continent and the Evangelical Awakening in England and America were necessary before the church could launch out on its worldwide mission. Before Carey's time there were stirrings of missionary interest in England. In 1719 Isaac Watts wrote his great missionary hymn, "Jesus Shall Reign Where'er the Sun." Several of Charles Wesley's compositions also bear a missionary theme. In 1723 Robert Millar of Scotland wrote *A History of the Propagation of Christianity and the Overthrow of Paganism,* in which he advocated intercession as the primary means of converting the "heathen." The idea soon caught on. Twenty years later prayer groups were to be found all over the British Isles. Their chief petition was for the conversion of the heathen world.

In 1746 a memorial was sent to Boston inviting the Christians of the New World to enter into a seven-year "Concert of Prayer" for missionary work. The memorial evoked a ready response from Jonathan Edwards, who the following year issued a call to all believers to engage in intercessory prayer for the spread of the gospel throughout the world.

Almost forty years later, in 1783, Edwards' pamphlet was introduced to the churches in England by John Sutcliff in the Northamptonshire Ministerial Association. Following the reading of the pamphlet he made a motion that all Baptist churches and ministers set aside the first Monday of each month for united intercession for the heathen world. It read:

> Let the whole interest of the Redeemer be affectionately remembered, and the spread of the Gospel to the most distant parts of the habitable globe be the object of your most fervent requests. We shall rejoice if any other Christian societies of our own or other denominations will unite with us, and we do now invite them to join most cordially heart and hand in the attempt. Who can

tell what the consequences of such a united effort in prayer may be?[5]

About this time William Carey (1761-1834) came on the scene. Strangely enough it was the reading of *The Last Voyage of Captain Cook* that first aroused in Carey an interest in missionary work. Thereafter he read every book that had any bearing on the outside world, including Guthrie's *Geographical Grammar*. It is certain that he read Jonathan Edwards' *Life and Diary of David Brainerd*. He was familiar with the Danish-Halle Mission, John Eliot of New England, and the Moravian missionaries. He made his own map of the world on which he inscribed every bit of pertinent information he could find.

In 1792 Carey published his eighty-seven-page book, *An Enquiry into the Obligations of Christians to Use Means for the Conversion of the Heathens*. Believed by some to be the most convincing missionary appeal ever written, Carey's *Enquiry* was certainly a landmark in Christian history and deserves a place alongside Martin Luther's Ninety-five Theses in its influence on subsequent church history.

Carey was no armchair strategist. He was concerned with action, not theory. His immediate aim was the formation of a society that would send missionaries abroad. This was not easy, for the Baptists among whom Carey moved were staunch Calvinists. At a ministerial meeting in Northamptonshire when Carey proposed that they discuss the implications of the Great Commission, Dr. John C. Ryland retorted: "Young man, sit down. When God pleases to convert the heathen, He will do it without your aid or mine."

On May 30, 1792, at the Baptist Ministers' Association at Nottingham, Carey preached his epochal sermon on Isaiah 54:2-3, in which he coined the now familiar couplet: "Expect great things from God; attempt great things for God." The sermon had a profound effect on his hearers. The following day Carey pled for immediate action; but the brethren, while acknowledging the "criminality of their supineness in the cause of God," faltered when they faced the immensity of the task.

Four months later Carey again pressed for action, and again the brethren wavered. After all, who were these men, ministers of poverty-stricken churches, to undertake a mission so beset with difficulty, so fraught with uncertainty? At the crucial moment, when all hope seemed gone, Carey took from his pocket a booklet entitled *Periodical Account of Moravian Missions*. With tears in his eyes and a tremor in his voice he said: "If you had only read this and knew how these men overcame all obstacles for Christ's sake, you would go forward in faith." That was it. The men agreed to act. The minutes of the

---

[5] H. B. Montgomery, *Prayer and Missions* (West Medford, MA: The Central Committee of the United Study of Foreign Missions, 1924), p. 78.

meeting record their decision to form The Particular Baptist Society for Propagating the Gospel among the Heathen.

It was one thing to pass a resolution to form a mission; it was another to get the mission under way. Difficulties abounded on all sides pertaining to family, finance, and field. Carey's father considered him mad. His wife refused to accompany him. But one by one the problems were solved, and after some delay and not a little discouragement William Carey sailed for India on June 13, 1793. He was accompanied by a reluctant wife, four children, and two companions. Five months later he arrived in India, the land to which he gave forty years of unbroken service.

Back home in Europe and America, largely through the labors and letters of Carey, missionary societies came into existence: the London Missionary Society (1795), the Scottish and Glasgow Missionary Societies (1796), the Netherlands Missionary Society (1797), the Church Missionary Society (1799), the British and Foreign Bible Society (1804), the American Board of Commissioners for Foreign Missions (1810), the American Baptist Missionary Union (1814), and the American Bible Society (1816). It is difficult to exaggerate the influence of William Carey on the missionary enterprise of the nineteenth century. Few will wish to deny him the title of "father of modern missions."

About this time there was a quiet but far-reaching movement of the Spirit of God on this side of the Atlantic. The call to preach the gospel to all nations came to Samuel J. Mills while he was following the plow on his farm in Connecticut one day in 1802. Four years later, in obedience to the heavenly vision, he entered Williams College at Williamstown, Massachusetts, to prepare for the Christian ministry. There he kindled a fire whose sparks were destined to be carried to the ends of the earth. A group of kindred spirits—James Richards, Francis Robbins, Harvey Loomis, Gordon Hall, and Luther Rice, known as the Society of the Brethren—met frequently in a grove of maples near the campus for prayer and discussion. One day on their way to prayer they were caught in a sudden thunderstorm. Taking refuge in the lee of a nearby haystack they had their usual time of prayer for the heathen world, following which they stood to their feet and said, "We can do it if we will." They thereupon resolved to become America's first foreign missionaries and signed a pledge to that effect. Henceforth they were known as "the Haystack Group."

After graduation several of them went to Andover Seminary, founded in 1808 by the Old Calvinists and the followers of Samuel Hopkins because of dissatisfaction with the liberalism of Harvard. This young school, the inheritor and preserver of New England Puritanism and the evangelical tradition of Jonathan Edwards, became the fountainhead not only of evangelicalism in New England but also of Christian missions overseas. Here they were joined by Adoniram Judson from Brown University, Samuel Newell from Harvard University, and Samuel Nott, Jr. from Union College. Under the leadership of Judson, the brilliant valedictorian, they formed the Society of Inquiry on the Subject of Missions.

On June 28, 1810, Judson, Mills, Nott, and Newell walked six miles to Bradford to present to the General Association of the Congregational Ministers of Massachusetts a memorial in which they offered themselves for missionary service and solicited the advice, direction, and prayers of the "Reverend Fathers." The young men gave their testimonies, after which the matter was referred to a committee of three. The following day the committee approved the purpose of the young men and recommended the formation of a foreign mission board. The report was immediately and unanimously adopted. Nine men were appointed to constitute the original Board of Commissioners for Foreign Missions. The first annual meeting of the board was held at Farmington, Connecticut, on September 5, 1810, with five commissioners present. They discussed and adopted a constitution of fourteen articles and elected officers for the following year, including a Prudential Committee of three members. They also prepared an *Address to the Christian Public* to enlist support for the new enterprise. Such was the humble beginning of the American foreign missionary movement, which today provides almost 70 percent of the worldwide Protestant missionary force and about 80 percent of the finances.

It was at the second annual meeting of the board that the four young men, Judson, Nott, Newell, and Hall, were actually appointed as missionaries. As usual finances were a problem. Only fourteen hundred dollars had been received and this was not enough to pay the cost of passage. The committee deliberated anxiously. Should they proceed with their plans or wait for additional support? At last, on January 27, 1812, they voted to send the four men but to detain the wives until sufficient funds were on hand. It was a brand-new venture. They oscillated between faith and fear; but their fear was shortlived. When it became known that the young missionaries had actually booked passage gifts flowed in from all quarters. Within three weeks more than six thousand dollars was received, enough to provide for outfit, passage, and a year's salary in advance!

The first party consisted of eight missionaries: Judson, Newell, and Nott with their wives, Gordon Hall, and Luther Rice. The five men, all graduates of Andover Theological Seminary, were ordained in the tabernacle in Salem on February 6, 1812. It was a most impressive service. The church was crowded, and at times the entire assembly "seemed moved as the trees of the wood are moved by a mighty wind."

Two weeks later the Judsons and the Newalls set sail from Salem on the *Caravan*. The other members of the party left from Philadelphia on the *Harmony* on February 24. It took them four months to reach India. The first American mission had been launched.

Expansion of Protestant Missions in the Nineteenth Century

In his monumental seven-volume *History of the Expansion of Christianity* Kenneth Scott Latourette devoted three volumes to the nineteenth century, which he referred to as "The Great Century." Indeed it was. Never before in the history of the Christian church had such a concerted, organized, herculean effort been made to take the gospel to the ends of the earth.

Protestant missions from England got under way during the closing years of the eighteenth century. The first foreign mission board in the United States was organized in 1810. As the century progressed one after another of the Protestant countries began sending missionaries to the "heathen world." By the end of the century every Protestant country in the world was represented on the mission field.

In Latin America the Spanish colonial system broke up between 1810 and 1824; but in other parts of the world—Asia, Africa, Oceania, and the Middle East—the missionary advance coincided with the rapid expansion of European power. Three major groups were involved in the invasion—the diplomat, the merchant, and the missionary. In the eyes of the nationals they came to represent three forms of imperialism—political, economic, and cultural.

Geographically the cross followed the flag. The very first Protestant missionaries of the Danish-Halle Mission went to Tranquebar, at that time a Danish colony on the east coast of India. Later on, in the nineteenth century, British missionaries followed the Union Jack to India and Africa. Dutch and German missionaries were found in large numbers in the East Indies. The Scandinavian countries had no colonies; consequently their missionaries did not concentrate in any one region. American missionaries represented the widest spread of all. They ended up in all the major regions of the world, but were particularly numerous in the Far East. In Latin America, apart from one or two small Anglican missions, they had the continent to themselves.

From a chronological point of view the shoe was on the other foot; the flag followed the cross. The missionaries were well established in Oceania long before Britain and France imposed their colonial rule on that part of the world. It was the missionaries, not the colonialists, who explored the vast unknown areas of Central Africa and there opened "a path for commerce and Christianity." In fact, it was the missionaries who invited the European powers to intervene in Africa to stop the iniquitous slave trade carried on by the Arabs. And in areas already under some form of colonial or quasi-colonial rule the missionaries often chafed at the bit to extend their endeavors beyond the areas regarded as safe by the colonial administrators.

Interestingly enough, North Africa was the last major region of the world to attract the attention of the churches in the West. For over 150 years missionaries passed North Africa on their way to the Middle East, India, and Southeast Asia. It was not until the 1880s that the first Protestant missionaries took up work in North Africa.

As the modern missionary enterprise got under way several different kinds of mission emerged. The earliest societies were interdenominational. The London Missionary Society and the American Board of Commissioners for Foreign Missions were in this category, though later on they became, for all practical purposes, congregational boards. The earliest societies in Germany were also in this category. Later, as the missionary movement gained momentum, each denomination organized its own board of missions, supported and controlled by the denomination. In a class by itself was the Church of England, that ended up with ten or eleven independent societies, none of which was the official society of the denomination.

A third kind of mission, the faith mission, came into existence about the middle of the century. These missions appeared first in the British Isles. The earliest was the Zenana and Medical Missionary Fellowship (now the Bible and Medical Missionary Fellowship) in 1852, followed by the British Syrian Mission (now the Lebanon Evangelical Mission) in 1860, and the China Inland Mission (now the Overseas Missionary Fellowship) in 1865. Others followed in rapid succession. By the end of the century there were some two dozen of these faith missions in Britain.

On this side of the Atlantic the earliest faith mission was the Woman's Union Missionary Society (now merged with the Bible and Medical Missionary Fellowship) in 1860. The Christian and Missionary Alliance was established in 1887, and the China Inland Mission opened a North American branch in 1888. Other well-known missions followed: The Evangelical Alliance Mission (1890), the Sudan Interior Mission (1893), and the Africa Inland Mission (1895).

Though their organizational structure and their patterns of support were quite different, these three kinds of missions had much in common so far as methods of work were concerned. All three engaged extensively in evangelistic, medical, and educational work. In this way they had a well-balanced program and tried to meet the needs of the whole man—body, mind, and soul.

In time a fourth kind of mission emerged—the specialized mission. These missions usually ministered to a certain class of people, such as the Jews, the Indians, the Eskimos, the deaf, the blind, the military, orphans, women, children, leprosy patients etc.; or they engaged in some particular kind of work: literacy, literature, radio, aviation, social service, relief work, etc. Some of these were sending missions; others were simply supporting agencies.

The *Encyclopedia of Modern Christian Missions,* published in 1967, lists 1437 missionary agencies based in the West. The tenth edition of the *Mission Handbook: North American Protestant Ministries Overseas,* published in 1973, lists 487 sending and supporting agencies in North America alone. Such has been the growth of the missionary movement in the past 250 years.

Special mention should be made of the Bible societies, without which the missions would have been greatly handicapped. In time each of the Protestant countries of the world organized its own Bible society; today fifty-six of them belong to the United Bible Societies with headquarters in London. Through the years four of these Bible societies have made an enormous contribution to Christian missions around the world; the British and Foreign Bible Society (1804), the National Bible Society of Scotland (1809), the Netherlands Bible Society (1814), and the American Bible Society (1816).

These Bible societies are unique. Never before in the history of the world have so many organizations been dedicated solely to the translation, publication, and distribution of one book. Through the years they have worked very closely with the various missions regardless of their ecclesiastical affiliation, their theological orientation, or their geographical location. Actually the Bible societies are responsible only for the publication of the Scriptures. The translation work is done by the missionaries, with the advice and supervision of the Bible societies' linguistic experts. When it comes to distribution, the Bible societies depend quite heavily on the missionaries at the local level, though they also hire their own colporteurs to sell the Scriptures.

The Scriptures are always published without note or comment, and are sold rather than given away. The first makes possible almost total cooperation on the part of the missions. The second ensures that the Scriptures will be read rather than used for other purposes. The Scriptures are always sold considerably below cost, at a price that the people in the Third World can afford. The Bible societies, like the missionary societies, depend for support on the contributions of the churches in the homelands.

During the nineteenth century the missions were all based in the Western world and had their headquarters in London, Edinburgh, Stockholm, Berlin, Geneva, Toronto, or New York. This meant that the major policy decisions were made at the home end, sometimes by men who had little or no personal experience with missionary work and problems overseas. As might be expected, such an arrangement often created as many problems as it solved, and caused confusion at home and frustration abroad. In some instances the situation became so bad that the missionaries on the field simply went their own way and ignored the directives from headquarters.

> Most disagreements between missionaries and directors concerned money. Although directors regularly denied funds to their missionaries for various new projects, the missionaries themselves often went ahead regardless, or juggled their station accounts in order to provide what they themselves assumed to be essential. Sometimes in exasperated tones, directors explained that funds were short. They counselled the missionaries to be patient and long-suffering.[6]

There was one happy exception—the China Inland Mission. Its headquarters was in Shanghai and all decisions were made there by the general director and his headquarters staff, all of whom were missionaries with long experience. This, of course, was made possible by the fact that the CIM had all its work and workers in one country. Even so, it was not without its internal problems.

What was the caliber of the nineteenth-century missionaries? From an academic point of view they represented a wide spectrum, all the way from semiliterate artisans to university graduates. Missionaries from Germany and Scotland were much better trained, many of them being university men. The same was true of the early missionaries from the United States. Most of them were graduates of the finest colleges and seminaries on the East Coast; and they established some of the most prestigious educational institutions on the mission field, especially in the Middle and Far East.

On the other hand the missionaries from England were not so well educated. From 1815 to 1891 the Church Missionary Society sent out 650 missionaries, of whom only 240 were college graduates. Moreover, most of them were laymen, not ordained ministers. The first band of London Missionary Society missionaries sailed for the South Seas in 1796. There were thirty in the party; only four of them were ordained; the rest were artisans. It should be remembered, however, that then as now colleges were not nearly as numerous in England as in the United

---

[6] Robert I. Rotberg, *Christian Missionaries and the Creation of Northern Rhodesia, 1880-1924* (Princeton: Princeton University Press, 1965), p. 158.

States; consequently there were fewer college graduates to offer for missionary service.

In general missionaries with a higher education were sent to Asia, while those with less education found their way to Africa.

> The majority of the two hundred missionaries who went to Northern Rhodesia before 1924 possessed a minimum of formal education and were predominantly of working-class background. Fewer than thirty-five had received a university education. The others had usually left school at an early age, worked at a trade, and perhaps studied at a Roman Catholic seminary or a Protestant Bible-training institute.[7]

The author goes on to explain:

> Society directors believed that mission fields in Asia were more deserving than those in Africa, and they wanted the better educated candidates to be sent to China and India, where more sophisticated heathen and "superior" cultures would, they believed, be encountered. Since Africa was widely thought to be devoid of history and civilization, its conversion could safely, so they thought, be entrusted to missionaries of "second rank."[8]

When the faith missions came on the scene in the latter half of the century they contributed greatly to the number of missionaries with an inferior education. Very few of them were university graduates. For the most part they were the products of the Bible schools that started about the same time.

What about their spiritual qualities? What they may have lacked by way of intellectual prowess they made up for in Christian character. Almost without exception the missionaries of the nineteenth century were men and women of deep conviction and compassion. They believed that the heathen were lost without a knowledge of Jesus Christ. They spared no pains to take the gospel to the lost and dying "before it was too late." Pearl Buck, whose biographies of her missionary parents would not lead one to believe that she was exactly in sympathy with missionary work, had this to say about missionaries:

> The early missionaries were born warriors and very great men, for in those days religion was still a banner under which to fight. No weak or timid soul could sail the seas to foreign lands and defy death and danger unless he did carry religion as his banner; under which even death itself would be a glorious end. To go forth, to cry out, to warn, to save others, these were frightful urgencies upon the soul already saved. There was a very madness of necessity—an agony of salvation.

What kind of reception did the missionaries receive? In the con-

---

[7] *Ibid.*, p. 161.
[8] *Ibid.*, p. 162.

duct of their work they encountered indifference, suspicion, hostility, persecution, and imprisonment. Times without number their homes were looted, their buildings burned, their churches desecrated, and their lives threatened. Thousands returned home broken in health. Other thousands died prematurely of tropical diseases. Hundreds became martyrs. And all of this they endured without reserve and without regret. Their compassion knew no bounds. They literally fulfilled the words of Christ: "Love your enemies, bless them that curse you, do good to them that hate you, and pray for them that despitefully use you and persecute you" (Mt 5:44, KJV), They were neither saints nor angels; but they were fine Christians. They were the salt of the earth and the light of the world.

The hardest thing of all to bear was the reaction to their message. As a rule the missionaries were not wanted, not liked, and not trusted; consequently their message was rejected. It is a mistake to think that the "heathen in his blindness" is just waiting for the missionary to bring him the light. He is blind all right, but he doesn't know it; consequently he is in no hurry to embrace the light. In country after country the missionaries had to wait years for the seed to take root in good ground. It required endless patience and stamina to win the day.

Adoniram Judson, America's first and greatest missionary, landed in Rangoon in 1813. From the beginning his life was beset with difficulties and frustrations calculated to break the strongest spirit; but in spite of all the adversities he persevered until, after six long years, he won his first convert. Robert Morrison, the first Protestant missionary to China, took seven years to win his first convert. The Primitive Methodists in Northern Rhodesia (Zambia) labored for thirteen years before the first African came forward for baptism. In Thailand it was even worse. The American Congregational missionaries arrived in 1831 and labored for eighteen years without baptizing a single convert. They became weary in well-doing and withdrew in 1849. The American Baptists had a similar experience. They baptized a few Chinese converts but not a single Thai. After seventeen years of futile effort they withdrew. The American Presbyterians entered in 1840 and refused to leave; but it took them nineteen long years to win their first Thai convert!

Death claimed an abnormal number of missionaries, especially in Africa. The big killers were malaria, yellow fever, typhus, and dysentery. The story of missions in Africa was an amazing tale of adventure, endurance, privation, sickness, weakness, and death. The pioneer missionaries penetrated the heart of that great unknown continent through peril, toil, and pain; and the trail they blazed was marked by blood, sweat, and tears.

In his farewell address to the Church Missionary Society before setting out for Uganda, Alexander Mackay said, "Within six months you will probably hear that one of us is dead. When the news comes, do not be cast down; but send someone else immediately to take the vacant place." How prophetic his words were. Within three months one of the party of eight was dead; within a year five had died; and at the end of two years Mackay himself was the sole survivor. In the face of overwhelming odds he struggled on for twelve years until he too was felled by the fever.

West Africa came to be known as "the white man's grave." When Adlai Stevenson II visited Africa in the 1960s he was dumbfounded at the number of missionary graves he saw. His reaction was: "My God, I didn't know this many missionaries died here." In Sierra Leone the Church Missionary Society lost fifty-three missionaries in the first twenty years. In Liberia the losses were even higher. The first American Methodist missionary, Melville B. Cox, arrived in Liberia in 1833 but died within four months of his arrival. His last words were: "Let a thousand fall before Africa be given up."

Not a few missionaries were called upon to seal their testimony with their blood. Strangely enough not many violent deaths occurred in Africa, for the simple reason that the European powers stopped the intertribal warfare and imposed their own form of peace on the entire continent. The colonial presence provided the missionaries with a certain degree of protection. The same was true of India, where apart from the Sepoy Mutiny there were few missionary martyrs. Not so with China, where almost every decade there was a major antiforeign outbreak. The businessmen and the diplomatic corps in the treaty ports were under the protection of the foreign concessions; but the missionaries upcountry were exposed to the fury of the Chinese mobs as they went on the rampage. In the Boxer Year of 1900 no fewer than 189 missionaries and their children lost their lives. Nobody knows how many Chinese Christians were killed. Certainly China proved to be the most resistant of all the major fields of the world, with the single exception of the Muslim world.

As the century wore on and more and more missionary societies appeared on the scene it became necessary to draw up comity agreements to eliminate overlapping and competition, and to ensure a wise and equitable distribution of the available resources, both men and money. Comity was the term used for a gentleman's agreement whereby one mission agreed not to intrude in the territory or interfere in the work of another mission in the same country. To begin with it sounded rather negative in its connotation; but with the passing of time it came to take on many positive features. It came to involve mutual recognition of and common agreement in the employment of national workers, salary scales, standards for church membership, arrangements for the transfer of membership, church discipline. etc.

Comity had several achievements to its credit: (1) It permitted the most economic use of missionary resources. (2) It offered the quickest and most effective means of evangelizing a given country, and ultimately the world. (3) It helped to avoid confusion on the part of converts. (4) It tended to eliminate, or at least to reduce, denominational rivalry. (5) It helped to standardize as far as possible the principles and practices of the various missions.

From time to time attempts were made to set up a board of arbitration to settle disputes when comity was violated; but these did not succeed. To the end comity remained a gentleman's agreement. Comity worked better in some countries than in others. It worked beautifully in the Philippines but was virtually ignored in Japan. Nor was it observed by all missions. The Seventh-day Adventists, Jehovah's Witnesses, and the Mormons have never paid any attention to comity. The Southern Baptists have likewise been a law unto themselves and have established churches in cities where other denominations have existed for decades.

One reason for calling the nineteenth century "The Great Century" is because it produced so many great missionaries. Certainly no other period in Christian history produced such a galaxy of missionary giants. *An Initial Bibliography of Missionary Biography*, published by the Missionary Research Library of New York in 1965, lists 2,286 full-fledged biographies; most of them belonged to the century under review. There is room here to mention only a few of the truly outstanding missionaries in different areas of the world.

We would have to begin with William Carey, the father of modern missions, who spent forty years in India, during which time he translated the Scriptures into thirty-five languages and dialects of India and Southeast Asia. Adoniram Judson, the first American missionary, spent thirty-seven years in Burma, during which time he translated the Bible into Burmese and completed his monumental *Burmese-English Dictionary*. By the close of his life the church in Burma had seven thousand members and Judson had the oversight of 163 missionaries. Robert Morrison, the first Protestant missionary to China, spent twenty-seven years preparing the way for the evangelization of the most populous nation on earth. His great life's work was the translation of the Bible into the ancient Wenli language of China and the publication of his massive six-volume *Chinese Dictionary*. These three men, Carey, Judson, and Morrison, by their prodigious literary labors placed all later missionaries forever in their debt.

Of the various countries of the world, China led the way with a group of missionary giants second to none. The list is a long one. It includes S. Wells Williams, James Legge, W. A. P. Martin, Karl Gützlaff, Hudson Taylor, Griffith John, David Hill, Timothy Richard, and Karl Reichelt, to mention only a few.

India, likewise, was blessed with some outstanding pioneers: Alexander Duff, Reginald Heber, John Scudder, James Thoburn, William Miller, and others.

Three outstanding missionaries laid the foundations of the Christian church in Japan—James Hepburn, Guido Verbeck, and Samuel Brown. Verbeck was a born linguist who spoke Japanese with a fluency and accuracy that amazed his missionary colleagues and charmed his Japanese friends. He was at once educator and evangelist, orator and translator, brilliant statesman and humble Christian worker. He helped the Japanese government build a modern system of education based on Western learning. He assisted in framing the Meiji Constitution. A man without a country, he was awarded the highest of all decorations—the Order of the Rising Sun—and when he died he was given a state funeral.

Horace Underwood and Henry Appenzeller, one a Presbyterian and the other a Methodist, landed in Korea on Easter Sunday, 1885. Together they laid the foundations of the two great churches that emerged in Korea. A third-generation member of the Underwood family acted as an interpreter for the United States Army during the armistice negotiations at Panmunjom in the early 1950s.

In the South Seas three Johns stand out from the rest: John Paton, John Patteson, and John Geddie. The famous Ludwig Nommensen spent fifty-six years in Sumatra, during which he witnessed the birth and growth of the great Batak Church whose early members had been cannibalistic headhunters.

In the Middle East the American Congregationalists built some of the finest educational institutions on the mission field and thereby made a significant contribution to the cause of Arab nationalism. Cyrus Hamlin founded Robert College in Istanbul. Daniel Bliss established the Syrian Protestant College, which later became the American University of Beirut. Speaking in 1920, Emir Feisal bore testimony to the influence of that institution when he said: "Dr. Daniel Bliss, the founder of the college, was the grandfather of Syria; his son, Dr. Howard Bliss, the present president, is the father of Syria. Without the education this college has given, the struggle for freedom would never have been won. The Arabs owe everything to these men." Two other giants were Eli Smith and C. V. VanDyck who together translated the Bible into the difficult classical Arabic language.

And what shall be said about Africa? The best-known missionary of all time was David Livingstone who, by his travels in Central Africa, exposed the Arab slave trade as "the open sore of the world" and managed to "open a path for commerce and Christianity" in that unknown continent. His father-in-law, Robert Moffat, became "the apostle to Bechuanaland," where he spent fifty years. His chief task was the translation of the entire Bible and the founding of the great church in that land. Other well-known pioneers in Africa include Dan Crawford, François Coillard, James Stewart, Donald Fraser, Alexander Mackay, Mary Slessor, and a host of others.

By all odds the missionaries of the nineteenth century were a special breed of men and women. Single-handedly and with great courage they attacked the social evils of their time: child marriage, the immolation of widows, temple prostitution, and untouchability in India; footbinding, opium addiction, and the abandoning of babies in China; polygamy, the slave trade, and the destruction of twins in Africa. In all parts of the world they opened schools, hospitals, clinics, medical colleges, orphanages, and leprosaria. They gave succor and sustenance to the dregs of society cast off by their own communities. At great risk to themselves and their families they fought famines, floods, pestilences, and plagues. They were the first to rescue unwanted babies, educate girls, and liberate women. Above all, they gave to the non-Christian world the most liberating of all messages—the gospel of Christ. They converted savages into saints; and out of this raw material they built the Christian church, which is today the most universal of all institutions. By the end of the century the gospel had literally been taken to the ends of the earth. "Never before in a period of equal length had Christianity or any other religion penetrated for the first time as large an area as it had in the nineteenth century."[9] The emissaries of the cross were to be found in all parts of the habitable globe, from the frozen wastes of Greenland to the steaming jungles of Africa. Churches, chapels, schools, and hospitals were scattered with great profusion from Turkey to Tokyo, from Cairo to Cape Town, from Monterrey to Montevideo, from Polynesia to Indonesia. There were, to be sure, a few areas of the world where there were no resident missionaries; but that was because of government restrictions, not because the church lacked either the will or the power to press forward with the task of world evangelization. Included in the Christian church, for the very first time, were representatives of "every tribe and tongue and people and nation" (Re 5:9). Latourette was right when he called it "The Great Century."

---

[9] Kenneth Scott Latourette, *The Great Century in the Americas, Australasia and Africa* (New York: Harper, 1953, p. 469.

Development of Protestant Missions In the Twentieth Century

The turn of the century marked the development of three important movements destined to have an important bearing on the course of Christian missions: the Faith Mission Movement, the Bible Institute Movement, and the Student Volunteer Movement. All three started during the latter half of the previous century but did not come to full fruition until the 1900s. All three came in time to be predominantly North American phenomena. The first two are still with us; the third petered out in the 1930s.

The term *faith mission* has been applied to a number of inter-denominational agencies which, because they have no "captive constituency," must to an unusual degree look to the Lord for the supply of their needs. They themselves, however, would be the last to claim that they have any monopoly on faith. Their missionaries have no guaranteed income, though they do have a support scale which they try to maintain. They do not go into debt, nor do they solicit funds. They prefer to make their needs known to the Christian public and look to the Lord to move in the hearts of His people.

The faith missions have never regarded themselves as being in competition with the mainline denominations. The latter, however, have tended to regard the faith missions as something of a Cinderella and refer to them as "sects." Every faith mission has a statement of faith which each member is expected to sign. In this way they preserve their conservative, evangelical stance.

One of the outstanding characteristics of the faith missions has been their enduring quality. Several of them are over one hundred years old and are still going strong. Others are close to the centennial mark. Not a single mission brought into existence in the nineteenth century has folded.

Another feature has been their steady and dynamic growth. Today the faith missions are among the largest in the world, some with a membership pushing the one-thousand mark. Wycliffe Bible Translators has three thousand members; Campus Crusade for Christ has over four thousand on its staff, of whom eight hundred are located overseas.

Still another feature has been their creativity. Most of the innovations of the twentieth century have been introduced by the faith missions, including radio, aviation, Bible correspondence courses, gospel recordings, tapes, cassettes, saturation evangelism, and theological education by extension.

Through the years the faith missions have derived most of their support from the independent Bible, Baptist, and community churches and their recruits from the Bible schools. In their overseas work they have concentrated on evangelism and church planting. In the medical field they have maintained scores of hospitals and hundreds of clinics. In the educational field they have established and maintained thousands of elementary schools, especially in Africa, but very few high schools and no colleges. In theological education they have been content with Bible schools. Only in recent years have they established a few seminaries.

The Bible School Movement got under way in the 1880s and even more than the Faith Mission Movement became overwhelmingly a North American phenomenon. S. A. Witmer in his book, *The Bible School Story*, published in 1962, listed 247 Bible institutes and colleges in the United States and Canada. Today the figure is considerably higher, with over fifty reported in Canada alone. The earliest schools were Nyack (1882), Moody (1886), Toronto (1894), and Providence (1900). From the beginning the Bible schools emphasized home and foreign missions as well as evangelism and Bible.

In recent years many of these schools have added sufficient liberal arts subjects to the curriculum to enable them to grant the B. A. degree. Today there are fifty-four colleges that are full members of the Accrediting Association of Bible Colleges and ten that are associate members. Total enrollment in the AABC schools in the fall of 1973 was 25,686, an increase of 5.37 percent over the previous year.

In spite of the changes that have come about, the Bible colleges continue to provide the lion's share of candidates for the faith missions. Schools such as Columbia Bible College, Nyack College, Multnomah School of the Bible, Prairie Bible Institute, Ontario (Toronto) Bible College, and others have through the years sent a steady stream of missionaries to the foreign field. Moody Bible Institute, the granddaddy of them all, has chalked up a fantastic record. Since 1890 almost 5,000 Moody alumni have served under 245 mission boards in 108 countries of the world. Of this number 2,327 were still in active service in 1973. This means that 1 out of every 13 American missionaries in the world today is an alumnus of Moody Bible Institute. And the flow continues unabated; 105 Moody students actually left for the field in 1973.

Another mighty movement of the Holy Spirit was the Student Volunteer Movement. It too began in the 1880s. Its inception and much of its early success were due to the missionary vision of Robert P. Wilder, a graduate of Princeton University; the spiritual power of D. L. Moody, the greatest evangelist of the nineteenth century; and the organizing genius of John R. Mott, then a student at Cornell University. It all began in the summer of 1886 when one hundred university and seminary students at Moody's conference grounds at Mt. Hermon, Massachusetts, signed the Princeton Pledge, which read: "I purpose, God willing, to become a foreign missionary." In 1888 the movement was officially organized in New York City as the Student Volunteer Movement for Foreign Missions, with John R. Mott as chairman and Robert Wilder as traveling secretary. In no time at all the movement spread to colleges and universities all over the United States and Canada and even to foreign countries. The watchword of the movement, coined by Wilder, was: "The evangelization of the world in this generation."

One of its outstanding features was the quadrennial missionary convention, the first of which was held in Cleveland, Ohio, in 1891. Through the years tens of thousands attended these conventions, hearing the call of Christ to missionary service and signing the Princeton Pledge. The Des Moines Convention of 1920 was the highwater mark, after which the movement began to decline. The last convention was held in Indianapolis in 1936, by which time it was virtually a spent force; but in fifty years it had been instrumental in sending 20,500 students to the foreign mission field, most of them from North America.

Two world wars played havoc with missions in various parts of the world. German missions were particularly hard hit. During World War II, had it not been for the aid given by mission boards of the United States and her allies through the good offices of the International Missionary Council, German missionary work would have come to a halt. Only now, after thirty years, are the German missions beginning to recoup their losses; but as long as East Germany remains under Communist rule full recovery will be impossible.

Two events in the 1930s had an adverse effect on missionary work. One was the Depression, which was worldwide; the other was the Laymen's Foreign Mission Inquiry, which was an American operation. The first precipitated a general retrenchment right across the board, from which some missions never did fully recover. Income dropped off drastically, and so did recruits. Significantly, the China Inland Mission at the depth of the Depression issued a special appeal for two hundred new workers in two years—and got them.

The Laymen's Inquiry was an examination made by a commission of fifteen laymen of the overall program of seven American boards working in the Orient. Many of its findings were discerning, constructive, and helpful. Conservatives, however, were understandably perturbed when they read that the aim of Christian missions is: "To seek with people of other lands a true knowledge and love of God, expressing in life and word what we have learned through Jesus Christ, and endeavoring to give effect to his spirit in the life of the world."[10] Equally disturbing was the statement that "ministry to the secular needs of men in the spirit of Christ, moreover, *is* evangelism, in the right sense of the word.[11] Out of this came a recommendation that "direct and conscious" evangelism be divorced from medical and educational work. The published report, as might be imagined, created a stir in missionary circles in the United States and did not a little to accelerate the process of secularization already at work in the missionary movement.

The Sino-Japanese War (1937-1945) brought Christian missions in China to a stop in all but three or four of the eighteen provinces. The final *coup de grâce* was administered by the Communists when they came to power in 1949 after twenty-two years of intermittent civil war. By 1953 all Protestant missionaries and most Roman Catholic missionaries were out of China. Without doubt the China debacle of the 1950s was the greatest single reverse ever suffered by the modern missionary movement.

Since World War II more than seventy-five countries have received their independence and joined the United Nations. Most of these are located in the Third World, where missions have always operated. The collapse of the vast colonial system in Asia and Africa has been the most significant event of the twentieth century. It has not only changed the balance of power in the United Nations and around the world, but it has profoundly affected the cause and course of Christian missions at home and overseas. Specifically three major changes have occurred: The image of Christianity has changed; the status of the national church has changed; the role of the missionary has changed.

Christianity in the Third World has always been regarded as a "foreign religion," but worse still it was identified with colonialism. Now that the colonial system no longer exists that millstone at last has been removed. The missionaries entered with the colonialists. It is just as well they did not leave with them or else the identification would have been complete. Now Christianity can stand on its own feet, free from the "entangling alliances" with the European empires of yesteryear. No longer can the missionaries be accused of "cultural imperialism," nor can the national Christians be called the "running dogs of foreign imperialism."

The status of the national church has likewise changed. The churches, with few exceptions, have received their independence. They are no longer tied to the "mother" churches in the West. For the first time they are free to act as they wish. Their leaders are now on

---

[10]William Ernest Hocking, *Re-Thinking Missions: A Laymen's Inquiry After One Hundred Years* (New York: Harper, 1932), p. 326.
[11] *Ibid.*

a basis of absolute equality with the missionaries. Indeed, they can refuse to accept missionaries if they want to. The church leaders are now masters in their own house, subject only to the authority of the Holy Spirit, not to the directions and dictates of the missionaries.

This, of course, means that the role of the missionary has also changed. He began by being the master. Then he was reduced to the role of partner. Now he is the servant, not only of the Lord but of the national church. This will not be an easy role to play; but play it he must, for the hour has come.

With the advent of independence the great ethnic religions of the East have taken a new lease on life. They are passing from the defensive to the offensive. Some are demanding that they be declared the official religion of the country. Others are calling for the expulsion of the foreign missionaries. Still others are urging their governments to pass anticonversion laws designed to cripple the witness of the national church. Some are even sending missionaries to the West to convert us. As a result there is a great and growing interest in our country in Oriental mysticism, transcendental meditation, yoga, and Zen Buddhism.

Since World War II Communism, the implacable foe of all religion, has made important gains in Asia and is infiltrating Africa and Latin America. China, Mongolia, North Korea, and North Vietnam are all closed to missionary work. It remains to be seen what happens in Laos and Cambodia. Even South Vietnam may yet fall to the Communists. Both Russia and China are fishing in troubled waters in the unstable countries of Africa. As for Latin America, the countries there have long since been ripe for revolution. In some countries Roman Catholic priests are flirting with guerrilla bands attempting to overthrow the reactionary governments. Wherever the Communists extend their rule, both church and mission are bound to suffer. Communism is not the monolithic international superstructure we once thought it was; but it is still too early to pronounce its demise.

A major twentieth-century event which affected Christian missions was the emergence after World War II of the United States as a superpower, along with the USSR, and the subsequent development of the Cold War. With military bases all over the world, and with military alliances with some forty countries, the United States is in world politics up to the eyes. In and out of the United Nations Uncle Sam has been the whipping dog of international politics. Time was when an American passport was an asset; now it is more likely to be a liability.

When the Six-Day War took place in June 1967 the Arab nations blamed the United States and broke off diplomatic relations. The American missionaries who evacuated at that time have not been able to return. Several Arab countries have recently resumed diplomatic relations with the United States and others are likely to follow in the near future. When India liberated Bangladesh in 1971 the United States sided with Pakistan. As a result America's stock soared in Pakistan but plummeted in India and Bangladesh.

Because of her immense power and her worldwide interests, the United States, directly or indirectly, is involved in international disputes in all parts of the world. Whatever side she takes she is likely to offend one of the disputants, and American missionaries in that country are in for trouble. Thus it comes about that the American missionary is caught in the crossfire of international politics.

This recent postwar period has seen a marked decline in missionary interest and activity on the part of the mainline denominations in the West. With few exceptions they have retreated all along the line. The following statistics tell the story for six of our largest denominations:

OVERSEAS TASK FORCE	1958	1971
American Baptist Convention	407	290
United Presbyterian, USA	1,293	810
Presbyterian Church, US	504	391
United Methodist Church (including EUB)	1,453	1,175
Protestant Episcopal Church	395	138
United Church of Christ	496	356
TOTAL	4,548	3,160[12]

The United Presbyterians announced in 1971 that they intended to drop another two hundred missionaries over the next two years.

There have been several contributing factors in this situation. (1) Now that the national churches have achieved both independence and maturity, the missions, as a matter of policy, have gradually and purposely reduced their overseas forces. (2) With nationalism making life and work on the mission field more and more difficult, to say nothing of the problem of closing doors, the home boards are not recruiting candidates in the same numbers as before. (3) With a lower enrollment in the liberal seminaries candidates for pastoral ministry and for missionary service are both in short supply. (4) Many of the mainline denominations have experienced a marked drop in contributions to the administrative budget to the point where staff members have been laid off. The more conservative church members are opposed to the increasing commitment on the part of the leaders to civil rights, social action, nation building, and even revolution. They have decided for the time being to withhold their gifts. (5) Theological liberalism, especially neo-universalism, is slowly but surely cutting the

---

[12] "The Missionary Retreat," *Christianity Today* (November 19, 1971), p. 26.

nerve of the Christian mission. If it is true that all men are already saved without a knowledge of Jesus Christ, there is no compelling reason why the church should break its neck to share the gospel with the world, especially when our own needs are so great.

It should be noted that not all mainline denominations are in retreat. The more conservative churches are holding their own and some of them, such as the Southern Baptists, are forging ahead, which would confirm the conviction that theology plays a major role in Christian missions.

While the mainline denominations are in retreat the conservative evangelicals, with few exceptions, are doing well. The older and larger missions, with a membership around one thousand, find it difficult to go much beyond that point. The main reason for this is the fact that every year the rolls are reduced by death and retirement, which just about offsets the influx of new members. The younger and smaller missions continue to grow, some of them rather rapidly. The New Tribes Mission, founded in 1942, now has 950 missionaries. Wycliffe Bible Translators, founded in 1935, has 3,125 workers. Some missions were not established until after World War II. Already they have a membership of between one and two hundred. In this category are the Greater Europe Mission and the Far Eastern Gospel Crusade.

Two new programs were developed during the 1960s: short terms abroad and the summer missionary project. The former goes back long before 1960, but only in recent years has the program really burgeoned. Both programs have attracted a good deal of attention. Both seem to fit the mood of today's youth. Both have been made feasible by the rapid transportation of the jet age and the affluence of American society. So popular are these programs that in some missions half the new recruits each year are short-termers. In fact three of the mainline denominations and one faith mission will no longer accept career missionaries when they first apply. Only after they have served a term or two on the field are they eligible to become career missionaries. In 1973 there were four thousand short-term missionaries from North America. *Opportunities 1974*, published by Short Terms Abroad, listed sixty-eight hundred opportunities as compared with fifty-six hundred in 1973.

The summer missionary project is even more popular than short terms abroad. Every summer thousands of college students serve overseas under the auspices of some mission board. They pay their own transportation and sometimes are responsible for their own room and board. They serve in scores of different capacities and usually manage to make a solid contribution. Upon their return to campus at the end of the summer they share their experiences and enthusiasm with their fellow students. Some Christian colleges report that the summer missionary project has completely changed the attitude of the student body towards foreign missions. It is still too early to make an accurate evaluation of these two programs, but there is reason to believe that an increasing number of short termers are signing up as career missionaries.

For almost a hundred years the church in its missionary meetings has been singing, "Give the winds a mighty voice." These familiar words took on new meaning when the first missionary radio station, HCJB in Ecuador, went on the air on Christmas Day 1931 with a tiny 250-watt transmitter which barely covered the city of Quito. Since those humble beginnings we have progressed to the place where there are now some sixty radio stations owned and operated by various missionary agencies, to say nothing of tens of thousands of Christian programs aired every week over commercial stations. Some of these stations are among the most powerful in the world.

The Far East Broadcasting Company based in Manila is typical of what is being done in missionary radio today. Founded in 1945, FEBC is presently using twenty-two transmitters to broadcast the gospel for 1,428 program hours each week in sixty-three major languages and dialects of Asia and Latin America. Broadcasting facilities are located on the island of Luzon in the Philippines, the Seychelles in the Indian Ocean, Cheju Island off the coast of Korea, and San Francisco. FEBC has its own recording studios in Tokyo, New Delhi, Bangalore, Bangkok, Jakarta, Hong Kong, and Singapore. Some thirty-five additional cooperating studios belonging to other missions throughout Asia make tapes in the languages of their respective countries and send them to Manila for broadcasting. Mail is received at an average of eighteen thousand letters a month from a hundred countries around the world. And FEBC is only one of sixty missionary radio stations!

A similar story could be told of other stations: ELWA in Liberia (Sudan Interior Mission), HCJB in Ecuador (World Radio Missionary Fellowship), RVOG in Ethiopia (Lutheran World Federation), HLKY (National Council of Churches) and HLKX (The Evangelical Alliance Mission), both in Korea, and Trans World Radio in Monte Carlo, Swaziland, Cyprus, and Bonaire. In Japan the Pacific Broadcasting Association prepares radio and television programs that are aired over commercial stations.

Along with radio broadcasting are the Bible correspondence courses. Many of the broadcasting stations operate their own Bible Institute of the Air. Through the years millions of persons have enrolled in these courses. The Light of Life Correspondence School, which promotes Bible studies in twenty-four languages of India, has itself enrolled over a million students since it began back in the 1940s. These courses have two great advantages. They are usually offered free of charge and can be studied in the secrecy of the home. Even in Muslim lands, where people would not dare enter a church, there are tens of thousands now studying the Word of God by means of Bible correspondence courses.

During that same period, the 1960s, three important developments took place—Church Growth, Evangelism-in-Depth, and Theological Education by Extension.

The first of these grew out of the Institute of Church Growth originally in Eugene, Oregon, and later transferred to Fuller Theological Seminary in Pasadena, California. Dr. Donald A. McGavran, former missionary to India, was the founder and for many years the director of the Institute of Church Growth. He has done more than any other missiologist to arouse both the home churches and foreign missions to the paramount importance of *growth* in Christian work. Growth with McGavran is always spiritual growth. He is not interested in more and bigger budgets, buildings, or bureaucracies. Growth to him is making converts, discipling the nations, multiplying churches—in a word, *church* growth. That to him is the end and aim of all missionary work worthy of the name. Other forms of work are valuable and have their place; but preaching the gospel and building the church should always be given first place.

Three auxiliary enterprises have been brought into existence: a monthly publication entitled *Church Growth Bulletin,* the Church Growth Book Club, and the William Carey Library. Many of the Masters' theses produced at Fuller are published by the William Carey Library. Every year Church Growth Workshops are organized in various parts of the United States for the benefit of missionaries on furlough.

The second development—Evangelism-in-Depth—was the brainchild of Dr. R. Kenneth Strachan, former General Director of the Latin America Mission. Expressed in simple terms EID is an attempt to mobilize the entire resources of the churches in a given country to take the gospel in verbal or written form to every family in that country. The idea caught fire and spread to other parts of the world, where it was called by various names: New Life For All (Nigeria), Christ For All (Zaire), Mobilization Evangelism (Japan), Evangelical Advance (Guatemala). Dr. George Peters of Dallas coined the phrase "Saturation Evangelism" and used it to describe all these various movements.

The philosophy underlying EID is based on four presuppositions: (1) Abundant reaping results from abundant sowing. (2) Christians can and must work together in evangelism. (3) When Christians pool their resources God multiplies them. (4) A dedicated minority can make an impact on an entire nation.

The genius of EID is summed up in the word *mobilization*. Dr. Strachan, after making an intensive study of the propaganda methods of the Communists, Jehovah's Witnesses, and other dynamic groups, enunciated the following principle: "The growth of any movement is in direct proportion to the success it obtains in the mobilization of the totality of its membership for the constant propagation of its beliefs."

Mobilization, according to EID, involves four principles: (1) Mobilization of every Christian in witness. (2) Mobilization within the framework of the church. (3) Mobilization by local leadership. (4) Mobilization with global objectives.

The program of EID develops progressively: organization of committees, establishment of prayer cells, training of leaders who will then train church members, visitation, local campaigns, special efforts, regional campaigns, national campaigns, and follow-up. In the smaller countries this program can be completed in a year. In larger countries it may take three or more years.

The stated objectives of EID are twofold: General objectives are: (1) Total mobilization of the Christian community. (2) Total evangelization of a given area. Particular objectives are: (1) Awakening of pastors and missionaries to the potential that lies dormant in the local church and a practical demonstration of what can be done when this potential is tapped. (2) Development of strong national leadership. (3) Development of a strong national church. (4) Evangelization of all levels and classes of society.

The third movement was Theological Education by Extension. This was not a beautiful theory developed in a spiritual vacuum in the homeland and exported to the mission field. Rather it grew out of an existential situation in Latin America where, because of rapid church growth, the existing seminaries were not doing an adequate job, with the result that some sixty thousand pastors were without any formal training in Bible or theology. Obviously something different, something drastic, had to be done.

These pastors were older men who already had churches and could not leave their farms, shops, and families for any extended period of time. If they were to get any kind of training, the seminary would have to go to them; they could not go to the seminary.

It all began with the Presbyterians in Guatemala in 1960. From there it spread to other countries of Latin America and eventually to Africa and Asia. During the past five or six years scores of TEE workshops have been conducted on three continents. CAMEO (Committee for Assisting Missionary Education Overseas) has assisted in the organizing and financing of these workshops.

The cornerstone of the decentralized seminary is the programmed textbook. This enables the student-pastor to study in his own way, on his own time, and at his own pace. Periodically he and the other student-pastors meet with the seminary professor in some central place for a short period of counsel, encouragement, supervision, and testing —not for learning; that is supposed to have been done by the student beforehand.

In the middle sixties there was a time when missionary interest, especially on the college campus, was very low. Mission leaders were having to beat the bushes for recruits; but in the past few years the situation seems to have improved. Once again the Christian mission has become a viable option.

This welcome change is due to a number of factors, one of which is the famous Urbana Missionary Convention convened every three years by Inter-Varsity Christian Fellowship. These conventions are the true successors of the Student Volunteer Movement conventions of an earlier period. In 1973 over fourteen thousand college students gave up their Christmas vacation to attend five days of missionary meetings. Five thousand signed the missionary pledge.

Another factor is the fine work done among university students by such groups as Inter-Varsity Fellowship and Campus Crusade for Christ. An increasing number of seminary freshmen come each year from this source. Many of them come from a pagan background and were introduced to Jesus Christ for the very first time after they got to college. These young people often make better disciples than the youth reared in evangelical homes and churches to whom Christianity is "old hat." These new converts are still in the glow of their first love and are willing to follow Christ to the ends of the earth.

Probably the most potent factor is the gracious moving of the Holy Spirit among the youth of our nation. No one can study the Jesus Movement that is sweeping the country without thanking God that He has once again visited His people. Everywhere there is a new interest in religion, even in intellectual circles. The charismatic movement has invaded the mainline denominations, including the Roman Catholic Church. As a result, Bible study groups are meeting not only in Christian homes but in shops, schools, factories, offices, banks, etc., all over the country. Bibles by the millions are being sold every year. And the amazing thing is that all this has happened without any human leader or any man-made organization. In the next ten years thousands of these Jesus People will find their way to Bible college and seminary; many of them will end up on the mission field. Missions and revival have always gone together. It will be the same again. The revival now taking place is bound to result in more recruits for the mission field. Indeed, the vanguard has already arrived. Several mission boards now report that they have more accepted candidates than they can send out.

The modern missionary movement based on the Western world has always been a multinational undertaking involving all the Protestant countries of Christendom. In the early part of the century only one out of every three missionaries in the world was an American; today the ratio is two out of three. The reason is not far to seek. German missions were hard hit during World War II and to date have not recouped their losses. Great Britain, which used to be one of the larger sending countries, is in the throes of a religious depression not seen since before the Wesleyan Revival. Moreover, Britain, robbed of her empire, is economically unable to sustain her overseas commitments on anything like the former scale. It is only proper that the United States with her vast resources in men and money should shoulder the lion's share of world evangelization. We can thank God that it has "come to the kingdom for such a time as this."

In this connection it should be noted that certain faith missions which formerly were based in Britain have in this postwar period opened branches in North America. Included in this category are the Bible and Medical Missionary Fellowship, Japan Evangelistic Band, Scripture Union, North Africa Mission, and the Red Sea Mission Team. In other instances the traffic has moved in the opposite direction. Several faith missions originally based in the United States have recently branched out into other parts of the world and now have supporting and recruiting offices in several Western countries. Wycliffe Bible Translators, Mission Aviation Fellowship, Gospel Recordings, and Trans World Radio belong on this list.

Several specialized agencies which began in, and for many years were confined to, the United States have in recent years become international in scope. The list is a long one: Bible Club Movement, Youth for Christ, the Gideons, Christian Businessmen's Committee, Child Evangelism Fellowship, Word of Life Fellowship, High School Evangelism, Young Life, Navigators, and Campus Crusade for Christ. Some of these are engaged in direct missionary work, others are only indirectly involved; but all are making a significant contribution to the cause of Christ throughout the world.

Time and again we have been told that the missionaries taught the people to read but the Communists gave them literature. This is one of those half-truths that can be so misleading to the uninformed. Missionaries have always given high priority to the printed page. William Ward, Carey's colleague in Serampore, was a professional printer and operated the first mission press in North India. The first thing the American missionaries did when they arrived in the Middle East in the early 1820s was to write home for a printing press. Shortly after the Communists came to power in Russia, Arthur J. Brown could report: "Today one hundred and sixty presses are conducted by the Protestant mission boards in various parts of the world, and they issue annually about four hundred million pages of Christian literature."[13] From that day to this in all parts of the world mission presses have been pouring out a veritable Niagara of Christian literature.

And the work goes on. Today several agencies are engaged solely in the production and distribution of Christian literature overseas: Christian Literature Crusade, Evangelical Literature Overseas, Literature Crusades, World Literature Crusade, and Moody Literature Mission. The last-mentioned is now producing and distributing gospel literature in 184 different languages in over a hundred countries. In addition, Moody Institute of Science has made its science films available in twenty-one languages to missionaries in 120 countries.

Several well-known evangelical publishing houses, such as Scripture Press, David C. Cook, and Gospel Light, are now sponsoring Christian education programs on the mission field, and giving technical assistance to Christian publishers overseas. In addition, several highly technical research agencies have come into existence in the last few years, among them Interchristo and Missions Advanced Research and Communication Center. In a word, there is at the present time an enormous amount of missionary work of all kinds based in the United States but reaching around the world. And it is growing with every passing year.

Missions and the Ecumenical Movement

The Ecumenical Movement of our day is the direct outcome of the missionary enterprise of the nineteenth century. "Missions and ecumenism are inseparable. Revival, missions, Christian unity, is an inevitable series."[14] The roots of the Ecumenical Movement go back to Zinzendorf and the Moravians in the first half of the eighteenth century.

The origin of the Moravian Church dates from 1467, when the followers of John Huss, with certain Waldensians and Moravians, banded together to form the United Brotherhood. Count Nicholaus Ludwig von Zinzendorf was the greatest missionary statesman of the eighteenth century. Under his leadership the Moravians started more missions in twenty years than the Anglicans and Protestants had

---

[13] Arthur J. Brown, *The Why and How of Foreign Missions* (New York: Missionary Education Movement, 1921), p. 127.
[14] Ruth Rouse and Stephen Neill, *A History of the Ecumenical Movement* (Philadelphia: Westminster Press, 1968), p. 310.

started in two hundred years. In his religious affections Zinzendorf embraced all "Followers of the Lamb," regardless of their denominational affiliation. He enjoyed close fellowship with evangelicals in all denominations, including the Roman Catholic Church.

During the first half of the nineteenth century half a dozen German missions were formed: Berlin, Rhenish, Gossner, Leipzig, and Hermannsburg. These missions accepted men and money from both Lutheran and Reformed Churches. The Basel Missionary Society brought together in Germany and Switzerland both Lutherans and Reformed in the common task of missions. Basel sent out its own missionaries; it also furnished missionaries for the Church Missionary Society and the London Missionary Society of England, and supplied pastors for the Reformed, Lutheran, and Evangelical Churches in the United States. So from the very beginning the modern missionary movement cut right across denominational lines and embraced all who had a concern to share the Christian message with the "heathen world."

The missionary movement in Britain grew out of the Evangelical Awakening under Wesley and Whitefield, who in turn were greatly influenced by the Pietists and the Moravians. The connecting link was Wesley's contact with Zinzendorf and Whitefield's study of the works of Francke.

The famous London Missionary Society when founded in 1795 was interdenominational. One of its purposes was "an increase of union and friendly intercourse among Christians of different denominations at home." At its founding an Anglican preached the sermon. "The whole world comprised the mission field," he said, "and in the kind of united endeavor for which the London Missionary Society stood, different kinds of church order should lose their identity under the greater name 'Christian.'" The stated policy of the new mission was "not to send Presbyterianism, Independency, Episcopacy or any other form of Church Order and Government . . . but the glorious gospel of the blessed God to the Heathen."[15]

The Church of England founded the Church Missionary Society in 1799; but the first two candidates were neither British nor Anglican. They were German Lutherans. Indeed, of twenty-four missionaries sent out during the first fifteen years, seventeen were German Lutherans.

On this side of the water the first foreign mission to be established was the American Board of Commissioners for Foreign Missions. The year was 1810. It was based in Boston and drew most of its early missionaries from New England. Like the London Missionary Society,

---

[15] Richard Lovett, *The History of the London Missionary Society* (London: Henry Frowde, 1899), Vol. I, pp. 49-50.

it was predominantly Congregational in polity; but from the beginning it accepted candidates from other denominations.

As the missionary movement progressed six ecumenical streams emerged. In time these streams converged to form the mighty river now known as the ecumenical movement.

1. Missionary conferences in the nineteenth century in India, China, and Japan, and later in Africa and the Middle East. India led the way. The earliest conference was a modest affair, held in 1825 in the city of Bombay. The participants were four missions working at that time in Bombay. Madras followed in 1827 and Calcutta in 1830. These were all city-wide conferences. Regional conferences began in North India in 1855 and in South India in 1858. In 1872 the first All-India Conference was held in Allahabad with 136 missionaries representing nineteen societies. Twenty years later the conference in Bombay attracted 620 missionaries belonging to forty mission boards. Thereafter an All-India Conference was held every decade. Similar conferences were held in China and Japan.

In the early years these conferences were for inspiration and fellowship, but as time went on more thought was given to solving problems and transacting business. A significant feature of these conferences was a growing sense of oneness in Christ and in the cause of Christian missions. As early as the Ootacamund Conference (1858) it was suggested that denominational differences, while meaningful in the West, were devoid of significance in mission lands where converts were content to be Christians, not Methodists, Baptists, Anglicans, etc. They also acknowledged at that conference that God "may create in India a church differing in many respects from any existing Christian communities in Europe and America."[16] Some twenty years later in Bangalore they went so far as to speak of a day when there would be one "Church of Christ in India."[17]

At the Lahore Conference (1862) they prefaced their report with the familiar prayer of our Lord—"That they all might be one." To prove that they meant business they conducted a Communion Service in which Anglicans, Methodists, Presbyterians, and Baptists joined. From the hands of Presbyterian clergymen Baptist deacons took the elements and passed them to the assembled delegates.

When we remember that at the founding Assembly of the World Council of Churches at Amsterdam in 1948—eighty-five years later— it was not possible to hold a Communion Service attended by all, one begins to realize how far ahead of their time these early missionaries

---

[16] William Richey Hogg, *Ecumenical Foundations* (New York: Harper, 1952), p. 20.
[17] *Ibid.*, p. 21.

were. From their inception the churches on the mission field were far more ecumenical in outlook than the "mother" churches in the West. The first church in Japan was organized in 1872 in Yokohama with eleven young men as charter members. They called their church "The Church of Christ in Japan" and included in the constitution this statement:

> Our church does not belong to any sect whatever; it believes only in the name of Christ in whom all are one; it believes that all who take the Bible as their guide and who diligently study it are the servants of Christ and our brethren. For this reason all believers on earth belong to the family of Christ in the bonds of brotherly love.[18]

2. **Intermission conferences, councils, and associations in the homelands, also in the nineteenth century.** The earliest effort at intermission cooperation at home began in England in 1819, when the secretaries of four mission boards with headquarters in London agreed to come together to form an association for "mutual counsel and fellowship." Their first meeting was held at the Baptist Missionary Society House October 29, 1819. Thereafter they met monthly until World War II. Three of England's greatest interdenominational missionary conferences were sponsored by the London Secretaries' Association— Liverpool in 1860, London in 1878, and London in 1888.

An even more influential group was the Evangelical Alliance in London formed in 1846. Its primary concern was with evangelical unity; but from the first it was strongly missionary and tried to foster cooperation among the various missionary societies. Its monthly journal, *Evangelical Christendom,* from its first issue in 1847 carried missionary news from all parts of the world. It held annual conferences in different parts of the British Isles. It sponsored the first of the general missionary conferences in England, the London Conference in 1854.

The first great Missionary Conference on this side of the water was the New York Missionary Conference in 1854. Alexander Duff, educator, missionary statesman, and orator, dominated the conference and left a lasting impression on all who heard him. A second great conference was held in New York in 1900. The word *ecumenical* had been used before to describe the missionary conferences. Now it was used officially for the first time. For sheer size it was the largest missionary conference ever held. No fewer than 162 mission boards were represented—64 from North America, 50 from Europe, 35 from the British Isles, and 13 others. A total of 175,000 persons attended the ten-day conference. Most of the missionary giants of that day were

---

[18] Harlan P. Beach, *Geography and Atlas of Protestant Missions* (New York: Student Volunteer Movement, 1901), p. 219.

present—Bishop Thoburn, Hudson Taylor, Timothy Richard, John Paton, John R. Mott, Robert E. Speer, and others.

From many points of view the London Conference of 1888 was the most significant, for it was at that conference that Gustav Warneck, the great German missiologist, in a paper on international cooperation proposed a general missionary conference each decade "to bring about gradually, by such fraternal alliances, a certain amount of unity in Protestant missionary labours." To this end he suggested the formation of a Standing Central Committee, with headquarters in London, composed of delegates from all the Protestant missionary societies. To strengthen and support this Central Committee, missionary councils should be formed in all Protestant countries. A third suggestion was the founding of a general scientific journal of missions.

In a remarkable manner Warneck anticipated two of the most far-reaching results of the Edinburgh Conference of 1910, the formation of a Central Committee and the founding of a Journal of Missiology.

The earliest interdenominational conferences in Europe were missionary in character. Some were national (Germany); some were regional (Scandinavian); others were continental. The earliest permanent councils in these countries were all missionary councils. Later they developed into national Christian councils.

3. **Bible Societies.** The first of these was the British and Foreign Bible Society founded in 1804. Three others had a worldwide ministry: the Netherlands Bible Society (1814), the American Bible Society (1816), and the National Bible Society of Scotland (1809). In time all the Protestant countries of the world formed their own Bible societies. Today there are fifty-six of these societies in the United Bible Societies. No religious organization in the Western world has commanded such widespread support, moral and material, as have the Bible societies. Take the American Bible Society as an example. At home it enjoys the active support of practically every denomination in the country. No fewer than sixty-five denominations are represented on its Advisory Council. Overseas it is working in 170 countries and territories, where it is actively cooperating with every church and mission that has a stake in the publication and dissemination of the Scriptures. No other religious organization has a broader base at home or a wider outreach on the field.

How are we to account for this kind of universal support? Several factors should be noted: (1) The Bible society is not a church; hence church polity never becomes a problem. (2) The Bible society, far from being in competition with the churches, is actively engaged in advancing their cause. (3) The Bible is the one thing that all denominations have in common. The Bible is not a sectarian book so long as notes and comments are omitted—which the Bible society has always done.

4. Student Christian Movement. This is the name applied to a number of Christian and missionary student movements that got under way during the latter half of the nineteenth century and which made such an enormous contribution to the missionary and ecumenical movements of the twentieth century. Included in the SCM were the following: Young Men's Christian Association (1844), Inter-Collegiate YMCA (1877), Inter-Seminary Alliance (1880), Student Volunteer Movement (1886), and the World Student Christian Federation (1895).

From the beginning the SCM was organized on a wide inter-denominational basis. This was inevitable since the students involved had been taken out of their denominational isolationism and introduced to the wider, looser fellowship of college life. For this reason many of the churchmen, certainly in the early years, took a rather dim view of the ecumenical overtones of the SCM. They spoke derisively of what they called "the YMCA mind." They considered the students to be inexperienced in ecclesiastical matters and naive in their approach to the theological problems of Christian unity.

The SCM made a significant contribution to the ecumenical movement. One of its most far-reaching achievements was persuading the High Church wing of the Anglican Communion to abandon its isolationism and participate in the Edinburgh Conference of 1910. The SCM produced a group of outstanding young men who were destined to play an enormously significant role in both the foreign missionary movement and the ecumenical movement of the twentieth century. Included in this group were such men as John R. Mott, Robert P. Wilder, Luther Wishard, Henry Drummond, John Forman, Robert E. Speer, J. E. K. Studd, Robert Mateer, D. L. Moody, Joseph H. Oldham, William Temple, and Nathan Söderblom. Many of these men became missionaries. Others were actively engaged in promoting missions at home and around the world. All of them were genuine ecumenists.

5. The various worldwide alliances, councils, and federations organized along denominational or confessional lines. Included in this category are the Lambeth Conference of Bishops of the Anglican Communion, the Lutheran World Federation, the World Methodist Council, the World Alliance of Reformed and Presbyterian Churches, the Baptist World Alliance, the World Conference of Pentecostal Churches, the General Conference of Seventh-day Adventists, the Mennonite

World Conference, the World Convention of Churches of Christ (Disciples), and the Friends World Committee for Consultation.

The Protestant Communion is by far the most fragmented of the three great Christian Communions. In the United States alone we have almost three hundred Protestant denominations, large and small. Most of these, however, fall into rather well-defined groups or families such as Baptist, Presbyterian, Episcopal, Pentecostal, etc. Since they have found it difficult to get together across denominational lines, they have felt the need for denominations within the same "confessional family" to form some kind of alliance or federation on a worldwide basis. Most of the mainline denominations in all parts of the world are now members of their appropriate worldwide alliances.

When these world alliances were first formed in the nineteenth century their member denominations were found almost exclusively in the Western world. In the twentieth century, and particularly since World War II, many of the churches on the mission field have received their independence. They are now no longer part of the "mother" church in the West. Instead, they have full membership in one of these world alliances and are making an increasingly important contribution to them. Indeed, they are responsible for most of the church growth reported by them.

6. The National Christian Councils in all parts of the world. Here again we discover a close connection between missions and unity. Here in the United States the earliest group was the Foreign Missions Conference of North America founded in 1893 under the influence of John R. Mott. This became the Federal Council of Churches in 1908, and in 1950 it was reorganized and enlarged to form the National Council of Churches. In Great Britain the earliest council was the United Council for Missionary Education founded in 1907. Not until 1942 did the British Council of Churches come into existence. Since 1952 these last two councils have been in association with each other.

Following Edinburgh Conference 1910 John R. Mott made a world tour in the interest of missions and unity. In India, China, Japan, and other Asian countries he organized national and regional councils which later developed into the present-day Christian councils. When the International Missionary Council came into existence in 1921 these national councils joined the IMC.

This brings us to the Edinburgh Conference which in a unique way brought missions and ecumenics together.

> By general consent of all competent judges the World Missionary Conference in June, 1910, was one of the most creative events in the long history of the Christian Church. Its significance is all the more clear in the perspective of fifty years after. In many

respects unique in itself, it was also unique in the impetus it
gave to Christian activity in many directions. It opened a new
era in the missionary enterprise, but it was also the beginning of
what we now call "the ecumenical movement." Edinburgh 1910
was in fact a fountain head of international, inter-church cooperation on a depth and scale never before known.[19]

As early as 1806 William Carey proposed the holding of a conference "once in about ten years" between the missionaries "of all denominations of Christians from the four corners of the World." The
place he suggested was the Cape of Good Hope; the time, 1810. His
proposal was dismissed as "the pleasing dream of an enlarged mind."
Exactly one hundred years later his dream came true when 1,355 delegates from 153 missionary societies around the world gathered in
Edinburgh for a conference destined to change the course of world
Christianity.

The conference itself was a missionary conference from beginning
to end, and the eight topics discussed all had to do with various aspects
of the worldwide mission of the church. Significantly, the first topic
was "Carrying the Gospel to all the World." The last topic was "Cooperation and Promotion of Unity." An enormous amount of work
went into preparation. Eight commissions were appointed to prepare
papers on the eight topics mentioned above. Each commission had
twenty members. They drew on the vast experience of retired missionaries and missionaries on furlough. They also sent questionnaires to
thousands of missionaries overseas. John R. Mott's commission (the
first one) enlisted the help of six hundred correspondents in all parts
of the world. One report alone ran to 140 typewritten pages.

But the most significant thing to come out of Edinburgh 1910 was
the formation of a Continuation Committee. It was the only official
action taken at the conference and it passed unanimously, whereupon
the delegates spontaneously broke into the Doxology. John R. Mott
became President of the Continuation Committee and Joseph H. Oldham its full-time secretary. Owing to the vicissitudes of World War I
the Continuation Committee almost foundered; but it was revived
and reorganized in 1921 at which time its name was changed to the
International Missionary Council.

Of equal significance was the development of two other important
movements that came into existence in 1920, both of them the direct
result of Edinburgh 1910. One was the Faith and Order Movement
fostered by Bishop Charles H. Brent, missionary to the Philippines,
and the other was the Life and Work Movement fathered by Bishop
Nathan Söderblom.

---

[19] *Beginning at Edinburgh: 50th Anniversary 1910-1960* (London: Edinburgh
House Press, 1960), p. 3.

These three movements held world assemblies about once a decade. The International Missionary Council sponsored five world conferences: Jerusalem, 1928; Madras, 1938; Whitby, 1947; Willingen, 1952; and Ghana, 1957-58. Faith and Order was responsible for Lausanne, 1927 and Edinburgh, 1937; Life and Work for Stockholm, 1925 and Oxford, 1937. Life and Work and Faith and Order merged in 1938 to set up the Provisional Committee of the World Council of Churches in Process of Formation. Owing to world conditions during the 1940s the World Council of Churches was not inaugurated until 1948 at Amsterdam. Since then the WCC has convened four world assemblies: Evanston (1954), New Delhi (1961), Uppsala (1968), and Nairobi (1975).

When the WCC was initially set up in 1938 no effort was made to unite with the International Missionary Council though the IMC leaders had been among the most active participants in drawing up the plan for the WCC. At the Madras Assembly in late 1938 the IMC took official notice of the formation of the WCC but added a word of caution: "In welcoming the appearance of this Council we consider that the distinctive service and organization of the IMC should be maintained. It is of particular importance that nothing should be done to undermine the confidence in the IMC that has been built up during the years."[20]

The centripetal force of the WCC proved too much for the IMC; consequently the two merged at New Delhi in 1961. The merger was a cause of real concern, especially in IMC circles. There were those who feared that the missionary emphasis of the IMC would be swamped by the larger interests of the WCC. Those in the WCC said that the latter body needed the missionary zeal of the IMC to keep it from getting bogged down in the meshes of its own ecclesiastical machinery. In the intervening years the fears of the IMC supporters seem to have been confirmed. Today the IMC, now known as the Division of World Mission and Evangelism, is only one of twelve divisions of the world body. Since becoming part of the WCC the DWME has held two world assemblies: Mexico, 1963, and Bangkok, 1973. It is rather difficult for the DWME to hold its own with the other divisions of the WCC when many of them have bigger budgets and larger staffs. It seems fair to say that the DWME is not nearly as influential today as the old IMC was before New Delhi.

The ecumenical movement started on the mission field. For many years it drew its inspiration from the missionary enterprise. Mission and unity went hand in hand. Unity was not an end in itself but a means to an end—the evangelization of the world in the shortest possible time. In recent years this important distinction has been lost. Con-

---

[20] *Tambaram, Madras, Series,* Vol. IV, p. 375.

sequently the ecumenical movement is in danger of losing the reason for its existence.

One thing should not be overlooked. The mainline denominations as represented in the World Council of Churches have no monopoly on ecumenism. The conservative evangelicals have their own missionary associations. There are two large associations—the Evangelical Foreign Missions Association and the Interdenominational Foreign Mission Association. The first is the missionary arm of the National Association of Evangelicals and comprises some sixty-six societies with a total of 8,000 missionaries. The latter is an independent organization of so-called faith missions and dates back to 1917. It includes in its membership forty-five missionary societies representing 9,250 missionaries. These two organizations have much in common and work closely together. They have established half a dozen joint committees. Together they maintain the Evangelical Missions Information Service in Wheaton, Illinois, whose publications include *Missionary News Service, Evangelical Missions Quarterly,* and five regional editions of *Pulse.* Every three years EFMA and IFMA hold a joint retreat. Another group is the Fellowship of Missions, an ultraconservative, separatist association with ten member missions representing 1,850 missionaries.

In 1958 the evangelicals in Great Britain organized the Evangelical Missionary Alliance, which comprises seventy missionary societies, mostly faith missions, and seventeen Bible and missionary training schools. *Missionary Mandate* is published bimonthly.

Several characteristics of this evangelical ecumenism are worth noting. (1) It is based on common life in Jesus Christ made possible through the gospel. Every truly born-again person is a brother to every other born-again person, regardless of denominational background or affiliation. (2) It is rooted in the Scriptures and based on a statement of faith which includes the essential doctrines of historic Christianity as expressed in the major creeds of Christendom. It repudiates the idea that "service unites while doctrine divides." (3) It is not particularly interested in organizational unity. The unity we have in Christ is essentially spiritual. All true believers are one in Christ even though they may belong to different churches. (4) It presents a kind of grass-roots ecumenism that is free and natural. It is not something imposed from above. Rather it has grown up over the years through personal contacts at the local level. (5) While it doesn't blow its own horn or make a big fuss about it, there is a great deal of active cooperation across church and mission lines. Without doubt there is more grass-roots fellowship between individuals and churches in conservative circles than in ecumenical circles.

In spite of the commendable progress made in the higher echelons of the ecumenical movement, there is comparatively little fellowship or cooperation at the local level. We still hear rumblings about "Baptist money for Baptist missions," or "Methodist preachers for Methodist pulpits." It is still very difficult for a graduate of a Presbyterian seminary to get into a Methodist church, or vice versa. And if students want financial aid from their churches, they had better go to one of their own denominational colleges or seminaries. This kind of thinking is not nearly so common among conservatives. In fact it is practically nonexistent. Conservative churches will accept a graduate of any seminary provided he knows the Lord, preaches the gospel, and can deliver the goods. His denominational label is not important. There is much to be said for this kind of pragmatic ecumenism.

The ecumenical movement has in recent decades made great gains in the Third World, where Christian missions have traditionally operated. In Asia there is the Christian Conference of Asia founded in 1959. Today it comprises 79 churches and fourteen National Christian Councils in sixteen countries. The well known Daniel T. Niles was its outstanding leader until his death in 1970. The All-Africa Conference of Churches was organized in 1963. It has 102 churches on its roll. The most recent group is the Pacific Conference of Churches, organized in 1966. The oldest of all such councils is the Near East Council of Churches, dating back to 1929.

These councils and conferences, while not organically related to the World Council of Churches, are closely affiliated with it and receive a good deal of help, moral and material, from it. For example, the WCC has a Secretary for Africa who works very closely with the All-Africa Conference of Churches. In fact he would not think of dealing with the churches in Africa except through the AACC. The same is true for Asia. As yet there is no permanent ecumenical organization in Latin America. All they have at present is UNELAM—Provisional Committee for Evangelical Unity in Latin America. The WCC is working on this problem but is meeting with stiff resistance on the part of the conservative evangelicals, who are very strong in that part of the world.

The conservative evangelicals have only recently begun to organize in the Third World. The Association of Evangelicals of Africa and Madagascar was organized in 1966. Only nine of Africa's fifteen evangelical fellowships are members. Churches are not eligible to join. The AEAM is an attempt to counteract the strong and growing influence of the All-Africa Conference of Churches. Its members are not permitted to hold membership in the WCC or any affiliated groups. At their meeting in 1969 the AEAM issued a strongly worded statement against "current dangerous trends of the Ecumenical Movement as evidenced in the increased efforts of liberals and neo-universalists to capture Africa and Madagascar."

In Latin America conservative evangelicals have convened several major congresses on theology and evangelism. In 1969 the Latin American Theological Fraternity was formed. The Evangelical Fellowships in various parts of the world come to focus in the World Evangelical Fellowship, with headquarters in London. The WEF has never been very active. At present its most viable program is the Theological Assistance Programme, which is seeking to advance and strengthen the cause of theological education among conservatives in the Third World. Dr. Clyde W. Taylor, for more than twenty-five years the General Director of the National Association of Evangelicals (USA), has recently been appointed International Secretary of the WEF. Doubtless under his dynamic leadership it will expand its worldwide program. However, it is only fair to say that the WEF is in no sense the counterpart of the World Council of Churches.

There is a natural desire on the part of the newly independent churches of the Third World to associate with regional associations or councils. The larger and stronger Ecumenical Conferences exercise a strong centripetal influence on these national churches, many of which are numerically small, financially weak, and vexed with all kinds of problems that call for help. If the conservative churches overseas are to hold their own against the growing influence of the Ecumenical Conferences, they will need more help from the West than they have received up to this point.

5

Cultural Penetration

In the parable of the sower (Mt 13:1-9) Jesus spoke of four kinds of soil into which the good seed of the gospel falls. In each instance the deciding factor was not the sower or the seed—for they were the same in each case—but the soil. The soil can be taken to represent the kind of response found in the heart of the individual as he is exposed to the gospel. It may also be interpreted as referring to the different kinds of cultural or religious soil found in various regions of the world where the gospel has been taken by the Christian missionary.

In each case the sower (the missionary) is the same and the seed (the gospel) is the same. How then are we to account for the disparity in results? Some parts of the mission field have remained hard and barren in spite of the toil and tears of the missionaries. Other regions have been much more productive, and today the church in those parts is a flourishing and growing institution. Surely the parable of the sower is intended to throw light on this problem. This chapter is an attempt to show how the different kinds of soil have produced a different kind of harvest in different parts of the world.

The Muslim World

"The explosion of the Arabian peninsula into the conquest and conversion of half the Mediterranean world is the most extraordinary phenomenon in medieval history."[1] So said Will Durant. Certainly the greatest threat ever faced by the Christian church came from the sudden rise and rapid spread of Islam in the seventh century.

Mohammed, the founder of Islam, died in A.D. 632. After his death his followers conquered and unified the warring tribes of Arabia, and in the flush of easy and rapid victory they went out on their mission of conquest and conversion.

With lightning speed they conquered Damascus, Antioch, Jerusalem, Caesarea, and Alexandria. By 650 the Persian Empire had been destroyed. They then turned west and swept across North Africa, where they destroyed nine hundred Christian churches—one quarter of all the churches in Christendom. By 715 the greater part of Spain was in their hands. Crossing the Pyrenees and penetrating into France, they were stopped by Charles Martel in 732 at the Battle of Tours. Later they made significant gains in the East, penetrating into Central Asia and through the Khyber Pass into the Punjab in northwest India. Then came a five-hundred-year stalemate.

A second tide of Muslim conquest occurred in the thirteenth and fourteenth centuries when the Ottoman Turks and the Mongols of Central Asia became followers of the prophet. They went on the rampage, pillaging and destroying everything in their path. By the fifteenth century the Ottoman Turks had invaded Greece and the Balkans. Constantinople fell in 1453. By a series of incursions the Muslims overran North India and in the sixteenth century established the famous Mogul Empire, which endured until the arrival of the British.

From India Islam spread down the peninsula of Malaya and across the straits to the East Indies. From there it spread east and north to the Philippine Islands, where its northern march was stopped on the island of Mindanao by the Roman Catholics moving south. Islam is still in possession of the lands it conquered centuries ago. More recently, in the twentieth century, Islam has made great progress in East and West Africa, where it is competing with Christianity for the soul of the continent.

Several factors make Islam unique among the religions of the world: (1) With some six hundred million adherents, it is the largest of the non-Christian religions. (2) It is the only non-Christian religion that makes any claim to being universal. (3) It is the only non-Christian religion that has any sense of world mission. (4) It is the only great ethnic religion that is younger than Christianity. The origin of Hinduism is lost in antiquity. Buddhism, Confucianism, and Taoism all appeared several hundred years before Christ. (5) It is the only religion that has fought and conquered Christianity in certain large

---

[1] Will Durant, *The Age of Faith* (New York: Simon and Schuster, 1950), p. 155.

areas of the world. In none of those areas has Christianity recouped its losses. (0) Through the years it has proved to be by far the most resistant of all the non-Christian religions. Apart from the island of Java, converts from Islam have been few and far between. In the parable of the sower in Matthew 13 Jesus speaks of four kinds of soil into which the seed of the gospel falls. If we apply this parable not to the soil of the individual heart but to the soil found in different regions of the non-Christian world, surely the Muslim countries would represent the first kind of soil (wayside) that proved to be completely barren.

Certainly it is correct to say that of all the non-Christian peoples in the world today the Muslims are the hardest to win to Christ. The Scottish Presbyterians have labored in Arabia for over eighty years and today they have a church of about thirty-five members. In North Africa, after ninety years of work, there is not one organized, indigenous church. In fact, there are more missionaries' graves in North Africa than there are converts.

R. Park Johnson, a Presbyterian missionary in the Middle East for many years, said: "So confined is the Muslim that in some countries of the Middle East a follower of Islam who changed his religion would in effect be tearing up his birth certificate, citizenship papers, voting registration, and work permit, and would become like a man without a country."[2]

WHY MUSLIM SOIL IS SO BARREN

A number of factors enter into the picture. Most of these are inherent in Islam itself. Some are historic facts that relate to Christianity.

1. Islam is younger than Christianity. This made it possible for Mohammed to borrow heavily from both Judaism and Christianity. Consequently it has more in common with Christianity than any of the other great religions. It has just enough of Christianity to inoculate it against the real thing.

According to Islam God has given to mankind one hundred and four separate revelations, only four of which have been preserved; the others have all been lost. The four extant revelations are the Law of Moses, the Psalms of David, the Gospels of Jesus, and the Koran of Mohammed. This means that the Muslims accept the Old Testament and the Four Gospels as divine revelations. That should be to the missionary's advantage, because it affords him a valuable point of

---

[2] R. Park Johnson, *Middle East Pilgrimage* (New York: Friendship Press, 1958), p. 142.

contact; but the Muslims believe that each succeeding revelation is greater than the preceding one. This makes the Gospels of Jesus more authoritative than the Law of Moses; but it also makes them less authoritative than the Koran of Mohammed. If the Koran differs from the Gospels, the Koran is correct and the Gospels are wrong.

If both revelations came from God, why should the Gospels and the Koran not agree? The answer is simple; we Christians have tampered with the Bible. That's why the Gospels don't agree with the Koran. And the fact that our Bible has been translated into hundreds of languages and now appears in scores of different versions in the English language alone only serves to strengthen their contention. On this point they are adamant.

They believe that the contents of the Koran were revealed to Mohammed, who passed them on orally to his disciples. Shortly after his death all his sayings were brought together in an "authorized" collection at which time the "canon" was fixed, never to be changed from that day to this. The Koran was originally given in Arabic, the holy language of Islam. To translate it into any other language would be an act of desecration.

2. Islam denies the deity and the death of Christ. He is mentioned many times in the Koran, as the son of Mary, as a great prophet, even as a sinless person. The Koran acknowledges that Jesus worked miracles. But the Jesus of the Koran differs from the Jesus of the Gospels in two very important respects: His deity and His crucifixion are both denied.

The doctrine of the deity of Christ is utterly and completely abhorrent to the Muslim. For God to have a Son, He must have a wife; so goes the argument. The very suggestion is blasphemous. Moreover, there can be only one God, not two. The worship of any God but Allah is idolatry. If the missionary but mentions the deity of Christ the Muslim is likely to spit on his shadow to show his contempt for such a blasphemous statement.

The Koran teaches that Jesus did not end His life on a cross; that too is unthinkable. God, the sovereign ruler of the universe, would never permit His prophet to come to such an ignominious end. Such a tragedy would be libelous to the character of God. He would not, He could not, tolerate such a diabolical deed. Therefore Jesus did not die on the cross. At the last minute a substitute appeared and Jesus was raptured away.

The deity of Christ and the death of Christ are the two great stumbling blocks to the Muslim. And there appears to be no way around these two obstacles. The missionary can find many points of contact and similarity between Christianity and Islam, and certainly he will want to exploit these for all he is worth; but sooner or later he must come to the central theme of the gospel—the cross. At that point he runs into a stone wall. He can remove many offending things; but he can never do away with the offense of the cross. That and the deity of Christ are hurdles that can never be removed.

3. **Islam treats defectors harshly.** All religions, including the broadest of them—Hinduism—look with disfavor on the devotee who changes his religion. But it remained for Islam to devise the Law of Apostasy, which permits the community to kill the adherent who defects from the faith. This law, of course, is not found in the Constitution, nor is it applied by the government; but it has the sanction of the Koran. "Whoso shall apostatise from his religion, let him die for it, and he is an infidel."[3] In Islam conversion is a one-way street. A person can convert *to* Islam but not *from* Islam.

> The law of apostasy has also been a stabilizing element in Islamic conversions. While it was easy for a man to become a Moslem once he had adopted the faith, no return to Christianity was possible. The mere repetition of the creed of Islam made a man a Moslem for life. If after that he changed his religion he was liable to the death penalty under this very rigid law of apostasy. The elements of compulsion and fear thus entered into the question from the moment the short confession of faith had been repeated.[4]

It is difficult to believe that such a law is still in effect in the twentieth century; but such is the case. As recently as 1970 a young eighteen-year-old Muslim girl in Pakistan confessed Christ. To save her life the missionaries took her into their home and never allowed her out of their sight. After six months, when they thought the storm of protest had blown over, they left her alone for two hours while they attended a funeral. When they came home they found her in a pool of blood on the living room floor. In a case of this kind the government will go through the motions of trying to apprehend and punish the culprit; but nothing ever comes of the investigation. Everyone, including the government officials, recognizes that according to the Koran the community has the right to inflict this kind of punishment on all those who depart from the faith.

4. **The solidarity of Muslim society is a deterrent.** In Islam there is no such thing as the separation of church and state. Religion is inextricably bound up with politics. To convert to Christianity is to be an apostate from the faith and a traitor to one's country. In the Middle

---

[3] *The Koran: Surah* 2:214.
[4] W. Wilson Cash, *Christendom and Islam* (New York: Harper and Brothers, 1937), p. 51.

East to be an Arab is to be a Muslim. To become a Christian is to cease to be both.

Although we are apt to think of Islam as a religion, it is probable that Mohammed regarded it as a nation:

> Islam is more than a religion. It is a complete code of life, a political system, an economic system. It is everything. Islam is a great practical religion because it is complete. A Muslim is one who has surrendered himself to God and to God's laws, and who has formed a society with other Muslims.[5]

There is no doubt that this solidarity acts as a deterrent to the Muslim contemplating conversion to Christianity.

> There is a great group solidarity among Moslems and this is welded by a fanatical devotion to the religion which may be likened to faith and patriotism combined. It is not difficult for any one of us to realize how hard it would be should we become, in the eyes of our fellow nationals, traitors to our country. Add to this the shame of becoming an apostate in the eyes of our co-religionists, and we get a picture of what it means for a Moslem to leave the faith of his fathers, and adopt a religion which has been considered an implacable enemy of all that from infancy the Moslem has been taught to hold most dear and sacred.[6]

It was because of this solidarity of religion and patriotism that in some former colonies the British did not allow missionary work among the Muslim part of the population. This was true in British India and Malaya. To baptize a Muslim convert would almost certainly lead to a communal riot, and this is what the British colonial authorities wanted to avoid. Hence they played it safe and kept the missionaries away.

It is true, of course, that in the Muslim countries of the Middle East there are Christian churches, some of them dating back to the early centuries of the Christian era. They were already there when the Arabs invaded that part of the world in the seventh century. Consequently they are recognized as legitimate religious minorities and as such enjoy certain rights and privileges. They are permitted to preserve their religious and cultural heritage. They are free to practice their religious rites within the precincts of the church. They may baptize their children, marry their young, and bury their dead. But if there is any attempt to convert Muslims to the Christian faith there is trouble. For this reason the Christian churches there have kept pretty much to themselves and through the centuries have developed a sort of "ghetto" complex. They have made no attempt to share their faith

---

[5] Freeland Abbott, *Islam and Pakistan* (New York: Cornell University Press, 1968), p. 181.

[6] Nazmul Karim, "Pakistan and the Islamic State," *Muslim World*, Vol. 43, Number 4 (October 1953), p. 254.

with their Muslim neighbors, nor do they look with favor on such activities on the part of Protestant missionaries from the West.

5. The public practice of religion in Muslim lands deters the spread of Christianity. We in the West know all too well that one can be a Christian in our society and travel incognito. Religion, if we have any at all, is confined to one hour on Sunday morning, and then we make a beeline for home to watch the Dallas Cowboys play the Green Bay Packers. Moreover, religion with us is a very private and personal affair. Even the few who say grace at mealtime in their own homes seldom have the courage to do the same when they dine out. The solemn warning of Jesus against the hypocrites who performed their religious rites "before men" is hardly needed in our society today. We have our hypocrites to be sure, but they don't perform in public.

Not so with the Muslim, who wears his religion on his sleeve. Islam is a religion that permeates all of life and is practiced more in public than in private.

> No one acquainted with Moslem peoples can fail to be impressed with the large place which religion occupies in their life. It is doubtful whether any people, unless it be the Jews, have taken religious observances as seriously as have the Moslems. In the case of the Mohammedan world, religion has seemingly affected every detail of life with its prescriptions and requirements.[7]

One of the Five Pillars of Islam is prayer. There are five stated times for prayer every day, beginning at dawn and ending after sunset. When the call to prayer goes out from the minaret every Muslim gets out his prayer mat, faces Mecca, and prays, regardless of where he is or what he is doing at the time. The peasant in the field, the teacher in the classroom, the merchant in the market, the traveler on the road, the prisoner in the jail—all fall on their knees, bow their heads to the ground, and recite their prayers. It is a moving sight to observe fifty thousand Muslims, all dressed in white robes, kneeling together in an act of public, corporate prayer.

This is not something that occurs once or twice a year on high days or holy days. It happens five times a day every day of the year. The lone individual who remains standing when all his compatriots are kneeling is sure to invite attention. There is no way for the Christian convert, or the person contemplating becoming such, to be lost in the crowd. He cannot travel incognito.

Once a year there is a special season known as Ramadan, when for a whole month the people neither eat nor drink from sun up to

---

[7] Charles Watson, *What Is This Moslem World?* (New York: Friendship Press, 1937), p. 53.

sun down. They make up for lost time, however, by feasting and merry-making during the night hours. Understandably religious feelings run high at such a time. The few Christians in such a society, especially recent converts, find the social pressures almost more than they can bear.

It is the hope of every devout Muslim that once in his lifetime he will be able to make the pilgrimage to Mecca. Many will spend the savings of a lifetime to achieve this goal. Those who succeed dye their beards red upon their return. In this way they let it be known that they have been to the holy city. No Muslim would dream of hiding his religion.

6. The Crusades are a serious stumbling block to the Muslims in the Middle East. To Christians in the West the Crusades were a bad dream of which we have only the faintest recollection; but to the Arabs they are the greatest proof of the Christian's hatred for Islam. Eight hundred years of history have failed to obliterate the Crusades from the memory of the Arabs. To this day they continue to fester in the body politic in that part of the world.

The Crusades were perhaps the greatest blunder ever made by the Christian church. The most calamitous result was the alienation of the entire Muslim world. The fact that the church would resort to war to regain the holy places of Palestine was itself a denial of its own faith. Once the victim of Muslim aggression, the church now became the aggressor. Such a course of action was a denial of the teaching of Christ and contrary to the practice of the early church.

Moreover, the atrocities committed by the Crusaders in the name of Christ left an indelible scar on the Muslim mind. When Jerusalem was liberated in 1099 the Crusaders, not content with wiping out the one-thousand-man garrison, proceeded to massacre some seventy thousand Muslims. The surviving Jews were herded into a synagogue and burned alive. The Crusaders then repaired to the Church of the Holy Sepulchre, where they publicly gave thanks to Almighty God for a resounding victory. To this day Christianity's reputation for cruelty and revenge is a millstone around the neck of the Christian missionary in the Middle East. Some Arab writers still refer to Christians as Crusaders.

7. American support of the State of Israel affects Christian missions in the Muslim world. This, of course, is quite recent and doubtless will pass when the Arab-Israeli conflict comes to an end. In the meantime Arab leaders hold the United States responsible for the existence of Israel. Moreover, they know that we have consistently supported Israel both morally and materially. The fact that many of the missionaries in that part of the world are Americans does nothing to ameliorate the situation. Christianity is not only associated with the West in general but with the United States in particular. Consequently the American missionary finds it doubly difficult to propagate his faith in the Middle East.

CRACKS APPEARING IN MUSLIM SOIL

In spite of the hardness of the soil in the Muslim world, there are signs, however small, that cracks are beginning to appear.

1. All of the Muslim countries are members of the United Nations and are anxious to play their part in the modern world. Many of them have signed the Universal Declaration of Human Rights drawn up by the Social and Economic Council of the United Nations, Article Eighteen of which deals with the problem of religious liberty. A stronger statement one could hardly wish to find:

> Everyone has the right of freedom of thought, conscience, and religion; this right includes freedom to change his religion or belief, and freedom, either alone or in community with others, and in public or private, to manifest his religion or belief, in teaching, practice, worship, and observance.

This does not mean that the Muslim countries are prepared to implement that particular article. For a long time there has been a breach between the promise and the performance. However, the fact remains: they have signed the statement and sooner or later they will have to come to terms with reality if they want to stay abreast of the modern world. There can be no doubt about it, religious freedom is the wave of the future.

Arnold Toynbee has argued that the time has arrived when the intelligent man has the information and ability to choose his own religion regardless of his inheritance, and that he will increasingly make his own choice. This being so, Muslim governments cannot continue very long to treat their nationals like children. The time will come when they will be forced to make concessions to religious liberty. Already Article Eighteen has been used to secure freedom for the preaching of the gospel in Northern Nigeria, where hitherto such freedom was denied.

2. An increasing number of Muslims, mostly students, have come to the West for travel, business, and higher education. While here they see our open society, our spirit of tolerance, our sense of fair play, and, above all, our freedom of religion. They cannot but be impressed with the pluralistic society found here in the West. The world over, educated people tend to be more tolerant than their uneducated compatriots. With more and more Muslims getting a higher education, the spirit of tolerance is bound to spread to Muslim countries. If it were not for the power of the mullahs in the smaller towns and villages, freedom of religion would be much greater than it is. High government officials are often embarrassed when public opinion forces them to crack down on Christian activities in their countries. Muslim missionaries are free to carry on their activities in Christian countries. How long can they refuse to allow Christian missionaries to do the same in their countries?

3. In years past it was possible for Muslim governments to keep their people from all contact with the outside world. This is no longer true. The Christian gospel is now being beamed into Muslim countries by radio. Powerful broadcasting stations in Addis Ababa, the Seychelles, Manila, Monaco, and Monrovia have daily programs aimed at the Muslim world. Muslims who would not be caught dead in a Christian church are only too eager to listen to the Christian message in the seclusion of their own homes. Every week letters of appreciation are received telling of interest and blessing.

4. In the past decade missionaries have had phenomenal success with Bible correspondence courses in the Muslim countries of the world. In 1960 the Gospel Missionary Union in Morocco placed an ad in the local newspapers offering a free correspondence course on the Christian religion. It was the first time anything like this had been done. The missionaries had no idea what kind of response they would get. Imagine how surprised they were when eighteen thousand people signed up. A few years later the North Africa Mission used the same plan in Tunisia and twenty thousand responded. When the government got word it closed the bookstore which housed the correspondence school. The operation was moved to Marseilles, France, where it continues unabated.

Operation Mobilization had a similar experience after a summer of work in Iran. Thousands signed up for a Bible correspondence course; so heavy was the work that missionaries had to be taken from other jobs to grade papers.

This is a strong indication that under the surface there is a deep hunger for spiritual reality in the Muslim world. Given complete freedom of religion, how many Muslims would embrace the Christian faith? Obviously their governments do not want to run the risk. But they cannot keep the lid on forever.

5. In some parts of the Muslim world the political climate is changing. Bangladesh is a good example. When it was part of Pakistan it was a Muslim state, based on Koranic law. As soon as independence was achieved Mujibur Rahman, the new prime minister, declared that Bangladesh is a secular state. Several of the more fanatical Muslim parties were dissolved. If genuine freedom of religion comes to Bangladesh, will we see large numbers turning to Christ? It is difficult to say; but the chances are good.

The process of secularization is going on in all parts of the world. Fewer and fewer governments are willing to support religion in general, much less any one religion in particular. Granted, this process is just beginning in the Muslim world; but it is likely to pick up momentum in the years ahead.

6. In one Muslim country there is genuine freedom of religion: Indonesia. The ideological basis of the state is expressed in the five principles known as *Pantjasila*: belief in a Supreme Being, just and civilized humanity, the unity of Indonesia, guided democracy, and social justice. Although Islam is the dominant religion (85 percent) the government recognizes three other religions: Hinduism, Buddhism, and Christianity.

Islam in Indonesia tends to be rather tolerant. Indeed, the Muslims in East and Central Java belong mostly to the nominal group. Several hundred thousand of them have been converted to Christianity. There are two reasons for this unprecedented phenomenon. The farther a Muslim community is removed from the heartland of Islam—the Middle East—the less fanatical it is. Secondly, throughout history the people of Indonesia have changed religions several times. Animism gave way to Hinduism; Hinduism to Buddhism; Buddhism to Islam. Now Islam is yielding converts to Christianity. There is an underlying feeling that Islam, like the other religions, is a foreign import, which, of course, it is. For whatever reason, Indonesia has produced more converts from Islam than all the rest of the world together.

7. While some Muslim countries, such as Libya, Iraq, and Syria, have recently expelled missionaries, others have opened their doors for the first time. Two missions were permitted to enter Somalia in the early 1950s; but missionary work was terminated twenty years later. During the 1960s several missions were permitted to begin work in Yemen. The situation there is rather precarious and anything could happen tomorrow. Saudi Arabia is the one Muslim country that has never at any time allowed missionaries to reside within its borders.

Afghanistan is another Muslim country which for centuries remained closed to missions. More recently it too has opened up to the point where nonprofessional missionaries under the International Afghan Mission have been able to engage in medical and educational work. All religious work is strictly forbidden. Recently certain members of IAM were expelled and the church in Kabul, the only one in the country, was demolished by government order. At this writing, some thirty members of IAM remain in the country. What the future holds no one knows. With a more liberal government in power, present restrictions may be lifted.

In conclusion it may be said that Christianity's impact on the Muslim world has been minimal. Apart from Indonesia our efforts have been almost fruitless so far as converts are concerned. In the Middle East our educational institutions, all of them founded by missionaries, have wielded considerable influence but resulted in very few converts. The same may be said for the many mission hospitals in that part of the world. We did win converts by the thousands; but they came not from Islam but from the Eastern Orthodox Churches and the Coptic Church in Egypt.

Asia

Before discussing the progress and problems of Christianity in this part of the world it might be helpful to make some general observations.

1. It is the most densely populated portion of the globe. Half the world's population lives between Karachi and Tokyo. Two countries have enormous populations, China with 800 million and India with 600 million. Since the Communists came to power in 1949 the population of China has *increased* by at least 220 million people, which is 10 million more than the total population of the United States. Some of the largest, and surely the most crowded, cities in the world are found in this region. The 1970 census gave metropolitan Tokyo a population of 22 million—twice that of Greater New York. Shanghai has ten million and Bombay seven. These cities are not only large, they are congested beyond anything known in the West. In Calcutta 750,000 people live and die in the alleys, without so much as a roof over their heads.

2. Asia is the home of the great ethnic religions of antiquity. Hinduism is the dominant religion of India. Buddhism died out in the land of its birth (India). In its Theravada form it spread south and east to Sri Lanka, Burma, Thailand, and Indo-China. Mahayana Buddhism spread north and east to China, Korea, and Japan. Today it is the most widespread religion in Asia. Taoism is native to China and Shinto to Japan. Confucianism, which began in China, spread to all parts of the Far East, where it has greatly influenced the culture of the entire region.

3. **Asia was the scene of the earliest and greatest missionary efforts.** The apostle Thomas is said to have reached India in A.D. 52 and labored there for twenty years before his martyrdom near Madras. The Mar Thomas Church in South India is named after him. The great Nestorian Church took the gospel first to India and later to China, where it flourished for two hundred years during the T'ang Dynasty (618-907). The earliest Roman Catholic missionaries went to this area of the world. The Franciscans were in China during much of the fourteenth century. The first Jesuit missionaries landed in India in 1542, labored in Japan in the sixteenth century, and gained entrance to China in the seventeenth century.

When Protestant missions got under way their first missionaries also went to Asia. The Danish-Halle Mission worked in India during most of the eighteenth century. William Carey, the first missionary from the English-speaking world, spent almost forty years in India. The first American missionary, Adoniram Judson, served in Burma. The first Protestant missionary to China, Robert Morrison, began work in Canton in 1807. When China opened five treaty ports in the 1840s a dozen Protestant societies entered China during the first decade.

During the 1920s there were some sixteen thousand missionaries in China, half of them Roman Catholic and half Protestant. This was more than in any other country in the world. In India the figure was only slightly lower. Through the years Asia has attracted more missionaries than Africa or Latin America. Tens of thousands of missionaries have lived and died in Asia, and literally hundreds of millions of dollars of missionary money have been invested in that part of the world.

4. **Asia has been the least productive of all the major areas of the world, with the exception of the Muslim camp.** After centuries of missionary endeavor only 2.4 percent of India's population is nominally Christian, and that includes Roman Catholics, Protestants, and Syrian Orthodox Christians, whose churches have been there for over fifteen hundred years. After more than a century of Protestant work in Japan there are fewer than one million professing Christians, including some 350,000 Roman Catholics. In China the results were even more meager. The latest reliable figures are those for 1949, when there were reported to be almost 1 million Protestants and 3 million Roman Catholics —4 million out of a total of 550 million. This represents about .7 percent of the population. After 140 years of missionary work in Thailand,

Protestant church members represent only .1 percent of the total population.

Here as elsewhere the picture is spotty. As indicated above we did poorly in the larger countries; but we did much better in the smaller ones. The Roman Catholics, after four hundred years of work, claim 72 percent of the Philippines and about 10 percent of South Vietnam. Protestants achieved their greatest results in Korea, where today slightly over 12 percent of the population is Christian. Indonesia and the Philippines are two countries where the Protestants also did fairly well. In each case we now have about 10 percent of the population within the Protestant fold. In the whole of Asia today there is only one nominally Christian country, the Philippines.

At the present time the population of East Asia (Pakistan to Japan) is approximately two billion. The estimated Christian population of this area, including Roman Catholics, Eastern Orthodox, and Protestants, is about sixty million. This works out at 3 percent of the total population—after almost five hundred years of missionary effort. We are not even keeping up with the population growth. There are three times as many non-Christians in India today as when William Carey arrived in 1793. The statistics for China and Japan are even higher. We must conclude then that after the Muslim world, the continent of Asia has been the least productive of all the major areas in which Christian missionaries have worked.

5. Christian converts in this part of the world have come mostly from the lower classes. This is especially true in India, where 80 percent of the Christians came originally from the Untouchables, now known as the *Scheduled Classes*. They are the result of mass movements that took place much earlier. Even as Hindus these outcastes were denied access to their own temples and to the village wells. Hence they had nothing to lose and much to gain by becoming Christians. Many of them have greatly improved their lot in life, but they are still poor even by India's standards. Their presence in the churches helps to explain, at least in part, the great poverty that plagues the Indian church today.

Over 95 percent of all the Christians in Burma have not come from the Burmese, who are Buddhists, but from the tribespeople, who are animists. A similar situation exists in Indonesia, where the great Batak Church of Sumatra is made up almost entirely of tribespeople who formerly were animists. In China the situation was better, but not much. Very few of the literati, or Mandarin class, ever embraced the Christian faith. Most of the church members came from the humbler walks of life. Japan was an exception to the rule. There the early Christians were members of the military elite—the *samurai*—who left their stamp on the Japanese church. Today the churches there are made up mostly of middle and upper middle classes.

REASONS FOR THE PAUCITY OF RESULTS

1. **In this part of the world the Christian missionaries encountered ancient, well-developed civilizations that go back three, four, or five thousand years.** These people are justly proud of their cultural heritage and are not about to give up without a struggle. Indeed, they regard their civilization as superior to ours in everything but technology; and they are not persuaded that technology is an unmixed blessing.

China is proud of three things: her long history, her advanced civilization, and her enormous population. In all three she leads the world. For well over a thousand years China shed the light and luster of her ancient civilization over most of Asia. She lent to everyone; she borrowed from nobody. Even Japan owes her civilization to China. Once a year tribute-bearing missions from all over Asia made their way to Peking, where they performed the *kowtow* and presented their tribute to the emperor. This was their way of acknowledging their debt to China's beneficent rule.

When King George III in 1793 wanted to improve trade relations with China, Emperor Ch'ien Lung, then close to the end of his sixty-year reign, refused to receive Lord McCartney in audience unless he performed the *kowtow*. On his return home he bore a very revealing letter from the emperor to the British monarch which read:

> You, O King, live beyond the confines of many seas, neverthe-less impelled by your humble desire to partake of the benefits of our civilization you have dispatched a mission respectfully bear-ing your memorial. . . . In consideration of the fact that your am-bassador and his deputy have come a long way with your me-morial and tribute I have shown them high favor and have allowed them to be introduced into my presence. . . . Strange and costly objects do not interest me. . . . Our celestial Empire possesses all things in prolific abundance, and lacks no product within its own borders. I . . . have no use for your country's merchandise.[8]

So far as the Chinese were concerned there was only one civilized country in the world, the Middle Kingdom. All others were beyond the pale of civilization; hence they were called "barbarians." China's civil-ization reached its highest point during the Dark Ages, when the lights all over Europe were going out. Changan, the capital of the T'ang Dynasty, was probably the most sophisticated city in the world of that day. With such a history and such a civilization, China can be forgiven if she entertained ideas of her own greatness.

---

[8] Helmut G. Callis, *China: Confucian and Communist* (New York: Henry Holt, 1959), p. 168.

When the missionaries from the West arrived in China they found themselves up against a stone wall. Their physical appearance alone—blue eyes, blonde hair, and white skin—was enough to scare the wits out of the illiterate peasantry. For want of a better term they called them "foreign devils." As for the literati, they regarded the missionaries with undisguised contempt because their Western learning posed a threat to their own power and prestige as leaders of the people. With every weapon at their disposal they fought the presence of the missionaries in China. As a result approximately once a decade there was an antiforeign outbreak of one kind or another. Worst of all was the Boxer Rebellion of 1900 when 189 missionaries and their children lost their lives. This is not to suggest that all the blame for the Boxer Rebellion is to be laid at the door of the literati. The fact remains that the literati time and again exploited the xenophobia of the Chinese people and thereby exacerbated an already explosive situation.

2. The Christian missionaries came into direct conflict with ancient, highly developed religious systems which antedated Christianity. These great ethnic religions have their own founders, philosophers, teachers, and reformers. They have their own beautiful and richly adorned temples, stupas, pagodas, and monasteries. People from all parts of the world travel to India to see its famous temples. The Taj Mahal is one of the most strikingly beautiful edifices in the world. Moreover they have their sacred rivers, their sacred mountains, and their sacred scriptures. They also have their holy men: fakirs, swamis, yogis, and gurus. And of course they have their gods and goddesses by the millions. They even have their own saviors and bodhisatvas.

The Hindus believe that their ancient scripture, the Rig Veda, was revealed by God to the seers. So sacred is this book, according to the ancients, that if a Sudra—a member of the lowest caste—were to take its words on his lips his tongue was to be cut out. And if he allowed himself to listen to its words, his ears were to be filled with molten lead. It comes then as no surprise that the Hindu is satisfied with his Bhagavad Gita and the Buddhist with his Lotus Gospel. Frankly our Gospel of Mark does not impress either the Hindu or the Buddhist.

The same is true of the Confucian scholars in China. On one occasion the literati memorialized the throne, requesting the emperor to outlaw the Christian religion. After studying the New Testament for himself the emperor replied: "There is no need to outlaw this religion. To say that the salvation of the world can be effected by the death of a criminal is sheer nonsense. No Chinese will believe such a doctrine. We have nothing to fear."

3. The missionaries encountered deep-seated, longstanding social

and religious practices and prejudices which were inimical to the Christian gospel. It seemed that in every culture there was at least one great stumbling block to the acceptance of Christianity.

In India it was the caste system. For thousands of years the outstanding feature of Indian social life was the caste system, by which Hindu society was divided into four broad socio-occupational groups. At the top were the *Brahmins,* the traditional priests and intellectual leaders; next were the *Kshatriyas,* the warriors and rulers; then the *Vaisyas,* the traders and merchants; and finally the *Sudras,* the servants and laborers, who performed all the menial tasks for the other three groups. Below this structure were the *Pariahs,* better known as the Untouchables.

Caste is a closed system, as rigid and irrevocable as the law of gravitation. A Hindu is a member of a particular caste by accident of birth. Throughout his entire life he remains a member of the caste in which he was born. He can go neither up nor down in the scale. His only hope of improving his condition is in the next reincarnation. The only way to do that is to accept his *karma* and fulfill his duty—*dharma* —to the best of his ability. By accepting his fate in this life he may possibly improve it in the next.

Along comes the Christian missionary, who declares that all men have been created in the image of God and are, therefore, members of the one great human family. Moreover, in Christ there is neither Jew nor Greek, slave nor free, male nor female, circumcised nor uncircumcised, barbarian nor Scythian; all are one in Jesus Christ.

This concept has not yet been universally accepted in the so-called Christian world. In Hindu society it is absolutely anathema. All men are *not* equal. Some are higher and others are lower in the social scale, and this by the law of *karma.* Scavengers can never associate with scholars; butchers can never associate with Brahmins—any time, any place, for any purpose. To do so would break caste; and to break caste is to become an outcast. And the Sudra is just as desirous as the Brahmin to stay within his caste, for only by so doing can he hope eventually to effect his own salvation. To break caste in this life is to set himself back and hinder his progress towards Nirvana. From this it can readily be seen that in India the greatest single obstacle to the acceptance of Christianity has been its egalitarianism. If somehow the missionary could have omitted that part of his message he would doubtless have been more successful. This is precisely what some people are now advocating. They say that caste in Indian society is cultural and not religious and should have been accepted by the early missionaries.

In China the great stumbling block was ancestor worship, which goes back thousands of years. In the Confucian ethic the greatest single virtue was filial piety. On one occasion the sage said, "If a person will not revere his father, he will not revere anyone." And filial piety extends to the dead as well as to the living, for both are members of the extended family. The souls of the departed are dependent for their sustenance on the food and other offerings made to them by the living, principally the eldest son. If he neglects his duty their souls perish. To neglect the dead is the same as to murder the living. To the average Chinese the idea is utterly repugnant.

The early missionaries regarded ancestor worship as a form of idolatry. They therefore preached against it. The Chinese church leaders did the same. The first criticism thrown at a new convert by his friends and relatives was, "So, you no longer want your elders." That was the last word in defamation. For a son to neglect his father, living or dead, was to commit the unpardonable sin in the eyes of the Chinese.

If the missionaries could have found some suitable substitute for ancestor worship, the number of converts to Christianity would doubtless have been far greater than it was.

The Japanese added emperor worship to ancestor worship and thereby compounded the difficulty. Shinto is the national religion of Japan. In 1889 Shinto was divided into two parts. One, known as Sect Shinto, was regarded as a religion. It dealt with ritual, prayers, divination, and charms. The other was State Shinto, which was not supposed to be a religion but a national cult which every patriotic Japanese was required to accept. State Shinto was supported by the government, enforced in the schools, and later exploited by the militarists. Shrines were converted into national monuments. Priests were civil servants under the Home Office. According to Japanese mythology the first emperor, Jimmu Tenno, was the great-great-grandson of the Sun Goddess, hence divine. All his successors likewise were divine. Thus State Shinto culminated in emperor worship.

Consequently in Japan the Christian convert had to reject both ancestor worship and the worship of the emperor, thereby incurring the wrath of the government as well as that of his relatives. Few people in the homelands have any idea what it costs to be a Christian in Japan, China, or India.

4. Christianity was closely identified with colonialism, and nobody liked colonialism. In the whole of East Asia only one country did not become the victim of imperialism—Thailand. Britain, France, Spain, Holland, and the United States all had colonies. Even before the Western governments moved in and took over, the powerful East India Companies had staked out their claims and made their fortunes. India, Pakistan, Bangladesh, Sri Lanka (Ceylon), and Burma were all at one time part of the British Empire. France occupied the three countries of Indo-China. Holland had the Netherlands East Indies. The Spanish empire in the Philippines gave way to American rule. China never became the colony of any one power. Instead she was carved like a melon into slices—spheres of influence they were called. Japan was never occupied but she did agree to extraterritoriality. Later on she annexed Taiwan and Korea. Some countries came under the rule of several European powers. Ceylon had three different colonial masters (Portuguese, Dutch, and British) over a period of four hundred years, all of them so-called Christian nations.

Western imperialism, always a distasteful thing, was particularly galling to the countries of Asia, with their long history and their ancient civilizations. A case can be made for colonialism in Africa, where intertribal warfare and the slave trade were decimating the population; but what can be said for colonialism in the highly developed civilizations of India, China, and Japan? Almost without exception the intellectuals in these countries regarded the intrusion of the white man as injurious to the national interest and an insult to their superior civilization. Only now, after several decades of independence, is the stigma of imperialism being removed from Christianity.

5. **The exclusiveness of Christianity made it unacceptable to the Asians.** We must remember that Asia was the homeland of the great ethnic religions of antiquity. If Christianity had posed as one religion among many it would have found greater favor; but Christianity presented itself as the only true religion and thereby dismissed all other religions as false. Such a view was totally unacceptable to the religious leaders of Asia.

Hinduism, the most tolerant of all religions, would gladly have made room for Christianity. It already had thousands of gods in its pantheon; to add one more was neither here nor there. In fact many Hindus were quite willing to regard Christ as one of the many *avataras* of Vishnu, along with Krishna. But to insist on the uniqueness of Christ was not only in poor taste, it was completely foreign to their way of thinking. Mahatma Gandhi had the greatest admiration for Christ as a person and was quite willing to acknowledge Him as one of the world's greatest teachers, but never as the Son of God. He was unable, he said, to place Jesus on a "solitary throne." Gandhi likened truth to a tree and the various religions to branches of the tree. As many branches are required to make a tree, so it takes many religions to express the full truth regarding God, man, sin, and salvation. "For me the different religions are beautiful flowers from the same garden, or they are branches of the same majestic tree."[9]

The same was true, though to a less extent, with Buddhism and Confucianism. Buddha never claimed to be inspired, nor did he leave

---

[9] M. K. Gandhi, *Christian Missions: Their Place in India* (Ahmedabad: Navajivan Press, 1941), p. 126.

behind any infallible guide for faith or morals. Original (Theravada) Buddhism had neither gods nor saviors. Every man was to work out his own salvation as best he could. The Chinese, for all their xenophobia, were not against a new religion simply because it was foreign. "The concept of a universal order on earth had made the Chinese tolerant of *any* religion as long as it posed no threat to that order. Thus, they found it difficult to grant to the Christian faith the uniqueness that it claimed."[10] Another aspect of Christianity that appeared strange to the Chinese was its emphasis on the sinfulness of man. For over two thousand years Confucianism had taught that human nature is essentially good and requires only self-cultivation to bring it to perfection.

Little wonder then that Christianity, with all its strange doctrines and its claim to uniqueness, should have been rejected by the vast majority of the people in Asia.

THE IMPACT OF CHRISTIANITY ON ASIA

To what extent did Christianity influence the culture of Asia? This is a big question and one that is difficult to answer in a few pages. Christian leaders, especially missionaries, are apt to exaggerate the impact that Christianity made on the continent of Asia. On the other hand antiforeign nationalists go to the other extreme and deny that Christianity has had any appreciable affect on Asia.

Obviously Christianity made its greatest impact where it has been the longest and where it made the largest number of converts, in the Philippines. The Christianization of the Philippines began with the arrival in 1564 of Father Legaspi and the Augustinian friars, followed later by the other religious orders. They opened schools at all levels and taught the doctrines of Christianity and the arts of Western civilization. The women were raised from practical slavery to virtual emancipation by the introduction of the Christian concept of the family. Spanish officials married Filipino women and the children were reared in the Christian faith. A combination of religious passion and military conquest enabled the Roman Catholics to effect the conversion of the Islands during the first century of occupation. Some of the credit for this achievement belongs to Philip II of Spain, who made the spread of the faith the chief aim of the colonization of the islands named after him. To the Roman Catholic Church must go the credit for stopping the spread of Islam from Indonesia through the archipelago. The Muslims advanced from the south, the Roman Catholics

---

[10] Charles Corwin, *East to Eden? Religion and the Dynamics of Social Change* (Grand Rapids: Wm. B. Eerdmans, 1972), p. 83.

from the north. They met on the island of Mindanao, where today there are two million Muslims known as Moros.

Beginning with 1900 American Protestant missions added to the Christianization of the Philippines. Today the Christian population of the Islands stands at about 84 percent, making the Philippines the only Christian country in Asia, Spanish culture and American influence remain strong. The modern Filipino is a mixture of Western and Oriental, with the Oriental predominating.

It is difficult to assess the impact of Christianity on a country as large and diverse as India with 600 million people, fourteen major language groups and over five hundred smaller ones. Christianity has made its greatest impact in the south, where the Orthodox churches have been for well over fifteen hundred years. Many of their members came originally from high-caste Hindu background and still enjoy a certain degree of prestige in the community. The strength of the Christian community varies greatly from state to state. Nagaland is almost 100 percent Christian, but the Nagas are a small tribe and have no influence outside their own restricted community. Goa is 36 percent Christian—entirely Roman Catholic. Kerala is next with 21 percent and Manipur with 20 percent.

In some states the number of Christians doubled between the census of 1951 and that of 1961. Similar growth occurred in the following decade; but their ratio to the total population is still rather small. About 70 percent of all the Christians in India live in the four southern states and Goa. Of these, 75 percent live in villages, which makes the Indian church predominantly rural.

It is largely to British influence that India owes its open society with its democratic institutions; but to what extent are these the result of Christianity? It is difficult to say. Modern Hinduism has seen three major attempts at reform, the Brahmo Samaj, the Arya Samaj, and the Ramakrishna Movement. All three were directly influenced by Christianity.

Ram Mohun Roy, founder of the Brahmo Samaj, never became a Christian; but he was on friendly terms with Alexander Duff and William Carey and through them was introduced to the Christian religion. After searching Sanskrit, Arabic, Greek, and Hebrew literature, he wrote: "The consequence of my long uninterrupted researches into religious truth has been that I have found the doctrines of Christ more conducive to moral principles and better adapted for the use of rational beings than any other which have come to my knowledge."[11]

---

[11] Daniel J. Fleming, *Building with India* (New York: Missionary Education Movement, 1922), p. 75.

And what about Mahatma Gandhi, the most influential person in India in the present century? He had close contact with evangelical Christians in England, South Africa, and India and his knowledge of Christian doctrine was considerable. His concept of nonviolence *(satyagraha),* which he used so effectively against the British Raj, he got directly from the Sermon on the Mount, not the Bhagavad-Gita.

No missionary knew India better or loved it more than E. Stanley Jones. Most of his sixty-year ministry was spent among the intellectuals of India. From his two books, *The Christ of the Indian Road* and *Christ at the Round Table,* one gets the impression that Christianity had deeply influenced the thinking of India and was at the bottom of its reforms. "Call the roll of the reforms that are sweeping across India, and whether they be economic, social, moral, or religious, they are all tending straight toward Jesus Christ and his thought. Not one of them is going away from him, that is, if it be a reform and not a reaction."[12]

He quotes a Hindu professor of modern history who said: "My study of modern history has shown me that there is a Moral Pivot in the world today, and that the best life of both East and West is more and more revolving about that center—that Moral Pivot is the person of Jesus Christ."[13] On one occasion he heard a Hindu lawyer give an address on "The Inescapable Christ" in which he said: "We have not been able to escape him. There was a time when our hearts were bitter and sore against him, but he is melting them by his own winsomeness. Jesus is slowly but surely entering all men in India—yea, all men."[14]

It is correct to say that nowhere in the non-Christian world is Jesus Christ more highly revered than in India. Somehow His gentleness, His integrity, and His spirituality have appealed to the soul of India. It is not too much to say that Jesus Christ is more highly regarded in India than in some circles here in the West.

K. N. Panikkar in his book *Asia and Western Dominance* was highly critical of Christian missions and predicted their demise once the colonial era came to an end. India has been independent now for over twenty-five years, and while the missionary forces have been greatly reduced, the Christian church is as viable as ever. Stephen Neill is correct when he says:

> It is true that numbers are small. . . . Yet these small minorities are
> well grounded and show every sign of having taken root in the
> soil of the subcontinent. It can be maintained with some confi-

---

[12] E. Stanley Jones, *The Christ of the Indian Road* (New York: Abingdon Press, 1925), p. 212.
[13] *Ibid.,* p. 217.
[14] *Ibid.*

dence that if every foreign missionary and every cent of foreign support were withdrawn, the churches, though weakened at certain points, would still maintain their existence, and would continue to expand, though perhaps more slowly than in the past. The number of fully independent and self-governing churches has increased rapidly in recent years. Most of the leading positions in the churches are filled by nationals. The faith of the village Christian is in many cases unenlightened, but it is real; it is most unlikely that he will ever forsake this religion in favor of any other.[15]

Christianity was introduced into China on four separate occasions. Not once did it take root permanently. Opposition came mostly from the scholar-gentry class, the most powerful segment of Chinese society. The closest that China ever came to becoming Christian was during the Taiping Rebellion in the middle of the nineteenth century. The Rebellion, which lasted almost fifteen years and took at least twenty million lives, was a quasi-Christian movement led by a "convert" named Hung Hsiu-ch'uan. The Roman Catholics, who might have been expected to support that kind of movement, opposed it because its leader was a Protestant. The Protestants repudiated Hung because he resorted to violence and included in his theology many bizarre doctrines which could only be regarded as heretical. Finally the Western powers helped the Central Government to suppress the movement and Hung and his cohorts came to an untimely end. It is interesting to speculate what might have happened to China had the Rebellion succeeded. Would China have become Christian? If so would it have been a good thing under the circumstances? Charles P. Fitzgerald, one-time cultural attaché to the British Embassy in Peking, thinks Christian missions missed the boat when they failed to support Hung and the Taipings. "Protestants temporized, sent emissaries to inquire, doubted and debated, and finally rejected the T'ai P'ing prophet as an imposter, and so lost their share in the only Christian movement which ever had a chance of converting the mass of the Chinese people."[16]

The impact of the West on China in the nineteenth century was enormous, all the more so because her civilization was so old and her population so large. The gospel as well as the gunboat was responsible for that impact. By the turn of the century China was ready to come to terms with the West and institute the reforms necessary to bring her into the family of nations. K'ang Yu-wei (1857-1927), one of China's greatest scholars and reformers, took a leading role in those reforms. Though he never became a Christian he acknowledged on one occa-

---

[15] Stephen Neill, *The Story of the Christian Church in India and Pakistan* (Grand Rapids: Eerdmans Publishing House, 1970), p. 167.

[16] Charles P. Fitzgerald, "Opposing Cultural Traditions, Barriers to Communication," Jessie G. Lutz, *Christian Missions in China: Evangelists of What?* (Chicago: D. C. Heath, 1965), p. 97.

sion: "I owe my conversion [to reform] chiefly to the writings of two missionaries, the Reverend Timothy Richard and the Reverend Doctor Young J. Allen."[17]

Sun Yat-sen, who was instrumental in bringing down the ancient empire, was a baptized Christian. It was his belief that the Republic of China could not long endure unless the righteousness for which the Christian religion stands was at the center of its national life. Curiously enough, Dr. Sun is claimed by both the Nationalists and the Communists as "the Father of the Republic."

From a numerical point of view the Christian mission in China was not very successful; the number of professing Christians was very small. But their influence was out of all proportion to their numbers. In the early 1930s 35 percent of those listed in *Who's Who in China* received at least part of their education in a Christian school. In the 1920s 90 percent of all registered nurses were Christians.[18] In line with this is the testimony of a non-Christian foreign newspaper correspondent who had many opportunities for wide observation. He said that "Christianity had produced a special type of human being in China, more alert, more modern, and more committed to the public welfare."[19]

Another experienced foreign newspaperman who described himself as a "friendly sceptic," declared that "Christianity provided the impetus for most of the really constructive social work in China in the 1930s."[20]

Chiang K'ai-shek was a devout Christian and used his influence to promote Christian ideals in Chinese society. When Chiang launched his New Life Movement in the 1930s he appointed a missionary to be in charge. Alas, Chiang K'ai-shek never had a fair chance. The Sino-Japanese War broke out just as he was beginning to effect his reforms. Given two decades of peace there is no telling what Chiang, with his Christian ideals, might have done for China.

There are those who believe that even the Chinese Communists were influenced by Christian missions. Fitzgerald states:

> The Chinese Communists took these things at second hand from the practice of the Russian Party, but in other respects they sought to imitate the work of missions, and have at long last, in the fulness of power, acknowledged the debt. . . . It is hard to doubt that

[17] Cyrus H. Peake, *Nationalism and Education in Modern China* (New York: Columbia University Press, 1932), p. 15.
[18] Kenneth Scott Latourette, *A History of Christian Missions in China* (New York: Macmillan, 1929), p. 362.
[19] George E. Sokolsky, *The Tinder Box of Asia* (Garden City, N.Y.: Doubleday, Doran & Co., 1932), p. 21.
[20] H. J. Timperley, *The China Quarterly* (Summer 1936).

some of these characteristics come from Christian examples, not from the manners of the Russian Communist Party.[21]

At one time it was thought that the last vestiges of Christianity were swept away by the Great Proletarian Cultural Revolution of 1966; but that judgment may have been premature. After almost twenty-five years of pathological hate for Uncle Sam, China is once again turning her face to the West. As a result there seems to be a loosening-up process going on. The English language, which went out in 1949, is today in such demand at all levels that there are not enough teachers to meet the need. Western missionaries are not likely to get back to China so long as the Communists remain in power; but there are increasing signs that religious freedom might be restored. Two former Canadian missionaries to China visited that country in the early part of 1973 and brought back encouraging reports regarding the situation now developing in that intriguing country.

> In conversations with Chinese clergy, church leaders, and former friends, these visitors learned that Christians in various parts of the country continue to practice their faith quietly but openly, usually meeting in their homes or in neighborhood gathering places, rather than in church buildings. Services are held regularly in both on Sundays and weekdays, in [two] Protestant and Catholic churches in Peking. Retired Christian workers are receiving pensions. Few young people are seen in church services. Bishop K. H. Ting, President of the Nanking Theological College, expressed the hope that the seminary would receive its first class of new students since 1966 early next year. Church leaders spoke with pride of the achievements of the new China, the guarantees of freedom of religious belief, and the independence and self-reliance of the churches. There was no mention of restoration of direct institutional ties with the churches of the West, or with ecumenical agencies of the churches.[22]

What about Japan, the most dynamic society in Asia? The early missionaries were very influential people. Thirty percent of their converts were from the powerful *samurai*, the military and intellectual elite who were interested in all kinds of social reform. To this day the Japanese church comprises the middle and upper middle classes, in contrast to the church in India, which represents the other end of the social spectrum. For over a hundred years Christians have been in the vanguard of reform movements. Many of them were decorated by the government. Outstanding among them was the world-famous Toyohiko Kagawa, who devoted his entire life to social action. He was one of the founders of the trade union movement in Japan.

Some thought that our use of the atomic bomb on Hiroshima and

---

[21] Charles Fitzgerald, *op. cit.*, p. 102.
[22] Division of Overseas Ministries, NCC/USA, *China Notes*, Vol. XI, No. 3 (Summer 1973), p. 25.

Nagasaki would have forever doomed Christianity's prospects in Japan. Such has not been the case. Following the war there was widespread interest in Christianity. Ten million copies of the Scriptures were distributed and tens of thousands of Japanese attended evangelistic meetings. In 1958 the secretary of the Bible Society wrote: "The Bible is becoming the Book of the people. It has been placed by the newspapers at the head of our classical literature."[23]

When it comes to the reception of the gospel, however, the Japanese must be numbered among the more resistant people of the world. From 1945 to 1963 Protestant church membership doubled from 200,000 to 400,000. According to the latest census almost three million persons listed Christianity as the religion of their choice. Obviously there are more "Christians" in Japan than appear on the church rolls. Most recent statistics show 560,000 Protestants, 360,000 Roman Catholics, and 25,000 Eastern Orthodox, making a total of 945,000, slightly less than 1 percent of the population—after 114 years of work.

The local churches are without exception small even by Asian standards. There are no mass meetings, no thronging crowds. The average church has fifty members. For many years the church in Japan was universally regarded as a foreign institution. This is changing, though rather slowly. To date Christianity has not succeeded in penetrating Japanese culture to a great extent. On the whole it has made little impact on Japanese society.

> The heritage of Japan's past, of course, can hardly be expected to be changed entirely by legal fiat in this or any other aspect; the old customs and ways of thinking are but in the process of change. Yet the nation has apparently committed itself irrevocably to the principle of true religious freedom and a secular state, and the rate of inward change seems rapid. The Christian church in Japan now has full freedom in life and witness. What it does from this point forward will depend largely upon its own resources of vision and spiritual power under God. There is good reason to believe that the Christian faith and church are now accepted by the nation as an authentic part of Japanese life. Christianity probably no longer appears as something spiritually alien, at least not to most people in the cities.[24]

It is in Korea that Protestant missions have made their greatest gains. Not only is the number of Christians high (slightly more than 10 percent of the population), but the quality of church life is also very high. Many of the leading educators and politicians are practicing Christians. In recent years a mass movement has been taking place in the army. In the summer of 1973 the Chief of Chaplains reported that

---

23 *Worlds Apart*, p. 98.
24 Richard H. Drummond, *A History of Christianity in Japan* (Grand Rapids: Eerdmans Publishing Company, 1971), p. 364.

250,000 officers and men—half the entire army—are now Christians. The Billy Graham Crusade in June 1973 attracted four and a half million people in six cities. Dr. Graham was overwhelmed by his reception and declared the Crusade to be the greatest in his twenty-five years of preaching on six continents. If the present growth rate continues it is quite possible that by 1980 Korea may be a predominantly Protestant country, the only one in Asia.

Africa

The continent of Africa is divided into two clearly defined regions, North Africa and Sub-Sahara Africa. North of the Sahara Desert the people are Arab and Berber by race and Muslim by religion. For this reason the five states in the north have more in common with the Middle East than with Africa. Together they have a combined population of about seventy-five million. Everything south of the Sahara is known as Sub-Sahara or Black Africa. In this section we are concerned only with Black Africa.

The population of Black Africa is approximately 300 million, divided among forty independent countries plus three colonies yet to get their independence. Most of these countries are small and have a population of 10 million or less. Six countries may be considered large: Nigeria (58), Ethiopia (26), South Africa (21), Zaire (18), Sudan (17), and Tanzania (14). Together these six countries represent one half of the 300 million people in Black Africa.

In the last fifteen years the political configuration of Black Africa has changed almost beyond recognition. In the heyday of Western imperialism all of Africa except Ethiopia and Liberia was parceled out among the European powers. Germany lost her colonies after World War I, which left Britain and France as the two colonial giants, each with a dozen or more colonies. Belgium had the Congo and Ruwanda-Burundi and Portugal had Angola and Mozambique. All thirteen French colonies received their independence in 1960. The British colonies were granted independence one by one over the period of a decade, beginning with Ghana in 1957. Today only three large colonies remain—Angola, Mozambique, and Southwest Africa (Namibia). The last-mentioned is governed by South Africa under a mandate granted originally by the League of Nations.

These three colonies plus Rhodesia and South Africa pose serious problems for Christian missions. Whether we like it or not religion and politics cannot be separated. Both the Western missionaries and the national Christians in these countries have to walk the tightrope. One false step and down they go. The nationals are sent to jail; the missionaries are expelled from the country. In either case the church suffers.

During the 1960s missionaries coming home on furlough were not permitted to return to Angola and Mozambique; consequently only a handful remain. Guerrilla warfare continues, churches have been destroyed, and refugees by the thousands have been created. In protest against the repressive colonial administration two mission boards, the United Church (USA) and the United Church of Canada, have removed all their missionaries from Angola. The recent coup in Portugal may lead to early independence for the colonies in Africa.

In Rhodesia and South Africa the situation is somewhat different. Neither of these two countries is a colony, but both have repressive regimes which have virtually reduced the nationals to colonial status. Missionaries are welcome, but they are expected to do nothing to upset the status quo. Some missionaries, feeling impelled to speak out against racism, have been expelled. The majority, equally distressed over existing conditions, have decided to stay, thinking that by so doing they can make their best contribution in a difficult and delicate situation. It takes more courage, wisdom, and patience to work within the establishment than to sound off and be expelled.

The earliest missionaries to Africa were Roman Catholics who accompanied the Portuguese explorers along the coast of Africa during the fifteenth century under Prince Henry the Navigator. They served as chaplains to their own compatriots and as missionaries to the Africans. They established thriving missions in West Africa and as far south as Congo and Angola. On the east coast they penetrated inland as far as present-day Rhodesia. For a time these missions thrived, but by the end of the eighteenth century they had all but disappeared.

When the Protestant missions got under way about the turn of the nineteenth century, they approached the vast continent from four different routes.

1. From the west. The earliest attempt was made by the Baptist Missionary Society, which sent William Carey to India. The place was Sierra Leone and the year was 1795. Other British societies followed. Missionary work in Liberia began in 1833; the missions there were American. Ghana was entered in 1828 by the Basel Mission of Switzerland and in 1834 by the English Methodists. The Church Missionary Society also had work in several countries of West Africa. In Nigeria the Church Missionary Society and the Southern Baptists pioneered about the middle of the century.

2. From the south. Here the leader was the London Missionary Society, in 1799. The two most famous missionaries were Robert Moffat and David Livingstone.

3. From the east. The Church Missionary Society led the way into the heart of East Africa via Mombasa. The year was 1844. Pioneer John Ludwig Krapf died after nine months and was followed by John Rebmann, both Germans. Another pioneer society in these parts was the Universities' Mission to Central Africa, which owed its origin to Livingstone's visit to Oxford and Cambridge Universities in 1857, after he had been seventeen years on the mission field.

4. Via the Congo River. Central Africa was opened to "commerce and Christianity" by David Livingstone and Henry M. Stanley, though neither of them actually did any missionary work there. The Baptist Missionary Society (England) was the pioneer in Congo (Zaire) in 1878, followed by the Christian and Missionary Alliance and the American Baptists.

In the early years the going was hard, deaths were numerous, and results were meager.

> The European arm of this missionary movement . . . was a costly business. In the first twelve years of its work from 1828 at Christiansborg, Accra, the Basel Mission lost eight of nine men from fever. The CMS lost fifty-three men and women in Sierra Leone between 1804 and 1824. The Methodists in the fifteen years following 1835 had seventy-eight new appointments, men and wives, in the Gambia, Sierra Leone and the Gold Coast; thirty of these died within a year of arrival.[25]

The story of missions in Africa in the nineteenth century was an amazing tale of adventure, endurance, privation, sickness, weakness, and death. With such crippling casualties the missions during the latter half of the century were able to do little more than maintain a holding operation. Under such conditions it is little wonder that converts came slowly.

> Each of the pioneer missions was disheartened by its inability to make numerous and lasting conversions. The Primitive Methodists [in Northern Rhodesia] for example waited thirteen years to make their first convert. Moreover, he, and five other students who followed him, soon lapsed into apostasy, and the Primitive Methodists were compelled to wait patiently until a new group of catechumens could be prepared slowly for baptism. For all missions, these were the barren, pioneer years.[26]

The period of rapid growth began about 1900. From 1900 to 1950 the Christian population increased about sixty times. From 1950 to 1970 the growth rate has been even faster. Today the whole of Black

---

[25] T. A. Beetham, *Christianity and the New Africa* (London: Pall Mall Press, 1967), p. 11.

[26] Robert I. Rotberg, *Christian Missionaries and the Creation of Northern Rhodesia, 1880-1924* (Princeton: Princeton University Press, 1965), p. 42.

Africa is on the move spiritually, away from animism, which has nothing to offer to an educated person, to something more satisfying to mind and soul.

The educated African today has really only two choices, Christianity or Islam, both of which are world religions and present a viable option as opposed to animism, which has long since lost its appeal. We often hear that Islam is making converts three and four times faster than Christianity. It is doubtful if this was ever true. Certainly it is not true at the present time. In some parts of the continent the Muslims may have a slight edge on us; but in other parts we are way ahead of them in the race for the mind of Africa.

Islam crossed the Sahara by the desert trade routes. Early in the eleventh century isolated Muslims were found in the region of the Niger River. The first forcible conversions came with the conquest of the old kingdom of Ghana in 1076. By the fourteenth century Islam had reached eastward to Katsina and Kano in what is now Nigeria. The great empires of the forest belt broke down in the seventeenth and eighteenth centuries. During this period Muslim traders and clerics were to be found in most towns; but the mass of the people remained animists. The nineteenth century saw the development of the "theocratic" states, with an emphasis on the uniqueness of Islam and its unwillingness to tolerate other religions. From the Wolof in Senegal to the Hausa in Nigeria and Cameroon, the Islamization of the common people became rapid, its consolidation being helped by the protective policy of religious neutrality on the part of the colonial governments of France and Britain.

In the past fifty years the rate of penetration has been much greater, more by migration than by conversion. In most of the coastal towns today a mosque is a common sight. At the same time Pakistani missionaries of the militant Ahmadiyyah Mission have spread along the coasts in English-speaking countries. Many of their converts are from nominal Muslims and Christians. Only one-third have been from the animists. Taking their cue from Christian missions the Muslims are now opening schools and clinics as well as mosques, and engaging in social service on an unprecedented scale. They are making an all-out bid for Africa's soul.

In East Africa the spread of Islam had two distinct stages. The first impact was made by the Arab and Persian traders of the coastal fringe in the thirteenth and fourteenth centuries. This resulted in the founding of Swahili culture groups in East Africa but left the Bantu untouched. The second period coincided with the extension of European trade and rule into the interior in the nineteenth century. One reason for the expansion was the fact that the Europeans recruited all their guides, servants, police, and carriers from among the Muslims of the coast. This period reached its height between 1880 and 1930. Today there are only eight countries in Black Africa that are predominantly Muslim; six of them are small countries in West Africa. The largest Muslim country is Sudan, with seventeen million people. Together these eight countries represent a total population of forty million. Nigeria, the most populous country in the whole of Africa, is the one country where Christian-Muslim competition is the keenest. Twenty years ago Nigeria was predominantly Muslim and no evangelistic work was permitted in the Northern Region. Today it is 44 percent Muslim and 46 percent Christian. The rapidly diminishing animists now account for only 10 percent.

Several Muslim countries in Black Africa are closed to Christian missions. Mauritania has never permitted missionaries to reside in its territory. Sudan expelled all missionaries from the southern part of the country in 1964, allowing only a few to remain in Khartoum and Omdurman. Following the conclusion of a sixteen-year civil war in 1972, several missions have been permitted to return to engage in relief and rehabilitation. It remains to be seen if they will be allowed to resume their church work. For almost twenty years two missions were permitted to do medical and educational work in Somalia, but in 1972 all mission work was terminated by the government.

Since 1950 the growth of Islam in Black Africa has tapered off considerably. Today it is not much greater than the natural population growth rate and is almost totally confined to West Africa and the northern part of Cameroon.

Although the growth of Islam has slowed down in recent years, it remains Christianity's greatest enemy in Africa. It still makes a strong appeal, for the following reasons: (1) It poses as the "black man's religion"—supposedly indigenous to Africa. This is in contrast to Christianity, which is identified with the West. (2) Islam was not identified with the European colonial system though through the Arabs it was connected with the slave trade of an earlier era. (3) Islam has made good use of lay missionaries, principally teachers and merchants who settle down and become part of the local community. (4) Islam makes fewer moral demands on its adherents. Polygamy, a veritable millstone around the neck of the Christian church, is no problem to Islam, for all devout Muslims are permitted to have four wives. (5) Some branches of Islam are now extensively engaged in social and humanitarian service, taking a leaf from the missionary's book.

Christianity has made more converts in Black Africa than in all the rest of the Third World combined. In spite of the fact that we got off to a late start in Africa as compared with Asia, we have made converts much faster. Accurate statistics are difficult to obtain. Moreover, church growth is so rapid that any estimate is out of date in a year or two. According to reliable estimates the population of Black Africa is around 300 million. Of this figure 150 million are Christians, 85 million are Muslims, and about 65 million are still animists. This means that 50 percent of the people in Black Africa are professing Christians, compared with about 2 percent for the continent of Asia. It should be noted that for the first time Christians outnumber Muslims.

The ratio of Christians to the total population is highest in South Africa, lowest in West Africa, and somewhere in between in Central and East Africa. Countries with the highest ratio, including Roman Catholics, are: Congo, 99 percent; Central African Republic, 90 percent; Lesotho, 87 percent; Zaire, 86 percent; Swaziland, 83 percent; South Africa, 83 percent; Namibia, 84 percent; and Angola, 83 percent.

In West Africa the ratio drops drastically. In seven countries the ratio is below 10 percent. The "Big Five" include: Ghana, 63 percent; Nigeria, 46 percent; Liberia, 42 percent; Togo, 30 percent; and Dahomey, 20 percent.

The Christians are broken down into four major groups: Roman Catholics with sixty-five million, Protestants with sixty million, Coptic Christians with ten million, and Separatists or Independents with fifteen million.

Of the four groups of Christians the oldest and most decadent are the Copts, who belong to the Ethiopian Orthodox Church, which dates back to the fourth century. The ex-emperor, reputed descendant of King Solomon by the Queen of Sheba, was the titular head of the church. Its ritual includes Jewish as well as Christian elements. Numbered among its saints are such strange figures as Balaam and his ass, Samson and his jawbone, and Pontius Pilate and his wife. Until 1900 all education in the country was provided by the church; nevertheless the literacy rate today is one of the lowest in Africa. Only since 1959 has the Ethiopian Church been independent of the Coptic Church in Egypt. Like the other Orthodox Churches it has been content to live in isolation without making any concerted effort to win either the Muslims or the pagans to Christianity. "It seems to have exerted no direct influence on, nor taken part in any extension of the Christian faith to, the rest of the continent."[27] The Ethiopian Orthodox Church is the state church and wields considerable political as well as economic power. Spiritually it remains moribund. Through the years many of its priests and monks have been illiterate and degenerate. In recent years there have been welcome signs of renewal. The membership figure of ten million is only an estimate. Indeed the population of Ethiopia

---

[27] T. A. Beetham, *op. cit.*, p. 7.

has never been established with scientific accuracy; that figure also is an estimate.

Another group is the African Independent Churches, sometimes referred to as Separatist Churches. Today there are seven thousand of these denominations found among 330 different tribes in thirty-five countries, with an estimated Christian community that may run as high as fifteen million. This movement is unique to Africa and is one of the outstanding features of Christianity in that continent.

The movement dates back to 1819; but the first noticeable surge took place in 1885, the year of the Berlin Conference. Since then the movement has expanded at a remarkably even rate, involving an average of three new tribes each year. About 10 percent of all the bodies formed since 1819 are now defunct. The average size of these churches is only 1,400 adherents; but many have over 50,000 members. The largest is the Church of Jesus Christ on Earth through the Prophet Simon Kimbangu (Zaire), which is estimated to have 500,000 adult members or a total Christian community of 3,000,000.

These Independent Churches are found all over Black Africa, but the largest concentrations are in South Africa (3,000), Nigeria (800), Zaire (600), Ghana (200), and Kenya (180). They are divided into two groups, Ethiopian and Zionist. The Ethiopian type is due in large measure to the color bar and emphasizes the African character of the church. The Zionist type is a much more significant and elaborate expression of the African mind. Both types have developed an indigenous form of ritual which includes hand-clapping, dancing, native music, and faith healing.

The purely Christian element varies from group to group. Some are definitely more Christian than others. Some are only semi-Christian; others tend to be anti-Christian. They are a strange mixture of animism, native customs, and magic, with certain Christian elements added and the whole embellished with the external symbols of Christianity. Some of the churches were indigenous from the beginning; many of them, however, broke off from the historic churches and missions, both Roman Catholic and Protestant. There are signs that some of these churches are beginning to move back into the mainstream of Christianity. Their leaders are requesting and receiving theological training and other forms of assistance from the historic denominations. Several of them have been admitted to the World Council of Churches, including the Kimbanguist Church of Zaire.

The third and largest group is the Roman Catholic Church, which now represents a total Christian community of 65 million souls. Through the years the Roman Catholics have had a big stake in Christian missions in Africa. Three religious orders carried the lion's share of the work: the White Fathers, the Holy Ghost Fathers, and the ubiquitous Jesuits. The vast majority of missionaries came from Europe. A small minority—at the present time about eleven hundred—are from the United States. Eighty-seven percent of these Americans are working in the countries once ruled by the British and where English is still the *lingua franca*.

Roman Catholic missions have achieved their greatest numerical success in those countries which were once colonies of France, Portugal, and Belgium, all Roman Catholic countries. The colonial administrators in those countries naturally favored Roman Catholic missions and often discriminated against Protestant missions, with predictable results. There are, however, three former British colonies—Tanzania, Zambia, and Uganda—where the Roman Catholics significantly outnumber the Protestants. Many of the independent countries maintain diplomatic relations with the Vatican and this always confers a certain degree of prestige on the Roman Catholic Church. In Ethiopia and Liberia Roman Catholic missions have only token forces and no church to speak of.

The Protestants, who through the years have lagged behind the Roman Catholics, have in recent years been making phenomenal strides. The total Protestant community in Black Africa is now in the neighborhood of sixty million, and in the near future it is likely to overtake the Roman Catholic community. This is due largely to the great emphasis that has been placed in recent years on mass evangelism, which under various names has been carried on with excellent results in Nigeria, Zaire, Ghana, and other countries. Everywhere churches have been revived, pastors and leaders have been given special training, and laymen at all levels have been mobilized for mass evangelism. A huge investment has been made in evangelism and the investment is paying off.

Along with evangelism goes Bible translation, an area in which Protestant missionaries have always excelled. Bible translation can be a nightmare in a continent with eight hundred tribes each speaking its own language. In most cases the language had to be reduced to written form before translation could begin. When translation was completed and the book published, the people had to be taught to read the script invented for them by the missionaries. It was a long, laborious, and costly operation, requiring infinite patience and not a little linguistic skill. By December 1972 the entire Bible was available in 89 languages of Africa, the New Testament in another 126, and Portions in still another 230, making a grand total of 445 languages for the entire continent.

An African girl was once asked what she thought of the Bible. She replied, "Well, it begins with Genesis and ends with Revolutions." Indeed it does! The Bible is the most revolutionary book in the world, far more revolutionary than *Das Kapital* or the *Communist Manifesto.* Wherever it goes it emancipates men as well as women and children. For millions of Africans the only book they possess is the New Testament. It has done more than any other book to bring Africa out of its Dark Ages into the full light of the twentieth century.

FACTORS THAT MADE FOR GROWTH

1. Christian missions made an enormous investment in Black Africa. There are more missionaries per capita in Africa than anywhere else in the world. To begin with, Black Africa attracted missions from *all* the major sending countries—England, Scotland, Ireland, Germany, Switzerland, Scandinavia, United States, Canada, Australia, and New Zealand. Moreover, in this part of the world we find all *kinds* of missionary agencies—main line denominations, faith missions, Pentecostals, Seventh-day Adventists, Quakers, and indigenous movements. Before the evacuation of the turbulent sixties there were over two thousand Protestant missionaries in Congo (Zaire), which had a population of only 12 million. Paul reminded the Corinthians of a fundamental principle of agricultural growth: he that sows bountifully will also reap bountifully. This has certainly been the case in Africa.

2. Colonialism, which proved so disastrous in Asia, was a blessing in disguise in Africa. In spite of its many shortcomings, colonialism in Africa had some things in its favor. It terminated the intertribal warfare and the slave trade, both of which were decimating the population, and imposed a much needed peace on the entire continent. Moreover, the colonial government favored missionary work in many ways. In the early years they made land grants for schools and mission stations and later on subsidized mission schools. Without such aid the missions would never have been able to maintain all their Christian schools. The colonial officials, representing as they did the paramount power in the colonies, enjoyed a good deal of personal prestige in society. Some of this prestige rubbed off on the missionaries, for they too belonged to the white race.

3. The social structure of African society made it easy for the missionaries to acquire more power than they otherwise might have had. For centuries all the major decisions were made by the African chiefs and the members of the tribe simply obeyed orders. When the Africans became Christians and were detribalized, it was only natural that they should transfer their allegiance to the missionaries. Hence the great power of missionaries in Africa. This should be borne in mind when the nineteenth-century missionary in Africa is criticized for acting like the Great White Father.

4. Christian missions invested a huge amount of time and money in education. This added burden was thrust upon them by the failure of the colonial authorities to provide education for the Africans. For many decades the missions were the sole purveyors of education. The British did as good a job as anybody in Africa; but in 1923 only one hundred of the six thousand schools in British Africa were government schools. As late as 1961, 68 percent of all the school children in Africa were still in mission schools.

This imposed a heavy burden on the missions and tied down thousands of missionaries who might have been engaged in direct evangelism. Nevertheless it afforded them a unique opportunity to mold the character of several generations of Africans. The connection between the school and the church was very close. In the bush schools the evangelist was also the teacher. He taught not only the three Rs but also the Bible and Christian doctrine. Today there is hardly a leader in any walk of life who did not receive at least part of his education in a mission school. With so many people being exposed to Christianity over such a long period of time during the most formative years of their lives, it is no wonder that so many of them embraced the Christian faith in one form or another.

5. The missionaries encountered no opposition from existing religious systems. No such opposition developed in Africa, for the simple reason that such systems did not exist. Animism is found in all parts of the world, usually as an accretion to the great ethnic religions; but Africa is the heartland of animism and the people there knew nothing else until the coming of Islam and Christianity.

Reduced to its simplest form, animism is the belief in spirits. Spirits abound everywhere—in the atmosphere, in trees, mountains, houses, and in human beings. There are two kinds, good and evil. The evil spirits are by far the more active; consequently they must be constantly placated or they will inflict all manner of pain and misfortune on human beings.

Animism has no books and no temples; nor has it produced any great leaders, thinkers, or scholars. Of course, it has its medicine men, its witch doctors, and its devil dancers; and while these are powerful figures in the local tribe, they are no match for the missionary doctors and teachers. Hence animism's inability to stand up to the insights of Western learning. People with a modern education find it difficult to continue to practice the superstitious rites connected with animism.

Little wonder that modern Africans are deserting animism by the millions every year.

6. The missionary was held in high esteem. We have noted that in Asia the missionary was looked down on by the Brahmins of India and the Confucian scholars of China. In Africa, however, the situation was reversed. There he was regarded as belonging to a superior race. Even the simple trinkets he used to pay his carriers and guides—beads, shells, nails, calico, and combs—were objects of the greatest curiosity; and their possession marked the proud owner as a person on his way to "civilization." And what shall be said of the more ingenious inventions of Western civilization which were introduced by the missionary: reading, writing, and arithmetic, not to mention agricultural tools, medical instruments, alarm clocks, rifles, typewriters, adding machines, etc.? When the simple, illiterate Africans saw the missionary and all the accoutrements of Western civilization he brought along, they must have felt like the Lycaonians of Paul's day when they exclaimed, "The gods have come down to us in the likeness of men!" (Acts 14:11). The nineteenth-century missionary did not have to *act* like a tin god, he *was* a tin god!

7. The Africans, in spite of their primitive animism, believed in a Great Spirit, a factor that helped to pave the way for the introduction of Christianity to Africa. He was called by different names in different tribes; but his existence was recognized by all. Indeed, his presence was never far away, for the Africans live close to nature and the veil between the seen world and the unseen world is paper thin. They have no hang-ups regarding the supernatural. They are not like the Theravada Buddhists, who deny the existence of all gods. Nor are they like the Pantheistic Hindus who believe that everything is god. Nor are they like Western men of science, who are locked into a closed system. The African carries religion in his soul and constantly communes with the unseen powers of the universe. In the vicissitudes of his daily life he may be preoccupied with spirits and demons; but in his more sober moments he recognizes the presence and power of the Great Spirit who lives in the sky, who sends the sunshine and the rain, who watches over crops and cattle, who can both protect and punish man. When the missionary, therefore, brought to the African a clear knowledge of the One True God, Maker of Heaven and Earth, and Jesus Christ His only Son, the African mind found it easy to embrace such a doctrine.

To what extent has Christianity affected the culture of Africa? When a powerful, highly developed civilization comes into contact with a less highly developed civilization, the former tends to swamp the latter. This is what has happened in Black Africa.

When that higher civilization is backed up by all the apparatus of a colonial government system based on economic and military power, it is bound to have an injurious effect on the indigenous culture.

Moreover, when education, the most potent instrument for the molding of the national character, is in the hands of the representatives of that higher civilization, the less-developed culture is sure to be undermined.

In most non-Christian countries Christians tend to have an influence out of all proportion to their numbers. And not without reason. They are often better educated than their compatriots. They are usually conscientious and trustworthy. They make good neighbors and loyal citizens. They are fair and honest in their business dealings. It is true that in the higher echelons of business and politics they may suffer some form of discrimination. This is especially true where they are in the minority. Even then, business clerks or government workers, they are often preferred before their non-Christian neighbors.

When Christians form more than half the population, which they now do in many African countries, their influence is all-pervasive. Because they are better educated and more trustworthy than non-Christians they often have access to better jobs and higher posts in government. In not a few countries the highest government officials are practicing Christians. They are making an honest effort to bring Christian principles to bear on the social, economic, and political problems of the day. Nigeria has made a spectacular recovery from thirty-two months of civil war with the Eastern Region of Biafra. There have been no reprisals and the country is united as never before. Best of all the economy is booming. President Gowon is a Christian, the son of a pastor. Is there any connection? We would like to think so.

Many Africans fear that their culture will in time be completely swamped by Western culture. They are making every effort to preserve all that is good. The Christian church is doing the same. It is trying to indigenize its liturgy, music, and other features of its corporate life. The next ten or fifteen years will be crucial to the future image of Christianity in Africa.

FACTORS THAT MILITATE AGAINST CHRISTIANITY

In spite of the phenomenal progress that Christianity has made in Black Africa there are warning signs that turbulent weather may be ahead.

1. **Political instability often results in chaotic conditions.** There is hardly a country that has not had one or more coups, successful or

abortive, in the past fifteen years. Democracy has been tried and found wanting. In very few countries did the two-party system of government last more than a couple of years. In some countries even the one-party government has been dissolved and a military regime installed in its place. Economic stagnation abounds and corruption is a way of life. Several countries have been through the horrors of a major civil war: Zaire, Nigeria, Sudan, and Burundi.

2. **Tribalism is on the increase.** There are over eight hundred tribes in Africa, each with its own language and customs. The colonial system put an end to intertribal warfare and forced the tribes to live together in some semblance of unity. Now that the colonial system is gone, tribalism is on the increase and threatens to tear some of the countries apart. Tribalism has been in the blood of the Africans for centuries and the pressure is steadily rising. Tribal rivalry was really at the bottom of the civil wars mentioned above. In Burundi 300,000 persons were slaughtered in six months. Although the Christians were not directly involved in the feud between the two tribes—the Tutsi and the Hutus—their losses were staggering. One missionary society lost nine of its ten national leaders. The largest church, the Anglican Church, lost thirteen of its thirty-five pastors. It will take a generation to replace them.

To the present time some tribes have successfully resisted all attempts to "civilize" them. The solidarity of their social structure is such that Christianity has been unable to gain a foothold. The Masai in East Africa are a classic example. "It is at present almost impossible for an individual within the Masai community to become a Christian. A young man who refuses to join the other warriors for a cattle raid will be beaten and have his cattle confiscated. A young girl who does not submit to intercourse on demand will be punished."[28]

3. **Nationalism is also on the increase.** This in itself need not be bad; but if it gets out of hand there can be trouble. In Zaire Christian parents cannot give their children Christian names; they must be African names. To help unify the country the president decreed that all the churches must unite to form the Church of Christ in Zaire. In Uganda President Amin in 1972 ordered forty thousand Asians to leave the country within ninety days. Later he outlawed twelve "religious sects" which he found undesirable, among them Campus Crusade for Christ. Hundreds of Christian leaders are in hiding in neighboring countries. Religious freedom is being sacrificed on the altar of nationalism.

---

[28] Richard and Helen Exley, *In Search of the Missionary* (London: Highway Press, 1970), p. 29.

4. Materialism is having its effect on the Christian church in Africa. Materialism is not unique to the affluent countries. In fact, the developing nations have an even bigger problem with it. For the first time they can now have more of the good things of life and they want them in a hurry. Young men with a college education want good jobs with high wages. The churches cannot afford to pay what the government and industry pay. Consequently few bright young men feel called to the Christian ministry when they can make five times as much money elsewhere. The greatest crisis facing the African church is the paucity of trained leaders, and with a mammoth influx of new believers each year the problem is getting worse by the month.

5. Racism at home and abroad is giving Christianity a bad name in Africa. Africans who have never heard of Chicago know all about Little Rock and Birmingham. Racism in "Christian" America is a millstone around the neck of the missionary in Africa. *Apartheid* in South Africa is a burning issue in most African countries, and South Africa is looked upon as a "Christian" country. The Ian Smith regime in white-dominated Rhodesia is another thorn in the flesh. In spite of the opposing forces Christianity is definitely making headway in Africa. There are those who predict that by the year 2000 Black Africa will be a predominantly Christian continent.

Latin America

A good deal is heard these days about the population explosion; but nowhere in the world is the population increasing faster than in Latin America, where the growth rate is around 3.5 percent as compared with the world rate of 2 percent. In some of the countries it is a whopping 4 percent or more. This high growth rate is due in part to Catholic influence and the continued opposition to birth control on the part of the Catholic Church.

The trend is away from the unproductive rural areas into the big cities. Almost 50 percent of the Latins now live in cities. Four of the world's largest cities are there: Mexico City (8,590,000), Buenos Aires (8,350,000), Sao Paulo (8,062,000), and Rio de Janeiro (7,094,000). On the outskirts of these cities are shanty towns which house hundreds of thousands of poverty-stricken people who have moved to the cities in search of a better life, only to find their lot has worsened. Living conditions in these shanty towns make the ghettos in other parts of the world look like the Garden of Eden.

The people of Latin America, now numbering 275 million, can be divided into three major groups: people of pure Spanish blood; people of pure Indian blood; and people of mixed blood, known as mestizos. There are about thirty million Indians. In the Andes countries of Peru, Bolivia, and Ecuador they constitute the bulk of the population. Two countries in Central America have large Indian populations— Guatemala and Mexico. On the other hand there are countries like Argentina and Uruguay, whose population is almost entirely European in descent. In Brazil a fourth of the population is mulatto, a mixture of Portuguese and Negro blood.

The Indians have never been assimilated by Spanish culture. They retain their own customs, traditions, and languages and live mainly by agriculture, which they carry on by methods both primitive and unproductive. Illiteracy among them is extremely high; and medical services are practically unknown. Housing is wholly inadequate. Three centuries of Iberian rule, while it brought many material benefits to Latin America, resulted in untold sufferings to the Indians, sufferings which to this day have not been redressed. Though nominally Roman Catholic, these Indians are still more pagan than Christian.

In recent years increasing attention is being paid to the plight of the Indians. In 1970 the World Council of Churches sponsored a Consultation on South American Indians in Barbados. Strangely enough, the Declaration which came out of the Consultation faulted the missionaries for the exploitation of the Indians and called for the immediate termination of all missionary work among them!

South America is the only continent that is completely dominated by the Roman Catholics. The Roman Catholic Church has been there ever since the Spanish and the Portuguese arrived at the beginning of the sixteenth century. Until the Protestant missionaries arrived about the middle of the nineteenth century the Catholics had the field entirely to themselves.

The first missionaries to the New World were Franciscans and Dominicans. The former arrived in Brazil with Cabral in 1500, in Haiti two years later, and in Mexico in 1523. The Dominicans began their missionary work in Haiti in 1510, in Cuba in 1512, in Colombia in 1531, and in Peru in 1532. They were joined by the Augustinians at an early date. In 1549 the Jesuits began to arrive in Brazil. By 1555, in the wake of the explorers and conquistadors, Roman Catholic missionaries had taken Christianity to the West Indies, Mexico, Central America, Colombia, Venezuela, Ecuador, Chile, Peru, and Brazil.

Due to the cruel treatment of the red man by the Spanish, the indigenous population of the West Indies completely disappeared, and Negro slaves from Africa were brought in to take their place. During the seventeenth century one thousand slaves landed each month at Cartagena. For three centuries the nefarious traffic continued unabated, during which time, it is estimated, Brazil alone received between six and eight million slaves for the sugar plantations. The only voice raised against this form of genocide was that of the friars. Most famous of these was Father Bartholomew de Las Casas (1474-1566), a Dominican missioner who made seven voyages to Spain to plead the cause of the oppressed Indians.

Some of these missionaries were worthy disciples of Loyola and Xavier and faced hardship, danger, disease, and persecution in a heroic spirit deserving of high praise. Yet they were part of the military, ecclesiastical, and political system of the times and their ardent evangelism and humanitarian service were strangely mixed with the slaughter and subjugation of the Indians and the extortion of their land and wealth. Conversion was often forced and occurred en masse, resulting in baptized pagans entering the church in large numbers with consequences all too familiar in Latin America.

Roman Catholic missions in South America suffered two catastrophic setbacks. Beginning with Brazil in 1759, some three thousand Jesuits were expelled from various countries. Other orders tried to fill the gap, but they had their own missions to man. No adequate effort was made to train the Indians for the priesthood, and to this day the shortage of well-trained native-born clergy is one of the greatest problems facing the Roman Catholic Church in that part of the world.

The second setback came with the wars of independence between 1810 and 1824. Until then church and state were one and most of the administrators were either Spanish or Portuguese. Thus the church possessed immense power and prestige; but when the revolutionists went on the rampage their hatred of colonialism was not confined to the civil authorities; it spilled over to the religious hierarchy as well. With the fall of the Spanish Empire in Latin America Catholic missions were deprived of the moral and economic support of the Spanish kings. Moreover, the new governments were anticlerical, some of them extremely so. Many of the missionaries, including some bishops, returned to Spain, leaving their flocks to fend for themselves. Under these conditions the patronage system broke down; and the Vatican was obliged to come to terms with the new regimes on an individual basis. These agreements, known as concordats, differed from country to country; but in nearly every case the Roman Catholic Church managed to secure preferential treatment.

Today the Catholic Church in Latin America is numerically large but spiritually weak. In strength and numbers it varies from country to country. In Peru the Church claims 99.3 percent of the population. At the other end of the spectrum is Haiti with only 65.7 percent. The Vatican has diplomatic relations with nineteen of the twenty republics in Latin America, Mexico being the single exception.

According to Father Albert J. Nevins, associate editor of *Mary-*

knoll Magazine, the church is strong and vital in Mexico, Costa Rica, Colombia, El Salvador, Cuba, Chile, Venezuela, Peru, and Uruguay. It is dying in Bolivia, Paraguay, Brazil, Ecuador, Panama, Honduras, Dominican Republic, and Haiti. Altogether the Church claims 90 percent of the people of Latin America, but confesses that fewer than 10 percent are practicing Catholics.

WEAKNESS OF ROMAN CATHOLICISM

1. There has never been a sufficient number of priests to provide adequate spiritual oversight for so large a population. The ratio of priests to the Catholic community is one to seven thousand, and this ratio continues to worsen. In 1900 it was one to five thousand. In Cuba there is one priest to twenty-eight thousand people. In Chile it is one to twenty-eight hundred—much better, but still a far cry from Europe, where the ratio ranges from one to five hundred in Switzerland to one to sixteen hundred in Portugal. While Latin America has almost 35 percent of the world's Catholics, it has only 8 percent of its priests.

2. The caliber of the priesthood in Latin America has never been very high. The vast majority of priests came from Spain, hardly the most progressive of the Catholic countries of the world; and they did not improve with the ocean voyage. They were not the best-educated priests in the service of Rome, nor were their morals always beyond reproach. In the best of circumstances celibacy is not an easy way of life. In the backward, isolated villages of Latin America the priests did not always keep themselves pure.

3. The Catholic Church failed to train a well-educated, indigenous clergy. Even today, after 450 years of work, 40 percent of the priests are foreigners, nearly half of them from Spain.

4. The Catholic Church has been too deeply immersed in politics. During the colonial period church and state were one. After the various republics gained their independence the Church demanded and received preferential treatment that was spelled out in concordats drawn up by the Vatican. In return the Catholic hierarchy supported military dictatorships and oppressive regimes. It did nothing to solve the problems or redress the grievances of the downtrodden masses.

The situation, however, has been improving in recent years. Cardinal Cushing of Boston took a personal interest in Latin America, and largely as a result of his influence more and more American priests have been going there. In 1972, 45 percent of all American Catholic missionaries were serving in Latin America. As a result the image of the Catholic Church is changing. Now the Church is making an attempt to identify more closely with the common people in their poverty and oppression. Many of today's priests are progressive. A few are even revolutionary. In some countries they have left the Church to join guerrilla forces fighting to overthrow the government. Several Maryknoll missionaries were recalled from Guatemala for this reason.

Following Vatican II the winds of change began to blow through Latin America. As a result relations between Catholics and Evangelicals have greatly improved in the last decade. There are veteran missionaries in this part of the world who still bear in their bodies the scars of Roman Catholic persecution. As recently as the 1950s some three hundred Evangelicals were killed in Colombia. Now it is possible for them to organize public parades and conduct open-air meetings in the plaza in the heart of downtown Bogota. In some of the larger city churches the priests are now using gospel films lent to them by Protestant pastors. Moody Institute of Science films are shown in the high schools. Some priests have invited Protestant clergymen and missionaries to speak in their pulpits. Such things were unthinkable ten short years ago. For the first time in history Evangelicals are respected in Latin America.

Most significant of all is the changed attitude of the Catholic Church to the reading of the Scriptures. In times past Bible colporteurs in Latin America were hunted and hounded from pillar to post and not a few of them wound up in prison. That day is gone. The Church itself is now encouraging its own people to read the Bible. As a result Bible sales are soaring in all parts of the continent.

The ecumenical overtures of the Roman Catholic Church have posed problems for the Evangelicals, who are divided into three camps at this point. There is a rather small group that welcomes the new stance and is happy to cooperate with the Catholics in many matters, including Bible translation. There is a second group of ultra conservatives who cannot believe that recent changes are anything but a facelifting operation designed to catch the Evangelicals off guard. No major dogmas have been changed one iota; therefore the new image is false. Between these two extremes are to be found the majority of Evangelicals, who at this point are simply confused. They left the Catholic Church when they became Evangelicals and for this they paid a high price. Yesterday they were "heretics." Today they are "separated brethren." In the meantime they have done nothing to merit the new name. They are thankful that persecution has ceased; they are not sure that cooperation is the right thing; and besides, they do not know where it will lead. They are rather uneasy about the whole thing.

While Roman Catholicism is the dominant religion of Latin

America and one-third of all the Catholics in the world are found there, the religious climate differs from country to country. The Catholics themselves identify four forms of Catholicism: formal, nominal, cultural, and folk.

The formal Catholic is one who seriously accepts the doctrine and discipline of the Church as given through her official representatives, the bishops and priests, and who seeks to express his faith in all aspects of his life—religious, social, economic, and political. Nominal Catholicism is an identifiable acceptance of membership in the Church, involving some allegiance but with little effort to follow faithfully those rites and proscriptions expected of the practicing Catholic. Cultural Catholicism is a further watered-down version that does not involve church membership but still retains an appreciation for the fringe benefits—art, music, literature, architecture—usually associated with institutionalized religion. Folk Catholicism is an intricate blending of native religion with orthodox Catholicsm. It is the kind found everywhere among the Indians and mestizos, whose conversion to Christianity was very superficial to begin with.

> We can find very easily all four Catholicisms in each of the twenty Latin American countries, but never in the same degree or in the same relation to one another. What can be affirmed of Peru and Bolivia, cannot be said of Chile and Argentina; and what may be observed in Colombia and Ecuador will be distinct from that noted in Mexico and Guatemala. Greater unity in greater diversity cannot be found in any area—religious, social, economic, or political—than can be found in Latin America.[29]

Uruguay is the least Catholic of all the countries and can be described as a secular state. By government decree Christmas is called "Family Day," and Holy Week is known as "Tourist Week." It is a democratic, open, peaceful nation with strong guarantees of civil rights. The people are largely unchurched and without any religious conviction.

Mexico, likewise, is a secular state. The Revolution of 1910 robbed the Catholic Church of most of its power. Since then Roman Catholicism has been on the defensive. The president is not permitted by the Constitution to attend mass during his six-year term of office. It is forbidden for the Catholic Church to engage in politics. All church property belongs to the state. No foreign priests or ministers have the authority to perform ecclesiastical functions.

The situation in Cuba is different again. Ever since Fidel Castro came to power in 1959 the Catholic Church has suffered various forms of opposition and persecution. In the early years of "liberation" some

---

[29] William J. Coleman, *Latin-American Catholicism: A Self Evaluation* (Maryknoll, N.Y.: Maryknoll Publications, 1958), p. 3.

six hundred priests either left the country or were deported to Spain. Some of these have been permitted to return. Cuba is the only Communist country in the world that maintains diplomatic relations with the Vatican.

PROTESTANT MISSIONS IN LATIN AMERICA

1. **Protestant missions in this part of the world got off to a late start.** Our earliest missionaries went to Southeast Asia, the Far East, and the Middle East long before they thought of taking the gospel to the lands south of the border. It was not until the middle of the nineteenth century that the first Protestant missionaries went to South America, and it was not until the 1870s that the movement built up any momentum. The Big Three were the United Presbyterians, the United Methodists, and the Southern Baptists. To this day these three boards have a huge investment in Latin America.

2. **Through the years American missions have enjoyed a virtual monopoly in Latin America.** One exception is the South American Missionary Society, an independent society of the Church of England, which maintains an important work in Argentina, Paraguay, and Chile. Another is the Canadian Baptists, who have had a strong mission in Bolivia ever since the turn of the century. Still another is the English Baptists in Brazil. There were several reasons why British and European missions never got deeply involved in Latin America. One, of course, was the fact that our Monroe Doctrine kept the European powers from meddling in the Western Hemisphere. Inasmuch as the cross often followed the flag, it was natural that British and European missions should avoid this part of the world. Another reason was the fact that in some circles Latin America was regarded as a Christian continent because the Roman Catholic Church had been there for four hundred years. Indeed, at the Edinburgh Missionary Conference in 1910, at the insistence of the Anglicans, it was clearly stated that Latin America was not to be considered as a mission field. Robert E. Speer and other American leaders opposed the idea, but the view prevailed.

3. **Latin America has attracted an abnormal number of conservative missionaries.** This differs from other major regions of the mission field where liberals and conservatives are found more or less in equal numbers. Conservative missionaries are found not only in the faith missions, but also in the main-line denominations. Consequently the churches they brought into existence are among the most conservative in the world. C. Peter Wagner, in his book *Latin American Theology,*

estimates that as many as 95 percent of the Protestants in Latin America are conservative evangelicals. This is one reason, doubtless the main reason, why the Ecumenical Movement has not been able to make much headway in Latin America.

4. The Pentecostal Movement, which got under way about the turn of the century, now has its adherents in all parts of the world; but Latin America is the continent where it has achieved their most spectacular results. In 1900 there were approximately fifty thousand Protestants in Latin America. By 1950 the number had climbed to the ten million mark. Twenty years later the figure had doubled to twenty million. Referring to an exhaustive study called *Church Growth in Latin America* published in 1969, Peter Wagner says:

> When this information was made available, one of the findings that surprised many observers was that 63.3 percent of all Latin American Protestants were Pentecostals of one kind or another. This proportion has undoubtedly increased since 1969, and is likely well above the two-thirds figure by now.[30]

According to Wagner the Pentecostals are the largest group of Protestants in ten of the twenty republics of Latin America. In Chile they outnumber all the other Protestants by nine to one. In Brazil the largest church, with 1,050,000 members, is the Assemblies of God. The second largest, with 500,000 members, is the Church of Christ in Brazil, another Pentecostal church. They are also the strongest group in Argentina, Peru, Ecuador, Colombia, Panama, El Salvador, Honduras, and Mexico. "Whether you are a Pentecostal or not, you have to admit that the Pentecostals are doing something right in Latin America."[31]

5. Latin America presents a unique situation vis-a-vis Protestant-Catholic relations. It is common knowledge that on the mission field there was no love lost between the Catholics and the Protestants. The rivalry between them was sometimes quite fierce, for they were competing for the same converts—the so-called heathen. But in Latin America the situation was different. There the two groups came into open, head-on conflict. It was not simply a case of competition but of direct opposition. When the Protestant missionaries appeared on the scene there were very few "heathen" to convert. More than 90 percent of the population was already "Christian." The Indians in some countries, like Colombia, were regarded as wards of the Roman Catholic Church and therefore off bounds to the Protestant missionaries. The Protestant missionaries, therefore, sought converts wherever they

---

[30] C. Peter Wagner, *Look Out! The Pentecostals Are Coming* (Carol Stream, IL: Creation House, 1973), p. 26.
[31] *Ibid.*, p. 26.

could find them—usually among the nominal Roman Catholics. Naturally the Roman Catholic Church looked upon these activities as "proselytizing" and persecution ensued.

However one looks at the situation, the fact remains that today there are some twenty million Protestants in Latin America, most of them converts from Roman Catholicism. These Protestants are divided into two distinct groups. The first is represented by the Lutheran and Waldensian churches located in the southern countries of Argentina, Uruguay, and Brazil. The Catholic Church has no quarrel with this small group, which is the result of European immigration. The second group comprises those Evangelical churches resulting from Protestant missionary work over the past century and the indigenous Pentecostal churches which have developed largely on their own. The Roman Catholic Church is *not* happy with this group, which the hierarchy claims is the result of "proselytizing."

Catholic leaders acknowledge their failure to properly educate their own people; at the same time they recognize that the Protestant missionary movement was characterized by "ample economic resources, very efficient technical methods, and systematic planning." Moreover, they accuse the missionaries of using unworthy methods to entice Catholics to defect from the church. These include economic benefits at the local level and scholarships for study in the United States. These favors, they claim, are given on condition that the beneficiaries join the Protestant faith.

Before we condemn the Catholics out of hand, we must remember that every Christian group regards its own constituency as composed of *bona fide* Christians and is resentful of any attempt on the part of others to take them away. The mainline denominations tend to resent the activities of the faith missions, sometimes referred to as "sects." The faith missions, on their part, resent the intrusion of charismatic groups who invade their ranks and run off with "their" Christians. This being so, it is not surprising that the Roman Catholic Church in Latin America should look with disfavor on the "proselytizing" activities of the Protestant missionaries. Given their political clout, as well as their ecclesiastical power, it is not difficult to understand why the Catholics proceeded to persecute the Protestants.

The Protestants, for their part, felt quite justified in their activities when they saw the low level of spiritual life manifested by the Catholics, the vast majority of whom never bothered to go to church except at Christmas and Easter. Speaking of Latin America Stephen Neill has remarked:

> It is not surprising that Protestant churches have regarded this
> as a field in which they may legitimately work; attempts to meet

the needs of those who have been left in such total spiritual desti-
tution can hardly be regarded as "proselytization" in any bad
sense of that word.[32]

6. **Much attention has been paid to church growth in this part of
the world.** This has been particularly true since the appearance of
Church Growth in Latin America in 1969. It is estimated that the
Protestant community throughout Latin America is growing at the rate
of 10 percent a year, which means it doubles every eight years. If this
continues Latin America could easily become a predominantly Protestant continent by the year 2000.

The growth pattern, however, has not been uniform. Some countries have registered higher gains than others. The fastest growth has
come in Brazil, Chile, and Colombia in South America; and in Mexico,
El Salvador, and Guatemala in Central America. Other countries
have not done so well, particularly Panama, Honduras, and Nicaragua.
In spite of recent growth four countries still have a Protestant population of less than 1 percent: Equador, Peru, Colombia, and Venezuela.

Nor have all the churches participated equally in the growth. In
most countries the Pentecostals have outdistanced everyone else. In
some countries the Seventh-day Adventists have done well. One denomination in Colombia, after 115 years of work, has a small church
of only sixteen hundred members. Another in Honduras, after seventy-
five years of work, reports a membership of only two thousand.

Particularly disappointing has been the lack of growth among the
faith missions. In 1969 they represented 32.4 percent of the missionary
force but only 1.5 percent of the communicant members. There are
several extenuating circumstances that should be borne in mind: (1)
They got a late start as compared with the mainline denominations.
(2) Many of the faith missions have done extensive work among the
Indians, who have proved to be much more resistant than the Latins.
Some of them are working *exclusively* among the Indian population.
(3) One very large faith mission, Wycliffe Bible Translators, is engaged in a technical form of missionary work, namely Bible translation, which only indirectly contributes to church growth.

7. **Missionaries are active among thirty million Indians.** In other
parts of the world, particularly in Southeast Asia, the greatest response
came from the aborigines. In Burma the tribespeople have produced
more than 95 percent of the Christian converts. Not so in Latin America. The Indians there, like the Indians in North America, have proved
to be impervious to the gospel. Missionaries have labored among them
for years with little or nothing to show for their efforts. Their languages

---

[32] Stephen Neill, *Call to Mission* (Philadelphia: Fortress Press, 1970), p. 86.

have been difficult to learn and Scripture translation has not kept pace with that in other parts of the world. Most of the translation that has taken place has been done by Wycliffe Bible Translators. Many of these Indian tribes are extremely primitive, live in isolated jungle areas of Amazonia and Mexico, and are wild and warlike, defying even government forces to subdue them. Through the years there has never been a people movement among them. Only recently has there been a moving of the Holy Spirit among the Quechuas of Ecuador, where some twenty-five hundred are reported to have turned to Christ in the last few years. This is the first major breakthrough in the evangelization of the Indians of Latin America.

8. Latin America has been the spawning ground for several important developments. One of these was Evangelism-in-Depth, which was the brainchild of R. Kenneth Strachan, the former general director of the Latin America Mission. The first crusade was held in Nicaragua in 1960. Since then EID has spread to over a dozen countries in Latin America and more recently has expanded, under different names, to Africa and Asia.

A second development was Theological Education by Extension, which began with the Presbyterian Seminary in Guatemala in 1960 and spread rapidly to all parts of the world. In Latin America alone more than ten thousand students are enrolled in seven hundred extension programs. Most of these men are pastors, many of whom have never before had any formal theological training. Seldom if ever in the history of theological education has an innovation received such overwhelming support.

A third development that augurs well for the future is known as the Venezuelan Experiment. It is a three-year in-depth approach to the problem of planting new churches. The first workshop was held in 1972, at which time forty-seven pastors and missionaries, in an act of faith, decided to work and pray towards the planting of fourteen new churches in four years. At the second workshop in 1973 they reported nineteen new churches in *one* year; whereupon they set a new goal of twenty-four new churches by 1977. There is every reason to believe they will far exceed their goal. Other countries in Latin America and Africa have requested similar workshops. Emphasis in these workshops is not simply on gospel preaching and soul saving, but on the planting of new churches. Too often in the past evangelistic crusades have generated enthusiasm and have registered a large number of first-time decisions, but they have not resulted in long-term church growth. The Venezuelan Experiment is a move in the right direction.

9. **Liberals and conservatives are divided into two separate and distinct camps.** Though the former are outnumbered nine to one they are better educated, better organized, and certainly more vocal than the conservatives. In the past decade there has been a rapid development in theological thinking, from theology of development to theology of liberation, and now to theology of revolution. The last-mentioned finds its highest and most cogent expression in Latin America.

The liberal theologians are deeply concerned about the deplorable social and economic conditions in Latin America and are thoroughly convinced that the present-day mission of the church is to right the wrongs that plague society. So deep-seated and long-standing are these evils that they can be eradicated only by the overthrow of the existing political systems. Given the political and military clout of the powers that be, liberation in Latin America can be achieved only by revolution.

The gulf between the liberals and the conservatives in Latin America is rather wide. The liberals consider the conservative churches to be lacking in social concern, altogether too "spiritual," and interested only in personal salvation. They are grateful for the contribution made by North American missionaries in years gone by but have grave doubts about the value of their continued presence in Latin America. The "gringos" can hardly be expected to understand, much less solve, the problems of Latin American society.

Their point of view, however, is not entirely correct. The conservatives, including the Pentecostals, are increasingly concerned about the social implications of the gospel and are speaking out against all forms of exploitation. At the grass roots they are engaging in social action and seeking to solve the problems of society, though understandably they are reluctant to adopt the radical methods of the new left. They believe they have theological as well as pragmatic reasons for wanting to work within the existing system rather than trying to overthrow it. But the gulf remains and it weakens the witness of the Protestant church.

10. **Nowhere in the world has the Ecumenical Movement had harder sledding than in Latin America.** One of its own leaders has confessed:

> The very term "ecumenical" tends to be a word of abuse in Latin America. The fact is that the enemies of the Movement got in first, and queered the pitch with their calumnies. Their chief accusations are that the World Council is pro-Communist, liberal in theology, guilty of the heresy of Universalism, activist instead

of spiritual, and friendly to the Catholic Church. Of these sins, the last is the worst.[33]

The above quotation is basically true. Rightly or wrongly that is what the Evangelicals think of the Ecumenical Movement, and not altogether without reason. The fact that 95 percent of the Evangelicals are conservative in their theology makes it possible for them to present a united front against what they consider to be a harmful influence. For that reason it has been very difficult for the Ecumenical Movement to make much headway in Latin America. Even the Presbyterians, who in other parts of the world have been in the vanguard of the Ecumenical Movement, are antiecumenical. The only denomination that is active in ecumenical matters is the Methodist Church.

There are half a dozen continent-wide ecumenical organizations. Two of the more important ones are ISAL (Church and State in Latin America) and UNELAM (Provisional Committee for Evangelical Unity in Latin America). Though not an integral part of the World Council of Churches these two organizations work closely with the world body. Seven National Councils are affiliated with the Division of World Mission and Evangelism of the WCC. That is the only organizational connection at present. ISAL is concerned almost exclusively with social and political action and works closely with progressive Roman Catholic priests and Marxists.

11. **It is impossible to speak of Latin America without making special mention of Brazil, the giant of the Southern Hemisphere.** According to the latest count there are three thousand missionaries in Brazil and more Evangelicals than in all the rest of South America combined. The four mainline denominations with their respective membership figures are the Lutherans (520,000), Baptists (400,000), Presbyterians (290,000), and Methodists (75,000). The Lutheran Church is made up largely of immigrants from Germany. The other three are the result of the work of American missionaries. Large as these churches are, they are dwarfed by three huge Pentecostal churches: the Assemblies of God, Congregacao Crista, and Brazil for Christ. Church growth in Brazil is unbelievably rapid.

12. **Several factors account for the phenomenal growth of the Pentecostals in Latin America:** (1) The churches have been largely indigenous from the beginning. Only a handful of missionaries are working with these huge churches. (2) These churches have been encouraged to pay their own way and manage their own affairs without the use of foreign funds. (3) They have made good use of lay

---

[33] Victor Hayward, "Latin America—An Ecumenical Bird's Eye View," *International Review of Mission* (April 1971), p. 176.

witness. Every Christian is expected to share his faith with his unsaved neighbors. Even the pastors are for the most part unordained
men. (4) Their lively church services, with plenty of music, hand-
clapping, and testimonies, appeal to the emotional nature of the Latins.
(5) They make their pitch to the lower classes, who make up the
bulk of the population; consequently these people feel at home in
the churches. (6) They have taken the gospel into the highways and
byways. Open-air meetings, Scripture distribution, and public parades
are a regular feature of their corporate witness. (7) They have emphasized the fullness of the Holy Spirit as an experience to be sought, not
simply as a doctrine to be believed. Faith healing is widely practiced
and has proved to be a great drawing card.

Europe

Ever since the beginning of the Holy Roman Empire, about A.D. 800,
Europe has been regarded as a Christian continent. This is no longer
true. Kenneth Scott Latourette, Hans Lilje, and other prominent
churchmen and historians have warned that Europe is rapidly becoming de-Christianized.

Several factors have contributed to this sad state of affairs. Secularism and humanism were spawned by the Renaissance. German
rationalism and higher criticism undermined the veracity and authority of the Holy Scriptures. Two world wars among the so-called Christian countries of the West and the failure of the Christian church in
Germany to offer more than token resistance to Nazism hardly enhanced the image of Christianity in Europe. The rise of the USSR and
the emergence of Communist governments in Eastern Europe have
imposed severe restrictions on the activities of the church in those
countries. The new theology and the new morality espoused by some
Protestant leaders in Western Europe have removed the ancient landmarks and left nominal church members in a spiritual vacuum. Vatican II and the rapid changes taking place in the Roman Catholic
Church have thrown the faithful into confusion. Non-Christian religions from the East, particularly Buddhism and Hinduism with their
mysticism and esoteric rites, are attracting a good deal of attention.
Muslims from Pakistan and North Africa are emigrating in large numbers to Europe in search of employment, higher wages, and a better
way of life. As a result mosques are being erected in the larger cities.

An estimated 160 million people in Europe make no profession of
religion. Among those who still claim allegiance to Christianity there
are few who take their religion seriously. France, though nominally
Roman Catholic, is the most pagan country in Europe. Fear and super-

stition abound, especially in the rural areas, and more and more people are turning to spiritism; so much so that the Roman Catholic Church now regards France as a mission field. In England 66 percent of the population are baptized by the Church of England; 26 percent go on to Confirmation; but only 9 percent remain as regular churchgoers. In the state churches of Europe the situation is even worse. Only 5 percent of the German Lutherans and 3 percent of the Swedish Lutherans attend church on a regular basis. By no stretch of the imagination can Europe be called a Christian continent. Oddly enough, the most virile form of Christianity is found in the Communist countries of Eastern Europe and the USSR.

It is difficult for Americans to understand and appreciate the difference between the religious situation in Europe and that in the United States. In the whole of Europe there is only one Christian radio station, and that was erected and is maintained by an American mission, Trans World Radio. It is possible to buy time on Radio Luxembourg and Radio Monte Carlo; but prime time is almost impossible to secure and when available is extremely expensive. Even in England the local churches cannot buy time on the British Broadcasting Corporation network. The Bible, available in so many editions and versions in the United States, is a rare book in many countries of Europe. The Bible school movement of the United States and Canada, which has done so much for the cause of evangelical Christianity at home and overseas, is practically unknown in Europe. The few Bible schools that do exist are largely the result of American initiative in this postwar period. During the last two centuries Europe has produced no great evangelists such as Charles G. Finney, Dwight L. Moody, or Billy Graham. In fact, mass evangelism as we understand it is an American phenomenon and not particularly appreciated by most European church leaders. The two largest confessional groups in Europe are the Anglicans and the Lutherans, both of which believe in baptismal regeneration. The emphasis is on religious education rather than individual conversion. The Methodists and the Baptists, who have traditionally preached repentance and faith as an integral part of the conversion experience, form a very small minority in Europe.

It was not until recent years that Europe came to be regarded as a mission field; and even today the historic denominations in the United States are reluctant to accept this point of view. The only large historical denomination with missionary work in Europe is the Southern Baptist Convention. Most of the American groups now working in Europe are evangelical and evangelistic and understand the missionary mandate to include all unregenerate persons regardless of their ecclesiastical connections. Nominal Christians have as much need for the gospel as the so-called pagans of the non-Christian world.

At present there are over eighty American societies in Europe. Together they account for 1,535 missionaries. In addition there are several hundred missionaries from Great Britain and the Commonwealth countries. The idea of Europe as a mission field did not really catch on until after World War II, when there was a sudden influx of missions from North America. Prior to that, however, there were several well-established America-based missionary societies in Europe.

Special mention should be made of the radio ministry of Trans World Radio, which began broadcasting from Monaco in 1960. Today it is beaming the gospel in thirty-one languages into all parts of Europe, Russia, North Africa, and the Middle East. TWR broadcasts seven days a week over medium, short, and long wave transmitters with a total of more than half a million watts. Studios in various parts of Europe and the Middle East furnish tapes which are mailed to Monte Carlo. A German branch, Evangeliums-Rundfunk, is now part of TWR and, with a staff of fifty full-time workers, produces five daily programs in German. The German branch is a work of faith and is entirely self-supporting. In some countries behind the Iron Curtain the German programs are the only spiritual nourishment available to German Christians.

In the state churches theological education is at the university level and seminary graduates usually know more about Barth, Brunner, and Bultmann than they do about the Bible. Among the free churches there are 29 indigenous Bible schools in the United Kingdom and 20 on the continent, of which six belong to the Pentecostal churches. Additional Bible schools have been established in this postwar period by American missions. A leader in this field is Greater Europe Mission. If the people of Europe are ever to be reached with the gospel, it will have to be by Europeans themselves. An unsolved problem is the reluctance of the state churches to accept the humble Bible school graduates as "men of the cloth." This too is changing as an acute shortage of pastors is forcing some state churches to accept Bible school graduates as assistant pastors.

What is the best way to evangelize Europe? To work through the existing churches, many of which are state or quasi state churches, or to start new churches? Most people would agree that the former is the more desirable; but is it feasible? When Protestant missionaries first went to the Middle East in the early part of the nineteenth century it was with the idea of reviving the Eastern churches and through them evangelizing the Muslim population. The attempt was not very successful because the Orthodox churches did not wish to be revived and resented any attempt on the part of the Western missionaries to infiltrate their ranks. Something of the same situation exists in the state churches of Europe. It has not proved easy to cooperate with them for reasons which are both theological and cultural.

For the most part, missionaries involved in church planting are working outside the state churches. Among the free churches and some independent groups they have been more successful. In some parts, where the free churches do not exist, the missionaries have had to start from scratch and build churches of their own. Most of the inter-denominational missions in Europe are devoting considerable time and energy to church planting.

Missionary work in Europe differs in many respects from that in other parts of the world. Illiteracy is no problem. Mission schools, which played an important role in the evangelization of Africa, are nonexistent. The same is true of medical work. Bible translation is no problem, since the Bible has been available in most of the languages of Europe for many years. Indeed, many of the European countries for decades have had their own Bible societies. In some countries schools for missionaries' children are not needed; the children attend local public schools. This sets the missionaries free for evangelism, church planting, radio broadcasting, and theological education.

There are approximately 110 million Protestants in Europe. The two largest groups are the Lutherans (60 million) and the Anglicans (30 million). The Lutherans are found in Germany and the four Scandinavian countries, Denmark, Norway, Sweden, and Finland. About 80 percent of the people of East Germany and some 50 percent of the West Germans are Lutherans. In Scandinavia it is anywhere from 90 percent to 97 percent. Of the thirty million Anglicans, almost twenty-eight million are found in England; the other two million are divided among Scotland, Wales, and Northern Ireland. There are no Anglican churches on the continent and no Lutheran churches in the United Kingdom, except for expatriates.

The remaining Protestants, made up of Baptists, Methodists, Pentecostals, Mennonites, Presbyterians, and Reformed, are found in relatively small groups in various parts of Europe. The Waldensian Church, the oldest Protestant church in the world, is located in Italy. It has a constituency of thirty-five thousand.

Many of the Protestant churches are state churches, supported by state funds and subservient to government control. Under such a system all citizens, Christian and non-Christian, are required to support the church. Such an arrangement is a source of irritation to the non-Christians and a serious detriment to the initiative of the church members, who feel no obligation to give to the support of the church. The pastors on their part have no great urge to seek the lost, to preach the gospel, or even to fill the pews. Their position is secure and their income is guaranteed regardless of performance. In England both church membership and seminary enrollment are decreasing rapidly. Religion is at its lowest ebb since the days of John Wesley. The situation is much better in Scotland and Northern Ireland, where the Presbyterians are numerically strong and church attendance is high. Even so, England is much better off than the Lutheran countries. In the Anglican Church there is a strong evangelical wing. In addition there are some six million non-Conformist church members in Great Britain, and church attendance among them is much higher than is the case with the Anglicans. Among the non Conformists there are evangelical denominations; and in all denominations there are some evangelical churches and preachers.

Europe with 252 million Roman Catholics is still a predominantly Roman Catholic continent. Fifty million of these 252 million, however, are behind the Iron Curtain, leaving roughly 200 million Roman Catholics in Free Europe. The three largest concentrations are in France, Italy, and Spain, which account for 127 million of the 200 million Catholics in Free Europe. These are the three countries which have attracted the largest number of missionaries from North America: France (372), Italy (174), and Spain (202).

While strife within the church is increasing, tension between Catholics and Protestants is on the wane. Ever since John XXIII substituted the term "separated brethren" for "heretics," a general *rapprochement* has been taking place between Roman Catholics and Protestants in all parts of the world. Two archbishops of Canterbury have visited the Vatican, but the pope has not returned the compliment. There is a growing spirit of cooperation between the Roman Catholic Church and the World Council of Churches. The General Secretary of the WCC has more than once visited the Vatican, and Pope Paul paid a historic visit to Geneva in June 1969. A Joint Working Committee is only one of many cooperative ventures of the two world bodies. While it is still too early to talk about the RCC joining the WCC, the RCC is now definitely part of the ecumenical movement.

The winds of change blowing through the Vatican have been felt to the ends of the earth, and Protestant missionaries in Roman Catholic countries are grateful for an increasing measure of religious liberty. This is particularly true in Italy and Spain, and to a lesser degree in Portugal. The coup in 1974 brought new freedom to Portugal.

Besides the USSR there are eight Communist countries in Eastern Europe. They are East Germany, Poland, Rumania, Czechoslovakia, Hungary, Bulgaria, Yugoslavia, and Albania. Three of these countries are predominantly Roman Catholic in religion: Poland, Hungary, and Czechoslovakia. Three are predominantly Eastern Orthodox: Bulgaria, Rumania, and Yugoslavia. Albania is 70 percent Muslim. In the USSR there are probably 40 million members of the Russian Orthodox

Church and perhaps as many as 5 million evangelicals. So when we think of Communist Europe we must not assume that all, or even a majority, of the people are Communists. Only a small fraction of the population are card-carrying Communists, even in the USSR. In all nine countries there are probably not more than 25 million Communists out of a total population of 375 million.

According to orthodox Marxism, religion is the opiate of the people; the church is an anachronistic, reactionary institution; and full-time religious workers are parasites on the body of society. This being so, one would not expect the church to fare very well under a Communist government. On the other hand, Communists the world over pose as the authors and guardians of genuine democracy and are careful to include in their constitution an article guaranteeing religious freedom. However, there is always a gap between the promise and the performance. Liberty, as we in the West understand the term, simply does not exist in a Communist country. Sooner or later every organization and institution is required to toe the party line. This is the price of survival. The church has usually been the last and the most difficult institution to bring under control.

The picture in Eastern Europe is spotty. The degree of religious freedom varies from country to country. Indeed, it may well vary from place to place within a given country; or it may change overnight without any apparent reason. The most predictable thing about the Communists is their unpredictability. One thing, however, seems certain. The Communists have not changed their view of religion. It is a bourgeois invention and will completely disappear when scientific socialism becomes universal. In the meantime the church will be permitted to exist but not grow. It can worship but not witness. Religious services must be confined to church buildings. To hold a meeting in a private home is to invite trouble. Open-air meetings are out of the question. However, there will be no persecution. The state will not make martyrs. If certain influential leaders must be removed, it will be on trumped-up charges with a moral or political complexion. Under these conditions, so they think, the church will gradually wither and die.

The church, like all other organizations, must be completely subservient to the state. It must agree to support the establishment of socialism leading to Communism; and this must be done under the leadership of the Communist party.

After more than fifty years of repression religion is by no means dead in the Soviet Union. The largest church is the Orthodox Church, with some 40 million members. The All Union Council of Evangelical Christians-Baptists, which includes Mennonites, Plymouth Brethren, and Pentecostals, represents a community of about 5 million. In recent years a rift has appeared among the Evangelicals, with a militant group known as the Initiators demanding full religious freedom and accusing their leaders of collaboration with the government. Some members of this dissident group have been arrested and others have been sent to labor camps in Siberia. In some instances their children have been placed in state institutions where they are indoctrinated with Communist ideology. Lutherans, found mostly in Latvia and Estonia, number approximately 1 million. The Roman Catholic Church reports 3,200,000 members. There are also small groups of Methodists and Adventists.

There is ample evidence that the Russian government has recently stepped up its persecution of both Jews and Christians. In November 1969, sixty-two members of the Council of Evangelical Christians-Baptists addressed an open letter "to all Christians of the world," in which they clearly documented the many instances of persecution and imprisonment, giving names, dates, and places. Towards the end the letter states:

> We accept the ever-increasing persecutions and sufferings as from the hands of our heavenly Father. They cannot separate us from the love of God in Christ Jesus. . . . We are condemned as in the days of Esther; all, one after another, to be sent to prison, harsh camps and exile. We have carefully studied the findings of investigations, the interrogation of witnesses at trials, sentences; and we declare before all the world that our relatives have been sentenced and are suffering for professing faith in God. Proof of this is provided by the universal offers of freedom in the camps and prisons in return for apostasy; by the denying of Bibles to prisoners; by the constant and universal confiscation of spiritual and religious literature.

The letter closes with an earnest plea:

> Dear children of God! The intention of our appeal to you is a heartfelt request to take warm part in prayer to our omnipotent Father, that He might look upon the threats of our persecutors and give His servants strength to speak the Word of God with all boldness (Acts 4:29).

Doubtless the most effective outside aid now being given to the evangelical Christians behind the Iron Curtain is the radio ministry. The gospel is beamed into Russia, including Siberia, from powerful short-wave transmitters in Monte Carlo, Quito, Addis Ababa, Manila, and Seoul. So effective are these broadcasts that they have attracted the attention of the Soviet authorities and been denounced in *Pravda*. In many isolated communities these Christian programs are the only spiritual nourishment available to the evangelicals.

Christian leaders from the West are now permitted to pay short visits to most of these Communist countries. In some cases they have been invited to preach in the churches. Billy Graham held a short rally in Yugoslavia. In all cases they reported a warm reception from the church leaders and a deep hunger for the Word of God on the part of the Christians. Doubtless it will be some time before missionaries from the West are permitted to resume normal operations in that part of the world.

6

Political Involvement

The missionary carries with him two important documents, a Bible and a passport. Both are essential to his life and work in a foreign country.

The Bible identifies him as an ambassador for Christ. As such he is a citizen of the world. He is a true internationalist. He represents a universal king—Jesus Christ. He belongs to a universal body—the church. He preaches a universal message—the gospel. In this capacity he would like to think of himself as being above national and even international politics.

But he also carries a passport and that links him irrevocably with an earthly kingdom. For better or worse his fortune and destiny are linked with those of his own country. When it performs well he is happy and proud. When it fails to perform well he is distressed and ashamed. Never for a moment is he permitted to forget that he is an American, or a Canadian, or an Englishman, as the case may be. When war breaks out he is expected to take orders from his consul general or bear the consequences. Even in time of peace it is impossible for him to disassociate himself completely from his own government, its foreign policy, and its international obligations.

The apostle Paul had no such problem. He was a Roman citizen and functioned within the confines of the Roman Empire. When he got into trouble he had only to appeal to the local authorities for justice and protection. But the modern missionary has not had it quite so easy. Many of them have been caught in the crossfire of the Sino-Japanese War, the Arab-Israeli War, the Indian-Pakistani War, as well as civil war in Nigeria, China, Vietnam, Zaire, and Burundi, to say nothing of the Cold War that has a way of heating up from time to time.

So it comes about that the Christian mission at certain times and in certain places has been caught in the coils of colonialism, nationalism, and Communism.

Missions and Colonialism

Modern colonialism began with the Vasco da Gama era about the year 1500. The first European powers to be involved were Portugal and Spain, followed some time later by Holland, France, and Great Britain. In time all the great powers of Europe were engaged in empire building. Finally, about the turn of the twentieth century, the United States got in on the act and acquired the Philippines after the Spanish-American War.

The colonial period reached its zenith in the nineteenth century, by which time most of Asia and Africa was parceled out among the European powers. It was that same century which K. S. Latourette called "The Great Century" of modern missions in all parts of the world. Missions and colonialism not only ran a parallel course but they operated in the same regions of the world. It was inevitable, therefore, that these two great forces should meet and mingle.

The relationship between missions and colonialism was by no means uniform in all parts of the world. In some countries there was active and cordial cooperation. In others there was mutual distrust and recrimination. Colonial governments did not always look with favor on the missionaries. Quite often they opposed them.

The alliance between missions and colonialism was much greater in Roman Catholic countries. The popes of Rome and the kings of Portugal and Spain worked hand in glove. There was no separation of church and state, at home or overseas. The French colonial governments regarded themselves as the guardians of Christianity and acted accordingly. The Dutch, and more especially the British, were inclined to remain neutral, sometimes antagonistic to Christian missions. The British East India Company went out of its way to make life miserable for the missionaries, often denying them passage on its boats and residence in its territories. Its officers made no attempt to disguise their contempt for this new breed of men:

The sending out of missionaries into our Eastern possessions is the maddest, most extravagant, most costly, most indefensible project which has ever been suggested by a moonstruck fanatic. Such a scheme is pernicious, imprudent, useless, harmful, dangerous, profitless, fantastic. It strikes against all reason and sound policy; it brings the peace and safety of our possessions into peril.

Actually there were three kinds of imperialism: political, represented by the diplomat; economic, represented by the merchant; and cultural, represented by the missionary. As far as the indigenous population was concerned there was little to choose among these three forms of imperialism. All came from the same source; all shared the same ambitions; all were bent on conquest of one kind or another.

From the very beginning these three forms were inextricably bound together. From its founding in 1603 the Dutch East India Company directed its governors in Java to "develop trade in the Indies to the profit of the great name of Christ and the salvation of the pagans."[1] The Sierra Leone Company was founded "to introduce trade, industry and Christian knowledge"[2] to that part of Africa. Other large trading companies had similar statements written into their charters. Bartholomew Ziegenbalg in 1705 and Alexander Duff in 1829 both carried with them letters of introduction to the colonial authorities in India.

In the early years in Africa the missionaries themselves engaged in various kinds of trade with the "natives." They introduced a primitive form of commerce to offset the appeal of the lucrative slave trade, described by Livingstone as the "open sore of the world." In time they came to control the economic, social, and political life of the people who sought refuge in their residential mission stations. In the beginning most of these people were ex-slaves, refugees, and other hapless persons who looked to the missionaries for safety and sustenance. The missionaries took them in, fed them, clothed them, disciplined them, and tried—not too successfully—to teach them the rudiments of Christianity.

Everywhere—at home and overseas—it was taken for granted that there was an essential connection linking commerce, civilization, and Christianity. In his great speech in Albert Hall on July 5, 1895, Lord Roseberry, in reply to the question, "What is liberal imperialism?" replied:

Liberal imperialism implies, first, the maintenance of the Empire; secondly, the opening of new areas for our surplus population; thirdly, the suppression of the slave trade; fourthly, the develop-

---

[1] R. C. Delavignette, *Christianity and Colonialism* (New York: Hawthorn Books, 1964), p. 104.

[2] Max Warren, *Social History and Christian Mission* (London: SCM Press, 1967), p. 23.

ment of missionary enterprise; and fifthly, the development of
our commerce, which so often needs it.[3]

In the missionary literature of the nineteenth century the three
words "commerce," "civilization," and "Christianity" occur again and
again as if they belonged together. Livingstone, in his famous address
to the Senate House of Cambridge University in December 1857, appealed for young men to go to Central Africa "to open a path for
commerce and Christianity." One is not surprised to read that the
Universities' Mission to Central Africa, which resulted from that visit
to Cambridge, stated that its plan of action was to "establish centers
of Christianity and civilization for the promotion of true religion, agriculture, and lawful commerce."[4]

What was the result of this approach? The mission stations in
East Africa developed into full-fledged economic and political units
governed and directed by the missionaries.

In most countries there was a good deal of mutuality between the
missionaries and the colonial administrators. The latter provided the
missionaries with protection, gave them preferential treatment, and
often subsidized their schools. The missionaries returned the compliment. By their educational and medical work they made a significant
contribution to the difficult work of "civilizing the natives," which in
turn aided the government in the administration of its affairs.

The average church member in America has little conception of
the extent to which Christian missions in the nineteenth century were
tied in with the vast worldwide colonial structure. Almost without
exception the missionaries of the nineteenth century lived and worked
under colonial systems of one kind or another. With or without com-
punction they had to accept the realities of the situation as they
found it.

In the Near East the American missionaries worked in such close
collaboration with the State Department that J. L. Grabill, writing
about the situation in 1971, called his book *Protestant Diplomacy and
the Near East: Missionary Influence on American Policy, 1810-1927*. In
the Pacific Islands the missionaries helped to write the laws. At different times they acted as prime ministers, foreign ministers, presidents
of the court of appeal, and agents general for the crown.

A British Government Commission of Inquiry in 1884 described
the situation in Tonga as follows:

> Though possessing a King and a nominally constituted form of
> Government, all power is practically vested in a Wesleyan clergy-

---

[3] *Ibid.*, p. 30.
[4] Roland Oliver, *The Missionary Factor in East Africa* (New York: Longmans,
Green and Co., 1952), p. 13.

man named Baker, whose influence is paramount and closely re-
sembles ... in the causes to which it is due and the mode in
which it is exercised, that of some political churchman in the
Middle Ages.[5]

In the British colonies of Africa the Anglican bishops of the Church
Missionary Society flew the Union Jack on their limousines. Of course,
they had access to Government House anytime they wished. Some
missionaries acted as official representatives of the queen. From time
to time missionaries submitted memorials to the foreign secretary
urging him to take certain actions designed to facilitate the missionary
cause. When the British Government in the 1880s could not extend
its diplomatic connections to Mombasa and Lake Nyasa, both the
Church Missionary Society and the Free Church of Scotland asked
that vice-consular status be granted to two of their leading missionaries.

When in 1888-89 the East Africa Companies engaged in war with
the Arabs, the Scottish Presbyterian missionaries as a body were adamantly in support of the war, and some of them actually took up arms
against the Arabs.

The colonial administrators in Africa had good reason to look with
favor on the activities of the missionaries.

> Except for the relatively small class of educated Swahilis at the
> coast, there was no other source than the mission centers to which
> they could look for their minor officials, clerks, interpreters and
> policemen, for their semi-skilled builders and joiners, or even for
> reliable unskilled labor, messengers, orderlies and domestic serv-
> ants. At a time when law and order, the introduction of currency,
> the promotion of local trade and the beginning of taxation were
> the main preoccupations of government, mission employees and
> adherents stood out from the rest as prosperous and orderly.
> They paid their taxes and they understood the new regime. Until
> private European settlement became extensive, the mission planta-
> tions alone produced the sorely needed cash crops.[6]

It would be a mistake, however, to accuse the missionaries of being
merely an auxiliary of the imperial expansion.

> There is no evidence from either of the British territories in East
> Africa to suggest that this early community of interests between
> missions and governments was regarded by either side as any-
> thing more than a happy accident. Neither agency had any idea
> of deviating from its own natural course in order to form a more
> powerful combination with the other.[7]

Nowhere in Asia was the tie-in between the gospel and the gun-

---

[5] Norman Goodall, *Christian Missions and Social Ferment* (London: Epworth
Press, 1964), p. 24.
[6] Oliver, *op. cit.*, p. 177.
[7] *Ibid.*, p. 179.

boat closer than in China. For centuries China managed to keep out the unwanted foreigners—known as "barbarians." During the first decades of the nineteenth century there were misunderstanding, arrogance, and threats on both sides. The Western powers were determined to open China with her teeming population to Western trade. China was equally determined she would have nothing to do with the barbarians except in the one port of Canton. The issue finally erupted in the Opium War between Britain and China (1839-1842). The Treaty of Nanking which followed the war forced China, among other concessions, to open five treaty ports. Who entered these ports but the merchants with their opium and the missionaries with their Bibles.

To make matters worse, missionaries acted as interpreters when the treaties were drawn up. Particularly galling to the Chinese was the matter of extraterritoriality, which placed all foreigners under the legal protection of their respective consuls rather than under the Chinese courts. They also promised protection from persecution for the converts as well as the missionaries. It was not until 1943 that Great Britain and the United States agreed voluntarily to abolish extraterritoriality. By this time, of course, the damage was done. For exactly one hundred years these unequal treaties were a millstone around the necks of the missionaries. It was one thing to open inland China to foreign trade and residence; it was quite another to open the hearts of the Chinese people to the influence of the gospel. The first could be effected by military might; the second was not amenable to force of any kind. The Chinese people can be forgiven if they had difficulty in understanding why the same "Christian" government was interested in forcing both opium and religion on China at the same time. Little wonder that the Communists when they came to power talked incessantly about religion being the opiate of the people!

During the latter half of the nineteenth century Protestant and Roman Catholic missionaries appealed to their own governments times without number to force the Manchu-Chinese officials to crack down on those responsible for anti-Western riots. Doubtless the missionaries meant well; but the impression created was far from good.

> The appeals unto Caesar for assistance in promoting the Christian gospel were defended by the missionaries as necessary to bring the government to maintain order; and order, they declared, would benefit the Chinese quite as much as the missionary. Thereby the missionaries inextricably identified themselves with the governments of Western nations with the inevitable result that the Chinese considered them part and parcel of Western imperialism.[8]

[8] Paul A. Varg, *Missionaries, Chinese and Diplomats: The American Protestant Missionary Movement in China, 1890-1952* (Princeton University Press, 1958), p. 41.

In China, as elsewhere, the missionaries lent their services when needed to their respective governments. As already mentioned the missionaries acted as interpreters when the unequal treaties were drawn up. More than that, several of them accepted official positions in the various embassies. In 1856 Dr. Peter Parker, first medical missionary to China, left missionary service to become the American Commissioner to China. Another missionary, S. Wells Williams, became Secretary of Legation. And the last American ambassador accredited to Chiang Kai-shek's Nationalist Government in Nanking in 1949 was a veteran missionary, Dr. Leighton Stuart. Consequently the Chinese Communists had plenty of ammunition when they declared war on the missionaries in the early 1950s.

It must be said, however, that for the most part the missionaries were law-abiding aliens and had no need to invoke the extraterritoriality clause in the unequal treaties. But the very fact that it was there was offensive to the Chinese. On the other hand, it is worth noting that the missionaries in China lived under conditions that were extremely irritating. Chinese xenophobia accused them of all sorts of atrocities, including kidnapping and killing babies, and gouging out their hearts and eyes to make medicine. As a result there were more missionary martyrs in China than in any other single mission field in the world.

The clause regarding the persecution of Christian converts dealt with a very complex problem. There was, of course, a good deal of persecution, which was a violation of the treaties. On the other hand, it must be acknowledged that many Chinese, not all of them genuine converts, abused the clause for their own selfish reasons. Missionaries were not always wise in the way they handled these cases of persecution.

Nowhere was missionary influence on politics greater than in the Pacific Islands. An official statement issued by the British Consul in Tahiti stated clearly: "The laws are framed by the missionaries, and brought forward by the chiefs at their meeting."[9] The laws were based on the Scriptures and the ethical code was taken largely from the Bible. It is no exaggeration to say that the missionaries were the legislators of the islands.

Korea was the one country in the world where colonialism was Oriental and not Western. There both the missionaries and the Christian leaders vigorously opposed the efforts of the Japanese to subjugate the Korean people and plough under the indigenous culture. As a result the missionaries, almost all of them American, became

---

[9] Aarne A. Koskinen, *Missionary Influence as a Political Factor in the Pacific Islands* (Helsinki: Suomalaisen Tiedeakatemian Toimituksia Annales Academiae Scientiarum Fennicae, 1953), p. 58.

persona non grata. By the time Pearl Harbor occurred there were no missionaries left in Korea.

As a general rule the mission boards in the homelands frowned on any attempt by the missionaries to meddle in politics, and frequently gave instructions to that effect. The missionaries, however, could not altogether extricate themselves from the political milieu in which they found themselves. What seemed like a noble ideal in London or New York did not always appear to be a wise course of action in Africa or Asia. Faced with the disintegration of the old social order on the one hand and with the intrusion of a powerful political dynamism from the West on the other, the missionaries could not always remain aloof.

How are we to account for the close association of Christianity and colonialism in the nineteenth century? And what was the gut reaction of the missionaries to a system which was essentially immoral?

1. In those days imperialism was a way of international life. All the great powers of Europe had their colonies, and because everybody was in on the act nobody thought it was wrong. At the turn of the century the concept of Manifest Destiny so gripped the American people that we too came to believe that Almighty God had chosen us to be the world's great benefactor.

Albert J. Beveridge, running for the United States Senate after the outbreak of the war with Spain, summed it up pretty well:

> Fate has written our policy for us; the trade of the world must and shall be ours. . . . Our institutions will follow our flag on wings of commerce. And American law, American order, American civilization, and the American flag will plant themselves on shores hitherto bloody and benighted but by those agencies of God henceforth to be made beautiful and bright.[10]

Like everyone else, the missionaries were and are the product of their age—no better and no worse than their peers.

2. Even those missionaries who had misgivings tended to regard colonialism as the less of two evils. Intertribal warfare and the slave trade in Africa were decimating the population. The missionaries were on the spot and had first-hand experience with the indescribable sufferings of the African peoples. They themselves were helpless to stop either the wars or the trade. That required the kind of military force that only some outside power could provide. Faced with this dilemma, the missionaries decided that a colonial administration would be better than a continuation of the iniquitous slave trade. Hence their decision to invite the European powers to take over.

---

[10] Frederick Merk, *Manifest Destiny and Mission in American History* (New York: Knopf, 1963), p. 232.

3. **Many missionaries regarded colonialism, evil though it was, as an instrument by which God was working out His sovereign purpose in the world.** They argued that if God could make the wrath of man to praise Him, and used pagan nations to chastise Israel, surely He could use colonialism to achieve His purpose. This was certainly true in China.

> That the [opium] war was unjust, the missionary S. Wells Williams admitted, but the results of injustice in this case led him to observe that "it is the prerogative of the Governor of nations to educe good out of evil, and make the wrath, the avarice, and the ambition of men to serve his purpose and advance his own designs, although their intentions may be far otherwise."[11]

This kind of reasoning was easy to accept when imperialism opened the door for the proclamation of the gospel in the most ancient, most populous kingdom in the world.

We in this enlightened day find it hard to believe that the missionaries of the nineteenth century could have had such a blind spot. But before we condemn them out of hand let us remember that we are in grave danger of doing the same thing only in a different context. There are not wanting today people who tell us that God is just as surely working through the secular movements of our day as He is through the established church. Indeed, we are told that Communism was God's judgment on Chiang Kai-shek and the Kuomintang in China. If we can believe that Communism with its kangaroo courts, its firing squads, its bloody purges, its concentration camps, and its totalitarian system of government can be used by God to establish a more just and equitable social system, can we not also believe that the colonial system of a bygone age was also part of His plan and purpose in the unfolding of human history?

4. **The missionaries were among the first to detect and detest the evils of the colonial system under which they lived.** The China missionaries openly advocated the abolition of the unequal treaties long before either the foreign diplomat or the foreign merchant were in favor of such a move. When in January 1926, eighteen missionary bodies advocated treaty revision, the business point of view was strongly expressed by the British-owned *North China Herald,* which lashed out at the National Christian Council for its stand on political questions. J. V. A. MacMurray, the American Minister in Peking, likewise took a strong stand against the missionaries. When the treaties were finally revised in 1943 no group was happier than the missionaries.

It should also be noted that while the missionaries were content to live with the colonial system, they invariably spoke out against all

---

[11] Varg, *op. cit.,* p. 5.

forms of discrimination and exploitation involving the indigenous population. They objected when the colonial government in Kenya decided to take the best land in the Highlands away from the Africans and sell it to the white settlers. They protested to the Government House in Nairobi and the Colonial Office in London. They wrote letters to the leading newspapers in England. They persuaded influential friends at home to contact members of Parliament. In short, they did everything in their power to prevent the takeover. In China the missionaries carried on a running battle with their own governments regarding the opium traffic. In the South Pacific they exposed the atrocities committed by the whalers and other unscrupulous white men.

Where the missionaries thought colonial rule would be the less of two evils—as was the case in Central Africa—they encouraged the European powers to intervene. In other instances they opposed imperialism.

> The Anglican missionaries in New Zealand were the strongest opponents of imperial expansion, and yielded only when it seemed apparent that, if the British did not come in, the French would do so. If Basutoland is today an independent and self-governing country, that is largely due to the labours of the great French and Swiss missionaries, who held the Boers at a distance, and kept alive the soul of a people under the shelter of a British protectorate which genuinely gave protection.[12]

Was colonialism good or bad? It depends on who answers the question. To the fiery nationalist colonialism was an unmitigated evil with no redeeming features. To the colonialist it was an unmixed blessing for which the "natives" should have been devoutly thankful. Doubtless the truth lies somewhere between the two extremes. Not all colonial systems were equally enlightened or progressive. It seems fair to say that the British type was perhaps the best of all. Certainly Great Britain left behind in India a political legacy for which the Indian people today are grateful. French colonialism was likewise fairly progressive. Italian and Belgian colonialism was considerably less enlightened; and the Portuguese brand was the most repressive and reactionary of them all.

If the missionaries had to live under a colonial system, naturally they preferred their own kind. Protestant missionaries were horrified at the thought of coming under the domination of a Roman Catholic power; and the Catholic missionaries, though with less reason, similarly feared a Protestant power.

5. The missionaries always believed that their first allegiance was

12 Stephen Neill, *Colonialism and Christian Missions* (New York: McGraw-Hill, 1966), p. 414.

to Jesus Christ and not to any government, good or bad. When colonial policy was obviously wrong, they said so. When incompetent and corrupt officials were allowed to remain in office, they objected. In times of war or civil war, when the consuls advised their missionaries to leave for safer regions, almost to a man they preferred to remain, especially if by so doing they could assist or protect their beloved people, Christian and non-Christian alike.

> From the days of Las Casas in New Spain to the days of the Anglican bishops in East Africa at the time of the enforced labour ordinances, there has been a memorable succession of missionaries who were not afraid to fight their own governments, and to jeopardize their own comfort and reputation for the sake of what they understood to be justice to those for whom they could speak and who could not speak for themselves.[13]

In the final analysis the Christian missionary is an ambassador for Christ. Consequently he takes his orders from his Commander-in-Chief. Jesus Christ is not only the Head of the church. He is also the Lord of history and the King of nations. The missionary must always be a law-abiding citizen of the host country, and he will surely think twice before ignoring or rejecting the advice of the American counsul; but his ultimate allegiance is always to Jesus Christ.

6. The missionaries have remained at their posts. In spite of the restrictions imposed upon them by the newly independent governments, the missionaries as a group have elected to carry on—business as usual. If it was a mistake to go in with the colonialists, it would have been a bigger mistake to come out with them. And this fact has not been lost on the political leaders in the Third World. At long last they seem to be drawing a distinction between missionaries and other groups who live and work abroad. It would appear that these leaders have come to realize that the missionaries, in spite of their failings and shortcomings, are their best, if not their only, friends. In many instances following independence missionary residences and Christian churches have been spared when United States government buildings have been burned to the ground. Even the popular Peace Corps has been expelled from half a dozen countries of Africa and Asia; yet those same countries have taken no action against the missionaries.

7. Few missionaries have mourned the passing of the colonial era. The stigma of "cultural imperialism" has been removed. The missionary now stands or falls on his own merit. No longer is he embarrassed by the Union Jack or the Stars and Stripes fluttering in the breeze. No longer does he have to apologize for the foreign gunboat in the harbor. He is now free to be an ambassador for Christ.

---

[13] *Ibid.*, p. 415.

Missions and Nationalism

If colonialism was the greatest force in the nineteenth century, surely nationalism has been the most potent force in the twentieth century. Nationalism existed long before the Communist Manifesto took shape in the mind of Karl Marx, and it will endure long after Communism has ceased to be a force in the world. We once thought that Communism was a mammoth monolithic system; but in recent years we have had second thoughts about the matter. Events in Poland, Hungary, East Germany, Yugoslavia, and Czechoslovakia provide ample evidence that nationalism runs far deeper in the human spirit than Communism. Even states that are not prepared to give up Communism demand that they be permitted to develop their own brand of national Communism. If anyone wants proof of this he need only look at the rift in the 1960s between Moscow and Peking.

Modern nationalism—nationalism in the Third World—was the direct result of colonialism. Had it not been for the colonialism of the nineteenth century we would not have had the nationalism of the twentieth century, certainly not to the same extent.

There is nothing wrong with nationalism *per se*. It is a natural and inevitable stage through which all people must pass on their way from colonialism to independence. It corresponds to the period of adolescence in the development of the individual. Adolescence does not last forever; it soon gives way to the maturity of adulthood, which is characterized by interdependence. Nations likewise pass through three stages—colonialism, nationalism, and independence. The period of nationalism, like adolescence, is usually a very turbulent time; but if properly handled it can prove to be both peaceful and productive. It becomes destructive only when it is thwarted by its opponents or distorted by its proponents. Every person wants to be master in his own house. Every nation wants to be in charge of its own affairs. Good rule is no substitute for home rule.

U Nu, Prime Minister of Burma, speaking in 1955 at the National Press Club in Washington, aptly described the genius of nationalism:

> First of all Burma has a long history. We had a great and flourishing civilization in Burma, based on one of the great religions of the world, Buddhism, at the time when William the Conqueror was crossing the English Channel.
>
> This civilization, passed on to us by our forbears, has now become our national heritage. It is our way of life. We prefer it to any other way of life on this earth. We do not say that it cannot be improved or that it cannot be adapted to suit modern conditions; but we do not wish to change its basis. We are not prepared to exchange it for any other way of life.

This is not a matter of conceit. We do not claim that our way of life is better than that of other people. We merely say that it is different, that it suits us better, and that we cannot therefore be induced to give it up in exchange for some other way of life, be that the Communist way, the West European way, the American way, or any other way.

When the Philippines was agitating for independence from the United States its national leaders developed what came to be known as Mabini's Decalogue:

Thou shalt love thy country after God and thine honor more than thyself; for she is the only Paradise which God has given thee in this life, the only patrimony of thy race, the only inheritance of thine ancestors, and the only hope of thy posterity. Because of her thou hast life, love, and interests, happiness, honor, and God.

Thou shalt strive for the independence of thy country for only thou canst have any real interest in her advancement and exaltation, because her independence constitutes thine own liberty; her advancement thy perfection; and her exaltation thine own glory and immortality.

Surely no one would want to quarrel with such reasonable and noble sentiments.

Strange as it may seem, the missionaries were the ones who sowed the seeds of nationalism. By opening schools, reducing hundreds of languages to writing, translating books, especially the Bible, they did more than anyone else to promote the ideas and ideals of democracy, including such concepts as the dignity of labor, the worth of the individual, social justice, personal integrity, freedom of thought and speech, etc. Their educational institutions produced the intellectual elite who eventually provided leadership for the independence movement. Mr. Sithole, an African nationalist, in his book *African Nationalism*, makes bold to say that all unconsciously the missionary movement was the mother of African nationalism. Almost without exception today's leaders in Black Africa received at least a part of their education in a mission school. In Kenya half of Jomo Kenyatta's first Cabinet came from one leading mission school. In Nigeria, Africa's largest nation, the story was much the same. Speaking of the period following World War I, E. A. Ayandele states:

Henceforth the missions ... devoted their energies to evangelization. Nevertheless their activity continued to produce results, indirectly through their schools, which continued to serve as nurseries for practically all the nationalists of note in Southern Nigeria until the achievement of independence. It was not an accident that when in 1923 the elective principle was introduced into the Legislative Council of Nigeria only the elite in the citadels of Christianity, Lagos and Old Calabar, were given the franchise. It is also in the logic of things that all the Nigerian sixteen elected and twenty-seven nominated members of the Council from 1923 to 1946 were professed Christians, including many ministers of religion and journalists who fanned the embers of national awakening in the country. Even until this day the development of the Southern half of this country is largely in the hands of Christian adherents.[14]

The same was true to a less extent in Asia. It was commonly said in China, "After all, the revolution began when Robert Morrison landed on Chinese soil!"

In 1912, while the great Baptist missionary, Timothy Richard, was attending a conference in Shantung, a large company of non-Christians asked for the loan of a church building in order that a public meeting might be called to testify to their indebtedness to the Christian Church for every reform that had been introduced. Over a thousand gathered.... Moslems and Manchus included, and teachers and scholars from government schools. A military band came to play and officials made speeches.[15]

Mahatma Gandhi did more than any other person to win independence for India. Almost single-handedly and without resorting to violence, he brought the British Raj to its knees. Gandhi, of course, was not a Christian, but he had close connections with Christianity in England, South Africa, and India. Missionaries such as E. Stanley Jones and Charlie Andrews, both strong advocates of independence, were close friends of Gandhi and frequently visited his ashrams. After the Bhagavad Gita, the New Testament was Gandhi's favorite Scripture. He had great admiration for the character and teachings of Jesus Christ. It is difficult to say precisely to what extent Gandhi's independence movement was influenced by Christian ideals; but one thing we know, his concept of *satyagraha*—soul force—he got not from the Gita but from the Sermon on the Mount.

From a statistical point of view Christian missions were the least successful in the Muslim world; but even there they had a profound effect on the development of Arab nationalism.

George Antonius, famed historian of the Arab awakening, was eminently right when he ascribed the modern Arab revival more to the influence of the Protestant missionaries than to any other single factor. No foreign-born educator has yet succeeded as Presbyterian Cornelius W. A. Van Dyck did in identifying himself with the Middle East. For his Christian piety, learning and

---

[14] E. A. Ayandele, *The Missionary Impact on Modern Nigeria, 1842-1914* (New York: Humanities Press, 1967), p. 342.
[15] Goodall, *op. cit.*, p. 59.

espousal of their common cause, the Arabs regard him as one of their foremost luminaries.[16]

While it is true that the missionaries sowed the *seeds* of nationalism, neither they nor the indigenous churches actively participated in the struggle for independence. There were individual Christians who joined the independence movement; but they acted largely on their own. The churches *as churches* did not play a significant role in the liberation of their people. How do we explain the failure of the churches in this matter? There were several contributing factors:

1. Their immediate benefactors, the missionaries, were all Westerners and by virtue of that fact were themselves part and parcel of the colonial system. To rebel against it was to rebel against them. Very few Christians wanted to rebel against the missionaries who had brought them the gospel in the first place and to whom they owed their education and their advancement in society.

2. The missionaries, with their pietistic bent, were not particularly interested in politics. They considered they had more important things to do. Moreover, even in the homeland politics was not regarded as the highest and noblest of all vocations. They had no reason to believe that politics in the Third World would be an improvement on the homeside variety. Consequently they did nothing to encourage their converts to enter politics. Some of them definitely discouraged the idea. Little wonder that the rank and file of the converts felt no great urge to revolutionize the "present evil world," of which Satan is said to be both "god" and "prince."

3. In most countries of the Third World the Christians were a small, feeble, sometimes persecuted minority whose ostracism by society forced them to develop a "ghetto complex." They said to themselves: "If independence comes, what will happen to us?" Many of them had become so Westernized in life and thought that they preferred the known stability of the colonial system to the unknown blessings of independence.

4. Many of the nationalist movements were related to or supported by one or other of the non-Christian religions. If independence came, could the Christians be sure of a continuation of the freedom they enjoyed under colonialism? What good is political freedom if religious freedom is taken away? For the Christians the latter was more im-

---

[16] Edward J. Jurji, "Christianity in the Middle East," *Theology Today* (April 1951).

portant than the former. With the coming of independence the indigenous religions were almost sure to prosper. What would this do to Christianity?

5. The majority of church members were illiterate, or at best only semiliterate. Consequently they had little understanding of, or interest in, anything as complicated as politics. They were not sophisticated enough to know the difference between home rule and foreign rule. All they wanted was to be left in peace to plough their fields and ply their trades. Any government that could give them that would have their support.

6. The church leaders, who had some worldly wisdom and could therefore be expected to join the independence movement, were supported with mission funds. It was difficult for them to bite the hand that fed them.

There were, of course, exceptions to the above. In a few instances the churches and their leaders were actively engaged in the resistance movement in their respective countries. In Indonesia the great Batak Church lent its full support to the fight against Dutch colonialism. The situation in Korea was unique. There the Christian leaders, with the wholehearted backing of the American missionaries, were in the vanguard of the resistance movement against the Japanese. In the Conspiracy Case of 1912, 123 Koreans were arrested. Ninety-eight of them were Christians. When the Koreans defied the Japanese authorities in 1919 by issuing a Declaration of Independence, sixteen of the thirty-three signatories were Christians—at a time when only 4 percent of the population was Christian.

> In many countries the Christian, because of his association with the West, was suspect and in danger of being regarded as a second-class citizen. In Korea exactly the opposite was the case; to be a Christian was to be a patriot; the Churches were widely identified with the Korean national cause.[17]

What about the missionaries? Did they do any better than their converts? The answer is No. Here again there were exceptions; but it must be said that the missionary body as a whole failed to identify itself openly with the national aspirations of the peoples of the Third World in their desire for independence. What were the reasons for this?

1. The missionaries were by no means convinced of the evils of colonialism, especially their own brand. The colonial governments, certainly the more progressive ones, did an enormous amount of good

---

[17] Neill, *op. cit.*, p. 219.

for the people under their care. The British in India did an outstand-ingly good job. Besides building railways, highways, harbors, airports, etc., they established the Indian Civil Service, which was second to none in efficiency and integrity. The colonial administrators were impeccable and could not be bought for any price. In these days when national sentiments are so easily offended it may be indiscreet to say it, but there was far less corruption in India before independence than there has been since. Naturally the missionaries were aware of the British contribution to India and they were in no hurry to call for the end of the British Raj.

2. The missionaries were unaware of the gathering strength of the independence movement. In few places was that movement stronger than in China, yet the missionaries there seemed to be oblivious to the impending storm.

> Not until 1924 did the missionaries perceive the danger of their reliance on the treaties. Their failure to recognize the strength of Chinese nationalism until so late seems strange. At the peace conference at Versailles in 1919 and again at the Washington con-ference in 1921 Chinese delegates had made a determined stand for China's rights as a sovereign nation and many an outburst of patriotic sentiment among Chinese students should have indicated to them the emergence of a Chinese national spirit. Recognition of this fact by the missionaries was delayed by their myopic concern with the daily routine of their mission stations, by their failure to look beyond the civil strife created by war lords and bandits, and by their theological bent, which taught them to accept Saint Paul's dictum that the wisdom of this world is fool-ishness with God.[18]

3. The missionaries feared that if independence ever came their work would be adversely affected. They would certainly be shorn of their power. They might even be asked to leave the country. Indeed many missionaries took for granted that this would be the case. On furlough they spoke gloomily of having "three more years" or "five more years" in a given country. They can be faulted for not taking the right stand on the issue of nationalism and leaving the consequences to the providence of God; but like other people they were human and therefore reluctant to advocate a course of action likely to spell their own doom. Winston Churchill was not the only person who did not wish to preside over the liquidation of his own empire!

4. In most cases the missionaries did not consider the people ready for independence. In this they unconsciously shared the view of the

---

[18] Varg, *op. cit.*, p. 194.

colonial administrators. In the case of India, Great Britain never gave Gandhi and the National Congress the concessions they wanted *when they wanted them*. It was always too little, too late. Though the missionaries tended to drag their feet in the matter of political independence, at which point they had a blind spot, in many instances the churches were given their independence before the governments received theirs.

Let no one think that nationalism in the Third World has been directed solely against the white man, though for obvious reasons he bore the brunt of it. In Korea it was directed against the Japanese. In Southeast Asia it has been directed mainly against the large and influential Chinese minorities. Some of these Chinese families have been there for three or four generations, during which they worked hard and acquired wealth. As laborers they were industrious and frugal. As businessmen they were shrewd, enterprising, and highly successful, to the point where they came to control, if not monopolize, certain important segments of the economy, such as banking, imports, exports, etc. They further alienated themselves by keeping to themselves, speaking their own language, publishing their own newspapers, and maintaining their own schools. As a people they have stubbornly resisted all attempts to assimilate them. In recent years the governments of these countries, especially Malaysia and Indonesia, have begun to crack down on the Chinese, forcing them, among other things, to give up dual citizenship.

Anti-Japanese sentiment in Southeast Asia goes back to the atrocities committed during World War II, after which all Japanese nationals were repatriated. Japanese businessmen and tourists are now swarming into these parts again. Already there is building up a resentment against the aggressive economic policies of Japan, known as neocolonialism.

Doggedly dedicated to the "Burmese Way of Socialism," the government of Burma has nationalized banks, business houses, import and export enterprises, schools, and hospitals. As a result tens of thousands of Indians, Pakistanis, and Chinese left the country during the 1960s.

The same kind of thing is taking place in East Africa, where Asian nationals are fast becoming *persona non grata* with the newly independent governments in that part of the world. Kenya is unhappy with the large number of Indians who have been there since the turn of the century and today control most of the small businesses. In 1972 President Amin of Uganda summarily ordered the expulsion of forty thousand Indians who had failed to apply for citizenship. In the Middle East Arab nationalism is directed against the Jews, most of whom were expelled from the Arab countries after the war of 1948.

Nationalism is directed against any foreign ethnic group that poses a threat to the political, economic, or cultural autonomy of the host country.

Nationalism has a way of cooling off once independence has been achieved. The white man was a convenient whipping dog during the last days of the colonial era when the politicians wanted to unify the country and galvanize the people into action. Politicians of every stripe can always be sure of a following so long as they denounce the evils of colonialism; but once colonialism is a dead issue the politicians quickly change their tune. They and the people soon discover that not *all* the problems can be blamed on the colonialists. They realize that it is one thing to overthrow the colonial government; it is quite another thing to run the country. For that they need massive aid from the outside—investment capital, raw materials, technical know-how, tools, and even weapons to keep the peace. Former colonies, such as Zaire and Indonesia, which expelled thousands of white settlers, businessmen, and colonial officials, have already invited many of them back. Of course these expatriots are now on an entirely different footing; nevertheless it is interesting to note that they are there.

Independence, the war cry during the colonial period, soon gives way to interdependence. One of the first official acts of a new sovereign state is to apply for membership in the United Nations, a tacit admission that independence is only a stepping-stone to interdependence.

Nor has nationalism always lived up to its own expectations. It promises the people a new life with all kinds of freedom—personal, economic, and political. In many instances civil rights, social justice, and personal freedom have not been fully achieved. The white sahibs have been replaced by brown and black sahibs. Democracy has given way to military dictatorships. India is the only ex-colony in Asia that has been able to achieve and maintain a genuine form of parliamentary democracy over a quarter of a century. In 1975 it too succumbed to totalitarian rule. In the past fifteen years coups, countercoups, civil war, and military dictatorships have plagued the continent of Africa.

Of particular interest to the student of missions is the marked erosion of religious liberty that has taken place in the Third World during the past ten or fifteen years. Most of the new nations have incorporated into their constitutions a clause which guarantees full religious liberty. In some instances the clause has been taken from the United Nation's Universal Declaration of Human Rights, which has a very strong statement regarding freedom of religion, which includes freedom to practice, propagate, and even to change, one's religion. But in practice this has not always been done. Missionaries are barred from certain countries. In other countries church leaders are restricted in their movements. In Chad some missionaries have been expelled and

church leaders have been jailed. In Zaire youth meetings have been outlawed and all religious publications have been banned by government action. In Malaysia missionaries are allowed to remain only for ten years. In
Thailand all missionaries without permanent visas have to leave the
country every seventy days. In Afghanistan the only church building
in the country was demolished by government action in the spring of
1973. President Amin of Uganda banned twelve "religious sects," calling them "dangerous to peace and order." In the Muslim world missionaries have been expelled from Syria, Iraq, and Algeria. The
government of Burma will not allow church leaders to leave the
country, even for large international and ecumenical conferences. In
many countries the national church has less liberty than it enjoyed
under the colonial system. Even Korea has disappointed us in this respect.

With the advent of independence certain major changes have
occurred *vis-à-vis* the Christian church.

1. The role of the missionary has changed. In most places he is
still needed and still wanted; but he is no longer the leader. Instead
he is the servant. If he is able and willing to fill this new role he will
find a warm welcome and a fruitful ministry. If not, he might as well
remain at home. The day is gone when the missionary was the Big
Shot who could tell the "natives" what to do.

2. The status of the church has changed. It is no longer under the
control of the mission, nor is it part of the "mother" church in the
West. It enjoys full autonomy with its own constitution, organization,
and membership. It is in no way subservient to the Western mission
that brought it into existence. It has reached maturity. It has declared
its independence. It now stands on its own feet. Where such a church
exists the missionaries should be prepared to live and work not only
with the church but under the church.

3. The image of Christianity has changed. No longer can Christianity in the Third World be identified with Western imperialism.
The unholy alliance between the gospel and the gunboat is forever
broken, and Christianity is free to chart its own course, develop its own
structures, and project its own image without reference to Western patterns of thought. Church leaders can now hold their heads high. No
longer are they regarded as second-class citizens whose first allegiance
is to Rome, London, Geneva, or Washington.

All of this is to the good and bound to augur well for the future
of Christianity in the Third World.

All is not sweetness and light, however. There are liabilities as well as assets so far as the Christian church is concerned. Since the advent of independence there has been a notable resurgence in the non-Christian religions. Immigration laws have been tightened and Western missionaries find themselves denied access to countries which previously were open to missionary work. Bureaucratic red tape has increased to the point where missionaries are frustrated to tears by difficulties and delays which are costly in both time and money. One missionary had to wait two years to get his driver's license. Another had to wait six months to get his car through customs. In former days missionaries paid neither personal income taxes nor duty on their household effects. Now they pay both. In some countries the duty on an American car may run as high as three or four thousand dollars.

Mission schools and many mission hospitals have been nationalized. In Africa, where Christian missions had a virtual monopoly on education, only a few institutions remain under Christian control. Some governments have passed laws against what they call proselytizing, making it a capital offense to convert anyone under eighteen years of age.

Finally, the coming of independence has sometimes resulted in increased tension between church and mission. In some instances the missions were to blame. They were too slow to see the handwriting on the wall and come to terms with the realities of the developing situation. They kept the church waiting too long for independence. In other cases the church leaders were to blame. Their new-found power went to their heads, and they made unrealistic demands which the missions could not conscientiously accept. So great has been this problem that a special conference on Church-Mission Tensions was called at Green Lake, Wisconsin, in the fall of 1971. Nearly four hundred mission leaders attended. The greatest weakness of the conference was the fact that only ten or twelve church leaders from the Third World were present.

But in spite of the liabilities, and they are many, the situation is improving. Given wisdom and patience on both sides, church-mission tensions should decrease. In spite of all its attendant circumstances nationalism is essentially good, right, and proper. In the long run it can only advance the spread of the gospel and the growth of the church.

Missions and Communism

Twentieth-century Communism has posed the greatest single threat to Christianity since the Muslim hordes swept out of the Middle East in the seventh century and destroyed nine hundred churches in North Africa. To this day we have not recouped our losses in that part of the world. With the single exception of Chile, wherever Communism has come to power it has turned out to be the implacable foe of religion; and the only reason why it did not run true to form in Chile was that Salvador Allende came to power by way of the ballot and endeavored to introduce Communism by democratic means.

Until the Russian Revolution in 1917 Communism was simply another ideology to be discussed and disseminated by liberals and other intellectuals in Europe. The October Revolution gave the Communists a power base from which to operate not only in Europe but elsewhere in the world. As early as 1919 Lenin founded the Communist (Third) International, also known as the Comintern, for the purpose of exporting Communism to other parts of the world. During the 1920s the Comintern was instrumental in founding Communist parties in various countries in Asia. As a gesture of good will to the Allies the Comintern was officially dissolved in 1943; but it was revived again in 1947 in the form of the Cominform.

Today there are two great centers of Communist power—Moscow and Peking. Of the eighty-eight Communist parties in the world, thirty-nine are oriented towards Moscow and five to Peking; thirty are split into two factions, and fourteen are neutral or independent.

Modern Communism is an outgrowth of Marxism as it developed in the latter half of the nineteenth century. Marx, of course, was against all forms of religion. He declared that "the criticism of religion is the foundation of all criticism." Again he stated, "I hate all gods." He referred to religion as the "opiate of the people," a phrase he borrowed from Kingsley. He regarded religion as a tool in the hands of the ruling classes to exploit the hard-working peasants and laborers. Law, morality, and religion he lumped together as "bourgeois prejudices." To Karl Marx religion was a threat to society and a barrier to progress.

However, he did not believe in persecuting religion. He regarded religion as a form of superstition which would vanish under the impact of scientific education. When everyone is properly educated no one will be foolish enough to believe in the supernatural. Moreover, when the classless society is achieved religion, the tool of oppression, will serve no further purpose. It is not necessary to persecute religion.

Marx is not altogether to blame for his negative attitude towards religion. He came of a long line of Jewish rabbis, and Jews the world over had for centuries been persecuted in the so-called Christian countries of the world. In Lenin's case the only form of Christianity with which he was personally acquainted was that represented by the Russian Orthodox Church, which was closely allied with the oppressive Russian state.

While Communist regimes have vehemently denied that they persecute religion, it is a well-documented fact that they do everything in their power short of outright persecution to oppose it. As a rule Christians are subjected to various forms of discrimination, some petty and some not so petty.

Communism purports to be the purest and highest form of democracy. A Communist country is generally referred to as a "People's Democracy." In theory everything belongs to the people—the government, the army, the banks, the railways, the factories, and the farms. This means that every Communist regime has to pay lip service to the generally accepted principles of democracy, including freedom of speech, press, assembly, domicile, and religion. The constitutions of Soviet Russia and Communist China include an article on freedom of religion. Both governments take great pains to draw attention to this fact whenever the question of religious persecution is brought up. Other Communist countries have the same kind of statement. This, however, does not mean what it does here in the West. It is really a matter of toleration rather than freedom. The church is given legal status and is allowed to perform certain religious rites for its members, but always within the precincts of the church building. Religion must be confined to the churches. It has no place in the home, the school, or the marketplace. Freedom of religion does not include freedom to propagate, but simply to practice, religion. In China the expression is freedom to "believe in religion."

Along with the clause that speaks of freedom of religion is another clause that speaks of freedom to oppose religion. The latter freedom is much broader than the former. The churches are at a great disadvantage. They can practice their religion only within the confines of their church buildings; but the government is free to use every means at its disposal—school, press, radio, and television—to oppose religion. Christian parents are not permitted to give religious instruction to their own children under eighteen years of age; but during those same impressionable years the children in school are exposed to an incessant barrage of Communist propaganda against religion.

The situation *vis-à-vis* religion differs from country to country. It even differs within some countries. In Poland, where 93 percent of the people are professing Catholics, the Communist regime must of necessity use kid gloves in dealing with the situation; otherwise it might be faced with massive opposition sufficiently strong to undermine if not overthrow the government. In other countries, where the Christians represent 2 or 3 percent of the population, the destruction of the church can be effected with great ease.

It is significant that fifty-six years after the October Revolution the Soviet government, with all its massive power and propaganda, has not been able to stamp out religion in the USSR. The great Russian Orthodox Church still claims at least forty million adherents, while the evangelicals probably number at least five million. In fact, the number of evangelicals is greater today than at any time in Russian history! In spite of all that the government has done to suppress religion, it is still a viable option for millions of Soviet citizens who have nothing to gain and doubtless something to lose by clinging so tenaciously to an ideology which is so offensive to the powers that be. It is generally assumed that religion is dying out in the USSR and that its present adherents are mostly old people on the wrong side of fifty. That is not so. There is plenty of evidence to prove that Soviet youth are showing an increased interest in religion.

In all Communist countries the church is required to be completely subservient to the state. It must wholeheartedly support the establishment of socialism leading to Communism. It is expected to toe the party line at home and support Soviet policy abroad.

The Russian Orthodox Church suffered greatly under Stalin; but when the church supported the government in its war against Hitler the situation improved. Now the Orthodox Church enjoys a measure of freedom. For a long time it was completely isolated from the rest of Christendom; but in 1961 it was permitted to join the World Council of Churches and since that time its leaders have been active in the ecumenical movement. These leaders, of course, have never been known to disagree with government policy, not even when Czechoslovakia was invaded in 1968. Even the churches in Czechoslovakia failed to speak out against the invasion of their own country. An exception was Dr. Joseph L. Hromadka, winner of the Lenin Peace Prize, who courageously wrote a letter to the Soviet ambassador in which he described the invasion as a "tragic error" and called for the speedy withdrawal of the occupying forces. But we must bear in mind that this is the price of survival. When the issues are political and not religious, Christian leaders take the path of least resistance and support the party line. Only those who have lived under a Communist regime can possibly appreciate the enormous pressures that a totalitarian government can exert on its hapless citizens.

To add insult to injury, the churches in a Communist country are required to tell the world that they enjoy complete freedom of religion, when all the time their members are enduring various kinds of discrimination, if not persecution. Christians outside the Communist orbit find this abject subservience to an atheistic regime difficult to understand. There is nothing very mysterious about it. It is the price of survival, both for the individual Christian and for the church as an organized body.

In the USSR and the Communist countries of Eastern Europe the Communist governments had to deal only with the Christian church. When we move into the Third World we find a different set of circumstances and the situation is much more complicated. There the governments have had to deal with two separate and distinct movements —the indigenous church and the Western mission. This fact posed special problems for both church and state.

At the present time nine Communist countries are located in Europe. Seven more are found in Asia. These include China, Mongolia, North Korea, North Vietnam, South Vietnam, Cambodia and South Yemen. There is one in Latin America, Cuba. Other countries in the Third World teetered on the brink of the Communist orbit only to be rescued, some of them at the last minute, by dictators of various sorts. Included in this list are Guinea, Mali, Ghana, and Central African Republic in Africa; Syria and Iraq in the Middle East; Sri Lanka and Indonesia in Asia. Cambodia became Communist in 1975. While various factions in Laos have settle for a coalition government that may well be the prelude to a Communist takeover. Even South Vietnam, into which the United States poured such enormous quantities of blood and treasure, has now fallen to the Communists.

The one part of the world where Christian missions and militant Communism have had their greatest confrontation is the People's Republic of China. In its relation to Christian missions surely China stands in a class by itself, and for good reasons: (1) It has by far the largest population in the world. (2) It absorbed the largest number of missionaries of all the countries of the Third World. (3) It provided the greatest number of Christian martyrs, national and missionary. (4) It proved to be the most resistant of all the countries outside the Muslim world. On four separate occasions Christianity was planted in China, and each time it died out.

The first attempt was made by the great Nestorian Church in the seventh century. The mission prospered for two hundred years and died when Emperor Wu Tsung in A.D. 845 issued a decree dissolving all monasteries and ordering all monks to return to private life.

The second attempt was made by the Franciscan missionaries under the leadership of John of Monte Corvino, who arrived in Peking about 1294. The Roman Catholic faith spread down the east coast to Fukien, some eight hundred miles south of Peking. When John died there were about one hundred thousand converts. When in 1368 the Chinese again became masters in their own house, the Ming rulers expelled the missionaries and Christianity died out.

Two hundred years later the Roman Catholics made another attempt to Christianize China. The leader that time was Matteo Ricci of the Society of Jesus. After almost twenty years of patient planning Ricci reached the capital in 1601. Because Ricci adopted Chinese culture and appeared in the guise of a Confucian scholar intellectuals flocked to converse with the great scholar from the West. Many of them embraced the new religion. By 1650 there were 250,000 converts. Later a controversy arose between the emperor and the missionaries over the term for God. The emperor took offense when the matter was decided by the pope, and edicts of persecution were issued in 1724 and again in 1736. All but a handful of missionaries were expelled. Once again Christianity suffered a major defeat.

The fourth and last attempt was the combined efforts of Roman Catholic and Protestant missionaries from 1842 to 1949. During the heyday, in the 1920's, there were eight thousand Protestant missionaries and an equal number of Roman Catholic missionaries in China, by far the largest concentration of missionaries in any country.

When the Communists came to power in 1949 most of the Protestant missionaries and all the Roman Catholic missionaries remained at their posts. They were not at all sure that the Communists meant what they said when they proclaimed "religious freedom" in liberated areas; but they decided to stay to see what developed. When the new Constitution was adopted in the fall of 1949, sure enough, Article 88 guaranteed "freedom of religious belief." The missionaries were grateful and entertained the hope that maybe they could do business with the new government. But as time went on it became abundantly clear that there was a gap between the promise and the performance—as is the case in every Communist country. When the Communists came to power in 1949 they had two hostile forces to deal with, the Western missions and the Chinese churches. Naturally they tackled the missions first.

It goes without saying that the Chinese Communists had no reason to love the missionaries after their long association with Western imperialism, as noted in an earlier section of this chapter. There is no doubt that they regarded the missionaries as wolves in sheep's clothing. They accused them of being political agents of their respective governments, all the while using religion and philanthropy as a cloak for their real intentions, intrigue and espionage. To make matters worse, the United States supported Chiang Kai-shek right up to the end and continued to speak of overthrowing the Communist regime after it came to power.

The first intimation of impending trouble came suddenly with the publication in the national press on September 23, 1950, of a manifesto signed by 1,527 church leaders. It read in part as follows:

> Christianity was first introduced into China more than 140 years ago. During that time it has made a significant contribution to Chinese society. Unfortunately, however, shortly after the coming of Christianity, imperialism also commenced activities. Since the missionaries came chiefly from these imperialistic countries, wittingly or unwittingly, Christianity has been associated with

imperialism.... Christian churches and organizations in China must, by utmost effort and effective means, enable the masses in the churches to clearly recognize the crimes committed by the imperialists in China, and also the fact that imperialism in the past made use of the Christian church. They must wipe out all traces of imperialistic influences in the church. They must be on the alert against any conspiracy on the part of the imperialists, especially American imperialists, to use religion to foster the growth of reactionary forces.[19]

Though signed by church leaders the manifesto was really the result of a meeting they had in Peking with Chou En-lai. It expressed the sentiment of the government rather than the church, though the church leaders were by no means ignorant of the history of Christianity in their own country. By 1952 the manifesto had been signed by four hundred thousand Christians belonging to seventy-nine denominations. As such it was supposed to represent "the will of the people," a concept always important to Communist strategy.

The government actually expelled very few missionaries. The rest became *persona non grata* and left more or less of their own accord when the situation became untenable. Several circumstances contributed to this development. (1) All foreign funds were frozen in the banks by government order. This was in retaliation for a similar move by the American government against Chinese assets in America. This meant that the missionaries were completely cut off from their supply base at home. (2) Foreigners were not permitted to travel in China except for emergency reasons, and even then permits were sometimes withheld. (3) Mission schools and hospitals were taken over by the government, thus relieving some of the missionaries of their duties. (4) Church services were gradually reduced to one a week, the Sunday morning worship service. Evangelism was out. (5) For the first time in a hundred years mission and church property was taxed, and taxed heavily, making it virtually impossible for the missions to meet their tax bills.

The final blow came when the government called in the church leaders and told them that the Chinese churches must be thoroughly indigenized, which meant getting rid of all foreign men and money. Only then would the government implement Article 88 that guaranteed religious freedom. This put both the missionaries and the church leaders in a very difficult situation.

By this time it was apparent that the presence of the missionaries in China was self-defeating. By prolonging their stay they were embarrassing the very people they wished to help. After an agonizing reappraisal the mission leaders concluded that the time had come for

---

[19] The author's translation.

the missionaries to withdraw and thus free the church of the stigma of imperialism. It was recognized by both groups that so long as the missionaries remained the church would be obliged to fight a war with Communism on two fronts, the political as well as the religious. It was believed that the church would stand a better chance if it were free from all incriminating connections with the West.

A general evacuation got under way early in 1951. For the most part it proceeded smoothly, with only minor irritations and delays. Some missionaries were placed under house arrest, others spent time in jail. On the whole the casualties were few. Given the history of Christianity in China and the pathological hate of the Communists for the United States, it is a miracle that the vast body of missionaries got out alive.

With the missionaries out of the way the government addressed itself to the task of cleaning up the church, which was required to purge itself of all "reactionary elements." Its leaders must "change their thoughts" and rid themselves and their people of all "bourgeois thinking." The agent appointed to carry out this task was the Three Self Patriotic Movement, made up of YMCA and church leaders. It was expected to accept orders from the Bureau of Religious Affairs and convey them to the churches.

The first task of the Three Self Movement was to supervise the housecleaning process by which the churches were to purge themselves of all imperialism, feudalism, and bourgeois thinking. The chief instrument of torture was the denunciation meeting. Initially the denunciations were aimed at the missionaries, some of whom had already taken their departure. Others had to stand trial. The government was determined to debunk the entire missionary movement by exposing the "crimes" of the missionaries. During 1951 no fewer than 228 denunciation meetings were held in 133 cities. Leading missionaries were singled out for special attention. Two prestigious church periodicals, *Tien Feng* and *Hsieh Chin,* devoted issue after issue to a blow-by-blow account of the various denunciation meetings all over the country. Not satisfied with that, they delved into history and carried on a veritable tirade against the leading missionaries of the past—Robert Morrison, Karl Gützlaff, S. Wells Williams, Timothy Richard, and Hudson Taylor, all of whom were accused of "imperialist designs" on China.

If the denunciations had been confined to the missionaries it would have been bad enough; but following that the church leaders were called on to confess their sins. It was assumed that anyone who had had any contact with American missionaries was infected with bourgeois thinking and was therefore "reactionary." This clearly called for radical reform action. Consequently all church leaders, teachers, doctors, and others were forced to attend study sessions once or twice a year, during which they studied Marxism, the Communist party line, and, of course, the evils of the capitalist system and American imperialism. At the end of these study sessions, which usually lasted for three months, each person was expected to give public testimony to the fact that he had undergone a genuine transformation of life and thought and was now prepared to support wholeheartedly the establishment of socialism in China. And, of course, he was expected to denounce American imperialism in vitriolic terms. And the testimony had to be genuine or the person was sent back for another period of study.

With their hands clean and their thoughts changed these leaders returned to their churches, where they were expected to conduct discussion and confession meetings designed to purge the churches of all "reactionary elements." One after another church members confessed their wrong thoughts and evil deeds. If they could not recall such wrongs they were helped by others. Usually these meetings degenerated into mutual accusation sessions, with elders accusing deacons and deacons accusing elders, and sometimes deacons and elders accusing pastors of all kinds of antisocial misdemeanors. Communist cadres were always on hand to see that instructions were properly carried out. Newspapers carried lurid accounts of the proceedings to make sure that the local populace in each town was made aware of the "crimes" committed by the Christians. Throughout the proceedings, however, the Communists were careful not to make any martyrs. The charges brought against church leaders were ethical, moral, or political rather than religious. In this way the government could not be accused of persecution.

As each church and organization successfully completed its accusation meeting it was given a clean bill of health and allowed to join the Three Self Patriotic Movement. This gave it a certain measure of security. It was then regarded as "reliable" and could function as a "free" institution in a "democratic" society. Those leaders who could not go through with this ghastly piece of hypocrisy were placed on the official black list. Some were brainwashed; some were imprisoned; some were sent to labor camps; some were executed. Most tragic of all was the final end of the leaders of the Three Self Movement, who had supported the party line and even participated in the destruction of their fellow believers. When their services were no longer needed by the state they were tossed aside and ignored.

The churches which survived the mutual accusation ordeal and gained legal status were never given the religious freedom promised to them by the constitution. They were reduced to one service a week, Sunday morning. Week-night meetings and special services were banned. Sunday schools continued for a time; but parades, demonstrations, and theatricals, all of a patriotic character, were usually held on Sunday, and all school children were expected to attend. Consequently Sunday school attendance at best was very uncertain.

The demise of the organized church in China coincided with the Great Proletarian Cultural Revolution launched by the Red Guards in August 1966. Armed with a little red book, *Quotations from Chairman Mao Tse-tung*, and provided with free transportation on the state-owned railways, the Red Guards, a hundred million strong, went on the rampage, physically attacking all institutions and organizations which harbored any one of the Four Olds—old ideas, old culture, old customs, and old habits. The few remaining churches which had survived the previous purges were entered and desecrated. Bibles, hymnbooks, pictures, images, and other religious symbols were removed and burned. The houses and shops of Christians were ransacked. In the process property was destroyed and persons were molested, sometimes humiliated. By the summer of 1967 the visible church in China had ceased to exist, killed by a regime that professed to believe in religious freedom.

In recent years, and especially since the visit to China of President Nixon, there have been encouraging reports concerning the church inside China. It is by no means dead; in fact there are signs of revival in many parts of the country. Mr. David Wang, a research man, who spent a month in China in 1972, reported:

> I saw China's living church—a dynamic, witnessing, worshipping church in China is far from exaggeration. I met them, I talked with them. I prayed with them. Five of my closest childhood friends have been won to Christ in the last two years. The young people have a distinct longing for truth and reality.[20]

Since that time two or three ex-China missionaries, all of them Canadians, have been permitted to visit China and speak rather freely with Christians and non-Christians. Each of these men was favorably impressed with what he saw.

In the spring of 1973 E. H. Johnson, Secretary for Research and Planning of the Board of World Mission of the Presbyterian Church in Canada paid a three-week visit to China, and returned with a rather optimistic report of the Protestant Church in that land.

He spent three days in Nanking and had ample opportunity to converse freely with an old friend, Bishop K. H. Ting, who requested Mr. Johnson to secure for him air-mail subscriptions to a wide variety of Christian periodicals. There is no censorship of mail, and the bishop said he would have no fear of negative articles that might appear in

---

[20] Coordinating Office for Asian Evangelism, *Newsletter* (February 1973).

the periodicals. Obviously the mass tension that existed during the Cultural Revolution has been largely dissipated.

From Bishop Ting and others he got the impression that the Christians heartily support the Communist government and are grateful for its accomplishments on the domestic and international scenes. Naturally they are very happy with the developing rapprochement between China and the United States. For the first time in history the Christians are directly engaged in the political life of the country, having representatives in the People's Congress at all levels. A huge portrait of Sun Yat-sen, a Christian, appears in the great Tien An Men Square in Peking, along with portraits of Marx, Engels, Lenin, Stalin, and Mao.

It is estimated that there are five hundred Protestants in Nanking and an equal number in Peking. In the latter city only two churches, one Protestant and the other Catholic, are open. They minister almost exclusively to the expatriates in the capital. In Nanking the Christians are meeting regularly in four different meeting places, often on Sunday but also at other times, depending on their work schedules. Denominationalism, that used to characterize the Protestants, has disappeared. So also have the differences between clergy and laity. Protestants and Catholics, however, still have little or no fellowship. Ordained professional ministers are considered nonessentials in the Christian community, as are church buildings. Church services are being resumed in various parts of the country, but for the time being they are held in halls. This relieves the Christians of the burden of upkeep; at the same time it avoids identification with former days when Christianity was Western in flavor and closely associated with church buildings. Nor are they sure that a Christian program centered in a church building is necessarily the proper expression of Christian life in a socialist society.

While the Three Self Patriotic Movement still exists, Christianity for the most part is congregational and local, and will probably remain that way for a long time to come. Since the government has taken over all schools and hospitals and provides for the general welfare of the people, there are very few "activities" in which the Christians can engage. Moreover, a six-day workweek and all kinds of study and political meetings in the evening hours leave them little time for church or family life. The Christianity that remains in China today is largely pietistic. One whole county in Chekiang is reported to have as many Christian services as it did prior to liberation. In that county the pastor is working as a tailor.

The question is often asked: "Will missionaries get back into China?" It is most unlikely that missionaries will be allowed back into China so long as the Communists remain in power. Diplomats, businessmen, professional groups, journalists, and even tourists will eventually be welcomed in China. It would take a miracle, however, to get missionaries back. This leads to a second question: "How long will the Communists remain in power?" There is every reason to believe they will remain in control of China for the foreseeable future.

In the case of North Korea, no missionaries were permitted to return after World War II; hence there was no occasion for a confrontation. There was, however, a strong Protestant church. At first the church leaders leaned over backwards to cooperate with the Communist regime, for they too were interested in peace and progress; but the tide turned after the Communist attack on South Korea in June 1950. Thousands of Christians were among the five million refugees who fled to South Korea at that time. Persecution broke out; many pastors went to prison and others were executed. When the Communist armies retreated from Seoul in the summer of 1950 they took with them three hundred Christian pastors whose fate is still unknown. The visible church in North Korea has been completely destroyed.

Christianity has fared somewhat better in North Vietnam than in either China or North Korea. All foreign missionaries were compelled, on one pretext or another, to leave the country; but the churches were permitted a modicum of liberty. Of the one million refugees who fled south after the Geneva Agreement in 1954, three-quarters were Roman Catholics. In 1962, the last year for which there are reliable statistics, there were 833,000 Catholics still in North Vietnam. Diplomatic relations with the Vatican were severed. Since 1960 the North Vietnam Church has been under the jurisdiction of the Vietnamese hierarchy. Good news was received in 1973 regarding the fate of the Protestant churches once associated with the Christian and Missionary Alliance. The three-thousand-member Evangelical Church of North Vietnam has a dozen pastors and preachers. Most of the churches are able to hold two services on Sunday and an evangelistic service on Thursday. Pastors are employed full time and their salaries are paid by the local congregations. Conversions are reported and six to eight months of training is given before baptism. There is an ample supply of Bibles, though a new translation is needed.

In Cuba the situation is quite different. There the dominant religion has been Roman Catholicism ever since the discovery of the New World. In June 1961 Fidel Castro nationalized 350 Roman Catholic schools. In September he expelled the archbishop and 135 priests. By that time large numbers of foreign religious had left the country. There are still some six million Roman Catholics there. Freedom of worship and religious instruction is limited to the confines of the churches. Organized social work is forbidden. The church is permitted to survive under constant surveillance in a condition of sufferance. Despite the animosity between church and state diplomatic relations with the Vatican have not been severed. The Protestants, a small minority compared with the Catholics, are barely tolerated. There has been no open, organized persecution of the church. The policy has been one of opposition, harassment, and suppression. There was a period in 1963 when the Evangelicals were singled out by Castro as "undesirable reactionaries" and a crackdown was ordered. In 1965 more than fifty Baptist pastors were arrested simultaneously. Thirty-four of them were brought to trial and sentenced for a variety of reasons. During the first years of the Castro regime there was a falling away; but as confidence was restored many returned to the church. The mass exodus of half a million Cubans in the mid-sixties included many Christians and some pastors. Their departure was a great blow to the church. In recent years, in spite of continual harassment by the government, the churches have not only held their own but have actually shown signs of virility and growth. A report in the summer of 1973 indicated that the church is still very much alive. It is a miracle, but churches are filled with young people in spite of strong government opposition.

Both church and missions have suffered more from Communism in Asia than in Latin America. How are we to account for this? There are three contributing factors. (1) Christianity never succeeded in becoming truly indigenous in Asia. It has always been regarded as a foreign religion. (2) Not only was it foreign, but it bore the stigma of imperialism, with which is was associated. (3) With the exception of the Philippines Christianity in Asia was embraced by only a small fraction of the population—in India by 2.4 percent, China and Japan by less than 1 percent. In Korea and Vietnam the percentage, though much higher—about 10 percent—was still low.

The Missionary Movement: An Evaluation

No enterprise known to man has ever been 100 percent successful. Man is a finite, fallen creature and his most noble efforts are marred by imperfection and failure. The modern missionary enterprise is no exception. Stephen Neill expressed it well when he said:

> Christian missionary work is the most difficult thing in the world. It is surprising that it should ever have been attempted. It is surprising that it should have been attended by such a measure of success. And it is not at all surprising that an immense number of mistakes should have been made.[21]

To hear some people talk one would conclude that the entire

[21] Stephen Neill, *Call to Mission* (Philadelphia: Fortress Press, 1970), p. 24.

missionary enterprise has been a total disaster. But before we can talk of disaster or even failure, we must understand clearly what the missionaries were supposed to do. If they failed to do what they were supposed to do, then, of course, they failed; but they can hardly be faulted for failure in a given task if that task was never really part of the missionary mandate.

For instance, the missionary enterprise in China was described in the 1950s as a complete failure. It was stated that the Communists did more for China in ten years than the missionaries did in a hundred. Our reply is: "Yes, that is perfectly true; but were the missionaries expected to do what the Communists did? Were they expected to shoulder a gun and join the Eighth Route Army? Or eliminate corruption from government? Or overthrow the Kuomintang? Or push through a program of land reform? Or negotiate a 300 million dollar loan from the USSR?" To ask these questions is to answer them.

The Communists have done many good things for China; but they were not the kind of things that Western missionaries could have done even if they had wanted to. Good though they were, they were not part of the missionary mandate. To fault them for failure is to miss the mark completely.

Having said that, we must go on to confess that the missionaries did fail in certain important respects.

WHAT MISSIONARIES DID WRONG

1. The missionaries had a superiority complex. Almost without exception they considered Western civilization superior to any other. Worse still, they unashamedly equated civilization with Christianity. They referred to the people as "natives," and in their letters home depicted them as lazy, dirty, dishonest, irresponsible, and untrustworthy. Henry Fowler, a Methodist bishop, speaking of the Chinese nation, said:

> This moral mummy is embalmed and wrapped in superstitions four thousand years old and more than ten thousand layers deep. These superstitions touch every act of life, and every word and every secret thought. They are victims of luck, fortune-tellers, and necromancy. They live in a world packed to the very stars with powerful spirits, which must not be offended. All ranks and classes, from the emperor down to the poorest coolies, are steeped and boiled and parboiled in superstition. By these superstitions the university men and the priests govern and rob and torment all classes.[22]

It is only fair to state that there were other missionaries in China

---

[22] Varg, *op. cit.*, pp. 113-114.

who had an altogether different view of the Chinese. Arthur Smith wrote:

> The Chinese have many and conspicuous virtues, among which are their faithfulness to duty, their sobriety, their unfailing industry, their unequalled patience, their inexhaustible cheerfulness, manifesting itself in blooming flowers, in warbling birds, and smiling faces, even in the midst of deep poverty, gloomy prospects, and heavy hearts. All these are wonderful and admirable endowments.[23]

Smith, of course, was much closer to the truth than Fowler. A Chinese writer complained that even the most sanguine missionaries were guilty of a superiority complex:

> Their experience of China may be lifelong; their information accurate. But their viewpoint is never that of the people they describe. Underlying everything that is written or spoken about China is the foregone conclusion that the Chinese are "inferior" and their ways of doing things are wrong.[24]

If the missionaries had such a view of Chinese civilization—certainly one of the highest in history—what must they have thought of the more primitive forms of civilization encountered in other parts of the world?

In defense of the missionaries, several observations are in order. The missionaries were not the only ones with a superiority complex. There were very few persons in the nineteenth century who did not share this point of view. Professors, clergymen, politicians, men of letters—all had a blind spot at this point. They assumed that Western civilization was superior to all others and expressed their views freely. In the United States this came to focus very sharply in the doctrine of "Manifest Destiny."

Modern Europeans have no monopoly when it comes to a superiority complex. All higher forms of civilization have produced the same effect. The ancient Greeks divided the world into Greeks and barbarians, the Romans into citizens and slaves, the Jews into Jews and Gentiles. To be a barbarian, a slave, or a Gentile was to be beyond the pale. For thousands of years the Chinese have called their country the "Middle Kingdom." All outsiders were barbarians. Lin Yutang's brilliant book, *My Country and My People,* which attracted so much attention in the 1930s, was a powerful, albeit somewhat humorous, apologetic for Chinese civilization. In reading the book one got the impression that Chinese vices are really virtues and, conversely, Western virtues are actually vices.

---

[23] Arthur H. Smith, *Chinese Characteristics* (New York: Revell, 1894), pp. 136-137.
[24] Lowe Chuan Hwa, "The Christian Peril in China," *The Nation* (February 7, 1923).

In the conduct of their daily work the missionaries were usually in contact with the lower classes who formed 80 to 90 percent of the population. In all honesty it must be said that these people, through no fault of their own, *were* poor, ignorant, dirty, superstitious, undernourished, and often diseased. When the missionaries wrote home they simply told it like it was. Their mistake was not in what they said but in what they left unsaid. They spoke only of the seamy side of life—the side they knew best.

Few people today realize what it meant for the early missionaries to cast in their lot with these underprivileged people. Curiously enough modern, well-educated nationals have difficulty in identifying with their poor, illiterate compatriots living in the rural areas of their own countries. Very few of them, having completed their education in the West, settle down in the small towns and villages "to serve the people." Instead they tend to congregate in the larger cities where they can enjoy the amenities of modern civilization.

2. The missionaries took a dim view of the "pagan" religions. They were unnecessarily negative in their attitude towards these religions and often preached against idolatry in terms that were quite offensive to the listeners. The same truths could have been expressed in less abrasive terms. Without sufficiently investigating the indigenous religions they assumed that they were wholly false and rejected them out of hand. Later on they discovered that such tactics were self-defeating and abandoned them. In the meantime the deed was done, and the reputation lingers.

Two factors were at work here. With few exceptions the pioneer missionaries were ignorant of the philosophical and theological foundations of the great ethnic religions. The sacred books of the East had not yet been translated, or if translated they were unknown to the missionaries. Hence they had no intelligent grasp of their major doctrines. All they knew was that they were man-made religions which involved idolatry and often immorality, the two great sins of the pagan world. In addition they judged these religions by the character and conduct of the devotees, many of whom were not exactly an advertisement for their religion. This was both unfortunate and unfair. How would we like it if Christianity were judged, not by the character and teachings of Christ, but by the history of the church and the behavior of its members? Obviously Christianity would not win many laurels.

3. They failed to differentiate between Christianity and Western culture. They took along with them a large amount of excess luggage: moral and social taboos, personal prejudices and predilections, ethical and legal codes, economic and political institutions—everything from

the Magna Carta to Robert's *Rules of Order*. In so doing they placed
on the necks of their converts a yoke that was more than they could
bear. Christianity as it developed in the Third World ended up with a
"Made in the U.S.A." stamp on it. Little wonder that it came to be
known as a "foreign religion" in Asia and the "white man's religion" in
Africa. Certainly it bore all the earmarks of a Western institution.

The mistake was a natural one. As far back as the fourth century
the church began to take on the complexion of its environment. Ever
since the beginning of the Holy Roman Empire, about A.D. 800,
Christianity has been the dominant religion of Europe. At the height
of its power the Roman Catholic Church was the wealthiest, most
powerful organization on the continent. For a thousand years Christianity provided both the matrix and the motif of Western civilization,
including art, music, sculpture, literature, philosophy, and, of course,
theology. Medieval history is largely church history. Religion has always been an integral part of culture; and when the two elements have
been together for hundreds of years it is virtually impossible to separate
them. It would be as easy to extract the salt from the sea as to remove
Christianity from Western culture. This fact should be borne in mind
when one is tempted to castigate the missionaries for their failure to
do a better job.

**4. The missionaries exported denominationalism along with the
gospel.** In the beginning they said they would not do this; but they
soon forgot their good intentions, and before they got through they
reproduced every major denomination and many of the minor ones in
the West. It was particularly confusing to the Chinese when the
Southern Baptist churches were in *North* China and the Northern
Baptist churches in *South* China!

Denominational divisions and distinctions naturally have historic
significance for us in the West; but many of them are practically meaningless to the emerging churches in the Third World. The convert
from Hinduism, Buddhism, or Islam has probably paid a high price for
his allegiance to Jesus Christ. It may have cost him his wife, family,
and livelihood. He becomes an outcast among his own people. He
naturally expects that his new-found faith will be his passport to the
Christian church—any branch of it. He is surprised and disappointed
when he is told that it is not enough to be a Christian; he must also be
a Presbyterian, or a Lutheran, or a Baptist, as the case might be. And
when missions compete with one another for the converts the scandal
is increased.

Here again we must be careful not to overstate the case. No less an
authority than Stephen Neill reminds us that "in point of fact Christian
divisions have wrought less harm than might be expected. Both Hindu-

ism and Islam are themselves religions of many sects."[25] He might have added Buddhism to the list, for it likewise is divided into scores of sects.

5. The missionaries failed to encourage the indigenization of Christianity. It never entered their minds that Christianity could retain its essential core while at the same time being expressed in Oriental forms. They seemed to think that the form was essential to the substance and must remain forever Western in motif. They erected church buildings replete with spire, bell, and cross. They introduced hymns with Western words and Western tunes. Drums and dances, so dear to the African soul, were taboo. Instead they used musical instruments imported from the West. The liturgy was Western in style. The Roman Catholics were the greatest offenders at this point. They insisted that the Mass be said in Latin in every Roman Catholic church in the world. The Anglicans translated the Book of Common Prayer along with, sometimes before, the Scriptures. Vestments worn by officiating priests and bishops were the same as those worn in the West. An Anglican church service in Patagonia was identical with one in London. Even theological education was patterned after the classical kind so common in the West. The curriculum included Hebrew, Greek, sometimes Latin, but never the ancient classical languages of the East —Sanskrit, Pali, and Arabic. Church history was Western church history with little or no mention of Christian missions around the world. The teaching of apologetics was geared to Western thought, not to the Oriental mind.

6. The missionaries were guilty of paternalism. It is easy to make a case against the missionaries on this score. The unhappy details are well known to everyone remotely interested in Christian missions. It should be remembered, however, that paternalism is not *always* bad. In the beginning it was natural, necessary, and inevitable, given the circumstances of the nineteenth century. This was especially true in Africa, where most of the early converts were fugitive slaves and miscreants from tribal society. The missionaries took them into their "residential" stations, after which they became virtual wards of the mission. The missionary in charge provided them with food, clothing, shelter, and security; taught them to read and write; gave them land, seed, and tools to make a garden; and taught them a trade. All they asked in return was obedience. If they did not accept the discipline of the community they were chastised. In rare cases they were even flogged. The greatest punishment was expulsion from the community.

---

25 Neill, *Call to Mission*, p. 37.

That was paternalism with a vengeance; but it is difficult to see how else the missionaries could have acted in those early years.

Moreover, the converts themselves offered no objections. They accepted the authoritarian approach of the missionary without question. It seemed to be the natural thing to do. "In the early days of the missions, tension rarely arose between missionaries and converts. The convert had little desire to concern himself with questions of administration and finance and was quite happy to leave these to his missionary friends."[26]

The real problem came when paternalism was continued long after it had served its purpose. It is simply a matter of record that the missionaries held on to power much too long. They can be forgiven for their treatment of the first generation of converts; but what about the second and third generations? They were educated men with ability and experience and wanted to be masters in their own house. It was at this point that the missionaries completely missed the boat. They continued to think of the Christians as children to be pampered, prodded, and protected, not as mature adults capable of holding office, exercising discipline, and administering the affairs of the church.

7. **The missionaries were unwise in their use of Western funds.** Too often they allowed their hearts to run away with their heads. Western funds were used all too freely and over too long a period of time, to the detriment of the developing churches. This situation, however, was not as simple as it might appear on the surface. To begin with, charity is a Christian virtue. Our Lord told us that it is more blessed to give than to receive. Again He said, "Freely ye have received, freely give." So if the missionary was generous with his money, he can hardly be faulted for being unchristian in his conduct. Secondly, the Christians were usually very poor, at least by Western standards; and often their profession of Christianity barred them from getting or holding jobs. Beverley Nichols in his book, *Verdict on India,* says that the people of India are so poor that they can live on the smell of an oil rag. This obviously is an overstatement, but it does dramatize the grinding poverty of rural India. Thirdly, the missionaries, though woefully underpaid by stateside standards, were regarded as fabulously well off on the mission field. In some instances the missionary's tithe, if all of it had gone into the local church, would have taken care of the total budget. In these circumstances the temptation to solve problems by handing out money was exceedingly great. Most of us would have done the same thing.

Later on, when the churches began to grow in size and strength

---

[26] *Ibid.,* p. 106.

and the missionaries tried to curb their generosity, they were given little encouragement by the church leaders. They had been on the dole so long that they verily believed they could not survive without it. It was here that the missionaries ran into opposition. The national churches have been notoriously slow to accept and implement the principle of self-support. When the Communists came to power in China in 1949 most of the large denominations, some of them almost a hundred years old, were still dependent on funds from the "mother" churches in the West. To this day there are large churches in India that find themselves in the same fix. If the government were to cut off foreign funds they would be in a bad way.

8. The missionaries were too closely identified with the colonial system. Through no fault of their own the missionaries were part and parcel of the gigantic outward thrust of the European nations in the nineteenth century whereby they acquired empires in all parts of Africa, Asia, and the South Seas. The colonial administrators and the Christian missionaries traveled on the same ships, served under the same flags, worked in the same countries, and were mutually helpful. The missionaries carried on a "civilizing" mission among the "natives." They helped to create a middle-class bourgeois society susceptible to Western influence and amenable to Western laws, thereby making it easier for the colonialists to administer the territories under their rule. The colonial governments reciprocated in kind, giving the missionaries land for their stations, subsidies for their schools, and protection in times of danger. From many points of view this was the greatest mistake made by the Christian missions in the nineteenth century.

The degree of wrongdoing on the part of the missionaries was not as great as some twentieth-century nationalists have maintained. Certainly it was not as great as the Communists have made it out to be. Nevertheless the link between the gospel and the gunboat was sufficiently close to give the whole missionary movement a black mark in the eyes of the Third World. Only now, after the collapse of the colonial system, is the stigma of imperialism being removed from Christianity. There are, of course, pockets of colonialism here and there throughout the world, but these are in various stages of liquidation. Whether the colonial authorities in these places are aware of it or not, their days are numbered. In the meantime both church and mission are lined up pretty solidly on the side of liberation.

It is true, however, that the missionaries, because of their association with the colonial system, failed to identify themselves with the national aspirations of the people in their struggle for independence. They avoided politics as much as possible. Then as now politics was not regarded as the noblest vocation in which a Christian could engage.

That was left for others with weaker ethics and fewer scruples. This attitude the missionaries conveyed to their converts. Moreover, they taught them that the powers that be are ordained of God and should be obeyed. Consequently the national Christians were content to support colonial rule, especially when times were good and life was easy. It is not surprising, then, to learn that the church *as a church* was not in the vanguard of the independence movement. There were individual Christians who joined the various liberation movements, but they usually drifted away from the church.

Having documented the faults and failings of the missionaries, we should also discuss their victories and successes. Obviously they did *some* things right or we would not be where we are today.

When one remembers the paucity of their numbers; the scarcity of their resources; the raw material with which they had to work; the incredible problems pertaining to food, health, climate, language, and culture, to say nothing of the indifference, ingratitude, opposition, and persecution they encountered, one is astounded at the progress made and the victories won. The famous words of Winston Churchill after the historic Battle of Britain in 1940 can be applied with equal truthfulness to the missionaries of the nineteenth century: "Never was so much owed by so many to so few." What then were some of their successes?

WHAT THE MISSIONARIES DID RIGHT

1. **The missionaries loved the people among whom they worked.** Even their paternalism was born of love. In all modesty they could say of their converts what Paul said of his: "So, being affectionately desirous of you, we were ready to share with you not only the gospel of God but also our own selves, because you had become very dear to us" (I Th 2:8).

They loved them as they loved their own children. In sickness and in health, in peace and in war, in adversity and in prosperity, in life and in death, the missionaries were always there—loving, caring, helping, sharing. To be with their converts they were willing to be separated from their own children nine months of the year. They had many faults; but lack of love was not one of them. Of all the people who went to the East in those early days, the missionaries were the only ones who went to give and not to get.

> The great Thomas Gajetan Ragland, pioneer of itinerating evangelism in South India, died in 1858. More than forty years after his death a missionary asked a pastor who had been trained by him about Ragland's methods in the preparation of his students for the ministry. The old man thought for a few moments, and

then said quietly, "He loved us. He loved us very much. Yes, very much he loved us."[27]

Their self-sacrificing love carried them to great lengths. Time and again they placed their own lives in jeopardy to protect the lives of others. When typhus, yellow fever, bubonic plague, and other dreadful epidemics swept the community missionary doctors and nurses remained at their posts to tend the sick and bury the dead.

2. The missionaries developed a genuine appreciation for the indigenous cultures. Missionaries have often been accused of undermining the local culture and replacing it with Western culture. It is true that they introduced Western learning; and in some cases, notably China, it ultimately undermined the old classical system of education. But it is not true to say that the missionaries set out to destroy the indigenous culture. They more than anyone else tried to preserve the best in those cultures.

In many cases it took time for the missionaries to become accustomed to a strange culture; but once the adjustment was made they soon acquired an appreciation for it. William Carey did for the Bengali language what the famous Chinese scholar Hu Shih did for the ancient Wenli of China. He invented a beautiful, free-flowing colloquial style that replaced the old classical form, thereby making it more intelligible and attractive to modern readers. Carey also showed his appreciation for Indian culture by translating the two great Hindu epics, *Ramayana* and *Mahabharata,* into English. James Legge, missionary to Hong Kong, did the same with the *Four Books* and the *Five Classics* of China.

Long before the modern anthropologists began to roam the world the missionaries were studying the cultures of the people among whom they worked. One such missionary was the English bishop, Robert H. Codrington, who studied the Melanesians of the Pacific. He wrote several books on their languages and cultures, including his famous classic, *The Melanesians.* Codrington is especially known for his discussion of *mana,* belief in a supernatural power which is both nonphysical and nonpresent, being unrelated to spirits or gods. This phenomenon is found in many parts of the world, but Codrington's study greatly clarified it, and his work in this area marks an important base line in the anthropological study of religion. Edwin W. Smith, missionary in South Africa, became president of the Royal Anthropological Institute and author of several books, including *African Ideas of God* and *The Golden Stool.*

---

[27] *Ibid.,* p. 49.

3. The missionaries learned the indigenous languages. The greatest compliment anyone can pay a people is to learn their language. Here again the missionaries showed the way, for they more than any other group took pains to acquire a knowledge of the language. In primitive parts of the world this was no easy task. In many instances the language had no written form. After learning the oral language the missionaries, starting from scratch and without the aid of primers or dictionaries, invented a written script; then they taught that script to their converts. This was a long, painful process and required many years of arduous intellectual work.

Many missionaries learned more than one language. After mastering the trade language they set to work to learn the tribal dialect. Some ended up speaking three or four languages. One European missionary who spoke seven languages fluently was asked which language she used in prayer. After a moment's reflection she replied, "I pray in German; that's the language I was converted in!"

There are 860 known languages and dialects in Africa. A hundred years ago fewer than twenty had a written form. Since then five hundred have been reduced to writing—all the work of missionaries. Let no one imagine that all African languages are primitive. Dan Crawford discovered in Central Africa a language that had nouns in twelve genders and verbs with thirty-two tenses!

4. The missionaries translated the Scriptures. Few people know what a gargantuan task Bible translation can be. It takes the average missionary the best part of ten years to become proficient enough to undertake translation work. He must know not only the finer points of the language, including grammar, syntax, and morphology, but he must be thoroughly acquainted with the culture of the people. That is why the British and Foreign Bible Society will not consider the publication of a manuscript unless the translator has lived in that particular culture for ten years.

The first book to be translated is the Gospel of Mark. It is the shortest of the four Gospels and has the most action and the fewest abstract terms. It is also the simplest and easiest to understand. After Mark they do Genesis, Acts, John, Psalms, and Romans, usually in that order. It takes approximately ten years to complete the translation of the entire New Testament, and another twenty to complete the Old Testament. In the meantime the original translator may himself have been translated to higher service, in which case it will be necessary to find a successor with the ability, interest, and time to do the job. The recently published Lisu Bible for the seventy-thousand member Lisu Church in North Burma was the work of three successive translators and required over forty years to complete.

The technical problems of translation are legion. Take a simple verse like Proverbs 17:3: "The crucible is for silver, and the furnace is for gold, and the Lord tries hearts." What does the missionary do when neither silver nor gold is used in that culture, and when the people have never seen a crucible or a furnace? For "hearts" he may have to substitute "bowels," "kidneys," "liver," or some other organ. Bible translation requires the wisdom of Daniel, the patience of Job, and the longevity of Methuselah.

Today Bible translators are trained linguists; but in the early days they had no technical expertise at all. They had to do the best they could with the tools and talents they had. Their monumental achievements are nothing short of a miracle. Today the entire Bible is available to 90 percent of the world's population. The New Testament is available to another 5 percent. At least one book of the Bible is available to still another 3 percent. This leaves only 2 percent of the world's population without any portion of the Word of God; and Wycliffe Bible Translators, with more than thirty-five hundred members on the job, are hoping to finish the task by 1985. As of December 31, 1975, the Scriptures had been translated into exactly 1,577 languages and dialects of the world. If the missionaries had done nothing more than translate the Holy Scriptures they would have put the world forever in their debt.

5. The missionaries provided modern scientific education for the peoples of the Third World. In country after country the first schools to be opened were mission schools. In other countries the missions were the first to offer Western learning, which in no time at all was in great demand all over Asia. It was in female education that the missions blazed a trail. In the nineteenth century such education was unknown east of Suez and all kinds of opposition developed. When Isabella Thoburn opened the first school for girls in India she had to go from door to door, imploring the parents to permit their daughters to attend her school. One indignant Hindu father retorted: "You want to educate my daughter? Next you'll want to educate my *cow*." Today the prime minister of India is a woman! Indira Gandhi owes more than she would care to acknowledge to the missionaries of the nineteenth century. In China the story was much the same. Unrelenting opposition came from the literati, who felt that Western education posed a threat to their favored position. But the missionaries persevered even when their buildings were ransacked by rampaging nationalists. They operated thousands of elementary schools and hundreds of high schools, plus thirteen full-fledged Christian universities. In Africa they were the sole purveyors of education. In Black Africa today there is hardly a leader in any walk of life who did not receive part of his education in a mission school.

6. The missionaries opened hospitals, clinics, and medical schools. Along with education they introduced modern scientific medicine. In the beginning they had to fight the witchdoctor and the medicine man, to say nothing of the fear and superstition of the illiterate populace. One missionary doctor in Cameroon waited eight long years before the first African had the courage to commit himself to the tender mercies of the white doctor. But patience paid off and perseverance won the day. One or two successful surgical operations broke down opposition and dispelled all fear. After that the people came in droves, many of them in the last stages of disease.

In the bush country missionaries opened clinics and dispensaries. Half the time they didn't bother with a building. Under the open sky they pulled teeth, set bones, lanced boils, washed wounds, and dispensed pills. In the larger cities they established some of the finest hospitals in the world. In China they operated 270 hospitals—not many for a population of 500 million; but they accounted for more than half of the hospitals in the country. In the 1930s 90 percent of all the nurses in China were Christians while less than 1 percent of the population was Christian. Today India has 450 hospitals in the Christian Medical Association.

The capstone of the medical work was the medical schools founded by the various mission boards. For many years the foremost and best-equipped medical school outside Europe and America was the Peking Union Medical College in China. Its founder was Dr. Thomas Cochrane, who conceived the idea of a medical school after the Boxer Rebellion when he was carrying on his medical work in a dilapidated stable in the ruins of Peking. Through the years it produced some of China's finest physicians and surgeons. It is still one of China's outstanding medical institutions; but its name has been changed to Anti-Imperialist People's Hospital.

The Christian Medical College and Hospital in Vellore, India, is one of the most prestigious institutions of its kind in the world. It was founded by Dr. Ida Scudder, who began her work in 1900. Her first building was a vacant shed. Her original equipment consisted of two books, a microscope, and a few bones. On its staff today are 391 full-time doctors, 418 graduate nurses, and 207 paramedical workers. In training are 376 medical students, 276 nursing students, and 147 postgraduate students.

7. The missionaries introduced social and political reforms. This they did by indirect rather than direct methods. Like the early church they did not, indeed they could not, launch a frontal attack on the social and political systems of the day. Quietly, consistently, unobtrusively, they went about their business of teaching and preaching the most revolutionary message the world has ever known. By precept and example they inculcated the ideas and ideals of Christianity—the sanctity of life, the worth of the individual, the dignity of labor, social justice, personal integrity, freedom of thought and speech—which have since been incorporated into the Universal Declaration of Human Rights drawn up by the United Nations.

Untouchability and widow-burning in India, footbinding and concubinage in China, and the destruction of twins in other parts of the world have all been outlawed by government decree; but it was the missionaries who first inveighed against these evils, often at great cost to themselves.

In political reform no less than in social reform the missionaries played an important role, albeit behind the scenes. In China Sun Yat-sen, himself a Christian, counted greatly on Christian support. Many of the leading members of the Chinese Republic after the Revolution of 1911 were graduates of the Anglo-Chinese College in Tientsin. "The College won the enthusiastic support of Yuan Shih-Kai, the President of the Republic, and its missionary founder—Dr. Samuel Lavington Hart—was tutor to Yuan Shih-Kai's son."[28]

W. H. P. Faunce, president of Brown University, visited China shortly after the 1911 Revolution. There he met Timothy Richard. This was his report:

> The work of Dr. Timothy Richard, secretary of the Christian Literature Society, has for forty-five years been a leavening force throughout all China. The writer recently saw him at his desk in Shanghai, surrounded by his Chinese assistants and translators, in a small office that is as influential as the headquarters of any foreign embassy in Peking. On the shelves were the Chinese versions, made by the society, of some two hundred standard English books, religious, scientific, historical, medical, philosophical, economic. These, with almost innumerable smaller works, have been scattered for four decades through the empire, and studied by Chinese students and literati. The world sees the revolution and the republic—it does not, cannot, see the causes behind the event. It sees the explosion, not the planting of the mine. It sees the Manchus driven out; it cannot see the great economic and religious truths driven in by half a century of silent, ceaseless publication. But when ten thousand Christian women in China united in presenting to the Empress Dowager on her sixtieth birthday a magnificent copy of the Bible, and when the young Emperor eagerly began to read it, then at last the heedless world began

---

[28] Goodall, *op. cit.,* p. 51.

to realize that even the haughty Middle Kingdom stood on the brink of change.[29]

The missionaries' contribution to reform in Africa has been enormous. It is no exaggeration to say that without the groundwork laid by them, especially in education, not a single country in Black Africa would be independent today. No one knows this better than the Africans themselves.

The earliest country to achieve independence was Ghana in 1957. Its first president in one of his early announcements said: "We owe much to the missionaries, and we will continue to welcome them to our country." Prime Minister Balewa of Nigeria, in his Motion for Independence made in parliament in January 1960 said: "We are grateful to the missionaries who have done so much to assist in the independence of Nigeria. . . . Missions can look back with satisfaction on many notable educational successes, and indeed, there are, I am sure, some honorable members present who are a living testimony to this." Jomo Kenyatta, one-time leader of the terrorist Mau Mau Movement, later president of Kenya, more than once went on public record, thanking the missionaries for their contribution to Kenya's independence and inviting them to stay and help him build a better country.

8. The missionaries formed a bridge between East and West and helped to bring the two together. World understanding is essential to world peace, especially in this nuclear age when it is possible to destroy an entire civilization in a matter of minutes. Kipling declared that East and West would never meet, but they have; and the missionaries made the greatest contribution. They not only carried Christianity and Western civilization to the ends of the earth, they also brought the great civilizations of the East to the peoples of the West.

Lord Macaulay, one of England's greatest literary lights in the nineteenth century and author of the Minute on Education of 1835, which determined India's educational course for more than a century, took a very dim view of Indian civilization. After confessing that he had no knowledge of Eastern languages he went on to say:

> I have never known one among them [Orientalists] who could deny that a single shelf of a good European library was worth the whole native literature of India and Arabia. The intrinsic superiority of the Western literature is, indeed, fully admitted by those members of the Committee who support the Oriental plan of education.[30]

---

[29] W. H. P. Faunce, *The Social Aspects of Foreign Missions* (New York: Missionary Education Movement, 1914), pp. 113-114.

[30] Michael Edwardes, *A History of India: From the Earliest Times to the Present Day* (Norwich: Jarrold and Sons, 1961), p. 261.

Contrast with this the attitude and understanding of William Carey, whose appreciation of Indian culture led him to produce his monumental *Dictionary of All Sanskrit-derived Languages.*

In China the missionary's admiration for Chinese civilization was great indeed. Bishop James W. Brashford ranked Confucius, along with Socrates, Epictetus, and Marcus Aurelius, as one of the greatest teachers of mankind. In his book, *The Lore of Cathay,* W. A. P. Martin went to the defense of Chinese civilization, stating: "Never have a great people been more misunderstood." S. Wells Williams' famous book, *The Middle Kingdom,* remains to this day a standard work on nineteenth-century China. On his return from China Williams became Yale University's first Professor of Chinese literature. James Legge, translator of the Confucian Classics, on his return to England became the first Professor of Chinese at Oxford University, a position he held for twenty years.

Paul Varg of Princeton, not particularly sympathetic to missionary work, had this to say:

> Westerners would have known little about China had it not been for the missionaries. Those who would dismiss them with scorn out of a feeling of revulsion for their obscurantist theological views do them an injustice. Anyone seeking to understand the Orient will find in the many articles written by missionaries, for instance those published in journals of the Royal Asiatic Society, excellent scholarship and will likewise benefit by a reading of their books.[31]

M. Searle Bates, former Professor of Missions at Union Theological Seminary, observed that in linguistics, history, ethnology, archaeology, and the social sciences Far Eastern missionaries have made studies of lasting value, not only to cultural understanding but also in the fields of exact science.

Thinking largely of Africa, Professor E. A. Hootan of Harvard said:

> As an anthropologist, I have completely reversed my opinion of missionaries. These men and women have contributed more to our knowledge of the peoples of the world than have the entire ruck of professional travellers and explorers. They may have done more than the anthropologists themselves.[32]

Sir H. H. Johnston said: "Huge is the debt which philologists owe to the labors of British missionaries in Africa. Many of these tongues were on the point of extinction and have since become extinct, and we owe our knowledge of them solely to the missionaries' intervention."[33]

[31] Varg, *op. cit.,* pp. 120-121.
[32] *Christian World Facts* (New York: Foreign Missions Conference of North America, 1941), p. 96.
[33] H. H. Johnston, *British Central Africa* (London: Methuen, 1897), p. 205.

Missionary scholars were not the only ones to increase our knowledge of the world. The ordinary missionary by his letters and his furlough ministry added greatly to our fund of knowledge. Henry L. Stimson, Secretary of State under President Roosevelt, made the following statement:

> Our most general information of China came through the great missionary movement. . . . The breadth and influence of that movement have not always been adequately appreciated by historians. . . . The news of the work of these missionaries coming through their reports and letters reached a large number of our people living in almost every quarter of the land. To many of them the progress of this work was one of their keenest interests.[34]

Many wars, large and small, have been fought between Eastern and Western nations; but they occurred not because of, but in spite of, the presence of the missionaries.

> The cause of world peace owed more to the ambassadors of the Christian faith than to any other single agency. Among savage tribes they have gone repairing the damage done by the white man's rum, his vices, his cruelties. But among the older and stronger peoples the missionary has constantly been mediator and interpreter.[35]

During World War II President Roosevelt sent Wendell Willkie on a fact-finding world tour. On his return he made this report:

> I came home certain of one clear and significant fact; that there exists in the world today a gigantic reservoir of good will towards the American people. Many things have created this enormous reservoir. At the top of the list go the hospitals, schools, and colleges which American missionaries, teachers, and doctors have founded in the far corners of the world.[36]

9. The missionaries planted the church in nearly every country in the world. At the beginning of the modern missionary era the church was a Western institution, confined entirely to Europe and America. Today it is the most truly universal institution in the world, thanks to the work of the missionaries.

When the first German Lutheran missionaries, Ziegenbalg and Plütschau, went to India in 1705 they took on a humanly impossible assignment. They were followed by the Moravians, who went to the West Indies in 1732 and Greenland in 1733. Beginning with the nineteenth century, first in Britain and later in the United States, the movement began to come to life in all parts of the world. Within a period of

---

[34] Henry L. Stimson, *The Far Eastern Crisis* (New York, London: Published for the Council on Foreign Relations by Harper & Bros., 1936), pp. 153-154.
[35] W. H. P. Faunce, *op. cit.*, p. 197.
[36] Wendell Willkie, *One World* (New York: Simon and Schuster, 1943), p. 158.

thirty years missions had been founded in the South Sea Islands, Burma, China, Africa, and the Middle East. By the beginning of the twentieth century missionaries were found in every land that would receive them.

Wherever they went they opened hospitals and schools; but their prime purpose was the founding of churches. To this end they devoted all their resources and energies. Their schools, at least in the beginning, were auxiliary enterprises designed to contribute to the building of strong churches with an educated ministry. Everywhere the gospel was preached, the Bible was translated, Christian literature was disseminated, catechists were instructed in the faith, converts were baptized, pastors, evangelists, and Biblewomen were trained, churches were organized, and the sacraments were administered.

The raw material out of which the churches were built differed widely from place to place. It included the Brahmins of India, the literati of China, the samurai of Japan, the Hottentots and Bushmen of Africa, the Eskimos of Greenland, the aborigines of Australia, the Indians of South America, the headhunters of New Guinea, the cannibals of the South Seas. All walks of life and all classes of men were included in the gospel invitation. Old and young, rich and poor, literate and illiterate, captains and coolies, soldiers and slaves, tribal chiefs and medicine men, fakirs and philosophers, princes and paupers, scholars and scavengers—all found their way into the Christian fold; all became members of the Body of Christ.

Today there are not more than half a dozen small, inaccessible countries without an organized Christian church; and even in those countries there are individual Christians who are shining as lights in a dark place. After two thousand years the Church of Jesus Christ has become truly universal and is fast approaching the day when in deed and in truth it will include in its membership "every tribe and tongue and people and nation" (Re 5:9).

And so it goes. To most of the world the missionary remains something of an enigma even to this day. Is it possible to strike a balance on such a controversial figure? Kenneth Scott Latourette, former Professor of Missions and History at Yale University, has probably come closer to the truth than anyone else:

> The missionaries were the one group of foreigners whose major endeavor was to make the impact of the West upon the Middle Kingdom of benefit to the Chinese. Bigoted and narrow they frequently were, occasionally superstitious, and sometimes domineering and serenely convinced of the superiority of Western culture and of their own particular form of Christianity. When all that can be said in criticism of the missionaries has been said, however, and it is not a little, the fact remains that nearly always at considerable and very often at great sacrifice they came to China, and in unsanitary and uncongenial surroundings, usually

with insufficient stipends, often at the cost of their own lives or the lives that were dearer to them than their own, labored indefatigably for an alien people who did not want them or their message. Whatever may be the final judgment on the major premises, the methods, and the results of the missionary enterprise, the fact cannot be gainsaid that for sheer altruism and heroic faith here is one of the bright pages in the history of the race.[37]

---

[37] Kenneth Scott Latourette, *A History of Christian Missions in China* (New York: The Macmillan Company, 1929), pp. 824-825.

7

Methodological Imperatives

The Christian missionary is first of all an evangelist. His primary task is to preach the gospel to every creature and make disciples of all nations. And everything he does is expected to contribute, directly or indirectly, to that end.

Wherever he went he preached the gospel, translated the Scriptures, won converts, and established churches. But he soon discovered that there were other forms of service that he was required to render if he was to follow in the steps of his Master, who went about all Galilee, teaching and healing as well as preaching the gospel (Mt 4:23).

It was not possible for him as a Christian to close his eyes to the appalling nonspiritual needs around about him. With the parable of the Good Samaritan ringing in his ears he had no choice; he had to do something to meet the physical and material needs of his constituency.

Man has three parts to his nature—body, mind, and soul. All three parts were affected by the Fall; all three must be included in the redemptive process (1 Th 5:23). The soul must be saved (Ja 1:21); the mind must be renewed (Ro 12:2); even the body is to be redeemed (Ro 8:23). The gospel of Jesus Christ is designed to meet the needs of the whole man. It is not simply grace abounding in the past (Ro 5:20), or glory by and by (Ro 8:18), but love here and now expressed in deed as well as word (1 Jn 3:17-18).

Having preached the gospel and saved their souls, the missionary could not say to his desperately needy brothers and sisters, "Go in peace, be warmed and filled" (Ja 2:16). The compassion of Christ compelled him to give them those things that were needed for the body. He was obliged then by the nature of the gospel and by the circumstances of his own calling to share everything he had. So the missionary opened hospitals and schools, thus paving the way for a full-orbed ministry to the whole man.

Evangelistic Missions

Evangelism is at the heart of all missionary endeavor. Missionary work that does not include evangelism is not missionary work at all.

> The very heart of the gospel lies in its mission to the world. The church's main task is to stand on the street corners of the world and shout, "The good news has come!" We cannot escape this obligation by ignoring it. Neither can we delegate it to others. Church and mission are one, and cannot in any way be broken apart. . . . Mission can never be thought of as only one of the marks of the church. It is *the* mark of the church. All other so-called marks, if legitimate, are but explication of mission. The only power which Christ through the Holy Spirit promises to the church is power to witness. All other church activities are derived from this essential task and must be judged by it.[1]

This applies with equal force to what we might call the auxiliary enterprises of the Christian mission—hospitals, schools, and other institutions. A school or a hospital is a *mission* institution only when it has a strong Christian witness. Without that it is simply humanitarian service.

What do we understand by evangelism? The definitions are legion. The Madras Conference of the International Missionary Council came up with no fewer than thirty-one definitions of evangelism. Michael Green defines evangelism in the strict sense of "proclaiming the good news of salvation to men and women with a view to their conversion to Christ and incorporation in his Church."[2] J. I. Packer suggests a very simple definition: "Evangelism is just preaching the gospel, the evangel."[3] In a word, evangelism is that activity of the Christian church by which it communicates the gospel of Jesus Christ to a lost world.

Underlying the concept of evangelism are three presuppositions, all of which have the support of the Scriptures. (1) All men are lost and

---

[1] John E. Skoglund, *To the Whole Creation* (Valley Forge, Pa.: Judson Press, 1962), p. 94.
[2] Michael Green, *Evangelism in the Early Church* (Grand Rapids, Mich.: Wm. B. Eerdmans Publishing Company, 1970), p. 7.
[3] J. I. Packer, *Evangelism and the Sovereignty of God* (London: Inter-Varsity Fellowship, 1961), p. 41.

need to be saved. (2) There is only one way of salvation and that is through Jesus Christ. (3) In order to be saved one must understand and believe the gospel.

It must be emphasized that evangelism is not an end in itself. Rather, it is a means to an end. On the mission field it has a twofold purpose. The immediate purpose is the conversion of the individual to Jesus Christ. The ultimate purpose is the establishing of strong spiritual, indigenous churches.

Both of these concepts—the conversion of the individual and the growth of the church—are under attack today. In ecumenical circles salvation is no longer personal but societal. Reconciliation is not between man and God but between man and man. Humanization and not redemption is the mission of the church.[4] To further complicate the situation "conversion" is a dirty word in some parts of the Third World, where it is equated with "proselytism." Several states in India have passed anticonversion laws designed to hinder the work of Christian missions. Hinduism professes to be the most tolerant of all the religions in the world. It will tolerate everything—except conversion! Some countries, such as Nepal, Afghanistan, Somalia, et al, have made it a capital offense for any citizen to change his religion.

This makes it very difficult, if not dangerous, for the Christian missionary to carry on his work. But in spite of all the difficulties he must always bear in mind that he is an ambassador for Christ and his chief task is to call upon all men everywhere to be reconciled to God through Jesus Christ (2 Co 5:19, 20; Acts 17:30, 31).

But conversion to Christ is only one of two goals. The other is the establishing of indigenous churches in all parts of the world. Here again we run into opposition. An increasing number of Christian leaders are telling us that the best thing for the church to do is to close its doors and go into liquidation. The church, they say, should be like the grain of wheat in John 12 that falls into the ground and dies. For all such leaders talk of church growth is not only erroneous, it is deplorable. The church should penetrate the world, take its agenda from the world, and lose its identity in the world.

If evangelism is the main task of the church, the church is the ultimate goal of evangelism. There *is* a difference between the church and the world. The church may be feeble, fragmented and unfaithful; it is still the body (Co 1:18) and bride (Eph 5:32) of Christ. In spite of its obvious incompleteness the church is "the fulness of Him who fills all in all" (Eph 1:23). As such it should not be downgraded or despised. The missionary, therefore, makes no apology for the fact

---

[4] For an excellent treatment of this problem see Peter Beyerhaus, *Missions: Which Way? Humanization or Redemption* (Grand Rapids, Mich.: Zondervan Publishing House, 1971).

that he is interested in the internal growth and the worldwide expansion of the church. Every person converted to Christ becomes a member of the universal church; and individual churches are local expressions of that one church. Persons are added to the church only as they are joined to Christ by faith (Acts 2:47).

Today we speak of three kinds of evangelism: presence evangelism, proclamation evangelism, and persuasion evangelism. As usual the Christian church is divided over the matter. On one hand we have some liberals who emphasize presence evangelism and all but deny or neglect proclamation evangelism. On the other hand we have some conservatives who believe in proclamation evangelism but deny the validity of presence evangelism and shy away from persuasion evangelism.

Presence evangelism refers to that nonverbal witness which the Christian church gives simply by virtue of its presence in the community. This is the kind of evangelism that is becoming more and more popular in ecumenical circles. Mahatma Gandhi favored this kind of evangelism. He took a dim view of any religion that requires articulation. Religion, he argued, should be like a rose that makes its presence known simply by giving off a pleasant odor. He said, "I do not believe in people telling others of their faith, especially with a view to conversion. Faith does not admit of telling. It has to be lived and then it becomes self-propagating."[5]

Presence evangelism is not the kind found most prominently on the pages of the New Testament, and it is a mistake to advocate it as *the* most desirable method. Nevertheless it is not wrong. It does have some validity. There is a twofold witness that the Christian gives—one by lip and the other by life. They belong together. Jesus clearly taught that His disciples were to be as salt in the earth and as light in the world (Mt 5:13-16). The emphasis there is on the quality of life. "Let your light so shine before men that they may *see your good works* and glorify your Father who is in heaven." It is absolutely essential that Christian behavior square with Christian belief. Otherwise the world will not be impressed.

In every culture there are those who remain unmoved by argumentation. They will be won not by precept but by example. The apostle Peter makes this very clear when he says, "Likewise you wives, be submissive to your husbands, so that some, though they do not obey the word, may be won *without a word* by the behavior of their wives, when they see your reverent and chaste behavior" (1 Pe 3:1-2). As every student of Christian missions knows, there are countries in the Third World where it is not possible to engage in proclamation

---

[5] M. K. Gandhi, *Christian Missions: Their Place in India* (Ahmedabad, Navajivan Press, 1941), p. 35.

evangelism. To do so is to break the law and run the risk of being expelled from the country. A classic example here would be the countries that make up the Muslim world, particularly those in North Africa and the Middle East. A missionary passing through Afghanistan on his way home on furlough gave a Gospel of Luke to the proprietor of a bazaar in Kabul. The incident was reported to the police. In a matter of minutes he was arrested and spent several months in jail. Obviously in all such situations the only form of evangelism possible is presence evangelism. The missionaries must be prepared to be patient, to take the long view, and to serve the people in the name and spirit of Christ, hoping for the day when all nations will honor Article Eighteen of the Universal Declaration of Human Rights drawn up by the United Nations, which guarantees full religious freedom, including the freedom to change one's religion.

The second kind of evangelism is proclamation evangelism. This is the kind found most frequently in the New Testament. This is the kind that Archbishop Whately had in mind when he said, "If our religion is wrong we ought to change it; if it is true we ought to propagate it." Christianity by its very nature is missionary. It has a message of life and hope for the whole world. This message called the gospel contains certain propositional truths concerning the person and work of Jesus Christ. These truths must be articulated, line upon line and precept upon precept. Before a person can exercise saving faith in Christ he must be made acquainted with the historical facts concerning the life, death, and resurrection of Christ. Only then can he decide for or against Christ.

This is the kind of evangelism associated with "preaching" found so frequently in the New Testament. John and Jesus both came "preaching." Peter and John preached so successfully in Jerusalem that they were accused of filling the city with their doctrine and were forbidden to teach or preach again in the name of Jesus (Acts 4:18). And what shall be said of the apostle Paul, the greatest preacher of all? Immediately upon his conversion he preached Christ in the synagogue in Damascus (Acts 9:20). A whole generation later we find the last chapter in Acts leaves Paul a prisoner in his own hired house in Rome, preaching the Kingdom of God (Acts 28:31). To the Corinthians he wrote: "Christ did not send me to baptize but to preach" (1 Co 1:17). Again he said: "Woe to me if I do not preach the gospel!" (1 Co 9:16).

Persuasion evangelism goes one step beyond proclamation evangelism in that it tries to induce men to *accept* the gospel. It is not content to "preach" the gospel and leave it at that. A concerted effort is made to "persuade" them to come to terms with Jesus Christ. Preaching the gospel is serious business. Certainly it was for Paul and his fellow apostles. The message is a savor either of life unto life or death unto death. To hear the gospel and reject it is worse than not hearing it at all. Little wonder that Paul exclaimed, "Who is sufficient for these things?" (2 Co 2:16).

There are those who assert that the missionary is responsible only for the proclamation and not for the reception of the gospel, and that no effort should be made to "get results." It is difficult to believe that Paul was not interested in results. His passion for souls was so great that he could say, "I have great sorrow and unceasing anguish in my heart; for I could wish that I myself were accursed and cut off from Christ for the sake of my brethren, my kinsmen by race" (Ro 9:2, 3). He also said, "I have become all things to all men, that I might by all means save some" (1 Co 9:22).

John the Baptist was not the only New Testament preacher who called for a verdict (Mt 3:7-12). Peter and Paul did the same. To both Jews and Gentiles they offered forgiveness of sins and life everlasting. They also warned of judgment to come (Acts 17:31) and they called for repentance (Acts 2:38; 3:19). They were not content to preach the gospel and leave it at that. They did their best to bring men to Christ. Paul made his position crystal clear. "Knowing the fear of the Lord, we persuade men" (2 Co 5:11). He goes on to say, "We are ambassadors for Christ, God making his appeal through us; we beseech you on behalf of Christ, be reconciled to God" (2 Co 5:20).

There are those who eschew this kind of evangelism as being unworthy of the Christian cause. They argue that religion is a private matter and no one has a right to impose his religious convictions on another. It must be acknowledged that this kind of evangelism can easily be abused. Persuasion, if carried too far, can easily become coercion. This is especially true on the mission field, where evangelism and philanthropy often go hand in hand. There is always the temptation to take unfair advantage of the adverse circumstances in which a person may find himself by pressing upon him the claims of Christ. More than once missionaries, Roman Catholic and Protestant, have been accused of "buying" converts with famine relief money. When patients in a mission hospital are *required* to listen to a presentation of the gospel before being admitted to the doctor's office, is this a form of coercion?

On the other hand it must be remembered that the missionary doctor knows that every patient who comes to him has *two* kinds of disease, one physical and the other spiritual. In the long run the spiritual disease, if not attended to, will prove more disastrous than the physical. For the missionary doctor to heal a patient's body and do nothing for his soul would not only be a denial of his missionary vocation, but would certainly be a disservice to the patient. The fact that the patient is not aware of his spiritual disease is all the more reason why the missionary doctor should point it out to him.

The Laymen's Foreign Missions Inquiry in the early thirties drew attention to this problem. In its report on medical work it stated: "The use of medical or other professional service as a direct means of making converts, or public services in wards and dispensaries from which patients cannot escape, is subtly coersive, and improper."[6]

Our Lord affords us a worthy example at this point. He rightly expected His miracles to produce repentance on the part of the nation (Mt 11:20-24) and faith on the part of the individual (Jn 10:38); but He did not force people to accept spiritual healing in order to get physical healing. Never once did He say to a healed person: "I have healed your body; now you must follow Me." He was Savior as well as Healer. He desired that all men should be "made whole." He offered them healing for body *and* soul. They were free to accept either or both or neither. At the same time He warned them that the soul is infinitely more important than the body (Mk 9:47), and that when a person loses his soul he loses all (Mk 8:36). Nevertheless it is a safe assumption that most persons were content to settle for physical healing. Nine of the ten lepers healed by Jesus fell into this category (Lk 17:12-19). Christian missionaries, in their desire to save souls, must resist the temptation to use humanitarian service simply as a "bait" to win converts to the faith. Persuasion by all means, but not coercion.

In any discussion of evangelism we must make sure that we adhere faithfully to the Biblical meaning of the term. The word *evangelism* is often used to describe a large number of activities which have little or no relation to the proclamation of the gospel. In some circles all activities other than medical and educational are lumped together and called evangelism. Many of these activities are right and proper and serve a worthwhile cause. They should not, however, be called evangelism. This is particularly true on the mission field where humanitarian services have always been an integral part of the modern missionary enterprise.

Two words in the New Testament are pertinent to our study of evangelism. One is a noun, the other a verb. The noun is *euangelion* and means "good news." It occurs seventy-five times. The verb is *euangelizomai*. It means "to publish good news." It appears twenty-four times. *Euangelion* is the word from which we get our English word *evangelism*. The gospel is the evangel, the good news. Evangelism is the act of proclaiming the good news.

Nor are we left in any doubt concerning the exact nature of the

---

6 The Commission of Appraisal, *Re-Thinking Missions* (New York: Harper and Brothers, 1932), p. 201.

good news. In its broadest sense the word *gospel* can be used to include the sum total of the teaching of Christ, including the Sermon on the Mount. This would certainly be its meaning in Mark 1:1, where we read: "The beginning of the gospel of Jesus Christ, the Son of God." It also ties in with the words of Christ in the Great Commission: "Teaching them to observe *all* that I have commanded you" (Mt 28:20).

In its narrowest sense the word *gospel* refers to the good news of the reconciling work of Christ accomplished through His atoning death and His victorious resurrection. Paul makes this clear when he defines the gospel in 1 Corinthians 15:1-3. This is the kernel of truth at the heart of the gospel. This is the irreducible minimum that a person must know and believe in order to be saved. The missionary may preach more; he dare not preach less.

After 250 years of modern missionary history it is pertinent to ask: "Is the evangelization of the world the white man's burden?" In the beginning it was necessary for the churches in Europe and North America to assume full responsibility for the evangelization of the rest of the world. But after 175 years of missionary work the Student Volunteer Movement, whose watchword was "The evangelization of the world in this generation," was entirely a Western phenomenon. We still thought of evangelization as the white man's burden.

The same psychology developed on the mission field. Too often the Western missionary created the impression that he and he alone was responsible for world evangelization. He did this all unconsciously by his method of work. Wherever he went he won converts, trained leaders, and organized churches. As soon as the church could manage its own affairs, the missionary moved on to another place to repeat the performance. To be sure, before he left he trained pastors, teachers, evangelists, and Biblewomen; but he did not train missionaries. They must come from the West!

The churches he left behind were supposed to be self-governing, self-supporting, and self-propagating; but in many instances this was only partially true. The churches were far more interested in governing themselves than in propagating the faith. By the second and third generation many of them were completely devoid of all evangelistic zeal and completely preoccupied with their own existence. They had no burden for the unreached areas of their own country, much less the evangelization of the world. The missionaries would take care of that.

The national churches are not altogether to blame for this state of affairs. The missionary, by always being on the move, always blazing trails, always penetrating into unreached territory, created the impression in the minds of the church leaders that he and not they were responsible for world evangelization. This was a great mistake. From the beginning he should have encouraged the church leaders to accompany him on his journeys into virgin territory and thus have inculcated in them the missionary spirit.

During this postwar period a new and encouraging development has taken place. National churches throughout the Third World are waking up to their responsibility not only for the evangelization of their own country but of countries overseas. So important is this development that a fuller treatment of the subject is given in chapter 8: Christianity in the Third World.

It is imperative that the churches of the Third World assume responsibility for the evangelization of their own people. Other things being equal it is better for a person to hear the gospel *for the very first time* from the lips of one of his own people. This has several advantages: (1) He will understand it more easily. (2) He will accept it more readily. (3) He will not be so likely to regard it as a foreign religion. (4) He will be more likely to share it with his neighbors. It is simply a matter of fact that Western missionaries do not make the best communicators in a cross-cultural situation. National evangelists are much better at communicating the gospel to their own people. With them language is no problem, culture is no barrier, life-style is no deterrent.

From the beginning Christian converts should be encouraged to witness for Christ on a voluntary basis. No convert should be *paid* to share his faith. This was one of the four principles laid down by John L. Nevius, Presbyterian missionary in China. He advocated that each convert abide in the calling wherein he was called. At the same time he was to be an individual worker for Christ, living for Christ in his own neighborhood and supporting himself by his trade.

This was certainly the pattern laid down by the early church. Even secular historians have remarked upon this phenomenon. In an effort to explain the rapid growth of Christianity in the Roman Empire, Gibbon wrote: "It became the most sacred duty of a new convert to diffuse amongst his friends and relations the inestimable blessing which he had received."[7] Will Durant made the same observation: "Nearly every convert, with the ardor of a revolutionary, made himself an office of propaganda."[8]

With no weapon but truth and no banner but love, the single-minded, warm-hearted followers of Jesus traveled by land and sea to all parts of the empire; and wherever they went they gladly shared their new-found faith with friends, relatives, neighbors, and strangers. As slaves, traders, and, later on, soldiers, they used their secular calling to advance the cause of Christ. Even as exiles they carried the conta-

---

[7] Edward Gibbon, *The Decline and Fall of the Roman Empire* (New York: Harcourt, Brace and Company, 1960), p. 147.

[8] Will Durant, *Caesar and Christ* (New York: Simon and Schuster, 1944), p. 602.

gion of their faith to distant shores and into inhospitable regions.

This does not rule out full-time, fully paid evangelists. They have their place. They are not, however, a substitute for, but a supplement to, the laymen who, in the course of their daily routine, speak of Christ to their friends and neighbors. Preferably these evangelists should be in the employ of the church, not the mission, though there might be exceptions.

In some countries, especially Muslim countries, it is not possible to engage in direct evangelism. In some instances it is against the law; in others public opinion will not tolerate it. In all such countries the only kind of evangelism possible is presence evangelism. Missionary work in the Middle East has been confined pretty much to medical and educational institutions. The influence of these institutions has been enormous. If there is any residue of good will towards the United States in the Arab world today it is due largely to the part played by these institutions, particularly the famous American University in Beirut, which for almost a hundred years was a missionary school. Missionaries working in the Muslim world must be endowed with a double portion of faith, hope, love, and patience.

The question naturally arises: Should missionaries remain in these countries decade after decade with little or nothing but good will to show for their endeavors? The question is a good one. It is not easy to answer. There are two schools of thought in the matter. One school advocates a strategy that would concentrate most if not all of our forces in responsive areas. The other school regards the unresponsive Muslim countries as being an integral part of the world for which Christ died. Certainly they are to be included in the "all nations" referred to by Jesus in the Great Commission. This being so, they cannot be left out. The Christian church has no choice but to obey the command of her Lord.

Evangelism has been most successful among primitive peoples. This should not surprise us. The New Testament reminds us that certain classes are difficult to win. Jesus said, "It is easier for a camel to go through the eye of a needle than for a rich man to enter the kingdom of God" (Mt 19:24). Paul indicated that intellectuals have certain hang-ups that hinder acceptance of the simple gospel (1 Co 1:18-23). Paul's experience with the philosophers in Athens supported his view. Jesus also recognized that worldly wisdom is more of a liability than an asset when it comes to understanding spiritual truth (Mt 11:25).

The history of missionary work in India bears this out. Sherwood Eddy made the statement that 80 percent of India's Christians came from a background of untouchability. At the other end of the social spectrum is the Brahmin caste. Comparatively few of them have embraced Christianity. The same was true to a lesser extent in China.

Most of the opposition, especially in the nineteenth century, came from the scholar-gentry class. In Burma well over 05 percent of the Christians are tribespeople in the hill country. Only a small number of Burmans from a Buddhist background have become Christians. Black Africa, the heartland of animism, has yielded more converts than all the rest of the Third World put together.

Is the evangelistic missionary on the way out? Is it not true that the developing countries prefer missionaries with professional and technical skills who can make a contribution to nation building? This is a widely held view, and it is basically true; but it is not universally applicable. There is no evidence that evangelistic or church-planting missionaries are singled out for discrimination. Many countries are trying desperately to get nationals into positions of leadership in all walks of life including the church. Anyone going to India today must prove to the government that among India's 600 million people there is not one who has the skills necessary to do the job he is going there to fill. That applies to all expatriates, missionary and nonmissionary alike.

Contrary to popular opinion, in some countries, at least, the church-planting missionary may be the last to leave. Most mission schools have long since been taken over by the government. In many countries socialized medicine is rapidly supplanting missionary medicine. None of these governments shows any signs of getting involved in religion. Consequently they are not likely to take over the purely religious institutions, such as churches, Bible schools, and seminaries. It is quite possible that the missionary working in these institutions may be the last to leave.

Evangelism, which seems to be dragging its feet in the homelands, is certainly on the march throughout the Third World. Evangelism-in-Depth, first launched in 1960, has covered more than a dozen countries in Latin America. The Berlin Congress on Evangelism in 1966 spawned regional congresses in Nigeria, Singapore, Zaire, Bogota, India, and Minneapolis. A second conclave, the International Congress on World Evangelization, was convened in Lausanne in July 1974.

In all parts of the world the Holy Spirit is raising up national evangelists who are conducting city-wide campaigns, often with free radio and television coverage. They include Luis Palau and Hermano Pablo in Latin America, Bakht Singh in India, Akira Hatori and Koji Honda in Japan, and Peter Octavianus in Indonesia—to mention only a few. The largest outdoor stadiums are not large enough to accommodate the crowds that press in to hear the gospel. The Assemblies of God have conducted Good News Crusades in dozens of countries. The Southern Baptists have held large evangelistic campaigns in Japan, Brazil, Spain, Korea, and North America. Organizations heavily engaged in mass evangelism include Overseas Crusades, African Enterprises, and World Vision International.

Gospel literature and Scripture distribution, both the handmaidens of evangelism, have greatly increased their output in recent years. Last year the American Bible Society distributed 163 million Scriptures. Operation Mobilization, with its good ship *Logos,* is seeking to saturate large areas of Europe and Southeast Asia with gospel literature. Gospel Recordings has given away free more than 7 million gospel records in almost four thousand languages and dialects. The latest innovation is gospel cassettes.

So far as the Third World is concerned, now is the day of salvation (2 Co 6:2).

Medical Missions

Christianity, in contrast to the Oriental religions, is a world-affirming religion. It is interested in the here-and-now as well as the life to come. It is interested in ministering to the whole man—body as well as soul. Jesus went about healing as well as teaching and preaching. His most common question was: "Wilt thou be made whole?" The word *whole* comes from the Anglo-Saxon root *hal* from which we get our two words *health* and *holiness.* Health is the well-being of the body. Holiness is the well-being of the soul. They belong together. Both are necessary if the person is to be "made whole."

When Jesus sent out the Twelve and again when He sent out the seventy, He instructed them to heal the sick. The first recorded miracle in the early church was the healing of the lame man in Acts 3.

The modern missionary movement, taking its cue from Jesus, has actively promoted medical missions, including clinics, dispensaries, sanitoria, rest homes, hospitals, and in a few cases medical schools. In fact, modern scientific medicine and surgery were introduced to the Third World by Christian missionaries. Some of the outstanding pioneers were medical men: Dr. John Scudder in India, Dr. Peter Parker in China, Dr. Paul Harrison in Arabia, Dr. Daniel Bradley in Thailand, and, of course, Dr. David Livingstone in Africa. Some missionaries became personal physician to the royal family in the countries where they served.

BENEFITS OF MEDICAL MISSIONS

1. It brings healing to the body. Unlike the Oriental religions, Christianity attaches great importance to the body. Salvation in its fullest sense includes the body as well as the soul. According to Genesis 2, the body as well as the soul of man was made by God. God has as much interest in the one as in the other. The body was made for health, not for sickness. It is obvious that man functions best when he is in good health. No one finds a throbbing toothache particularly conducive to either work or prayer. Disease is an aberration introduced by the Fall. It is therefore part of the kingdom of darkness that Jesus came to destroy (Mt 12:22-30; 1 Jn 3:8). That is why He "went about doing good and healing all that were oppressed of the devil" (Acts 10:38).

Even today in mission lands there is an enormous amount of unrelieved sickness and pain that cries out for healing. The church cannot turn a deaf ear to those cries. To do so would be a denial of our faith. Jesus, speaking of the believer, said, "He who believes in me will also do the works that I do" (Jn 14:12). Again he said, "As the Father has sent me, even so I send you" (Jn 20:21). The missionary, like his Master before him, is desperately concerned for the healing of the body. The healing of the body is not simply a means to an end —the healing of the soul. It is a good work in and of itself. Certainly the healing ministry, which has been an integral part of the missionary enterprise, falls within the guidelines given by Paul to Titus: "This is a faithful saying, and these things I will that thou affirm constantly, that they which have believed in God might be careful to maintain good works. These things are good and profitable unto men" (Ti 3:8).

2. It disarms prejudice and creates good will. This was especially true in the nineteenth century when antiforeign feeling ran high in most parts of the Third World, particularly in the Orient. In one of his letters from North China, Charlie Studd wrote: "For five years we never went outside our doors without a volley of curses from our neighbors."[9] It was said of Peter Parker that he "opened China at the point of the lancet." Xenophobia was by no means confined to China. In the 1880s the pioneer missionaries were in grave danger of being expelled from Korea. The situation changed almost overnight when in 1884 Dr. H. N. Allen successfully treated the wounds of a member of the royal family. Dr. Dan Bradley, personal physician to Thailand's famous King Mongkut, so ingratiated himself with the king that he became the king's advisor on foreign affairs and the translator of important government documents. In this capacity it was said that "Bradley's influence on the Thai government was incalculable."[10] No Asian country has had more cordial relations with the United States than Thailand—thanks to Dr. Bradley.

---

[9] Norman P. Grubb, *C. T. Studd: Cricketer and Pioneer* (London: Religious Tract Society, 1934), p. 95.
[10] Donald C. Lord, *Mo Bradley and Thailand* (Grand Rapids: Wm. B. Eerdmans Publishing Company, 1969), p. 176.

3. It demonstrates Christian compassion. Jesus was moved with compassion when He saw the multitudes as sheep without a shepherd. On at least one occasion He refused to send them away without meeting their physical needs "lest they faint on the way" (Mt 15:32). The missionary doctor feels the same way when he comes face to face with sickness and pain which only he can relieve. His heart goes out to the unfortunate sufferers and longs to show them compassion. Usually he charges no fee for his services. Major surgical operations which would run into hundreds of dollars in this country are performed for a few dollars, just enough to cover the costs of the equipment and materials used. His only reward is the lasting gratitude of his patients.

4. It often leads to conversion. Most mission hospitals do their best to give a Christian witness. Where possible this witness is verbal. In Muslim countries it is often necessary to settle for a nonverbal form of witness expressed in loving service beyond the call of professional duty. Some of the larger hospitals have a full-time evangelist and/or Biblewoman as a permanent member of the staff. Others arrange for such a person to spend several hours each day going from bed to bed ministering to the spiritual and emotional needs of patients. In this way a clear Christian witness is given.

In the case of outpatients, who often number two to three hundred a day, arrangements are made for them to hear a clear presentation of the gospel while waiting to see the doctor.

It is impossible to ascertain with any degree of accuracy the percentage of patients who come to Christ as a result of their stay in a mission hospital. It is one thing to be impressed with the compassion and skill of the doctors and nurses; it is quite another to embrace their religion. Nevertheless, it is a known fact that many Christians have testified that their first contact with Christianity came during their stay in a mission hospital. Others have confessed that their attitude towards Christianity was completely changed as a result of the loving care they received at the hands of the staff members, national as well as missionary. Moreover, it is a known fact that persons are more likely to be favorably disposed towards religion when they are sick than when they are well. A week in a hospital affords ample time to reflect on the great issues of life and death, time and eternity, heaven and hell.

5. It lends prestige to the church. In most countries of the Third World the Christian church is not exactly a prestigious institution. With few exceptions the Christians come from the lower strata of society. Their identification with the "foreign religion" does nothing to enhance their position in the eyes of the local populace. Years of ostracism, in some cases persecution, may have developed in them a ghetto complex. To make matters worse they may be hopelessly out-numbered by non-Christians, ten to one, twenty to one, fifty to one, a hundred to one, in some countries a thousand to one. But if in the same city there is a mission hospital, some of its reputation will rub off on the Christian church. Usually the missionary doctor is on speaking terms with the city officials, the local gentry, the wealthy citizens, and other prestigious persons in the community. Naturally his connection with the church does much to enhance its image.

PROBLEMS OF MEDICAL WORK

1. **Personnel.** Medical work requires highly qualified personnel, both foreign and national. Both are difficult to get; both are difficult to hold.

Medical training in the United States is long, arduous, and very costly. To begin with, only one out of three applicants ever gets into medical school. After four back-breaking years of graduate work the young intern must serve for one or two years in a hospital before he can hang out his shingle. In the meantime he has invested some forty thousand dollars in his education and may be head-over-heels in debt by the time he is ready to practice medicine. Unless he has a rich father or uncle who is willing to bail him out, it will take him four or five years to liquidate his debt. By this time he will have bought a house, established a practice, and begun to raise a family. With his roots so far down in American soil it is very difficult to pry himself loose. And if he does offer for missionary service it is with the knowledge that his income will be cut from fifty thousand to ten thousand dollars a year. No other missionary candidate takes such a heavy pecuniary loss. Little wonder that missionary doctors are so difficult to recruit.

Hospitals in this country are well equipped and well staffed. The Highland Park General Hospital, the one closest to the author's home, has three hundred beds and 175 doctors on the staff. On the mission field many hospitals have only one doctor and he must be physician and surgeon both. In some parts of Africa one doctor is responsible for two or three institutions twenty to thirty miles apart. Several years ago the Sudan Interior Mission sent out an urgent call for doctors. The notice read: "The death of Dr. Troup has been a severe blow to the mission's medical department, currently very short of doctors. We may have to close one of our hospitals in order to adequately cover the others unless other doctors come out right now. We need five doctors in West Africa right away, some to come on a short-term basis to cover furloughs."[11]

---

[11] *Africa Now* (May-June 1970).

National doctors are in even shorter supply and will remain so until the educational standards in the Third World are raised. When Zaire (Congo) received its independence in 1960 there was not a single doctor, lawyer, architect, or engineer in the whole country!

Missionaries train nationals to be doctors and nurses, only to have them leave mission employ to set up in business for themselves or join the staff of a government hospital. In either case they make more money. Worse still, they join the "brain drain" and come here to the United States, where the fringe benefits are greater than anything they can enjoy in their own country. In 1971 India lost 821 of its physicians to the United States. Korea has only thirteen thousand doctors for a population of 33 million; yet there are two thousand Korean medical graduates in the United States and more pour in each year. There are more graduates of Thailand's medical schools now in New York than there are serving that country's rural population of 28 million.[12]

2. Finance. Time was when land, labor, and materials were dirt cheap in most parts of the Third World. That is no longer true. Medical costs are soaring on the mission field. Buildings are dilapidated and equipment is obsolete. A survey made by the World Council of Churches in 1968 revealed that of one hundred hospitals in seven states in India, seventy were more than forty years old and twenty-five were more than seventy years old. All were obsolete and nonfunctional. To completely modernize these hospitals would have cost well over twenty million dollars.

Mission boards are finding it more and more difficult to operate hospitals overseas. They would gladly turn them over to the churches; but few churches have the necessary resources to maintain them. The problems are legion. Should hospital fees be raised if it means excluding the poor for whom the hospitals were designed in the first place? Should the rich be expected to pay more and thus subsidize the services rendered to the poor? What about church members who expect to get free treatment at "their" hospital when everyone else is required to pay? And what about high government officials who run up a large bill at the hospital and leave without paying? Should an attempt be made to collect these bills or should they be written off to good will?

3. Administration. Under the colonial system of government, hospital administration was in the hands of the mission doctors. This is now rapidly changing. Some hospitals have been taken over entirely by the government. Sometimes the mission doctors remain; sometimes they don't. When hospitals are thus nationalized seldom is anything

---

[12] *U.S. News & World Report,* July 1, 1973, p. 48.

said about compensation. The government reasons that the money was originally given by the Christians of America for the purpose of ministering to the physical needs of poor people overseas. This purpose is still being served under the new regime; hence the question of compensation is not raised.

Even when the hospitals remain nominally under mission control, standards are set and reports required by the government. This involves an enormous amount of red tape, paper work, the making and filing of reports, etc. In some instances medical supplies must be ordered through the Department of Health and this often results in serious shortage due to bureaucratic snafus, endless delays, clerical mistakes, and even pilfering.

4. Competition. In prior years missionary medicine had the field to itself. This too has changed. Most of the developing countries have opted for a socialist form of economy. This means, among other things, socialized medicine. Each year large amounts of tax money are allocated to government programs designed to encourage personal hygiene, public sanitation, family planning, pest control, etc. Clinics, day-care centers, and hospitals are springing up in all the larger cities. The buildings are new; the equipment is modern; the service is usually free. By comparison the old mission hospitals are not very attractive, though it must be said that for major medical care many patients still prefer the mission hospital, where they will be sure of the skill of a foreign doctor. Another consideration is the dedication and loving care shown by the Christian nurses, which the government institutions do not begin to match.

In January 1972 the Bible and Medical Missionary Fellowship announced the closing of its Lady Kinnaird Hospital after seventy-five years of service to the people of Lucknow. The announcement went on to say: "Rising costs have placed the running of a city hospital beyond the resources of the BMMF. . . . Over the years it has become increasingly clear that the government is well able to provide necessary health services in the cities of modern India and that the place where medical missions should make their contribution in developing countries is in the rural areas."[13]

An increasing number of missions are content to minister to the physical needs of the patients. They prefer to settle for a nonverbal witness and hope that somehow the patients will be sufficiently impressed with the "Christian atmosphere" to inquire about the Way. One mission house organ carried the following comment:

---

[13] Raymond Windsor, "One Door Closes," *Go* (January 1972).

> Development should be the primary concern. Give people enough
> to eat first—then start talking about religion. . . . Send elec-
> tricians and plumbers who can teach people how to install wir-
> ing or bathroom facilities. . . . Teachers, doctors, and agricul-
> turalists are desperately needed. If you can preach Christianity
> on the side, fine. But the physical and social welfare should
> come first.[14]

In line with this kind of thinking, some hospitals have long ago
ceased to share the gospel with the inpatients; and even in hospitals
run by the more conservative groups there is always a danger that the
pressure of time and the day-by-day demands of the work will gradually crowd out the spiritual ministry of the institution.

5. Ignorance and superstition. In the more primitive areas of the
world the peasants are the victims of age-old superstitions that prevent
them from coming to a mission hospital. Only as a last resort, when all
other methods have failed and they have nothing to lose and possibly
something to gain, do they consent to be treated by strange foreigners
with white skin, blue eyes, and blond hair. By that time many of them
are beyond help and have to be sent home to die. Many women patients
are filled with fear at the sight of a male doctor. They would sooner
die than be examined by a member of the opposite sex. This is especially true in Muslim lands, where many of the women still observe
purdah. In such parts of the world a woman doctor is worth her
weight in gold.

6. Specialization. Unlike his counterpart here at home, the mission
doctor must be a general practitioner. Many hospitals have only one
doctor; consequently he must be physician and surgeon all in one. He
may have to treat several hundred outpatients in the morning, perform
half a dozen operations in the afternoon, and visit the wards in the
evening. Nor can he refer the difficult cases to a specialist. He must
handle them himself as best he can. In addition he is ultimately responsible for all departments of the hospital. When the generator
breaks down, or the roof caves in, or the plumbing springs a leak, he
must supervise the repairs. One doctor in Niger had to build his own
hospital from the ground up. In missionary life the greatest of all
assets is versatility.

Dr. Paul E. Rodriguez, of Gospel Missionary Union refers to himself as a jack-of-all-trades. He writes:

> When a couple decides to marry, they come to me for premarital
> counseling. When the wedding day arrives, I perform the cere-
> mony. I preach to them on Sundays, baptize them after conver-

---

14 *The Missionary Herald Newsletter* (Spring 1970).

sion, and share with them the Lord's Supper. When they have spiritual problems, I give spiritual counsel. When the wife is expecting a child, I provide prenatal care. When the time comes, I deliver the baby. When they need surgery, I perform it. When they die, I sign the death certificate. I also officiate at the funeral. When they need permission for burial in the evangelical cemetery, I sign the authorization papers. After the funeral, I comfort the mourners. I am a jack-of-all-trades. I am a missionary doctor.

WEAKNESSES OF MEDICAL MISSIONS

1. **Tendency to concentrate in large cities.** In the nineteenth century the strategy was to open mission stations in the cities, where the people were found in large numbers. This was both logical and proper. But before we got around to entering the rural areas we ran out of men. Hence the vast majority of mission institutions in the Third World are today located in the cities. The governments of the developing countries are making the same mistake. They too are locating their medical facilities in the centers of population. Communist China is a notable exception. It has sent its "bare foot doctors" into the rural areas where they are most needed.

2. **Tendency to minister to the middle and upper classes.** This grew inevitably out of the first weakness. The upper and middle classes have always been found in the cities; so this tendency was a natural one. Nevertheless we patterned our larger hospitals on similar institutions in the United States. Naturally as funds permitted we were interested in bigger and better institutions, and ended up in some instances with large, impersonal institutions whose appointments, modest though they were by stateside standards, doubtless attracted the upper classes and discouraged the lower classes. Interestingly enough, one of the criticisms that the Chinese Communists made of Christian missions in China was that our institutions were too closely identified with the bourgeoisie. As institutions and movements expand and grow it is easy for them to lose the common touch.

3. **Failure to train fully qualified doctors.** Christian missions did an excellent job in training nurses. In the 1930s 90 percent of all the nurses in China were Christians—at a time when less than 1 percent of the population was Christian.

In many parts of the Third World nurses need have only a high school education. To be a full-fledged doctor one needs a college education plus three or four years of graduate school. Until recently many countries did not have a single four-year college, much less a graduate school. How then could the missions train doctors in those countries? The best they could do was to take the talent they had and do their best to fashion it into something resembling a medical practitioner. When the American Presbyterians in 1960 turned their seven hospitals in Cameroon over to the national church they did not have a single national doctor. This is no reflection on the American Presbyterians. The low educational standards in Cameroon made it impossible to produce doctors. The fact remains, however, that to this day many mission hospitals are staffed only by Western doctors; and this must be regarded as a serious weakness.

In the more advanced countries the record has been better. In China there were six graduate medical schools owned and operated jointly by various mission boards. In India there were two. These, however, were the exception, not the rule.

4. Failure to engage in effective follow-up work. Not every patient who heard the gospel in a mission hospital responded affirmatively, but many did. Those who do respond, however, often do not get the kind of spiritual oversight and counsel that they need. Inevitably some fall away who might otherwise be shepherded into the Christian fold.

There are several reasons for this: (1) The hospital staff is usually grossly overworked and cannot possibly be expected to take on this responsibility. (2) Many of the patients return home to towns and villages where there is no Christian church to nurture their new-found faith, and in their isolation they fall away. (3) Even churches in the same city as the hospital do not have a well-organized program of follow-up for the patients who profess Christ during their stay in the hospital.

5. Failure to enlist the active cooperation and support of the national church. With very few exceptions mission hospitals have been the responsibility of the mission. The Christians are happy to take advantage of the medical facilities, and, of course, they are proud to be remotely connected with such a prestigious institution as a mission hospital; but the national church has tended to look upon the mission hospital as belonging solely to the mission. It is something quite outside their sphere of interest or control. This is not altogether strange, for the church has neither the men nor the money to make much of a contribution to the operation of the hospital. Too often there has been an almost complete separation of church and hospital, to the detriment of both. The only contact between the two is when the hospital staff attends church on Sunday morning or when the pastor gets appendicitis!

MODERN TRENDS IN MEDICAL MISSIONS

1. Government restrictions are on the increase. Foreign-trained doctors coming to the United States must take a written medical examination in English before being permitted to practice. In retaliation the governments of the developing countries now oblige Western doctors to pass stiff examinations overseas, often in the vernacular. The same applies to nurses. Most foreign-trained doctors coming to this country already have a working knowledge of English. The reverse, however, is not true. American doctors going abroad know nothing of Thai, Tagalog, or Tyringia. To learn all the technical terms as well as the language of the common man is an enormous task. Some of the older doctors who came out of China after the debacle of 1950 found themselves unable to pass the medical examinations in other Far Eastern countries to which they went. Their only recourse was to go into general missionary work.

2. As medical facilities increase mission hospitals will decrease in both number and effectiveness. Not only are socialist governments allocating more funds to health services, the World Health Organization and a host of American secular enterprises are now engaged in medical work overseas. Dr. Doolittle in Laos achieved worldwide fame by his "bush" hospitals. Consequently he received large support from medical foundations and pharmaceutical firms in this country. Very few new mission hospitals have been opened in the last decade. On the contrary, several hospitals have been closed and others have been taken over by the government.

3. More emphasis is being placed on mobile clinics working in the rural areas. Government hospitals are being built mostly in the larger cities, to the neglect of the rural areas. Private doctors do the same. When the missions find themselves unable to cope with competition in the cities, instead of closing down entirely they switch over to rural work. Rather than build costly hospitals they prefer to use mobile clinics. In this way they can bring modern medicine right to the poor peasants at the village level.

Since 1960 the Latin America Mission has used Goodwill Caravans to take medical, dental, and other services—and the gospel—to isolated areas of Costa Rica. During 1972 some twelve thousand people received treatment.

4. More importance is being attached to preventive medicine. In the past missionary doctors were content to "heal the sick" and many of their patients came to them in the last stages of tuberculosis or some other contagious disease. Now they see the importance of preventive medicine and are doing what they can to provide health services designed to reduce the incidence of disease. There are, however, serious limits to what a mission hospital or even a mobile clinic can do along this line; but at least an effort is being made.

> Perhaps the greatest obstacle to improving health care in an area such as ours occurs in the field of preventive medicine. . . . We are looked upon with amusement when we fuss about all sorts of invisible creatures like bacteria and tiny worms. Nepalese prepare and serve their meals on mud floors and eat with their hands. Their water supply is usually contaminated, and they resist boiling their water because it flattens the taste and uses up their already limited firewood. Latrines and outhouses are a curiosity, and the progressive citizen who ventures to construct such a facility usually abandons the whole project after a week because the place stinks so badly.[15]

5. Greater use is being made of short-term personnel. Jet travel makes it possible for a doctor or surgeon to spend two weeks or a month overseas during his summer or winter vacation. In some instances the difficult surgical cases are held over for the visit of the specialist from America. An eye specialist may spend a month at the famous Eye Hospital in Kano, Nigeria, during which time he may perform hundreds of very delicate operations quite beyond the competence of the mission doctor.

A recent letter from Zaire tells of a short visit by a specialist. "Dr. Don Madsen, orthopedic surgeon from Minneapolis, operated on 40 patients at Tandala and taught us some valuable techniques for polio deformities. It's good that we had plenty of plaster because the wards were full of casts, tractions, and people walking on crutches."[16]

Educational Missions

Education has always been an integral part of the missionary movement. Teaching held an important place in the public ministry of Christ. It was included in Christ's instructions to His disciples as recorded in the Great Commission in Matthew 28:19, 20. Teaching played a large role in the development of the early church. Paul was known as a teacher long before he was recognized as an apostle (Acts 13:1). Among the gifts given by the ascended Lord to His church was that of teacher (Eph 4:11), though the early church did not establish schools as we understand the term today.

---

[15] *Prayer Letter,* November 1971, Tom and Cynthia Hale, Nepal.
[16] *Tandala Newsletter* (May 1973).

Modern scientific education was introduced to the Third World by the missionaries. In Africa the missionaries were for many decades the sole purveyors of education. In Black Africa today there is hardly a leader in any walk of life who did not receive his education in a mission school, Protestant or Catholic.

In some countries education, at least in the early years, was the only method open to the missionaries. This was true in Japan, where the public edicts against Christianity were not removed until 1873. For the first fifteen years missionary work was confined largely to the education of the bright young *samurai* who had been disfranchised by the Meiji Restoration. In the Muslim countries of the Middle East education has had to serve as a substitute for more direct forms of evangelism.

Some of the early pioneers were intellectual and spiritual giants who left their mark on the countries where they served. Outstanding among these were Guido F. Verbeck in Japan, Alexander Duff in India, Cyrus Hamlin and Daniel Bliss in the Middle East, Timothy Richard in China, James Stewart in South Africa, and a host of others whose names cannot be mentioned here.

Schools of all kinds were established, beginning with elementary schools and going up through colleges and universities. In Africa mission education remained at lower levels owing to the primitive conditions on that continent in the nineteenth century, and also to the educational policies of some of the colonial powers, notably Belgium in what used to be called the Belgian Congo (Zaire). In the larger countries of Asia there were thousands of elementary schools, but the emphasis was on secondary and tertiary education. In the heyday of missions there were 340 middle schools and 13 colleges in China; 421 middle schools, 291 high schools, and 37 colleges in India; 65 middle schools, 74 high schools, 34 junior colleges, 16 colleges, and 6 graduate schools in Japan. All of them were Christian at least in name and intent.

The situation differed from country to country. In India mission schools were subsidized by the government; in China and Japan they were not. In India they were prestigious institutions and attracted the finest students. In Japan they were quite inferior to the government schools and got the leftovers from them. The situation in China was somewhere between the other two. Mission schools in China were all taken over by the government after the Communists came to power in 1949.

In Africa the colonial governments showed little interest in education; that was left largely to the missions. They did, in time, support mission schools with grants. Britain and France did a better job in Africa than did Belgium and Portugal. In 1923 there were in the British colonies in Africa some six thousand schools; only one hundred of them were government schools. As late as 1961, 68 percent of the children in Africa were in mission schools, most of them at the elementary level. In Africa the missions concentrated on elementary education for various reasons and in this area they did yeoman service. In Zaire alone the Protestants had several thousand schools and the Roman Catholics had many more. Very few students went beyond the fifth grade, for the simple reason that there was nothing higher. High schools were very scarce and Christian colleges were all but nonexistent.

On the whole it is correct to say that mission schools enjoyed a good reputation and attracted more students than they were able to accommodate. There were several reasons for this: (1) The academic standards were high and discipline was good. (2) The parents appreciated the emphasis on character training. (3) Western education, especially the English language, was in great demand as a passport to good government positions and travel abroad.

There were two schools of thought among the missionaries with regard to the use of English in mission schools. The Vernacularists, led by William Carey and Serampore College, were in favor of teaching English as a subject, but laid chief emphasis on the development of the vernaculars, the translation of proper books into these languages, and their use as the chief instrument. The Anglicists, headed by Alexander Duff, insisted that English be the chief medium of communication, especially at the higher levels. English, they said, would open to the students the whole world of Western thought. Moreover it would serve as a unifying factor in India, with its fourteen major languages and hundreds of dialects. And, of course, after 1835 English became the language of government in India. So enamored of English was Duff that he said on one occasion. "Only use English as the medium and you will break the backbone of caste."[17]

The missionary body was likewise divided on the purpose of mission schools. There were those who believed that mission schools should be employed primarily, if not exclusively, for the education of the children of Christian parents and the preparation of men for the Christian ministry. There were others who took a broader view and wished to include non-Christian students, in which case the mission school would become an evangelistic agency. Its chief aim would be to lead the non-Christian students to personal faith in Christ. There were still others who regarded the mission school simply as a leavening agent in a pagan society. Enlightenment and Christianity were considered inseparable if not synonymous. The colleges, they said, were necessary if Christianity were to make an appeal to the intellectuals. According

---

[17] Robert E. Speer, *Some Great Leaders in the World Movement* (New York: Fleming H. Revell, 1911), p. 116.

to this view conversion was not to be sought. In fact the mission school was intended to be primarily an academic institution and no direct effort was made to convert the students. Dr. Daniel Bliss, founder of the Syrian Protestant College, which in 1920 became the American University in Beirut, made this quite clear when he said:

> A man white, black or yellow; Christian, Jew or Mohammedan, or heathen, may enter and enjoy all the advantages of this institution for three, four, or eight years; and go out believing in one God, in many gods, or in no God. But it will be impossible for one to continue with us long without knowing what we believe to be the truth and our reasons for that belief.[18]

Except in Africa, where everybody got in on the act, the vast majority of mission schools were the responsibility of the old-line denominations. The faith missions never had a large stake in educational missions, nor did they establish a single prestigious institution. There were several reasons for this: (1) They got a late start after the groundwork had been laid. (2) Their missionaries for the most part were not university graduates and consequently lacked the necessary qualifications. (3) Apart from the famous China Inland Mission, which at one time had over thirteen hundred missionaries in China, very few faith missions were attracted to the continent of Asia, where the denominational missions had most of their institutions. (4) They were interested in more direct forms of evangelism.

Different levels and kinds of education were offered by the mission schools. At the lowest level were the kindergartens, confined mostly to Japan. Above that were the elementary schools, which usually included grades one through five. These were found in all parts of the mission field but were particularly numerous in Africa. Indeed, until after 1945 education in Africa did not go above this level.

Secondary education included middle schools and high schools. In some cases these were boarding schools. Many of the so-called colleges were, in fact, high schools. Some of these high schools became very prestigious institutions, drawing students from other countries. The better ones usually had more applicants than they were able to accept. Most of the high schools were in Asia; Africa was far behind. As late as 1960 there was only one high school in Kenya. For every student who was accepted, dozens were turned away. When Zaire received its independence in 1960 there was not a single high school in the country. This was not the fault of the missions. The Belgians did not want to educate the nationals to the point where they might make trouble for their colonial masters.

Teacher training schools played a major role in the educational

---

[18] United Church Board of World Ministries, *Calendar of Prayer and Directory* (1968-1969), p. 112.

process in Africa, where high schools and colleges were very few. As national teachers were trained in these schools the missionaries withdrew from teaching at the lower levels and concentrated on the training of teachers.

Technical schools were also maintained. Some of them, such as Lovedale in South Africa, achieved worldwide fame. Indeed, most of the other schools included in their curriculum such practical subjects as carpentry, agriculture, sewing, home economics, handcrafts, and so on.

At the top of the pyramid were the colleges and universities. These were found mostly in India, China, Japan, and the Middle East, where they gave a certain degree of prestige to Christianity. Yenching University in Peking was the Harvard of China. The American University in Beirut, founded originally as a missionary institution, has been described as America's best investment in the Arab world. At the founding of the United Nations in 1945 there were more graduates from that one university than from any other educational institution in the world. Robert College in Istanbul is another famous Christian college in that part of the world.

Schools often overlooked in the study of educational missions are the schools for missionaries' children. The greatest single *personal* problem of the missionaries is the education of their children. It is also the problem that mission executives wrestle with most often. In the larger countries there is one, sometimes two or three, of these schools, usually operated by one of the larger missions, sometimes as a joint effort by several missions. Some of these provide only elementary education; others take the student through high school. They are both costly to operate and difficult to staff. In Europe they are quite unnecessary for obvious reasons. In the more primitive parts of the world they are absolutely essential. In other parts they serve a real need but are not, strictly speaking, necessary. The children could conceivably attend the public schools in the more advanced countries though this too has serious problems, since they must be sure of a good education with a thorough mastery of English language and literature to get into college in the homeland. Teaching in these schools is both a privilege and a challenge. On the whole the students are usually brighter than those found in the average school at home or abroad. An extraordinarily high percentage of them go on to college and upon graduation the vast majority go into the various professions. Not a few of them return to the field as missionaries. Only a handful end up in business.

PROBLEMS IN EDUCATIONAL MISSIONS

Private education is today fighting with its back to the financial wall. Education is becoming increasingly costly in all parts of the world. Even in the affluent West church related schools are hurting for lack of financial support. On the mission field the problem is much greater.

In Africa, India, and a few other countries mission schools received grants from the government. In other countries, such as China and Japan, they were obliged to pay their own way. To do this they had to charge fees. This put them at a serious disadvantage *vis-à-vis* the tax-supported government schools.

Another problem is personnel. It has always been difficult to get qualified personnel, both missionary and national. In the nineteenth century, especially in Africa, the missionaries had no pedagogical training. They simply imparted what knowledge they had. Even today at the higher levels it is very difficult to secure the services of qualified Christian teachers. In some colleges in Asia only 60 percent of the teachers are Christians; the others are Hindus, Buddhists, Muslims, or agnostics. This naturally vitiates the Christian thrust of the institution.

In many parts of the world pastors, missionaries, and evangelists must do double duty, dividing their time and strength between the church and the school. This results in poor performance in both areas. "Ways should be sought for disengaging pastors and missionaries from such administrative involvement so that their training and experience can be used effectively."[19]

In Africa the situation is particularly bad.

> The church must face up to the problem of finding teachers to serve in Christian schools. This is not only a problem of training sufficient teachers but also of persuading them to remain in the teaching profession. All over Africa the loss of graduates and trained teachers from the schools to administration, commerce and industry undermines education systems.[20]

Government control has been a problem almost from the beginning. The governments not only set high standards—which was good—but they prohibited religious instruction and chapel services. In a few instances they were permitted on a voluntary basis; in that event attendance dropped drastically. Without religious instruction in what sense is the school a mission institution? As usual the missionary body was divided on the matter. Some missions complied; others did not. They preferred to close rather than discontinue religious instruction. In many instances the missions treated the government regulations with benign neglect as long as they could get away with it. Sooner or later, however, they were all forced to comply.

---

[19] All Africa Churches Conference, *Christian Education in Africa* (London: Oxford University Press, 1963), p. 51.
[20] *Ibid.*, p. 65.

Students the world over are known for engaging in mass demonstrations to get what they want. They have toppled governments in Korea, Japan, Turkey, Pakistan, and elsewhere. Whenever student unrest takes on antiforeign overtones, mission schools become the object of attack. This was especially true in China in the 1920s when a wave of antiforeign sentiment swept the country. From Peking to Canton mission schools were attacked by students, Christian and non-Christian, who went on the rampage, molesting teachers, destroying records, and even burning buildings.

In all mission schools Christian witness has been a perennial problem, so much so that some persons have questioned the value of mission schools from a purely practical point of view. Have the spiritual results been commensurate with the vast amount of time and money invested? Almost to a man educational missionaries have defended the system. Evangelistic and church-planting missionaries have had grave doubts. Much depends on one's point of view and what part of the world is under consideration. In China some 30 percent of all the persons whose names appeared in China's *Who's Who* received part of their education in a mission school and 90 percent of all registered nurses were Christians. On the other hand the record was not nearly so good in Japan; and in Muslim countries the number of converts was almost nil.

RECENT TRENDS
IN EDUCATIONAL MISSIONS

Increasingly mission schools are being secularized. Sometimes this is the result of government action; in other instances it is the result of indifference on the part of the missionaries and their national colleagues. They are more concerned with nation building than with character development, more dedicated to social betterment than to personal conversion, more interested in humanization than in redemption. Some mission schools have become hotbeds of revolutionary fervor. In these institutions the distinctly spiritual emphasis has all but disappeared. Such schools are Christian in name only.

Increasingly mission schools are being nationalized. One of the earliest governments to take this kind of action was Iran, when in 1939 all mission schools in the country were seized. Not long afterwards Egypt followed the same course. The Bantu Education Act of 1953 promulgated by the government of South Africa with a stroke of the pen removed fifty-three hundred schools from Protestant auspices. Since 1960, when some seventeen countries in Africa got their independence, thousands of mission schools have passed under government control. One of the first things a newly independent government does is to nationalize all private schools. They feel that education is too powerful an instrument for the molding of national character to be left in the hands of foreigners, no matter how high minded they might be. It is only a matter of time when all mission schools will be under government control.

The nationalization of mission schools is not an unmitigated tragedy. Indeed, it may be a blessing in disguise. It relieves the missions of an enormous financial burden and the missionaries of onerous administrative chores, setting them free for work more directly connected with the spread of the gospel and the growth of the church. When there were no schools the mission boards had no option. They had to engage in education. Now that the governments have the willingness, the expertise, and the funds, it is only right and proper that the missions should retire from the field. Our resources in men and money are limited; they must be used where they are needed the most.

It is interesting to note that in recent years new avenues have opened for missionaries desiring to engage in a teaching ministry. In most countries of the Third World religion is not the "hot potato" it is in educational circles here in the United States. Even in tax-supported government schools religious knowledge is compulsory at all levels from first grade through college. In two countries—South Africa and Indonesia—missionaries were engaged to write the curricula for the teaching of this important subject throughout the entire system.

THEOLOGICAL EDUCATION

Two generations ago John R. Mott stated that the greatest weakness of the missionary movement was our failure to produce well-trained leaders for the national churches. Half a century has come and gone and the problem is still with us. In spite of all that has been said and done in the intervening years, the national churches in most parts of the mission field are still without adequately trained pastors and evangelists. We have made millions of converts. We have established thousands of churches. We have not trained nearly enough leaders. Only three countries—Japan, Korea, and Taiwan—have anything like an adequate number of trained pastors. In other parts of the world it is not uncommon to find a pastor who is responsible for anywhere from ten to twenty congregations.

Peter Savage of the Andes Evangelical Mission wrote: "Of 16,000 Brazilian pastors, only 4,500 have received any form of Bible school or seminary training. Forty thousand additional workers are not even included in this figure." The statistics for all of Latin America are no better. "Of 75,000 Latin American church leaders, only 15,000 have had what might be called adequate theological training."[21]

Theological education is offered at various levels: short-term Bible schools, long-term Bible schools, Bible colleges, theological seminaries, Bible correspondence courses, and theological education by extension. Most of the two hundred seminaries operate on two, sometimes three, levels: postprimary, posthigh, and postcollege. In some of the more advanced countries—India, Japan, Philippines, and Indonesia—the seminaries offer a *bona fide* B.D. program.

PROBLEMS OF THEOLOGICAL EDUCATION

It is universally recognized that theological education has been woefully neglected. Bruce J. Nicholls of Union Biblical Seminary, Yeotmal, India, writes: "Theological education has been the Cinderella of missionary aid in terms of personnel and finance."[22] Norman A. Horner has said virtually the same:

> With notable exceptions, seminaries have long been the weakest link in the entire chain of educational work in the Protestant missionary outreach. Bishop Stephen Neill, Charles Ranson, Yorke Allen, Jr., and others who have made recent studies of the training of the ministry in Africa, Asia, and Latin America bear eloquent testimony to the fact that this is still widely the case. By and large the seminaries are small, ill-equipped, understaffed "stepchildren" of the churches.[23]

1. **Proliferation.** On the mission field as well as at home each denomination wants to train its own future leaders to make sure they have the correct orientation. Even in this heyday of ecumenism a Presbyterian ministerial student had better get his training in a Presbyterian seminary if he wants to serve in a Presbyterian church. Maybe we can afford this kind of luxury at home. It is doubtful if we can justify it on the mission field. There we have ended up with an inordinate amount of proliferation which has resulted in a shameful waste of time, money, energy, and talent. For example, in Korea there are no fewer than forty-eight Bible schools. In Taiwan nineteen new schools were founded between 1951-1961. Each mission, it would seem, insists on maintaining its own Bible school. In some cases the Bible schools are founded by individual missionaries.

The largest and strongest theological schools are union schools found in the more advanced countries such as India, Philippines, and

21 *Andes Evangelical News Release*, October 24, 1968.
22 Bruce J. Nicholls, "Toward an Asian Theology of Mission." *Evangelical Missions Quarterly*, Winter 1970, p. 65.
23 Norman A. Horner, *Cross and Crucifix in Mission* (New York: Abingdon Press, 1965), p. 105.

Japan. These schools, however, tend to be liberal in their theological
orientation.

2. Small enrollment. Among the two hundred seminaries in the
Third World the average enrollment is only twenty-five. This makes
the teacher-student ratio the highest in the world—almost one teacher
to every three students. This in turn makes theological education extremely costly in terms of both men and money. The small enrollment
is due to several factors: (1) In most countries of Asia the Christian
community is very small to begin with. (2) Most parents, Christian
as well as non-Christian, are reluctant to see their sons go into a
vocation which will not permit them to take care of their parents when
they get old. (3) Even without parental restraint, not many young men
feel called to the ministry when it has so little to offer by way of
worldly rewards. (4) As long as each denomination insists on having
its own seminary, there will not be enough students to go around.

3. Inadequate library facilities. Only a few of the union seminaries
have anything like adequate library holdings. The average library would
certainly not have more than five thousand volumes and many of these
would be in English. Scores of small Bible schools are struggling along
with only the few books the missionary teachers might have. The
average pastor here at home probably has more books in his study than
can be found in many Bible school libraries on the mission field.

4. Paucity of qualified teachers. This is especially true in the faith
missions, many of whose missionaries until recent years were only
Bible college graduates. To have a strong seminary men with seminary
training, preferably with a doctorate, are needed.

We are producing more and more men in the United States with
advanced degrees in Bible and Theology, but few of them feel called
to teach on the mission field. They want to be where they can engage
in research and writing. To do this they must teach in a prestigious
school with good facilities or at least be near enough to such a school
to be able to use its facilities. To go to the mission field is a "waste" of
one's time and talents. Or so it seems to many of our seminary
graduates.

5. Placement. Several questions are pertinent to a discussion of
this problem: (1) Will the seminary graduate with all this education
under his belt be willing to go where he is needed or will he insist
on getting a large church in a big city? Three or four years in the
academic atmosphere of an urban institution can easily incapacitate a
man for the very work to which he was originally called. He may find

it impossible to go back to his own town where life is simple and where the people are unsophisticated. To retain his services the church may have to create a special administrative or ecclesiastical position for him. (2) Will the church that invites him be able to pay him a salary commensurate with his training? With the same amount of education he could command a handsome salary in business or government, where he would enjoy a far greater degree of prestige. (3) Will he be accepted by the older pastors with more experience but less education? This is a very acute problem in Africa, where the faithful old pastors with only three or four years of education but twenty or thirty years of experience are reluctant to welcome the younger but better-educated men. Naturally, they pose a threat to the older pastors.

Humanitarian Service

The average American has a very distorted view of the Christian missionary. He is pictured as a religious zealot whose sole ambition is to save the souls of the heathen from the damnation of hell. He wears a pith helmet, Bermuda shorts, and knee socks and always carries a Bible under his arm. He lives in a "big bungalow" and never gets dirt on his hands. Particularly offensive is the way he "rams religion down the throats" of the benighted heathen who are perfectly happy as they are. When he manages to get a convert, he proceeds to make him into a "little American," replete with clothes on his back, shoes on his feet, and a small American flag in his hand.

Nothing could be farther from the truth. Doubtless there have been a few missionaries who fitted this picture; but they surely belonged to the "lunatic fringe" found in any large group of people. To identify the tens of thousands of missionaries with the occasional oddball is to do a disservice to the most magnificent, magnanimous enterprise the world has ever seen.

By all odds the early missionaries were a special breed of men. Single-handedly and with great courage they attacked the social evils of their time—child marriage, the immolation of widows, temple prostitution, and untouchability in India; the opium trade, gambling, footbinding, and infanticide in China; the slave trade, the liquor trade, and the destruction of twins in Africa. In all parts of the world they opened schools, hospitals, medical colleges, clinics, orphanages, and leprosaria. They gave succor and sustenance to the dregs of society cast off by their own people. At great risk to themselves and their families they fought famines, floods, pestilence, and plagues. They were the first to rescue unwanted babies, educate girls, and liberate women. They reduced languages to writing, translated the Scriptures, and taught the people to read, thereby opening to them a whole new world of ideas.

In the conduct of their work they encountered indifference, suspicion, hostility, persecution, and imprisonment. Times without number their homes were looted, their buildings burned, their churches desecrated, and their lives threatened. Thousands returned home broken in health. Other thousands died prematurely of tropical diseases. Hundreds became martyrs. And all this they endured without reserve, without regret, and without reward.

Nowhere was the humanitarian work of the missionaries more conspicuous than in the area of medicine. Dr. Peter Parker had many *firsts* to his credit. He was the first medical missionary to China. His famous eye hospital in Canton was the first modern hospital in the Far East. He was the first person to introduce medical education under Christian auspices. He was the first to use anesthesia.

Dr. Dan Bradley had the distinction of introducing smallpox vaccine into Thailand as early as 1836. He got his vaccine from America via the Cape of Good Hope before the Suez Canal was built and long before the days of refrigeration. Later, in the 1890s, Dr. James McKean developed his own vaccine from calves and manufactured his own quinine. He trained two hundred paramedical personnel and sent them into the surrounding counties to check the spread of the two dreadful scourges, smallpox and malaria. In no time at all he rid that part of Northern Thailand of smallpox. The king decorated him with the Order of the Crown.

Dr. Nelson Bell was for many years in charge of the largest mission hospital in China. During the turbulent 1930s when the countryside was overrun by bandits, warlords, and other antisocial elements, he stayed by the stuff and ministered to the bandits and their victims as well as soldiers, civilians, officials, and others. He made a special study of kala-azar (black fever) and was instrumental in helping to isolate the sandfly as its carrier, thus conferring an inestimable blessing on the people of the Orient and at the same time making a significant contribution to medical science.

Whatever emancipation the women of the Third World enjoy today they owe to the educational work of the pioneer missionaries. Modern scientific education was introduced to Asia and Africa by the missionaries; but it was in female education that the mission schools led the way. In the nineteenth century such education was unknown and all kinds of opposition developed. When Isabella Thoburn opened the first school for girls in India she had to go from door to door imploring the parents to permit their daughters to attend her school. The women of India have come a long way in the last one-hundred years, thanks to Isabella Thoburn, Ida Scudder, Clara Swain, Amy Carmichael, Edith

Brown, and a host of other equally beautiful characters who voluntarily gave up the prospect of marriage and a family in order to share the gospel of Christ with the women of India.

In an effort to raise the standard of living the missionaries in all parts of the world engaged in agricultural and industrial missions. Pioneering in this area was the Basel Mission of Switzerland. As early as 1846 it opened an industrial school in India where young men were taught carpentry, weaving, lockmaking, bookbinding, printing, and other equally useful trades. When the school could not compete with cloth imported from Europe, the mission set up a small factory with twenty-one European looms and a dyehouse. The master weaver, Haller, invented the fast-brown dye called *khaki* which later became a household word around the world. The wagons and carts made in the Basel workshops in Ghana were to be seen in all parts of Sierra Leone and the Cameroons. In one year the mission exported thirty-five tons of rubber and seventeen million pounds of cocoa; while in its savings bank were deposited by national Christians 575,000 francs.

Agriculture is obviously important in the Third World, where to this day 75 to 80 percent of the people live on the land. Here too the missionaries made a significant contribution. Besides teaching agronomy in their schools they drained swamps, cleared forests, planted trees, introduced new and better seeds, livestock, fruits, and vegetables, and new methods of irrigation, fertilization, and cultivation. They brought with them all kinds of agricultural implements designed to reduce labor and increase production. The work of Sam Higginbottom in India, James Stewart in Africa, and Frank Price in China is well known to all students of Christian missions.

Even the missionary bishops got in on the act. Bishop Charles Brent in the Philippines wrote of the Moros:

> The Moro is by nature aggressive.... The only way to convert him is to convert his energies, to teach him the joy of productivity, and to inspire him with self-respect. This we plan to do by teaching him to build roads, railways, bridges, houses, to market his crops and improve his land, to lead in our modern sport instead of his ancient piracy, to develop himself and his resources in normal, ideal, and beneficial ways.[24]

Some missions formed trading companies for the benefit of their converts. One such was the Uganda Company Limited, established in 1903 by the Church Missionary Society. Similar companies were established in West Africa.

In all such endeavors the missionaries had two goals in view. One was to provide a means of support for their converts, many of whom

---

[24] W. H. P. Faunce, *The Social Aspects of Foreign Missions* (New York: Missionary Education Movement, 1914), pp. 161-62.

lost their jobs because of persecution. The larger goal was to improve the economic well-being of the community. In either case it was the missionary's aim to help the people help themselves, not just give them handouts.

The missionaries were not content simply to improve the lot of the individual. They were equally concerned about the social, economic, and political structures and institutions which condemned certain segments of the populace to misery, poverty, and starvation. Many of them became crusaders against the inhumane social customs of their adopted countries.

The Christian missionaries from the earliest days in India have been aggressive social workers. William Carey led the way. For more than thirty years he carried on a crusade against the social evils of India. Time and again he addressed memorials to the government on child marriage, infanticide, and *suttee*—the self-immolation of widows on the funeral pyres of their husbands. One of the happiest days of his life was Sunday, December 5, 1829, when he received a summons from the Governor General to translate the official document outlawing *suttee*.

Another social evil of India was temple prostitution, which involved innocent but helpless young girls being "married to the gods" and thereafter living a life of utter misery and degradation. Amy Carmichael, founder of Dohnavur Fellowship, gave half a century of tender loving care to thousands of temple girls whom she personally rescued from a life of shame.

Then there was the caste system, sometimes described as the greatest example of man's inhumanity to man. Keshub Chunder Se, himself a Hindu, said: "Caste has completely and hopelessly wrecked social unity, harmony, and happiness, and for centuries has opposed all human progress."[25] Untouchability, for centuries an integral part of the caste system, was in direct conflict with the Christian gospel, which makes all men one in Christ. Naturally the preaching of the gospel aroused opposition, especially among the higher castes. When a storm of protest blew up against the missionaries Sir George Barlow sent Carey a brief message: "The Governor General does not interfere with the prejudices of the natives and he must request Mr. Carey and his associates to abstain likewise from any interference with them."[26] Untouchability has been outlawed since Independence; but caste, which is at the very heart of Hinduism, is still securely entrenched in Indian society. Even the Christian church has not been able to eradicate it.

---

[25] *Ibid.*, p. 175.
[26] F. Deaville Walker, *William Carey: Missionary Pioneer and Statesman* (Chicago: Moody, 1925), p. 208.

In the great land of China the missionaries crusaded against infanticide, foot-binding, gambling, and the use of opium. The first two involved women and girls, and the second two the menfolk for the most part. The missionaries not only spoke out against these evils, they did what they could to stop the practices altogether, or at least to ameliorate the problems. As early as 1874 Dr. John MacGowan of Amoy persuaded nine brave women to sign a pledge not to bind the feet of their daughters. That was the beginning of the Heavenly Foot Society. Here and there throughout China Christian mothers joined the society. Other mothers soon followed. It was not until thirty years later that the Empress Dowager issued a decree discouraging foot-binding.

Year after year the various missions in their house organs crusaded for the abolition of the opium trade in China. When they proved unsuccessful they established opium refuges in which tens of thousands of opium addicts were cured, though only a small number ever embraced the Christian faith.

Likewise the missionaries were powerless to abolish infanticide, which in the nineteenth century averaged 40 percent of all the baby girls born in China. Instead they opened foundling institutions and orphanages which took in the baby girls discarded by their parents. There they were fed, clothed, housed, educated, and introduced to the Christian way of life. When they reached adolescence many of the girls married Christian husbands and established Christian homes. The Roman Catholic missionaries, with their celibacy and their more austere life style, outdid the Protestants in this particular form of work.

Regardless of how busy they were the missionaries could always be depended on to come to the rescue in time of famine, flood, pestilence, plague, earthquake, or war. At the height of disaster they laid aside their "spiritual" work and gave all their time to the business at hand. Not a few missionary doctors and nurses lost their lives fighting cholera epidemics. In the affluent West "famine" is a word found only in the dictionary. For centuries in India and China it has been a specter to be dreaded. One poor harvest—and famine ensued. In the China famine of 1911-12 over a hundred missionaries gave one to six months to famine relief work. Following World War II the United Nations Relief and Rehabilitation Administration undertook massive relief work in war-devastated China. Mountains of material, left over from the American war effort in the South Pacific, were unloaded on the docks in Shanghai. Upcountry it was the missionaries who administered the program at the grass roots.

And what shall be said of the endeavors of the missionaries to alleviate the sufferings of those persons whose disease is so offensive that they have been cast off by their own relatives and friends—the leprosy patients. Indeed, so dreadful is the disease and so repulsive is the victim that the very word "leper" is no longer in good form. Christians at home have been known to close their eyes when leprosy patients were suddenly thrown on the screen at the annual missionary conference. What must be the dedication of the missionaries who live day by day in the leprosarium with the patients, changing their beds, serving their meals, and washing and dressing their suppurating sores!

Slavery has all but disappeared from the world; but in the nineteenth century, especially in Africa, it was referred to as "the open sore of the world." When David Livingstone on his first missionary journey saw for himself the horrendous effects of the infamous slave trade, he burned with indignation and vowed to do everything in his power to end the nefarious traffic. On his return to England in 1857 he made a strong plea for "an open path for commerce and Christianity" as the best way to root out the slave trade in Central Africa. The entire Protestant world was greatly moved by his appeal. But Livingstone and his fellow missionaries realized that the slave trade could not be curbed so long as the Arabs had free access to inland Africa; and the only way to drive the Arabs out of Africa was for the European powers to move in and establish colonies. This was the less of two evils and the missionaries concurred. It is not too much to say that Livingstone's verbal attack on the Arab slave trade in Central Africa led directly to the extirpation of that devastating institution.

Another area of humanitarian service is relief work among refugees. It is estimated that since World War II some thirty million persons have been rendered homeless if not stateless, and that does not include the millions of refugees on the mainland of China during the Sino-Japanese War in the late 1930s. The best-known group are the Palestinian refugees, who have received a great deal of attention in and out of the United Nations. Not so well known are other groups, from the five million refugees created by the Partition of India in 1947 to the ten million refugees that fled from Bangladesh to India in 1971. In Africa there have been large numbers of refugees from Southern Sudan, Burundi, Biafra, Angola, and Mozambique. And the end is not in sight.

In every case Christian organizations came to the aid of the refugees: Inter-Church Aid, Refugee and World Service (WCC), World Relief Commission (NAE), Church World Service (NCC), Mennonite Central Committee, Lutheran World Federation, World Vision International, and others. Millions of dollars are raised every year by these organizations and sent to the affected areas of the world. But who does the actual work at the local level? The missionaries and their national colleagues. In times of emergency they suspend their normal operations to give themselves full time to relief and rehabilitation.

It should be understood that in all their humanitarian endeavors the missionaries never lost sight of their primary goal, the evangelization of the non-Christian world. They would share the benefits of Western civilization, but not without the blessings of the gospel. Livingstone said: "The end of the geographical feat is only the beginning of the missionary enterprise."[27]

Dan Crawford, of Central Africa fame, said:

> No doubt it is our diurnal duty to preach that the soul of all improvement is the improvement of the soul. But God's equilateral triangle of body, soul, and spirit must never be ignored. Is not the body wholly ensouled, and is not the soul wholly embodied? ... In other words, in Africa the only true fulfilling of your heavenly calling is the doing of earthly things in a heavenly manner.[28]

Never was the bravery of the missionaries more prominently displayed than in time of war. Where possible they acted as intermediaries and did their best to prevent war. Sometimes they succeeded; sometimes not. When war did come they gave themselves unreservedly to the care of the innocent victims, throwing their homes, churches, hospitals, and compounds open to refugees, mostly women and girls fleeing from rapacious soldiers bent on raping and killing. When the war was over they helped with the gargantuan task of relief and rehabilitation.

Nowhere were missionary achievements more spectacular than in the Pacific Islands, where they were responsible for the abolition of cannibalistic wars. In ten short years they changed the life-style of the "natives." One missionary wrote:

> I often wish that some of the cavillers who are forever sneering at Christian missions could see something of their results in these islands. But first they would have to recall the Fiji of ten years ago, when every man's hand was against his neighbor, and the land had no rest from barbarous intertribal wars, in which the foe, without respect of age or sex, were looked upon only in the light of so much beef, the prisoners deliberately fattened for the slaughter ... limbs cut off from living men and women and cooked and eaten in the presence of the victim. ... Then further, think of the sick buried alive, the array of widows who were deliberately strangled on the death of any great man, the living victims who were buried beside every post of a chief's new house.
> Now you can pass from isle to isle, certain everywhere to find the same cordial reception by kindly men and women. ... Can you realize that the first sound that greets your ear at dawn, and the last at night, is that of hymn-singing and the most fervent

---

[27] Faunce, *op. cit.*, p. 233.
[28] Dan Crawford, *Thinking Black* (New York: Doran, 1913), p. 444.

worship arising from each dwelling at the hour of family worship?[29]

Fifty years later our American GIs landed at Guadalcanal and fought their way island by island in World War II. They expected to find headhunters; instead they discovered Christians who took them in, hid the paratroopers from the Japanese, bound up their wounds, and gave them food and shelter until they could get back to their own lines. Lowell Cutler, a serviceman from Boone, Iowa, wrote: "The missionaries have really done a job over here and can never get enough credit for their work. . . . They are usually the last to leave a Japanese-infested area. They go out the back door as the Japanese come in the front."[30] Another wrote:

> Well, Mom, believe me . . . more miracles have happened than seemed possible. In all fairness I must say the missionaries have done absolutely marvelous work among the natives of these islands. As a result of that work the lives of scores of fliers have been saved. They come back after being missing for weeks with unbelievable tales of nursing care that the natives have given them. Believe me, the real heroes of this war never get their names in the paper.[31]

A naval seaman wrote: "Our missionary service is one to be proud of. I wish some of our skeptical people back home, who frown every time money is collected for the missionary service, could see what their filthy lucre has done for these natives."[32]

During the same period—World War II—missionaries in China were conducting themselves in the traditional humanitarian manner. As the Japanese armies swept inland they remained at their posts and did what they could to shield Chinese women and girls from the unspeakable atrocities of the Japanese soldiers. Whenever a large city fell to the Japanese all hell broke loose. As a reward for their "bravery" the Japanese soldiers were given seventy-two hours of complete freedom during which time there was no military discipline whatever. The atrocities committed during those days beggar description. Until Pearl Harbor was attacked in December 1941, Americans were regarded as neutrals and treated with a good deal of civility by the Japanese soldiers and officers. After Pearl Harbor, of course, all Allied personnel in China were placed in concentration camps for the duration.

When the capital city of Nanking fell on December 12, 1937, only twelve foreigners remained in the city, all of them missionaries. In all

---

[29] John Liggins, *The Great Value and Success of Foreign Missions* (New York: Baker & Taylor, 1888), pp. 72-73.
[30] Henry P. Van Dusen, *They Found the Church There* (New York: Scribners, 1945), p. 37.
[31] *Ibid.*, p. 43.
[32] *Ibid.*, p. 42.

parts of Occupied China the missionaries opened their compounds to the women and girls and saved them from the depredations of the drunken soldiers, some of them brandishing pistols. In Showchow Mabel Jones, a Southern Presbyterian missionary, was the only foreigner in the city. When it fell some five thousand women and girls stampeded into the mission compound. At the risk of her own life Miss Jones stood at the compound gate with an American flag in her hand. When the Japanese soldiers tried to brush her aside she said: "This is American property. You cannot enter this compound." The soldiers replied, "Get out of the way; we want the girls you have in there." The missionary replied: "You enter this compound only over my dead body!" The soldiers left in disgust. It was five months before the last of the girls left the mission compound to return home.

During those troublous times missionary stock in China rose dramatically. President Chiang Kai-shek publicly acknowledged the brave humanitarian endeavors of the missionaries, Roman Catholic and Protestant. Randall Gould, owner and editor of the *Shanghai Evening News*, wrote:

> Japan's attack on China raised hundreds, nay thousands of Christian missionaries from the status of nice, devoted but rather humdrum workers in the vineyard of the Lord to that of true heroes and heroines. . . . It was a time of supreme test which Christian missions met superbly. They braved Japanese bombs and bayonets to save hundreds of thousands of Chinese lives. . . . No honest person of any race or nationality could watch the Christian missionaries during Japan's brutal onslaught and feel anything but fervent admiration.[33]

More recently still, during the rape of Bangladesh in 1971, most of the missionaries remained at their posts. At great risk to themselves and their families they again manifested the love of Christ for the victims of war, regardless of class, color, or religion. It was estimated that during the nine-month holocaust three hundred thousand girls were raped by the invading soldiers, ten million refugees fled to India, and thirty million persons were rendered homeless. The problems were enormous, far beyond the power of the missionaries to cope with; but with their meager resources they stayed behind and did what they could to save human life.

The savagery of the Pak soldiers and the sufferings of the civilian population were incredible. The soldiers marched from one Hindu village to another searching for Mukti Bahini, gunning down fleeing civilians, grabbing girls, setting fire to bamboo homes. Father Goedert, thirty miles north of Dacca, had 10,407 refugees under his care. He wrote to CORR, a relief agency in Dacca:

---

[33] Randall Gould, *China in the Sun* (New York: Doubleday, 1946), p. 285.

We have so many problems that, at times, we even forget to be afraid. One bullet case has died. He has the distinction of being the only Hindu to be buried in our cemetery in 280 years, though he probably does not appreciate it. . . . We have had five deliveries, one case of typhoid, and hundreds of dysentery. We need everything: food, clothes, medicine; and we need it yesterday.[34]

Later he wrote:

The condition in Baira is appalling. Forty-nine people are dead, and the number is rising; 174 homes totally destroyed; 86 more partially destroyed; about 500 tons of rice, their entire food supply for the year, either burned or stolen. Most of them have only one piece of clothing that they fled in, bled in, and sweat in since May 14th.[35]

More than once Father Goedert almost lost his life. His colleague, Father Evans, did not survive. On November 13, 1971, he was accosted on his way to a rural mission station by five Pakistani soldiers, They ordered him to sit in a ditch. Then they struck him with their rifles, slashed him with their bayonets, shot him twice, and kicked his body into a river.

The Protestant missionaries also had some tense moments. On one occasion a group of Mukti rebels turned up at a hospital and demanded guns and ammunition. Dr. Viggo Olsen said, "You'll use our hunting guns to kill people. It isn't right for us to get involved. We're here to save lives, not take them."[36]

Mission hospitals are particularly vulnerable in time of civil war for the simple reason that they insist on remaining neutral and caring for the wounded of both sides. But it isn't easy. On one occasion a Pakistani officer appeared at a mission hospital and demanded of the doctor in charge: "Why have you been treating our enemies?" Dr. Ketcham replied: "Major, you have your military code. We respect that. We Christian physicians have our code. It calls for us to help anyone hurt or sick regardless of politics or religion. We'll help you and your men just as we'll help the local people."[37]

The mission doctor then secured from the officer a guarantee that he would protect the Hindu members of the hospital staff. That granted, he requested the same for all the Hindus living near the hospital. The officer's only remark was, "We'll see."

Wherever missionaries have gone the story has been the same. They have consistently followed in the steps of their Master, who "went

---

[34] James and Marti Hefley, *Christ in Bangladesh* (New York: Harper, 1973), p. 47.
[35] *Ibid.*, p. 47.
[36] *Ibid.*, p. 27.
[37] *Ibid.*, p. 31.

about doing good" (Acts 10:38). In good times and bad they could always be depended on to be in the right place at the right time, healing, helping, serving, saving.

8

Christianity in the Third World

The Christian Church is the only truly universal institution in the world. It was not always so. In fact until the beginning of the nineteenth century Christianity was pretty well confined to Europe and America. Then came "The Great Century" when the Christian Church, like a mighty army with its banners flying, moved into Asia, Africa, the Middle East, and the Pacific Islands. Today the Christian Church is firmly rooted in all six continents. There are still half a dozen small countries that do not have an organized church of any kind; but there isn't a single country in which there are no Christians.

While it is generally recognized that the field is the world, and that any attempt to divide the mission field into home and foreign is arbitrary and artificial, it is true that the emphasis in Christian missions is still in the Third World. This does not mean that Africa and Asia are any more needy than Europe or North America. The fact remains that the opportunities for hearing the gospel are much greater in the so-called Christian countries of the world. It is only fit and proper that special attention should be given to those areas where the name of Christ is still largely unknown, and where the Christians represent less than 10 percent of the population.

Every student of missions should be vitally interested in the progress of Christianity in the Third World. That is where the action is. And what happens there may well determine the future course of Christianity. In the past in the study of Christian missions too much time and thought have been given to the Western missions and not enough to the national churches. After all, the missions exist for the churches, not the churches for the missions. What happens to the churches is much more important than what becomes of the missions. Conceivably the missions could cease to exist while the churches continued to grow and prosper.

Identification: Problem
of Western Missionaries

The Christian mission takes the missionary across geographical and cultural boundaries. When he arrives at his destination he finds himself among an alien people with an unknown language, a foreign religion, and an exotic culture. For the first time in his life the missionary discovers that *he* is the foreigner. As such he is not likely to attract people to himself unless, of course, he can somehow identify himself with the host country, its people, and its culture.

PRINCIPLES OF IDENTIFICATION

1. Identification is at the heart of the Christian faith. John tells us that "the Word became flesh and dwelt among us" (Jn 1:14). Paul makes a similar statement. Speaking of Christ, he says, "Who, though he was in the form of God, did not count equality with God a thing to be grasped, but emptied himself, taking the form of a servant, being born in the likeness of men" (Ph 2:6, 7). The incarnation remains the greatest miracle and the most profound mystery of Christianity; for in the incarnation God, the eternal, the immortal, the invisible, wrapped Himself round with the mantle of our humanity and appeared on earth in the humble guise of a human being. So complete and perfect was His identification with us that one must look a second time to discover His divinity.

2. Identification was a fundamental principle in the ministry of Paul, the greatest missionary of all time. He said: "To the Jews I became as a Jew, in order to win Jews; to those under the law I became as one under the law, that I might win those under the law. To those outside the law I became as one outside the law. . . . I have become all things to all men, that I might by all means save some" (1 Co 9:20-22). This comes out very clearly in The Acts and in Paul's epistles. On the fundamentals of the faith there was no room for compromise or concession (Ga 1:6-9); but on all other matters Paul was willing to settle for anything that would facilitate the preaching of the gospel or contribute to the growth of the church. As far as salvation was concerned "neither circumcision nor uncircumcision is of any avail" (Ga 5:6); but in order to make Timothy, a Christian evangelist, more acceptable to his Jewish compatriots Paul arranged to have him circumcised (Acts 16:3).

For the sake of the gospel Paul carried his identification to great lengths. He could say, "If food is a cause of my brother's falling, I will never eat meat, lest I cause my brother to fall" (1 Co 8:13). If Paul had been a missionary to the Muslims, he would not have eaten pork. If he had been a missionary to the Hindus, he would not have eaten beef. Paul was some missionary!

3. Missionaries have not, as a group, done all they might have done by way of identification. To be sure, they did better than any other group that ventured into the Third World; but on the whole their performance was disappointing, at least to the nationals. There were, of course, some noble exceptions. Hudson Taylor and the early China Inland Mission missionaries not only lived in Chinese houses and ate Chinese food; they adopted Chinese dress, including the despised "pigtail," which was a symbol of Chinese subjugation to the Manchus. But in so doing they incurred the wrath of the foreign community, including other missionaries.

As a rule missionaries have tended to live apart from the people in houses whose architectural style and interior decoration were as American as apple pie. The pictures on the wall, the dishes on the table, the carpets on the floor—everything was exactly like homeside. There was no attempt to conceal their foreignness.

Referring to the situation in India *vis-à-vis* the problem of conversion, Charles W. Forman said: "The foreignness of missionaries is a problem which is today confused with that of freedom of conversion. In fact, there are suggestions that it is foreignness which is the real problem."[1]

4. Identification is more difficult in some cultures than in others. Missionaries to Europe will not find identification to be any great problem. We have our roots in European culture and when we go to Europe we are really returning home. But once the missionary goes east of Suez he finds himself in an entirely different world. There identification becomes more difficult. In nineteenth-century Africa or in

---

[1] Blaise Levai, *Revolution in Missions* (Vellore: The Popular Press, 1957), p. 101.

twentieth-century New Guinea the missionary encountered living conditions so primitive that his attempts at identification necessarily had to be limited. After all, the missionary can hardly be expected to live without any of the amenities of modern civilization. But in the more advanced countries of Asia with their rich and ancient civilizations the missionaries might easily have done a better job of identification.

5. Identification is more important in missionary work than in any other kind of overseas vocation. The missionaries were not the only ones to live abroad. Two other groups did the same—the merchants and the diplomats. They never made any concerted effort to identify with the "natives." For the most part they despised them. Not one in a hundred ever bothered to learn the language. Their purpose for being there was different from that of the missionary. They were not interested in making friends or influencing people. They were there to buy and sell, to make a profit, and to protect Western interests. This they could do quite successfully without ever stopping to make friends. The missionary, on the other hand, was there to win men to Christ; and this he could not do unless he first won them to himself. Moreover, the average businessman remains overseas for only two or three years; whereas the missionary, until recently at least, was prepared to spend the rest of his days in the land of his adoption. Identification becomes a *sine qua non* for the missionary.

6. Identification in the final analysis is an attitude as much as an activity. It is possible to identify outwardly and remain aloof inwardly. It is possible to live in a hut with and like the people and yet not really identify with them in spirit. On the other hand, it is possible for the missionary to possess many things not available to the nationals and yet successfully identify with them. Much depends on the missionary's attitude toward his possessions. Are they so valuable or precious that he will not share them with his friends? Does he truly believe that a "man's life does not consist in the abundance of his possessions"? (Lk 12:15).

7. Identification is costly but rewarding. This is what Jesus had in mind when He spoke of losing one's life in order to find it again (Mt 10:39). He also spoke of the grain of wheat that falls into the ground and dies. "If it dies," He said, "it bears much fruit" (Jn 12:24). In this as in everything else He practiced what He preached. Identification was a supremely costly thing for Christ. "For you know the grace of our Lord Jesus Christ, that though he was rich, yet for your sake he became poor; so that by his poverty you might become rich" (2 Co 8:9). No one in China carried identification farther than Hudson Taylor. For fifty years he gave himself without regret and without reserve to the people of China. When it was all over he said, "If I had a thousand lives, I'd give them all to China."

8. Identification can never be 100 percent complete. The greatest missionary will have to be content with something less than perfection. Even if he were to go so far as to give up his American citizenship, he would not cease to be a white man with all the connotations that belong to that term. There are some marks he cannot remove. His fair skin, his big nose, his blond hair will betray him.

Tony Idle, working in the slums of Nairobi, put it this way: "Try though we may, live in a mud hut though we may, we will never cease to be anything but Europeans. We know this. We have been told this by well-meaning African friends."[2]

9. Very few nationals can appreciate the difficulties inherent in identification. In recent years, especially since nationalism became such a force in the Third World, the missionaries have been criticized by their national colleagues for their failure to live at the level of the people. In some instances this criticism has led to harsh words and strained relations.

It has already been said that the missionaries failed to achieve that degree of identification which was expected of them. On the other hand, it is only fair to discuss the other side of the problem. It is natural for the national worker to look with envy at the missionary with his higher salary and his bigger house, to say nothing of motorcycles, automobiles, record players, and other things that are quite beyond the reach of the pastor.

The national worker is acutely aware of the economic gulf that exists between the missionary and himself. He has no way of knowing what the missionary's standard of living was in the homeland. He knows what the missionary brought with him; he doesn't know what he left behind. More than one national worker has changed his mind regarding the missionary's "affluence" after he has had an opportunity to visit the United States in person. Most of them return with a deeper appreciation of the "sacrifices" in missionary life. In this connection it is interesting to note that quite frequently well-educated national workers have a harder time adjusting to a subculture in their own country than the missionary has in adjusting to the dominant culture in the same country.

---

[2] Helen and Richard Exley, *In Search of the Missionary* (London: Highway Press, 1970), p. 24.

PROBLEMS OF IDENTIFICATION

1. **Problems presented by a stratified society.** All societies, including Communist societies, are stratified. In many parts of the Third
World this phenomenon is most pronounced. The missionary desires to
identify as closely as he can with the people; but the question arises:
Which section of the people? To identify with the poor is to alienate
the rich. The opposite is also true. In India the caste system poses an
enormous problem at this point. It is impossible in most societies to
identify with *all* the people.

2. **Problems occasioned by the domestic life of the missionary.**
Roman Catholic missionaries with their celibate life-style and their
clerical garb tend to be much more isolated from the community than
Protestant missionaries with their wives and children. Children the
world over never fail to attract attention and create good will. It is
not always possible for missionary families to keep open house; but if
they can it will go a long way towards bridging the gap between
the foreign missionary and the national.

3. **Problems involved in a multiracial situation.** Some countries,
such as China and Japan, have a homogeneous society. They make an
ideal mission field. India, on the other hand, with fourteen major
languages and over five hundred dialects, is the most variegated society
in the world. Or take Malaysia for example. There are three racial
groups, each with its own language, religion, and culture: The Malays
who are Muslims, the Chinese who are Buddhists, and the Tamils who
are Hindus. In such a situation the missionary must decide among
which group he will work; he will then do his best to identify with
that particular group. He cannot successfully identify with all three.

4. **Problems involved in the economic disparity between the East
and the West.** Two-thirds of all the Protestant missionaries in the world
come from North America, the most affluent part of the globe. This
poses a real problem. Can a person accustomed to the affluence of
urban America ever get down to the economic level of a country such
as India, where the average per capita income is around a hundred
dollars per year? Of course, in the larger cities of India he will find
wealth alongside poverty. If he settles down in one of them he can
live quite comfortably. But what about the smaller towns and villages?
Still worse, what about such primitive, poverty-stricken areas of the
world as West Irian, the Amazon Valley, and Central Asia? In all such
regions identification on the economic level is virtually impossible.

Some well-meaning missionaries have tried to go the whole way and have cracked up.

5. Problems involved in the value system of non-Christian cultures. With few exceptions (Europe being one) the missionary goes to non-Christian people whose value system may be entirely different from his own. He may sincerely desire to identify with the culture but he can go only so far and then he runs into trouble. What about the inferior status of women and girls? Is he expected to go along with that? What about the rigid caste system of India, which favors those on the top but condemns to perpetual poverty those at the bottom? What about the almost universal practice of graft? Should he bribe an official to get a driver's license? What about male and female attendance at the public baths in Japan? Should he and his wife indulge? Becoming all things to all men in a non-Christian culture poses some vexing problems for the Christian missionary.

6. Problems involved in religious rites. Here in this country religion is pretty well confined to the eleven o'clock hour on Sunday morning. Not so in other parts of the world where religion is so closely interwoven with the pattern of daily life that it is virtually impossible to separate the two. Such ceremonies as weddings and funerals are particularly troublesome. Is ancestor worship really a form of worship or is it simply an expression of filial piety? Is it right for the Chinese to perform the *kowtow* when announcing the death of a parent? Is it all right to set off a string of firecrackers at the close of a baptismal service? What about bowing to a portrait of the emperor? Is this an act of worship or is it equivalent to our saluting the flag? In all such matters it requires great tact and wisdom to maintain a Christian position and at the same time avoid offending the sensibilities of the people.

SPHERES OF IDENTIFICATION

1. The physical realm. Three items are important here: food, clothing, and housing. Paul said he would not eat meat if it caused his brother to fall. Eating pork is definitely offensive to the Muslim. Eating beef is equally repugnant to the Hindu. Should the missionary in Pakistan avoid the one and the missionary in India the other? Is this not what Paul had in mind? If not, what did he mean? Many missionaries do not feel that their converts have really come through for Christ until they have broken their vegetarian habits. Is this necessary? Must a convert from Hinduism eat a plateful of meat to prove to the world that he is now a good Christian?

It is not simply a matter of *what* the missionary eats, but also *how* he eats it. In India they use their fingers. In China and Japan they use chopsticks. We use knives and forks. When invited to the home of friends, of course, the missionary uses what is provided; but what about at home? Does he there revert to Western habits? When the Indians and the Japanese eat, they sit on the floor. The missionary does the same in their homes. But what does he do when friends come to his house? Does he sit with them on the floor or does he expect them to sit on chairs? This may sound like a trivial matter; but one need only to put himself in the other fellow's place to know how it feels. Suppose a Buddhist missionary came to the United States to convert us to his religion but insisted on our sitting on the floor in his home. How would we respond? Would this be the way to make friends and influence people?

Then there is the matter of clothing. To what extent is it wise and proper for the missionary to adopt national dress? In most cultures women are more conservative in dress than men. In India and Japan many of the men have adopted Western dress but the womenfolk still cling to the beautiful sari and kimono. They even wear them when they go abroad. And why not? They are among the most beautiful costumes in the world. It seems wise then for the missionary to take his cue from the nationals. If the men have long since adopted Western dress, it would be foolish for male missionaries to adopt Oriental dress. On the other hand, the women missionaries might be wise to wear the national costume, especially if it pleases the womenfolk. Right up to the general evacuation of 1950 the women missionaries of the China Inland Mission all wore Chinese dress. It was a small gesture but it meant a great deal to the conservative people of inland China. As a rule very few missionaries in any land adopted national dress. It was not simply a matter of convenience or inconvenience. There was deep-seated prejudice against it even on the part of missionaries. When Amy Carmichael decided to adopt Indian dress the home board threatened to cut her off!

Housing can be a problem too. In mission circles everyone has heard of the "big bungalow." Most missionary residences have been foreign in style, large in size, and rather pretentious in appointments. The trend today is away from the "compound" to rented quarters. In the larger cities such houses are often Western or semi-Western in style, so the problem does not arise. In the smaller towns and rural areas, where many missionaries still function, the Western-style house appears luxurious in the eyes of the people. It is still customary for national workers to live in much humbler houses than the missionaries.

What about interior decorations? Do they conform at all to the national culture, or are they wholly American in motif? And what about all the household stuff that the present-day missionary takes with him to the field? No one objects to the necessities that cannot be acquired in the host country. Perhaps a case can be made for such luxury items as electric washers, dryers, stoves, etc. But why is it necessary to take bedroom, dining room, and kitchen furniture? Must every stick of furniture bear a "Made in U.S.A." stamp on it? It may come as a surprise to some to learn that missionaries are still doing this; but they are.

2. The economic realm. Missionaries are certainly not overpaid by homeside standards; nevertheless by the standards of the host country they appear to be very wealthy. In some countries, such as Japan, the missionary may very well be less affluent than his Japanese counterpart; but that is the exception and should not be used as a yardstick to measure the magnitude of the problem. In most cases the missionary gets several times as much salary as the national pastor. He may spend as much on his annual vacation as the pastor gets in a whole year. In many cases the missionary has his own car. This widens the gap between the missionary and the national worker.

How can identification be achieved when the gap is so great? Should the church raise the salary of the pastor or should the mission lower the salary of the missionary? Both methods present difficulties. Here the Peace Corps presents a challenge to Christian missions. Its volunteers are expected to live at the level of the people. They are not permitted to own vehicles of any kind. When traveling they go second class—third if there is one. Can we learn a lesson from the Peace Corps? Of course, the volunteers are overseas for only twenty-one months and one can endure almost anything for a short period of time. Moreover, most of them are single, so children are not involved. But when all is said and done it is a fact that the greatest single focal point of tension today between the sending mission and the receiving church is related to money.

3. The social realm. All missionaries *work* with the nationals. Few of them *play* with the nationals. In their professional capacity as missionaries they have many contacts with the people; but in their personal life, especially in their leisure time, they tend to restrict their contacts to other missionaries or Westerners in the same city. In the large, cosmopolitan cities they may even belong to a tennis or a swimming club that is predominantly, if not exclusively, white. It is difficult for the missionary to persuade the nationals that he loves them if his only contacts with them come in the course of his missionary work. They invite him and his family frequently to their homes. Does he return the compliment or is he satisfied to be always on the receiving end? Above all, does he love them as human beings, as friends, as brothers, or simply as fellow workers in the vineyard of the Lord? Does he enjoy their company during his leisure time?

An area of great sensitivity is the education of missionaries' children—known as MKs. Not one MK in a hundred attends a local school. Instead they attend special schools for MKs or they are sent home for their education. Has the time come to consider the possibility of sending MKs to local schools, especially in the more advanced countries where the educational standards are as good as, or better than, ours? This is being done in Europe; but in the Third World it is still a rare phenomenon.

Two English journalists who visited Africa in 1970 had this to say about the matter: "Very few of them send their children to African secondary schools. Many Africans we spoke to felt hurt and bewildered by this; the missionaries talked about the value of African culture yet when it came to the crunch over the education of their children, they opted for the West."[3]

And what shall we say about furlough which now comes, in some countries, every two years? Some nationals are asking: "Must the missionaries have furloughs so frequently? If so, must they always go home to America? Could they not get rest and relaxation in our country?" It *can* be done. Amy Carmichael served in India for almost fifty years without a furlough.

At the World Missionary Conference in Edinburgh in June 1910, V. S. Azariah of South India made a courageous speech which disturbed many of his hearers. His own relations with Western missionaries had been "simply delightful" but he was sure, generally speaking, that there was need for a deep readjustment of personal relationships. What was wanted was friendship. He concluded with these words: "Through all ages to come the Indian Church will rise up in gratitude to attest the heroism and self-denying labors of the missionary body. You have given your goods to feed the poor. You have given your bodies to be burned. We also ask for love. Give us *friends!*"[4]

There is no doubt that we have come a long way since Edinburgh 1910; but we still have a long way to go. The appeal is still pertinent— Give us friends!

Stephen Carr, an agricultural missionary in Africa, summed it up pretty well when he defined involvement as:

> Entering into the life of the people rather than offering impersonal advice or service. This means learning a language (or several languages) and social customs. It means adapting yourself

---

3 Helen and Richard Exley, *In Search of the Missionary* (London: Highway Press, 1970), p. 21.
4 United Council for Missionary Education, *Beginning at Edinburgh* (London: Edinburgh House Press, 1960), p. 29.

to other people's eating habits and food. It means ordering your home so that people feel entirely at ease in it. It means using your leisure among the people you live with rather than your own compatriot group.[5]

4. The cultural realm. This is perhaps the most difficult area of all. It is comparatively easy to pick up the social habits of the people; it is much more difficult to appreciate their art forms, to understand their thought patterns, to master their linguistic nuances. This is not achieved in "Ten Easy Lessons."

Culture has been defined as the sum total of all the learned behavior patterns of a particular people. Some peoples, such as the Chinese, are very numerous and have been around for a long time. To become acquainted with all their behavior patterns will require a lifetime of effort.

The most important aspect of culture is language. Without a thorough understanding of the language it is quite impossible to get to the heart of any culture.

In contrast to other groups that have lived abroad, the career missionary has always made an effort to learn the language. On the whole he has done a fairly good job. According to a survey made by the Missionary Research Library of New York, only .8 percent of missionary dropouts are attributable to failure to learn the language. This should come as an encouragement to the fainthearted.

Most missionaries, however, seldom go on to become experts in the language. They are content to complete the required course of language study laid down by the mission. Everything beyond that point is acquired not by concerted study but by a process of osmosis. As a result most missionaries have a good theological vocabulary because that is the area in which they do all their teaching and preaching; but their general vocabulary leaves much to be desired. All career missionaries should continue to work at the language as long as they remain on the field.

And what about the missionary's reading habits? After acquiring the language does he use it only for teaching and preaching or does he use it in his intellectual pursuits? Does he subscribe to newspapers and magazines in the vernacular? Does he write his own letters in the vernacular, or does he get his language teacher to do this for him? Does he listen to radio broadcasts in the vernacular or does he stay pretty much with the Voice of America or the British Broadcasting Corporation?

Has he acquired a genuine appreciation for indigenous art, including music, painting, sculpture, and so on? A missionary friend of

---

[5] Exley, *op. cit.,* p. 10.

the author's made a hobby of writing the difficult Chinese characters with a brush. For years he spent hours every night practicing the difficult art. He became so adept at it he was asked by Chinese friends, Christian and non-Christian, to write scrolls for them. Quite an accomplishment! In time he became a connoisseur of Chinese art. He had a special collection of Chinese ink, paper, and brushes, and would sit for hours showing these to his Chinese friends. He would go into a shop or a home and see a rare scroll on the wall and go into ecstacies about its fine points. His missionary friends didn't know what it was all about. His Chinese friends loved it!

5. The political realm. Before ever going to the field the missionary is warned by his board not to interfere in the internal politics of the host country. This is good advice. It is virtually impossible, however, to heed the advice in the face of colonialism, nationalism, and Communism; and there are few countries in the Third World not affected by one or other of these three forces. Whether he wants to or not, the present-day missionary will be asked questions relating to politics either in the United States or the host country or some other part of the world. This is particularly true if the missionary is working among students, for students in the Third World take their politics very seriously. They will insist on asking questions. Such questions can be embarrassing, especially to the American missionary; but they deserve an honest answer.

Woe betide the missionary whose attitude is, "My country right or wrong." During the past decade United States involvement in Southeast Asia has given Americans around the world a black eye. Our failure to side with Bangladesh in its struggle for independence did not sit well with either Bangladesh or India. We will be mending our fences in that part of the world for some time to come. Fortunately the missionaries in Bangladesh supported "their" country in her hour of trial.

The Jews, speaking of the Roman centurion in Capernaum, said: "He loves our nation" (Lk 7:5). Does the missionary love the nation, not just the people? Does he wish the nation well? Does he want to see it prosper? Does he speak well of it whenever he can? Is he willing to identify himself with the national aspirations of an oppressed people? On national holidays does he fly the Stars and Stripes or the national flag? Does he celebrate the national Independence Day with the same enthusiasm as he celebrates the Fourth of July? Is he critical of corruption in the host government but willing to overlook corruption in his own?

By and large missionaries in the past have not been very sympathetic to the cause of nationalism or the desire for independence. The author spent five months in India in 1944-45 when Gandhi was carrying on his "Quit India" campaign against the British. He did not find a single missionary who was in favor of independence for India. Doubtless they feared that the coming of independence would mean the end of the missionary era; and this they did not want.

And what about the missionary's most prized possession—his American citizenship? If the situation requires it, would he be willing to give up his citizenship? In the last few years a score of missionaries in India have applied for naturalization papers in the hope that by this means they might be permitted to remain in the country. To date it has not worked out; but at least they made the try.

If Christianity is to hold its head high and make its appeal to the intelligentsia of the Third World, its emissaries will have to be on the side of civil rights, social justice, and political independence.

Indigenization: Problem of National Churches

Christianity began in Asia. It was carried to Europe by Paul. There it took root and, in the words of the parable of the mustard seed (Mt 13:31-32), it grew into a large tree in which the birds built their nests. After the conversion of Constantine Christianity became popular and millions of persons flocked to its banners. Later on it became the state religion. By A.D. 800 there had emerged the Holy Roman Empire, in which church and state were one. Europe was Christianized and the church was paganized.

Now the tree has been transplanted back into the soil of Asia; but along with the tree we have taken the "birds" and the "nests" which were never really part of the tree. We failed to separate Christian doctrine from Western culture. With what results? In Asia Christianity has always been regarded as a "foreign religion" and in Africa it is known as the "white man's religion." In a word, we have failed to make Christianity indigenous.

What is an indigenous church? The Madras Conference of 1938 adopted the following definition: "An indigenous church, young or old, in the East or in the West, is a church which, rooted in obedience to Christ, spontaneously uses forms of thought and modes of action natural and familiar in its own environment."[6] If this definition is correct,

---

[6] International Missionary Council, *The World Mission of the Church* (London and New York: Madras Conference Report, 1939), p. 26.

the modern missionary movement has failed miserably to produce an indigenous church. There are several major areas where the failure to adapt Christianity to the culture of the Third World is evident.

FACTORS WHICH MILITATED
AGAINST INDIGENEITY

1. **Denominationalism.** The charter of the famous London Missionary Society, founded in 1795, stated clearly that its missionaries would "not send Presbyterianism, Independency, Episcopacy, or any other form of Church Order and Government . . . but the glorious Gospel of the blessed God."[7] The churches in mission lands were to have the liberty to develop in their own way. At the Bangalore Conference in 1879 the missionaries in India went on record as saying that they looked forward to the day when God would do a new thing and there would be one "Church of Christ in India."[8]

This was a noble ideal. Alas, it was honored more in the breach than in practice. We did precisely what we said we would not do; we exported our denominationalism to the mission field. In some of the larger countries we ended up with 150 different missionary societies each reproducing its own little church or denomination, which in nearly every respect resembled the "mother" church back home.

Denominationalism is not *all* bad. After all, the Plymouth Brethren would find it difficult to worship with the Episcopalians. But surely half a dozen denominational groups would have been sufficient. Did we need such vast proliferation, especially when much of our denominationalism in the West was historically and culturally conditioned?

2. **Organization.** The early church had little by way of organization and what it had was the result of natural growth. Beginning with the second century church organization assumed greater proportions until it eventually grew into the gigantic Roman Catholic Church. It was not enough that we exported our denominationalism to the mission field; we foisted on the emerging churches our own elaborate form of church structure long before they were able to assume responsibility for, or to profit by, it. To make matters worse, the non-Caucasian peoples of the world do not have our flair for organization. And they never heard of Robert's *Rules of Order* until the missionaries introduced it. "The missionaries imposed the Western patterns of

---

[7] Ruth Rouse and Stephen Charles Neill, A *History of the Ecumenical Movement 1517-1948* (Philadelphia: The Westminster Press, 1968), p. 150.
[8] William Richey Hogg, *Ecumenical Foundations* (New York: Harper and Brothers, 1952), p. 21.

church organization cultus, thought, and support firmly upon the emerging churches."[9]

3. Architecture. The early church met in the homes of its members. It was several hundred years before the church invested in real estate and erected stately buildings known as "churches." When we took the gospel to the mission field, we organized the first group of converts into a church and proceeded to erect a church building, when it might have been better to meet in homes or even in the open air. We went further; we built the churches along Western lines, exact replicas of what we have here at home. Interior and exterior, all was the same, including the appointments. Then we attached foreign names to the churches, calling them the "Judson Memorial Church" or the "American Presbyterian Church" or the "English Methodist Church." And we wondered why Christianity was regarded as a foreign religion!

The nationals, especially the non-Christians, would have found it much easier to attend church had the institution been more indigenous in format and atmosphere. Church architecture should in general conform to the style indigenous to the country. John L. Nevius made this plain in his four-point Nevius Plan which worked so well in Korea; but outside Korea Nevius was a voice crying in the wilderness. *Must* a church in China have a spire? *Must* a church in India have pews? *Must* the preacher stand behind a pulpit? *Must* the musical instrument be an organ?

There were, of course, exceptions to the rule. "The magnificent cathedral of Dornakal, inspired by both Moslem and Hindu forms and yet genuinely Christian in every respect, is an example of what can be accomplished in this field."[10]

Moreover, the churches which we built were so costly that the indigenous church in many places could not afford to keep them in repair. So we built foreign churches with foreign money designed for foreign worship!

4. Worship. Here again we missionaries slavishly followed the Western pattern. The worship service is always on Sunday morning and the format seldom varies. It begins with the invocation and ends with the benediction. The entire order of service is identical with that in the homeland. The sermon is the most important part of the service. With few exceptions the hymns are translations of the great majestic hymns and gospel songs of the church in the West. The

---

[9] R. Pierce Beaver, *The Missionary Between the Times* (Garden City: Doubleday, 1968), p. 131.
[10] Willis Church Lamott, *Revolution in Missions* (New York: The Macmillan Company, 1954), p. 104.

tunes are usually familiar Western tunes played on a piano or organ. Only in recent years have indigenous hymns and tunes in any significant numbers been included in the hymnals. We are still reluctant to make use of musical instruments familiar to the people.

5. Paid clergy. In the first century Christianity was spread largely by laymen who gossiped the gospel as they went about their daily duties. It was not long before the clergy began to emerge as a distinct and somewhat elevated group in the church. By the end of the second century the episcopal form of church government was fully developed. Thereafter there was a clear line of demarcation between the clergy and the laity. This has continued down to the present time, though in very recent years there are signs of a change in this respect.

A church in the West must have a pastor; he must work full time and be fully supported by the congregation. He does most of the work; that's what he is paid for. This system of a one-man, fully paid, ordained ministry we exported to the mission field. In the early years we used foreign funds to pay the pastors. More recently we have tried to shift this burden to the churches. Some of them can support a full-time pastor; many cannot. And the paid pastors are woefully underpaid. Consequently few young men feel called to the ministry. *Must* every church have a paid pastor? *Must* every pastor be ordained? Can the Plymouth Brethren teach us something at this point? By giving the impression that a church cannot be a genuine church without a full-time, fully paid pastor, we have created a false impression, raised an unattainable standard, and placed on the necks of the Christians a yoke which they are unable to bear. Would it have been better to allow the national church to develop its own form of ministry more in keeping with its economic resources, its social pattern, and its cultural mores? After almost two hundred years of missionary work in India there are still local churches that cannot support their pastors without help from the mission.

6. Church discipline. In the early years discipline was exercised by the missionaries. The moral and ethical standards were those accepted in the "Christian" West. They often had higher standards for converts on the mission field than for church members here at home. Sabbath observance was rigidly enforced even if it meant financial loss for the new convert. Polygamy was considered to be an unmitigated evil and had to be eradicated root and branch in the first generation. The social and economic implications of polygamy were either unknown or overlooked. Discipline was often administered in a legal fashion with little or no consideration given to extenuating circumstances—spiritual immaturity, social pressures, cultural mores, etc.

7. Theological education. It began in a simple way with the first seminarians attending Bible classes in the missionary's home. As numbers increased new and larger facilities were needed. Short-term Bible schools were opened. These soon channeled students into long-term Bible schools and ultimately into seminaries. Unfortunately these seminaries were patterned after similar institutions in the West. Curriculum building, course content, grading system, class schedules, teaching methods—all were identical with those in the homeland. The textbooks were of Western origin. And, of course, the missionaries did the teaching. No attempt was made to adapt the instruction to the background of the students or the needs of the national church. After four or five years in that kind of environment the students were more Western than Oriental in their outlook. "Time and again graduating students have returned enthusiastically to their regions with real and great visions for the future. Sad to say, they are now foreigners! Their people suspect them, detest their 'foreignness' and finally reject them."[11]

The story is the same in Africa. Bishop Tucker Theological College in Uganda, one of the more prestigious seminaries in Africa, is reported to be turning out priests in an atmosphere of Western education, urgently teaching them English, giving them running water and all modern amenities. Recent visitors remarked: "We felt that the Bishop Tucker staff is teaching a thoroughly Western life style and theology to people who will go back to a mud hut and a community that speaks no English."[12]

HOW MISSIONARIES CAN ACCELERATE THE PROGRESS OF INDIGENIZATION

1. Missionaries must recognize the evils of paternalism. Paternalism, like colonialism, was not wholly evil. In the pioneering stage paternalism was inevitable, given the primitive conditions that prevailed at the time. When the national churches were in their infancy, and even up through childhood, they requested and received support and supervision from the missionaries. This was both necessary and desirable. We need to bear this fact in mind when we thoughtlessly pass judgment on the missionaries of the nineteenth century. Had we been in their shoes we probably would have done much as they did. But times have changed and the missionaries must change with them. We are rapidly approaching the last quarter of the twentieth century. Paternalism simply does not work.

The old paternalism is dead, or should be; but the specter still

---

[11] Peter Savage, "A Bold Move for More Realistic Theological Training," *Evangelical Missions Quarterly* (Winter 1969), p. 67.
[12] Exley, *op. cit.*, p. 23.

lingers. Perhaps the hardest task for the modern missionary is to avoid the label of paternalism when he is in the number two spot and is obviously having to prop up number one. This very often leads to difficulties on both sides, difficulties that were probably exacerbated in the first place by a premature appointment.

2. Missionaries must acknowledge the right of the national churches to order their own affairs. Most of the churches established by the ecumenical missions have long since received their independence. Those brought into existence by the conservative missions are still on their way. Some of them have already arrived; but many are in that turbulent period known as adolescence, halfway between the dependence of childhood and the interdependence of adulthood.

This period is characterized by independence. Right or wrong, they want their own way. They have come of age and insist on asserting their independence, and woe betide anyone who gets in the way. Governments overseas have received their independence from colonial rule. Churches overseas are demanding independence from mission control. Missions, like parents, are sometimes possessive and unwilling to see their offspring break free from their control. In many instances mission leaders have been like the colonial administrators—reluctant to give the nationals what they wanted *when they wanted it*. It was always "too little and too late."

The situation was further complicated by the fact that the national churches and the Western missions both had their own point of view. The churches identified independence with self-government, and they were all for that. The missions, on the other hand, equated independence with self-support, and they pushed for that. In the hassle that ensued both churches and missions lost sight of the most important thing of all—self-propagation.

Be that as it may, the time has come for all mission leaders to take the initiative in arranging for the transfer of power from the mission to the church. And when this is done, let the missionaries at the grass roots beware of back-seat driving!

3. Missionaries must be patient and sympathetic during the period of transition. In the first years of independence mistakes will be made; but hopefully the national leaders will learn by their mistakes. At least, they have the right to make them! Worse still, the missionaries will have to stand by and see some of their cherished plans and schemes blown away by the winds of change. Some of the excess baggage will be jettisoned to make room for new commodities with "Made in Africa" or "Made in Asia" labels on them. Not all the new items will be good; but they will doubtless be better than the "Made in U.S.A."

articles introduced by the missionaries. The real test of the missionary's spirituality will come when he is asked to step down to make way for a national leader whose qualifications might not be as great as his own. It will afford an excellent opportunity for him to give heed to the admonition of Paul: "Do nothing from selfishness or conceit, but in humility count others better than yourselves" (Ph 2:3). Winston Churchill was not the only man who did not want to preside over the liquidation of his own empire. Missionaries have that problem too. It is natural to want to hold on to power. He is a rare person who will relinquish power voluntarily. Happy is the missionary who understands the signs of the times and has the grace to make the necessary adjustments with patience and good will.

4. **Missionaries must be willing to commit the national church and its leaders to the Lord.** In the early days of independence many a missionary feels like Uzzah, who put forth his hand to steady the ark of the covenant (2 Sa 6:6-8). But the ark of the covenant was also "the ark of God" and He was well able to take care of His own ark. The same is true of the church. The church is His church, not theirs. He is at work building His church and Jesus Christ has declared that "the gates of Hades shall not prevail against it" (Mt 16:18). The missionaries must do what Paul did with his converts—commend them to God and to the word of His grace (Acts 20:32). And he did this even though he knew beforehand that fierce wolves would come among them and scatter the flock.

5. **Missionaries must trust the Holy Spirit to work through the church as He did through the mission.** The word of the Lord to Zerubbabel is pertinent at this point: "Not by might, nor by power, but by my Spirit, says the Lord of hosts" (Ze 4:6). Paul may plant and Apollos may water, but only God can give the increase (1 Co 3:6). The missionary enterprise began with the coming of the Holy Spirit at Pentecost. Without His power and presence there would have been no mission. He and He alone can convert the sinner. He and He alone can sanctify the saint. He and He alone can purify and edify and beautify the church in both East and West. The missionaries taught these truths to the nationals. Now they must learn the lesson for themselves.

6. **Missionaries must rejoice in, and if possible cooperate with, indigenous movements outside the mainstream of Christianity.** In many countries there have grown up Christian groups which from the beginning were purely indigenous. The Little Flock and the Jesus Family in China were in this category. So also is the Bakht Singh Movement

in India. In Africa there are some seven thousand indigenous groups, sometimes called Separatist Churches, whose Christian community may run as high as fifteen million.

For the most part these movements have remained completely outside the more traditional churches. Two factors have contributed to this aloofness. In the first place many of the leaders have been less than friendly in their attitude toward Western missionaries. They tend to be ardent nationalists and have shown no great desire for outside help. On the other hand the Western missions and the churches which they brought into existence have often been jealous of the success of these indigenous groups and opposed them as much on ecclesiastical as on theological grounds.

In some cases these indigenous groups have, wittingly or unwittingly, espoused heretical views which would naturally alienate them from the mainstream of Christianity. It must be said, however, that quite frequently the real root of the trouble has been the fact that these indigenous groups often grow at the expense of the main-line churches. Because they are thoroughly indigenous, and also because they offer some emphasis, doctrine, or experience that is either missing or neglected in the main-line churches, they are able to attract Christians away from these churches. This is known as "sheep stealing." In some instances large churches have been split wide open in this way.

There are, of course, serious problems to be solved. Sometimes doctrinal error is involved, in which case cooperation would be difficult if not impossible. On the other hand missionaries must beware of jealousy and make sure they do not oppose these groups simply because they have lost members to them. John the Baptist must have found it difficult to say, "He must increase, but I must decrease" (Jn 3:30) at a time when his disciples were leaving him and going over to Jesus.

The apostle Paul had a similar experience. Some of his colleagues were engaging in Christian work out of envy and rivalry. They even proclaimed Christ out of partisanship, not sincerity, with a view to hurting Paul. But Paul refused to return the coin in kind. Rather he declared that so long as Christ was preached he would rejoice (Ph 1:15-18).

Time is running out. Church-mission tension is on the increase. The churches in the Third World are seeking for their own identity. They want to be authentic churches in their own right. They want to stand on their own feet, manage their own affairs, and project their own image. Somehow Christianity in the Third World must shed its foreignness if it is to survive.

> This is the essence of the problem which every missionary organization faces today. It is at the root of church-mission tensions, and an adequate answer to the question must be found if the

world is to be effectively evangelized. Foreignness is an increasing liability in the work of the Lord, and our allegiance to the Great Commission may prove to be only lip service unless missions learn how to become more thoroughly rooted in the culture which they seek to serve.[13]

Evangelization: Problem of National Missions

Too long have we subscribed to the notion that the evangelization of the world is the "white man's burden." In the beginning of the modern missionary period it was necessary for the churches in the West to take the gospel to the non-Christian parts of the world. There was no other way to get started. But now that the church has been planted in all the major regions of the world, world evangelization should no longer be regarded as the sole responsibility of the churches in the West.

Some of the great pioneer missionaries had the good sense to realize that the non-Christian peoples of the world could never be adequately evangelized by the efforts of Western missionaries, no matter how numerous they were or how hard they worked. William Carey said that India would be evangelized only by her own sons. David Livingstone said the same thing about the continent of Africa. Yet as time went on the missionaries seemed to lose sight of this fact and began to act and think as if the Great Commission applied only to the Christians in the West.

There were, of course, shining examples of missionary-minded churches in the Third World; but these were the rare exception, not the rule. By and large it is true to say that we did not plant *missionary* churches. The churches were supposed to be self-governing, self-supporting, and self-propagating. The churches emphasized the first, self-government. The missions attached great importance to the second, self-support. Neither church nor mission attached equal importance to the third, self-propagation. The vast majority of churches have been content to maintain their own existence. This is especially true of second- and third-generation churches, many of which have long since lost any evangelistic zeal they had. The result is that much of today's so-called growth is biological.

The churches are not altogether to blame for this state of affairs.

---

[13] Horace L. Fenton, Jr., "Latinizing the Latin America Mission," *Church-Mission Tension Today*, ed. C. Peter Wagner (Chicago: Moody Press, 1972), pp. 147-48).

The missionaries themselves did much to foster the idea that pioneer evangelism was the work of the mission, not the church. The word *missionary* was applied only to Westerners. Nationals engaged in spreading the gospel were called "evangelists." The distinction between the two terms was very clear.

By definition the missionary was a frontiersman, always on the move, penetrating deeper and deeper into virgin territory with the gospel of Jesus Christ. He was never supposed to "settle down." If he did he ceased to be a missionary in any genuine sense of the term. He had a twofold goal: to preach the gospel and to plant churches. As soon as a church was able to manage its own affairs—sometimes even sooner—he moved on to virgin territory and began the process all over again.

The missionaries started Bible schools and theological seminaries to train leaders for the indigenous churches. They taught the usual run of subjects: Old Testament, New Testament, church history, Bible geography, apologetics, homiletics, music, English, Greek, and Hebrew —everything but missions! As a result the church leaders in India knew all about the Holy Roman Empire, the Protestant Reformation, the Evangelical Awakening, and all the other highlights of Western church history; but they knew nothing of *missionary work* in China or Japan, much less Nigeria or Brazil. Little wonder that the churches in the Third World knew little and cared less about the Great Commission. If they had a blind spot it was no fault of theirs.

Rightly or wrongly the churches got the idea that pioneer evangelism (missionary work) was the responsibility of the *mission,* not the *church.* When the missionaries moved on the churches they left behind were content simply to manage their own affairs and thus perpetuate their own existence; and that task consumed most of their energies and resources.

Here and there there were exceptions to this rule. The classic example was the churches in the Pacific Islands. The gospel was first introduced to Tahiti in 1797 and to Tonga in 1822 by Western missionaries. But the first missionaries to Samoa were not Europeans but Polynesian teachers from Tahiti and Tonga. As early as 1828 a Samoan on a visit to Tonga learned of Christianity and became a Christian. On his return to Samoa he shared the gospel with his own people.

Friends and neighbors believed and churches sprang up everywhere. In 1830 John Williams of the London Missionary Society paid a visit to Samoa to strengthen the churches there. On his departure he left behind eight Tahitian teachers. Five years later there was a Christian church with a membership of over two thousand. In two more years the number had increased to thirteen thousand. In a matter of a few years the entire population embraced Christianity. The same thing took place in the Fiji Islands. The first missionaries were two Tahitian teachers placed on the island of Onoatu by the London Missionary Society in 1830. The same procedure was repeated in New Hebrides in 1839.

Through the years hundreds of indigenous missionaries, called teachers, moved back and forth across the main islands in the Southwest Pacific area. A report in 1970 gave the following statistics (excluding wives):[14]

SENDING ISLANDS			RECEIVING ISLANDS		
Fiji	269	missionaries	Papua-New Guinea	561	missionaries
Samoa	209	"	Solomon	98	"
Cook	197	"	New Hebrides	73	"
Solomon	139	"	Gilbert/Ellice	38	"

From this it can be seen that Fiji and Samoa have been the great and continuing source of missionaries, the first for the Methodists and the second for the Congregationalists. By far the largest receiving area has been New Guinea. It is the largest and most populous of all the islands. It was also the last to be reached as the missionary movement traveled from east to west. Two main streams of indigenous missionaries converged on New Guinea: the Congregationalists from Samoa, Cook, and Loyalty Islands and the Methodists from Fiji, Tonga, and Solomon Islands.

Not included in the above figures are over one thousand members of the Melanesian (Anglican) Brotherhood in the Solomon Islands who served as foreign missionaries in Malaita, Guadalcanal, and Santa Cruz. Another group of indigenous missionaries are the Lutheran evangelists in New Guinea, who took the gospel to the vast hinterland of their island, some four hundred miles from home. In 1935 these numbered eight hundred; by 1961 the number had risen to twelve hundred. "The total number of these Lutheran foreign missionaries up to the present time certainly reaches several thousands."[15]

The indigenous missionaries were not one whit behind their Western counterparts when it came to dedication, courage, sacrifice, and willingness to serve in hard places. Many of them died from malnutrition and disease. Not a few were killed and eaten by the cannibals they sought to win to Christ. During World War II many of them remained at their posts when the Western missionaries had to leave.

If the indigenous churches planted by Western missionaries in Africa, Asia, and Latin America had followed the pattern developed

---

[14] Charles W. Forman, "The Missionary Forces of the Pacific Island Churches," *International Review of Missions,* Vol. LIX, No. 234 (April 1970), p. 215.
[15] *Ibid.,* p. 220.

in the Pacific area the story of Christian missions in the last 150 years would have been vastly different. The fact that the Pacific Islanders had to cross large bodies of water to reach their destination only makes their achievements all the more remarkable. In recent years there has been increasing evidence that the national churches in the Third World are waking up to their missionary responsibility. For 150 years they have been on the receiving end; now they are beginning to send out their missionaries to various parts of the world.

As might be expected the churches in Asia led the way. In 1884 the Methodist Conference of South India sent its first missionary to Singapore. The National Missionary Society of India, the brainchild of K. T. Paul and Bishop Azariah, was founded in 1905. Two years later the first Korean missionary went to Cheju Island. In 1912 the first Korean missionaries landed in China. By 1940 the Korean churches had sent a hundred missionaries to various parts of the Far East.

Some of the larger churches in the Third World have long ago established their own home and foreign mission boards. The Mar Thoma Church of South India now has 250 missionaries working in a cross-cultural context in the subcontinent of India. The Brazilian Baptist Convention has an equal number of missionaries serving in five foreign countries. The Evangelical Churches of West Africa have 115 missionary families engaged in pioneer work among the many unreached tribes of Nigeria. The Seventh-day Adventist Church in the Philippines has sent 175 missionaries to various parts of the world. The United Church (Kyodan) in Japan now has 20 missionaries in nine countries, including the United States and Canada. These are only a few of the many missionary agencies now operating in the Third World.

A recent survey by a research team of Fuller's School of World Mission revealed that there are now 201 non-Western agencies with a combined total of 2,971 missionaries. If all the questionnaires had been returned the total figure would doubtless have been considerably higher.

Not all of these agencies are engaged in overseas work. Many of them work in a cross-cultural context within their own country. This is especially true of India, where there are fourteen major language groups and over five hundred smaller tribal groups. Any work that takes the evangelist across political or cultural boundaries is missionary work. These persons then are genuine missionaries in every sense of the word.

As might be expected, the vast majority of these mission agencies are working within the confines of their own continent. This is especially true of Latin America and Africa. Of the 917 African missionaries only two are working outside that continent—and they are in London and New York!

There is a natural tendency for national churches to be concerned for their own compatriots who have migrated in significant numbers to other countries. The fifteen million Chinese in Southeast Asia are the concern of Chinese churches in Hong Kong, Taiwan, Singapore, and even the United States. Indians from India have migrated in large numbers to East Africa, Malaysia, and the Fiji Islands. It is only natural that the missionary agencies in India should be concerned for their spiritual welfare. Ten agencies in Japan have sent Japanese missionaries to the large concentration of Japanese in the Sao Paulo region of Brazil. These missionaries have to cross geographical and political boundaries; but there are few cross-cultural problems when they get there.

In Asia the spread of missionary agencies is pretty evenly divided among the countries, both sending and receiving. This is not true in Latin America and Africa. In Latin America Brazil carries the lion's share and is responsible for 75 percent of all the missionaries from that continent. The same is true in Africa. Only six countries report missionary activity and Nigeria accounts for almost 90 percent.

The numbers involved are very small, but it is noteworthy that some Third World missionaries are now working in the so-called Christian countries of the world: the United States, Canada, Britain, France, Portugal, Greece, and Australia.

Four countries are at the top of the list so far as the number of missionaries is concerned: India, Philippines, Brazil, and Nigeria. These are the four countries that have received a large number of Western missionaries. Is there any connection between sending and receiving? We would like to think so. To whom much is given of him shall much be required.

In the Third World we are beginning to see the same kind of proliferation that has plagued the Western missionary movement. Instead of sending a substantial number of missionaries to one country where they could make a solid impact there is a tendency to scatter them over many countries. For instance, the United Church of Christ in Japan has twenty missionaries overseas; but they are distributed among nine different countries. The National Council of Churches in the Philippines has sent missionaries to no fewer than thirteen countries. Though Japan has sent only ninety-seven missionaries to other countries there are in Japan thirty-two sending agencies, which works out at about three missionaries per agency. Ten of these agencies are now members of the Japan Overseas Missions Association, which was formed in 1971. Its purpose is "to seek cooperatively more efficient ways of promoting foreign missions among evangelical churches in Japan."

The vast majority of the Third World missionaries are engaged in evangelism and/or church planting. The figure actually stands at 89 percent, which is much higher than the figure for Western missions.

As already indicated, some of these agencies have a history going back to the beginning of the century. The period of greatest growth, however, has been from 1960 to the present. That means that many of the societies are young and therefore small. It will be some time before they make their presence felt. The Evangelical Free Church in Japan, not yet twenty years old, has sent six missionaries overseas and has another couple waiting to go. The Dani tribe in West Irian, which received the gospel for the first time in 1957, has sent over one hundred missionaries to other areas and tribes in a spontaneous missionary movement.

In several countries the national churches have both home and foreign missionaries on their rolls. The Evangelical Church in South Vietnam not only has missionaries in Laos, Cambodia, and Thailand, but also among the Montagnard tribes in the highlands of Vietnam.

In recent years there has been an increase in the number of undenominational, or interdenominational, agencies such as the Indonesian Missionary Fellowship, India Evangelical Mission, Philippine Missionary Fellowship, Korea International Mission, Malaysia Evangelistic Fellowship, and the Thai Overseas Missionary Society. The Philippine Missionary Fellowship has sent fifty-four missionaries to various unreached areas of the islands. In the same country Grace Gospel Church alone has sent out forty-seven missionaries in the last seven years. The churches of Taiwan have sent more than twenty missionaries to other parts of Asia.

Some Western missions have encouraged the national churches overseas to form their own mission agencies. The Christian and Missionary Alliance has done exceedingly well in this respect. Six autonomous Churches of C&MA background in Asia got together in March 1970, for an Asian Missionary Consultation. Out of this grew the C&MA Fellowship of Asia, whose purpose is "to fulfill the command of Jesus Christ by promoting the program of foreign missions in Christian and Missionary Alliance churches throughout Asia." To date these Churches have sent out forty-eight missionaries to various parts of the world. The Assemblies of God Churches in Asia have sent out thirty-two couples to other parts of Asia. All these missionaries are fully supported by their national Churches. The overseas national Churches of the Seventh-day Adventists in 1972 gave almost nine and a half million dollars (United States) to foreign missions.

In many respects the Chinese are in a class by themselves. They were reported to be the strongest national group from the Third World at the Madras Conference in 1938. The evacuation of Western missionaries from China in the early 1950s and the subsequent destruction of the Christian church were a body blow to Chinese Christianity. Nevertheless there are some fifteen million Chinese in Taiwan and another fifteen million scattered all over Southeast Asia. The overseas Chinese, as they are called, have been more receptive to the gospel than any other ethnic group in Asia. Even here in the United States there are many practicing Christians among American-born Chinese and also among Chinese students who have come here for graduate work. Among the Chinese are great spiritual leaders such as Andrew Gih, Moses Chow, Calvin Chao, Philip Teng, John Pao, and a host of others.

These Chinese leaders are deeply concerned for the evangelization of their compatriots and also for the strengthening of Chinese churches all over Southeast Asia. They are a very able group of men and are making a determined effort to shoulder their responsibility along these lines. In recent years the Chinese have established several very important organizations: Evangelize China Fellowship, Chinese Christian Literature Association, China Evangelical Seminary, Chinese Congress on Evangelism, Association for the Promotion of Chinese Theological Education, China Graduate School of Theology, North American Congress of Chinese Evangelicals. They are engaged in a new translation of the Chinese Bible. They have also launched *Cosmic Light*, a magazine to take the place of *Dengta*, a mission venture which folded several years ago.

There is a higher percentage of Christians among the Chinese in the United States than among any other non-Western group. At present there are two hundred Chinese Bible study groups. There are so many Chinese students studying theology that in March 1973, they began the publication of a *Bulletin* to be circulated among themselves. At the Urbana Convention every three years they are always the largest group of overseas students. Every summer the Chinese students organize their own Bible conferences in various parts of the country. Ambassadors for Christ in Washington, D.C., and Chinese for Christ in Los Angeles are working among Chinese graduate students in our universities.

This large group of well-educated, highly dedicated Chinese Christians could be a mighty force for world evangelism if they were to hear the call of God to be missionaries to their own people in Southeast Asia. No other expatriate group in the Western world has the spiritual potential of this group.

There is no doubt that the Holy Spirit is appealing to the churches of Asia as He did to the church in Antioch when He said, "Set apart for me Barnabas and Saul for the work to which I have called them" (Acts 13:2). Something big is brewing in the great continent of Asia, where two-thirds of the world's population lives. We can hope and pray that the churches there will not be insensitive to the promptings of the Holy Spirit.

When Billy Graham returned from speaking to over one million persons in Seoul, Korea, in the summer of 1973, he remarked that the religious center of gravity might be shifting from the Western world to the Eastern world. That may be a slight exaggeration but there is enough potential truth in the statement to make us sit up and take notice.

An important development was the Asia—South Pacific Congress on Evangelism in Singapore in 1968. Out of that grew the Coordinating Office for Asian Evangelism with Bishop Chandu Ray as executive director. A monthly *Newsletter*, now in its fifth year, keeps the Asian churches abreast of the developing situation *vis-à-vis* evangelism and missions in that part of the world. In country after country Congresses on Evangelism are being held; and the churches are rising to the occasion. A Chinese Congress on Evangelism in Taiwan in 1970 attracted 390 participants.

Practically every country now has its own Evangelical Fellowship and these are expanding rapidly. At the 1973 annual meeting of the Evangelical Fellowship of India eleven new groups were admitted, bringing the total to ninety-six. The Union of Evangelical Students in India, formed in 1953, held its first National Missionary Conference in Madras in December 1972 with over 360 delegates from all over the country.

Campus Crusade for Christ International is the fastest growing Christian organization in the world. It now has 2,000 national staff members serving in eighty countries. For the most part these staff members are serving in their own countries, so technically they might not qualify as "missionaries," but they are surely on the cutting edge of the worldwide Christian mission. CCC has plans to greatly expand its overseas commitments between now and 1980. Expo '74 in Korea was attended each day by 300,000 trainees. The public meetings in the evenings attracted almost a million persons each night. Most of CCC's converts are college students. Given their emphasis on evangelism and missions, there is no telling how many of these young people from the Third World will one day become missionaries.

Several Western missions have opened their membership to nationals of the Third World on a basis of absolute equality. Included in this group are the Latin America Mission, Overseas Missionary Fellowship, Overseas Crusades, Navigators, and others. In this way they hope to induce nationals to become missionaries in their own part of the world. To date the results have not been very encouraging. After eight years the OMF has only fifteen non-Caucasians on its staff. This would seem to indicate that if Asians are to become missionaries to other countries they prefer to be identified with an indigenous mission rather than a Western organization.

Horace Fenton, General Director of LAM, said: "I believe that LAM cannot be really effective in its evangelistic objective until fully rooted in Latin America. . . . There are only a limited number of Latins who will continue to honor us with their membership in our mission unless there are basic and deep changes in our whole structure."[16] Dennis Clark offered a likely explanation when he wrote: "It seems almost too late for Western societies to recruit the national because with very few exceptions the stigma of being labeled a 'stooge' or 'puppet' reduces usefulness. The more likely pattern of development will be the strengthening of existing missionary societies in Third World nations and proliferation of others."[17]

Another step in the right direction is the placing of Third World nationals in charge of Western-based organizations. Too long these positions have been held exclusively by Westerners, mostly Americans. When the Latin America Mission was reorganized in 1971 it became the Community of Latin American Evangelical Ministries, with Dr. George Taylor, a Latin American, as president. When Stacey Woods stepped down as executive secretary of the International Fellowship of Evangelical Students, he was succeeded by Chua Wee Hian, a Chinese from Singapore. When Inter-Varsity Christian Fellowship wanted a new general director for Canada, they chose Dr. Samuel Escobar from Latin America. These innovations are long overdue and, therefore, doubly welcome.

One of the most exciting developments in recent mission history was the All-Asia Mission Consultation held in Seoul, Korea, in the summer of 1973. This was the first time that the word *mission* was used in such a context. Up to this time the congresses and consultations have all been on evangelism. This in itself was significant. The initiative for the Consultation came entirely from the Asians themselves. The moving spirit behind the gathering was David J. Cho, Director of the Korea International Mission.

Twenty-five delegates from fourteen Asian countries unanimously adopted the following statement:

> We appeal to the Christian churches in Asia to be involved in the preaching of the Gospel, specially through sending and receiving Asian missionaries to strengthen the witness to the saving power of Christ.
>
> We are compelled by the Holy Spirit to declare that we shall

---

[16] *Latin American Evangelist*, 1971:2.
[17] Dennis Clark, *The Third World and Mission* (Waco, Tex.: World Books, 1971), p. 45.

work towards the placing of at least two hundred new Asian missionaries by the end of 1974.

These missionaries will be involved primarily in evangelism in the power of the Holy Spirit in order that men and women may come to believe God's work of grace through Jesus Christ and in turn be agents of evangelism in the fellowship of His Church, the body of Christ. These missionaries will also be sent to plant evangelistic churches where they do not already exist.[18]

In keeping with this new emphasis was the first All-Asia Student Missionary Convention which took place in Baguio (Philippines) in December 1973, attended by eight hundred students.

A unique and most encouraging event took place in 1973 when missionaries and overseas pastors studying at Fuller Theological Seminary School of World Mission launched the Lafricasia Mission Advance Fellowship (LAMAF). The purpose of the organization is to encourage and assist the expansion of missionary outreach from Africa, Asia, and Latin America. Samuel Kim of the Korea International Mission was elected chairman. The new Fellowship will seek to become a communication bridge among churches and mission agencies throughout the Third World. Publication of a newsletter and the development of research and training programs are planned.

It is generally assumed that Asians have little trouble when they become missionaries to other Asian countries; but this is not so. They have many minor problems and several major ones as well.

The Asian churches have not yet developed close working relations with one another, nor do they have the apparatus to facilitate the recruitment, appointment, and movement of missionaries. Most of their contacts have been with the "mother" churches or missions in the West. Doubtless the missions in the Orient will have to feel their way and work things out as they go along by the trial-and-error method. They are not averse to studying our methods and benefiting from our mistakes. Along the way they will probably make a few of their own.

Missionaries sent out by the ecumenical groups usually go at the request of the receiving church. When they get there they are immediately absorbed into the existing organizational structure. Most of these missionaries end up in educational institutions. Missionaries sent out by the conservative groups, many of them undenominational, usually go into pioneer evangelistic and church planting work, with or without cooperation with a church in the host country.

Recruitment and orientation are major problems. Recruitment is not yet on an active, organized basis. The ecumenical missions have an annual orientation program in Manila. As yet the conservatives have nothing along this line.

---

[18] *Missionary News Service,* September 17, 1973.

Financial support is another serious problem. One of the major differences between Asian and Western missionaries is found in the area of support. Almost without exception Western missionaries are wholly supported by the sending churches in the West. Not so the Asian missionaries. In the ecumenical camp some missionaries are supported by the sending churches; some by the receiving churches; some by both; and some by funds from the West. The Christian Conference of Asia has established a Missionary Support Fund in cooperation with mission boards in the United States, Britain, and Germany. One stipulation is that the sending church must provide at least 25 percent of the support. The Fund will not grant more than a thousand dollars per year.

The Asian missionaries sent out by the various Evangelical Missionary Fellowships are on a somewhat different basis. They are fully supported by their own churches or by the undenominational fellowships and therefore do not expect to receive support from the receiving churches. One reason for this is that they are engaged mostly in pioneer evangelism and so are not connected directly with any church in the host country.

Another problem relates to government restrictions. In this postwar period nationalism in Asia has posed serious problems for Western missionaries. It is generally assumed that Asian missionaries would be immune; but this is not so. Nationalism is not directed solely against the white man. If Western missionaries have a hard time getting into India—and they do—Asian missionaries would fare no better. The same rules would apply to them.

Chinese missionaries from Taiwan will find it difficult, if not impossible, to gain entrance into countries which have diplomatic ties with Communist China. Also throughout Southeast Asia there is a feeling of resentment against the powerful Chinese minorities. That resentment is likely to be transferred to any missionary from Taiwan. The same thing applies to Japanese missionaries. In Southeast Asia the most recent form of imperialism was Japanese; consequently the Japanese are not the most popular people in that region of the world. During the confrontation between Indonesia and Malaysia it would have been difficult for national missionaries from either country to go to the other country. Japan accepts American missionaries, but rejects Korean missionaries.

There is also the problem of orientation and adjustment. The Asian missionary will experience his share of culture shock. Japanese culture has no more in common with Indian culture than it has with American culture. In fact a missionary from Nebraska may find life in rural India more to his liking than would a missionary from Tokyo. There is nothing to support the view that Orientals adjust to a strange culture more easily than Americans do. The average Japanese finds it exceedingly difficult to get along without his rice and fish.

Then again, the people of these countries don't make the same allowance for Oriental missionaries that they do for missionaries from the West. Western missionaries have white skin, blue eyes, and blonde hair. Obviously they are foreigners and allowance has to be made for them; but Orientals look pretty much alike wherever they originate, and because they look alike they are expected to think and act alike. Consequently the people are less patient with Oriental missionaries when they make mistakes than they are with Western missionaries.

One missionary doctor who went from the Philippines to Thailand was given such a rough time that she had a nervous breakdown and was invalided home. The people expected her to speak Thai *perfectly*. When patients came to the mission hospital they expected to be treated by a "foreign" doctor, only to find a Filipino instead!

The missionary movement has always encountered cross-cultural problems in the past. The future will not be any different. The problems will remain whether the missionaries be Oriental or Occidental; but the time has come to internationalize the movement.

9

Recent Developments

The modern missionary movement, now over 250 years old, is one of the most dynamic enterprises of the twentieth century. Other programs come and go. The League of Nations endured for twenty years. President Truman's Point Four Plan lasted for about a dozen years. The Peace Corps, now just over ten years old, is showing signs of slowing down. But not the missionary movement. Far from dying, it is developing new and exciting programs.

The Short-term Missionary

One of the most dramatic breakthroughs in modern missions is a new program known as Short Terms Abroad. Some main-line denominations have had such a program for a long time. The United Presbyterians have made use of short-term missionaries for over half a century. Most of their short-termers were employed as teachers in their many educational institutions around the world. Until recently their numbers were not large. About 1960 the program was greatly expanded. By the mid 1960s two out of three missionaries were short-termers. In 1968 the denomination decided to make no more life-time appointments. Since then two other denominations have done likewise—the Protestant Episcopal Church and the United Church of Christ. In 1973 the Central American Mission announced similar plans.

371

The United Methodists began their STA program in 1948. By the mid-1960s they had sent out over one thousand short-term missionaries Another pioneer in this area was the Mennonite Central Committee. Its first group of twenty Paxmen went to Europe in 1951 to serve for two or three years in the refugee camps. Since then almost one thousand Paxmen have served in Asia, Africa, Latin America, and the Middle East. They work in such diverse fields as agriculture, mechanics, construction, maintenance, radio, teaching, relief goods distribution, and office work. Beginning in 1962 the MCC introduced a second program for teachers only, known as Teachers Abroad Program (TAP). Working almost exclusively in Africa, TAP in the past nine years has placed 250 teachers in strategic short-term positions.

One by one the other missions got in on the act. Today there is hardly a mission that does not have its own STA program. The Protestant Episcopal Church has its Volunteers for Missions. The American Baptists have their Volunteer Services. The Southern Baptists have two STA programs: the Missionary Associates Program, launched in 1961, and the Missionary Journeymen Program, begun four years later. The former makes it possible for men and women between thirty-five and fifty-nine years of age to serve a term overseas in projects that do not involve the learning of a foreign language. The second program is designed to enlist young people under twenty-seven years of age who want to use their talents to meet critical spiritual, educational, and physical needs overseas. Both programs offer one- or two-year terms of service. In 1975 the Southern Baptists sent out 265 new missionaries, of whom 107 were short-termers.

For some time the conservative evangelicals, represented by the Interdenominational Foreign Mission Association and the Evangelical Foreign Missions Association, tried to buck the tide. They held out as long as they could, but by 1960 they too were forced to come to terms with STA. Why the sudden change? The answer is simple. They had no choice; they were not getting enough career missionaries to maintain their existing work, much less initiate new work. No mission *prefers* short-termers, but half a loaf is better than none. The universal law of supply and demand has been with us for a long time; and to date no one has been able to circumvent that law.

Thus it came about that the evangelical conservative boards began accepting short-term workers. One of the earliest to launch its STA program was the Sudan Interior Mission. In January 1962, it issued an appeal for twenty-five college graduates to proceed to Nigeria on a thirty-month program designed to provide qualified teachers for teacher training colleges. "Our need," the mission said, "is for many *missionary* teachers who have at least minimum qualifications. We underline 'missionary' because it is a prime qualification. We would be unable to use in our work individuals who are not first missionaries having mature Christian faith and a sound understanding of the Bible."

The Conservative Baptist Foreign Mission Society, the Christian and Missionary Alliance, and the Evangelical Free Church all launched their own STA programs. Other mission boards followed in rapid succession. Today there are only a few of the nearly one hundred missions in the two associations that do not accept short-term missionaries.

The program takes on various forms. The usual term is three years, though quite frequently the period of service is one or two years and sometimes as high as four years. Some missions have several programs from which the volunteer can choose—one-, two-, or three-year programs.

Short-termers consist mostly of young people just out of college. Sometimes they take a year or two out of their college program and spend the time abroad. Most of them are single. Girls as well as fellows volunteer; indeed the girls usually outnumber the men, as they do among career missionaries. A second group of short-termers represent people at the other end of the age spectrum. These are retired persons who still have five or ten good years ahead of them and want to serve the Lord on the mission field. Indeed, some of them choose to retire early in order to lengthen their short-term missionary career. These people are known as second careerists, and their number is growing with every passing year. These older folks have several things going for them. At that advanced age married couples as well as single persons are free from family responsibilities. Most of them have a pension which renders them financially independent. Those who are sixty-five or older usually have Social Security benefits as well.

These people are usually able to pay their own way and take care of room and board on the field. In this as well as other respects, they represent a handsome "gift" to the missions under which they serve. Most of the single people in this category are teachers. On the mission field there are scores of schools for missionaries' children; most of them are hurting for lack of qualified teachers. With twenty-five or thirty years of teaching experience behind them, these second careerists are able to fill a vital role in the missionary ranks. Even without missionary experience, these older "missionaries" make wonderful hosts and hostesses in mission homes, or houseparents in schools for missionaries' children. Others with experience in bookkeeping, accounting, typing, filing, etc., are able to fill vacant posts in mission offices, at home or abroad, thus setting career missionaries free for more direct forms of missionary service. There is no end to the helpfulness of these second careerists.

Not a few older couples, as well as widows and widowers, visit their children and grandchildren on the mission field, fall in love with the people and the work, and decide to stay on for a year or two to help out in various capacities.

Still other short-termers go abroad to perform a specific task; when the task is completed they return home. A building contractor spent a year in Pakistan where he built a mission hospital. A Canadian doctor spends his annual vacation in a mission hospital in Monrovia, Liberia.

THE POPULARITY OF THE SHORT-TERM PROGRAM

How are we to account for the sudden popularity of the STA? Several factors readily come to mind.

1. Our American society is increasingly mobile. Time was when a family living in Maine would remain there for several generations. If a member of the family ventured as far west as Boston, he was regarded as a world traveler. Today the members of the younger generation are leaving Maine and not stopping until they get to California. If they don't like the smog there, they can always move to Florida. If they don't like the hurricanes there, they can migrate to Colorado. By the time the second generation arrives on the scene, the family may be scattered over half a dozen states of the Union. It is estimated that one of every four families moves every year.

Nor is it simply a matter of geography. People are forever changing jobs. Young executives on the way up may work for three or four firms before finding their niche. Few of them are willing to make a long-term commitment to any one firm, even General Motors. If Ford or Chrysler comes along with a better offer, away they go.

2. The attitude of youth has changed greatly since World War II. They want to look before they leap. They want to canvass all the options before making up their minds. They want to get acquainted with the field and the work, as well as the mission, before making their final decision regarding their lifework. For this they have often been criticized. But are they very different from the pastors here at home?

Very few pastors are extended a call sight unseen. In fact, such a practice is almost unknown in this country. What is the procedure? A church without a pastor gets in touch with a preacher seeking a change. Arrangements are then made for the preacher to "candidate" in the church. The candidate and his family will spend a Sunday in the church, during which time he and the church will have an opportunity to find out as much as possible about each other. Only when the church is satisfied that he is "their" man will it issue a call. Only when the candidate is persuaded that the call comes from the Lord as well as from the church will he accept.

If this is the universal practice in the homeland, why should the procedure for service on the mission field be different?

3. Transportation is much cheaper and faster than it was in the nineteenth century. Hudson Taylor took five months from Liverpool to Shanghai in 1853. Today it is possible to reach any city in the world in a day or two. Jet travel, almost at the speed of sound, has made STA not only a possibility but a live option.

4. The unsettled conditions in many parts of the world cause young people to think twice before committing themselves to a lifetime of service in a particular country. Since World War II there have been well over fifty wars of one kind or another, and literally hundreds of coups and countercoups. In some parts of the world governments rise and fall almost with the barometer. Whole continents, such as South America, are seething with unrest. In Africa some forty countries have achieved independence since 1960; one could number on the fingers of one hand the countries that have not experienced at least one coup, successful or abortive.

All this is in stark contrast to the situation that prevailed in Africa under the colonial system. For all its evils, colonialism did impose peace on the entire continent. Once the colonial system was established there were very few missionary martyrs. In fact, there were more martyrs in Congo 1960-64 than in the whole of Africa up to that time. This being so, it is hardly surprising that our young people are reluctant to commit themselves to Africa or Latin America for life.

5. There is no doubt that the Peace Corps has caught the imagination of youth in all parts of the world. On the whole, the Peace Corps has been fairly successful; it has been well received in all but a few of the sixty countries in which it has worked. If the Peace Corps volunteer can do a good job in twenty-one months overseas, why can't the short-term missionary do the same?

THE ADVANTAGES OF THE SHORT-TERM PROGRAM

1. The short-term program appeals to today's youth. For the most part, young people are freedom-loving and easygoing, and do not want to be tied down to any one plan or program for any length of time. Moreover, it offers an opportunity to engage in missionary work without the "stigma" of being a missionary. They can return home after one term without being counted among the "casualties." Also, it satisfies a legitimate desire to see the world and to enrich one's life and experience by serving the Lord in a completely different social and cultural milieu.

2. The short-term program helps to solve a major problem on the mission field—manpower shortage. In some places this problem is so acute that career missionaries have had to postpone retirement or furlough because there was no one to take their place. In some instances it has been necessary to close a hospital during furlough for lack of qualified personnel. Evangelism and church planting are different. If the program stops when the missionary comes home on furlough, no great loss is incurred. The work can be resumed when the missionary returns. Institutional work, by its very nature, has to go on; and personnel *must* be found to fill positions that fall vacant.

3. The short-term program is not only valuable in and of itself; it often leads to a lifetime of service. In some of the historic denominations, more than 50 percent of their present career missionaries began as short-termers. Three denominations no longer accept career missionaries to begin with. All new missionaries are expected to serve for one or two short terms before making up their minds to become career missionaries.

The STA program is still comparatively young, and reliable statistics are difficult to obtain. To further complicate the matter, the situation differs from mission to mission; but it is generally believed that 20 percent of the short-termers become career missionaries after one term abroad. Of those who spend two or more short terms abroad, 50 percent sign up for life, which means that in the long run STA is a good thing for the cause of missions.

Of course, there is no guarantee that the volunteers will be favorably impressed with what they find overseas. Most of them are "turned on" and come back with glowing reports. Others are "turned off" and do great harm on their return to this country. But even the ones who are "turned off" are by no means a total loss to the cause. If they could not adjust to missionary life and work in three years they would almost certainly have become casualties if they had signed up for life. If missionary work is not their "cup of tea," they might as well find this out early as late. Mistakes are made. To err is human. Divine guidance is never 100 percent certain—not after it has filtered through the human mind.

Every person is emotionally involved in his own understanding of the Lord's will for his life. Consequently it is impossible for him to be completely objective in his appraisal of a given situation involving his own interests, ambitions, and desires. The author is personally acquainted with several wonderful students who in their college days were enthusiastically dedicated to missionary work and were leaders in the Foreign Missions Fellowship; but they were disillusioned by a visit to the mission field. One of these is now a waitress in a Howard Johnson's restaurant. Another married a truck driver. Missionary work is not for everyone. We can only assume that those who are "turned off" by a visit to the mission field were never called to missionary work in the first place. It is good, both for the candidate and for the mission, that this fact be discovered as early as possible to avoid loss of time, money, and face.

4. The short-term program frees career missionaries for other duties. We hear a good deal these days about specialization; but the truth is that most missionaries, including specialists, are required to do double or triple duty, not because it is mission policy but simply of necessity. There are too few missionaries and too many jobs to fill. For instance, the medical missionary will be physician, surgeon, and administrator all in one. When the electrical equipment breaks down, he repairs it. When an epidemic of cholera breaks out, he becomes a public health officer in the community. The teaching missionary cannot confine his teaching to the Old Testament or the New Testament. There are not enough teachers for that kind of specialization. Sometime or other he will be required to teach nearly every subject in the catalog. In addition, he may be asked to act as dean of men or registrar. When the business manager goes on furlough, he may be asked to do the bookkeeping on the side.

In all such situations the short-termer is a veritable godsend. He can fill the gap and relieve the career missionary of the extra chores for which he has neither the time nor the training.

5. The short-term program brings a reflex blessing to the home constituency—churches and colleges alike. The vast majority of short-termers return with glowing accounts of their time abroad. Almost to a man they affirm that the experience was an eye-opener. Even if they don't get back to the field, they will never be the same again. They are now sold on missions and will help sell missions to others. In this capacity they can do more for missions than career missionaries on furlough. Indeed, college students are more impressed with the reports of their fellow students than by anything the missionary might say. After all, most missionaries are over thirty! Besides, they have a vested interest in their own vocation; whereas the returning short-termer is believed to be more objective if not more impartial. Many Christian colleges have noticed an increased interest in missions since they launched their summer missionary programs.

6. The short-term missionaries provide enthusiasm and idealism. Short-termers are almost all under twenty-five years of age, with all the freshness, initiative, and idealism of youth. They have none of the hang-ups that blur the vision and impede the progress of the veteran missionaries. One of their strengths is the mobility and adaptability that usually go with a person whose stay is temporary. Being young, they are more apt to be footloose and fancy-free. Being single, they can afford to run greater risks. Certainly they are able to identify with the youth of the host countries, adapt to their customs, and respond to their needs in a way that some of the older missionaries have not been able to do. Their free and easy manner, the informality of their dress, their practice of sitting on the floor, their desire to just "rap," their experiments in communal living, all enable the short-termer to get close to the people. After all, that's what missionary work is all about.

PROBLEMS RELATED TO THE
SHORT-TERM PROGRAM

Like every other program, STA has its problems, some of which are rather serious.

1. Lack of experience. Experience is a valuable asset in any endeavor; it is doubly valuable in a cross-cultural situation. Of course, the career missionary has the same problem at first, but by the time he returns for his second term, his mistakes are mostly behind him. He is now ready to make a *real* contribution to the spread of the gospel and the building up of the church. But the short-termer comes home just when he is beginning to function like a seasoned missionary. This is hard on everyone concerned, particularly the national Christians and leaders, who patiently endure the bluff and blunder of the young missionary in the hope that he will learn by his mistakes and be more of a blessing and less of a burden during his second term. But if there is no second term, they are doomed to another round of bluff and blunder. After breaking in nine or ten of these short-termers, they become weary in well-doing.

2. Acculturation. It is of the utmost importance that missionaries understand and appreciate both the people and the culture of the land in which they serve. This takes time. It cannot be learned in "thirteen easy lessons." It is naive in the extreme to imagine that a three-hour course in general psychology will enable a person to understand the Oriental mind, and that a study in American sociology will enable one to understand and appreciate such exotic cultures as are found in many parts of the Third World. It usually takes a year or two to really feel at home in a culture other than one's own. The body can be transported to another part of the world in a matter of hours. It may take years for the soul to catch up. This is especially hard on the short-term worker who is just beginning to make his way and feel at home when his term is up.

3. Communication. Most missionary work involves some form of cross-cultural communication. To do effective work, the short-term volunteer should be able to speak the vernacular accurately and fluently. It is difficult to acquire fluency through a crash program of five or six weeks. Indeed, veteran missionaries constantly find themselves making blunders, especially in tonal languages. The right word expressed in the wrong tone will not only create misunderstanding, but in some cases will result in downright embarrassment to both speaker and hearer.

Short-termers who speak only English should be sent to English-speaking countries. They will get along fairly well in ex-British colonies where English is still the *lingua franca* if not the official language. One great advantage attaching to STA launched from the United States or the Commonwealth countries is the fact that English is the most widely understood language in the world. It comes closer than any other language to being the world's *lingua franca*. When the Dalai Lama fled as a refugee from Tibet to India and was greeted by Prime Minister Nehru, the two conversed in English! Most of the speeches in the United Nations are made in the English language.

Persons going to Francophone Africa should be able to speak French. Those going to Latin America will find Spanish spoken in all countries but Brazil. Language is not usually a great problem for medical missionaries. The nature of their work does not require them to do much talking. If the medical tests reveal appendicitis, the surgeon goes to work and removes the offending member with little or no conversation. Also, in many countries nationals who study medicine are required to learn the medical terms in English. Fluency is a must for all teaching and preaching missionaries.

Interpretation, of course, is always a possibility, but it has its detractions. Can an interpreter be found? If so, is he fluent enough to pick up idiomatic expressions and translate them accurately? Then there is the time factor. To use an interpreter cuts the speaker's time in half. One or two lectures can be translated without much difficulty, but what about a series of thirty or forty lectures in a Bible school? It can and has been done; but it requires much patience on the part of the speaker and just as much perseverance on the part of the listeners.

4. High cost. Regular air fare from Chicago to Johannesburg is $1,186.00 round trip; to New Delhi and back it is $1,478.00. If this amount is amortized over thirty-six months, it works out at $41.00 per month; but if the worker stays only one year, it averages out at $123.00 per month—just for transportation. Fourteen hundred dollars may not sound like a lot of money to affluent Americans; but it represents a mammoth sum to the Christians in India, where the per capita income is less than one hundred dollars a year. Whatever else may be said for the STA program, it isn't cheap.

5. The difference in age, outlook, manners, and insights of the two groups, the short-termers and the long-termers. The average age of the former is about twenty-six years; that of the latter is much higher. This alone can create problems. Added to this is the fact that the career missionary is wiser, more mature, more experienced, and more patient than his younger counterpart. The newcomer, in his youthful enthusiasm, may criticize his senior colleague for his failure to initiate change, improve methods, correct mistakes, and hand over responsibility to others. The career missionary on his part may secretly resent the idealism, enthusiasm, and passion for action and reform that characterize today's younger generation. He has been around long enough to know that it is easier to see than to solve the major problems of the mission field. The older missionary may feel that his very seniority invests him with a certain degree of authority and prestige; while the short-termer may consider himself to be a "second class citizen." Under such conditions it is quite possible that a kind of "pecking order" may develop between the two groups.

6. Lack of continuity. Change is good; but it is possible to get "too much of a good thing." We want change by all means; we also need stability, and stability cannot be achieved without a high degree of continuity. When we extol the virtues of the STA program, we are generally thinking in terms of the mission and its recruiting problems. Seldom do we consider the needs and wishes of the national Christians and the church leaders on the mission field. To get some idea of their perspective, one need only imagine a church in the United States that undergoes a change of pastor every year or two. No church would voluntarily vote for that kind of arrangement. In rare circumstances it happens, but always without the approval of the church concerned. If the pastor is any good at all, the people will want him to stay for five or six years at least. If the church has more than two hundred families, it will take the new minisiter a year or two to really get to know his people, their names, their needs, and their notions.

It goes without saying that Christian work, abroad as well as at home, suffers from frequent interruption. What is needed on the mission field is more, not less, continuity. Indeed, with career missionaries coming home on furlough every four years, the problem of continuity is already acute. Short-termers only make it worse. A problem that mission executives have always had to grapple with is how to provide substitutes for missionaries on furlough. Not infrequently positions have been left vacant and the work has suffered accordingly. On occasion it has been necessary to take a general missionary out of his work to fill the personnel needs of a school or hospital when a missionary goes on furlough. With more and more short-term workers joining the missionary ranks, the problem of continuity is greater than ever.

National church leaders have never been happy with the concept of furlough. Many of them have considered it unnecessary, certainly undesirable. Time and again they have asked the question: "Why do missionaries and their families have to go home to the United States every four or five years? They seem to be quite well in body and mind. Why the prolonged vacation? And if they must have a rest, could they not get it here in our country?" To add to their troubles, they are never sure that if and when the missionary returns, he will be reassigned to the same position. If they have these feelings with regard to career missionaries, what must be their attitude to the short-term missionary? They *know* he will not be back; nor will the one after him, nor the next one after him. No, the national church leaders do not take kindly to all the comings and goings of the missionaries, short or long term.

7. Balance in the missionary force. Even the most ardent supporters of STA do not suggest that the short-termer is a substitute for the career missionary. If the career missionary needs the short-termer, certainly the short-termer needs the career missionary. Indeed, he could hardly function without him. With the sudden and expanding popularity of the short-term program there is a real danger that certain missions will find themselves with a serious imbalance in their roster. To work effectively the short-termer needs the counsel and guidance of the veteran missionary. A given mission can profitably absorb only a certain number of short-termers. If they become too numerous, the whole program is likely to get out of kilter.

In the early stages of STA, the mission stands to gain; but after five or ten years the homebound traffic gets pretty heavy. Then the home office has to send out an ever-increasing number of new workers to keep the roster at full strength. More and more time must be spent filling the many vacancies created by returning short-termers. After a while the problem begins to snowball, and the mission, instead of needing a hundred new workers each year, needs two hundred.

CONDITIONS OF SUCCESS

The STA is no panacea. There is no guarantee that it will work. Certain conditions must be met if the program is to succeed.

1. Great care should be exercised in the choice of the short-termer. One must not assume that casualties do not occur in a short period of time. (The Peace Corps term of service is only twenty-one months, yet its casualty rate is 17.2 percent.) The candidate should be required to pass most if not all the tests demanded of the career missionary. It is for the volunteer's own good if he is kept home because of deficiencies. He should also be required to attend candidate school and benefit by the orientation given to the other missionaries. Moreover, as a short-termer he is susceptible to motives not usually present in the career missionary. Is he going along just for the ride, or to see the world, or to be exposed to an exotic culture, or even to enrich his own life? As fringe benefits these all have a legitimate place in his thinking; but they should never be the prime factor in his motivation.

2. Equal care should be shown in the choice of the field. A young person who would undoubtedly make the grade in Japan might easily fall flat on his face in Jordan. The person's health, education, interests, and skills should all be taken into consideration when assigning him to a specific country. If there is reason to believe that he will not feel at home in a primitive society, he should not be assigned to New Guinea. On the other hand, if he is a medical doctor, he should not be sent to Japan, where medical missions are practically nonexistent. If he is a died-in-the-wool capitalist and equates the free enterprise system with the Kingdom of God, he may not be happy in India, Ghana, or Sweden.

3. The short-term worker should be assigned to a country where communication is not a problem. If he cannot speak the language with a fair degree of fluency he will most certainly be frustrated. If he knows Spanish, he ought to go to Latin America. If he can speak French, he will feel most at home in Francophone Africa. If he is familiar only with English, he can be sent to Anglophone Africa or any large city where English is understood by the people.

4. The particular skills of the short-termer should be matched with the existing needs on the field. The career missionary can afford to spend two or three years in search of a niche that he can fill with satisfaction to himself and profit to the church and mission; but not so the short-term worker. He has no time to "look around" or to "find a job." The job should be waiting for the volunteer. For this reason it is advisable to place the volunteer in a highly structured program, usually in an institution, where he will know exactly what to do, can go to work immediately, and will have the satisfaction of making a worthwhile contribution. It is no accident that teaching has claimed the largest number of short-termers. They can arrive one day and start teaching the next. This is why it is important that the short-termer have a particular skill. He does not usually make an effective general missionary.

SUMMER MISSIONARY PROGRAM

A rapidly developing phase of STA is the Summer Missionary Program adopted now by practically every mission board in the country. Not all American students who go to Europe each summer go to bask in the sun and sleep in the parks. An increasing number of them engage in missionary work.

One of the oldest and largest programs is Operation Mobilization, sponsored by Send the Light, Incorporated. The first venture took place in 1958, when George Verwer and twenty-one Moody students spent Christmas vacation distributing gospel literature in Mexico. From Mexico OM moved into Europe and today sends summer missionaries all over the world. Last summer over a thousand young people engaged in literature distribution in Europe.

Cooperating with the mission boards are the various Bible schools and Christian colleges. The Foreign Missions Fellowship usually sponsors the program on the local campus, providing moral and financial support for the volunteers. Some of the larger colleges send as many as forty or fifty students overseas each summer. The program lasts about ten weeks, allowing the students plenty of time to get back for the opening of school in September. Upon their return the students share their experiences with their fellow students. On some campuses the entire spiritual climate has been changed as a result of this kind of Summer Missionary Program.

A fairly high percentage of the SMP students later sign up for the STA program, and from the STA program go on to become career missionaries. In recent years the Summer Missionary Program has become exceedingly popular, with thousands of young people joining in. A questionnaire was filled in by sixty-five of the ninety-five missions in the EFMA/IFMA groups. In 1966 they reported a total of 308 who participated in the Summer Missionary Program. By 1969 the figure had jumped to 974. In 1974 the total reported by all missions was 3,975.

AN EVALUATION

It is still rather early to make a final evaluation of the STA program, but in recent years three separate surveys have been made.[1] From these certain broad outlines are discernible.

Much depends on the person making the evaluation—the short-termer himself, mission boards, fellow missionaries, or nationals. Naturally they don't all agree. Those whose goals were vague and general reported the greatest measure of success—over 80 percent. The percentage drops drastically when specific goals or projects were under review. Only 57 percent who worked on their own, 54 percent who engaged in technical assistance, and 42 percent of those engaged in evangelism reported that they were "successful" or "very successful" in attaining the goals they had set for themselves.

On the whole the mission boards took a more charitable view of the short-termer's work than he did. On the other hand the nationals on the receiving end were not so optimistic. Two-thirds of the missionaries said the short-termer was "helpful." Only 40 percent of the nationals concurred. One-third of them felt that the short-termer was "adventurous," compared with only 22 percent of the missionaries. Over 9 percent of the nationals thought the short-termer was primarily a "tourist," 10 percent that he was "naive," and 7 percent that he was "ineffective."

Regardless of the measure of success there is no doubt that there is a burgeoning interest on the part of Christian youth in all forms of short-term missionary service. In 1965 there were 580 short-termers working with some 85 predominantly evangelical missions. By 1970 the number had increased to 4,000. At the present time there are some 120 mission boards that make short-term appointments. Short-termers represent almost 12 percent of their total missionary force. In some cases more than half the new recruits going out each year are now short-termers.

The Nonprofessional Missionary

The number of Americans living abroad has increased dramatically since World War II. Much of this is due to the military alliances we

---

[1] For complete statistical analysis see W. Meredith Long, *Pulse: Special Report,* August 1973, Evangelical Missions Information Service, Box 794, Wheaton, IL: 60187.

have with forty other countries. In addition American business firms have greatly expanded their overseas operations. These overseas Americans may be divided into several categories: military personnel, government and diplomatic personnel, business and professional people, Peace Corps volunteers, and missionaries.

Fifty years ago almost all Americans in Africa were missionaries. Today they are outnumbered by persons in nonreligious occupations. This dramatic shift in the balance of American personnel overseas points up the vast potentialities of a nonprofessional missionary career.

Perhaps we should begin with a definition. Who or what is a nonprofessional missionary? A nonprofessional is any dedicated Christian who lives and works overseas under nonreligious auspices, and who uses his secular calling as an opportunity to give his personal witness to Jesus Christ.

GENERAL OBSERVATIONS

Some general observations are in order before we discuss the pros and cons of such an arrangement.

1. There is nothing new about the lay apostolate. In the first century there were no missionary societies such as we have today and there were few professional missionaries outside the apostolic group. The gospel was spread far and wide throughout the Roman Empire by laymen—soldiers, slaves, merchants, and even displaced persons. Luke informs us that those that were scattered abroad upon the persecution that arose about Stephen went everywhere preaching the gospel (Acts 8:2). Some of them went into nearby Judea and Samaria (Acts 8:1); others went as far afield as Antioch and Cyprus (Acts 11:19). Speaking of the converts in the mission church at Thessalonica, Paul said, "From you sounded out the word of the Lord, not only in Macedonia and Achaia, but also in every place your faith in God is spread abroad" (1 Th 1:8).

Edward Gibbon, in his *Decline and Fall of the Roman Empire,* explains the rapid growth of Christianity in the early centuries by the fact that it became the sacred duty of every convert to speak of his new-found faith to his friends and neighbors. Will Durant in his book *Caesar and Christ* makes the same point. "Nearly every convert, with the ardor of a revolutionary, made himself an office of propaganda."[2]

With no weapon but truth and no banner but love these single-minded, warmhearted followers of Jesus traveled by land and sea to all parts of the empire, and wherever they went they gladly shared their

---

[2] Will Durant, *Caesar and Christ* (New York: Simon and Shuster, 1944), p. 602.

faith with friends, neighbors, and strangers. As slaves, traders, and, later on, soldiers, they used their secular calling to advance the cause of Christ. Even as exiles they carried the contagion of their faith to distant shores and inhospitable regions.

Even in modern times, when missionary endeavor has been along organizational lines, we have not been entirely without nonprofessional missionaries. The first Protestant missionary to China, Robert Morrison, though a member of the London Missionary Society, was also for a time an official interpreter for the East India Company. William Carey supported himself and his colleagues by teaching at Fort William College in Calcutta. His salary of six thousand dollars a year helped to support the missionary enterprise at Serampore.

Other laymen, with no missionary society connections, have had a remarkable ministry in non-Christian countries. Outstanding among these was a military man, Captain Janes, who taught military science at Doshisha University in Japan. So dynamic was his witness that out of that university came the famous Kumamoto Band, composed mostly of samurai, which made such an impact on the emerging church in Japan.

2. There is nothing wrong or undesirable about the lay apostolate. Jesus Christ needs His witnesses in all walks of life. In the body of Christ there are various offices and ministries. Not all are apostles, prophets, or preachers. In fact, these professional classes represent a tiny minority of the whole church. The important thing is not whether one is a professional minister or missionary, but whether he is dedicated to the proposition that the gospel by its very nature must be shared with all the world. Whether a person becomes by profession a merchant or a missionary is for God to decide. The merchant is not a second-class citizen in the Kingdom of Heaven. So far as Holy Orders are concerned, many are called but few are chosen. Not every Christian is a missionary but every Christian is, or should be, a witness. To fail to witness is a denial of one's faith.

3. The lay apostolate is a supplement to, not a substitute for, regular missionary work. An exception, of course, would be the countries now closed to the professional missionary. Afghanistan is a classic example. Officially this country is tightly closed against all Christian missionaries; but it is common knowledge that today there are about thirty dedicated Christians in Afghanistan, most of them from the Christian countries of the West, who are serving the government and people in the name and spirit of Jesus Christ. But in other countries the nonprofessional missionary is not working in competition with the professional missionary. Where possible he will identify with the Christian church and channel his converts into the church.

There should be no rivalry between the two kinds of missionary. Both represent the same Lord; both serve the same cause; both seek to extend the same Kingdom. Where the professional missionary is present, the nonprofessional missionary fills a supporting role in church building. Where the professional missionary is absent, the nonprofessional missionary will have to carry the full load himself.

4. Members of the lay apostolate should be aware of the limitations of their calling. Few of them have had any theological training. Fewer still have any knowledge of the great non-Christian religions of the world. These two facts will put the nonprofessional missionary at a serious disadvantage when he comes to witness for Christ. One must have a thorough understanding of his own faith before he can explain it to a person of another faith. It is one thing to share one's faith with his fellow Americans, whose cultural background is similar to his own. It is quite another thing to present the claims of Christ to a Hindu, a Buddhist, or a Muslim. To do this successfully one must have a clear understanding of his own faith and at least a working knowledge of these other non-Christian religions. Otherwise the non-Christian is likely to get the best of the dialogue. Not every Christian layman can articulate his own faith in terms that are meaningful to non-Christians.

Moreover, the company for which he works, whether private firm or government agency, may place certain restrictions on the religious activities of its employees. He may be forbidden to "talk religion" during working hours. Even in his leisure time he may be expected to socialize with his own expatriate group. Such restrictions are not unknown in American communities overseas.

The nonprofessional missionary, no less than the professional missionary, is affected by the political climate prevailing in the host country. The United States is at once the best-loved and most-hated nation in the world today. Time was when an American passport was the most desirable in the world. This is no longer so. The Cold War, our voting record in the United Nations, our foreign aid program, our involvement in Indo-China, and the tensions between the "have" nations and the "have not" nations, directly affect the status of Americans overseas. If a government decides to discriminate against Americans residing in its territory, no distinction is made between missionaries and nonmissionaries. When restrictions are imposed, *all* Americans are involved. It is a mistake to assume that the nonprofessional missionary will fare better than the professional missionary.

5. The nonprofessional missionary will need to be a strong char-

acter with firm convictions and much courage. The professional missionary has many built-in safeguards. He is a member of a team and has all the advantages of Christian fellowship and counsel. He lives and works in an atmosphere conducive to holiness. He has many Christian friends, missionary and national; and in times of discouragement they may prove to be a tower of strength. But the nonprofessional missionary may have to stand all by himself. Certainly he lives and moves, for the most part, in a climate that is hostile to the Christian faith and inimical to spiritual growth. If he is to hold his own against the insidious influence of the world around him, he will have to be a person of sterling character and strong convictions. The pressure from his peer group to conform to the life-style of the non-Christian community of which he is a part will be enormous. Only with the utmost tenacity will he be able to maintain any kind of Christian witness. He will discover in no time at all that it is easier to drift with the current than to swim against it. More than one lay Christian has started out with high hopes and great expectations, only to fall by the way when the going got rough. Unable to "go it alone," he has ended up a moral and spiritual shipwreck.

6. **The teaching profession offers the best opportunity for the nonprofessional missionary.** The classroom situation has much to offer. To begin with, in the Orient and to a lesser degree in Africa, the teaching profession is held in high esteem; in Confucian culture the scholar occupies the highest station in society. Second, the teacher is the captain of his class, and can do pretty much what he likes in his own classroom. Third, the dialogue of the classroom provides a natural setting for a discussion of the Christian faith. Fourth, the teacher is dealing with young people who are still in the process of intellectual maturation. Their minds are not yet set; consequently they are open to new ideas. They are not averse to change. Fifth, the students of today are the leaders of tomorrow. As such they represent the greatest potential of all groups on the mission field. Sixth, there is less frustration in the classroom than in any other situation in which the nonprofessional missionary may find himself. In other vocations he is likely to be all tied up in official red tape, bureaucratic control, political rivalry, vested interests, community squabbles, social and religious taboos, and a host of other problems; whereas in a school system he has an established institution, a structured program, a captive audience, and a forward-looking and on-going community. Of course, he will make more money in business or government; but if it is an opportunity for effective Christian witness he is looking for, then the teaching profession is his best bet.

7. **When the political situation explodes, the nonprofessional missionary is no better off than the professional missionary.** The notion is growing that unless the Christian missionary is engaged directly in nation building he is not really making much of a contribution to the host country. Consequently he is the least desirable of all expatriates. From this it is deduced that when trouble breaks out the first person to be expelled is the professional missionary. But the events of the past twenty-five years do not bear this out.

According to *Time* magazine, in this postwar period almost one hundred buildings owned by the United States government in various parts of the world have been destroyed. And no one knows how many times the American flag has been burned in anti-American demonstrations. In contrast, very few mission buildings—churches, schools, hospitals, or missionaries' residences—have been destroyed. When embassy buildings have been attacked and USIS libraries burned to the ground, church and mission buildings in the immediate vicinity have often been spared. Apart from Zaire, relatively few missionaries have lost their lives by hostile action. In several countries the Peace Corps volunteers have been asked to leave, while the missionaries have been permitted to remain. It would appear that the peoples and governments of the world have in this postcolonial period come to realize that the missionaries are their best friends.

8. **Volunteers for the lay apostolate would do well to search their hearts to make sure that their motives are pure in God's sight.** No one who understands the treachery of the human heart will want to deny the fact that even the best of us are susceptible to temptation. When we are emotionally involved in our own decisions, it is easy to misinterpret the will of God. Man's capacity for self-deception is absolutely enormous; and none of us is free from this danger. It is just possible that a person may be called by God to full-time missionary work; but for reasons of his own he prefers to settle for the nonprofessional status.

This kind of temptation is extremely strong for several reasons. It affords the person involved an opportunity to serve the Lord outside The Establishment, which is under attack these days. Also, it makes it possible for him to be a missionary in fact without the stigma of being a missionary in name. Moreover, it enables him to function without the restrictions necessarily imposed by a mission board. With so many things going for it, the nonprofessional role is very attractive. Under such conditions it is easy for a dedicated person to assume that the more attractive role is God's will for him. It *may* be God's will. In that case he should be encouraged to pursue the matter with all the vigor at his command. Only let him be sure that he is not mistaking his own preferences and predilections for the will of God.

9. **Being a nonprofessional missionary is not an either/or proposition.** Here is one instance when a person can have his cake and eat it too. It is possible nowadays to be a member of a mission, with all the rights and privileges pertaining thereto, and at the same time hold a teaching position in a secular college or university. Many missions not only permit but encourage their members to accept teaching positions in nonmission institutions. The Sudan Interior Mission has made a commitment to the government of Nigeria to supply a certain number of teachers for the public schools. The Africa Inland Mission has done the same in Kenya. Alas, neither mission has been able to fill the quota it assumed. These teachers are members of their respective missions; at the same time they are employees of the government and are paid with state funds. The Overseas Missionary Fellowship, operating in East Asia, has seconded a number of its workers to secular colleges and universities. One of them is preparing the curriculum for the study of Christianity to be used in all government schools throughout Indonesia. The North Africa Mission has similar plans for dedicated Christians wishing to work in secular capacities in North Africa. If they wish, they may be members of the North Africa Mission. Arrangements differ from mission to mission and from country to country. In some instances these teachers are full members of the mission; in others they are associate members. In either case, they have the best of both worlds.

ADVANTAGES OF THE LAY APOSTOLATE

1. **Access into countries closed to the professional missionary.** The Universal Declaration of Human Rights, prepared by the United Nations, has a very strong article on religious freedom, including freedom to change one's religion. All but a handful of the 144 member nations have signed the Declaration. But in spite of all the fine talk about religious freedom there are still countries where it exists only in theory. This is especially true of the Muslim countries of the Middle East and North Africa. It was not until the 1950s that the professional missionary was admitted to Nepal and Somalia. Only recently has he been allowed into Yemen. He is still unable to enter Afghanistan and Saudi Arabia.

But in all of these countries there are large numbers of expatriates serving in various capacities, either with their own governments or with the government of the host country. Others are engaged in business enterprises, and still others are in the professions. Countries such as Syria and Iraq, which broke off diplomatic relations with the United States during the Six Day War in 1967, are for the time being out of bounds to all American missionaries.

Other countries in the near future may close their doors to the professional missionary. Such countries as India, Malaysia, Singapore, Surinam, and Thailand are tightening up on visa requirements; consequently the number of missionaries in those countries is gradually decreasing. In the light of this trend it is imperative that the Christian church seek other ways of getting the gospel to the ends of the earth. We must learn to be more flexible. If traditional methods fail, we should be prepared to adopt other modes of operation. There is nothing sacred about methods. Paul adopted one approach to the Jews and another to the Gentiles. He became all things to all men that by all means he might win men to Christ.

The nonprofessional missionary is a *missionary,* and as such deserves the support of the Christian community in the homeland. He will not require any financial aid; but he will stand in constant need of moral and spiritual support; and this the church should be ready and willing to give. His name and picture should appear on the missionary roster in the foyer. If he is wise, he will keep the home church informed of his ministry and movements. He no less than the professional missionary stands in need of prayer support. He too wrestles not against flesh and blood, but against demonic forces which are part of the kingdom of Satan which Jesus Christ came to destroy.

2. More glamor and prestige. The image of the professional missionary has been tarnished at home and overseas. He is not the hero he was in the nineteenth century. Moreover, because he is engaged largely in religious work, the government of the host country does not consider that he is making a contribution to nation building. The nonprofessional missionary has no such handicap. In the eyes of the host country he is a secular person with a secular calling, and anything he does contributes directly or indirectly to nation building. In this sense he enjoys a greater measure of prestige than the professional missionary, who gives all his time to gospel preaching and church planting.

Moreover, the nonprofessional missionary is free from the stigma of "proselytizing." Coming from a so-called Christian country, he is assumed to be a Christian; but he is not expected to talk about religion, much less try to make converts to the Christian faith. Most Americans living abroad would call themselves Christians, but their religious convictions are not strong enough to prompt them to share their faith with non-Christians. Most of them prefer to travel incognito. Hence they pose no threat to the established religions of the host country. This being so, the nonprofessional missionary, so far as his status is concerned, enjoys the freedom of action that comes from "neutrality." While he himself is a dedicated Christian, his official role is that of the businessman, the professor, or the diplomat. And when he talks about his religion, he does so in a casual, nonprofessional fashion. He has no axe to grind. He has no vested interests.

3. Greater financial remuneration. Church workers and school teachers have always been among the lowest paid professional groups. In the past ten or fifteen years the plight of the teachers has been greatly relieved. Pastors are still at the bottom of the scale. Even so, they are better off than the missionaries, many of whom go right off the graph! One missionary kid, when applying for a scholarship, was called in by the college financial officer and questioned about the annual income reported by his parents. When the missionary kid insisted that the figure was correct, the officer replied, "It can't be correct! No one in the United States today can live on that kind of salary." Which only proves that the upper half of society doesn't know how the lower half lives.

It is a crying shame that the Christian church in the United States has permitted its full-time workers to live so long on the border line of poverty. In some parts of the country Christian organizations are still paying their employees less than the minimum wage established by law. Even so, the pastor is better off than the missionary. If the pastor's salary is not in hand at the end of the month, the church board will call an emergency meeting and make up the difference. But no one is there to go to bat for the missionary when his remittance falls below the norm, and the norm barely enables him to keep body and soul together. Almost every mission has missionaries on its role for whom *full* support is not provided. The missionaries are expected "to live by faith," while the church members at home enjoy all the creature comforts of an affluent society. Some church members spend more on their summer (or winter) vacation than the missionaries get in a whole year.

In stark contrast to the missionaries are the business and professional people who are sent overseas by their companies. To induce them to live abroad their firms usually raise their salaries in addition to giving them a cost-of-living bonus that will provide them with all kinds of household servants to take the place of the time-saving mechanical gadgets they had at home. A special allowance is provided to take care of the education of the children. Fully paid furloughs come along every two or three years. And all these benefits are over and above the basic salary which, to begin with, may be three or four times what the missionary gets.

Thus the nonprofessional missionary, whether employed by an American firm or working for the host government, will be better off than the professional missionary. He will be able to provide himself and his family with the luxuries as well as the necessities of life. He will be able to pay all his bills and have something left over for travel, recreation, entertainment, and even investment. In these days when so many Americans are living "high on the hog" this is no mean advantage.

4. Opportunity to reach the elite. It is a well-known fact that most missionaries are working among the lower classes of society. Only a small number have access to the elite—and every country has its elite. Through the years the upper classes have been neglected, not so much by design as by necessity. There are several reasons for this. First, in a great many countries the elite represent a very small minority of 2 or 3 percent of the population. Second, in many non-Christian countries the stratification of society is so rigid that anyone working among the elite would automatically cut himself off from the rest of society. Third, the lower classes have the greatest needs and therefore get the most attention. Fourth, the lower classes are much more open to the gospel and therefore represent a better investment of time and money. Fifth, the missionaries themselves have often felt inadequate to deal with the elite. Few missionaries come from wealthy families and therefore feel out of place among the rich. Others, with only a Bible school education, tend to shy away from the intellectuals. So for one reason or another the upper classes have been neglected.

The nonprofessional missionary, on the other hand, finds himself in an entirely different situation. He belongs to one of the professions; and other things being equal, he will work with fellow professionals in the host country. Engineers team up with engineers, or at least with budding engineers; lawyers with lawyers; diplomats with diplomats; bankers with bankers; surgeons with surgeons. Even in the Peace Corps an attempt is made to have the host government provide a counterpart to the American volunteer, even if he be only the community social worker.

If the nonprofessional missionary turns out to be a professor in a university, the principle still holds good. He will be working among fellow intellectuals, either students or teachers. Not only will he be accepted; he will be looked up to and respected. His academic and professional qualifications are usually impeccable. He is a specialist in his field, or he wouldn't be there in the first place. Consequently he has no difficulty in holding his own with the elite in any country. He is among peers, not patrons.

Consequently he doesn't have to force his way into the upper echelons of society; that's where he belongs. That's where he functions best. In such circles he will meet some perfectly charming people whose need for the gospel is just as great as that of the lower classes. Here, by the grace of God, he can bear his quiet witness for Jesus Christ; and his testimony will be all the more forceful for the fact that it comes spontaneously from the heart, prompted by deep personal convictions and supported by professional credentials of the highest order. In these high circles he will find some inquiring minds, hungry hearts, and searching souls. And the persons thus won to Christ may be able, because of their position, to exercise an influence out of all proportion to their number.

DISADVANTAGES OF THE LAY APOSTOLATE

I wish it were possible to say that the lay apostolate has only advantages and no disadvantages; but this is not so. Nothing in this life is *all* good. The good is always tempered with the bad. There are, alas, some disadvantages, and these should be discussed.

1. Lack of Christian fellowship. We who live in a Christian country and have membership in an active local church do not fully realize what we owe to Christian fellowship. We have had it so long and enjoyed it so much that we have come to take it for granted. The Sunday morning worship, the evening evangelistic service, the Sunday school for all ages, the midweek prayer and praise service, the home Bible classes, the committee meetings, the social gatherings, the choir rehearsals, the women's missionary society, the men's fellowship, the various youth groups, the married couples' club, the annual missionary conference, the vacation Bible school, and a host of other activities provide us with an endless source of inspiration, edification, and consolation—to say nothing of the many and varied religious programs brought right into our living rooms by way of radio and television. Surely the lines are fallen unto us in pleasant places. We have indeed a goodly heritage.

The situation on the mission field is quite different. The size of the Christian community varies greatly from 50 percent in some countries in Africa to less than 1 percent in many of the countries in Asia. For the most part the local churches are small and the fellowship is correspondingly weak. Quiet, orderly services, good "meaty" sermons, hearty Christian music are among the many things the professional missionary misses. I shall never forget my feeling of exultation when, after ten consecutive years in inland China, I attended my first English language worship service in Bowen Memorial (Methodist) Church in Bombay. The preacher was a handsome, brilliant Anglo-Indian who had received his theological education at Drew University. Such a well-prepared and thought-provoking sermon I had not heard in ten years. And what shall be said of the beautiful order of service, the content of the pastoral prayer, the choice selections by the well-trained choir, and the quiet and reverent atmosphere that prevailed throughout the entire service? All came cascading over my parched spirit like a sparkling waterfall on a hot and humid day. I shall always cherish the memory of that first service of my five-month stay in India.

If the *professional* missionary misses Christian fellowship, what shall be said of the plight of his nonprofessional counterpart? He is not a member of a mission so he cannot look in that direction for fellowship. The little church in town will not offer much help unless he understands the vernacular, and very few do. If he is located in the capital city, he will doubtless find a union church where the services are held in English. There he may or may not find the kind of fellowship he wants. Many of these union churches are liberal in their theological orientation and cater to a motley group of expatriates, many of whom are Christians in name only. The weekly program, if there is one, may have more in common with a social club than a Christian church.

Come Sunday the nonprofessional missionary may have nothing to do and no place to go. This will be particularly hard on him if he resides in a small town where there are no recreational or cultural activities. Complete lack of Christian fellowship over a long period of time may rob him of his joy and render him useless in the service of Christ.

2. Restrictions placed on expatriates by the host country. Religious freedom, like all other forms of freedom, can never be 100 percent. Communist governments regard all religions as the opiate of the people and place severe restrictions on religious activities. Muslim countries favor Islam and make the practice of other religions difficult if not impossible. Some countries, such as Nepal, will allow foreign missionaries to operate in their territory but make it illegal for their own citizens to change their religion. Other countries, such as Burma and Syria, permit national churches to function but will not allow foreign missionaries to enter.

The nonprofessional missionary must not assume that because he is not a professional missionary he will be able freely to give his Christian witness in a given country. It stands to reason that countries which look askance on conventional missionary work are not likely to look with favor on the evangelistic efforts of the nonprofessional missionary. Peace Corps volunteers are warned by our government not to engage in religious activities overseas. They are free to attend church and to answer questions relating to their beliefs; but they are expected not to engage in any activities which might be construed as proselytizing.

In some instances the nonprofessional missionary is required to sign a statement agreeing not to engage in religious activities while overseas. Several such missionaries created a furor in Ethiopia when they held a Bible study class in their home in violation of their contracts. Only the timely intervention of Emperor Haile Selassie prevented their being expelled from the country. Muslim countries are especially sticky on this point. In most Muslim countries Islam is the state religion and Muslims are off bounds to the Christian missionary, professional or nonprofessional. Pagan peoples and animistic tribes are fair game but not Muslims. Conversion is a one-way street. A person may convert from Judaism or Christianity to Islam, but not from Islam to any other religion. It is true that in the Muslim countries of the Middle East religious minorities are tolerated and ancient Christian churches are permitted to exist; but only for the purpose of worship, not witness. An open attempt to convert a Muslim might easily lead to a communal riot.

In all countries where religious freedom is restricted the nonprofessional missionary will be at a serious disadvantage. He will need to be as wise as a serpent and as harmless as a dove. One false move and he may be asked to leave.

3. Limitations necessitated by time and strength. The first responsibility of the lay missionary is to his employer. He will be expected to give forty hours a week—sometimes more—to the work for which he is paid. The terms of his contract may not permit him to give an oral witness on the job, in which case his only opportunity to engage in Christian work will be after hours and on weekends. When the weekend rolls around, he may be so tired that he cannot face the extra effort required by Christian work. Either he or his wife may decide that the weekend is the only opportunity available for relaxation. We all know how difficult it is to get Christian laymen at home to give time to the church. People are too busy—or think they are—to attend the midweek prayer and Bible study. As for special week-night meetings, they have been eliminated in many churches for lack of support. If this is so on the home front, what reason is there to believe that the lay Christian on the mission field will act differently? He may start out with high resolve, but the limitations of time and strength may prove too much for him. It takes a very unusual Christian to stand up to the pressures of vocational life, the responsibilities of home and family life, *and* the demands of Christian service over a long period of time. Sooner or later lethargy sets in and he becomes weary in well-doing. When this happens, the first thing to suffer is Christian service.

4. Language barriers that make witness difficult. The average American remains overseas for two and a half years. During this time few ever bother to learn a foreign language; and even if they do, the time span is not long enough to ensure any degree of proficiency. Many expatriates carry on their professional work by means of interpreters provided either by the American firm or by the host government. These are available only for the eight hours each day when the person is on the job. They are not available for social contacts during the evening hours or the weekends. Without an interpreter the lay missionary is at a very serious disadvantage when it comes to witnessing for Christ. It is difficult enough to explain the Christian gospel to fellow Americans at home. How much more difficult it is to explain the gospel to non-Christian nationals of other countries! Of course many nationals, especially those in high positions, have a working knowledge of English and can be reached through that medium.

5. Limited contacts with the nationals. In most countries the expatriate tends to move in the narrow circles of the international community, where English is spoken. This is especially true of his free time. He may *work* with the nationals, but he *plays* with the Americans and other members of the international community. This unfortunate behavior on the part of Americans abroad has been graphically described in *The Ugly American,* in which the authors tell of the endless round of cocktail parties that go to make up the social life of the diplomatic corps in the large cities of Southeast Asia.

In the heyday of colonialism the expatriates kept pretty much to themselves in their social contacts. They had their own swimming pools, golf courses, and tennis courts from which the nationals were excluded. Their social life was confined to these exclusive clubs. It was enough that they had to spend the working day in a strange environment. When evening came they retired to the sanctuary of the international community. There was almost no contact with the nationals outside office hours.

In recent years some progress has been made. Segregated clubs are no longer traditional; but expatriates still tend to congregate with other expatriates. In some instances they live in a foreign enclave in the most affluent part of town and saunter forth only during the day. In a few countries the large oil companies provide housing for their American personnel on company property, making the isolation that much more complete. To keep in touch with life back home in the United States of America, they subscribe to the international editions of *Time* and *Newsweek.* For their day-by-day international news they listen to the Voice of America. They live and move and have their being in a little patch of the United States set down in the heart of Caracas, Cairo, Kabul, or Kathmandu. Their bodies are overseas, but their hearts and minds are back home in good old USA.

The nonprofessional missionary often finds himself part of such an international community. He can, of course, break away from the American ghetto and establish social contacts with the people of the country; but it will require a strong personality and a go-it-alone mentality on his part. The pressure to conform to the social patterns of his peer group will be enormous. He will require the wisdom of Solomon and the courage of Daniel to bridge the social gap between the two communities; and if he succeeds, he may incur the displeasure of the international community and the censure of the American firm for which he works.

If he cannot speak the local language—and few business and professional people can—his contacts with the national churches will be minimal. Listening to a sermon in an unknown tongue is not particularly edifying. Curiosity may prompt him to attend one or two services, but after that he and his family will probably gravitate to the Union Church, where the service is in English and the worshipers are mostly expatriates. Under these conditions he will have little contact with the nationals, Christian or non-Christian.

6. Frustration, a perennial problem. It is common knowledge that frustration has dogged the steps of the professional missionary from the very beginning. What is not so well known is that the same thing is true of the business and professional man. In fact, it is a greater problem with the latter than with the former. This is particularly true of the wives of business and professional men, who have nothing to do and all day to do it. Not a few businessmen have had to return to the States before their term of service was completed because their wives could not endure life in a foreign culture, where everything was so different from what they were accustomed to back home.

There are few persons more pathetic than the wives of American businessmen overseas. Without a knowledge of the language they have no way of communicating with the people. Shopping for the smallest item is an exercise in frustration. To make matters worse, they can't attend the movies or even watch television. With a staff of domestic servants to take care of the household chores they have all kinds of time on their hands, with nothing to do and no place to go. Little wonder that many of them spend their days playing cards and their evenings at cocktail parties.

Frustration is by no means confined to the wives; their husbands have their frustrations too! The American way of doing things may or may not appeal to the leaders in Africa, Asia, or even Latin America. They have their way of life and are in no great hurry to change. Promptness and efficiency, the hallmarks of American business, are not necessarily regarded as virtues in the Third World. Life there is lived at a leisurely pace. The business of making a living is not nearly so important as the art of living. As for improving life by newfangled gadgets and gimmicks, this has no great attraction for people who for centuries have been content with simple things. There are two ways in which a person can be rich. One is in the multiplicity of his possessions; the other is in the simplicity of his wants. Most persons in the Third World would cheerfully settle for the second. Consequently when American technicians try to introduce a better product or a more efficient method of production, they often encounter indifference. Such an attitude is the cause of deep frustration.

Even the Peace Corps has its problems with frustration. The people show little interest in new and better ways of doing things and are so loath to change. And if they do change under pressure from the volunteer, they frequently revert to type after the Peace Corps moves on. This is one reason why the casualty rate in the Peace Corps is 17.2 percent as compared with 2.5 percent for professional missionaries over the same period of time.

Is there a place for the nonprofessional missionary? Indeed there is. God needs His servants in all walks of life, at home and overseas. The Holy Spirit is sovereign. He chooses one person to be a professional missionary and another to be a nonprofessional. There should be no rivalry between them. Both are needed for the preaching of the gospel and the extension of the Kingdom. Only let the nonprofessional missionary take cognizance of the pros and cons of the situation and be fully aware of the pitfalls peculiar to his calling.

10.

Future Prospects

Predicting the future is always a risky thing to do. We are living in a rapidly changing world and anything could happen in the next five or ten years, including the return of Christ. Moreover, the Christian mission has traditionally operated in the Third World, where political stability is an unknown quantity. Even here in the United States we can't be sure what the future holds for us. Our own political institutions are being shaken to their foundations and the highest offices in the land are honeycombed with corruption. Every passing day brings additional ugly facts to light and we wonder where it is all going to end.

Developing Trends

Of one thing we can be sure: The Christian mission will continue to the end of the age in spite of the many changes that will take place. When Jesus Christ gave the Great Commission to His apostles He indicated quite clearly that the mandate was to extend to the end of the age (Mt 28:20). The Christian mission was not to terminate with the apostolic era, or the Middle Ages, or the Reformation period; it was to continue to the end of the age.

During the intervening period there would be wars and rumors of wars and all kinds of opposition and persecution. The disciples would

401

be hated of all men. The missionary enterprise would be involved in all kinds of difficulties and dangers. The messengers of the cross would be hunted and hounded from pillar to post. They would be scourged in the Jewish synagogues and beaten by Roman officials. Indeed, some of them would lay down their lives for the sake of the gospel. But the mandate would never be rescinded nor the mission aborted. If the disciples were persecuted in one city they were not to call it quits, but move on to the next city.

Neither the mischief of men nor the machinations of the devil were to deter them. They were taught to believe that they were engaged in a Holy War with an implacable foe who would not surrender without a life-and-death struggle. Casualties would occur and reverses come, but they were to press on in the full assurance that the Captain of their salvation would be with them to the end of the age. Many battles would be lost, but the war would be won. On that point there was no doubt.

We do well to bear this in mind when the prophets of doom are sounding the death knell of the Christian mission. The days are dark and doors are closing in various parts of the world. Some timid souls are afraid that we are about to witness the demise of the missionary enterprise; but such is not the case. Dictators come and go; kingdoms rise and fall; civilizations wax and wane; but the worldwide mission of the Church will continue to the end of the age in spite of all the vicissitudes of human history. When one door closes another will open. If Western missionaries become *persona non grata*, non-Western missionaries will be raised up to take their place. If *all* expatriate missionaries are expelled from a given country, the indigenous church will remain to carry on. If the indigenous church is forced to go underground, the Spirit of God, who dwells not in temples made with hands but in the hearts of His people, will be there. It is one thing to get rid of the visible Church; it is quite another to get rid of Almighty God. Heaven is His throne and earth is His footstool. It is impossible to banish Him from any part of His domain.

Problems will doubtless increase, difficulties will abound, costs will soar, but the mission will go on. God, who is able to make the wrath of man to praise Him (Ps 76:10) will see to that.

There is reason to believe that the rapid decline in missionary interest and activity on the part of the main-line denominations will continue in the days to come, As mentioned in chapter 4 the total number of missionaries in six large denominations dropped from 4,548 in 1958 to 3,160 in 1971. Their leaders give no indication that steps are being taken to reverse the downward trend. So we can expect the missions affiliated with the Division of Overseas Ministries of the National Council of Churches in the U.S.A. to assume less and less responsibility for the evangelization of the world. This means that the conservative missions will have to bear increasing responsibility for the worldwide mission of the Christian Church. This raises an important question: Can these missions get enough candidates year by year to expand their overseas operations? Between 1965 and 1973 the forty-five faith missions in the Interdenominational Foreign Mission Association reported an overall increase of 9.6 percent for the eight-year period, which is slightly more than 1 percent per year. This is not very encouraging in light of the fact that in recent years many of the candidates have been short-termers, not career missionaries. It should also be borne in mind that five additional missions joined the association during that period, and two have recently withdrawn.

Not all these faith missions are growing at the same rate. Some are barely holding their own. Most of them have registered modest gains. Two or three have actually fallen behind. Half a dozen have experienced large gains, in some cases well over 100 percent. The largest growth has occurred in the younger missions. The older and larger missions are finding it increasingly difficult to hold their own against the attrition occasioned by death and retirement. When they reach the 800- or 900-member mark they have a tendency to level off at that point. Only one IFMA mission is now above the 1,000-mark—the Sudan Interior Mission; and its membership has dropped by 146 to 1,127 since 1965.

What is true of the IFMA is also true in the EFMA—the Evangelical Foreign Missions Association. Its member missions have registered modest growth in the past eight years and hopefully will be able to maintain the momentum. Though most of these missions are denominational, they face the same problems as the faith missions.

There are, of course, many missions that do not belong to either of these organizations. Their rate of growth has been higher than that of the IFMA or the EFMA. Some of these missions have experienced rapid growth in the past decade. Outstanding among them are Wycliffe Bible Translators, Southern Baptist Mission, and New Tribes Mission. It remains to be seen if they can maintain comparable growth during the coming decade.

One aspect of the present situation that augers well for the future of the missionary movement is the obvious working of the Holy Spirit in recent years. There is no doubt that the Jesus movement, the charismatic movement, and similar movements are bringing renewal to the churches throughout the world, especially here in the United States. Prayer cells and Bible study groups are springing up all over the country, many of them outside the organized churches. Tens of thousands of students and young people, inside and outside the churches, have been "turned on" to Jesus Christ. Thousands of these in the glow of their first love will find their way into Christian training institutions of one kind or another, and hopefully hundreds, maybe thousands, of them will turn up on the mission field. In the history of the church revival and missions have always gone hand in hand. There is no reason to believe it will be different this time. Already this renewal is reflected in seminary enrollment, which is on the increase, especially in the more conservative seminaries. Even in the liberal seminaries the prospective students are now inquiring about the spiritual climate of the school and showing an interest in prayer groups, Bible study, and the parish ministry, in contrast to a few years ago when social action was the craze.

One interesting facet of the situation is the increased number of seminary students now coming from the secular colleges and universities, and a corresponding decrease in those coming from the Christian and Bible colleges.

Many of these students were virtual pagans when first confronted with the claims of Christ by Inter-Varsity Christian Fellowship, Campus Crusade for Christ, and other evangelical agencies engaged in student work. Their conversion experience is usually a clear-cut one which leaves them with a sense of appreciation and dedication often lacking in Christians who have come up through evangelical homes, churches, and colleges, to whom the gospel is "old hat." These new converts have none of the hang-ups that plague students from a fundamentalist background. The Christian life to them is new and beautiful, and they have a deep desire to share it with others. Consequently they make good seminary students, and later on will make excellent missionaries.

There is likely to be a significant increase in the number of short-term missionaries in the years ahead. At present there are between seven and eight thousand short-termers out of a total of some fifty-five thousand Protestant missionaries in all parts of the world. The program is obviously popular and is likely to attract an increasing number of youth in the coming decade. This will be prompted largely by two considerations: (1) The demand for career missionaries will certainly outstrip the supply and the gap will have to be filled by short-termers. (2) The thinking of today's youth is away from lifetime commitment in any area of endeavor. They want to look before they leap. They want to keep all options open. Recognizing this fact, some of the main-line denominations and at least one faith mission have already given up the idea of appealing for career missionaries, at least in the beginning.

During the coming decade the number of nonprofessional missionaries is likely to increase. Two factors will operate here: (1) With the rise of nationalism the professional missionary may become *persona non grata* in some parts of the world. If these countries are to continue to have a Christian witness it will be necessary for nonprofessional missionaries to take up the torch. This in turn will mean additional training. These nonprofessional missionaries, to be effective in their witness, should spend at least a year in a Bible college or seminary. With this new type of work in mind some of the more progressive schools are now offering a two-year course in Bible, Theology, Comparative Religions, etc., leading to a new degree known as Master of Arts in Religion. (2) Today's emphasis in the homeland on the role of the laity in Christian witness and worship is bound to encourage church members to think in similar terms with regard to overseas service. More and more churches, including the Roman Catholic Church, are experimenting with lay leadership and congregational participation in church services. If laymen can be persuaded to get involved in Christian service at home, they will find it easy to do the same overseas.

Today there are millions of Americans traveling and residing overseas. If all the dedicated Christians among them could be trained and persuaded to be effective witnesses for Jesus Christ, they would add a whole new dimension to the missionary movement. The spiritual potential here is enormous.

In the years ahead there will doubtless be more emphasis on evangelistic missions and less on medical and educational missions. The reason for this is that the governments in the Third World have nationalized most of the mission schools and are now in the process of doing the same with the hospitals. This is a move in the right direction. It is what the colonial governments should have done long ago but didn't. This will set the missionaries free to give more time, thought, energy, and money to the supreme task of "making disciples," which includes gospel preaching, church planting, theological education, Bible translation and revision, literature production and distribution, and mass communications, all of which contribute directly to the building up of the church and the extension of the kingdom. After all, that is what missions is all about. In the past we had no choice; we had to provide educational and medical facilities, first for o converts and later on for the public in general. This day is fast passing, and we should rejoice in our new-found freedom. Now we can concentrate on the job for which we are best qualified.

In the future we can look forward to more inter-mission cooperation on the part of evangelical boards. In the past there has been a tendency for each mission to do its own thing, and this has resulted in a certain amount of duplication and overlapping. This is particularly true in the area of theological education. Each mission wants to run its own Bible school to make sure its pastors and evangelists come out with the right "stamp" on them. In some countries there are twenty or thirty small, struggling Bible schools, each with a handful of students. There are indications that mission leaders are becoming aware of the problem and are prepared to do something about it. A classic example is Union Biblical Seminary in Yeotmal, India, which began in 1938 as a small Free Methodist school, but today is supported by some seventeen mission boards, all of them thoroughly evangelical.

It may even be that some mission mergers will take place. Several of them have already occurred; but in each case the prime consideration was financial. A small mission, rather than cease to exist, has requested to be taken over by a larger mission with more assets and personnel. There has not yet been a merger involving two viable missions on the basis of economy and efficiency of operation. Perhaps it is still too early to expect this kind of merger; but doubtless it will come before long. Already feelers have been put out with this in mind; but to date no merger of this kind has been consummated.

Denominational boards, of course, cannot merge with other boards unless and until the denominations themselves merge. Several mergers of this kind have taken place. The interdenominational missions are the ones that have the greatest difficulties. Each mission has its own history, tradition, image, constituency, and membership to think of; and the older the mission, the more cherished these things are.

Saturation evangelism and other forms of inter-mission cooperation are on the increase, and we shall see more of this in the future. If cooperation is desirable at home it is even more essential on the mission field. In two or three countries several missions have pooled their resources and have operated under one banner. The classic example of this kind of cooperation is the United Mission to Nepal, which comprises some thirty different mission boards all operating under one umbrella in Nepal. Another example is the International Afghan Mission.

In the past Roman Catholic and Protestant missions went their separate ways. In most parts of the world there was mutual hostility and opposition. In Latin America the Protestants were openly persecuted by the Roman Catholics. Since Vatican II this has all changed. The Roman Catholic Church is now actively cooperating with the United Bible Societies. Most of the Bible translation and revision now going on is being done by joint committees of Roman Catholics and Protestants. The Bibles are known as union Bibles, acceptable to both sides. The Apocryphal Books are included in the Bibles used by the Catholics, but always at their request and expense. This kind of cooperation was made possible by the decision of the Vatican to give the Bible for the first time to the laymen in the church.

The present openness of the Roman Catholic authorities in Latin America would have been unbelievable ten short years ago. Today gospel films produced by the Billy Graham Evangelistic Association and the Moody Institute of Science are being shown in Catholic schools and churches throughout Latin America.

Nowhere has inter-mission cooperation been more widespread than in Bible translation work. In the past four Bible societies carried the lion's share of Bible translation and publication: the British and Foreign Bible Society, the American Bible Society, the National Bible Society of Scotland, and the Netherlands Bible Society. In 1946 the United Bible Societies came into being. Today it has fifty-six member societies, all contributing in their own way to the translation and publication of the Scriptures in over a thousand languages of the world. Wycliffe Bible Translators, which has translated portions of the Scriptures into over three hundred languages, does not actively cooperate with the UBS. But apart from them, well over 90 percent of all Bible translation and publication is now being done under the auspices of the UBS. This is the kind of cooperation that missions in general might well emulate.

In the past the task of world evangelization rested on the churches of the West. It was taken for granted that this was part of the "white man's burden." In recent years a change has taken place. The "younger" churches of the Third World are beginning to take responsibility for the evangelization of the unreached peoples in their own countries and overseas. Indeed, some of them have sent missionaries to the so-called Christian countries of the West. Hard statistics are difficult to obtain, but reliable estimates indicate that well over three thousand missionaries are now being supported by the churches in the Third World. This is only a beginning. In the future we shall see a great expansion of this kind of missionary interest and outreach. One gets the impression that the "younger" churches are quite excited about the prospect of missionary work around the world. There is every indication that they intend to accept their full share of responsibility for world evangelization. With the rising standard of living in the Third World many of these churches now have the financial base for such an undertaking. This is especially true of the churches in the Far East.

In a pluralistic world it is becoming increasingly difficult for the Christian missionary to insist on the uniqueness of the Christian faith and the finality of Jesus Christ. This is occasioned by two factors: the increasing popularity of relativism in the West and the resurgence of the non-Christian religions of the East. In view of these two developments the missionary is going to look more and more like a relic of bygone days. If there are no absolutes in the moral realm, it is foolish to insist that one religion is true and all the other religions are in varying degrees false. Such a notion is equally repugnant in East and West. We always thought of the nineteenth-century missionary as being a person of great courage. The missionary of the future will need even more courage, but it will be moral rather than physical courage. It is embarrassing to live in a "global village" and insist that the neighbors' gods are false, especially when the neighbors are such fine folks.

Out of this situation grows a demand for dialogue. In the past the preaching of the gospel took the form of monologue. The missionary did all the talking; the others sat and listened, or they quietly walked away. That day has gone. The people in the Third World are not as docile as they once were. They have learned to stand on their own feet and to think for themselves. They are no longer content to listen. They have something to say and they want to be heard.

The devotees of the Eastern religions are by no means persuaded that theirs is a lost cause. Also they know enough about the moral bankruptcy of the West to have grave misgivings about the "superiority" of the Christian religion. They are still willing to listen to the claims of Christianity as expounded by the missionary, but with the expectation that the missionary will return the compliment and listen to them as they explain the claims of Hinduism, Buddhism, or Islam, as the case may be.

Dialogue has its advantages as well as its disadvantages, especially in the Muslim world. To engage in this kind of dialogue will require great tact, skill, understanding, and love on the part of the missionary. More than ever it will be necessary for him to be well versed in the major doctrines of the great ethnic religions as well as in the Christian Scriptures. It cannot be said too often: it is an act of consummate folly to go to the mission field without an understanding of the non-Christian religions. Indeed, if we at home want to hold our own against the inroads made by Hare Krishna, Soka Gakkai, and Transcendental Meditation, we had better take seriously the study of the Eastern religions.

One of the most hopeful signs on the horizon is the growing strength of the national churches in the Third World; but their very strength has posed serious problems that call for solution. It is no exaggeration to say that church-mission tension in many parts of the world is at an all-time high.

The problem stems in part from the colonial image that still clings to the sending missions of the West. It will be some time before they can live down the reputation of the past. Part of the problem lies with the receiving churches, which have not yet learned to cope with the problems of independence. In a matter of a few years they have gone from the complete dependence of childhood to the bewildering independence of adolescence. This second period is always turbulent; but hopefully it leads on to the interdependence of adulthood. In the meantime the "mother" missions are having a hard time trying to live with the "daughter" churches as they pass through the trial-and-error period of adolescence on their way to the full maturity of adulthood.

Naturally there is some distrust, even suspicion, on both sides, due largely to misunderstanding. If the distrust is to be eliminated there must be dialogue. If dialogue is to be fruitful there must be openness and honesty on both sides. This kind of honest openness will not come overnight. It will have to be cultivated over a period of time. Naturally, the missions should take the initiative. They should encourage the churches to speak their mind without fear of retaliation. There is still a fear in some quarters that funds may be cut off if the churches become too free in their speech. In such circumstances genuine dialogue is impossible. The churches must be persuaded that the missions are sincere in their desire for harmonious dialogue.

Another problem that must be solved in the near future is this: How can the sending missions best help the national churches to develop missionary strategy and structures as they move out to evangelize the unreached peoples of the world? So important is this question that a special study conference was convened in Overland, Kansas, in November 1973, to discuss the matter. Five or six leaders from the national churches were on hand to present their point of view.

It was agreed that the Western missions should stand ready to assist the Third World sending agencies if such assistance is requested. Cooperation between the two groups may or may not be desirable, depending on the needs and attitudes of the Third World leaders. We in the West should not assume that they need our help. It should be given only if requested. If requested, it should be given wisely, in a way that will not do injury to their authentic selfhood. In such instances the permanent authority should reside in the Third World sending agencies. We can easily do more harm than good if we insist on our patterns of work, or impose our organizational structures and financial policies, or become too generous with our money.

As more and more churches in the Third World achieve full maturity the sending missions will have to decide what relationship they will sustain to these churches. There are three possibilities: parallelism, partnership, and fusion. Many of the mainline denominations have already settled for fusion. Their missionaries are now known as "fraternal workers" and are under the supervision and control of the national church. The mission structure has been dismantled, except for the home end of the work.

The evangelical missions hesitate to go that far. They prefer either parallelism or partnership. In parallelism both the sending mission and the receiving church maintain their own work side by side, the one supplementing and complementing the other. In partnership the sending mission and the receiving church agree to work in close collaboration, with missionaries and national leaders sitting together on the same boards and administering joint programs to achieve common goals.

Whichever plan is adopted it is absolutely imperative that the national leaders be in on the decision-making. Otherwise all our fine talk about cooperation is meaningless. The time has come to recognize the full autonomy of the national churches and to treat their leaders as equals in every sense of the word. Tokenism is not good enough.

The sending missions must never forget that they are *missionary* agencies and as such are irrevocably committed to the evangelization of the world. They must never lose this vision or permit the cooperating national churches to forget it. Churches the world over have a tendency, especially in the second and third generations, to lose their first love and their evangelistic zeal and settle down to a comfortable existence with little or no concern for the fate of the unsaved.

Another trend has to do with indigenous theology which is developing in the Third World. Biblical theology is rooted in the Word of God and consequently has nothing to do with East or West *per se*. As it has developed in the West, however, it has acquired certain cultural overtones that have little if any relevance in the Third World. At the same time it is recognized that our theology is what we derive from the Scriptures, and that a Biblical theology is effective in any culture only in the measure in which it is expressed in concepts and terms that are relevant to the needs and aspirations of that culture.

An essential task of the church, therefore, is the careful study of the Scriptures in the context of the culture in which they are to be communicated and the development of a theology that can be successfully communicated to that culture. For such a task the help of Western missionary theologians is both needed and wanted in the Third World, provided they have some knowledge of cross-cultural communications and have lived long enough in the culture to understand and appreciate the nuances of that culture. There is probably no greater service that we can render to the emerging churches in the Third World. Alas, so few missionaries are theologians, and so few theologians are missionaries.

The greatest single focal point of friction between the sending missions and the receiving churches involves the use of foreign funds. The national church leaders have three gripes: (1) The missionary standard of living is usually considerably higher than that of the national worker. (2) Missions are willing to invest money in a given program so long as the missionary is on hand to supervise the use of funds; but when for any reason the missionary is removed the funds are withdrawn. In other words, the money is used to support the person (who is temporary), not the office (which is permanent). (3)

When foreign funds are given to the churches they usually have strings attached.

If church-mission tension is ever to be eliminated some way must be found to defuse this explosive issue. In years past the sending missions used foreign funds all too freely to the detriment of the developing churches. Now the pendulum is in danger of swinging to the opposite extreme and the churches are suddenly told they must sink or swim.

Some missions have done a better job than others. The Christian and Missionary Alliance has in the last decade achieved a remarkably harmonious working relationship with its overseas "daughter" churches, now really "sister" churches. They have settled for the partnership plan and have used foreign funds, not to support local churches and pastors, but as a catalyst to spark missionary giving and vision on the part of church leaders. Today the C&MA churches in Asia have their own missionaries, sent out by their own churches, and supported by their own funds.

There is a growing awareness among mission leaders that while the receiving churches should be fully self-supporting at the local level, there is justification for the use of foreign funds at higher levels of administration. Theological education, certainly at the graduate level, is very costly and in some countries quite beyond the financial capability of the local churches. The evangelical churches of Africa and Madagascar now have a continent-wide association with a full-time executive secretary. The present budget of thirty-five thousand dollars a year, modest though it is, is a big drain on the meager resources of the national fellowships that compose its membership. For the time being Western funds are being used to underwrite the program. This seems to be a wise use of foreign funds.

The role of the missionary is changing rapidly. In the heyday of colonialism he was a person of stature, a force to be reckoned with. At home he was a hero; on the field he was a leader. Now he is neither hero nor leader, but just a plain servant. This is a good thing, for it forces the missionary to come to grips with the words of the Master: "As the Father has sent me, even so I send you" (Jn 20:21). And we all know that Jesus Christ came not to be ministered unto but to minister, and to give His life a ransom for many (Mt 20:28).

Seldom in history have the followers of Christ rushed to fill the servant role. Like the early disciples, they have jostled for position and hankered after power. Few of them have taken kindly to the footwashing ministry commanded by our Lord (Jn 13:14).

Indeed, the role is changing. Yesterday the missionary was the leader. Today he is the partner. Tomorrow he will be the servant.

Opposing Forces

We are living in days of unprecedented opportunities; but along with the opportunities are opposing forces. This should not surprise us. The apostle Paul found the same thing true in his day. He said, "A wide door for effective work has opened to me, and there are many adversaries" (1 Co 16:9). Our Lord said as much when He sent out the twelve apostles: "Behold, I send you out as sheep in the midst of wolves. . . . Beware of men; for they will deliver you up to councils, and flog you in their synagogues, and you will be dragged before governors and kings for my sake" (Mt 10:16-18).

Mao Tse-tung, the greatest revolutionist of the twentieth century, said on one occasion that a revolution is not a tea party. Neither is the missionary enterprise. Missionary work has always involved all kinds of difficulties and dangers. As it was in the past, so it will be in the future. Opposing forces should not discourage or deter us; rather they should spur us on to greater effort.

Some of these opposing forces operate right here in the homeland; others are encountered only on the field. But whether here or there they are formidable foes of the gospel and should be recognized as such. Before moving on to the mission field we shall discuss certain obstacles in the homeland that militate against the worldwide Christian mission.

The first of these would have to be the moral decadence of Western civilization. The distinction between Christendom and heathendom, so marked in the nineteenth century, is rapidly disappearing. Europe is no longer a Christian continent; and North America is rapidly going down the same road. Western culture is becoming less and less Christian in its content. In fact we ourselves are now talking of a "post-Christian era." And well we might.

Our large metropolitan centers are controlled by gangsters. Our inner cities are jungles of violence and crime. Our entire political system, including the police and the courts, is honeycombed with corruption. X-rated movies and pornographic literature are flooding our sex-saturated society. Premarital sex, adultery, abortion (new name for infanticide), prostitution, divorce, cheating, shoplifting, and gambling —all have reached unprecedented heights in the past ten years. Less "sinful" but equally reprehensible have been our love of money, our penchant for war, our pursuit of happiness, and our preoccupation with material prosperity.

Fifty years ago the peoples of the Third World knew the United States largely through the missionaries residing in those parts. To this day they assume that all Americans are Christians. Now with worldwide, instantaneous mass communications, Uncle Sam (sometimes called Uncle Sham) stands naked and ugly before the non-Christian world.

It is a shame, but we must confess that the moral standards in the non-Christian countries are often higher than in our own. Many of the governments have taken action to keep out the various forms of pollution from the West. The most puritanical society in today's world is Communist China, which has abolished both God and religion.

All this makes it increasingly difficult for the Western missionary to preach the gospel in the Third World. They argue that if Christianity has failed so miserably in the West why should it be exported to the East? They can be forgiven if they say to the missionary: "Physician, heal thyself."

Particularly vexatious is the problem of racial prejudice in the United States. We are not the only country to have this problem; but we are the largest, strongest, and best known; and what we say and do today is prominently displayed in the world headlines tomorrow. We are indeed a city that is set on a hill and cannot be hid (Mt 5:14), which adds to the gravity of the situation.

If segregation were confined to American society it would be bad enough, but it is found in the Christian churches as well. Indeed the most segregated hour of the week is between eleven and twelve o'clock on Sunday morning. African Christians visiting this country have been mistaken for Afro-Americans and treated as second-class citizens, even by the churches. When the error is discovered profuse apologies are offered; but the damage has been done. There is no doubt about it; racial prejudice in this country is a millstone around the neck of the missionary in the Third World.

The assassination of President Kennedy and his brother Bobby and Martin Luther King, all within a few years, shocked not only the American people but the people of the entire world. In every country American missionaries were bombarded with a barrage of questions, some of them quite hostile. How could a so-called Christian nation descend to such barbarity? Needless to say, the missionaries had no satisfactory answers.

Following the death of Dr. King, Jack Robinson, missionary in Senegal, wrote: "We have sensed real cooling off in the attitude of the people since our arrival in Senegal three years ago because of the reports they get of the horrible racial situation in the United States. Many have the impression that our whole country is burning. Being an American is no longer to our advantage."[1]

And what shall be said of the Vietnam War, the longest and dirti-

---

[1] Jack Robinson, *Impact* (February 1969), p. 7.

est in our history? Fortunately the war is over—at least so far as Americans are concerned—and people have short memories, so the whole mess will soon be forgotten. But while it lasted it was a constant source of embarrassment to American missionaries overseas. Here again the missionaries were hard pressed for an explanation that would satisfy the questioners.

The presence of hundreds of thousands of American GIs overseas has done nothing to enhance the image of "Christian" America in the eyes of the Third World. Besides getting into drunken brawls and otherwise making a nuisance of themselves, the GIs in Japan, Korea, and Vietnam sired thousands of babies. Deserted by their fathers, unwanted by their mothers, and unable to hide their identity, these children are the most unfortunate in the world. World Vision International, the Pearl Buck Foundation, and other similar organizations have done what they could to alleviate the situation; but the problem was much too great for their meager resources. As long as they live these victims of modern warfare will carry with them the stigma of their origin.

Another developing force is neo-isolationism. Isolationism was the official policy of the United States between the two world wars. Following World War II the United States, through no fault of its own, had to assume the leadership of the free world. Our most successful venture was the Marshall Plan, that put Western Europe back on its feet and checked the advance of Communist power in that part of the world. President Truman's Point Four Plan was likewise very successful, for it kept Greece and Turkey from falling into the Russian orbit. In the last twenty-five years our foreign aid program has cost the American taxpayer over 100 billion dollars, and this does not include the enormously costly Vietnam War.

And what do we have to show for our generosity? Not very much. A good deal of our foreign aid found its way into the black markets that developed overseas. Some of it ended up in the pockets of the politicians. In the process we made as many enemies as friends. Now with mounting problems at home the American people are asking, "Why give to others when we don't have enough money for ourselves?" "Is it not time to put our own house in order?" This is what Senator McGovern had in mind when he closed his acceptance speech at the 1972 Democratic Convention with the plea, "Come home, America." A growing number of Americans are disillusioned with the United Nations and advocate that we pull out. In the United States Congress there is a growing sentiment in favor of withdrawing American troops from Europe. We are determined never again to get our fingers burned in overseas operations. This kind of "me first" psychology makes a strong appeal to the innate selfishness of human nature.

If this mood becomes widespread, it could easily have an adverse effect on Christian missions, for, whether we like to admit it or not, the church usually is only five or ten years behind the world. If the American government decides to abdicate its worldwide responsibilities the American church might well do the same with its worldwide missionary enterprise.

Another opposing force is the resurgence of the great non-Christian religions of Asia. Fifty years ago missionaries on furlough spoke hopefully of the breakup of the ethnic religions. No one talks that way today. With the advent of independence these religions have taken a new lease on life and are passing from the defensive to the offensive. Throughout the entire Muslim world the study of Islam is a required subject in all public schools from grade school through university. New mosques are being built and old ones are being refurbished; and attendance is on the increase. A missionary in Tunis in 1973 wrote: "A trend to more strict observance of Islam is noticeable, and it is common to see women and men, young and old, attending prayers at the mosques, whereas 10 years ago prayers were considered 'for mice and old men.'"

In India Hinduism is making a valiant effort to win back the hundreds of thousands of converts (former untouchables) lost to Christianity. Some of the more militant Hindus are calling for the expulsion of all missionaries. Two state governments were persuaded to pass anti-conversion laws; they were later struck down by the Supreme Court as unconstitutional. The Bhagavad-Gita has been translated into hundreds of languages, and a cheap paperback edition in English can be purchased in the corner drug store on Main Street, U.S.A. The Hare Krishna Movement, Transcendental Meditation, and Eastern Mysticism, all from India, are now invading the West and sweeping thousands of American youth off their feet. Buddhism, known through the centuries for its emphasis on meditation, has suddenly become both missionary and militant. In South Vietnam Buddhist monks helped to topple more than one Saigon regime during the 1960s. Buddhist scriptures are being translated into the major languages of Europe and Buddhist missionaries are to be found in all parts of the Western world. Outside the international airport in Colombo there is a huge poster exhorting the people to contribute money to send Buddhist missionaries to Europe.

Soka Gakkai in Japan, combining prayer and politics, has won over ten million families since 1950. Its religious exclusiveness, militant nationalism, forced conversions, political ambitions, and worldwide missionary aims make it Christianity's most formidable foe in Japan. More recently it has invaded the West, where it is making converts in significant numbers. Writing in the English-language *Seikyo Times* its leader, Mr. Ikeda, said: "We have a message! We are committed to the salvation of mankind. Our aim is to save the masses from misfortune and misery and to establish a happy life for every individual. We must create a peaceful world. Soka Gakkai is not only the hope of Japan, but the hope of the world."

Another opposing force that is gathering momentum today is syncretism. Visser't Hooft defines syncretism as "the view which holds that there is no unique revelation in history, that there are many ways to reach the divine reality, that all formulations of religious truth or experience are by their very nature inadequate expressions of that truth and that it is necessary to harmonize as much as possible all religious ideas and experiences so as to create one universal religion for mankind."[2]

This point of view is gaining wide acceptance in both East and West. The Vedanta school of thought in Hinduism maintains that it is possible to realize God by various ways—Jesus, Krishna, Mohammed, Zoroaster, and others. Gandhi said the same. Arnold Toynbee castigates Christianity for its "arrogance" and predicts that unless it rids itself of its exclusive spirit it will be rejected by modern man—East and West. He prefers to believe that "all the higher religions are also revelations of what is true and right. They also come from God and each presents some facet of God's truth."[3]

This problem has been with us for a long time, but it is particularly acute in these days when the national churches in the Third World are trying to make Christianity indigenous to the national culture. The Indian church wants to make Christianity indigenous to India and the African church wants to do the same in Africa. This is good and proper. This is what the early church did with Christianity in the Graeco-Roman world. But there is a serious problem: How far can the process of indigenization go without altering the hard core of Christian doctrine and practice?

Nowhere is the problem greater than in Africa, where some seven thousand independent churches (denominations) are trying to develop an African form of Christianity. Many of these churches are a strange mixture of animism, native customs, and magic, with certain Christian elements added and the whole embellished with the external symbols of Christianity. "Among the many independent churches and sects which have grown up in Africa there are those which simply seek to give a more specifically Christian [African] expression to the Christian faith without departing from that faith. But there are others which

2 W. A. Visser't Hooft, *No Other Name* (Philadelphia: Westminster Press, 1963), p. 11.
3 Arnold Toynbee, *Christianity Among the Religions of the World* (New York: Charles Scribner's Sons, 1957), pp. 99-100.

have gone so far in reintroducing traditional African religious ideas and practices (sometimes including magic) that they have become essentially syncretistic."[4]

The missionary finds himself in a very delicate situation. If he does nothing and allows the church to lapse into baptized paganism, he will be abdicating his responsibility. If he tries to point out the dangers inherent in the situation he may be accused of "theological imperialism." In either case he is in trouble. This is one reason why the evangelical missions should help to train national theologians, who will be able to cope with the problem better than we can.

Another opposing force is nationalism. As we have already seen, nationalism has been the greatest force in the Third World during most of the twentieth century. With the achievement of independence nationalism has a way of cooling off. Though the most turbulent phase is probably over it is by no means dead. With the passing of time nationalism will gradually give way to internationalism; but we still have a long way to go before we reach that stage. Inasmuch as nationalism is directed against outsiders and all missionaries are expatriates, it stands to reason that nationalism will pose a problem for years to come.

Now that these countries are sovereign, independent states they have every right to order their internal affairs and their foreign policies as they see fit. Their immigration authorities have a perfect right to exclude or expel anyone they consider undesirable. All foreigners are now guests; as such they enter, remain, and depart only with permission of the government. They have no rights, only privileges. This is in stark contrast to colonial times when the missionaries came and went and did as they liked.

To make matters worse many of these countries are under military dictatorships of the left or the right, which means that civil and political rights are shelved for the time being. Many of them have demographic and economic problems—too many people and too few jobs. Such governments do not want expatriates taking jobs away from their own citizens. Some governments, such as in Thailand, impose an annual quota on the number of foreigners to whom they will give permanent residence visas. Other governments will accept only citizens from "friendly" countries. Still other governments, such as Burma, are determined to get rid of all expatriates.

In the "good old days" all that missionaries needed was a passport; and British missionaries going to British colonies didn't need even that. Today they need residence permits in addition to passports and visas if they want to remain in the country longer than the usual time

---

[4] Visser't Hooft, *op. cit.,* p. 45.

allotted to tourists. In some countries these are difficult to obtain; and once obtained, they have to be renewed every year or two. Missionaries without a residence permit are treated like tourists and have to leave the country every month or so to have their permits renewed. They usually step over the border into a neighboring country, spend a day or two there, do some shopping or sightseeing, and return within forty-eight hours. This procedure, of course, is costly in time and money.

Many countries now require a work permit for all aliens holding a residence permit. This is even harder to get because of the high rate of unemployment in many of the underdeveloped countries. In some instances the applications get lost in the bureaucratic red tape while the missionaries wait patiently—or impatiently—for their permits. In 1973 some three hundred visas for missionaries going to Brazil were held up because of an interdepartmental feud between the Foreign Office and the Ministry of Labor. If the apostle Paul had encountered this kind of problem he would not have been able to support himself and his colleagues by tent-making.

Bernard Shaw once said that nationalism is like a cancer and when a person has cancer he can think of nothing else. This seems to be the case with certain dictators and demagogues who have seized power in recent years. Independence has produced a whole crop of politicians more interested in their own self-aggrandizement than in the welfare of the people. They build magnificent presidential palaces, surround themselves and their cronies with a platoon of bodyguards, outlaw all opposition parties, declare martial law, impose censorship on the press and radio, and apply various kinds of pressure on minority groups, especially aliens.

In 1973 President Amin of Uganda gave forty thousand Asians ninety days to leave the country; and they were not permitted to take their money with them. About the same time he outlawed twelve "religious sects" declared to be "dangerous to peace and order." Earlier fifty-eight missionaries were expelled, accused of having "entered the country illegally, were qualified military men dressed in religious habits and yet could not answer questions about the Bible."[5]

In Zaire President Mobutu is throwing his weight around. During 1973 he expelled the Roman Catholic cardinal, forced Christians to adopt Zairean names, and outlawed all uniformed youth groups, church business meetings, and religious periodicals. His actions were directed against the growing power of the Roman Catholic hierarchy; but Protestants were naturally included in all the directives.

In the past year several Muslim countries have cracked down on missionary activities. In Afghanistan the only church in the country

---

[5] *Afroscope* (November 1973), p. 3.

was bulldozed by order of the government, and half a dozen non-professional missionaries under the International Afghan Mission were expelled with no reason given for the action. Somalia opened to missionary work in 1954 but closed again in 1973.

Another opposing force is Communism. Communism is not the monolithic world structure we once thought it to be. Nor does it pose the same threat to world peace as it did in the fifties and sixties. Moreover the détente between the USSR and the United States and the exchange of diplomatic personnel between Communist China and the United States have resulted in a relaxed atmosphere. It is doubtful, however, if either the Soviet Union or Communist China has given up its ultimate goal of world revolution. In the 1960s both countries overplayed their hands in certain parts of the world and suffered embarrassing setbacks as a result. Both countries are actively engaged in extending their influence in certain strategic regions, the Russians in the Middle East and the Chinese in East Africa.

It is quite possible that a Communist regime might emerge in East Africa; in that event we should expect both church and mission work to suffer. After South Yemen turned Communist several years ago mission property was confiscated and all missionaries were expelled. South Vietnam, after many years of attack and infiltration from the North, fell under Communist control in April 1975, despite the prior involvement of Western nations. As predicted, missionary work there has come to an abrupt halt.

There is another opposing force the full extent of which is not yet known. This is the high cost of missionary work. The American people are rightly concerned about the rate of inflation in our economy; at least we can derive comfort from the fact that it is lower in the United States than in any other industrialized state. And if we think it is bad in Europe, it is many times worse in other parts of the world. In some countries the cost of living soars as much as 100 percent a year. In Chile inflation ran wild in 1973, rising almost 400 percent in the first six months!

Added to inflation abroad have been two devaluations of the American dollar, amounting to almost 20 percent. The inflation in Japan coupled with the devaluation of the American dollar reduced the purchasing power of the missionary's remittance by over 40 percent. In Japan steak runs as high as fifteen dollars a pound and an eight-ounce glass of orange juice costs three dollars. If it is true that "a day without orange juice is like a day without sunshine," the missionaries in Japan do not enjoy much sunshine!

Some governments are now trying to squeeze every dollar they can out of foreigners passing through or residing in their countries. Singapore has recently passed a law requiring all persons, including students, entering the country to make a deposit of $3,000. Jordan demands as much as $4,000 duty on a secondhand car and a $350 license fee. Some countries levy a head tax on everyone entering or leaving the country. Many, taking their cue from the West, have introduced the personal income tax; and missionaries along with other expatriates have to pay up. Others go so far as to charge duty on medical and relief supplies furnished free by missionary and humanitarian agencies in the West.

What shall be said about the price of land and buildings? In some countries the sky is the limit. "In the capital's [Tokyo] prestigious Minato section, a 1,245-square-foot apartment which sold new for $78,000 in 1970 now would cost $380,000. In other metropolitan centers such as Osaka and Nagoya, land prices have also jumped 200 to 300 percent in a single year."[6] Needless to say, mission boards don't have that kind of money. The problem could be solved by renting instead of buying; but rents are not cheap either. In some cities missionaries are paying $300 to $400 a month for a small apartment.

There is no doubt about it. The missionary enterprise is now a costly business; and unless the churches in this country get behind it and support it up to the hilt, there is bound to be a certain amount of retrenchment over the next decade. One mission board with fewer than seventy missionaries reckons that an extra $150,000 a year will be needed to maintain its present missionary force. Recently the author received a year-end letter from a mission asking for $53,000 to enable it to end the year in the black. During the past year some churches failed to meet their commitments to the missionaries; so the mission "borrowed" from other funds to prevent undue hardship on the part of the missionaries. Now these funds have to be replenished. Scores of letters of this kind come to the author's desk every December.

The United Presbyterian Church in the U.S.A. has recently announced a 35 percent reduction in its 1974 overseas mission programs, and the American Lutherans had to rely on a $250,000 special grant from a Lutheran insurance company to maintain their overseas personnel for the last months of 1973. Devaluation of the American dollar and falling income are given as reasons for the cutbacks.

Unlimited Opportunities

As indicated in the preceding section the Christian mission in this postcolonial period is facing many opposing forces. At the same time

---

6 *U.S. News and World Report* (October 8, 1973).

there are unprecedented opportunities; and the former should not be allowed to obscure the latter.

It is true that missionaries have a hard time getting into some countries and after they get there they have to endure petty annoyances of one kind or another; but upon their arrival they usually find the people friendly. Most of the ill will, mistrust, suspicion, and animosity that exist in the world today have been generated not by peoples but by governments. They are the ones that make laws, break treaties, and declare war. Trade barriers, immigration quotas, and other obstacles designed to keep the nations apart are established by the politicians, not the people. When people are left to themselves they usually manage to get along pretty well with other people.

When the missionary gets into a foreign country he invariably finds the people open and friendly on a person-to-person basis. For all the anti-American propaganda that was generated by the Cold War there is still an enormous reservoir of good will for the United States. It is no exaggeration to say that in spite of all our faults and failings America enjoys the confidence and admiration of most of the world. It is noteworthy in this connection that our two former enemies, Germany and Japan, both of whom we reduced to rubble, are today our strongest allies. When the chips are down even the Arabs in the Middle East prefer to do business with us rather than with the USSR, and that in spite of our consistent support of the State of Israel. This is not intended as a pat on the back for Uncle Sam; it is simply a recognition of the facts in international life.

In spite of administrative red tape many governments in the Third World are coming to see that the missionaries are their best friends and they are still willing to give them preferential treatment. The government of Thailand is urging religious leaders and missionaries to help solve some of the nation's problems. The country's new Alien Occupation Law, which restricts the practice of some fifty-eight occupations to Thai nationals, does not apply to teachers of religion. Missionaries have been told that the government considers their work beneficial to the country. They have been urged to win those committed to no faith and to "try to win the hearts of the young people."

David Wilkerson, during a recent crusade in Brazil, was invited to speak to the Legislative Assembly in session in Sao Paulo. The governor and other key officials met with him privately to discuss ways and means of combatting the growing drug problem. In every city that he visited, Wilkerson was swarmed by reporters seeking interviews regarding the critical youth problems now facing Brazil. The nation's largest leading magazine, *Manchete,* featured his crusades.

In country after country churches and missions are being given prime time on national networks for religious programs. The Africa Inland Mission produces over a hundred programs a month for broadcast over the powerful government station in Nairobi. In Zambia President Kenneth Kaunda has given the churches as much radio time on the national network as they are able to program. Each Sunday evening Monrovia's only television station telecasts a program, "New Life in Christ," prepared by the Sudan Interior Mission.

The government of Kenya recently gave the Assemblies of God a beautiful piece of property worth $100,000 in the most densely populated part of Nairobi. An influential Ethiopian offered the Sudan Interior Mission a tract of land if it could find the manpower to develop a mission center. Alas, the offer had to be turned down for lack of personnel. In Paraguay the Ministry of National Education recently gave permission for the Bible Society to place Scriptures in the hands of every school and college student in the country.

Far from wanting to get rid of the missionaries, some governments have recently gone out of their way to honor their work. The government of Korea has issued a commemorative postage stamp honoring World Vision for twenty years of child care and other forms of social service. The government of Liberia has conferred a similar honor on the Sudan Interior Mission. A special commemorative postage stamp was issued on January 18, 1974, to mark the twentieth anniversary of Radio Station ELWA. Two medical missionaries, Titus Johnson and Arden Almquist, on the staff of the Paul Carlson Medical Center in Zaire, were decorated by the government with the highest medal of honor for their "distinguished service to the nation." On August 31, 1973, Wycliffe Bible Translators in the Philippines received the Ramon Magsaysay Award for International Understanding, widely regarded as the Asian equivalent of the Nobel Peace Prize.

The missionary may have lost some of his glamor among his friends at home. He is still making a solid contribution overseas where his presence is appreciated by those who see him in action.

C. Stacey Woods, former General Secretary of the International Fellowship of Evangelical Students, writing in 1972, said;

> I see two worldwide, contradictory crosscurrents strongly flowing: First, there is the rushing torrent of godlessness, sensuality, secularism and violence, which is increasing everywhere. Second, there is what many of us believe may be the final great movement of God's Spirit just before the Day of God's grace ends and the awesome Day of the Lord begins. This is seen most significantly in the tremendous increase in the study of God's Word. Second, in the many movements worldwide, which are being used of God in the salvation of young and old.[7]

---

7 C. Stacey Woods, *Asia Pulse*, Vol. III, No. 3 (April 1972), p. 101.

There is no doubt that the Spirit of God in our day is working in strange ways and in most unexpected places. It is literally a worldwide movement embracing Christians and non-Christians alike, renewing the one and converting the other. The churches at home are being renewed and the churches overseas are growing by leaps and bounds, some of them doubling and tripling their total membership in the last decade.

After his 1973 crusade in Korea, attended by three million people, Billy Graham said, "I seriously doubt if my own ministry can ever be the same again." Dr. Myron Augsburger, President of Eastern Mennonite College, after a recent world tour said that he is convinced that the Third World is the cutting edge of the Christian church today. All who visit the mission field come back with the same observation. The words *fabulous* and *fantastic* are being used to describe the situation. Millions are turning to the Lord and tens of millions are being exposed to the Christian gospel for the very first time. And this quest for spiritual reality is not confined to the poverty-stricken masses, whose interest in religion might be suspect. It includes teachers, students, government officials, successful businessmen, and others whose hearts have been touched by the Holy Spirit.

Some Christian groups are finding that their overseas work is expanding so rapidly that the "daughter" churches in the Third World now have a larger cumulative membership than the "mother" church in this country. Among such groups are the Christian and Missionary Alliance, the Assemblies of God, the Seventh-day Adventists, and others. The Assemblies of God began work in Korea only in the 1950s. Today their largest church in Seoul has a membership of twenty thousand and last year its budget amounted to $500,000, much of which went to foreign missions.

Mass evangelism seems to have had its day in the homelands. Billy Graham is about the only evangelist who can attract and hold large audiences today. Not so on the mission field. Beginning in 1960 Evangelism-in-Depth brought the small, timid churches of Latin America out of their ghettoes and into the streets, parks, municipal auditoriums, and soccer stadiums for city-wide rallies. From Latin America the idea spread to Africa and Asia, where the program is known by various names: New Life For All (West Africa), Christ For All (Zaire), Evangelism Deep and Wide (South Vietnam), Total Mobilization (Japan), and Christ the Only Way (Philippines). In 1958 the Assemblies of God launched a mass evangelism program known as Good News Crusades. These have been held in scores of large cities in all parts of the world and have resulted in greatly accelerated growth. The Southern Baptists have likewise gone in for huge evangelistic campaigns with gratifying results.

The Argentine evangelist, Luis Palau of Overseas Crusades, has a burden for the 250 million Spanish-speaking people, whom he hopes to reach with the gospel in a ten-year period. He has held crusades in several of the Latin American countries with amazing response on the part of the people. Four crusades in Guatemala attracted 100,000 persons, with 3,000 first-time decisions. In addition he did simultaneous live talk shows over the nation's three television stations. In Lima, Peru, 103,000 persons attended the meetings in the Bull Ring. Over 4,500 indicated their decision to follow Christ. During the crusade Palau appeared on television thirteen times with messages, counseling sessions, and talk shows. Forty-five radio stations around the country carried news and excerpts from the crusade. A press conference in downtown Lima was attended by forty-two newsmen. It is estimated that thirty million Latin Americans have seen and heard Palau on television.

An amazing thing happened in Bolivia. Julio Cesar Rubial, a Roman Catholic layman, after a remarkable conversion experience began preaching simple Bible messages. Though a Roman Catholic, his Christ-centered preaching and the absence of any reference to the saints and the Virgin Mary gained him the enmity of the Catholic hierarchy. He began preaching in the Roman Catholic churches; but when banned he moved, like John Wesley, to the open air. In January 1973, he twice filled the La Paz soccer stadium (seating capacity twenty thousand) with an overflow of equal size outside. From there he moved on to Cochabamba, where his open-air services drew thirty thousand to sixty thousand persons. As a result revival has broken out and spilled over to the Protestant churches. One large church now holds morning and evening meetings every day of the week. A new suburban church with only four members two months ago now averages more than two hundred in each service.

In the spring of 1973 French evangelist Jacques Giraud was invited to Ivory Coast for a one-week evangelistic crusade. So powerful were the meetings in the capital, Abidjan, that the city council canceled all sporting events and gave the evangelistic team the use of the huge soccer stadium. Morning and evening for *six* weeks thirty to thirty-five thousand people crowded into the stadium. During the first part of the crusade the evangelist emphasized the power of Christ to heal. Hundreds were healed, including some high government officials and their relatives. By the end of the first week the crusade was the talk of the town. During the second part of the crusade Mr. Giraud emphasized the power of Christ to save. Having already witnessed the healing of the body, the people responded in droves.

In Abidjan over fifteen hundred were baptized. The Bible Society sold out its entire stock: twelve thousand New Testaments, two thousand Bibles, and twenty thousand Gospels. Never in the history of Ivory Coast had so much Christian literature been sold in so short a time.

As the meetings in the capital drew to a close government officials persuaded the evangelist to hold similar meetings in the interior. The minister of state insisted that he go to his hometown, Moumodi, for a week on his way to Bouake where he had been invited by the minister of the interior and the mayor of the city. From that point on the government took care of all arrangements, including hospitality and finances, something previously unheard of in Ivory Coast—or anywhere else.

In November 1972, Dr. Stanley Mooneyham of World Vision, accompanied by Anglican Archbishop Marcus Loane of Australia and Bishop Chandu Ray of Singapore, conducted a city-wide campaign in Phnom Penh, capital of the Khmer Republic (Cambodia). Every night the twelve-hundred-seat Municipal Music Hall was filled, with an overflow crowd on the closing Sunday. Altogether 2,681 persons publicly expressed their desire to know more about Jesus Christ. Were there any lasting results? The facts speak for themselves. In 1971 the Khmer Evangelical Church had only one congregation in Phnom Penh. In 1973 the number had risen to eleven, each with about 120 persons in attendance.

Similar stories of church growth come from all parts of the mission field. Churches are springing up with such rapidity that it is quite impossible adequately to shepherd the flock. The Sudan Interior Mission reports that prior to the civil war in Nigeria the Evangelical Church of West Africa had only four congregations in the Eastern Region, then known as Biafra. Today in that same region there are fifty churches, with over five thousand people in the Sunday services.

An even more thrilling report comes from the Wallamo people in Ethiopia. In a three-month period ten thousand adults renounced their spirit worship. Entire villages turned to Christ. Witch doctors were converted and joined the church. New congregations are growing up so rapidly that the Sudan Interior Mission hardly knows how to cope with the mushroom growth which threatens to get out of hand.

Dr. Clyde W. Taylor, after a visit in Africa in 1972, wrote: "In some areas where New Life For All campaigns have been held there has been a 50 percent church growth in one year. The results are fantastic but can only be preserved with thorough follow-up by the churches. This type of evangelism demands the total attention of the church while it lasts."[8] The New Life For All campaign in Central African Republic resulted in a 65 percent church growth in one year.

---

[8] Clyde W. Taylor, *Africa Pulse*, Vol. III, No. 5 (December 1972), p. 3.

And what shall be said about evangelism and church growth in South America? The Pentecostal churches in Brazil are growing at a rate of 20 percent a year. Some twenty-five hundred to three thousand new congregations are being formed there every year.

Even among the Indians of South America, who have proved in the past to be so resistant to the gospel, there is now a gracious moving of the Holy Spirit. The Gospel Missionary Union reports a breakthrough in the evangelization of the Quechua Indians in Ecuador. For over seventy years these descendants of the ancient Incas resisted all attempts at conversion. The first break came in 1967 when 116 professed faith in Christ and were baptized. There are now more than 2,500 baptized believers and many more who are undergoing instruction. In 1973 the American Bible Society published a new translation of the Quechua New Testament. The influence of the Quechua church is being felt in other parts of South America. At least ten groups of believers have sprung up in Colombia as a direct result of the evangelistic endeavors of the Quechua believers in Ecuador.

From Bolivia comes word of a similar movement among the Aymara Indians.

> Yesterday (May 15, 1973) I was handed the last report on the Aymara church growth on the Altiplano. It shows tremendous increase, even after the latest figures of February. Forty-one new churches have been raised up in three months! Four hundred and fifty new members have been baptized during the same time.... My life and ministry for the Lord will never be the same. Since I have seen the churches growing and expanding throughout the whole country, I will never try to do anything else in my life. Church planting is exciting! And contagious.[9]

Nowhere is Christian missionary work more thrilling than in the student world, where thousands are turning to Christ every year. Students the world over are known for their open-mindedness and their willingness to examine different points of view. More and more of them are becoming disillusioned with their own religions and are willing to examine the claims of Christianity. The International Fellowship of Evangelical Students, with headquarters in London, now has full-time staff workers in sixty countries serving forty national member movements, and from all of them except the Muslim world come reports of increased attendance and interest. It is still too early to report a breakthrough in student work; but we may be on the threshold of great things.

The General Secretary of IFES writes: "We are working toward the time when hundreds of graduates will cross national and cultural frontiers in obedience to the Lord's missionary mandate to 'go into all

---

[9] Bruno Frigoli, *Church Growth Bulletin*, Vol. IX, No. 6 (July 1973), p. 334.

the world and make disciples of all nations.' "[10] The Christian Union at Oxford University reported the conversion of more than 150 students at its February 1973 mission. That same month a training course was held at Concepcion in Chile. The leader reported:

> We've had a glorious manifestation of the Lord's presence at our camp. We expected 40 students to attend and actually 83 turned up! Some non-Christian students, who at first opposed us, met the Lord and were wonderfully converted. These were led to Christ by Christian students. On the day of departure, the Christian students preached the gospel openly at the railway station and some of the listeners professed faith in Christ.[11]

In November 1973, the Reverend John R. W. Stott conducted an evangelical mission at the University of Nairobi. The mission lasted for eight days. The average attendance was six hundred. Each evening students stayed behind and talked until midnight. A thousand students turned out for the closing meeting.

At Ahmadu Bello University in Zaria, Nigeria, the Fellowship of Christian Students organized a four-day evangelistic crusade with a Nigerian pastor as the featured speaker. The crusade theme was "Who Is Jesus?" On the opening night the crusade faced stiff competition from a troupe of dancers and musicians hired for a special party. But the fears of the crusade sponsors proved groundless. Only fifteen turned up for the party and eight of them left early and joined the crusade meeting. An estimated three thousand students were present each of the four nights of the crusade; some two hundred of them stayed for counseling.

If anyone is thinking seriously of going into student work, he or she should give serious consideration to service on the mission field. That's where the action is.

In this connection it is interesting to learn that the leading universities in Sierra Leone, Ghana, Nigeria, Zaire, Uganda, Kenya, and Ethiopia now have important departments in theological disciplines. Qualified missionary-theologians would find a challenging field in any of these universities. That religion has again come into its own on the college campuses of the United States is seen from the fact that two prestigious universities—Stanford and UCLA—have both introduced an undergraduate major in religious studies. Could any professor ask for a more exciting mission field?

Dr. Harold O. J. Brown, former Theological Secretary of the International Fellowship of Evangelical Students, after a tour of the Far East wrote to the dean of a well-known theological seminary in the United States:

[10] Chua Wee Hian, *IFES Newsletter,* October 1973.
[11] *IFES Prayer and Praise Bulletin,* April 1973.

> There are some very real opportunities for theological teaching,
> to a large extent in English, in seminaries in all of the countries
> of South East Asia. . . . In Singapore, Hong Kong, Malaysia, the
> Philippines, and even Taiwan and Indonesia, there are a num-
> ber of opportunities for a young man who is willing to devote
> several years of his life to the task. In many of these places
> there are relatively under-staffed theological schools facing a
> tremendous challenge. They have eager students, mostly with a
> rather low degree of background but with a high level of zeal
> and often with a tremendous faith. In all of these countries, the
> educational level and academic aspirations are rising rapidly.
> People with minimal academic theological training are no longer
> capable of filling the churches' need in many cases. Perhaps the
> greatest handicap for the existing evangelical schools is lack of
> faculty.[12]

That appeal is now four years old but the need still remains. In
fact it is greater than ever. Fully qualified theologians prefer to remain
in the States where, so they think, they can have wider scope for their
erudition. The need for better-educated pastors in the Third World is
ten times greater than it is here at home. The person who goes abroad
to teach theology has the satisfaction of knowing that he is filling a
role that few other people are qualified to fill. And he will not find
anywhere else in the world a more highly motivated group of students.
He will be their *guru* and as long as they live they will cherish the
memory of his name.

If teaching at the graduate level is too high for many missionaries,
there are ample opportunities to teach at the Bible college level. There
are hundreds of Bible schools on the mission field and they are always
in need of competent, dedicated teachers who love the Lord, know the
Word, and have the gift of teaching. Greater Europe Mission now
operates ten Bible schools with more to open in the next few years.
Total enrollment in these schools now stands at 445, an increase of
16 percent in the last year. The Assemblies of God maintain ninety-
five Bible schools in ninety-two countries of the world. Total enrollment is 4,675. Indeed there are very few missions that do not have
at least one Bible school. The opportunities here are endless.

Another opportunity, quite unknown in the United States, is the
teaching of Religious Knowledge in the government schools in many
parts of the Third World. In Anglophone Africa the governments require that all students study religion, either Islam or Christianity. The
African churches at this point do not have qualified teachers in sufficient numbers to meet the demand. Hence many missionaries are now
employed on the staff of the government schools teaching Christianity
and getting paid to do the job.

---

[12] Harold O. J. Brown, *Letter,* January 9, 1970.

Kagoro in Nigeria was for years a large Sudan Interior Mission educational center, with a mission-operated primary school, secondary school, teachers college, and Bible college. The mission now maintains only the Bible college with seven staff members; but it has six missionaries teaching Bible classes full time in the government-administered schools. One of the missionaries was thrilled with her new assignment. She wrote: "I am doing more direct missionary work now than I have done in my sixteen years in Nigeria."[13] Les Greer reports thirty-seven Bible classes a week in the government schools in the city of Kano and more opportunities for personal witness than he can handle. In addition to the Religious Knowledge classes, the teachers are often responsible for baptismal classes, leadership training courses, monthly Communion services, and the promotion of the Fellowship of Christian Students, which has branches in most of the high schools and colleges.

More strategic than teaching Religious Knowledge is the training of student teachers to teach the same subject. In this way the missionary-teacher is multiplying himself many times. A member of the Overseas Missionary Fellowship was asked by the government of Indonesia to prepare a complete syllabus for the teaching of Christianity in the public school system of Indonesia, which is a Muslim country. Another missionary was asked to undertake a similar assignment for the government of South Africa. One could hardly ask for a more strategic ministry.

The government of South Sudan is trying desperately to rehabilitate the devastated countryside after seventeen years of civil war which took tens of thousands of lives and drove at least 250,000 refugees into exile. Word has just been received that the minister of education wants nineteen qualified teachers and administrators to go to South Sudan to help set up several new high schools now on the planning boards. He prefers to have Christians and has asked the missionaries now working under the African Committee for the Rehabilitation of Southern Sudan to recruit them. It remains to be seen whether our Christian young people will rise to the challenge. In the 1960s similar calls came from Nigeria and Kenya, but neither of the two missions asked to do the recruiting was able to secure the required number of Christian teachers; so the government turned to the Peace Corps.

Another exciting opportunity is the translation and distribution of the Scriptures. Here in this country Bibles and New Testaments are "a dime a dozen," and we have more English versions than we can possibly read. But in many parts of the mission field the churches are still waiting for the Old Testament. Indeed, some of them do not have the complete New Testament.

---

[13] Jennifer Weller, *Africa Now* (September-October 1973), p. 12.

When the New Testament in the Bassa language of Liberia went on sale for the first time in 1971 the people danced in the streets, and the Christian Literature Crusade Bookstore had to lock the iron burglar grill across the doorway and sell the books through the grillwork. Missionary Dave Stull said, "It looked like the New York Stock Exchange. We sold 300 copies in the first fifteen minutes."[14] June Hobley, the missionary who translated the Bassa New Testament, was hugged and greeted by the buyers. Later the CLC bookmobile headed for an inland market and sold its entire supply of six hundred New Testaments in one day.

Never in the history of the Christian church has the demand for the Word of God been as great as it is today. Kenneth Taylor's *Living Bible* first appeared in July 1971. In five years time it has sold over twenty million copies. Four million additional copies are now on order and will be delivered in the next few months. *Good News for Modern Man*, the New Testament in Today's English published by the American Bible Society, first went on sale in the mid-1960s; already it has sold over fifty million copies.

In 1975 the American Bible Society distributed 191 million copies of the Scriptures. The Bible Society's latest plan is to raise sixty-three million dollars over the next twelve years to help newly literate people around the world improve their reading ability. *Good News for New Readers* will involve the production and distribution of 725 million Bible stories in four-page illustrated leaflet form. These were translated into more than two hundred languages by 1975. It is by far the most ambitious program ever undertaken by the Bible Society in its 160 years of history.

All around the world Scripture distribution is on the increase. In Malagasy distribution jumped from 125,000 copies in 1973 to 325,000 in 1975. In August 1975 a hundred college students distributed half a million Scriptures in Taiwan. Even behind the Iron Curtain, Bibles are being published and distributed in record numbers.

For the first time in history the Roman Catholic Church is actively engaged in Scripture distribution. In the Philippines more than two thousand persons, the majority of them Roman Catholics, participated in "Operation Philip" training courses conducted by the Bible Society's sixteen full-time distribution/promoters during 1971. As a result distribution increased almost 27 percent. Recently the Bible Society in Kenya received an order from the Roman Catholic Church for 160,000 Bibles in eight languages and 240,000 New Testaments in nine languages. Little wonder that sales jumped almost 100 percent in 1973.

A new and fascinating project has been promoted by Rochunga

---

[14] Dave Stull, *Africa Now* (September-October 1971), p. 12.

Pudaite, General Director of Partnership Missions. The idea is to send copies of the New Testament to all persons in the Third World whose names appear in the telephone directories. Already 1,350,000 New Testaments have been mailed to India. The attractive cover, with a picture of the beautiful Taj Mahal and the title *Love Is the Greatest*, makes a strong cultural appeal to the people of India. The response has been remarkable. The office in New Delhi is receiving a thousand letters of appreciation each day. On his last visit to India Mr. Pudaite placed a small ad in a New Delhi newspaper, inviting those who had received copies of the book to come to an auditorium to meet him and to hear the story of his life. Two hours ahead of time the large auditorium was packed out. These were all upper-class people, people in a position to afford telephone service. At the close of the address an invitation was given to all who wanted to know more about Jesus Christ and the Bible to come to the front. Half the audience responded. A unique feature of this New Testament is that the Gospel of John comes first because it, more than Matthew, appeals to the Hindu mind.

Another very fruitful form of missionary activity is Bible correspondence courses. One of the earliest courses was *Light of Life*, initiated by Dr. Don Hillis in India back in the 1940s. It began with one course in the Gospel of John in Marathi. Today its five basic courses (John, Acts, Galatians, Mark, and Luke) are available in 70 languages. To date three and a half million persons have received the initial lessons. Of these, 625,000 have completed one or more courses. The Emmaus Bible Correspondence School has produced sixty different courses which have been translated into 120 languages. Some six million persons have enrolled in these courses.

Bible correspondence courses are particularly effective in Muslim countries, where the people are afraid to identify with the Christian church. Over twenty thousand Muslims in Tunisia and an equal number in Morocco have signed up for courses sponsored by the North Africa Mission and the Gospel Missionary Union respectively. So popular were these courses that the government of Tunisia closed the bookstore from which the courses were sent. The operation was moved to France, where it became part of the Radio School of the Bible's outreach. In Iran the requests for Bible correspondence courses were so numerous that missionaries had to be taken off other jobs to cope with the mail. Since the liberation of Bangladesh over twelve thousand persons, most of them Muslims, have signed up for Bible courses. In six months time the missionary staff was increased from one to six. Even so it has not been possible to keep up with the demand.

Missionary radio is another exciting field in which to labor. There are today some sixty radio stations owned and operated by Christian missions in all parts of the world. Half a dozen of them are very large and powerful. These include Station ELWA in Liberia; Station HCJB in Ecuador; Far East Broadcasting Company in Manila, Korea, and Seychelles Island; Trans World Radio in Monaco, Bonaire, Sri Lanka, and Swaziland; Radio Voice of the Gospel in Ethiopia; and TEAM in Korea. Some of these stations have three hundred members on the staff, including nationals as well as missionaries. Two of them operate a hospital in connection with their work. Several of them have a Bible Institute of the Air by means of which they do follow-up work. In addition there are hundreds of missionaries and nationals producing radio and television programs for broadcasting over commercial and government stations. This is a wide-open field and one that requires highly trained technical personnel not always easy to recruit.

A new and rapidly developing field is Christian journalism. Most missions are weak in this area and the national churches are almost completely destitute of well-trained journalists. With tens of millions of new literates in the world every year, and with the governments of the Third World in some cases devoting 20 to 30 percent of the national budget to education, it goes without saying that both church and mission must produce more and better literature than in the past. The most desperate need is for professional missionary-journalists who can train nationals to produce good, attractive, well-written literature in the vernacular.

These are days of great opportunity. The doors that are open are *wide* open. People the world over are receptive as they have never been before. The fields are indeed white unto harvest. Bill Bright, President of Campus Crusade for Christ, has just returned from a world tour. This is what he says: "The more I see of what God is doing in the world, the more I am convinced that we stand today, *at this very hour,* on the threshold of the greatest spiritual advance the world has ever witnessed. Clearly God is telling us that tens of millions are ready and waiting to know Jesus Christ."[15]

Campus Crusade for Christ, the fastest growing Christian organization in the world, has five thousand staff members, almost half of them overseas. Its latest venture is the Agape Movement, a ministry that is designed to recruit and train 100,000 men and women to give two years or more of their lives to sharing God's love with the people in more than two million villages, cities, and university centers all over the world by 1980.

Another aggressive group is Wycliffe Bible Translators, whose missionaries are now at work in 665 tribes in twenty-five countries the world. There are still more than 2,000 tribes without any portion of the Word of God. WBT intends to zero in on those 160 million

---

[15] Bill Bright, *Christmas Letter,* 1973.

people. To this end they are expanding their work with every passing month. Their ultimate goal is aptly described in the phrase: "Every Tribe by Eighty-Five."

The Unfinished Task

Before we can decide whether a task is finished or unfinished it is necessary to define both its nature and extent. What is the extent of the Christian mission? It is coterminous with the world. It is a global task. We have been commanded by the Lord Jesus Christ to go into *all* the world, to preach the gospel to *every* creature, and to make disciples of *all* nations. And when we get through we shall have in the church converts "from every tribe and tongue and people and nation" (Re 5:9). This gospel must be preached in all the world. Then, and only then, will the end come (Mt 24:14). This is the extent of the task.

What is the nature of the task? Is it to civilize, to Christianize, or to evangelize the world? Obviously it is not to civilize, for large portions of the world were civilized long before we were. Nor is it to Christianize, for even that part of the world that we identify as Christendom has not been completely Christianized. There is nothing in Scripture or history to support the view that the entire world is going to be converted to Jesus Christ—at least not in this age. We are left, then, with world evangelization. That, without doubt, is the supreme task of the church.

But this poses another question. What are we to understand by the term "evangelization?" Or to put it more concretely: When is a country or a people evangelized? When they have heard the gospel once? Twice? Ten times? A hundred times? When the Bible has been translated? When a church has been established?

A people may be said to be evangelized when everyone has had the gospel presented to him often enough and clearly enough to enable him to make an intelligent response for or against Jesus Christ as Savior and Lord.

There are, of course, degrees of evangelization. Not everyone in a given society will be equally knowledgeable, even though all have the same access to knowledge. There are still some people in the United States who do not know who Henry Kissinger is and others who have never heard of Johnny Carson. The same applies to a knowledge of the gospel. Even here in the United States there are millions of persons who have never seen a copy of the Bible or attended a church service. Indeed, some have never heard the name of Christ except as a curse word. If this is true, then even the United States is still unevangelized even though the Bible is the best seller year after year and the Christian church is the largest and most influential institution in the country.

There is another aspect of the problem of world evangelization. It is not something that can be achieved once and for all. Every generation needs to be evangelized all over again, for every thirty years we have an entirely new group of people. One generation may be predominantly Christian while the following one is only nominally so. This in turn may be followed by a third generation that is more pagan than Christian. In the history of the church there have been times of renewal and advance and there have been periods of stagnation and decline. Nothing can be taken for granted. The candlestick may be removed and the church left without light. Or the church may be disobedient and allowed to go into captivity. The church that fails to live by the law of God will find itself under the judgment of God.

This may be happening right under our eyes. We are now talking about a "post-Christian era" here in the West. It may be that God's center of gravity is about to shift from the West to the East. By the end of this century it is quite possible that Africa may be a predominantly Christian continent and Europe virtually pagan. And the United States may not be far behind.

> In thinking about the Church it is easy to slip into the erroneous idea that, because a country or parish has once been Christian it will remain so until the end of time. . . . One generation succeeds to another, and that which comes is not naturally and inevitably Christian. . . . The task of the Church must always be unfinished, because so much energy must go into the endless business of winning the younger generation for Christ.[16]

So we see that the task of world evangelization has two aspects. It is perennial and universal at the same time. For this reason the task is never finished.

If the task remains unfinished, it is only right to ask: What remains to be done? The answer is: Plenty.

The population of the world now stands at 4.0 billion and is increasing at the amazing rate of 80 million every year. In round figures *approximately* one third of the world's population are professing Christians—more than half of them Roman Catholics. Another third has been exposed to the Christian message in one form or another but has failed to respond affirmatively. Another third has yet to hear the name of Jesus Christ for the first time.

Every concerned Christian must agree that there is little comfort to be derived from those statistics. In spite of the enormous amount of time, energy, and money that have gone into the Christian mission in the last 250 years we are not quite holding our own. In 1960 Christians

---

[16] Stephen Neill, *The Unfinished Task* (London: Edinburgh House Press, 1957), p. 35.

represented about 34 percent of the world's population. Today the ratio is closer to 30 percent, *and dropping slowly every year.* Black Africa is the only continent where we are making significant gains; but these are more than offset by the losses suffered in the vast continent of Asia, where more than half the world's population is located.

In the Muslim world, where there are some 600 million souls, we have yet to achieve anything resembling a breakthrough, except in Indonesia, where on the island of Java several hundred thousand Muslims have come to Christ. In all other Muslim countries converts are hand-picked, one by one, and a public baptism is a rare phenomenon. Bangladesh, the second largest Muslim country in the world, is now a secular state. It remains to be seen to what extent this will facilitate missionary work.

In Asia there is only one predominantly Christian country—the Philippines, where 72 percent of the people are Roman Catholics and 10 or 12 percent are Protestants. We are making significant progress in several other countries. We are doing well in Korea, Indonesia, and South Vietnam, where approximately 10 percent of the population are professing Christians. A people movement in Taiwan has brought most of the 250,000 animistic tribespeople into the Christian fold; but the Taiwanese, like Buddhists elsewhere, have not responded in anything like the same manner.

In the other countries of Asia we are barely holding our own; in some we are actually falling behind. In India, with 600 million souls, the Christians represent about 2.4 percent of the population. That ratio has not changed in the last twenty years. The situation in Communist China is difficult to evaluate precisely. In 1950, the last year for which we have reliable statistics, the total number of Christians was four million, of whom three million were Roman Catholics. During the last twenty-three years the population of China has increased by at least 220 million; but the number of Christians has probably decreased by a million or two. Here is one area—a rather large one—where, through no fault of ours, we are losing ground rapidly.

Another large country is Japan with 107 million people, of whom only 1 million are professing Christians. In Burma the tribal churches, without missionaries since 1966, are thriving; but the Burmese Buddhists, who form well over 95 percent of the population, are practically untouched. In Thailand, the only other large country in that part of the world, there is 1 Christian to every 999 Buddhists. Like Goliath of old the great ethnic religions of Asia are still defying the armies of the living God. We still have a long way to go before Asia's more than 2 billion people are evangelized.

In Africa the picture is much brighter. Here is the one major region of the world where Christianity is forging ahead with such vigor that some experts are predicting that by the year 2000 Africa will be a pre-dominantly Christian continent. Already Christians represent 50 per-cent of the total population of Black Africa—everything south of the Sahara Desert. We have often been told that the Muslims are making converts faster than we are. That may have been true ten or twenty years ago; it is true no longer. Christians in Black Africa now out-number the Muslims by 75 million. In some countries the Christians now represent anywhere from 75 to 95 percent of the population. In the largest country, Nigeria, the Christian ratio has climbed rapidly in the last decade to 46 percent, two percentage points ahead of the Muslims. Animism, now referred to as "traditional religion," is on the way out; and the battle for the soul of Africa is between Chris-tianity and Islam, with Christianity having the edge.

In Latin America the situation is unique. The Protestants, especially the Pentecostals, are registering fantastic gains in such countries as Brazil, Chile, and Colombia. In 1900 there were fifty thousand Protes-tants in Latin America. By 1950 the number had climbed to ten million. Twenty years later the figure had doubled to twenty million. Today it is closer to twenty-five million.

It must be remembered, however, that almost all of these con-verts have come from a nominally Catholic background; so the overall picture of Christianity versus "heathenism" is not appreciably altered by the tremendous growth of evangelical Christianity in Latin America. The Roman Catholic Church dominates the religious scene in that part of the world and claims 90 percent of the people as adherents; but by its own confession very few of them—perhaps 10 percent—are practicing Catholics. This has left them wide open to the overtures of the gospel as presented by the Evangelicals.

Europe and North America are also part of the mission field. They too should be included in the tally. An estimated 160 million people in Europe make no profession of religion. The two big denominations are the Lutherans on the continent and the Anglicans in the United Kingdom. In both Communions membership is down and the bottom has dropped out of church attendance. By no stretch of the imagination can Europe be called a Christian continent. This is one area of the world where Christianity seems to be losing ground.

In North America the scene is considerably brighter; but even here there is cause for concern. The main-line denominations, which repre-sent the majority of Protestants, are reducing their staffs and slashing their budgets, particularly that portion that relates to foreign missions. The conservative denominations and the many independent churches are growing; but because they are small their growth hardly makes up for the decline in the main-line churches. Church membership in the United States remains fairly steady year after year, about 63 percent;

and church attendance is high as compared with Europe—60 percent for the Catholics, 40 percent for the Protestants, and 25 percent for the Jews.

We are grateful to God for the growth of the Christian Church in many parts of the world; at the same time we are painfully aware of certain elements and areas of weakness. Many of the older churches stand in need of revival if they are ever to assume their role in the evangelization of the world. It is commonly known that the most zealous Christians are first-generation believers, whose conversion experience is generally very meaningful. There is often a noticeable cooling off in second- and third-generation Christians.

After describing the remarkable ministry of Bishop Azariah of Dornakal, Stephen Neill goes on to say: "The work in Dornakal was very far from perfect. As we have already seen, at the end of his life Bishop Azariah was distressed to find in the second and third generations of Christians so much less zeal and devotion than he had hoped for."[17]

After the second or third generation Christianity tends to take on cultural overtones, and its adherents lose all desire to share their faith with friends and neighbors. The churches then become so moribund that their chief preoccupation is not the salvation of the lost but their own survival.

In the older regions of the mission field there are thousands of such churches that need to be revived. If these churches with their well-educated pastors and their highly literate, and sometimes wealthy, congregations could be revived they could easily spearhead an evangelistic thrust that would be felt throughout the whole of the Third World. During the 1940s John Sung was mightily used of God to revive the older Chinese churches in Southeast Asia. In every church he formed an evangelistic band, which helped to keep the revival fires burning. To this day the older members of those churches still talk of John Sung and his powerful ministry. One revivalist like John Sung or Jonathan Goforth can do more for the evangelization of the world than ten evangelists who win converts but fail to revive the churches.[18]

The churches in the Third World are not the only ones that need to be revived. The sending churches in the West have the same problem. They too have a tendency to cool off in the second and third generations. Indeed, every movement secular or sacred tends to revert to type with the passing of time. Even the Communists are not immune to this kind of problem. The Cultural Revolution in China in 1966 was

---

[17] Stephen Neill, *The Unfinished Task* (London: Edinburgh House Press, 1957), p. 129.
[18] For the ministry of these two men see Leslie Lyall, *John Sung: Flame for God in the Far East* (Chicago: Moody Press, 1956); and Jonathan Goforth, *By My Spirit* (Grand Rapids: Zondervan, 1942).

an attempt on the part of Mao Tse-tung to stem the rising tide of bourgeois thinking that was beginning to reappear in Chinese society, after only seventeen years.

There is a good deal of dead wood in our American churches. It is not uncommon for a church with 2,500 members to have only 750 present on Sunday morning. In our larger denominations the average church member gives less than three dollars a year to world missions. On the other hand some of the younger and smaller denominations are giving ten and twenty times that much. Throughout history revival and missions have always gone together. When the former ceases, the latter is sure to languish. At home or overseas the churches stand in need of continuing renewal.

Closely allied to the revival of the churches is a crying need for a spiritual ministry to the pastors throughout the Third World. There are tens of thousands of these faithful men serving small, struggling, semiliterate congregations. Most of them are underpaid and over-worked. They are constantly giving out; seldom do they have an opportunity to take in. Their entire "library" may occupy less than two feet of shelf space. They shepherd small flocks in the midst of a pre-dominantly non-Christian culture. They have no one with whom they can share their burdens. Often they become weary and discouraged.

World Vision International has done more than any other group to minister to the spiritual needs of these pastors. In twenty-two years it has conducted eighty-one pastors' conferences with a total attendance of 56,268. Pastors from all denominations are invited to a central place for a week or ten days of rich ministry by such outstanding Bible teachers as Paul Rees, Chandu Ray, Carl Henry, and others. All travel expenses are paid; room and board are provided free. All the pastors have to do is to attend the meetings, enjoy the fellowship, and drink in the exposition of the Word. For many of these men a gathering of this kind is like a blood transfusion. They return to their churches refreshed and invigorated in body, mind, and spirit. Only eternity will reveal what has been accomplished by these conferences. This is a vital ministry that should by all means be continued in the future.

Another unfinished task is theological education. We rejoice when Dr. George Peters tells us that the non-Christian peoples of the world are more eager to hear the gospel than we are to preach it; but the mushroom growth in evidence in some countries is a cause for deep concern. In Latin America some sixty thousand leaders who function as pastors in the churches have had little or no Bible training. Only fifteen thousand out of the seventy-five thousand church leaders have had what might be termed adequate theological training. Only in half a dozen countries—Japan and Korea among them—is there anything like a sufficient number of trained pastors. In other countries it is not uncommon for one man to have the oversight of anywhere from one to ten congregations.

Only in recent years has a concerted effort been made to meet this appalling need. The new program known as Theological Education by Extension is discussed in section 3 of chapter 4. It is still too early to know how effective it will be; but preliminary reports are most encouraging. This is an ongoing task. It will take us many years to provide the Third World churches with a sufficient number of fully trained pastors.

Another part of the unfinished task is pioneer work. With today's emphasis on the rapidly developing national churches and the talk about urbanization and its effect on Christian missions, there is a prevailing notion that there is no more pioneer work to be done. Nothing could be further from the truth. Indeed, one outstanding missiologist reminds us that "the greater part of the missionary work that ought to be carried on is still pioneer work."[19] The General Secretary of New Tribes Mission writes:

> There are many, many tribes still outside the orbit of civilization and we would like to see many more missionary candidates recognize this. In the Sepik River area of Papua New Guinea, we have recently gone in. There are almost 200 tribes in that area and a few other missions are working with just a few of these tribes. . . . In the Solomon Islands we have knowledge of 40 tribes and work being carried on among only four of them. This is true of the larger islands in the South Pacific, also. While most of these tribes are not savages, nevertheless they live outside the realm of civilization and much work needs to be done among them.[20]

David Barrett reminds us that of 860 tribes in Africa, 213 are completely or heavily Muslim and have virtually no Christian witness. In addition there are still 236 tribes largely unevangelized, representing 13 percent of the population. There are still tribes in the great Amazon Basin that have yet to establish contact with the outside world.

There are infant churches in the pioneer areas without leadership that are calling for outside help. Such a plea came recently from Nagaland in northeast India:

> We send you greetings in the name of Jesus Christ. We are all fine. We have accepted the Faith since 1969. No one ever taught us about Christ. But we were hungry for the eternal message. Fourteen villages have accepted the Faith. The present membership is 1,112. There are still countless people who want to become Christian, but there is no one who knows the Bible well. . . . We have been looking for a missionary family who could live

---

[19] Stephen Neill, *Call to Mission* (Philadelphia: Fortress Press, 1970), p. 101.
[20] J. B. Knutson, *Personal Letter,* August 23, 1973.

with us and teach us daily. We are also looking for someone
who could help us in medical treatment. We have been waiting
such a long period for someone, but still not a single person has
come to teach us.[21]

There are still areas of the world where the Christian presence is
either very weak or nonexistent: Sikkim, Bhutan, Saudi Arabia, Mauritania, Afghanistan, Nepal, and Somalia. The Christian church should
not rest content until all these countries are open to the gospel. And
what shall be said about China with its 800 million souls living under a
Communist government that is bent on the ultimate destruction of all
forms of religion? Now that China seems to be turning its face once
again toward the West, the Christian church throughout the world
should make the evangelization of that immense country a matter of
long and earnest prayer.

Still largely neglected are the intellectuals in the Third World.
In the past missionaries, for reasons not altogether invalid, ministered
almost exclusively to the lower classes. This is one reason, though not
the only one, why so many national churches today lack well-educated
leaders. Now that higher education is available to the masses, it is
imperative that we give more attention to the evangelization of the
intellectual classes, especially the students on the university campuses.
In some of the large cities of the Third World, Tokyo, Manila, Jakarta,
and Calcutta, there are dozens of colleges and universities and tens of
thousands of students. The Christian witness in these institutions comes
almost entirely from the outside, sponsored largely by such groups as
Campus Crusade, Inter-Varsity Christian Fellowship, International
Fellowship of Evangelical Students, Navigators, and others. An IFES
staff worker reports that there are 700,000 students in forty-four universities in Italy; but committed Christians number fewer than fifty.
The ratio wouldn't be any better in France.

There are two ways to have an effective witness in these secular
universities of the Third World. Nonprofessional missionaries with
advanced degrees could seek teaching positions in these institutions.
Once on the faculty these dedicated Christians could have a most
effective ministry, to some extent in the classroom (depending on the
subjects taught) and certainly in social intercourse outside the classroom. A second method would be for the missions to establish hostels,
with or without boarding facilities, in close proximity to the universities. Christian students needing fellowship and moral support could
live at the hostel and study in the university. Others could visit the
hostel, play games, read periodicals, listen to good music, engage in rap
sessions, Bible study, etc. From the long-range point of view it is more

---

[21] *Church Growth Bulletin,* Vol. X, No. 1 (September 1973), p. 360.

advantageous to win one university student than to win half a dozen peasants who can neither read nor write.

No church can ever become permanently strong and virile without the Scriptures in its own tongue. This was one reason for the demise of the large church in North Africa at the time of the Muslim invasion. One of the greatest achievements of the missionaries has been the translation of the Scriptures into more than fifteen hundred languages. This represents a monumental piece of work, and the churches of the Third World are forever indebted to them and the Bible societies for giving them the Bible in their own tongue at a price they can afford to pay.

A closer look at the situation will reveal the fact that of these 1,577 translations, only 261 involve the entire Bible and another 384 the New Testament. The remaining 932 translations are single Books, called Portions. This means that in spite of all that has been done there are many large churches on the mission field that are still without the New Testament. It is difficult for us in the West to visualize a Church of ten thousand members without a complete Bible. But such a phenomenon is by no means uncommon on the mission field.

Wycliffe Bible Translators have done yeoman service in this area. They have translators in 665 tribes who have already produced Scriptures in four hundred languages; but most of these have been Portions. To date sixty-five complete New Testaments have been produced. WBT make it a practice to remain with one tribe only until the New Testament is translated, then they move on to another tribe and repeat the performance there. In this way they hope to cover every tribe by 1985. They still have more than two thousand tribes to go. It is estimated that these tribes represent about 160 million people. But even if they achieve their goal they will have given to these tribes only the New Testament; they will still need the Old Testament.

Whenever Bible translation is mentioned we naturally think of first-time translations. These, of course, are very important, but they are not the whole story. Languages change as we have good cause to know. When they change significantly a new translation of the Scriptures is needed. This is called revision rather than translation. At the present time the United Bible Societies are working with some three thousand missionary-linguists at work on some eight hundred different projects, most of them revisions of earlier translations. This is a never-ending task.

The production of Christian literature is another facet of the unfinished task. In addition to the Scriptures the churches and their leaders need a long list of helps: hymnbooks; commentaries; dictionaries; study, devotional, and expository books; Sunday school and Christian education materials; periodicals; audio-visual aids, and a hundred-and-one other helps that can be found in any Christian bookstore in the United States.

Here in this country every major denomination has its own hymnal, its own Sunday school materials, and in many cases its own publishing house. If a Sunday school superintendent runs out of materials he has only to drop a postcard in the mail on Monday and the desired materials will be on hand for the following Sunday. Would to God it were that simple on the mission field! The average American church member cannot possibly visualize what Christian work is like in many parts of the mission field. The difference between the services and facilities available there and those available here is like the difference between the old general store and the modern supermarket. There is no comparison.

Imagine trying to teach Sunday school without any helps at all, or trying to prepare a sermon without a single commentary or expository book. It's done all the time on the mission field, not by choice but of necessity. Many a pastor has only the notes he acquired in Bible school—if indeed he ever went to Bible school. In preparing for his Sunday morning service he must rely on his own knowledge of the Scriptures. Little wonder that some of them fall back on dreams and visions.

Is the task of world evangelization completed? From all four corners of the earth comes a resounding *No!* Far from being completed, we have hardly reached the halfway point. To quit now would jeopardize the entire enterprise.

Bibliography

(Arranged topically)

CHURCH GROWTH

Allen, Roland. *The Spontaneous Expansion of the Church.* Grand Rapids: Eerdmans, 1962.

Cook, Harold R. *Historic Patterns of Church Growth.* Chicago: Moody Press, 1971.

Hodges, Melvin L. *A Guide to Church Planting.* Chicago: Moody Press, 1973.

McGavran, Donald, et al. *Church Growth and Christian Mission.* New York: Harper and Row, 1965.

McGavran, Donald. *How Churches Grow.* New York: Friendship Press, 1955.

————. *Understanding Church Growth.* Grand Rapids: Eerdmans, 1970.

McQuilkin, J. Robertson. *How Biblical Is the Church Growth Movement?* Chicago: Moody Press, 1973.

Pickett, J. W. *Christian Mass Movements in India.* New York: Abingdon Press, 1933.

————. *The Dynamics of Church Growth.* New York: Abingdon Press, 1963.

————, et al. *Church Growth and Group Conversion* (5th ed.). South Pasadena, CA: William Carey Library, 1973.

Read, William R., et al. *Latin American Church Growth.* Grand Rapids: Eerdmans, 1969.

Tippett, Alan R. *Church Growth and the Word of God.* Grand Rapids: Eerdmans, 1970.

————. *God, Man and Church Growth.* Grand Rapids: Eerdmans, 1973.

CRUCIAL ISSUES

Beaver, R. Pierce. *The Missionary Between the Times.* Garden City, NY: Doubleday, 1968.

Boberg, John T. and Scherer, James A., (eds.). *Missions in the '70s*. Chicago: Chicago Cluster of Theological Schools, 1972.

Bridston, Keith R. *Mission Myth and Reality*. New York: Friendship Press, 1965.

Danker, William J., and Kang, Wi Jo. *The Future of the Christian World Mission*. Grand Rapids: Eerdmans, 1971.

Devanandan, P. D. *Christian Issues in Southern Asia*. New York: Friendship Press, 1963.

Fenton, Horace L., Jr. *Myths About Missions*. Downers Grove, IL: InterVarsity Press, 1973.

Kane, J. Herbert. *Winds of Change in the Christian Mission*. Chicago: Moody Press, 1973.

McGavran, Donald, (ed.). *Crucial Issues in Missions Tomorrow*. Chicago: Moody Press, 1972.

Street, T. Watson. *On the Growing Edge of the Church*. Richmond, VA: John Knox Press, 1965.

Wagner, C. Peter. *Stop the World I Want to Get On*. Glendale, CA: Regal Books, 1973.

Warren, Max. *Perspective in Mission*. New York: Seabury Press, 1964.

Winter, Ralph D. *The Twenty-Five Unbelievable Years, 1945-1969*. South Pasadena, CA: William Carey Library, 1970.

DICTIONARIES, DIRECTORIES, HANDBOOKS, REPORTS

Beaver, R. Pierce, (ed.). *The Gospel and Frontier Peoples: A Report of a Consultation, December 1972*. South Pasadena, CA: William Carey Library, 1973.

Buker, Raymond B. and Ward, Ted. *The World Directory of Mission-Related Educational Institutions*. South Pasadena, CA: William Carey Library, 1972.

Coxwell, H. Wakelin and Grubb, Kenneth, (eds.). *World Christian Handbook, 1968*. Nashville: Abingdon Press, 1968.

Dayton, Edward R., (ed.). *Mission Handbook: North American Protestant Ministries Overseas*, (10th ed.). Monrovia, CA: Missions Advanced Research and Communication Center, 1973.

Douglas, J. D. (ed.). *Let the Earth Hear His Voice: International Congress on World Evangelization, Lausanne*. Minneapolis: World Wide Publications, 1975.

Goddard, Burton L., (ed.). *The Encyclopedia of Modern Christian Missions*. Camden, NJ: Nelson, 1967.

Neill, Stephen; Anderson, Gerald H.; and Goodwin, John, (eds.). *Concise Dictionary of the Christian World Mission*. London: Lutterworth Press, 1971.

ENCOUNTER: CHRISTIAN/NONCHRISTIAN

Bavinck, J. H. *The Church Between Temple and Mosque*. Grand Rapids: Eerdmans, 1966.

————. *The Impact of Christianity on the Non-Christian World*. Grand Rapids: Eerdmans, 1948.

Corwin, Charles. *East to Eden? Religion and the Dynamics of Social Change*. Grand Rapids: Eerdmans, 1972.

Kraemer, Hendrik. *The Christian Message in a Non-Christian World.* New York: International Missionary Council, 1938.
———. *World Cultures and World Religions: The Coming Dialogue.* London: Lutterworth Press, 1960.
McKain, David W., (ed.). *Christianity: Some Non-Christian Appraisals.* New York: McGraw-Hill, 1964.
Neill, Stephen. *Christian Faith and Other Faiths.* New York: Oxford University Press, 1961.
Niles, Daniel T. *Buddhism and the Claims of Christ.* Richmond, VA: John Knox Press, 1967.
Stowe, David M. *When Faith Meets Faith.* New York: Friendship Press, 1963.
Subbamma, B. V. *Christ Confronts India.* Madras: Diocesan Press, 1973.
Toynbee, Arnold. *Christianity Among the Religions of the World.* New York: Scribners, 1957.
Warneck, Joh. *The Living Christ and Dying Heathenism.* Grand Rapids: Baker Book House, 1954.
Yamamori, T. and Charles R. Taber, (eds.). *Christopaganism or Indigenous Christianity.* South Pasadena: William Carey Library, 1975.

ENCOUNTER: ECUMENICAL/EVANGELICAL

Beyerhaus, Peter. *Missions: Which Way? Humanization or Redemption.* Grand Rapids: Zondervan, 1971.
———. *Shaken Foundations: Theological Foundations for Mission.* Grand Rapids: Zondervan, 1972.
Horner, Norman A., (ed.). *Protestant Crosscurrents in Mission: The Ecumenical-Conservative Encounter.* Nashville: Abingdon Press, 1968.
———. *Cross and Crucifix in Mission: A Comparison of Protestant-Roman Catholic Missionary Strategy.* New York: Abingdon Press, 1965.
McGavran, Donald, (ed.). *Eye of the Storm: The Great Debate in Missions.* Waco, TX: Word Books, 1972.
Winter, Ralph D., (ed.). *Evangelical Response to Bangkok.* South Pasadena, CA: William Carey Library, 1973.

EVANGELISM

Bradshaw, Malcolm R. *Church Growth through Evangelism-in-Depth.* South Pasadena, CA: William Carey Library, 1969.
Gerber, Vergil. *A Manual for Evangelism/Church Growth.* South Pasadena, CA: William Carey Library, 1973.
Green, Michael. *Evangelism in the Early Church.* Grand Rapids: Eerdmans, 1970.
Henry, Carl F. H. and Mooneyham, W. Stanley, (eds.). *One Race, One Gospel, One Task: World Congress on Evangelism—Berlin 1966,* (2 vols.). Minneapolis: World Wide Publications, 1967.
Lageer, Eileen. *New Life for All.* Chicago: Moody Press, 1969.
Latin America Mission. *Evangelism In Depth.* Chicago: Moody Press, 1961.
Packer, J. I. *Evangelism and the Sovereignty of God.* Chicago: Inter-Varsity Press, 1961.
Palmer, Donald C. *Explosion of People Evangelism.* Chicago: Moody Press, 1974.
Peters, George W. *Saturation Evangelism.* Grand Rapids: Zondervan, 1970.
Roberts, W. Dayton. *Revolution in Evangelism.* Chicago: Moody Press, 1967.

MISSIONARY APOLOGETIC

Batal, James. *Assignment: Near East.* New York: Friendship Press, 1950.
Broomhall, A. J. *Time for Action: Christian Responsibility to a Non-Christian World.* London: Inter-Varsity Fellowship, 1965.
Exley, Helen and Richard. *In Search of the Missionary.* London: Highway Press, 1970.
Griffiths, Michael. *Give Up Your Small Ambitions.* London: Inter-Varsity Press, 1970.
Neill, Stephen. *Call to Mission.* Philadelphia: Fortress Press, 1971.
———. *The Unfinished Task.* London: Edinburgh House Press, 1957.
Trueblood, Elton. *The Validity of the Christian Mission.* New York: Harper and Row, 1972.
Van Dusen, Henry P. *They Found the Church There.* New York: Friendship Press, 1946.

MISSIONARY LIFE AND WORK

Adolph, Paul E. *Missionary Health Manual.* Chicago: Moody Press, 1970.
Beck, James R. *Parental Preparation of Missionary Children for Boarding School.* Taipei, Taiwan: Mei Ya Publications, 1968.
Brown, Arthur J. *The Foreign Missionary.* New York: Revell, 1950.
Cannon, Joseph L. *For Missionaries Only.* Grand Rapids: Baker Book House, 1969.
Collins, Marjorie A. *Manual for Accepted Candidates.* South Pasadena, CA: William Carey Library, 1973.
———. *Manual for Missionaries on Furlough.* South Pasadena, CA: William Carey Library, 1973.
———. *Who Cares About the Missionary?* Chicago: Moody Press, 1975.
Cook, Harold R. *Missionary Life and Work.* Chicago: Moody Press, 1959.
Fleming, Daniel J. *Living as Comrades.* New York: Agricultural Missions, 1950.
———. *What Would You Do?* New York: Friendship Press, 1949.
Hillis, Don W. *I Don't Feel Called (Thank the Lord!).* Wheaton, IL: Tyndale House, 1973.
Isais, Juan M. *The Other Side of the Coin.* Grand Rapids: Eerdmans, 1966.
Kane, J. Herbert. *The Making of a Missionary.* Grand Rapids: Baker Book House, 1975.
Morgan, G. Helen. *Who'd Be a Missionary?* Fort Washington, PA: Christian Literature Crusade, 1972.
Phillips, J. B. *The Church Under the Cross.* New York: Macmillan, 1956.
Tuggy, Joy T. *The Missionary Wife and Her Work.* Chicago: Moody Press, 1966.
Williamson, Mabel. *Have We No Right?* Chicago: Moody Press, 1957.

MISSIONARY PREPARATION

Cable, Mildred, and French, Francesca. *Ambassadors for Christ.* Chicago: Moody Press, 1935.
Hogben, Rowland. *In Training.* Chicago: Inter-Varsity Christian Fellowship, 1946.
Houghton, A. T. *Preparing to be a Missionary.* London: Inter-Varsity Press, 1956.

Sargent, Douglas N. *The Making of a Missionary*. London: Hodder and Stoughton, 1960.
Soltau, T. Stanley. *Facing the Field*. Grand Rapids: Baker Book House, 1959.

MISSIONS AND COMMUNISM

Bush, Richard C., Jr. *Religion in Communist China*. Nashville: Abingdon Press, 1970.
A Christian's Handbook on Communism. Richmond, VA: John Knox Press, 1964.
Hoffman, Gerhard and Wille, Wilhelm, (eds.). *World Mission and World Communism*. Richmond, VA: John Knox Press, 1971.
Jones, Francis P. *The Church in Communist China: A Protestant Appraisal*. New York: Friendship Press, 1962.
Lyall, Leslie T. *The Church in Mao's China*. Chicago: Moody Press, 1969.
————. *Come Wind, Come Weather*. Chicago: Moody Press, 1960.
MacInnis, Donald E. *Religious Policy and Practice in Communist China*. New York: Macmillan, 1972.
Merwin, Wallace C. and Jones, Francis P., (eds.). *Documents of the Three-Self Movement: Source Materials for the Study of the Protestant Church in Communist China*. New York: Far Eastern Office, Division of Foreign Missions, National Council of the Churches of Christ in the U.S.A., 1963.
Mooneyham, Stan. *China: The Puzzle*. Pasadena, CA: World Vision International, 1971.
Patterson, George N. *Christianity in Communist China*. Waco, TX: Word Books, 1969.
Price, Frank W. *Marx Meets Christ*. Philadelphia: Westminster Press, 1957.
Saunders, J. R. *The Challenge of World Communism in Asia*. Grand Rapids: Eerdmans, 1964.

MISSIONS AND CULTURE

Bosch, David J., (ed.). *Church and Culture Change in Africa*. Pretoria: Kerk-Boekhandel, 1971.
Brown, Ina C. *Understanding Other Cultures*. Englewood Cliffs, NJ: Prentice-Hall, 1963.
Christianity Across Cultures: A Survey of Available Research. Monrovia, CA: Missions Advanced Research and Communication Center, 1970.
Luzbetak, Louis J. *The Church and Cultures*. Techny, IL: Divine Word Press, 1963.
Nida, Eugene A. *Customs and Cultures*. New York: Harper and Row, 1954.
————. *Message and Mission*. New York: Harper and Row, 1960.
————. *Religion Across Cultures*. New York: Harper and Row, 1968.

MISSIONS AND ECUMENICS

Beaver, R. Pierce. *Ecumenical Beginnings in Protestant World Mission*. New York: Nelson, 1962.
Fey, Harold E., (ed.). *A History of the Ecumenical Movement, 1948-1968*. Philadelphia: Westminster Press, 1970.
Hogg, William R. *Ecumenical Foundations: A History of the IMC*. New York: Harper and Row, 1962.
Johnston, Arthur P. *World Evangelism and the Word of God*. Minneapolis: Bethany Fellowship, 1974.

Neill, Stephen. *Brothers of the Faith.* New York: Abingdon Press, 1960.
Rouse, Ruth and Neill, Stephen, (eds.). *A History of the Ecumenical Movement, 1517-1948.* Philadelphia: Westminster Press, 1968.

MISSIONS AND POLITICS

Beaver, R. Pierce. *Envoys of Peace.* Grand Rapids: Eerdmans, 1964.
Deats, Richard L. *Nationalism and Christianity in the Philippines.* Dallas: Southern Methodist University Press, 1967.
Delavignette, R. *Christianity and Colonialism.* New York: Hawthorne, 1964.
Grabill, Joseph L. *Protestant Diplomacy and the Near East.* Minneapolis: University of Minnesota Press, 1971.
Koskinen, A. A. *Missionary Influence as a Political Factor in the Pacific Islands.* Helsinki: Academia Scientiarum Fennicae, 1953.
Liu, Kwang-Ching. *American Missionaries in China.* Cambridge: Harvard University Press, 1971.
Lutz, Jessie G., (ed.). *Christian Missions in China: Evangelists of What?* Boston: D. C. Heath, 1965.
Moorhouse, Geoffrey. *The Missionaries.* New York: J. B. Lippincott, 1973.
Neill, Stephen. *Colonialism and Christian Missions.* New York: McGraw-Hill, 1966.
Oliver, Roland. *The Missionary Factor in East Africa.* London: Longmans, Green and Co., 1952.
Rotberg, Robert I. *Christian Missionaries and the Creation of Northern Rhodesia, 1880-1924.* Princeton: Princeton University Press, 1965.
Thompson, James C. *While China Faced the West: American Reformers in Nationalist China.* Cambridge: Harvard University Press, 1971.
Varg, Paul A. *Missionaries, Chinese and Diplomats.* Princeton: Harvard University Press, 1960.

MISSIONS AND SOCIAL CHANGE

Abrecht, Paul. *The Churches & Rapid Social Change.* London: SCM Press, 1961.
Ajayi, J. F. Ade. *Christian Missions in Nigeria, 1841-1891: The Making of a New Elite.* London: Longmans, Green and Co., 1965.
Considine, John J. *The Missionary's Role in Socio-Economic Betterment.* Glen Rock, NJ: Newman Press, 1960.
Dennis, James S. *Christian Missions and Social Progress,* (3 vols.). New York: Revell, 1897.
Faunce, W. H. P. *The Social Aspects of Foreign Missions.* New York: Missionary Education Movement, 1914.
Goodall, Norman. *Christian Missions & Social Ferment.* London: Epworth Press, 1964.

MISSIONS AND THE STUDENT WORLD

Adeney, David H. *China: Christian Students Face the Revolution.* Downers Grove, IL: Inter-Varsity Press, 1973.
Barkman, Paul, et al. *Christian Collegians and Foreign Missions.* Monrovia, CA: Missions Advanced Research and Communication Center, 1969.
Howard, David M. *Student Power in World Evangelism.* Downers Grove, IL: Inter-Varsity Press, 1970.

MISSIONS IN CRISIS

Almquist, Arden. *Missionary, Come Back.* New York. World, 1970.

Cogswell, James A. *Response: The Church in Mission to a World in Crisis.* Richmond, VA: John Knox Press, 1970.

Dodge, Ralph E. *The Unpopular Missionary.* Westwood, NJ: Revell, 1964.

Fife, Eric S. and Glasser, Arthur F. *Missions in Crisis.* Chicago: Inter-Varsity Press, 1961.

Gerber, Vergil, (ed.). *Missions in Creative Tension: The Green Lake Compendium.* South Pasadena, CA: William Carey Library, 1971.

Kitagawa, Daisuke. *Race Relations and Christian Mission.* New York: Friendship Press, 1964.

Lamott, Willis C. *Revolution in Missions.* New York: Macmillan, 1954.

Neill, Stephen. *Creative Tension.* London: Edinburgh House Press, 1959.

Scherer, James A. *Missionary, Go Home! A Reappraisal of the Christian World Mission.* Englewood Cliffs, NJ: Prentice-Hall, 1964.

Wagner, C. Peter, (ed.). *Church/Mission Tensions Today.* Chicago: Moody Press, 1972.

MISSIONS IN THE LOCAL CHURCH

Cooper, Clay. *Your Home Church and Its Foreign Mission.* Chicago: Moody Press, 1963.

Garrett, Willis E. *A Successful Missionary Program in Your Church.* Lincoln, NE: Back to the Bible, 1965.

Griffiths, Michael C. *Who Really Sends the Missionary?* Chicago: Moody Press, 1974.

Harner, Nevin C. and Baker, David D. *Missionary Education in Your Church.* New York: Friendship Press, 1950.

How to Organize a Mission Program in the Local Church. Jenkintown, PA: Louis Neibauer Co., 1973.

Idea Notebook Promoting Missions in the Local Church. New York: Sudan Interior Mission, 1967.

Lewis, Norm. *Faith Promise for World Witness.* Lincoln, NE.: Back to the Bible Broadcast, 1974.

Pearson, Dick. *Missionary Education Helps for the Local Church.* Palo Alto, CA: Overseas Crusades, 1966.

Pierce, Robert. *Emphasizing Missions in the Local Church.* Grand Rapids: Zondervan, 1964.

Ranck, J. Allan. *Education for Mission.* New York: Friendship Press, 1961.

Richardson, Carol L. *Know Your Missionaries.* Portland, OR: Ronn House Publications, 1970.

Stowe, David M. *The Worldwide Mission of the Church.* Boston: United Church Press, 1966.

Webster, Douglas. *Local Church and World Mission.* New York: Seabury Press, 1962.

HISTORY OF MISSIONS

Aberly, John. *An Outline of Missions.* Philadelphia: Muhlenberg Press, 1945.

Carver, William O. *The Course of Christian Missions.* New York: Revell, 1912.

Kane, J. Herbert. *A Global View of Christian Missions.* Grand Rapids: Baker Book House, 1971.

Latourette, K. S. *A History of the Expansion of Christianity,* (7 vols.). Grand Rapids: Zondervan, 1937-45.
Mathews, Basil J. *Forward Through the Ages.* New York: Friendship Press, 1951.
Neill, Stephen. *History of Christian Missions.* Baltimore: Penguin Books, 1964.
Warren, Max. *The Missionary Movement from Great Britain in Modern History.* London: SCM Press, 1965.
————. *Social History and Christian Mission.* London: SCM Press, 1967.

PHILOSOPHY OF MISSIONS

Beaver, R. Pierce, (ed.). *To Advance the Gospel: Selections from the Writings of Rufus Anderson.* Grand Rapids: Eerdmans, 1967.
Beyerhaus, Peter, and Lefever, Henry. *The Responsible Church and the Foreign Mission.* Grand Rapids: Eerdmans, 1964.
Coggins, Wade T. *So That's What Missions Is All About.* Chicago: Moody Press, 1975.
Cook, Harold R. *An Introduction to Christian Missions.* Chicago: Moody Press, 1971.
Evangelical Alliance Commission on World Mission. *One World, One Task.* London: Scripture Union, 1971.
Lindsell, Harold. *A Christian Philosophy of Missions.* Wheaton, IL: Van Kampen Press, 1949.
Niles, Daniel T. *Upon the Earth.* New York: McGraw-Hill, 1962.
Warren, Max, (ed.). *To Apply the Gospel: Selections from the Writings of Henry Venn.* Grand Rapids: Eerdmans, 1971.

STRATEGY OF MISSIONS

Allen, Roland. *Missionary Methods: St. Paul's or Ours?* Grand Rapids: Eerdmans, 1962.
Bavinck, J. H. *An Introduction to the Science of Missions.* Philadelphia: Presbyterian and Reformed Publishing Co., 1964.
Chang, Lit-sen. *Strategy of Missions in the Orient.* Philadelphia: Presbyterian and Reformed Publishing Co., 1968.
Cook, Harold C. *Strategy of Missions: An Evangelical View.* Chicago: Moody Press, 1963.
Greenway, Roger S. *An Urban Strategy for Latin America.* Grand Rapids: Baker Book House, 1973.
Liao, David C. E. *The Unresponsive: Resistant or Neglected?* Chicago: Moody Press, 1972.
McGavran, Donald. *The Bridges of God.* New York: Friendship Press, 1955.
Pentecost, Edward C. *Reaching the Unreached.* South Pasadena, CA.: William Carey Library, 1974.
Subbamma, B. V. *New Patterns for Discipling Hindus.* South Pasadena, CA: William Carey Library, 1970.
Wagner, C. Peter. *Frontiers in Missionary Strategy.* Chicago: Moody Press, 1972.
Womack, David A. *Breaking the Stained-Glass Barrier.* New York: Harper and Row, 1973.

SURVEY OF MISSIONS

Bates, M. Searle and Pauck, W. *The Prospects of Christianity Throughout the World*. New York: Scribners, 1964.

Cook, Harold R. *Highlights of Christian Missions*. Chicago: Moody Press, 1967.

Harr, W. C. *Frontiers of the Christian World Mission*. New York: Harper and Row, 1962.

Lyall, Leslie T. *Missionary Opportunity Today*. Chicago: Inter-Varsity Press, 1963.

Thiessen, John C. *A Survey of World Missions*. Chicago: Moody Press, 1961.

Taylor, Clyde W. *A Glimpse of World Missions: An Evangelical View*. Chicago: Moody Press, 1960.

THEOLOGICAL EDUCATION BY EXTENSION

Covell, Ralph R. and Wagner, C. Peter. *An Extension Seminary Primer*. South Pasadena, CA: William Carey Library, 1971.

Ward, Ted. *Programmed Instruction for Theological Education*. Farmington, MI: Associates of Urbanus, 1971.

Weld, Wayne. *World Directory of Theological Education by Extension*. South Pasadena, CA: William Carey Library, 1973.

Winter, Ralph D., (ed.). *Theological Education by Extension*. South Pasadena, CA: William Carey Library, 1969.

THEOLOGY OF MISSIONS

Adeney, David H. *The Unchanging Commission*. Chicago: Inter-Varsity Press, 1955.

Allen, Roland. *The Ministry of the Spirit*. Grand Rapids: Eerdmans, 1962.

Anderson, Gerald H., (ed.). *Christian Mission in Theological Perspective*. New York: Abingdon Press, 1967.

————., (ed.). *The Theology of the Christian Mission*. New York: McGraw-Hill, 1961.

Blauw, Johannes. *The Missionary Nature of the Church*. New York: McGraw-Hill, 1962.

Boer, Harry R. *Pentecost and Missions*. Grand Rapids: Eerdmans, 1961.

Boyd, R. H. S. *An Introduction to Indian Christian Theology*. Madras: Christian Literature Society, 1969.

Carver, William O. *Missions in the Plan of the Ages*. Nashville: Broadman, 1951.

Champion, Richard, et al., (eds.). *Our Mission in Today's World*. Springfield, MO: Gospel Publishing House, 1968.

Davis, Lew A. *The Layman Views World Missions*. St. Louis: Bethany Press, 1964.

Fife, Eric S. *Man's Peace, God's Glory*. Chicago: Inter-Varsity Press, 1961.

Forman, Charles W. *A Faith for the Nations*. Philadelphia: Westminster Press, 1957.

Glover, Robert H. *The Bible Basis of Missions*. Chicago: Moody Press, 1964.

Gordon, A. J. *The Holy Spirit in Missions*. Harrisburg, PA: Christian Publications, 1968.

Hillis, Don W., (ed.). *The Scriptural Basis of World Evangelization*. Grand Rapids: Baker Book House, 1965.

Lindsell, Harold, (ed.). *The Church's Worldwide Mission*. Waco, TX: Word Books, 1966.

———. *An Evangelical Theology of Missions*. Grand Rapids: Zondervan, 1970.

Morgan, G. Campbell. *The Missionary Manifesto*. Grand Rapids: Baker Book House, 1970.

Newbigin, Lesslie. *The Finality of Christ*. Richmond, VA: John Knox Press, 1969.

———. *Trinitarian Faith and Today's Mission*. Richmond, VA: John Knox Press, 1972.

Peters, George W. *A Bibilcal Theology of Missions*. Chicago: Moody Press, 1972.

Rowley, Harold H. *The Missionary Message of the Old Testament*. London: Carey, 1944.

Sanders, J. Oswald. *What of the Unevangelized?* London: Overseas Missionary Fellowship, 1966.

Skoglund, John E. *To the Whole Creation*. Valley Forge, PA: Judson Press, 1962.

Tippett, Alan R. *Verdict Theology in Missionary Theory*. Lincoln, IL: Christian College Press, 1969.

Vicedom, Georg F. *The Mission of God*. St. Louis: Concordia, 1965.

Visser't Hooft, W. A. *No Other Name*. Philadelphia: Westminster Press, 1963.

Wagner, C. Peter. *Latin American Theology*. Grand Rapids: Eerdmans, 1970.

Warren, Max. *The Uniqueness of Jesus Christ*. London: Highway Press, 1969.

Webster, Douglas. *Unchanging Mission: Biblical and Contemporary*. Philadelphia: Fortress Press, 1965.

———. *Yes to Mission*. New York: Seabury Press, 1966.

Wolff, Richard. *The Final Destiny of the Heathen*. Ridgefield Park, NJ: Interdenominational Foreign Mission Association, 1961.

THIRD WORLD: CHURCH AND MISSION

Barrett, David B. *Schism and Renewal in Africa*. Nairobi: Oxford University Press, 1968.

Clark, Dennis E. *The Third World and Mission*. Waco, TX: Word Books, 1971.

Daniels, George M. *This Is the Church in the New Nations*. New York: Friendship Press, 1964.

Danker, William J. *Profit for the Lord*. Grand Rapids: Eerdmans, 1971.

Forman, Charles W., (ed.). *Christianity in the Non-Western World*. Englewood Cliffs, NJ: Prentice-Hall, 1967.

———. *The Nation and the Kingdom*. New York: Friendship Press, 1964.

Hodges, Melvin L. *On the Mission Field: The Indigenous Church*. Chicago: Moody Press, 1953.

The Indigenous Church: A Report from Many Lands. Chicago: Moody Press, 1960.

Manikam, Rajah B., (ed.). *Christianity and the Asian Revolution*. New York: Friendship Press, 1955.

Sundkler, Bengt. *Bantu Prophets in South Africa*. London: Oxford University Press, 1961.

Wong, James, et al. *Missions from the Third World*. Singapore: Church Growth Study Center, 1973.

URBANA CONVENTION REPORTS

1946 Convention: *Completing Christ's Commission.* Chicago: Inter-Varsity Press, 1947.

1948 Convention: *From Every Campus to Every Country.* Chicago: Inter-Varsity Press, 1949.

1951 Convention: *By All Means—Proclaim Christ.* Chicago: Inter-Varsity Press, 1952.

1954 Convention: *Changing World—Unchanging Christ.* Chicago: Inter-Varsity Press, 1955.

1957 Convention: *One Lord, One Church, One World.* Chicago: Inter-Varsity Press, 1958.

1961 Convention: *Commission, Conflict, Commitment.* Chicago: Inter-Varsity Press, 1962.

1964 Convention: *Change, Witness, Triumph.* Chicago: Inter-Varsity Press, 1965.

1967 Convention: *God's Men: From All Nations to All Nations.* Downers Grove, IL: Inter-Varsity Press, 1968.

1970 Convention: *Christ the Liberator.* Downers Grove, IL: Inter-Varsity Press, 1971.

1973 Convention: *Jesus Christ, Lord of the Universe, Hope of the World.* Downers Grove, IL: Inter-Varsity Press, 1974.

Index

455

266.09
K16
c.2

3 4711 00187 7242